A THEOLOGY OF THE FAMILY

A THEOLOGY OF THE FAMILY

Edited by Jeff Pollard & Scott T. Brown

NCFIC

WAKE FOREST, NORTH CAROLINA

Second Printing: January 2016

Copyright © 2016 The National Center for Family-Integrated Churches
All Rights Reserved

The National Center for Family-Integrated Churches
220 South White St., Wake Forest, NC 27587
www.ncfic.org

ISBN 978-1-624180-46-0

Book Design and Typography by Justin Turley

Cover Art: "St. Paul" by Pompeo Girolamo Batoni (1708-1787)
This founding figure of the Christian Church is from a group of eight pictures now in the Iliffe Collection that comes from a set of twelve pictures of God the Father and the Apostles, originally painted for the town palace of Count Cesare and Fra Giuseppe Merenda in Forlí. They were Batoni's most dedicated patrons, commissioning at least 32 paintings from him between about 1740 and 1750. Paul appears to address us in token of his great powers as a preacher. (This image was modified from the original).

Scripture references in this book are taken from the King James Version, originally published 1611. Used by permission. All rights reserved.

Printed in the United States of America

To
Myra Pollard and Deborah Brown
true and gracious helpmeets, our eyes and ears,
who have evaluated and embraced the doctrine of the family
articulated by the authors featured in this book

&

Steven and Linda Frakes
faithful servants of Christ at Mount Zion Bible Church
and Chapel Library; gifted fellow-elder and his wife,
a gifted proofreader

&

the precious saints of Mount Zion Bible Church and Hope Baptist Church,
who have searched the Holy Scriptures and looked heavenward for
their patterns for church and family life

&

Claudia Brown, Colton Neifert, James Fletcher, Connor Stearns,
Jonathan Njiragoma, Levi Hopkins, Joshua Wikman, and Tim Grissom

&

the Staff of Chapel Library—Lynn Benjamin, Greg Kelly, Thom LeBlanc,
Nate Maxson, Bonnie Reesman, Clarence Simmons, Laura Trayer, and
Winford Wilson; along with all our faithful helpers and volunteers, past and present

Now unto him that is able to do exceeding
abundantly above all that we ask or think, according to the
power that worketh in us, unto him be glory in the church by
Christ Jesus throughout all ages, world without end. Amen.
—Ephesians 3:20-21

Other Books from the NCFIC

A Weed in the Church

Early Piety

Counterfeit Worship

Family Reformation

Feminine by Design

It Can Be Done

Moment of Courage

Preparing Boys for Battle

Preparing for Marriage

"If we suffer the neglect of this, we undo all. What are we like to do ourselves to the reforming of a congregation, if all the work be cast on us alone, and masters of families will let fall that necessary duty of their own, by which they are bound to help us! If any good be begun by the ministry in any soul in a family, a careless, prayerless, worldly family is like to stifle it, or very much hinder it. Whereas, if you could but get the rulers of families to do their part, and take up the work where you left it, and help it on, what abundance of good might be done by it! (as I have elsewhere showed more at large). I beseech you, therefore, do all that you can to promote this business, as ever you desire the true reformation and welfare of your parishes!"

—Richard Baxter, The Reformed Pastor
(Morgan, PA: Soli Deo Gloria Publications, 2000), 384

TABLE OF CONTENTS

Endorsements for *A Theology of the Family* 21

Authors Featured in *A Theology of the Family* 25

Preface 33

Chapter 1—Family Worship

One Cause of the Decay of Religion in Our Day 44

Family Worship
Arthur W. Pink (1886-1952) 46

A Remedy for Decaying Religion
Oliver Heywood (1630-1702) 50

The Nature, Warrant, and History of Family Worship
J.W. Alexander (1804-1859) 53

What God Is to Families
Thomas Doolittle (c.1632-1707) 60

Motives for Family Worship
J.H. Merle D'Aubigne (1794-1872) 64

The Word of God and Family Prayer
Thomas Doolittle (c.1632-1707) 69

Seven Reasons Families Should Pray
Thomas Doolittle (c.1632-1707) 73

The Father and Family Worship
J.W. Alexander (1804-1859) 79

Women Leading Family Worship
John Howe (1630-1705) 85

Memories of Family Worship
John G. Paton (1824-1907).................................87

Implementing Family Worship
Joel R. Beeke..91

Heathens and Christians
John G. Paton (1824-1907)...............................100

Chapter 2—Godly Manhood

True Godliness Described
Benjamin Keach (1640-1704)..............................106

The Nature of an Upright Man
Richard Steele (1629-1692)..............................112

Signs and Character of a Godly Man
Thomas Watson (c. 1620-1686)............................116

Husbands, Love Your Wives
William Gouge (1575-1653)...............................126

The Conversion of Family Members
Samuel Lee (1627-1691)..................................137

A Godly Father's Anger
John Gill (1697-1771)...................................145

Threats to Godliness in Young Men
John Angell James (1785-1859)...........................147

How True Manhood Is Restored
Charles Haddon Spurgeon (1834-1892).....................156

Chapter 3—Virtuous Womanhood

Christianity's Influence on the Condition of Women
John Angell James (1785-1859)...........................164

Woman's Mission
John Angell James (1785-1859)...........................169

A Virtuous Woman Described
Charles Bridges (1794-1869).............................175

Christ's Call to Young Women
Thomas Vincent (1634-1678)..........................180

Grace for a Wife's Submission
William Gouge (1575-1653)...........................186

For Mothers, Experienced or New
John Angell James (1785-1859).......................195

Christ's Work and Single Women
W.K. Tweedie (1803-1863)............................206

To a Recent Woman Convert
Jonathan Edwards (1703-1758)........................209

A Grandmother in Glory
Jabez Burns (1805-1876).............................210

Chapter 4—Marriage

The Excellence of Marriage
Arthur W. Pink (1886-1952)..........................214

What Are the Duties of Husbands and Wives
Richard Steele (1629-1692)..........................223

Mutual Duties of Husbands and Wives
John Angell James (1785-1859).......................229

A Husband's Love for His Wife
Richard Steele (1629-1692)..........................237

A Wife's Submission
John Bunyan (1628-1688).............................242

A Wife's Respect for Her Husband
Richard Steele (1629-1692)..........................247

Duties That Preserve Marriage
William Gouge (1575-1653)...........................252

Thoughts on Finding a Marriage Partner
John Angell James (1785-1859).......................259

The Marriage of the Lamb
Charles Haddon Spurgeon (1834-1892).................267

Chapter 5—Bringing Up Children

Bringing Up Children for God
Edward Payson (1783-1827)..................................276

Nurture and Admonition
David Martyn Lloyd-Jones (1899-1981)....................279

Primary Obligations of Parents
J.C. Ryle (1816-1900)..285

General Duties of Parents to Children
John Bunyan (1628-1688)....................................292

Teaching Children about God
Philip Doddridge (1702-1751)...............................295

The Art of Balanced Discipline
David Martyn Lloyd-Jones (1899-1981)....................300

Children to Be Educated for Christ
Edward W. Hooker (1794-1875).............................305

Teaching Children Character
Philip Doddridge (1702-1751)...............................319

Principle Obstacles in Bringing Up Children for Christ
John Angell James (1785-1859)..............................325

The Calamity of Ungodly Children
Edward Lawrence (1623-1695)..............................333

Directions for Grieving over Ungodly Children
Edward Lawrence (1623-1695)..............................337

A Unique Opportunity of Witnessing to the World
David Martyn Lloyd-Jones (1899-1981)....................341

Chapter 6—Fatherhood

Father as Prophet, King, Priest
William Gurnall (1617-1679)................................344

Fatherhood: Responsibility and Privilege
Arthur W. Pink (1886-1952).................................345

A Father's Main Responsibility
John Calvin (1509-1564) 351

A Father's Oversight
John Bunyan (1628-1688) 354

Leading a Family for Christ
Richard Baxter (1615-1691) 361

A Father Must Be Godly
Nicholas Byfield (1579–1622) 367

Fathers Must Teach God's Word and Pray
Thomas Doolittle (1632-1707) 373

Fathers and Discipline
William Gouge (1575-1653) 377

How Fathers Can Provoke Their Children to Wrath
Thomas Watson (c. 1620-1686) 384

Counsel to Reforming Fathers
Richard Baxter (1615-1691) 387

A Father's Prayer
George Swinnock (1627–1673) 397

Chapter 7—Motherhood

The Dignity of Motherhood
Jabez Burns (1805-1876) 402

A Mother's Main Responsibility
Thomas Boston (1676-1732) 406

Keepers of the Springs
Peter Marshall (1902-1949) 408

Biblically Training Children, I
James Cameron (1809-1873) 414

Biblically Training Children, II
John Angell James (1785-1859) 421

The Mother's Legacy to Her Unborn Child
Elizabeth Joscelin (c. 1595-1622) 425

Loving, Wise Chastening
Richard Adams (c. 1626-1698) 438

A Mother's Encouragement
James Cameron (1809-1873) 441

A Gospel Call to Mothers
James Cameron (1809-1873) 446

Church and Motherhood
Charles Haddon Spurgeon (1834-1892) 449

Chapter 8—Childbearing

God's Image and God's Blessing
John Calvin (1509-1564) 452

Be Fruitful and Multiply
Martin Luther (1483-1546) 458

The Heritage of the Lord
Thomas Manton (1620-1677) 463

Loving and Caring for Babies
J. R. Miller (1840-1912) 468

Saved in Childbearing
Stephen Charnock (1628-1680) 475

Four Necessary Graces
Richard Adams (c. 1626-1698) 480

Sarah Gave Birth by Faith
Arthur W. Pink (1886-1952) 485

The Best Support in Childbearing
Richard Adams (c. 1626-1698) 489

When God Withholds Babies
Thomas Jacomb (1622-1687) 493

A Child Is Born
Thomas Boston (1676-1732) 495

Chapter 9—Abortion

Thou Shalt Not Kill
Ezekiel Hopkins (1634-1690)....................................502

The Silent Holocaust
Peter Barnes...505

The Bible and Sanctity of Life
R. C. Sproul..513

Mankind and the Death Factor
George Grant..519

Answers to Abortion Arguments
Joel Beeke..523

When Does Life Begin?
R. C. Sproul..528

Proclamations of God's Word and Abortion
Joel Beeke..534

Molech Is Alive and Well
Franklin E. (Ed) Payne..539

Great Forgiveness for Great Sin
Charles Haddon Spurgeon (1834-1892)...........................543

Chapter 10—Duties of Sons & Daughters

A Prayer for Readers, Especially Sons and Daughters
J. G. Pike (1784-1854)..548

Honor Your Father and Mother
Thomas Watson (c. 1620-1686)..................................553

The Duties of Sons and Daughters to Their Parents
John Angell James (1785-1859).................................557

Some General Responsibilities of Children to Parents
John Bunyan (1628-1688).......................................565

Children, Authority, and Society
David Martyn Lloyd-Jones (1899-1981)..........................569

Sins of Children and Youth
J. G. Pike (1784-1854) 578

Children, Seek the Good Shepherd
Robert Murray M'Cheyne (1813-1843) 586

Why Sons and Daughters Need Faith in Christ
Charles Walker (1791-1870) 591

Children Walking in Truth
J.C. Ryle (1816-1900) 594

To the Children of Godly Parents
Charles Haddon Spurgeon (1834-1892) 598

Chapter 11—Modest Apparel

Thinking Like a Christian about Modest Apparel
Robert G. Spinney 602

Christian Modesty Defined
Jeff Pollard 607

A Crying Sin of Our Age
Arthur W. Pink (1886-1952) 611

Symptoms of Bodily Pride
John Bunyan (1628-1688) 616

Avoiding Immodest Fashions
Vincent Alsop (1630-1703) 620

Accessories to Adultery
Robert G. Spinney 629

Your Clothing Reveals Your Heart
Richard Baxter (1615-1691) 632

Too Much, Too Little, Too Tight
Robert G. Spinney 637

Our Royal Apparel
Charles Haddon Spurgeon (1834-1892) 643

A Return to Modest Apparel
Jeff Pollard 647

Chapter 12—Thoughts for Young People

Thoughts for Young People
Archibald Alexander (1772-1851) 652

General Counsels for Young People
J.C. Ryle (1816-1900) 661

Youth Warned Against Sin
John Angell James (1785-1859) 669

Persuasions to Sober-mindedness
Matthew Henry (1662-1714) 675

Brothers and Sisters
John Angell James (1785-1859) 685

Standing Fast or Falling Away?
Thomas Vincent (1634-1678) 690

No Excuses: Believe the Gospel
Charles Haddon Spurgeon (1834-1892) 694

Chapter 13—The Lord's Day

Established at Creation
Arthur W. Pink (1886-1952) 704

Biblical Thoughts About the Lord's Day
J.C. Ryle (1816-1900) 709

The Fourth Commandment
Thomas Boston (1676-1732) 714

Foundations of the Lord's Day
Benjamin B. Warfield (1851-1921) 718

From Sabbath to Lord's Day
Archibald A. Hodge (1823-1886) 727

The Lord's Day in Public
Exekiel Hopkins (1634-1690) 733

The Lord's Day at Home
William S. Plumer (1802-1880) 736

Piety, Necessity, and Charity
Ezekiel Hopkins (1634-1690)..................................741

Honoring God on His Holy Day
Thomas Case (1598-1682) 744

A Most Precious Enjoyment
Jonathan Edwards (1703-1758) 748

Appendix A
Themes and History of the Free Grace Broadcaster...................753

Appendix B
History 757

Appendix C
About Chapel Library 761

Endorsements for
A THEOLOGY OF THE FAMILY

A Theology of the Family is an excellent anthology featuring a wealth of mostly-forgotten material from great Christian leaders of the past 500 years. Long before the era of television, child psychology, secularized public education, and commercial day-care centers, various heroes of the faith had much to say about home and family life. Their writings and sermons on the subject are full of practical, biblical wisdom about marriage, parenting, order and virtue in the home, family devotions, the training and discipline of children, and similar topics. They drew their principles from Scripture, so this is timeless wisdom—but it is as timely today as when it was first published. In fact, the current dearth of biblical wisdom, combined with the rapid decline of the family as an institution, illustrates precisely why the material in this book is more truly relevant and more desperately needed than ever.

—Phil Johnson, Executive Director of Grace to You, Sun Valley, California

This volume is a spiritual buffet for Christian family life, a delicious smorgasbord of short selections largely drawn from treasured Reformed writers. It dishes up biblical truth, loading the table with meaty explanation, sweet comfort, and well-spiced exhortation for fathers, mothers, children, and young people. You could use this book like an encyclopedia, finding an article on a specific question. Better yet, you could read it one article at a time for your devotions or family worship. However you read it, chew it well and take it into yourself, for it is full of nutritious truth.

—Dr. Joel R. Beeke, President of Puritan Reformed Theological Seminary, Grand Rapids, Michigan

There are many books on the family, so why another one? This is not "another one"! I commend A Theology of the Family because it is a compilation of some of the best articles on the subject of the family from proven teachers of the last five hundred years. The articles are short and full of rich practical pastoral counsel for both young and old. I also commend this book because it starts in the right place—the worship of God. Once we get that right the rest often falls into place!
—Conrad Mbewe, pastor of Kabwata Baptist Church, in Lusaka, Zambia, and author of *Foundations for the Flock: Truths About the Church for All the Saints*

We are all placed in great debt to those whose vision and labors have produced this amazing collage of godly wisdom concerning this all important issue. With God's blessing upon its pages, may the usefulness of this book in our day exceed our highest expectations and our most bold prayers. May the same be true for future generations, should our Lord delay his return.
—Albert N. Martin, served as a pastor of Trinity Baptist Church of Montville, New Jersey for forty-six years and is author of *Preaching in the Holy Spirit*; *Grieving, Hope, and Solace: When a Loved One Dies in Christ*; and *You Lift Me Up: Overcoming Ministry Challenges*

There is perhaps no greater need in our day than a return to godly family life. There is probably no greater threat to our culture than the demise of godly family life. There is no certainly greater resource for a godly family life (outside the Bible) than the vast and blessed legacy contained in the Reformed tradition of teaching on this subject. The present volume gives easy access to that vast resource for godly family life. It is, therefore, with gratitude to Jeff Pollard who compiled this volume by many years of labor that I pen this commendation and endorsement. May God be pleased through this volume to raise up godly families and through them to strengthen and stabilize godly churches.
—Sam Waldron, Dean and professor of Systematic Theology at Covenant Baptist Theological Seminary, and author of *A Man as Priest in His Home*

The godly Christian family faces unrelenting pressures from a fallen world (and sadly, sometimes from misguided churches) which threatens to dismantle it or at least redefine it on its own terms. In our own generation this antagonism seems to be steadily intensifying. We live in spiritually dark days in this regard—a darkness which may even be felt. For this reason I joyfully commend this wonderful anthology which brightly shines the light of God's truth on issues faced by this most basic yet vital unit of society. This book is a spiritual treasure chest filled with pure gold from proven writers both old and new. It touches on a variety of subjects beneficial for every family member. I heartily recommend it.

—Pastor Rob Ventura, Grace Community Baptist Church,
North Providence, Rhode Island,
Co-Author of *A Portrait of Paul* and *Spiritual Warfare*

Authors Featured in

A THEOLOGY OF THE FAMILY

1. **Richard Adams (c. 1626-1698):** 438, 480, 489
   English Presbyterian minister; born at Worrall, England.

2. **Archibald Alexander (1772-1851):** 652
   American Presbyterian theologian, first professor of Princeton Seminary; born in Augusta County, VA.

3. **J.W. Alexander (1804-1859):** 53, 79
   Eldest son of Archibald Alexander, the first professor of Princeton Theological Seminary. Attended both Princeton College and Princeton Seminary, later teaching at both institutions. His first love, however, was the pastorate, and he labored in churches in Virginia, New Jersey, and New York until his death in 1859.

4. **Vincent Alsop (1630-1703):** 620
   English Nonconformist minister; born in Northamptonshire, England.

5. **Richard Baxter (1615-1691):** 361, 387, 632
   English Puritan preacher and theologian; born in Rowton, Shropshire, England.

6. **Peter Barnes:** 505
   Minister of the Presbyterian Church of Australia; now serving in the parish of Macksville after ministering in Vanuatu (formerly New Hebrides).

7. **Joel R. Beeke:** 91, 523, 534
   Pastor of Heritage Netherlands Reformed Congregation in Grand Rapids, MI; theologian, author, and president of Puritan Reformed Theological Seminary, where he is Professor of Systematic Theology and Homiletics.

8. **Thomas Boston (1676-1732):** 406, 495, 714
   Scottish Presbyterian minister and theologian; born in Duns, Berwickshire.

9. **Charles Bridges (1794-1869):** 175
   A leader of the Evangelical party in the Church of England. Best known for *The Christian Ministry*, *Proverbs*, and *Psalm 119*.

10. **John Bunyan (1628-1688):** 242, 292, 354, 565, 616
    English minister, preacher, and author; born at Elstow near Bedford, England.

11. **Jabez Burns (1805-1876):** 210, 402
    English nonconformist theologian and philosopher; born in Oldham, Lancashire, England.

12. **Nicholas Byfield (1579-1622):** 367
    Anglican Puritan preacher and author; born in Warwickshire, England.

13. **John Calvin (1509-1564):** 351, 452
    French theologian, pastor, and important leader during the Protestant Reformation; born in Noyon, Picardie, France.

14. **James Cameron (1809-1873):** 414, 441, 446
    Scottish Congregational minister; born in Gourock, Firth of Clyde, Scotland.

15. **Thomas Case (1598-1682):** 744
    English Presbyterian minister and member of the West-minster Assembly; born in Kent, England, UK.

16. **Stephen Charnock (1628-1680):** 475
    English Puritan Presbyterian pastor, theologian, and author; born in St. Katherine Cree, London, England.

17. **J.H. Merle D'Aubigne (1794-1872):** 64
    Pastor, professor of church history, president, and professor of historical theology at the Ecole de théologie de Genève; author of several works on Reformation history including his well-known *History of the Reformation of the Sixteenth Century* and *The Reformation in England*.

18. **Philip Doddridge (1702-1751):** 295, 319
    English Nonconformist minister; prolific author and hymn writer; born in London, England.

19. **Thomas Doolittle (1632-1707):** 60, 69, 73, 373
    English Nonconformist minister; born at Kidderminster, Worcestershire, England.

20. **Jonathan Edwards (1703-1758):** **209, 748**
    American Congregational preacher. Regarded as America's greatest evangelical theologian and well-known for his preaching in the Great Awakening along with George Whitefield. Author of *Sinners in the Hands of an Angry God*, *A Treatise Concerning Religious Affections*, and numerous other titles. Born in East Windsor, Connecticut Colony.

21. **John Gill (1697-1771):** **145**
    Baptist theologian; born in Kettering, England.

22. **William Gouge (1575-1653):** **126, 186, 252, 377**
    Puritan minister for 46 years at Blackfriars, London; born in Stratford-Bow, Middlesex County, England.

23. **George Grant:** **519**
    Pastor of Parish Presbyterian Church, church planter, author, president of King's Meadow Study Center, founder of Franklin Classical School, and chancellor of New College Franklin.

24. **William Gurnall (1617–1679):** **344**
    An English author and clergyman born at King's Lynn, Norfolk. He was educated at the free grammar school of his native town, and in 1631 was nominated to the Lynn scholarship in Emmanuel College, Cambridge, where he graduated BA in 1635 and MA in 1639. He was made rector of Lavenham in Suffolk in 1644; and before he received that appointment he seems to have officiated, perhaps as curate, at Sudbury.

25. **Matthew Henry (1662-1714):** **675**
    Presbyterian preacher, author, and commentator; born at Broad Oak, on the borders of Flintshire and Shropshire, England.

26. **Oliver Heywood (1630-1702):** **50**
    Non-Conformist Puritan divine. Ejected from his pulpit in 1662 and excommunicated, Heywood preached mainly in private homes after the Great Ejection.

27. **Archibald Alexander Hodge (1823-1886):** **727**
    American Presbyterian pastor, theologian, and principal of Princeton Seminary; born in Princeton, NJ, USA.

28. **Edward W. Hooker (1794-1875):** **305**
    American Congregational minister, author, professor of rhetoric and church history; born in Goshen, Connecticut.

29. **Ezekiel Hopkins (1634-1690):** 502, 733, 741
Anglican minister and author; born in Sandford, Crediton, Devonshire, England.

30. **John Howe (1630-1705):** 85
Non-Conformist Puritan author and preacher; chaplain to Oliver Cromwell; born in Loughborough, England.

31. **Thomas Jacomb (1622-1687):** 493
English Presbyterian minister; a man of exemplary life and great learning; born in Melton Mowbray, Leicestershire, UK.

32. **John Angell James (1785-1859):** 147, 164, 169, 195, 229, 259, 325, 421, 557, 669, 685
English Congregationalist preacher and author; born at Blandford, Dorsetshire, England.

33. **Elizabeth Brooke Joscelin (c. 1595-1622):** 425
Granddaughter of Anglican theologian and bishop, William Chaderton (1540?-1608); born in Cheshire, England.

34. **Benjamin Keach (1640-1704):** 106
English Particular Baptist preacher, author, and ardent defender of Baptist principles, even against Richard Baxter. Often in prison and frequently in danger for preaching the gospel, he was the first to introduce singing hymns in the worship of English congregations. Prolific author of *Tropologia* (reprinted as *Preaching from the Types and Metaphors of the Bible*), *Gospel Mysteries Explained* (reprinted as *Exposition of the Parables*), and numerous other works; born at Stokeham, Buckinghamshire, England.

35. **Edward Lawrence (1623-1695):** 333, 337
Nonconformist English minister; born in Moston, Shropshire, England.

36. **Samuel Lee (1627-1691):** 137
Congregational Puritan minister of St. Botolph, Bishopsgate; born in London, England.

37. **Martin Luther (1483-1546):** 458
German monk, former Roman Catholic priest, theologian, and influential leader of the sixteenth century Protestant Reformation; born in Eisleben, Saxony.

38. **Thomas Manton (1620-1677):** 463
    Nonconformist Puritan preacher; born in Lawrence-Lydiat, county of Somerset, England.

39. **Peter Marshall (1902-1949):** 408
    Scottish-American Presbyterian preacher; twice appointed Chaplain of the U. S. Senate; born in Coatbridge, Scotland.

40. **David Martyn Lloyd-Jones (1899-1981):** 279, 300, 341, 569
    Perhaps the greatest expository preacher of the 20th century; Westminster Chapel, London, 1938-68; born in Wales.

41. **Robert Murray M'Cheyne (1813-1843):** 586
    Scottish Presbyterian minister of St. Peter's Church, Dundee; born in Edinburgh, Scotland.

42. **J. R. Miller (1840-1912):** 468
    Presbyterian pastor and gifted writer; Superintendent of the Presbyterian Board of Publication; born at Frankfort Springs, PA, USA.

43. **John G. Paton (1824-1907):** 87, 100
    Scottish Presbyterian missionary to the New Hebrides; began his work on the island of Tanna, which was inhabited by savage cannibals; later evangelized Aniwa; born in Braehead, Kirkmaho, Dumfriesshire, Scotland.

44. **Franklin E. (Ed) Payne, M.D.:** 539
    American physician; taught Family Medicine at the Medical College of Georgia for 25 years; has written helpfully and extensively on the subjects of biblical-medical ethics with Hilton Terrell, PH.D, M.D. (www.bmei.org), worldview (www.biblicalworldview21.org), and biblical-Christian philosophy (www.biblicalphilosophy.org).

45. **Edward Payson (1783-1827):** 276
    American Congregational preacher; pastor of the Congregational Church of Portland, ME; born in Rindge, NH, USA.

46. **J. G. Pike (1784-1854):** 548, 578
    Baptist minister; born in Edmonton, Alberta, Canada.

47. **Arthur W. Pink (1886-1952):** 46, 214, 345, 485, 611, 704
    Pastor, itinerate Bible teacher, author; born in Nottingham, England.

48. **William S. Plumer (1802-1880):** 736
    American Presbyterian minister and author; born in Greensburg, PA, USA.

49. **Jeff Pollard:** 607, 647
    An elder of Mount Zion Bible Church in Pensacola, Florida.

50. **J.C. Ryle (1816-1900):** 285, 594, 661, 709
    Anglican bishop; born at Macclesfield, Cheshire County, England.

51. **Robert G. Spinney:** 602, 629, 637
    Baptist minister and associate professor of history at Patrick Henry College, Purcellville, VA.

52. **R. C. Sproul:** 513, 528
    Presbyterian theologian and teaching elder; president of Ligonier Academy of Biblical and Theological Studies; founder and chairman of Ligonier Ministries.

53. **Charles Haddon Spurgeon (1834-1892):** 156, 267, 449, 543, 598, 643, 694
    Influential English Baptist preacher; born at Kelvedon, Essex, England.

54. **Richard Steele (1629-1692):** 112, 223, 237, 247
    Puritan preacher and author; born at Bartholmley, Cheshire, England.

55. **George Swinnock (1627-1673):** 397
    Puritan preacher and author; born in Maidstone, Kent, England.

56. **W.K. Tweedie (1803-1863):** 206
    Free Church minister and author; minister of the Tolbooth Kirk in Edinburgh, leader of the disruption in 1843 when the Free Church broke away from the Established Church in Scotland. Born in Ayr, Scotland.

57. **Thomas Vincent (1634–1678):** 180, 690
    English Puritan minister and author; born in Hertford, Hertfordshire, England.

58. **Charles Walker (1791-1870):** 591
    Congregational minister, burdened to teach God's truth to the young; born in Woodstock, Connecticut.

59. **Benjamin Breckinridge Warfeld (1851-1921):** 718
    Presbyterian professor of theology at Princeton Seminary; born near Lexington, KY, USA.

60. **Thomas Watson (c. 1620-1686):** 116, 384, 553
    English Nonconformist Puritan preacher and author; possibly born in Yorkshire, England.

PREFACE

In the mid 1990s, it began to occur to me that the modern Church had actually lost the biblical doctrine of the family. Biblical fatherhood was dead. Feminists owned womanhood. Motherhood was despised. Babies were marginalized as thieves of convenience and success. In America, we had aborted millions of children since 1973. Marriages were crumbling, and the very institution was being redefined. It was almost impossible to find men in the church who understood biblical manhood or fatherhood. The twentieth century was a bad time for the family; the trends were all running in the wrong direction, and biblical ignorance was speeding the family on its way to destruction.

Dark Age for the Family

The widespread biblical ignorance regarding the family was disturbing. And all the while came the unrelenting attacks of the sexual revolution, radical feminism, the birth control movement, cohabitation, welfare, homosexuality, post-Malthusian environmentalism, godless public education, and pornography. The deepening dark age of the family seemed impossible to reverse. I began to believe that Christ's Church would continue in its downward spiral unless we recovered three things: the true Gospel, the Word of God in the church, and biblical family life.

Meanwhile, Jeff Pollard was doing something about it. He was toiling into the night to document a correct theology of the family. He brought these doctrines together in an organized form for the ministry of Chapel Library. If you have known Jeff for any length of time, you know that the last twelve years of his life have been defined by his ministry to Mount Zion Bible Church and the unrelenting schedule to produce the *Free Grace Broadcaster*, a quarterly digest of Christ-centered sermons and articles from prior centuries. It is all about recovering sound doctrine and biblical practices. Jeff has produced dozens of booklets on subjects such as the Gospel, sin, repentance, the Holy Spirit, the blood of Christ, justification, sanctification, secret sins, and many other critical matters. Through Jeff's work at Chapel Library, there is a wealth of doctrinal resources that are being shipped all over the world. He brought them together in order to correct the lapses and heal the wounds, and to pass on a life-giving legacy to the rising generation. He worked for over a decade to identify the great authors and writings of the past that could meet the problems of our day. He went back in time. He returned to eras where a Christ centered view of the family was understood much better. He has revealed the doctrine locked in the literary treasure chests of the past. I am thankful that he also did this for the doctrine of the family.

What Does the Bible Say about the Family?

I once heard someone say that there is not much in the Bible about the family, especially in the New Testament. This is a common opinion. But, contrary to his impression, there is a rich doctrine of the family in the Bible. This book contains some long-forgotten elements of that doctrine.

We need to recover the belief that God's purpose for and instruction of the family is a vital aspect of life in this world. We need to affirm in our generation that God created the family as an important element in the outworking of His eternal purpose. First, God created the family to give structure and order to the human beings that He made in His image. Second, the family provides the essential labor of teaching and preparation of children for churches, communities, cultures, and nations. Third, God created the family in order to pass the gospel from one generation to the next. Finally, God designed the family to be a living demonstration of various aspects of the glory of the gospel and the embodiment of biblical truths.

This is why God has ordained that the family is the fountainhead of culture. It is the first place on earth that culture is made, and it is formational of all other cultures.

Redemptive History

It is no accident that the entire story of redemption is couched in family terminology. The Bible begins with the marriage of Adam and Eve (Gen. 2:20-24) and ends with the marriage supper of the Lamb, where the bride—the Church—is married to her husband (Rev.19:7-9). The story of Christ's love for the Church is summarized in a picture of a husband saving a bride, giving his life up for her, loving her, sanctifying her, and glorifying her. The apostle Paul delivers this imagery as he commands husbands to love their wives as Christ loved the Church and gave Himself up for her. Paul asserts that the love of Christ in the redemption of sinners is the pattern for the way husbands ought to love their wives. While no husband can save his wife's soul, his life with her is a picture of the redemption that is found in Christ.

Not only do marriages picture the gospel of God's grace on earth, but so do the relationships between children and their parents. God is a father (John 14:10; Eph. 4:6; Phil. 2:11; Col. 1:19; 1 Peter 1:2); His family is united (Deut. 6:41; Matt. 28:19; John 15:26; Gal. 3:20; 1 John 5:7); He has a son (John 3:16-17; 1 Cor.1:3; Eph. 1:3; Col.s 1:3; Heb.s 1:1-2; 1 Peter 1:3); and He has children who are born of the Spirit (Gal. 3:26; 1 John 2:28-3:3). These children are brothers and sisters and fathers and mothers in the family of God (Rom. 12:5; 1 Tim. 5:1-2; 1 John 3:14); they are members of God's household on earth (John 14:2-3); and Jesus makes the Church like a bride adorned for her husband (Rev. 19:1-10; 21:1-21).

Immediately after God created the heavens and the earth, He created an earthly husband and wife (Gen. 2:20-24). He instructed the husband and wife He had created to reproduce more families by being fruitful and multiplying (Gen. 1:27-28).

The relationships in the Trinity are an analogy of familial relationships. The covenantal activity among the Father, Son, and Holy Spirit is the very matrix from which the covenant of redemption issues forth, bringing erring children back to a loving and merciful Father. The members of the heavenly family daily bring sons and daughters into fellowship with the members of the Godhead and with one another. They are bringing "many sons to glory" (Heb. 2:10) as Jesus' disciples baptize others into this family, literally into "the name of the Father, the Son, and the Holy Spirit" (Matt. 28:16-28). When we take on the name of Christ in baptism, we are being welcomed into a new family.

When God Does Something Wonderful

When God does something wonderful in the world, He often uses a family. When God created the universe in all of its glory, He, His Son, and His Spirit happily went to work making all that there is (Prov. 8; John 1:1).

When God wanted to tend the garden and tame the wilderness, He instructed a family composed of Adam and Eve to take dominion over it (Gen. 1:28). When God wanted to preserve His righteous seed from destruction as He carried out judgment on a wicked world, He chose Noah and his family to preserve the human lineage that is in place to this day (Gen. 8-10). When He wanted to bless the world with the righteousness that is by faith alone, He appointed Abraham, in whose family all the families of the nations would be blessed (Gen. 12:1-3; 15; 17; 22:17; Hab. 2:4; Gal. 3:7-9; Rom. 3:21-26, 30; 4:1-4; 5:1). When God wanted to bring salvation to mankind, He sent His only begotten Son and His Son created a family—the family of God (Gal. 6:10). He established His Church, which is composed of spiritual brothers and sisters, mothers and fathers. This family is "the church of the living God," which is "the pillar and ground of the truth" (1 Tim. 3:15).

The family is a central aspect of God's purpose in redemptive history. Fathers who teach their families the Holy Scriptures are an important part of God's plan for saving the lost in the fulfillment of the Abrahamic covenant and the Great Commission. They preach the gospel to their families, and they deliver the whole counsel of God to their children as they bring them up in "the nurture and admonition of the Lord" (Eph. 6:1-4; Deut. 6:1-9; 11:18-21).

Family Reformation

Today, we are in need of a family reformation, or, rather, a reformation of biblical family life. A family reformation took place during the Protestant Reformation and later among the successors of the reformers—the Puritans. Because John Calvin was first and foremost an expositor and a pastor, he applied Scripture to every aspect of life—including the family. But that reformation did not die with Calvin because the successors of the reformers took up where Calvin left off and the family reformation continued, and it continues to this day. Most of the authors presented in this book are from the family reformation that took place during the Reformation and Puritan eras.[1]

During the Protestant Reformation, numerous theological and practical aspects of life were examined and reformed according to Scripture. While the doctrine of salvation was being reformed during the sixteenth century, so were marriage, manhood, womanhood, fatherhood, motherhood, courtship, child rearing, fertility, and almost every area that touches family life. John Calvin never wrote a book specifically about the family, but through his sermons, commentaries, systematic writings, and ordinances in Geneva, he ignited a family reformation that is still burning. As John Witte, Jr., notes, "John Calvin transformed the Western theology and law of sex, marriage, and family life…Calvin constructed a comprehensive new theology and law that made marital formation and dissolution, children's nurture and welfare, family cohesion and support, and sexual sin and crime essential concerns for both church and state. He drew the Consistory and Council of Geneva into a creative new alliance to guide and govern the reformation of the intimate

---

[1] Scott T. Brown, *Family Reformation: The Legacy of Sola Scriptura in Calvin's Geneva* (Wake Forest, NC: The National Center for Family-Integrated Churches, 2013), 29-83.

domestic sphere."² God appointed him to be the instigator of a massive restructuring of the most fundamental institution of society—the family. Calvin's instruction on the family was not only extensive in sheer quantity, but also comprehensive in its scope, speaking to almost every area of the family.

Like no other reformer, Calvin provided the exegetical precision that defined the terms for a biblical vision of family life. With crystal clarity, he explained the details of how the family had exchanged the truth of God for a lie.

It is striking to notice the simple means that God used to generate this family reformation. It was doctrinally oriented and arose from the rich soil of a vision of the majesty of God, a belief in the infallibility and sufficiency of Scripture, a practical and tenderhearted pastoral care, a devotion to expository preaching, and the real transformation of those who were reforming their lives to this biblical teaching.

The family reformation in Geneva needs to be understood in the twenty-first century because it sets before us a biblical vision for family life and reminds us of the upheaval that accompanies public family reformation.

This volume is an attempt to bring forth the fruits of the revival that took place during the Reformation and the Puritan era, as well as the legacy of those who embraced their doctrine and practice afterwards. During the Puritan era, there was a distinct revival of biblical family life. This reformation is clearly documented in the many detailed books they wrote on the subject.

Family worship was encouraged. Fathers were instructed to see themselves as the prophets, priests and kings of their households; wives were exhorted to be Titus 2 and Proverbs 31 women, and children were called to honor their parents--and the fragrance of beautiful family life rose up throughout England and Europe.

Attacked from the Beginning

In the Garden of Eden, the first attacks of the devil came against God's Word, which directly affected God's institution of marriage and the fruit of marriage—the family. The serpent convinced a wife that God was not good and undermined God's word. The husband did not protect his wife in her vulnerability, and the poison pill of sin entered the world. The bitter fruit of this appeared in the first generation of children: the first older brother in history murdered the first younger brother. And the devil continues to wage relentless war against the family to this very hour.

2John Witte, Jr., "Marriage and Family Life" in *The Calvin Handbook*, Herman J. Selderhuis, ed. (Grand Rapids, MI: Wm. B. Eerdmans, 2009), 455.

Why is there such an unceasing attack against the family today? Is it because the devil does not like the love and companionship in a family? Not primarily.

Hatred for the Gospel

The devil hates the family because he hates the gospel of Jesus Christ. A mangled marriage communicates a mangled gospel; an unloving, selfish husband declares a loveless faith and lies about Christ's love for the church; an un-submissive wife represents the falsehood of an antinomian church; a rebellious child images a disobedient individual child of God. The devil is on a mission, hell-bent to destroy the glory of God and His everlasting kingdom wherever it exists, so he aims at the most important target: the gospel. The gospel is the devil's bulls-eye because it reveals the Seed of the woman, Who crushed the serpent's head at Calvary.

The church becomes healthier when biblical family life flourishes. Furthermore, the world experiences blessing when fathers take up the mantle of family shepherd. As Christ's Church is the pillar and ground of the truth, the biblical family can be a biblical preservative of the gospel and a blessed field of evangelism. Further, the gospel truth is displayed by the very structure of the family. Because of these things, it should not be a surprise to us that the devil would hate God's design and purpose for families.

Generational Genocide

Satan wants to destroy Christian families because they are a conduit of the blessing of God for many generations. God's elect are born into families, and Christ Himself—the Savior of the world—entered this world from His mother's womb. The serpent's attacks on the Christian family always have broader implications that reach far beyond a single generation. Satan has been at war against the "seed of the woman" (Gen. 3:15) from the very beginning. The "seed of the woman" is a figure of Christ and all those in Him; is it any wonder that Satan is always trying to destroy that seed? He knows that sin is the only thing that can defeat the exponential impact of godly seed, multiplying across the generations. Sin is the reason families fall apart: "sin lieth at the door…and thou shalt rule over him" (Genesis 4:7). Cain rejected the Lord's counsel about the danger of sin when he pursued murderous thoughts toward his brother Abel. Sin has been the source of every family problem since Adam's fall into sin.

From that beginning, Satan has been in the family-destroying business. Cain did finally murder his brother, and this brutal, violent act fractured his family in the coming generations. Sin stands in the way of the blessings that

God has ordained for the families of the nations of the earth. This attack on the family is central to Lucifer's war against mankind; it is a global, transgenerational war against "the seed of the woman." In his attempt to wipe out the knowledge of God from one generation to the next, Satan attacks God's formational institutions: the church and the family. These attacks are rising. A response is required.

As cultures progress from one moral season to another, changes take place that require a biblical response. Movements often rise up attempting to respond to recover good things that are being lost. These reactionary movements are often vehement, but they are usually characterized by public responses through publishing. As the culture collapses, the writers pick up their weapons to sound the alarm. They are reactionary. They are often disruptive. One of the ways you can identify cultural degradation in a particular area is that you begin to see a wave of publishing on the subject that you had not seen for many years previously. When there is a major shift taking place, people write about it and talk about it. As we find ourselves in a period of history where the family is being attacked on all sides, we have seen a rise in publishing on the family. For many years there was very little activity, but over the past two decades the activity has increased dramatically.

I am grateful for Jeff Pollard, who picked up his weapons of war to do battle.

Beautiful things are declared in this volume. They are defining markers on "the old paths" (Jer. 6:16). This volume is dedicated to the preservation of these markers along the King's highway.

This Historical Moment

We present this volume at a time when many people in the cultures of the world have set aside the commands and godly patterns for family life that are revealed in Scripture, commands that they once obeyed faithfully. If you speak publicly about these matters, quoting the Bible, you will find that there is a broad rejection of them. Many genuinely hate the beautiful things God has ordained for family life. The devil himself hates beautiful things. But he will never be able to destroy them; "the gates of hell will not prevail" (Matt. 16:18) over the beauty and goodness of God's design for the church and the family.

As for Me and My House

Joshua boldly challenged the people of Israel to be faithful to the God Who had delivered them from bondage in Egypt: "And if it seem evil unto you to serve the LORD, choose you this day whom ye will serve; whether the gods which your fathers served that were on the other side of the flood, or the gods of the Amorites, in whose land ye dwell: but as for me and my house, we will serve the LORD" (Josh. 24:15). Joshua pressed them to make a life-changing decision: would they serve the true and living God or the false gods of other nations? The same decision faces God's people today. Many have courageously taken up Joshua's bold declaration, "As for me and my house, we will serve the LORD," only to discover that they do not know *how* to do this or *what* it looks like. The voice of faithful Christians that have gone before us can help us with both points. The articles in this book have been compiled precisely to instruct us how to "serve the LORD" as men, women, and children, according to God's infallible Word.

Chapter 1
FAMILY WORSHIP

If we ever hope to recover the biblical mission of the family, we must first restore its worship. People often try to fix their families by making surface changes in important areas, but until they deal with worship, they will find themselves like the men of Judah—healing "the hurt of [the] people slightly" (Jer. 6:14). So many maladies in family life can be traced to the abandonment of family worship.

You won't find the words "family worship" in the Bible, but you can trace its principles and practices from Genesis to Revelation. It is perhaps one of the most powerful forces in family life. I've seen remarkable transformations take place in families. They occur when a man does the simplest thing: he picks up the Bible and reads it to his family. This is transformational because the Word of God is powerful (Heb. 4:12; Ps. 19). When a man does this from the sincerity of his heart, it always changes his life. It also plants the flag of Christ's authority in the center of his home. Through the wellsprings of God's Word and the Holy Spirit, the family is refreshed and reformed.

Our church strives to prepare her people for this task. I have personally trained many men and women for it by utilizing a four-point training course on how to conduct family worship. It takes about thirty seconds to deliver. First, simply open your Bible and read it to your family. Second, after you have read it, you should ask your family to share the spiritual truths that stood out to them. Third, have your family earnestly pray for one another, making requests of God for His favor, for family, church, community, nation and world, and to cry out for the souls of the lost. Fourth, sing together as a family. For when God and the Word of His grace are exalted, the fountains of living water begin to flow. The following chapter lays out theological and practical instructions to enable you to perform this marvelous responsibility and thereby release the cleansing flood that God brings through worship. The worship of God is the only hope for the restoration of individuals, families, churches, and ultimately, nations.

—Scott Brown

One Cause of the Decay of Religion in Our Day

And oh, that other contentions being laid asleep, the only care and contention of all upon whom the name of our blessed Redeemer is called, might for the future be to walk humbly with their God and in the exercise of all love and meekness towards each other; to perfect holiness in the fear of the Lord, each one endeavoring to have his conversation[1] such as becometh[2] the Gospel; and also suitable to his place and capacity, vigorously to promote in others the practice of true religion and undefiled in the sight of God and our Father. And that in this backsliding day, we might not spend our breath in fruitless complaints of the evils of others, but may every one begin at home to reform in the first place our own hearts and ways; and then to quicken all that we may have influence upon to the same work; that if the will of God were so, none might deceive themselves by resting in and trusting to a form of godliness without the power of it and inward experience of the efficacy of those truths that are professed by them.

And verily there is one spring and cause of the decay of religion in our day, which we cannot but touch upon and earnestly urge a redress[3] of; and that is the neglect of the worship of God in families by those to whom the charge and conduct of them is committed. May not the gross ignorance and instability of many with the profaneness[4] of others be justly charged upon their parents and masters, who have not trained them up in the way wherein they ought to walk when they were young? But they have neglected those frequent and solemn commands which the Lord hath laid upon them so to catechize and instruct them, that their tender years might be seasoned with the knowledge of the truth of God as revealed in the Scriptures; and also by their own omission of prayer, and other duties of religion in their families, together with the ill example of their loose conversation, have inured[5] them first to a neglect, and then contempt of all piety[6] and religion? We know this will not excuse the blindness, or wickedness of any, but certainly it will fall heavy upon those that have thus been the occasion thereof. They indeed die in their sins; but will not their blood be required of those under whose care they were, who yet permitted them to go on without warning, yea led them

---

1 **conversation** – behavior; lifestyle.
2 **becometh** – in accordance with; suitable to.
3 **redress** – correction; reformation of something wrong
4 **profaneness** – contempt or irreverence for that which is sacred; disrespect towards God.
5 **inured** – hardened.
6 **piety** – reverence for God, love of His character, and devout obedience to His will; godliness.

into the paths of destruction? And will not the diligence of Christians with respect to the discharge of these duties, in ages past, rise up in judgment against, and condemn many of those who would be esteemed such now?

We shall conclude with our earnest prayer, that the God of all grace will pour out those measures of His Holy Spirit upon us, that the profession of truth may be accompanied with the sound belief and diligent practice of it by us that His name may in all things be glorified through Jesus Christ our Lord. Amen.

From the Preface to the *Second London Baptist Confession of 1677/1689*; reprinted by and available from Chapel Library.

Family Worship

ARTHUR W. PINK (1886-1952)

There are some very important outward ordinances and means of grace[7] that are plainly implied in the Word of God, but for the exercise of which we have few, if any, plain and positive precepts; rather are we left to gather them from the example of holy men and from various incidental circumstances. An important end is answered by this arrangement: trial is thereby made of the state of our hearts. It serves to make evident whether, because an expressed command cannot be brought requiring its performance, professing Christians will neglect a duty plainly implied. Thus, more of the real state of our minds is discovered, and it is made manifest whether we have or have not an ardent love for God and His service. This holds good both of public and family worship. Nevertheless, it is not at all difficult to prove the obligation of domestic piety.[8]

Consider first the example of Abraham, the father of the faithful and the friend of God (James 2:23). It was for his domestic piety that he received blessing from Jehovah Himself: *"For I know him, that he will command his children and his household after him, and they shall keep the way of the LORD, to do justice and judgment"* (Gen. 18:19). The patriarch is here commended for instructing his children and servants in the most important of all duties—*"the way of the Lord"*—the truth about His glorious person, His high claims upon us, His requirements from us. Note well the words *"he will command"* them, that is, he would use the authority God had given him as a father and head of his house to enforce the duties of family godliness. Abraham also prayed with as well as instructed his family: wherever he pitched his tent, there he built *"an altar unto the Lord"* (Gen. 12:7; 13:4). Now, my readers, we may well ask ourselves, Are we *"Abraham's seed"* (Gal. 3:29) if we do not *"the works of Abraham"* (John 8:39) and neglect the weighty duty of family worship?

The examples of other holy men are similar to that of Abraham's. Consider the pious determination of Joshua, who declared to Israel, *"As for me and my house, we will serve the LORD"* (Josh. 24:15). Neither the exalted station that he held nor the pressing public duties that developed upon him were allowed to crowd out his attention to the spiritual well-being of his family. Again, when David brought back the ark of God to Jerusalem with

---

7 **means of grace** – Any activities within the fellowship of the church that God uses to give more grace to Christians: teaching of the Word, baptism, the Lord's Supper, prayer for one another, godly fellowship, and others. (Grudem, *Systematic Theology*, 951)

8 **piety** – godliness.

joy and thanksgiving, after discharging his public duties, he *"returned to bless his household"* (2 Sam. 6:20). In addition to these eminent examples we may cite the cases of Job (Job 1:5) and Daniel (Dan. 6:10). Limiting ourselves to only one in the New Testament, we think of the history of Timothy, who was reared in a godly home. Paul called to remembrance the *"unfeigned faith"* that was in him (2 Tim. 1:5), and added, *"which dwelt first in thy grandmother Lois, and thy mother Eunice."* Is there any wonder, then, that the apostle could say *"from a child thou hast known the holy scriptures"* (2 Tim. 3:15)!

On the other hand, we may observe what fearful threatenings are pronounced against those who disregard this duty. We wonder how many of our readers have seriously pondered these awe-inspiring words: *"Pour out thy fury upon the heathen that know thee not, and upon the families that call not on thy name"* (Jer. 10:25)! How unspeakably solemn to find that prayerless families are here coupled with the heathen that know not the Lord. Yet need that surprise us? Why, there are many heathen families who unite together in worshiping their false gods. And do not they put thousands of professing Christians to shame? Observe too that Jeremiah 10:25 recorded a fearful imprecation[9] upon both classes alike: *"Pour out thy fury..."* How loudly should these words speak to us.

It is not enough that we pray as private individuals in our closets; we are required to honor God in our families as well. At least twice each day, in the morning and in the evening, *the whole household* should be gathered together to bow before the Lord—parents and children, master and servant—to confess their sins, to give thanks for God's mercies, to seek His help and blessing. Nothing must be allowed to interfere with this duty: all other domestic arrangements are to bend to it. The head of the house is the one to lead the devotions, but if he be absent, or seriously ill, or an unbeliever, then the wife would take his place. Under no circumstances should family worship be omitted. If we would enjoy the blessing of God upon our family, then let its members gather together daily for praise and prayer. *"Them that honour me I will honour"* is His promise (1 Sam. 2:30).

An old writer well said, "A family without prayer is like a house without a roof, open and exposed to all the storms of heaven."[10] All our domestic

---

9 **imprecation** – curse.
10 This quote has been attributed to Thomas Brooks (1608-1680) in Joel R. Beeke and Mark Jones, *A Puritan Theology: Doctrine for Life* (Grand Rapids, MI: Reformation Heritage Books, 2012), 876; William Jay (1769-1853), *Morning Exercises for the Closet for Every Day of the Year* (Baltimore: Plaskitt & Co. and Armstrong & Plaskitt, 1833), 14; William Burns (1769-1859) in "A Pastoral Letter to Heads of Families on Family Worship" in *The Scottish Christian Herald*, Vol. 3, No. 116, 305; and, Augustus Toplady (1740-1778) in "Excellent Passages from

comforts and temporal mercies issue from the lovingkindness of the Lord, and the best we can do in return is to gratefully acknowledge, together, His goodness to us as a family. Excuses against the discharge of this sacred duty are idle and worthless. Of what avail will it be when we render an account to God for the stewardship of our families to say that we had not time available, working hard from morn until eve? The more pressing be our temporal duties, the greater our need of seeking spiritual succor. Nor may any Christian plead that he is not qualified for such a work: gifts and talents are developed by use and not by neglect.

Family worship should be conducted *reverently, earnestly,* and *simply*. It is then that the little ones will receive their first impressions and form their initial conceptions of the Lord God. Great care needs to be taken lest a false idea be given them of the divine character, and for this the balance must be preserved between dwelling upon His transcendency[11] and immanency,[12] His holiness and His mercy, His might and His tenderness, His justice and His grace. Worship should begin with a few words of prayer invoking God's presence and blessing. A short passage from His Word should follow, with brief comments thereon. Two or three verses of a Psalm may be sung. Close with a prayer of committal into the hands of God. Though we may not be able to pray eloquently, we should earnestly. Prevailing prayers are usually brief ones. Beware of wearying the young ones.

The advantages and blessings of family worship are incalculable. First, family worship will prevent much sin. It awes the soul, conveys a sense of God's majesty and authority, sets solemn truths before the mind, and brings down benefits from God on the home. Personal piety in the home is a most influential means, under God, of conveying piety on the little ones. Children are largely creatures of imitation, loving to copy what they see in others.

"He established a testimony in Jacob, and appointed a law in Israel, which he commanded our fathers, that they should make them known to their children: That the generation to come might know them, even the children which should be born; who should arise and declare them to their children: That they might set their hope in God, and not forget the works of God, but keep his commandments" (Ps. 78:5-7). How much of the dreadful moral and spiritual conditions of the masses today may be traced back to the neglect of their fathers in this duty?

Eminent Persons," *The Works of Augustus M. Toplady*, Vol. 4 (London; Edinburgh: William Baynes and Son; H. S. Baynes, 1825), 418.
11 **transcendency** – God's distinction from His creation and His sovereign exaltation over it. He is not part of the universe, but is self-contained and self-existent.
12 **immanency** – God's indwelling His creation and its processes; in balance with His transcendency, God is very near to all of us.

How can those who neglect the worship of God in their families look for peace and comfort therein? Daily prayer in the home is a blessed means of grace for allaying those unhappy passions to which our common nature is subject. Finally, family prayer gains for us the presence and blessing of the Lord. There is a promise of His presence that is peculiarly applicable to this duty (*see* Matt. 18:19-20). Many have found in family worship that help and communion with God that they sought for with less effect in private prayer.

From *Family Worship*, available from Chapel Library.

Arthur W. Pink (1886-1952): Pastor, itinerate Bible teacher, author; born in Nottingham, England.

> *Family prayer and the pulpit are the bulwarks of Protestantism! Depend upon it, when family piety goes down, the life of godliness will become very low. In Europe, at any rate, seeing that the Christian faith began with a converted household, we ought to seek after the conversion of all our families and to maintain within our houses the good and holy practice of family worship.* —Charles Haddon Spurgeon.

A Remedy for Decaying Religion
OLIVER HEYWOOD (1630-1702)

For your sakes, dear Friends, I presume again to appear upon the public stage to be your faithful monitor,[13] to prompt you to your duty, and to promote the work of God in your souls and the worship of God in your families. And I know not how a minister can employ his time, studies, and pen better (next to the conviction and conversion of particular souls), than in pressing upon householders a care of the souls under their charge. This hath a direct tendency to public reformation. Religion begins in individuals and passeth on to relatives, and lesser spheres of relationship make up greater: Churches and commonwealths consist of families. There is a general complaint of the decay of the power of godliness and inundation[14] of profaneness,[15] and not without cause. I know no better remedy than domestic piety:[16] did governors teach their inferiors by counsels and examples; did they severely discountenance[17] and restrain enormities[18] and zealously promote holiness and then call on God unitedly and earnestly that He would efficaciously work what they cannot effect, who can tell what a blessed alteration would follow?

In vain do you complain of magistrates and ministers, while *you* that are householders are unfaithful to your trust. You complain that the world is in a bad state: what do *you* do to mend it? Do not so much complain of others as of yourselves, and complain not so much to man as to God. Plead with Him for reformation, second[19] also your prayers with earnest endeavors, sweep before your own doors, and act for God within your sphere. As you have more opportunity of familiarity with the inmates[20] of your house, so you have more authority over them from their dependence on you to influence them. And if you improve not this talent, you will have a dreadful account to give, especially as their blood will be required at your hands because their sin will be charged on your neglect.

Oh, sirs! Have you not sin enough of your own, but you must draw upon yourselves the guilt of your whole families? It is *you* that make bad times and

---

13 **monitor** – one who warns of faults or informs of duty.
14 **inundation** –flood; overwhelming in abundance.
15 **profaneness** – contempt or irreverence for that which is sacred; particularly the use of language that implies disrespect towards God.
16 **domestic piety** – reverence for God, love for His character, and obedience to His will in the home.
17 **discountenance** – view with disfavor.
18 **enormities** – monstrous offenses or evils; outrages.
19 **second** – support; assist.
20 **inmates** – persons who lodge or dwell in the same house with another.

bring down judgments on the nation. Would you rather see the agonies of your children and hear them crying amidst infernal torments, than speak a word to them for their instruction, hear them cry under your correction, or supplicate God for their salvation? Oh, cruel tigers and barbarous monsters! You may imagine yourselves to be Christians, but I cannot judge that man worthy to be a fit communicant[21] at the Lord's Table that maintains not the worship of God ordinarily in his family. And he deserves admonition and censure[22] for this sin of omission as well as for scandalous sins of commission; for he bewrays[23] his base hypocrisy in pretending to be a saint abroad, when he is a brute at home. For a right-bred[24] Christian [has respect] to all God's commandments. Such as are righteous before God *"walking in all the commandments and ordinances of the Lord blameless"* (Luke 1:6). Let these then go amongst the herd of the profane, and fare[25] as they do at the last, that make no conscience of family or relative godliness. Such as will not pray now will cry too late, *"Lord, Lord, open to us,"* when the door is shut (Matt. 25:11). Yea, they that now will not cry for a crumb of mercy shall in Hell cry out for a "drop of water, to quench their scorched tongues in those eternal torments" (Luke 16:22-24). To these self-destroying hypocrites, I recommend the serious consideration of Proverbs 1:24-31; Job 8:13-15; 27:8-10. O what an honor is it, that the King of Heaven gives you an admittance into His presence-chamber[26] with your families twice a day to confess your sins; [to] beg pardon and supplies of mercy; to give Him the glory of His goodness; and to lay your load on Him and get ease. I hope you will never be averse to it or weary of it. God forbid you should: you are not weary of meal times, if you be healthy. Know and keep these appointed times of coming to God. If you promise to meet a person of quality at such an hour when the clock strikes, you rise up, crave pardon, and tell the company [that someone] tarries for you, you must be gone. Oh, take not more liberty with God than you would do with men, and keep your hearts continually in a frame for duty.

From "The Family Altar," *The Works of Oliver Heywood,* Vol 4, reprinted by Soli Deo Gloria Publications.

---

21 **communicant** – person who receives the Lord's Supper.
22 **admonition and censure** – warning and spiritual judgment by the church
23 **bewrays** – betrays.
24 **right-bred** – well-mannered and refined.
25 **fare** – turn out.
26 **presence-chamber** – the room into which a great person receives company.

Chapter 1—Family Worship: A Remedy for Decaying Religion

Oliver Heywood (1630-1702): Non-Conformist Puritan divine. Ejected from his pulpit in 1662 and excommunicated, Heywood preached mainly in private homes after the Great Ejection.

The writer has met many people who profess to be Christians, but whose daily lives differ in nothing from thousands of non-professors all around them. They are rarely, if ever, found at the prayer-meeting, they have no Family Worship, they seldom read the Scriptures, they will not talk with you about the things of God, their walk is thoroughly worldly; and yet they are quite sure they are bound for heaven! Inquire into the ground of their confidence, and they will tell you that so many years ago they accepted Christ as their Savior, and "once saved always saved" is now their comfort. There are thousands of such people on earth today, who are nevertheless, on the Broad Road, that leadeth to destruction, treading it with a false peace in their hearts and a vain profession on their lips. —Arthur W. Pink

The Nature, Warrant, and History of Family Worship

J.W. ALEXANDER (1804-1859)

Family worship, as the name imports, is the joint worship rendered to God, by all the members of one household. There is an irresistible impulse to pray for those whom we love; and not only to pray *for* them, but *with* them. There is a natural as well as a gracious prompting to pray with those who are near to us. Prayer is a social exercise. The prayer which our Lord taught His disciples bears this stamp on every petition. It is this principle which leads to the united devotions of church assemblies and which immediately manifests itself in Christian families.

If there were but two human beings upon earth, they would be drawn, if they were of sanctified hearts, to pray with one another. Here we have the fountain of domestic worship. Time was, when there were but two human beings upon earth; and we may feel assured that they offered adoration in common. This was the Family Worship of Paradise.

That religion should specially pertain to the domestic relation is not at all wonderful.[27] The family is the oldest of human societies: it is as old as the creation of the race. Men were not drawn together into families by a voluntary determination or social compact according to the absurd figment of infidels: they were *created* in families.

It is not our purpose to make any ingenious[28] efforts to force into our service the history of the Old Testament or to search for Family Worship in every age of the world. That it has existed in every age, we do not doubt; that the Old Testament was intended to communicate this fact is not so clear. But without any indulgence of fancy, we cannot fail to discern the *principle* of Family Worship appearing and reappearing as a familiar thing in the remotest periods.

While all the church of God was in the ark, the worship was plainly Family Worship. And after the subsiding of the waters, when *"Noah builded an altar unto the LORD,"* it was a family sacrifice which he offered (Gen. 8:20). The patriarchs seem to have left a record of their social worship at every encampment. As soon as we find Abraham in the Promised Land, we find him rearing an altar in the plain of Moreh (Gen. 12:7). The same thing occurs in the vale between Hai and Bethel. Isaac not only renews the fountains which his father had opened, but keeps up his devotions, building an altar at Beersheba (Gen. 26:25). Jacob's altar at Bethel was eminently

---

27 **wonderful** – strange; astonishing.
28 **ingenious** – inventive skill and imagination.

a family monument and was signalized by his saying on the way unto his household, and to all that were with him, *"Put away the strange gods that are among you"* (Gen. 35:1-2). The altar was named EL-BETH-EL. This descent of religious rites in the family line was in correspondence with that declaration of Jehovah respecting the family religion which should prevail in Abraham's house (Gen. 18:19). The service of Job in behalf of his children was a perpetual service: he *"sent and sanctified them, and rose up early in the morning, and offered burnt offerings according to the number of them all…Thus did Job continually,"* or as it is in the Hebrew, "all the days" (Job 1:5). The book of Deuteronomy is full of family religion, as an example of which we may specially note the sixth chapter. The Passover, as we shall observe more fully in the sequel, was a family rite.

Everywhere in the Old Testament good men take cognizance[29] of the domestic tie in their religion. Joshua, even at the risk of being left with none but his family, will adhere to God: *"As for me and my house, we will serve the Lord"* (Josh. 24:15). David, after public services at the tabernacle where *"he blessed the people in the name of the Lord,"* returns *"to bless his household"* (2 Sam. 6:20). He had learned to connect God's service with domestic bonds in the house of his father Jesse, where there was *"a yearly sacrifice there for all the family"* (1 Sam. 20:6). And in the predictions of penitential[30] humbling, which shall take place when God pours on the house of David and the inhabitants of Jerusalem, the spirit of grace and of supplications, the suitableness of such exercises to families, as such, is not overlooked: *"And the land shall mourn, every family apart; the family of the house of David apart, and their wives apart; the family of the house of Nathan apart, and their wives apart; the family of the house of Levi apart, and their wives apart; the family of Shimei apart, and their wives apart; all the families that remain, every family apart, and their wives apart"* (Zech. 12:12-14).

In the New Testament, the traces of family religion are not less obvious. We gladly borrow the animated language of Mr. Hamilton of London and ask: "Do you envy Cornelius, whose prayers were heard, and to whom the Lord sent a special messenger to teach him the way of salvation? He was a *'devout man, and one that feared God with all his house, which gave much alms to the people, and prayed to God alway,'* and who was so anxious for the salvation of his family, that he got together his kinsmen and near friends, that they might be ready to hear the apostle when he arrived and share with himself the benefit (Acts 10:2, 24, 31). Do you admire Aquila and Priscilla, Paul's *'helpers in Christ Jesus,'* and who were so skillful in the Scriptures, that they were able to teach a

---

29 **cognizance** – recognition; conscious knowledge.
30 **penitential** – expressing sorrow for sin.

young minister the way of God more perfectly? You will find that one reason for their familiarity with the Scriptures was that they had a *'church that is in their house'"* (Acts 18:26; Rom. 16:5). It was doubtless recognized in regard to spiritual as well as in regard to temporal things, that *"if any provide not for his own, and specially for those of his own house, he hath denied the faith, and is worse than an infidel"* (1 Tim. 5:8). That spirit of social prayer which led disciples to join in supplication or praise, in upper chambers, in prisons, in the stocks, and on the sea beach could not but have manifested itself in daily household devotion (Acts 1:13; 16:25; Gal. 4:12; 2 Tim. 1:3).

Our records of primitive Christianity are so much distorted and corrupted by a superstitious tradition, that we need not be surprised to find a simple and spiritual service such as this, thrown into the shade by sacerdotal[31] rites. Yet we discern enough to teach us, that believers of the first ages were not neglectful of Family Worship.

"In general," says Neander[32] in a work not published among us, "They followed the Jews, in observing the three seasons of day, nine, twelve, and three o'clock, as special hours of prayer; yet they did not use these in a legal manner, such as militated against Christian liberty; for Tertullian[33] says, in regard to times of prayer, 'nothing is prescribed, except that we may pray at every hour, and in every place.' The Christians began and closed the day with prayer. Before meals, before the bath, they prayed, for as Tertullian says, the 'refreshment and nourishment of the soul must precede the refreshment and nourishment of the body; the heavenly before the earthly.' When a Christian from abroad, after brotherly reception and hospitality in the house of a brother Christian, took his leave, he was dismissed from the Christian family with prayer, 'Because,' said they, 'In thy brother thou hast beheld thy Lord.' For every affair of ordinary life they made preparation by prayer."

To this we may add the statements of a learned man, who has made Christian antiquities his peculiar study: "Instead of consuming their leisure hours in vacant idleness, or deriving their chief amusement from boisterous[34] merriment, the recital of tales of superstition, or the chanting of the profane songs of the heathen, they passed their hours of repose in rational and enlivening pursuits; found pleasure in enlarging their religious knowledge,

---

31 **sacerdotal** – pertaining to priests or priesthood; a reference to Romanism.
32 **Johann August Wilhelm Neander** (1789-1850) – German church historian and theologian; born David Mendel, a Jew; converted to Protestantism and took the name Neander (Greek for "new man"); author of the 6 volume *General History of the Christian Religion and the Church*.
33 **Tertullian** (c. 155-220)–early Latin father of the church; born a pagan, converted, finally left Roman Catholicism for Montanism; coined the term "trinity."
34 **boisterous** – loud, noisy, and lacking restraint.

and entertainment in songs that were dedicated to the praise of God. These formed their pastime in private, and their favorite recreations at their family and friendly meetings. With their minds full of the inspiring influence of these, they returned with fresh ardor to their scenes of toil; and to gratify their taste for a renewal of these, they longed for release from labor, far more than to appease their appetite with the provisions of the table. Young women sitting at the distaff[35] and matrons going about the duties of the household, were constantly humming some spiritual airs.

And Jerome[36] relates, of the place where he lived, that one could not go into the field without hearing the ploughman at his hallelujahs, the mower at his hymns, and the vinedresser singing the Psalms of David. It was not merely at noon and in time of their meals that the primitive Christians read the word of God, and sang praises to His name. At an early hour in the morning, the family were assembled, when a portion of Scripture was read from the Old Testament, which was followed by a hymn and a prayer, in which thanks were offered up to the Almighty for preserving them during the silent watches of the night, and for His goodness in permitting them to meet in health of body and soundness of mind; and at the same time His grace was implored to defend them amid the dangers and temptations of the day, to make them faithful to every duty and enable them in all respects to walk worthy of their Christian vocation. In the evening before retiring to rest, the family again assembled, when the same form of worship was observed as in the morning with this difference: that the service was considerably protracted beyond the period which could conveniently be allotted to it in the commencement of the day. Besides all these observances, they were in the habit of rising at midnight, to engage in prayer and the singing of psalms, a practice of venerable[37] antiquity, and which, as Dr. Cave justly supposes, took its origin from the first times of persecution, when not daring to meet together in the day, they were forced to keep their religious assemblies in the night."[38]

When we come down to the revival of evangelical piety at the Reformation, we find ourselves in the midst of such a stream of authority and example that we must content ourselves with general statements. Whatever may be the practice of their degenerate sons, the early Reformers are universally known to have set great value on family devotion. The

---

35 **distaff** – a stick or spindle onto which wool or flax is wound for spinning
36 **Jerome** (c. 347-419) – Biblical scholar and translator of the Latin translation of Scripture known as the Vulgate.
37 **venerable** – deserving honor and respect.
38 *The Antiquities of the Christian Church*, Lyman Coleman, 2nd edition, p. 375.

prayers of Luther in his house are recorded with warmth by his coevals[39] and biographers. The churches of Germany, in a better day, were blessed with a wide prevalence of household piety. Similar facts are recorded of Switzerland, France, and Holland.

But in no country has the light of the dwelling burned more brightly than in Scotland. Family Worship in all its fullness was coeval with the first reformation period. Probably no land in proportion to its inhabitants ever had so many praying families; probably none has so many now. In 1647, the General Assembly[40] issued a *Directory for Family Worship* in which they speak as follows:

> *"The ordinary duties comprehended under the exercise of piety, which should be in families, when they are convened to that effect, are these: first, prayer, and praises performed, with a special reference, as well to the condition of the Kirk[41] of God, and this kingdom, as to the present state of the family, and every member thereof. Next, reading of the Scriptures, with catechizing in a plain way, that the understandings of the simpler may be the better enabled to profit under the public ordinances, and they made more capable to understand the Scriptures when they are read: together with godly conferences tending to the edification of all the members in the most holy faith: as also, admonition and rebuke, upon just reasons, from those who have authority in the family. The head of the family is to take care that none of the family withdraw himself from any part of Family Worship; and seeing the ordinary performance of all the parts of Family Worship belongeth properly to the head of the family, the minister is to stir up such as are lazy, and train up such as are weak, to a fitness for these exercises."*
>
> *"So many as can conceive prayer, ought to make use of that gift of God; albeit, those who are rude[42] and weaker may begin at a set form of prayer; but so that they be not sluggish in stirring up in themselves (according to their daily necessities) the spirit of prayer, which is given to all the children of God in some measure: to which effect, they ought to be more fervent and frequent in secret prayer to God, for enabling of their hearts to conceive, and their tongues to express, convenient desires to God, for their family."* *"These exercises ought to be performed in great sincerity, without delay, laying aside all exercises of worldly business or hindrances, notwithstanding the*

---

39 **coevals** – contemporaries.
40 **General Assembly** – highest church court of various national churches, especially the Church of Scotland.
41 **Kirk** – Scottish form of "church," derived ultimately from the NT Greek adjective *kuriakos*, "of the Lord."
42 **rude** – ignorant; untaught.

mockings of atheists and profane men; in respect of the great mercies of God to this land, and of His corrections, whereby lately He hath exercised us. And to this effect, persons of eminency, and all elders of the kirk, not only ought to stir up themselves and families to diligence herein, but also to concur effectually, that in all other families, where they have power and charge, the said exercises be conscionably performed."

The faithfulness of private Christians in regard to this duty was made matter of inquiry by church courts. By the *Act of Assembly*, 1596, ratified December 17-18, 1638, among other provisions for the visitation of churches by presbyteries, the following questions were proposed to the heads of families:

"Do the elders visit the families within the quarter and bounds assigned to each of them? Are they careful to have the worship of God set up in the families of their bounds? The minister also is directed in his pastoral visits, to ask, 'Whether God be worshipped in the family, by prayers, praises, and reading of the Scriptures? Concerning the behavior of servants towards God and towards man; if they attend family and public worship? If there be catechizing in the family?'"[43]

When the *Confession of Faith* of the Westminster Assembly of Divines was adopted by the Church of Scotland, it contained this provision, which is still valid among ourselves: "God is to be worshipped everywhere, in spirit and in truth; as *in private families* daily, and in secret each one by himself."[44]

In conformity with these principles, the practice of Family Worship became universal throughout the Presbyterian body in Scotland and among all the Dissenters[45] in England. In Scotland especially, the humblest persons in the remotest cottages, honored God by daily praise; and nothing is more characteristic of the people at this day. I have sometimes seen Family Worship in great houses," says Mr. Hamilton, "but I have felt that God was quite as near when I knelt with a praying family on the earthen floor of their cottage. I have known of Family Worship among the reapers in a barn. It used to be

---

[43] Recited in "Overtures of General Assembly, A.D. 1705, concerning the method of proceeding in Kirk-Sessions and Presbyteries."

[44] *Confession of Faith*, Ch 21, para. 6

[45] **Dissenters** – persons who refuse to accept the authority of, or conform to, the laws of an established church. The term *Dissenters* was commonly used in 17th-century England, especially after passage of the *Toleration Act in 1689*, to denote groups who separated from the Church of England.

common in the fishing boats upon the friths[46] and lakes of Scotland. I have heard of its being observed in the depths of a coal pit."

The fathers of New England, having drunk into the same spirit, left the same legacy to their sons.

It is highly honorable to Family Worship, as a spiritual service, that it languishes and goes into decay in times when error and worldliness make inroads upon the church. This has been remarkably the case among some of the Protestant communities of the continent of Europe. As a general statement, it must be said that Family Worship is not so extensively practiced there; and of course, it cannot be so highly prized as in the churches of Great Britain and America. This is true even when the comparison is made between those in the respective countries whose attachment to the gospel appears to be the same. There are many, especially in France and Switzerland, who as highly value and as regularly maintain the daily worship of God as any of their brethren in England or the United States; but they constitute exceptions to the above statement, rather than any refutation of it. Christian travelers observe, however, that better views on this subject, as on the observance of the Sabbath, are decidedly on the increase in France and Switzerland and probably to a certain extent in Germany and other countries on the Continent. This is to be attributed to the translation of many excellent works from the English into French and their circulation in those countries within the last few years.

From what has been said, it is manifest that the universal voice of the Church, in its best periods, has been in favor of Family Worship. The reason of this has also become apparent. It is a service due to God in regard to His bountiful and gracious relation to families as such, rendered necessary by the wants, temptations, dangers, and sins of the family state; and in the highest degree fit and right, from the facilities afforded for maintaining it by the very condition of every household.

From *Thoughts on Family Worship*, reprinted by Soli Deo Gloria.

J.W. Alexander (1804-1859): Eldest son of Archibald Alexander, the first professor of Princeton Theological Seminary. Attended both Princeton College and Princeton Seminary, later teaching at both institutions. His first love, however, was the pastorate, and he labored in churches in Virginia, New Jersey, and New York until his death in 1859.

---

46 **friths** – narrow inlets of the sea

What God Is to Families
THOMAS DOOLITTLE (C.1632-1707)

Proposition 1

God is the Founder of all families: therefore families should pray unto Him— The household society usually is of these three combinations: husband and wife, parents and children, masters or servants: though there may be a family where all these are not, yet take it in its latitude,[47] and all these combinations are from God. The institution of husband and wife is from God (Gen. 2:21-24), and of parents and children, and masters and servants. And the authority of one over the other and the subjection of the one to the other is instituted by God and founded in the law of nature, which is God's law. The persons, singly considered, have not their beings only from God, but the very being of this society is also from Him. And as a single person is therefore bound to devote himself to the service of God and pray unto Him, so a household society is therefore bound jointly to do the same because a society is from God. And hath God appointed this society only for the mutual comfort of the members thereof or of the whole, and not also for His own glory, even from the whole? And doth that household society live to God's glory that does not serve Him and pray unto Him? Hath God given authority to the one to command and rule and the other a charge to obey only in reference to worldly things and not at all to spiritual? Can the comfort of the creature be God's ultimate end? No: it is His own glory. Is one, by authority from God and order of nature, paterfamilias,[48] "the master of the family," so called in reference to his servants, as well as to his children, because of the care he should take of the souls of servants and of their worshipping God with him as well as of his children? And should he not improve this power that God hath given him over them all, for God and the welfare of all their souls in calling them jointly to worship God and pray unto Him? Let reason and religion judge.

Proposition 2

God is the Owner of our families; therefore they should pray unto Him— God being our absolute Owner and Proprietor, not only by reason of the supereminency[49] of His nature, but also through the right of creation giving us our being and all we have, we ourselves and all that is ours (we and ours

---

47 **latitude** – extent; full range.
48 **paterfamilias** – a man who is the head of a household or the father of a family.
49 **supereminency** – superiority above all others.

being more His than our own) are unquestionably bound to lay out ourselves for God, wherein we might be most useful for our Owner's interest and glory. Whose are your families, if not God's then? Will you disclaim God as your Owner? If you should, yet in some sense, you are His still, though not by resignation and wholly devoting of yourselves to Him. Whose would you have your families to be—God's own or the devil's own? Hath the devil any title to your families? And shall your families serve the devil, that hath no title to you either of creation, preservation, or redemption? And will you not serve God, that by all this hath a title to you and an absolute, full propriety in you? If you will say your families are the devil's, then serve him. But if you say they are God's, then serve Him. Or will you say, "We are God's, but we will serve the devil?" If you do not *say* so, yet if you *do* so, is it not as bad? Why are you not ashamed to do that, which you are ashamed to speak out and tell the world what you do? Speak, then, in the fear of God. If your families, as such, be God's own, is it not reasonable that you should serve Him and pray unto Him?

Proposition 3

God is the Master and Governor of your families—therefore, as such, they should serve Him in praying to Him. If He be your Owner, He is your Ruler too: and doth He not give you laws to walk by and obey, not only as you are particular persons, but as you are a combined society? (Eph. 5:25-33; 6:1-10; Col. 3:19-25; 4:1) Is God, then, the Master of your family, and should not then your family serve Him? Do not subjects owe obedience to their governors? *"A son honoureth his father, and a servant his master: if then I be a father, where is mine honour? and if I be a master, where is my fear?"* (Mal. 1:6) Where, indeed? Not in prayerless, ungodly families.

Proposition 4

God is the Benefactor of your families—therefore, they should serve God in praying to Him and praising of Him. God doth not do you good and give you mercies only as individual persons, but also as a conjunct[50] society. Is not the continuance of the master of the family, not only a mercy to himself, but to the whole family also? Is not the continuance of the mother, children, and servants in life, health, and being, a mercy to the family? That you have an house to dwell together and food to eat together—do not you call these *family-mercies*? And do not these call aloud in your ears and to your consciences to give praises to your bountiful Benefactor together and

---

50 **conjunct** – joined together; united.

to pray together for the continuance of these and the grant of more as you shall need them? It would be endless to declare how many ways God is a Benefactor to your families conjunctly; and you are shameless, if you do not conjunctly praise Him for His bounty. Such an house is rather a sty for swine than a dwelling-house for rational creatures.

May not God call out to such prayerless families, as to them in Jeremiah 2:31? *"O generation, see ye the word of the LORD. Have I been a wilderness unto Israel? a land of darkness? wherefore say my people, We are lords; we will come no more unto thee?"* Hath God been forgetful of you? Speak, ye ungodly, prayerless families. Hath God been forgetful of you? No! Every morsel of bread [which] you eat tells you, God doth not forget you. Every time [that] you see your table spread and food set on, you see God doth not forget you. "Why, then," saith God, "will not this family come at me? When you have food to put into your children's mouths—when they do not cry for bread, [so that] you are constrained to say, 'I would, my poor hungry child! I would, but I have it not!'—Why then will you not come at me? Live together and eat together at my cost and care and charge, and yet be whole months and never come at me? And that your children have reason, raiment, limbs, not born blind, nor of a monstrous birth, and a thousand ways besides have I done you good," may God say, "Why then will you live whole *years* together and never together come at me? Have you found one more able or more willing to do you good? That you never can. Why then are you so unthankful as not to come at me?"

You see, when God is a Benefactor to a people (and there is the same reason for families) and they do not serve Him, what monstrous wickedness it is! God hath kept you all safe in the night, and yet in the morning you do not say, "Where is the Lord that did preserve us? Come, come, let us give joint praises to Him!" God hath done you and your families good so many years; and yet you do not say, "Where is the Lord that hath done such great things for us? Come! Let us acknowledge His mercy together." God hath carried you through affliction and sickness in the family: the plague hath been in the house, and yet you live—the smallpox and burning fevers have been in your houses, and yet you are alive—your conjugal companion[51] hath been sick and recovered, children nigh to death, and yet restored—and for all this you do not say, "Where is the Lord that kept us from the grave and saved us from the pit, that we are not rotten among the dead!" And yet you do not pray to nor praise this your wonderful Benefactor together. Let the *very* walls within which these ungrateful wretches live be astonished at this! Let

---

51 **conjugal companion** – spouse; husband or wife.

the very beams and pillars of their houses tremble! And let the very girders of the floors on which they tread and walk be horribly afraid! That such as dwell in such an house together go to bed before they go to prayer together! Let the earth be *amazed*, that the families which the Lord doth nourish and maintain are rebellious and unthankful, being worse than the very ox that knoweth his owner and of less understanding than the very ass (Isa. 1:2-3)!

From what hath been said, I reason in this manner: if God be the *Founder, Owner, Governor,* and *Benefactor* of families, then families are jointly to worship God and pray unto Him.

From "How May the Duty of Family Prayer Be Best Managed for the Spiritual Benefit of Every One in the Family?" *Puritan Sermons 1659-1689, Being the Morning Exercises at Cripplegate,* Vol 2, Richard Owen Roberts, Publisher.

Thomas Doolittle (c.1632-1707): Converted as a young man after reading Richard Baxter's *The Saints' Rest*; a gifted writer and preacher and one of the best-known Puritans of his day. Born at Kidderminster.

Motives for Family Worship

J.H. MERLE D'AUBIGNE (1794-1872)

As for me and my house, we will serve the LORD. —*Joshua 24:15*
Let me die the death of the righteous, and let my last end be like his!
—*Numbers 23:10*

We have said, my brethren, on a former occasion, that if we would die His death, we must live His life. It is true that there are cases in which the Lord shows His mercy and His glory to men who are already lying on the deathbed, and says to them, as to the thief on the cross, *"Today shalt thou be with me in paradise"* (Luke 23:43). The Lord still gives the Church similar examples from time to time for the purpose of displaying His sovereign power by which, when He is pleased to do so, He can break the hardest hearts and convert the souls most estranged[52] to show that all depends on His grace, and that He hath mercy on whom He will have mercy. Yet these are but rare exceptions on which you cannot rely absolutely; and if you wish, my dear hearers, to die the Christian's death, you must live the Christian's life. Your heart must be truly converted to the Lord; truly prepared for the kingdom; and trusting only in the mercy of Christ, desirous of going to dwell with Him. Now, my brethren, there are various means by which you can be made ready in life to obtain at a future day a blessed end. It is on one of the most efficacious[53] of these means that we wish to dwell today. This mean[54] is Family Worship; that is, the daily edification which the members of a Christian family may mutually enjoy. "As for me and my house," said Joshua to Israel, *"we will serve the LORD"* (Josh. 24:15). We wish, my brethren, to give you the motives which should induce us to make this resolution of Joshua and the directions necessary to fulfill it.

Why Family Worship?

1. To Bring Glory to God

But, my brethren, if the love of God be in your hearts, and if you feel that being bought with a price, you ought to glorify God in your bodies and spirits, which are His, where do you love to glorify Him rather than in your families and in your houses? You love to unite with your brethren in worshipping Him publicly in the church; you love to pour out your souls before Him in your closets. Is it only in the presence of that being with whom God has connected you for life and before your children that you cannot think of God? Is it, then, only that

---

52 **estranged** – alienated
53 **efficacious** – having the power to produce a desired effect.
54 **mean** – method by which something is accomplished.

you have no blessings to ascribe?⁵⁵ Is it, then, only, that you have no mercies and protection to implore? You can speak of everything when with them; your conversation is upon a thousand different matters; but your tongue and your heart can not find room for one word about God! You will not look up as a family to Him who is the true Father of your family; you will not converse with your wife and your children about that Being who will one day perhaps be the only Husband of your wife, the only Father of your children! It is the Gospel that has formed domestic society. It did not exist before it; it does not exist without it. It would, therefore, seem to be the duty of that society, full of gratitude to the God of the Gospel, to be peculiarly consecrated to it. And yet, my brethren, how many couples, how many families there are, nominally⁵⁶ Christian, and who even have some respect for religion, where God is never named! How many cases there are in which immortal souls that have been united have never asked one another who united them, and what their future destiny and objects are to be! How often it happens that, while they endeavor to assist each other in everything else, they do not even think of assisting each other in searching for the one thing needful, in conversing, in reading, in praying, with reference to their eternal interests! Christian spouses! Is it in the flesh and for time alone that you are to be united? Is it not in the spirit and for eternity also? Are you beings who have met by accident, whom another accident, death, is soon to separate? Do you not wish to be united by God, in God, and for God? Religion would unite your souls by immortal ties! But do not reject them; draw them, on the contrary, tighter every day, by worshipping together under the domestic roof. Voyagers on the same vessel converse of the place to which they are going; and will not you, fellow-travelers to an eternal world, speak together of that world, of the route which leads to it, of your fears and your hopes? *"For many walk,"* says St. Paul, *"of whom I have told you often, and now tell you even weeping, that they are the enemies of the cross of Christ"* (Phil. 3:18); but *"our conversation is in heaven; from whence also we look for the Saviour, the Lord Jesus Christ"* (Phil. 3:20).

2. To Protect Your Children from Sin

But if it be your duty to be engaged with reference to God in your houses for your own sakes, ought you not to be so engaged for the sakes of those of your households whose souls have been committed to your care, and especially for your children? You are greatly concerned for their prosperity, for their temporal happiness; but does not this concern make your neglect of their eternal prosperity and happiness still more palpable? Your children are young

---

55 **ascribe** – attribute as to a cause.
56 **nominally** – existing in name only.

trees entrusted to you; your house is the nursery where they ought to grow, and you are the gardeners. But, oh! Will you plant those tender and precious saplings in a sterile and sandy soil? Yet this is what you are doing, if there be nothing in your house to make them grow in the knowledge and love of their God and Savior. Are you not preparing for them a favorable soil, from which they can derive sap and life? What will become of your children in the midst of all the temptations that will surround them and draw them into sin? What will become of them in these troublous times, in which it is so necessary to strengthen the soul of the young man by the fear of God, and thus to give that fragile bark[57] the ballast needed for launching it upon the vast ocean?

Parents! If your children do not meet with a spirit of piety in your houses, if, on the contrary, your pride consists in surrounding them with external gifts, introducing them into worldly society, indulging all their whims, letting them follow their own course, you will see them grow vain, proud, idle, disobedient, impudent, and extravagant! They will treat you with contempt; and the more your hearts are wrapped up in them, the less they will think of you. This is seen but too often to be the case; but ask yourselves if you are not responsible for their bad habits and practices; and your conscience will reply that you are; that you are now eating the bread of bitterness which you have prepared for yourself. May you learn thereby how great has been your sin against God in neglecting the means which were in your power for influencing their hearts; and may others take warning from your misfortune, and bring up their children in the Lord! Nothing is more effectual in doing this than an example of domestic piety. Public worship is often too vague and general for children, and does not sufficiently interest them; as to the worship of the closet, they do not yet understand it. A lesson learned by rote, if unaccompanied by anything else, may lead them to look upon religion as a study, like those of foreign languages or history. Here as everywhere, and more than elsewhere, example is more effectual than precept. They are not merely to be taught out of some elementary book that they must love God, but you must show them God is loved. If they observe that no worship is paid to that God of whom they hear, the very best instruction will prove useless; but by means of Family Worship, these young plants will grow *"like a tree planted by the rivers of water, that bringeth forth his fruit in his season; his leaf also shall not wither"* (Ps. 1:3). Your children may leave the parental roof, but they will remember in foreign lands the prayers of the parental roof, and those prayers will protect them. *"If any,"* says the Scripture, *"have children or nephews, let them learn first to shew piety at home"* (1 Tim. 5:4).

---

57 **bark** – small ship.

3. To Produce Real Joy in the Home

And what delight, what peace, what real happiness a Christian family will find in erecting a family altar in their midst, and in uniting to offer up sacrifice unto the Lord! Such is the occupation of angels in heaven; and blessed are those who anticipate those pure and immortal joys! *"Behold, how good and how pleasant it is for brethren to dwell together in unity! It is like the precious ointment upon the head, that ran down upon the beard, even Aaron's beard: that went down to the skirts of his garments; as the dew of Hermon, and as the dew that descended upon the mountains of Zion: for there the Lord commanded the blessing, even life for evermore"* (Ps. 133). O what new grace and life piety gives to a family! In a house where God is forgotten, there is rudeness, ill-humor, and vexation of spirit. Without the knowledge and the love of God, a family is but a collection of individuals who may have more or less natural affection for one another; but the real bond, the love of God our Father in Jesus Christ our Lord, is wanting. The poets are full of beautiful descriptions of domestic life; but, alas! how different the pictures often are from the reality! Sometimes there is a want of confidence in the providence of God; sometimes there is love of riches; at others, a difference of character; at others, an opposition of principles. O how many troubles, how many cares there are in the bosoms of families!

Domestic piety will prevent all these evils; it will give perfect confidence in that God who gives food to the birds of the air; it will give true love toward those with whom we have to live: not an exacting, sensitive love, but a merciful love, which excuses and forgives, like that of God Himself; not a proud love, but a humble love, accompanied by a sense of one's own faults and weakness; not a fickle love, but a love unchangeable as eternal charity. *"The voice of rejoicing and salvation is in the tabernacles of the righteous,"* (Ps. 118:15).

4. To Console During Times of Trial

And when the hour of trial comes, that hour which must come sooner or later, and which sometimes visits the homes of men more than once, what consolation will domestic piety afford! Where do trials occur, if not in the bosoms of families? Where then ought the remedy for trials to be administered, if not in the bosoms of families? How much a family where there is mourning is to be pitied if it has not that consolation! The various members of whom it is composed increase one another's sadness. But if, on the contrary, that family loves God, if it is in the habit of meeting to invoke the holy name of God, from Whom comes every trial, as well as every good gift; then how will the souls that are cast down be raised up! The members of the family who still remain around the table on which is laid the Book of God, that book where they find the words of resurrection, life, and immortality, where they find sure pledges of the happiness of the being who is no more among them, as well as the warrant of their own hopes.

The Lord is pleased to send down the Comforter to them; the Spirit of glory and of God rests upon them; an ineffable[58] balm is poured upon their wounds, and gives them much consolation; peace is communicated from one heart to another. They enjoy moments of celestial bliss. *"Though I walk through the valley of the shadow of death, I will fear no evil: for thou art with me; thy rod and thy staff they comfort me,"* (Ps. 23:4). *"O Lord, thou hast brought up my soul from the grave…his anger endureth but a moment: in his favour is life; weeping may endure for a night, but joy cometh in the morning"* (Ps. 30:3, 5).

5. To influence society: And who can tell, my brethren, what an influence domestic piety might exert over society itself? What encouragements all men would have in doing their duty, from the statesman down to the poorest mechanic! How would all become accustomed to act with respect not only to the opinions of men, but also to the judgment of God! How would each learn to be satisfied with the position in which he is placed! Good habits would be adopted; the powerful voice of conscience would be strengthened: prudence, propriety, talent, social virtues, would be developed with renewed vigor. This is what we might expect both for ourselves and for society. Godliness hath promise of the life that now is, and of that which is to come.

From *Family Worship;* available as a small booklet from Chapel Library.

J.H. Merle D'Aubigne (1794-1872): Pastor, professor of church history, president, and professor of historical theology at the Ecole de théologie de Genève; author of several works on Reformation history including his well-known *History of the Reformation of the Sixteenth Century* and *The Reformation in England.*

---

58 **ineffable** – indescribable; incapable of being expressed.

The Word of God and Family Prayer
THOMAS DOOLITTLE (C.1632-1707)

Masters of families ought to read the Scripture to their families and instruct their children and servants in the matters and doctrines of salvation. Therefore, they are to pray in and with their families. No man that will not deny the Scripture can deny the unquestionable duty of reading the Scripture in our houses, governors of families teaching and instructing them out of the Word of God. Amongst a multitude of express Scriptures, look into these: *"And it shall come to pass, when your children shall say unto you, What mean ye by this service? that ye shall say, It is the sacrifice of the Lord's Passover, who passed over the houses of the children of Israel in Egypt, when he smote the Egyptians, and delivered our houses"* (Ex. 12:26-27). And there is as much reason that Christian parents should explain to their children the sacraments of the New Testament, to instruct them in the nature, use, and ends of baptism and the Lord's Supper: *"And these words, which I command thee this day, shall be in thine heart: and thou shalt teach [whet or sharpen] them diligently unto thy children, and shalt talk of them when thou sittest in thine house, and when thou walkest by the way, and when thou liest down, and when thou risest up,"* that is, morning and evening (Deut. 6:6-7; 11:18-19). *"And, ye fathers, provoke not your children to wrath: but bring them up in the nurture and admonition of the Lord"* (Eph. 6:4). And God was pleased with this in Abraham: *"For I know him, that he will command his children and his household after him, and they shall keep the way of the LORD"* (Gen. 18:19). This then is undeniable, if the Word is to be believed, received as our rule, and obedience to be yielded thereunto. And the Heathens taught a necessity of instructing youth betimes.[59]

The reason of this consequence, from family reading and instructions to family praying, is evident, (we need to beg of God the illumination of His Spirit, the opening of the eyes of everyone in the family,[60] the blessing of God upon our endeavors, without which it will be to no saving benefit) and will be more manifest, if we consider and lay together these things following:

1. Whose word it is that is to be read in the family together—the Word of the eternal, blessed, glorious God. And doth this call for and require preceding prayer, no more than if you were to read the book of some mortal man? The Word of God is that out of which God speaketh to us. It is that by which He doth instruct us and inform us in the highest and weightiest

---

59 **betimes** – speedily; soon.
60 "But, before everything else, address thy prayers to God, that the gates of divine light may be opened to thee. For these things can neither be perceived nor understood by any one, except by him on whom God and His Christ bestow this privilege."—Justin Martyr (110-165).

concernments of our souls. It is that from which we must fetch remedies for the cure of our spiritual maladies. It is that from whence we must have weapons of defense against our spiritual enemies that do assault our souls and be directed in the paths of life.[61] And is not prayer together needful then, that God would prepare all their hearts to receive and obey what shall be read to them of the mind of God? Is all the family so serious and so sensible of the glory, holiness, and majesty of that God that speaketh to them in His Word, that prayer is not needful that they may be so? And if it be needful, should it not first be done? And when it hath been read, and the threatenings, commands, and promises of the glorious God been heard, and your sins discovered and God's wrath against them, and duties enjoined, and precious privileges opened, and promises of a faithful God, both "great and precious promises," made to such as do repent, believe, and turn to God with all their hearts unfeignedly; for have you not all need together to fall down upon your knees, to beg and cry and call to God for pardon of those sins that by this Word you are convinced you are guilty of and to lament them before the Lord? And that when your duty is discovered, you might have all hearts to practice and obey, and that you might unfeignedly[62] repent and turn to God, that so you may apply those promises to yourselves and be partaker of those privileges? From this then, there is great reason, [that] when you read together you should also pray together.

2. Consider what great and deep mysterious things are contained in the Word of God which you are to read together. And there will appear a necessity of praying together also. Is there not in this Word the doctrine concerning God, how He might be known, loved, obeyed, worshipped, and delighted in? Concerning Christ, God-man, a mystery that the angels wonder at and no man fully understands or can express and fully unfold?[63]

---

61 "Holy scripture is (1) The *chair of God* from which He addresses Himself to us. (2) It is *God's school* in which He teaches us and communicates information. (3) It is *God's dispensary* and the spiritual office from which He distributes His healing medicines. (4) It is *God's armory* and grand collection of suitable weapons from which He furnishes us with defensive and offensive arms for our protection against enemies of every description. (5) It is *the hand of God* by which He leads us onward through the paths of faith and righteousness and safely conducts us unto life eternal."—Johann Gerhard (1582-1637).

62 **unfeignedly** – without hypocrisy; sincerely.

63 "Let every faithful and believing Christian devote his attention to the Sacred Scriptures. In them he will find wonderful exhibitions, worthy of the faith by which they were produced. He will behold the men of the world lying in their wickedness, the rewards of the godly, and the punishment of the wicked. He will also look with wonder on wild beasts overcome by religion, and their fierceness changed into mildness, and the souls of men recalled into their lifeless bodies. But a spectacle far surpassing all these will be displayed to his enraptured view—he will see that devil who wishes to triumph over the whole world, lying

Concerning the offices of Christ—Prophet, Priest, and King? The example and the life of Christ, the miracles of Christ, the temptations of Christ, the sufferings of Christ, His death, the victories of Christ, the resurrection, ascension, and intercession of Christ, and His coming to judgment? Is there not in the Scripture the doctrine of the Trinity, of the misery of man by sin, and his remedy by Christ? Of the covenant of grace, the conditions of this covenant, and the seals thereof? The many precious, glorious privileges that we have by Christ—reconciliation with God, justification, sanctification, and adoption? The several graces to be got, and duties to be done, and of men's everlasting state in heaven or hell? Are these, and such like, contained in the Word of God that you ought to read daily in your houses? And yet do not you see the need of prayer before and after your reading of it? Weigh them well, and you will.

3. Consider how much all the family are concerned to know and understand these things so necessary to salvation. If they are ignorant of them, they are undone. If they know not God, how shall they love Him? We might love an unseen God and an unseen Christ (1 Peter 1:8), but not an unknown God. If they in your family know not Christ, how shall they believe on Him? And yet they must perish and be damned, if they do not. They must for ever lose God and Christ and heaven and their souls, if they do not repent, believe, and be converted. And yet when that Book is read by which they should understand the nature of true saving grace, is not prayer needful? Especially when many have the Bible and read it, yet do not understand the things that do concern their peace!

4. Consider further, the blindness of their minds and their inability, without the teachings of God's Spirit, to know and understand these things. And yet is not prayer needful?

5. Consider, yet further, the backwardness of their hearts to hearken to these weighty, necessary truths of God, and their unwillingness naturally to learn, show prayer to be necessary that God would make them able and willing to receive them.

6. Once more, consider that prayer is a special means to obtain knowledge from God, and a blessing upon the teachings and instructions of the master of the family. David prayed that God would *"open thou mine eyes,"* that he might *"behold wondrous things out of thy law"* (Ps. 119:18). There are "wondrous things" in the Word of God. That fallen man should be recovered is a wondrous thing. That a holy God should be reconciled to sinful man is

---

as a vanquished foe under the feet of Christ. Brethren, what an appropriate, delightful, and necessary spectacle is this!"—Cyprian (200-258).

a wondrous thing. That the Son of God should take upon Him the nature of man, and God be manifested in the flesh, and a believer justified by the righteousness of another—these are wondrous things. But there is darkness upon our minds and a veil over our eyes, and the Scripture is a clasped, closed book that we cannot savingly understand these great wonderful things, to have our love chiefly upon them and our delight in them, except the Spirit of God take away the veil and remove our ignorance and enlighten our minds. And this wisdom is to be sought from God by fervent prayer. You that are masters of families, would you have your children and servants know these things and be affected with them? Would you have impressions made upon their minds and hearts of the great concernments of their souls? And therefore you do instruct them? But can *you* reach their hearts? Can *you* awaken their consciences? Can you not? And yet doth it not become you to pray to God with them, that He would do it? While you are a-praying jointly with them, God may be secretly disposing and powerfully preparing their hearts to receive His Word and your instructions from it.

From "How May the Duty of Family Prayer Be Best Managed for the Spiritual Benefit of Every One in the Family?" *Puritan Sermons 1659-1689, Being the Morning Exercises at Cripplegate,* Vol 2, Richard Owen Roberts, Publisher.

Thomas Doolittle (1632-1707): English Nonconformist minister; born at Kidderminster, Worcestershire, England.

Seven Reasons Families Should Pray
THOMAS DOOLITTLE (C.1632-1707)

Reason 1

Because we receive every day family-mercies from the hand of God. He loads us daily with His benefits (Ps. 68:19). When you wake in the morning and find your dwelling safe, not consumed with fire, not broken through by thieves, is not this a family-mercy? When you wake and find none dead in their beds, that news is not brought you in the morning, there is one child dead in one bed and another in another, and there is not a lodging-room in the house but the last night one or other died in it; but on the contrary you find all well in the morning and refreshed by the rest and sleep of the night—are not these and many more such mercies to the family, that when you rise you should call them all together jointly to bless God for? If it had been otherwise, [if] master or mistress [were] dead, children or servants dead, would not the rest say, "It would have been a mercy to us all, if God had spared him, her, or them?" If your house had been consumed by flames, and God had turned you all out of doors before morning, would you not have said, "It would have been a mercy, if God had safely preserved us and our dwellings and caused us to rest and sleep and rise in safety?" Why, Sirs, will you not acknowledge mercies to be mercies, till God hath taken them away from you? And if you do, should you not give the praise daily unto God? Was it not God Himself that watched over you while you did sleep, and could not, did not, watch yourselves? *Except the LORD keep the city, the watchman waketh but in vain…for so he giveth his beloved sleep* (Ps. 127:1-2).

And as you have had many family-mercies in the night to bless God for in the morning, so you have many family-mercies in the day to give thanks to God for at night before you go to bed. Methinks you should not quietly sleep till you have been together on your knees, lest God should say, "This family that hath not acknowledged My mercy to them this day, nor given Me the glory of those benefits of which to them I gave the comfort, shall never see the light of another day, nor have the mercies of one day more to bless Me for. What if God should say unto you when you are laid down in your beds, "This night your souls shall be required of you, you that went to bed before you had given Me the praise of the mercies that I had given unto you all the day, and before you had prayed for My protection over you in the night." Take heed: though God be patient, do not provoke Him.

Reason 2

You should pray to God daily in your families, because there are sins committed every day in your families. Do you indeed sin together, and will you not pray together? What, if you should be damned all together? Doth not every member of your family commit many sins every day? How great is the number then of all, when considered or put together? What! So many sins every day under your roof, within your walls, committed against the glorious, blessed God, and not one prayer? One sin should be lamented with a thousand tears; but you have not one tear shed by one, and another by another, in prayer together, for a thousand sins. Is this to repent daily, when you do not confess them daily? Would you have God to pardon all the sins of your family? Say, would you or no? If you would not, God might justly let you go to your graves and hell too, with the guilt of sin upon your souls. If you would, is not pardon worth asking for? Would you have it and not beg it at the hands of God? Would not all judge that man worthy of death, that being justly condemned, might yet have life for asking for and will not? How do you, how *can* you quietly go to your beds and sleep with the guilt of so many sins upon your souls and have not prayed to have them blotted out? What is your pillow made of, that your heads can rest upon it under the weight and load of so much guilt? Is indeed your bed so soft or your heart so hard, that you can rest and sleep, when to all the sins of commission in the day, you add this sin of omission in the evening? Lay to heart your daily family-sins, and you will feel a reason why you should pray to God in your families daily.

Reason 3

You should pray in your families daily unto God, because you have many daily family-wants, which none can supply but God. God[needs] not your prayers, but you and yours [need] God's mercies! And if you will have them, should you not pray for them? Can you supply your families' wants? If they want health, can you give it them? If they want bread, can you give it them except God first give it unto you? Why then did Christ direct us to pray, "Give us this day our daily bread" (Matt. 6:11). If they want grace, can you work it in them? Or do you not care though they die without it? Is not God the Giver of every good gift? *"Every good gift and every perfect gift is from above, and cometh down from the Father of lights"* (James 1:17).

Mercies are above and good things are from above, and prayer is a means appointed by God to fetch them down. *"If any of you lack wisdom, let him ask of God"* (James 1:5). Do you think you do not want wisdom to discharge your duties to God and man, that you do not want wisdom to manage your family for their temporal, spiritual, and eternal good? If you think so, you are fools. And if you think you want it not, by those very thoughts you may discern your [lack] of it. If you think you have enough, it is plain that you have none. And should you not ask it of God, if you would have it? If you and yours want health in your family, should you not ask it of God? Can you live without dependence upon God? Or can you say you have no need of God's help to supply your wants? Then you speak contradictions: for to be under wants and not to be dependent beings is a contradiction. To think you do not live in dependence upon God is to think you are not men nor creatures. And if you do depend on Him and want His help to supply your [needs], your own indigency[64] should bring you upon your knees to pray to Him.

Reason 4

You should pray in your families daily because of your families' daily employments and labors. Every one that puts his hand to work, his head to contrive, should set his heart to pray. For will not your trading be in vain and your laboring and working, your carking and projecting[65] for the world, be to no purpose without the blessing of God? Will you be convinced if God Himself doth tell you? Then read Psalm 127:1-2: *"Except the LORD build the house, they labour in vain that build it…It is vain for you to rise up early, to sit up late, to eat the bread of sorrows."* Bread of sorrows! What bread is that? Bread gotten with much care, and labor, and toil, is "bread of sorrows." Without God, you labor to get bread for yourselves and families in vain. You might miss of it after all your labors. And without God's blessing, if you eat it when you have got it with much toil and care, you eat it in vain; for without Him it cannot nourish your bodies.

And yet is it not necessary to pray to God to prosper and succeed you in your callings? Prayer and labor should both promote what you aim at. To pray and not to do the works of your callings would be to expect supplies while you are negligent. To labor and trade and not to pray, would be to hope for increase and provision without God. Religion that puts you upon holy duties doth not teach you to neglect your callings, nor yet to trust to your own endeavors without praying unto God. But both are to keep their place and have a share of your time.[66] Prayer is a middle thing betwixt God's

---

64 **indigency** – poverty.
65 **carking and projecting** – anxious toil and planning.
66 **Desiderius Erasmus** (c.1466-1536) – "We must not confide so much in our own industry as to neglect the Divine aid; nor, on the contrary, ought we so to depend upon that gracious aid as to remit our exertions, and to neglect our duty."

giving and our getting. How can you receive, if God does not give? And why do you expect that God will give, if you do not ask? *"Ye have not, because ye ask not"* (James 4:2).

What ye work for, pray for. And what ye pray for, work and labor for. And this is the true conjunction of labor and prayer. Or will you be like to them [whom] the apostle speaks to? "Go to now, ye that say, To day or to morrow we will go into such a city, and continue there a year, and buy and sell, and get gain" (James 4:13). You *will*? But will you not ask leave from God whether you shall or no? You will go? What! Though God cast you upon a bed of sickness or into your graves? Do, if you can. You will continue there a year? What! If death drag you out as soon as you come there? If death fetch your bodies to the dust and grave and devils fetch your souls to hell, after this will you "continue in such a city for a year?" If one part of you be in the grave and the other part in hell, what is left of you to continue in the city? You will buy and sell, will you? What if God give you neither money nor credit? With whom, I wonder? And you *will* get gain? You are resolved upon it; you will thrive, and prosper, and grow rich. What if God curse your endeavors and say, "You shall not?" You will all this, and you would have your will; but your power is not equal to your will. Here is much will, but not a word of prayer. You should not go unto your work nor to your shops and callings, till you have first prayed unto God.

Reason 5

You should pray to God in your families daily, because you are all every day liable to temptations. As soon as you wake, the devil will be striving for your first thoughts. And when you are risen, he will be urgent with you to do him the first service and attend you all the day to draw you into some heinous[67] sin before night. And is the devil a subtle, watchful, powerful enemy and unwearied? And do you not all need to get together in the morning that Satan might not prevail against any of you before night, till you come to God together again? How many temptations might you meet with in your callings and your company, which without God you will not be able to resist! And how might you fall and dishonor God, discredit your profession, defile your souls, disturb your peace, and wound your consciences! This Origen[68] bewailed in his lamentation. For, that day [in which] he omitted prayer, he heinously sinned: "But I, O unhappy creature! Skipping out of my bed at

---

67 **heinous** – grossly wicked; abominable.
68 **Origen** (c.185-c.254) – theologian and Biblical scholar of the early Greek Church.

the dawning of the day, could not finish my wonted[69] devotion, neither accomplish my usual prayer; [but] folded and wrapped myself in the snares of the devil."[70]

Reason 6

You should pray in your families daily because all in your families are liable to daily hazards, casualties, and afflictions. And prayer might prevent them, or obtain strength to bear them, and prepare you for them. Do you know what affliction might befall your family in a day's time or in a night's time, either in regard of sickness, death, or outward losses in your estate? Might not you hear of one man's breaking in your debt and gone away with so much, and another gone away with so much? And are you indeed so weaned from the world, that this shall not put you into a passion and cause you to sin against God, or that you can bear it without murmuring and discontent, that you need not pray for a composed frame of heart, if such things befall you? Do you know if you go abroad yourself or send a son or servant that you or they may return alive again? Though you go out alive, you may be brought back again dead. Had you not then need to pray to God in the morning, that He would keep you in your goings-forth and comings-in and bless Him together in the evening, if He do? How many evils is man exposed to, whether he be at home or abroad! Anacreon[71] lost his life by the kernel of a raisin going wrong down his throat. Fabius,[72] a senator of Rome, in a draught of milk swallowing a small hair, was strangled. Do not your daily sins cry aloud for daily punishments? And should you not in daily prayer cry as loud that God in mercy would prevent them? Or if they come upon you, to sanctify them for your good or remove them? Or, if they remain, to support you under them? Know indeed that you are nowhere safe without God's protection, night or day. If your houses were built upon foundations of stone, and the walls were made of brass or adamant, and the doors of iron, yet you would be no longer safe than [so long as] God protects you from all dangers. Pray, then.

---

69 **wonted** – accustomed; habitual.
70 **Eusebius of Caesarea** (c.260-c.339) – theologian, church historian, and scholar; quote is from his *Ecclesiastical History*.
71 **Anacreon** (c.587-c.485 BC) – ancient Greek poet born in Teos, Asia Minor.
72 **Quintus Fabius Pictor** (fl 200 BC) – one of the first Roman prose historians and member of the Roman Senate.

Reason 7

You must pray to God in your families daily, or the very Heathen will rise up against you Christians and condemn you. Those that never had the means of grace (as you have had), nor a Bible to direct and teach them (as you have), nor ministers sent to them (as you have had in abundance), do shame many that are called "Christians" and go for great professors too. When I have read the sayings of some Heathens, showing what they were wont to do, and consider and know the practice and negligence of many Christians in their families, I have been ready to conclude the Heathen to be the better men. It was their manner to sacrifice to their gods morning and evening, that they might have the favor of them and be successful in their outward estates as you may learn from their poets.

Do not the Heathen shame many of you? They were wont to say, "Now we have sacrificed, let us go to bed." You say, "Now we have supped, let us go to bed," or, "Let us play a game or two at cards and go to bed." Are you men or swine in the shape of men? Mr. Perkins[73] likened such to swine that live without prayer in their families, "Which are always feeding upon the mast[74] with greediness, but never look up to the hand that beats it down, nor to the tree from 'whence it falleth."

From "How May the Duty of Family Prayer Be Best Managed for the Spiritual Benefit of Every One in the Family?" *Puritan Sermons 1659-1689, Being the Morning Exercises at Cripplegate,* Vol 2, Richard Owen Roberts, Publisher.

Thomas Doolittle (1632-1707): English Nonconformist minister; born at Kidderminster, Worcestershire, England.

---

73 **William Perkins** (1558-1602) – Puritan preacher and theologian educated at Cambridge and sometimes called the "Father of Puritanism."
74 **mast** – nuts of forest trees accumulated on the ground, used especially as food for swine.

The Father and Family Worship

J.W. ALEXANDER (1804-1859)

There is no member of a household whose individual piety is of such importance to all the rest as the father or head. And there is no one whose soul is so directly influenced by the exercise of domestic worship. Where the head of a family is lukewarm or worldly, he will send the chill through the whole house. And if any happy exception occur, and one and another surpass him in faithfulness, it will be in spite of his evil example. He, who ought by his instructions and life, to afford a perpetual incitement[75] to his inferiors and his juniors, is made to feel in case of such delinquency, that they must look elsewhere for guidance, even if they do not weep in secret places over his neglects. Where the head of the family is a man of faith, of affection, and of zeal, consecrating all his works and life to Christ, it is very rare to find all his household otherwise-minded. Now one of the chief means of promoting such individual graces in the head is this: his daily exercise of devotion with the members. It is more to him, than to others. It is he who presides and directs in it, who selects and delivers the precious Word, and who leads the common supplication, confession, and praise. To him, it is equal to an additional act of personal devotion in the day; but it is more. It is an act of devotion, in which his affection and duty to his house are particularly brought before his mind; and in which he stands in the place and pleads the cause, of all that he holds dearest upon earth. No one need wonder then, that we place family-prayer among the most important means of reviving and maintaining the piety of him who conducts it.

Observation shows that families which have no household worship are at a low ebb in spiritual things; that families where it is performed in a cold, sluggish, negligent, or hurried way, are little affected by it and little affected by any means of grace; and that families where God is worshipped, every morning and evening, by all the inmates of the house in a solemn and affectionate service are blessed with increase of piety and happiness. Every individual is blessed. Each one receives a portion of the heavenly food.

Half the defects and transgressions of our days arise from want[76] of consideration.[77] Hence the unspeakable value of an exercise, which twice every day calls each member of the household at least to think of God.

---

75 **incitement** – stirring up of feelings.
76 **want** – lack; absence of.
77 **consideration** – mature thought; serious deliberation.

Even the most careless or impious[78] son, or servant, must now and then be forced to talk a little with conscience, and meditate a little on judgment, when the grey-haired father, bowed before God, with trembling voice pours out strong supplication and prayer. How much more mighty must be the influence on that larger number, who in ten thousand Christian families in the land are more or less impressed with the importance of divine things! And how peculiar and tender and forming must the same influence be, on those of the domestic group, who worship God in the spirit, and who often wipe the gushing tear, as they rise from their knees, and look around on husband, father, mother, brother, sister, child—all remembered in the same devotion, all clouded with the same incense of intercession!

Perhaps among our readers, more than one can say: "Times without number have I felt the influence of domestic worship on my own soul. When yet a child, no one means of grace, public or private, so awakened my attention, as when the children were prayed for day by day. In wayward youth, I was never so stung by conviction of my sin, as when my honored father earnestly besought God for our salvation. When at length in infinite mercy I first began to open the ear to instruction, no prayer so reached my heart, or so expressed my deep affections, as those which were uttered by my honored father."

The maintenance of domestic religion in every house is primarily entrusted to the head of the family, whoever this may be. If he is totally unfitted for the charge by an unbelieving mind or an ungodly life, the consideration is one which should startle and appall him; and it is affectionately submitted to any reader whose conscience may plead guilty to such an imputation. There are instances, where divine grace has so endowed some one of the household, even though not the parent or the senior, as plainly to devolve[79] on him the performance of this duty. The widowed mother, or the elder sister, or the actual guardian, may stand in the parent's place. But inasmuch as in a majority of cases, the service if rendered at all must be rendered by the father, we shall treat the subject under this supposition, premising that the principles laid down apply in most of their extent to all the other influences.

No man can approach the duty of leading his household in an act of devotion without solemn reflection on the place which he occupies in regard to them. He is their head. He is such by a divine and unalterable constitution. These are duties and prerogatives which he cannot alienate. There is

---

78 **impious** – not showing due respect for God; ungodly.
79 **devolve** – pass on or delegate to another.

something more than mere precedence in age, knowledge, or substance. He is the father and the master. No act of his and nothing in his character can fail to leave a mark on those around him. This he will be apt to feel when he calls them about him to pray to God. And the more devoutly he addresses himself to the work, the more will he feel it. Though all priesthood, in the proper sense, is now done away on earth and absorbed in the functions of the great High Priest, there is still something like a priestly intervention in the service of the Christian patriarch. He is now about to go before the little flock in the oblation of a spiritual sacrifice of prayer and adoration. Thus it is said respecting Christ: *"By him therefore let us offer the sacrifice of praise to God continually, that is, the fruit of our lips giving thanks to his name"* (Heb. 13:15). This perpetual offering, the head of the family is about to make. Until long perseverance in a deadening formality of routine shall have blunted all sensibility, he must yield to the solemn impression. It will sometimes lie like a burden at his heart; it will sometimes swell within his affections, like *"wine which hath no vent"* (Job 32:19). These are salutary and elevating emotions, which go to form the grave and lofty character which may be observed in the old peasantry of Scotland.

Though he be but a poor and unlettered man, who bows his hoary head amidst a band of sons and daughters, yet is he more sublimely honored than prayerless kings. His head is encircled with that *"crown of glory,"* which is found *"in the way of righteousness"* (Prov. 16:31). The father, who year after year presides in the sacred domestic assembly, submits himself to an influence which is incalculably strong on his own parental character.

Where is a parent so likely to admit the impression of his responsibility, as where he gathers his household for worship? It is true at all times that he is bound to watch for their souls; but now he is placed where he must feel it to be true. His family are met in a religious capacity and looking up to him for guidance. His eye cannot light on a single member of the group who is not committed to his especial charge. *Among all these there is not one for whom he shall not give account at the judgment-seat of Christ.* The wife of his youth! To whom shall she look for spiritual watch, if not to him? And how unnatural the family-relation, when this guardianship is repudiated and this relation reversed! The children! If ever saved, it will probably be in some degree consequent on his exertions. Domestics, and apprentices, and sojourners, are all committed for a term longer or shorter to his care. The domestic minister will surely cry, "Who is sufficient for these things?" and most of all when in the very performance of these duties. If his conscience is kept awake by personal acquaintance with God, he will never enter upon family-worship without sentiments which involve this very accountability; and such sentiments cannot but have their impression on the parental character.

Unspeakable good would ensue, if every father could feel himself to be the earthly but divinely-appointed head-spring of religious influence to his household. Is it not true? And is there any means of making him feel it to be true, which can be compared to the institution of Family-Worship? Now he has assumed his rightful place as an instructor, a guide, and an exemplar[80] in devotion. Now his mouth, even though he be a silent or a bashful man, is opened.

The hour of domestic prayer and praise is also the hour of Scriptural instruction. The father has opened God's word in the presence of his little flock. He thus admits himself to be its teacher and under-shepherd. Perhaps he is but a plain man, living by his labor, unused to schools or libraries, and like Moses, "slow of speech, and of a slow tongue" (Ex. 4:10). Nevertheless, he stands by the open well of wisdom, and like the same Moses, may draw water enough and water the flock (Ex. 2:19). For the time, he sits "in Moses' seat," and no longer "occupieth the room of the unlearned" (1 Cor. 14:16). This is encouraging and ennobling.[81] As the loving mother rejoices to be the fountain of nourishment to the babe which clings to her warm bosom, so the Christian father delights to convey, even by reverent reading, *"the sincere milk of the word"* (1 Peter 2:2). He has found it good to his own soul; he rejoices in an appointed means of conveying it to his offspring. The humblest master of a house may well feel himself exalted by recognizing such a relation to those who are under his care.

The example of a father is acknowledged to be all-important. The stream must not be expected to rise higher than the fountain. The Christian householder will feel himself constrained to say, "I am leading my family in solemn addresses to God—what manner of man should I be! How wise, holy, and exemplary!" This undoubtedly has been in cases innumerable, the direct operation of Family-Worship on the father. As we know that worldly men and inconsistent professors are deterred from performing this duty by the consciousness of a discrepancy between their life and any acts of devotion, so humble Christians are led by the same comparison to be more circumspect and to order their ways in such a manner as may edify their dependents. *There cannot be too many motives to a holy life, nor too many safeguards to parental example.* Establish the worship of God in any house, and

---

80 **exemplar** – one that is worthy of imitation.
81 **ennobling** – to make someone more noble or dignified.

you erect around it a new barrier against the irruption[82] of the world, the flesh, and the devil.

The master of the house in Family-Worship appears as the intercessor for his house-hold. The great Intercessor is indeed above, but *"supplications, prayers, intercessions, and giving of thanks"* (1 Tim. 2:1) are to be made below; and by whom, if not by the father for his family? The thought of this must bring solemn reflections. The parent, who with any sincerity, comes daily to implore blessings on his wife, children, and domestics, will bethink[83] himself as to what they need. Here will be an urgent motive to inquire into their wants, temptations, weaknesses, errors, and transgressions. The eye of a genuine father will be quick; his heart will be sensitive on these points; and the hour of devotion will gather these solicitudes together. From such a motive, as we have already seen, holy Job, after the festivities of his children, "sent and sanctified them, and rose up early in the morning, and offered burnt offerings, according to the number of them all: for Job said, It may be that my sons have sinned, and cursed God in their hearts. Thus did Job continually" (Job 1:5). Whatever may have been the effect on the sons, the effect on Job himself was, no doubt, an awakening of mind as to his parental responsibility. And such is the effect of Family-Worship on the head of a household.

The father of a family is under a wholesome influence, when he is brought every day to take a post of observation, and say to his own heart, "By this single means, in addition to all others, I am exerting some definite influence, good or bad, upon all who surround me. I cannot omit this service needlessly; perhaps I cannot omit it at all without detriment to my house. I cannot read the Word, I cannot sing, I cannot pray, without leaving some trace on the tender mind. How solemnly, how affectionately, how believingly, should I then approach this ordinance! With how much godly fear and preparation! My conduct in this worship may save or may kill. Here is my great channel for reaching the case of those who are submitted to my charge." These are wholesome thoughts, naturally engendered by a daily ordinance which too many regard as little better than a form.

The Christian husband needs to be reminded of his obligations; he cannot be reminded of them too often. The respect, the forbearance, the love, which the Scriptures enjoin towards the feebler and more dependent party in the conjugal[84] alliance, and which are the crown and glory of

---

82 **irruption** – breaking or bursting in.
83 **bethink** – cause oneself to reflect or consider.
84 **conjugal** – marital.

Christian wedlock, are never more brought into action, than when they who have plighted[85] their faith to one another years ago are brought day by day to the place of prayer and lift up a united heart at the feet of infinite mercy. As the Head of every man is Christ, so the head of the woman is the man (1 Cor. 11:3). His post is responsible, and that in spirituals. He can seldom feel it more sensibly than when he falls down with the partner of his burdens at the throne of grace.

From *Thoughts on Family Worship*, reprinted by Soli Deo Gloria.

J.W. Alexander (1804-1859): Eldest son of Archibald Alexander, the first professor of Princeton Theological Seminary. Attended both Princeton College and Princeton Seminary, later teaching at both institutions. His first love, however, was the pastorate, and he labored in churches in Virginia, New Jersey, and New York until his death in 1859.

---

85 **plighted** – pledged; betrothed.

Women Leading Family Worship

JOHN HOWE (1630-1705)

QUESTION: Some have desired to be informed, "Whether in case of the absence or sickness of a husband from or in the family, it be incumbent on the wife to keep up family duty in such a case?" And the case is the same as to widows, or others of that sex, who are sole governesses of families.

ANSWER: it must be said in general to this, that one rule cannot be suited to all cases. There may be very great variety as circumstances differ. But,

1. Nothing is plainer than that while the conjugal relatives remain, the female relation hath a real part in the government of the family. That is plainly enough asserted in 1 Timothy 5:14: that it is the woman's part to "guide the house." The word is *oikodespotein*, to have a despotical[86] power in the family, a governing power, which must be solely in her in the absence or failure of the other relative; and that must by no means be abandoned or quitted. And whereas all power and all order is from God, it cannot be denied or disowned or laid aside without an injury to Him.

2. Hereupon, if there be in a family a prudent pious son or a prudent pious man-servant, who may be assigned to this work, it may fitly enough be done by such a one by her appointment. And so the authority that belongs to her in her station is preserved and the thing done. That such a work as that is may be assigned to another, is out of all doubt and ought to be so, where it may most fitly and most duly be so. And none question the fitness of assigning such a work statedly to another, in such families where persons are kept on purpose for the discharge of family duties.

3. It is possible, there may be families that do entirely at present consist of those that are of the female sex; and concerning them there is no question.

4. Where the family is more numerous, and consists of the male sex, of whom none are fit or willing to undertake that business, and it cannot be done by the governess with decency or to edification; in that case she is to follow the example of Esther, (a very laudable one,) with her maidens and younger children still to keep up to this worship in her family; and, as much as in her lies, to warn and charge the rest, that they be not omissive for their part, (though they do not concur with them,) together or severally in calling on the name of the Lord daily.

---

86 **despotical** – literally from the Greek, "to command and give leadership to a household, to manage a home."

From Family Religion and Worship, Sermon 5.

John Howe (1630-1705): Non-Conformist Puritan author and preacher; chaplain to Oliver Cromwell; born in Loughborough, England.

Memories of Family Worship

JOHN G. PATON (1824-1907)

The "closet" was a very small apartment betwixt the other two, having room only for a bed, a little table, and a chair, with a diminutive window shedding diminutive light on the scene. This was the Sanctuary of that cottage home. Thither daily, and oftentimes a day, generally after each meal, we saw our father retire and "shut to the door"; and we children got to understand by a sort of spiritual instinct (for the thing was too sacred to be talked about) that prayers were being poured out there for us, as of old by the High Priest within the veil in the Most Holy Place. We occasionally heard the pathetic echoes of a trembling voice pleading as if for life, and we learned to slip out and in past that door on tiptoe, not to disturb the holy colloquy.[87] The outside world might not know, but we knew, whence came that happy light as of a new-born smile that always was dawning on my father's face: it was a reflection from the Divine Presence, in the consciousness of which he lived. Never, in temple or cathedral, on mountain or in glen, can I hope to feel that the Lord God is more near, more visibly walking and talking with men, than under that humble cottage roof of thatch and oaken wattles.[88] Though everything else in religion were by some unthinkable catastrophe to be swept out of memory, or blotted from my understanding, my soul would wander back to those early scenes and shut itself up once again in that Sanctuary Closet, and hearing still the echoes of those cries to God, would hurl back all doubt with the victorious appeal, "He walked with God, why may not I?"…

Besides his independent choice of a Church for himself, there was one other mark and fruit of his early religious decision, which looks ever fairer through all these years. Family Worship had heretofore been held only on Sabbath Day in his father's house; but the young Christian, entering into conference with his sympathizing mother, managed to get the household persuaded that there ought to be daily morning and evening prayer and reading of the Bible and holy singing. This the more readily, as he himself agreed to take part regularly in the same and so relieve the old warrior of what might have proved for him too arduous spiritual toils. And so began in his seventeenth year that blessed custom of Family Prayer, morning and evening, which my father practiced probably without one single omission till he lay on his deathbed, seventy-seven years of age; when even to the

---

87 **colloquy** – conversation, especially a formal one.
88 **wattle** – construction of poles intertwined with twigs, reeds, or branches, used for walls, fences, and roofs.

last day of his life, a portion of Scripture was read, and his voice was heard softly joining in the Psalm, and his lips breathed the morning and evening Prayer,—falling in sweet benediction on the heads of all his children, far away many of them over all the earth, but all meeting him there at the Throne of Grace. None of us can remember that any day ever passed unhallowed thus; no hurry for market, no rush to business, no arrival of friends or guests, no trouble or sorrow, no joy or excitement, ever prevented at least our kneeling around the family altar, while the High Priest led our prayers to God, and offered himself and his children there. And blessed to others, as well as to ourselves, was the light of such example! I have that, in long after years, the worst woman in the village of Torthorwald, then leading an immoral life, but since changed by the grace of God, was known to declare, that the only thing that kept her from despair and from the hell of the suicide, was when in the dark winter nights she crept close up underneath my father's window, and heard him pleading in family worship that God would convert "the sinner from the error of wicked ways and polish him as a jewel for the Redeemer's crown." "I felt," said she, "that I was a burden on that good man's heart, and I knew that God would not disappoint *him*. That thought kept me out of Hell, and at last led me to the only Savior."

My father had a strong desire to be a minister of the Gospel; but when he finally saw that God's will had marked out for him another lot, he reconciled himself by entering with his own soul in this solemn vow,—that if God gave him sons, he would consecrate them unreservedly to the ministry of Christ, if the Lord saw fit to accept the offering, and open up their way. It may be enough here to say that he lived to see three of us entering upon and not unblessed in the Holy Office;—myself, the eldest born; my brother Walter, several years my junior; and my brother James, the youngest of eleven, the Benjamin of the flock...

Each of us, from very early days, considered it no penalty, but a great joy, to go with our father to the church; the four miles were a treat to our young spirits, the company by the way was a fresh incitement, and occasionally some of the wonders of city-life rewarded our eager eyes. A few other pious men and women of the best evangelical type, went from the same parish to one or other favorite minister at Dumfries,—the parish church during all those years being rather miserably served; and when these God-fearing peasants "foregathered" in the way to or from the House of God, we youngsters had sometimes rare glimpses of what Christian talk may be and ought to be. They went to the church, full of beautiful expectancy of spirit—their souls were on the outlook for God; they returned from the church, ready and even anxious to exchange ideas as to what they had heard and received of the things of life. I have to bear my testimony that religion was presented to us with a great deal of intellectual freshness, and that it did not repel us but kindled our spiritual interest. The talks which we heard were, however, genuine; not the make-believe of religious conversation, but the sincere outcome of their own personalities. That, perhaps, makes all the difference betwixt talk that attracts and talk that drives away.

We had, too, special Bible Readings on the Lord's Day evening,—mother and children and visitors reading in turns, with fresh and interesting question, answer, and exposition, all tending to impress us with the infinite grace of a God of love and mercy in the great gift of His dear Son Jesus, our Savior. The Shorter Catechism was gone through regularly, each answering the question asked, till the whole had been explained, and its foundation in Scripture shown by the proof-texts adduced. It has been an amazing thing to me, occasionally to meet with men who blamed this "catechizing" for giving them a distaste to religion; every one in all our circle thinks and feels exactly the opposite. It laid the solid rock-foundations of our religious life. After-years have given to these questions and their answers a deeper or a modified meaning, but none of us have ever once even dreamed of wishing that we had been otherwise trained. Of course, if the parents are not devout, sincere, and affectionate,—if the whole affair on both sides is taskwork, or worse, hypocritical and false,—results must be very different indeed!

Oh, I can remember those happy Sabbath evenings: no blinds drawn and shutters up, to keep out the sun from us, as some scandalously affirm; but a holy, happy, entirely human day, for a Christian father, mother, and children to spend. How my father would parade across and across our flag-floor,[89] telling over the substance of the day's sermons to our dear mother, who, because of the great distance and because of her many living "encumbrances" got very seldom indeed to the church, but gladly embraced every chance, when there was prospect or promise of a "lift" either way from some friendly gig![90] How he would entice us to help him to recall some idea or other, rewarding us when we got the length of "taking notes" and reading them over on our return; how he would turn the talk ever so naturally to some Bible story or some martyr reminiscence, or some happy allusion to the "Pilgrim's Progress"! And then it was quite a contest, which of us would get reading aloud, while all the rest listened, and father added here and there a happy thought, or illustration, or anecdote. Others must write and say what they

---

89 **flag-floor** – stone floor.
90 **gig** – a light carriage with one set of wheels drawn by one horse.

will, and as they feel; but so must I. There were eleven of us brought up in a home like that; and never one of the eleven, boy or girl, man or woman, has been heard, or ever will be heard, saying that Sabbath was dull or wearisome for us, or suggesting that we have heard of or seen any way more likely than that for making the Day of the Lord bright and blessed alike for parents and for children. But God help the homes where these things are done by force and not by love!

John G. Paton and James Paton, *John G. Paton: Missionary to the New Hebrides* (New York: Fleming H. Revell Company, 1898 and 1907), 11-25.

John G. Paton (1824-1907): Scottish Presbyterian missionary to the New Hebrides; began his work on the island of Tanna, which was inhabited by savage cannibals; later evangelized Aniwa; born in Braehead, Kirkmaho, Dumfriesshire, Scotland.

Implementing Family Worship

JOEL R. BEEKE

Here are some suggestions to help you establish God-honoring Family Worship in your homes. We trust this avoids two extremes: an idealistic approach that is beyond the reach of even the most God-fearing home, and a minimalist[91] approach that abandons daily Family Worship because the ideal seems so out of reach.

Prepare for Family Worship

Even before Family Worship begins, we should privately pray for God's blessing upon that worship. Then we should plan for the *what*, *where*, and *when* of Family Worship.

1. What

Generally speaking, this includes instruction in the Word of God, prayer before the throne of God, and singing to the glory of God. But we need to determine more of the specifics of Family Worship.

First, have Bibles and copies of *The Psalter*[92] and song sheets for all the children who can read. For children who are too young to read, read a few verses from Scripture and select one text to memorize as a family. Say it aloud together several times as a family, then reinforce that with a short Bible story to illustrate the text. Take time to teach a stanza or two of a Psalter selection to such children, and encourage them to sing with you.

For young children, try using *Truths of God's Word*, which has a guide for teachers and parents that illustrates each doctrine. For children in grade four and up, try James W. Beeke's *Bible Doctrine* series with accompanying teachers' guides. In any case; explain what you have read to your children, and ask them a question or two.

Then sing one or two psalms and a sound hymn or a good chorus like "Dare to be a Daniel." Close with prayer.

For older children, read a passage from Scripture, memorize it together, then apply a proverb. Ask questions about how to apply those verses to daily life, or perhaps read a portion from the gospels and its corresponding section in J.C. Ryle's *Expository Thoughts on the Gospels*. Ryle is simple yet profound. His clear points help generate discussion. Perhaps you'd like to read parts of an inspirational biography. However, don't let the reading of edifying

---

91 **minimalist** – one who provides the minimum amount.
92 *The Psalter* – book containing psalms, or the Book of Psalms, used for singing in worship.

literature replace Bible-reading or its application.

John Bunyan's *Pilgrim's Progress* or *Holy War*, or daily meditations by Charles Haddon Spurgeon [such as Morning and Evening or Faith's Checkbook] are appropriate for more spiritually-minded children. Older children will also benefit from William Jay's *Morning and Evening Exercises*, William Mason's *Spiritual Treasury*, and Robert Hawker's *Poor Man's Morning and Evening Portions*. After those readings, sing a few familiar psalms and perhaps learn a new one before closing with prayer.

You should also use the creeds and confessions of your church. Young children should be taught to say the Lord's Prayer. If you adhere to the Westminster standards, have your children memorize the *Shorter Catechism* over time. [If your church uses the *Second London Baptist Confession*,[93] you can use Spurgeon's or Keach's *Catechism*.[94]] If the *Heidelberg Catechism* is used in your congregation, read on Sabbath mornings the Lord's Day of the Catechism from which the minister will be preaching at church. If you have *The Psalter*, occasional use can be made of the Forms of Devotion found in Christian Prayers. Using these forms at home will afford opportunity for you and your children to learn to use such forms in an edifying and profitable manner, a skill which will stand you all in good stead when the liturgical[95] forms are used as part of public worship.

2. Where

Family worship may be held around the supper table. However, it might be better to move to the living room, where there are fewer distractions. Whatever room you select, make sure it contains all of your devotional materials. Before you start, take the phone off the hook, or plan to let your answering machine or voice mail take messages. Your children must understand that Family Worship is the most important activity of the day and should not be interrupted by anything.

---

93 This *Confession of Faith* is the doctrinal standard of many Baptist churches. First published in 1677 and adopted in1689, it is known by many simply as the "1689." This and Spurgeon's *Catechism* are both available from Chapel Library.

94 As foreign as it may sound to modern Baptists, historically Baptists faithfully used confessions and catechisms for training their families and worshiping in their homes.

95 **liturgical** – means "of or relating to liturgy," which comes from the Greek word *leitourgia*. *Liturgy* means public worship according to set forms and rites (such as read texts and prayers, i.e., the Church of England's *Book of Common Prayer*), often with reference to the Lord's Supper. This is in contrast to worship which does not follow a formal structure.

3. When

Ideally, Family Worship should be conducted twice a day, in the morning and in the evening. That fits best with Scriptural directions for worship in the Old Testament economy in which the beginning and close of each day were sanctified by the offering of morning and evening sacrifices as well as morning and evening prayers, and [in] the New Testament church which apparently followed the pattern of morning and evening prayers. The *Westminster Directory of Worship* states, "Family worship, which ought to be performed by every family, ordinarily morning and evening, consists in prayer, reading the Scriptures, and singing praises."

For some, Family Worship is scarcely possible more than once a day, after the evening meal. Either way, heads of households must be sensitive to the family schedule and keep everyone involved. Practice the principle of Matthew 6:33 ("But seek ye first the kingdom of God, and his righteousness") in establishing a family schedule.

Carefully guard this time of Family Worship. If you know ahead of time that the normal time will not be suitable on a certain day, reschedule worship time. Don't skip it, however; that can become habitual. When you can keep to your appointed times, plan carefully and prepare beforehand to make every minute count. Fight every enemy of Family Worship.

During Family Worship, Aim for the Following

1. Brevity

As Richard Cecil said, "Let Family Worship be short, savory, simple, tender, heavenly." Family worship that is too long makes children restless and may provoke them to wrath.

If you worship twice a day, try ten minutes in the morning and a little longer in the evening. A twenty-five minute period of Family Worship might be divided as follows: ten minutes for Scripture reading and instruction; five minutes for reading a daily portion or an edifying book or discussing some concern in a Biblical light; five minutes for singing; and five minutes for prayer.

2. Consistency

It is better to have twenty minutes of Family Worship every day than to try for extended periods on fewer days—say forty-five minutes on Monday, then skipping Tuesday. Family worship provides us "the manna which falls every day at the door of the tent, that our souls are kept alive," wrote J.W. Alexander in his excellent book on Family Worship.

Don't indulge excuses to avoid Family Worship: If you lost your temper at a child a half-hour before Family Worship time, don't say, "It's hypocritical for me to lead Family Worship, so we'll skip it tonight." You don't need to run from God at such times. Rather, you must return to God like the penitent[96] publican. Begin worship time by asking everyone who witnessed your loss of temper to forgive you, then pray to God for forgiveness. Children will respect you for that. They will tolerate weaknesses and even sins in their parents so long as the parents confess their wrongdoings and earnestly seek to follow the Lord. They and you know that the Old Testament high priest was not disqualified for being a sinner but had first to offer sacrifice for himself before he could offer sacrifices for the people's sins. Neither are you and I disqualified today for confessed sin, for our sufficiency lies in Christ, not in ourselves. As Arthur W. Pink said, "It is not the sins of a Christian, but his unconfessed sins, which choke the channel of blessing and cause so many to miss God's best."

Lead Family Worship with a firm, fatherly hand and a soft, penitent heart: Even when you're bone-weary after a day's work, pray for strength to carry out your fatherly duty. Remember that Christ Jesus went to the cross for you bone-weary and exhausted but never shrunk from His mission. As you deny yourself, you will see how He strengthens you during Family Worship, so that by the time you finish, your exhaustion is overcome.

3. Hopeful Solemnity

"Serve the LORD with fear, and rejoice with trembling," Psalm 2 tells us. We need to show this balance of hope and awe, fear and faith, repentance and confidence in Family Worship. Speak naturally yet reverently during this time, using the tone you would use when speaking to a deeply respected friend about a serious matter. Expect great things from a great covenant-keeping God.

Let's Get More Specific

1. For the Reading of Scripture

Have a plan: Read ten or twenty verses from the Old Testament in the morning and ten to twenty from the New Testament in the evening. Or read a series of parables, miracles, or biographical portions. Just be sure to read the entire Bible over a period of time. As J.C. Ryle said, "Fill their minds with Scripture. Let the Word dwell in them richly. Give them the Bible, the whole Bible, even while they are young."

---

96 **penitent** – repentant; remorseful; regretting one's sins.

Account for special occasions: On Sunday mornings, you might want to read Psalm 48, 63, 84, or John 20. On the Sabbath when the Lord's Supper is to be administered, read Psalm 22, Isaiah 53, Matthew 26, or part of John 6. Before you leave home for family vacations, gather your family in the living room and read Psalm 91 or Psalm 121.

Involve the family: Every family member who can read should have a Bible to follow along. Set the tone by reading Scripture with expression, as the living, "breathing" Book it is.

Assign various portions to be read by your wife and your children: Teach your children how to read articulately and with expression. Don't let them mumble or speed ahead. Teach them to read with reverence. Provide a brief word of explanation throughout the reading, according to the needs of the younger children.

Encourage private Bible reading and study: Be sure that you and your children close the day with the Word of God. You might follow Robert Murray M'Cheyne's *Calendar for Bible Readings*[97] so that your children read the Bible on their own once each year. Help each child build a personal library of Bible-based books.

2. For Biblical Instruction

Be plain in meaning: Ask your children if they understand what you are reading. Be plain in applying scriptural texts. The 1647 *Church of Scotland Directory* provides counsel here:

"The Holy Scriptures should be read ordinarily to the family; and it is commendable, that thereafter they confer, and by way of conference, make some good use of what hath been read and heard. As, for example, if any sin be reproved in the word read, use may be made thereof to make all the family circumspect[98] and watchful against the same; or if any judgment be threatened that portion of scripture which is read, use may be made to make all the family fear lest the same or a worse judgment befall them, unless they beware of the sin that procured it: and finally, if any duty be required, or comfort held forth in a promise, use may be made to stir up themselves to employ Christ for strength to enable them for doing the commanded duty, and to apply the offered comfort in all which the master of the family is to have the chief hand; and any member of the family may propose a question or doubt for resolution" (par. III).

---

97 Available from Chapel Library.
98 **circumspect** – cautious; careful to consider all circumstances and possible consequence.

Encourage family dialogue around God's Word in line with the Hebraic procedure of household question and answer (cf. Ex. 12; Deut. 6; Ps. 78). Especially encourage teenagers to ask questions: draw them out. If you don't know the answers, tell them so; and encourage them to search for answers. Have one or more good commentaries on hand, such as those by John Calvin, Matthew Poole, and Matthew Henry. Remember, if you don't provide answers for your children, they will get them elsewhere—and often those will be wrong answers.

Be pure in doctrine: Titus 2:7 says, "In all things shewing thyself a pattern of good works: in doctrine shewing uncorruptness, gravity, sincerity." Don't abandon doctrinal precision when teaching young children; aim for simplicity and soundness.

Be relevant in application: Don't be afraid to share your experiences when appropriate, but do that simply. Use concrete illustrations. Ideally, tie together Biblical instruction with what you recently heard in sermons.

Be affectionate in manner: Proverbs continually uses the phrase "my son," showing the warmth, love, and urgency in the teachings of a God-fearing father. When you must administer the wounds of a father-friend to your children, do that with heartfelt love. Tell them you must convey the whole counsel of God because you can't bear the thought of spending eternity apart from them. My father often said to us with tears: "Children, I cannot miss any of you in heaven." Tell your children: "We will allow you every privilege an open Bible will allow us to give you—but if we say no to you, you must know that flows out of our love." As Ryle said: "Love is one grand secret of successful training. Soul love is the soul of all love."

Require attention: Proverbs 4:1 says, "Hear, ye children, the instruction of a father, and attend to know understanding." Fathers and mothers have important truths to convey. You must demand a hearing for God's truths in your home. That may involve repeated statements at the beginning like these: "Sit up, son, and look at me when I'm talking. We're talking about God's Word, and God deserves to be heard." Don't allow children to leave their seats during Family Worship.

3. For Praying

Be short: With few exceptions, don't pray for more than five minutes. Tedious prayers do more harm than good.

Don't teach in your prayer; God doesn't need the instruction. Teach with your eyes open; pray with your eyes shut.

Be simple without being shallow: Pray for things that your children know something about, but don't allow your prayers to become trivial.

Don't reduce your prayers to self-centered, shallow petitions.

Be direct: Spread your needs before God, plead your case, and ask for mercy. Name your teenagers and children and their needs one by one on a daily basis. That holds tremendous weight with them.

Be natural yet solemn: Speak clearly and reverently. Don't use an unnatural, high-pitched voice or a monotone. Don't pray too loudly or softly, too fast or slow.

Be varied: Don't pray the same thing every day; that becomes monotonous. Develop more variety in prayer by remembering and stressing the various ingredients of true prayer, such as: Invocation,[99] adoration,[100] and dependence. Begin by mentioning one or two titles or attributes of God, such as, "Gracious and holy Lord . . ." To that add a declaration of your desire to worship God and your dependence upon Him for His assistance in prayer. For example, say: "We bow humbly in Thy presence. Thou who art worthy to be worshiped, praying that our souls may be lifted up to Thee. Assist us by Thy Spirit. Help us to call upon Thy Name by Jesus Christ, in whom alone we can approach to Thee."

Confession for family sins: Confess the depravity of our nature, then actual sins—especially daily sins and family sins. Recognize the punishment we deserve at the hands of a holy God, and ask God to forgive all your sins for Christ's sake.

Petition for family mercies: Ask God to deliver us from sin and evil. You might say, "O Lord, forgive our sins through Thy Son. Subdue our iniquities by thy Spirit. Deliver us from the natural darkness of our own minds and the corruption of our own hearts. Free us from the temptations to which we were exposed today."

Ask God for temporal and spiritual good. Pray for His provision for every need in daily life. Pray for spiritual blessings. Pray that your souls are prepared for eternity.

Remember family needs, and intercede for family friends. Remember to pray in all these petitions that God's will be done. But don't allow that subjection to God's will stop you from pleading with God. Plead with Him

---

99 **invocation** – calling upon God for help.

100 **adoration** – perhaps the highest kind of worship, involving reverent contemplation of God's perfections and acknowledging them in words of praise and postures of reverence, i.e., Rev 4:8, 10, 11: "...and they rest not day and night, saying, Holy, holy, holy, Lord God Almighty, which was, and is, and is to come...the four and twenty elders fall down before him that sat on the throne, and worship him that liveth for ever and ever, and cast their crowns before the throne, saying, Thou art worthy, O Lord, to receive glory and honour and power: for thou hast created all things, and for thy pleasure they are and were created."

to hear your petitions. Plead for everyone in your family as they travel to eternity. Plead for them on the basis of God's mercy, His covenant relation with you, and upon the sacrifice of Christ.

Thanksgiving as a family: Thank the Lord for food and drink, providential mercies, spiritual opportunities, answered prayers, returned health, and deliverance from evil. Confess, "It is of Thy mercies that we are not consumed as family." Remember Question 116 of the Heidelberg Catechism, which says, "God will give His grace and Holy Spirit to those only, who with sincere desires continually ask them of Him, and are thankful for them."

Bless God for who He is and for what He has done. Ask that His kingdom, power, and glory be forever displayed. Then conclude with "Amen," which means "certainly it shall be so."

Matthew Henry said that the morning Family Worship is especially a time of praise and of petition for strength for the day and for divine benediction on its activities. The evening worship should focus on thankfulness, penitent reflections, and humble supplications for the night.

4. For Singing

Sing doctrinally pure songs: There is no excuse for singing doctrinal error, no matter how attractive the tune might be. [Hence the need for doctrinally sound hymnals such as the *Trinity Hymnal*.]

Sing psalms first and foremost without neglecting sound hymns: Remember that the Psalms, called by Calvin "an anatomy of all parts of soul," are the richest gold mine of deep, living, experiential scriptural piety available to us still today.

Sing simple psalms, if you have young children: In choosing Psalms to sing, look for songs that children can easily master and songs of particular importance for them to know. Choose songs that express the spiritual needs of your children for repentance, faith, and renewal of heart and life; songs that reveal God's love for His people, and the love of Christ for the lambs of His flock. Words such as righteousness, goodness, and mercy should be pointed out and explained beforehand.

Sing heartily and with feeling: As Colossians 3:23 says, "And whatsoever ye do, do it heartily, as to the Lord, and not unto men." Meditate on the words you are singing. On occasion, discuss a phrase that is sung.

After Family Worship

As you retire for the night, pray for God's blessing on Family Worship: "Lord, use the instruction to save our children and to cause them to grow in grace that they might put their hope in Thee. Use our praise of Thy name in song to endear Thy name, Thy Son, and Thy Spirit to their never-dying souls. Use our stammering prayers to bring our children to repentance. Lord Jesus Christ, breathe upon our family during this time of worship with Thy Word and Spirit. Make these life-giving times."

Joel R. Beeke: President and Professor of Systematic Theology and Homiletics for Puritan Reformed Theological Seminary. Pastor of the Heritage Netherlands Reformed Congregation in Grand Rapids, MI; has written, co-authored, or edited forty books and has contributed about 1,500 articles to reformed books, journals, periodicals, and encyclopedias.

Heathens and Christians

JOHN G. PATON (1824-1907)

The following is an excerpt from *John G. Paton: Missionary to the New Hebrides*, edited by James Paton. This remarkable autobiography displays the wonders of God's saving grace. After years of laboring among the cannibals, God used Paton's digging of a well to break the grip of paganism and bring the cannibals to bow before our sovereign God. Having been stunned by the sight of water coming out of the ground in the well, the old chief Namakei later gave this testimony in Paton's mission church:

> "My people, the people of Aniwa,[101] the world is turned upside down since the word of Jehovah came to this land! Who ever expected to see rain coming up through the earth? It has always come from the clouds! Wonderful is the work of this Jehovah God. No god of Aniwa ever answered prayers as the Missi's[102] God has done. Friends of Namakei, all the powers of the world could not have forced us to believe that rain could be given from the depths of the earth, if we had not seen it with our eyes, felt it and tasted it as we here do. Now, by the help of Jehovah God the Missi brought that invisible rain to view, which we never before heard of or saw, and,"—(beating his hand on his breast, he exclaimed),—
>
> "Something here in my heart tells me that the Jehovah God does exist, the Invisible One, whom we never heard of nor saw till the Missi brought Him to our knowledge. The coral has been removed, the land has been cleared away, and lo! the water rises. Invisible till this day, yet all the same it was there, though our eyes were too weak. So I, your Chief, do now firmly believe that when I die, when the bits of coral and the heaps of dust are removed which now blind my old eyes, I shall then see the Invisible Jehovah God with my soul, as Missi tells me, not less surely than I have seen the rain from the earth below. From this day, my people, I must worship the God who has opened for us the well, and who fills us with rain from below. The gods of Aniwa cannot hear, cannot help us, like the God of Missi. Henceforth I am a follower of Jehovah God. Let every man that thinks with me go now and fetch the idols of Aniwa, the gods which our fathers feared, and cast them down at Missi's feet. Let us burn and bury and destroy these things of wood and stone, and let us be taught by the Missi how to serve the God who can hear, the Jehovah who gave us the well, and who will give us every other

---

101 **Aniwa** — (ah-NEE-wah) tiny island among the New Hebrides in the Pacific Ocean.
102 **Missi** — the tribal term for *missionary*.

blessing, for He sent His Son Jesus to die for us and bring us to Heaven. This is what the Missi has been telling us every day since he landed on Aniwa. We laughed at him, but now we believe him. The Jehovah God has sent us rain from the earth. Why should He not also send us His Son from Heaven? Namakei stands up for Jehovah!"

This address, and the Sinking of the Well, broke, as I already said, the back of Heathenism on Aniwa. That very afternoon, the old Chief and several of his people brought their idols and cast them down at my feet beside the door of our house. Oh, the intense excitement of the weeks that followed! Company after company came to the spot, loaded with their gods of wood and stone, and piled them up in heaps, amid the tears and sobs of some, and the shoutings of others, in which was heard the oft-repeated word, "Jehovah! Jehovah!" What could be burned, we cast into the flames; others we buried in pits twelve or fifteen feet deep; and some few, more likely than the rest to feed or awaken superstition, we sank far out into the deep sea. Let no Heathen eyes ever gaze on them again!

We do not mean to indicate that, in all cases, their motives were either high or enlightened. There were not wanting[103] some who wished to make this new movement pay, and were much disgusted when we refused to "buy" their gods! On being told that Jehovah would not be pleased unless they gave them up of their own free will, and destroyed them without pay or reward, some took them home again and held on by them for a season, and others threw them away in contempt. Meetings were held; speeches were delivered, for these New Hebrideans are irrepressible orators, florid,[104] and amazingly graphic; much talk followed, and the destruction of idols went on apace. By-and-bye two Sacred Men and some other selected persons were appointed a sort of detective Committee, to search out and expose those who pretended to give them all up, but were hiding certain idols in secret, and to encourage waverers to come to a thorough decision for Jehovah. In these intensely exciting days, we "stood still" and saw the salvation of the Lord.

They flocked around us now at every meeting we held. They listened eagerly to the story of the life and death of Jesus. They voluntarily assumed one or other article of clothing. And everything transpiring was fully and faithfully submitted to us for counsel or for information. One of the very first things of a Christian discipline to which they readily and almost unanimously

---

103   **wanting**—lacking.
104   **florid**—very ornate; flowery.

took was the asking of God's blessing on every meal and praising the great Jehovah for their daily bread. Whosoever did not do so was regarded as a Heathen. (Query:[105] how many *white* Heathens are there?) The next step, and it was taken in a manner as if by some common consent that was not less surprising than joyful, was a form of Family Worship every morning and evening. Doubtless the prayers were often very queer, and mixed up with many remaining superstitions; but they were prayers to the great Jehovah, the compassionate Father, the Invisible One—no longer to gods of stone!

Necessarily these were the conspicuous features of our life as Christians in their midst—morning and evening Family Prayer, and Grace at Meat;[106] and hence, most naturally, their instinctive adoption and imitation of the same as the first outward tokens of Christian discipline. Every house in which there was not Prayer to God in the family was known thereby to be Heathen. This was a direct and practical evidence of the New Religion; and, so far as it goes (and that is very far indeed, where there is any sincerity at all), the test was one about which there could be no mistake on either side.

John G. Paton and James Paton, *John G. Paton: Missionary to the New Hebrides* (New York: Fleming H. Revell Company, 1898 and 1907), 190-194.

John G. Paton (1824-1907): Scottish Presbyterian missionary to the New Hebrides; began his work on the island of Tanna, which was inhabited by savage cannibals; later evangelized Aniwa; born in Braehead, Kirkmaho, Dumfriesshire, Scotland.

> *I trust there are none here present who profess to be followers of Christ, who do not also practice prayer in their families. We may have no positive commandment for it, but we believe that it is so much in accord with the genius and spirit of the Gospel, and that it is so commended by the example of the saints, that the neglect thereof is a strange inconsistency. Now, how often this Family Worship is conducted in a slovenly manner! An inconvenient hour is fixed; and a knock at the door, a ring at the bell, the call of a customer, may hurry the believer from his knees to go and attend to his worldly concerns. Of course, many excuses might be offered, but the fact would still remain that, in this way, we often restrain prayer.*
> —Charles Haddon Spurgeon

---

105 **query**—question.
106 **meat**—food in general; meal time.

Praise is certainly not at all so common in family prayer as other forms of worship. We cannot all of us praise God in the family by joining in song, because we are not all able to carry a tune, but it would be well if we could. I agree with Matthew Henry when he says, "They that pray in the family do well; they that pray and read the Scriptures do better; but they that pray, and read, and sing do best of all." There is a completeness in that kind of Family Worship which is much to be desired.
—*Charles Haddon Spurgeon*

We deeply want a revival of domestic religion. The Christian family was the bulwark of godliness in the days of the Puritans; but in these evil times hundreds of families of so-called Christians have no Family Worship, no restraint upon growing sons, and no wholesome instruction or discipline. How can we hope to see the kingdom of our Lord advance when His own disciples do not teach His Gospel to their own children?
—*Charles Haddon Spurgeon*

Would you keep up your authority in your family? You cannot do it better than by keeping up religion in your family. If ever a master of a family looks great, truly great, it is when he is going before his house in the service of God, and presiding among them in holy things. Then he shows himself worthy of double honor, when he teacheth them the good knowledge of the Lord, and is their mouth to God in prayer, blessing them in the name of God. —*Matthew Henry*

Happy is the household which meets every morning for prayer! Happy are they who let not the evening depart without uniting in supplication! Brethren, I wish it were more common, I wish it were universal, with all professors of religion to have family prayer. We sometimes hear of the children of Christian parents who do not grow up in the fear of God, and we are asked how it is that they turn out so badly. In many, very many cases, I fear there is such a neglect of Family Worship that it is not probable that the children are at all impressed by any piety supposed to be possessed by their parents. —*Charles Haddon Spurgeon*

Chapter 2
GODLY MANHOOD

There are times in human history when manhood gets mangled. In times like these, there is only one hope: the sovereign power of God, working through the Word of God by the Spirit of God. This is one of those times, and this is why a recovery of biblical manhood is pivotal. The task of recovery is arduous, challenging, and controversial. Furthermore, getting calibrated to the biblical vision for manhood is a lifelong task, which we cannot accomplish without the grace of Christ Jesus. Three powerful forces work continually to destroy this vision. First, the sons of the first Adam have been marred inwardly with a sinfully passive streak that deters them from the courageous and principled leadership they were designed to provide. Second, the most powerful institutions in the world today attempt to undermine and even usurp a man's role. The state, in particular, has mounted an all-out assault to diminish a man's leadership roles as teacher and provider, and the church often follows suit. Third, feminism has plagued modern man's sensibilities. Their minds have been pickled in feminist brine for so long they can hardly think straight about the mantle of manhood that Christ has laid upon them. The synapses of their brains are misfiring. This is why modern men almost feel guilty that they are men, that they think like men, and act like men.

Can these synapses be healed? Can all this be reversed? Yes. The articles ahead in this chapter will help you cleanse your mind of cultural lies, identify any syncretistic practices and reconnect your God-given male circuitry, to help you win back the role God intended. They will help you set your feet upon a gospel foundation, and make you fit for godly—and manly—service.

—Scott Brown

True Godliness Described

BENJAMIN KEACH (1640-1704)

True Godliness,[1] being a great stranger to most men and indeed known but by few, I shall in the first place, before treating of his travels and of the entertainment[2] he meets with, give you a description of him. Many persons are subject to so great an error as to take *Morality* for him; some have mistaken *Counterfeit Godliness* for him; and others, either through ignorance or malice, rail and ignominiously[3] call him *Singularity*,[4] *Stubbornness, Pride,* or *Rebellion.* These last declare him not fit to live, being a seditious[5] disturber of peace and order, wherever he comes. Yea, such a factious[6] and quarrelsome companion, that he is indeed the cause of all those unhappy differences, divisions, troubles, and miseries with which the world abounds. I conclude, therefore, that nothing is more necessary than to take off that mask which his implacable[7] enemies have put upon him and clear him of all the slanders and reproaches of the sons of Belial.[8] When he is thus made to appear in his own original and spotless innocency, it will be seen that none need be afraid of him, or be unwilling to entertain him, or ashamed to own him and make him their bosom companion.

Know, therefore, in the first place that Godliness consists in the right knowledge of divine truths or fundamental principles of the Gospel, which all men ought to know and be established in, that would be saved. *"And without controversy great is the mystery of godliness: God was manifest in the flesh, justified in the Spirit, seen of angels, preached unto the Gentiles, believed on in the world, received up into glory"* (1 Tim. 3:16). You see from this text that the great truths of the Christian religion are called Godliness.

Now, should any demand to hear more particularly what are those principles of divine truth or fundamentals of the Christian faith, which are the essentials of *True Godliness*, I answer,

---

1 [**Editor's Note**] In the late 1600s, Benjamin Keach wrote an allegory entitled *The Travels of True Godliness*, which is similar in style to Bunyan's *Pilgrim's Progress*. In this article, Keach portrays the Christian faith as a male character named "True Godliness."
2 **entertainment** – treatment.
3 **ignominiously** – shamefully; disgracefully.
4 **Singularity** – differing from others in matters of behavior or religion in order to draw attention to one's self. Keach's point is that the faithful Christian will be accused of acting peculiarly just to be noticed.
5 **seditious** – guilty of engaging in or provoking rebellion against the authority of the state.
6 **factious** – characterized by causing dissension and division.
7 **implacable** – cannot be satisfied or pacified; irreconcilable.
8 **Sons of Belial** – Belial means "wicked, worthless, lawless," and came to be used in Hebrew literature as a name for Satan. A Son of Belial then is a wicked and worthless person.

1. That there is one eternal, infinite, most holy, most wise, just, good, and gracious God, or glorious Deity, subsisting[9] in three distinct Persons—the Father, the Son, and the Holy Ghost—and these are one, that is, one in essence.

2. That this God, out of His great love and goodness, hath given us one sure and infallible rule of faith and practice, viz.,[10] the Holy Scriptures. By [these,] we may know, not only that there is a God and Creator, but the manner of the creation of the world, together with the design or reason wherefore He made all things. [We may also know] how sin came into the world and what righteousness it is that God requires to our justification[11] (or discharge from the guilt of sin), viz., by a Redeemer: His own Son, whom He sent into the world. There is no other rule or way to know these things so as for men to be saved but by revelation or the sacred records of the Holy Scriptures, the mystery of salvation being far above human reason and [cannot] be known by the natural light in men.

3. That our Redeemer, the Lord Jesus Christ, Who is the Surety[12] of the New Covenant and only Mediator[13] between God and man, is truly God (of the essence of the Father) and truly man (of the substance of the virgin Mary), consisting of these two natures in one Person—and that redemption, peace, and reconciliation are by this Lord Jesus Christ alone.

4. That justification and pardon of sin are alone by that full satisfaction which Christ made to God's justice and are apprehended by faith alone through the Holy Spirit.

5. That all men who are or can be saved must be renewed, regenerated,[14] and sanctified[15] by the Holy Spirit.

6. That there will be a resurrection of the bodies of all men at the Last Day.

7. That there will be an eternal judgment, that is, all shall be brought to the tribunal[16] of Jesus Christ in the great Day and give an account for all things done in the body, and that there will be a future state of glory and

---

9 **subsisting** – existing.
10 **viz.** – from Latin *videlicet*: that is to say; namely.
11 **justification** – Justification is an act of God's free grace, wherein He pardons all our sins and accepts us as righteous in His sight only for the righteousness of Christ imputed to us and received by faith alone. (*Spurgeon's Catechism*, Q. 32) See FGB 187, *Justification*, available from CHAPEL LIBRARY.
12 **Surety** – one who enters into a bond to undertake the responsibilities or debt of another.
13 **Mediator** – a go-between; one who intervenes between two hostile parties to restore them to a relationship of harmony and unity.
14 **regenerated** – born again; brought from spiritual death to spiritual life and union with Jesus Christ by the miraculous work of the Holy Spirit.
15 **sanctified** – made holy by the divine grace of the Holy Spirit; set apart for God's use.
16 **tribunal** – judgment seat.

eternal happiness of all true believers and of eternal torment and misery of all unbelievers and ungodly persons, who live and die in their sins.

Now, I say, in the true knowledge and belief of these principles (which comprehend the fundamentals of true religion or the Christian faith) does *True Godliness* consist as to his essential part.

Secondly, *Godliness* as to his inward parts is a holy conformity to these sacred and divine principles, which natural men understand not. *True Godliness* consists in the light of supernatural truths and life of grace, God manifesting Himself in the light of those glorious principles and working the life of supernatural grace in the soul by the Holy Ghost. It consists in the saving and experimental[17] knowledge of God and Jesus Christ [and] in having the evil qualities of the soul removed and heavenly habits infused[18] in their room or in a gracious conformity and affection[19] of the heart to God, cleaving to all truths made known to us and finding the powerful influences of the Gospel and Spirit of Christ upon us, whereby our souls are brought into the image and likeness of His death and resurrection. This is *True Godliness*. [It is] not a bare living up to the natural principles of morality nor an historical, notional, or dogmatical knowledge[20] of the sacred Gospel and its precepts; but a faithful conformity to the principles of the Gospel, discharging our duties with as much readiness[21] and faithfulness towards God as towards man, so that our conscience may be kept void of offence towards both (Acts 24:16).

It consists in forsaking sin and loathing it as the greatest evil and in cleaving to God in sincerity of heart, valuing Him above all, being willingly subject from a principle of divine love to all His laws and appointments. Godliness makes a man say with the Psalmist, *"Whom have I in heaven but thee?"* (Ps. 73:25). St. Austin[22] saith, "He loves not Christ at all, that loves him not above all." He that entertains[23] *True Godliness* is as zealous for the *work* of religion as for the *wages* of religion. Some there are who serve God that they may serve themselves upon God. However, a true Christian desires

---

17 **experimental** – having a personal experience of anything; experiential.
18 **infused** – to put into, as if by pouring; imparted by divine influence.
19 **affection** – the state of mind toward something; inclination.
20 **historical, notional, or dogmatical knowledge** – *historical* = being acquainted with the truth, but not believing it by the regenerating power of God's Spirit; *notional* = imaginary, existing in ideal only; and *dogmatical* = acknowledging something based on theological tradition without personally trusting it by the regenerating power of the Holy Spirit.
21 **readiness** – willingness.
22 **St. Austin or St. Augustine** (354-430) – Bishop of Hippo, early church theologian considered by many the father of orthodox theology; born in Tagaste, North Africa.
23 **entertains** – to hold in the mind with favor; to experience.

grace, not only that God would glorify him in heaven, but also that he may glorify God on earth. He cries, "Lord, rather let me have a good heart than a great estate." Though he loves many things beside God, yet he loves nothing above God. This man fears sin more than suffering, and therefore he will suffer rather than sin.

Thirdly, that you may have a complete and perfect knowledge of him, it may not be amiss if I describe his form (2 Tim. 1:13; 3:5) together with the habiliments[24] he continually wears. The external parts of *True Godliness* are very beautiful. No wonder that they are so, seeing he was fashioned by the wisdom of the only wise God our Savior, the works of Whose hands are all glorious. But this, viz., the formation of Godliness, being one of the highest and most admirable contrivances[25] of His eternal wisdom, must of necessity excel in glory and amiableness.[26] His form and external beauty, therefore, are such that he needs no human artifice[27] to adorn him or to illustrate or set off his comeliness[28] of countenance; for there is nothing defective as to his evangelical and apostolical form, as he came out of his great Creator's hands. As there is nothing from head to foot that is superfluous,[29] so every line and lineament,[30] vein, nerve, and sinew are in such an exact and admirable order placed, that to his beauty there can be no addition. Everyone, therefore, that adds to or alters anything touching the form of *True Godliness*, mars and defiles instead of beautifying. Besides, God hath strictly forbidden anything of this nature to be done. *"Add thou not unto his words, lest he reprove thee, and thou be found a liar"* (Prov. 30:6), by ascribing[31] that to God which is none of His. Do not the Papists call those superstitious and vain ceremonies used in their church by the name of God's worship? And what is this less than putting a lie upon Him? Besides, it reflects upon the wisdom of God, to attempt to change or alter anything in the form of Godliness, as if God did not know best how He Himself would be worshipped, but must be indebted to man for his help, wisdom, and contrivances, touching many things that are called decent and necessary. Does it not reflect upon the care and faithfulness of God, to suppose that He should not Himself take care to lay down in His blessed Word things that are all necessary to the form of Godliness, without

---

24 **habiliments** – the apparel or garments appropriate for any occasion.
25 **contrivances** – ingeniously, skillfully planning or accomplishing something.
26 **amiableness** – loveliness.
27 **artifice** – trickery.
28 **comeliness** – beauty.
29 **superfluous** – beyond what is required; excessively abundant.
30 **lineament** – contour of the body; distinctive feature.
31 **ascribing** – to attribute credit to; to reckon or account.

weak man's care and wisdom to supply what He should omit?

All, therefore, may perceive that *True Godliness* never changes his countenance. He is not altered in the least from the aspect he bore in primitive times. Nay, there is indeed nothing more foreign to him than those pompous garbs,[32] superstitious vestments,[33] images, crossings, salt, oil, holy water, and other ceremonies, which are by many thought necessary to his existence. Therefore, take heed you do not mistake the counterfeit form of Godliness for the true one. It is only necessary to note one thing more, viz., you must be sure to receive the *power* of Godliness with his form; for his form without his inward life and power will do you no good: it is but as the body without the soul, or the shell without the kernel, or the cabinet without the jewel. Neither [should] any slight his form, for you may remember what the Apostle speaks of the "form of doctrine" (Rom. 6:17) and of "the form of sound words" (2 Tim. 1:13); for as the true faith must be held fast, so must the profession of it also. You may, it is true, meet with a shell without the kernel; but it is rare to meet the kernel without the shell!

From *The Travels of True Godliness*, Solid Ground Christian Books: www.solid-ground-books.com.

Benjamin Keach (1640-1704): English Particular Baptist preacher, author, and ardent defender of Baptist principles, even against Richard Baxter. Often in prison and frequently in danger for preaching the gospel, he was the first to introduce singing hymns in the worship of English congregations. Prolific author of *Tropologia* (reprinted as *Preaching from the Types and Metaphors of the Bible*), *Gospel Mysteries Explained* (reprinted as *Exposition of the Parables*), and numerous other works; born at Stokeham, Buckinghamshire, England.

> *Let us so give ourselves to God, to be ruled by Him, and taught by Him that, contented with His Word alone, we may never desire to know more than we find therein. No! Not even if the power so to do were given to us! This teachableness, in which every godly man will ever hold all the powers of his mind, under the authority of the Word of God, is the true and only rule of wisdom.* —John Calvin

---

32 **pompous garbs** – characterized by an exaggerated display of self-importance; pretentious.
33 **vestments** – any of the ritual robes worn by members of the clergy or assistants at services or rites.

God knows what godliness is, for He has created it, He sustains it, He is pledged to perfect it, and His delight is in it. What matters it whether you are understood by your fellow men or not, so long as you are understood by God? If that secret prayer of yours is known to Him, seek not to have it known to anyone besides. If your conscientious motive is discerned in heaven, mind not though it is denounced on earth. If your designs— the great principles that sway you—are such as you dare plead in the great Day of Judgment, you need not stop to plead them before a jesting, jeering generation. Be godly, and fear not. And, if you be misrepresented, remember that should your character be dead and buried among men, there will be "a resurrection of reputations" as well as of bodies. "Then shall the righteous shine forth as the sun in the kingdom of their Father" (Mat 13:43). Therefore, be not afraid to possess this peculiar character, for though it is misunderstood on earth, it is well understood in heaven.
—Charles Haddon Spurgeon

The Nature of an Upright Man
RICHARD STEELE (1629-1692)

With an upright man thou wilt shew thyself upright. —Psalm 18:25

1. An upright heart is single without division. To a hypocrite, there are many gods and many lords; and he must have a heart for each. But to the upright, there is but one God the Father and one Lord Jesus Christ, and one heart will serve them both. The hypocrite fixes his heart upon the creature, for every creature he must have a heart; and the dividing of his heart destroys him (Hos. 10:2). Worldly profits knock at the door, and he must have a heart for them. Carnal pleasures present themselves, and he must have a heart for them also. Sinful preferments[34] appear, and they must have a heart too. Of necessary objects, the number is few; of needless vanities, the number is endless. The upright man has made choice of God and has enough.

A single Christ is enough for a single heart; hence, holy David prayed in Psalm 86:11: *"Unite my heart to fear thy name."* That is, "Let me have but one heart and mind, and let that be Thine."

As there are thousands of beams and rays, yet they all meet and center in the sun. So an upright man, though he has a thousand thoughts, yet they all (by his good will) meet in God. He has many subordinate ends—to procure a livelihood, to preserve his credit, to provide for his children—but he has no supreme end but God alone. Hence, he has that steadiness in his resolutions, that undistractedness in his holy duties, that consistency in his actions, and that evenness in the frame of his heart, which miserable hypocrites cannot attain.

2. An upright heart is sound without rottenness. *"Let my heart be sound in thy statutes; that I be not ashamed"* (Ps. 119:80). The more sincerity, the less shame. Integrity is the great author of confidence. Every frost shakes an unsound body, and every trial shakes an unsound soul. An upright man does not always have so pure a color as a hypocrite may have, but his color is natural: it is his own; it is not painted; his constitution is firm. The hypocrite's beauty is borrowed; the fire of trial will melt it off.

An upright man has his infirmities, his diseases; but his new nature works them out, for he is sound within. Leprosy overspreads the hypocrite, but he hides it. *"For he flattereth himself in his own eyes, until his iniquity be found to be hateful"* (Ps. 36:2). He endeavors to hide himself from God, more from men, but most from himself. He would fain[35] be in with himself howsoever, and this trade he drives *"until his iniquity be found to be hateful."* But an upright

---

34 **preferments** – preferences; desirable or favored choices.
35 **fain** – gladly; willingly.

man is always sifting³⁶ and trying himself: "Am I sound? Am I right? Are my services rightly done? Are my infirmities consistent with integrity?"

An upright saint is like an apple with rotten specks, but a hypocrite is like the apple with a rotten core. The sincere Christian has a speck of passion here, there one of worldliness, and there one of pride. But cut him up and anatomize him, and he is sound at heart: there Christ and Christianity live and reign. A hypocrite is like an apple that is smooth and lovely on the outside, but rotten within. His words may be exact, his duties devout, and his life blameless; but look within, and his heart is the sty of sin—the den of Satan.

3. An upright heart is pure without mixture. It is not absolutely pure, for that happy condition is reserved for heaven; but it is compared with the pollution and base mixture that constitutes a hypocrite. Though his hand cannot do all that God bids, yet his heart is sincere in all he does. His soul is bent for perfect purity, and so he has his name from that. *"Blessed are the pure in heart"* (Matt. 5:8). In his words he sometimes fails and in his thoughts and deeds also. But open his heart, and there is a love, a desire, a design, and an endeavor after real and absolute purity. He is not legally pure, that is, free from all sin; but he is evangelically pure, free from the reign of all sin, especially of hypocrisy, which is so flatly contrary to the covenant of grace. In this sense, the upright man is the Scripture Puritan, and so is further from hypocrisy than any other man. He is really glad that God is the Searcher of hearts, for then he knows that He will find His name and nature in His own [chosen people].

Yet the most upright man in the world has some hypocrisy in him. *"Who can say, I have made my heart clean, I am pure from my sin?"* (Prov. 20:9). But he detects, resists, and hates this hypocrisy; and so it cannot denominate him as a hypocrite in this world, nor damn him as one in another. His ends are generally purely for the glory of God; his frame of heart and thoughts are pure, and generally better than his outside; the farther you trace him, the better he is. He is pure from dishonesty in his dealings, purer yet in his family from all appearance of evil, purer still in his closet, and most pure in his heart. Though there is sin there, yet there is also there an antipathy³⁷ against it, so that it does not mingle with it.

The hypocrite chooses sin; the upright man would have no sin if he could choose. The traveler meets with dirt on his way, but he keeps it off as well as he can and does not mingle with it. If he gets soiled, he rubs it off as soon as may be. But the swine delights in it and cannot be well without it. It is just so between the upright man and the hypocrite. The most upright

---

36 **sifting** – examining and sorting carefully.
37 **antipathy** – a strong feeling of intense dislike; hostile feelings toward.

saint on earth is mired with sin sometimes, but he did not design it in the morning, nor does he sleep with it at night. But a hypocrite designs it and delights in it; he is never as well contented as in sin. In a word, the hypocrite may avoid sin, but no man can abhor sin save the upright man.

4. An upright man is perfect and entire without reservation. *"Mark the perfect man, and behold the upright"* (Ps.37:37). You may see them both at once. His heart is entirely devoted to the will and ways of God. The hypocrite ever has some exceptions and reservations. "Such a sin I must not leave; such a grace I cannot love; such a duty I will not practice. Thus far I will yield but no farther; thus far I will go. It is consistent with my carnal ends, but all the world shall not persuade me farther." The judgment of the hypocrite will drive beyond his will, his conscience beyond his affections; he is not entire, his heart is parted, and so he is off and on.

The upright man has but one happiness, and that is the enjoyment of God; he has but one rule, and that is His holy will; he has but one work, and that is to please his Maker. Thereupon he is entire and certain in his choices, in his desires, in his ways and contrivances.[38] Though there may be some demurs[39] in his prosecution of his main business, yet there is no hesitancy and wavering between two objects; for he is entirely fixed and resolved therein, and so may be said to be "perfect and entire, wanting nothing."

There is in every hypocrite someone fort or stronghold that has never yielded to the sovereignty and empire of God's will. Some lust fortifies itself in the will; but where integrity enters, it brings every thought into captivity to the obedience of Christ. "Lord," he says, "I am wholly Thine; do what Thou wilt with me. Say what Thou wilt to me. Write what Thou wilt upon me. *'O LORD our God, other lords beside thee have had dominion over us: but by thee only will we make mention of thy name'"* (Isa. 26:13). Here is the upright man.

5. An upright heart is plain without guile.[40] *"Blessed is the man unto whom the LORD imputeth not iniquity, and in whose spirit there is no guile"* (Ps. 32:2). Here is a blessed word indeed. Alas! We have great and many iniquities; would it not be happy for us to be as if we had never sinned? Why, nonimputation will be as well for us as if there had been no transgression; sins remitted are as if they had not been committed; the debt-book crossed as good as if no entries had ever been made. But who is this blessed man? *"In whose spirit there is no guile,"* that is, no fundamental guile. He is the man who has not deceitfully covenanted with his God. He has no approved guile, to approve and yield to any way of wickedness.

---

38 **contrivances** – plans.
39 **demurs** – delays; lingerings.
40 **guile** – cunning; deceit; treachery.

He does not juggle with God or men or with his own conscience. He does not hide his idols under him when God is searching his tent (Josh. 7:21). Rather, as it follows in Psalm 32:5, he acknowledges, hates, and leaves his sin.

When the upright man confesses his sin, his heart aches, and he is deeply troubled for it; he does not dissemble.[41] The hypocrite proclaims open war, but maintains secret intelligence[42] with his lusts. When the upright man prays for any grace, he earnestly desires it, and he takes pains to compass it too; for he is in good earnest and does not dissemble.

He who will dissemble with God will dissemble with any man in the world. See the wide difference between Saul and David. Saul is charged with a fault in 1 Samuel 15:14. He denies it, and the charge is renewed in verse 19. Still he minces[43] the matter and looks for fig leaves to cover all. But plain-hearted David is another man: he is charged, and he yields; one prick opens a vein of sorrow in his heart. He tells all, he makes a psalm of it, and therein concludes this in Psalm 51:6: *"Behold, thou desirest truth in the inward parts."* The plain-hearted man says, *"As for me, with the upright man I will show myself upright."*

From *The Character of the Upright Man*, Soli Deo Gloria, a division of Reformation Heritage Books: www.heritagebooks.org.

Richard Steele (1629-1692): Puritan preacher and author; born at Bartholmley, Cheshire, England.

> *Can a man be like to God? Ah, me! What a wide discrepancy there must always be between God and the best of men!…Yet grace does make us like God in righteousness, true holiness, and especially in love. Has the Holy Spirit taught thee…to love even those that hate thee?…Dost thou love even those that render thee no love in return, as He did who gave His life for His enemies? And dost thou choose that which is good? Dost thou delight thyself in peace? Dost thou seek after that which is pure? Art thou ever gladdened with that which is kind and just? Then art thou like thy Father Who is in heaven, thou art a godly man, and this text is for you: "Know that the Lord hath set apart him that is godly for himself " (Ps. 4:3).*
> *— Charles Haddon Spurgeon*

---

41 **dissemble** – disguise in order to conceal or deceive.
42 **intelligence** – communication; a good understanding between.
43 **minces** – makes little of; minimizes.

Signs and Character of a Godly Man

THOMAS WATSON (C. 1620-1686)

"For this shall every one that is godly pray unto thee." —Psalm 32:6

Who is the godly man? For the full answer whereunto, I shall lay down several specific signs and character of a godly man.

The first fundamental sign of a godly man is a man of knowledge: *"The prudent are crowned with knowledge"* (Prov. 14:18). The saints are called "wise virgins" (Matt. 25:4). A natural man may have some discursive[44] knowledge of God, but he knoweth nothing as he ought to know (1 Cor. 8:2). He knows not God savingly: he may have the eye of reason open, but he discerns not the things of God after a spiritual manner. Waters cannot go beyond their springhead; vapors cannot rise higher than the sun draws them. A natural man cannot act above his sphere. He is no more able to judge aright of sacred things, than a blind man is to judge of colors. 1. He sees not the evil of his heart: if a face is ever so black and deformed, yet it is not seen under a veil. The heart of a sinner is so black, that nothing but hell can pattern it, yet the veil of ignorance hides it. 2. He sees not the beauties of a Savior: Christ is a pearl, but a hidden pearl.

The knowledge of a godly man is *quickening*.[45] *"I will never forget thy precepts, : for with them thou hast quickened me"* (Ps. 119:93). Knowledge in a natural man's head is like a torch in a dead man's hand; true knowledge animates. A godly man is like John the Baptist, *"a burning and a shining light"* (John 5:35). He doth not only shine by illumination, but burn by affection. The spouse's knowledge made her *"sick of love"* (Song 2:5), [or] "I am wounded with love. I am like a deer that is struck with a dart; my soul lies a-bleeding and nothing can cure me but a sight of Him whom my soul loves."

The knowledge of a godly man is *appropriating*. *"I know that my redeemer liveth"* (Job 19:25). A medicine is best when it is applied; this applicative knowledge is joyful. Christ is called a Surety[46] (Heb. 7:22). O what joy, when I am drowned in debt, to know that Christ is my Surety! Christ is called an Advocate (1 John 2:1). The Greek word for *advocate* signifies "a comforter." O what comfort is it, when I have a bad cause, to know Christ is my Advocate, who never lost any cause He pleaded!

Question: But how shall I know that I make a right application of Christ?

---

44 **discursive** – rambling; rapidly passing from one subject to another.
45 **quickening** – animating; makes him alive spiritually.
46 **Surety** – one who assures the fulfillment of something; a guarantor.

A hypocrite may think he applies when he doth not.

Answer: He, who rightly applies Christ, puts these two together: *Jesus and Lord* (Phil.3:8). Christ Jesus my Lord: many take Christ as a Jesus, but refuse Him as a Lord. Do you join Prince and Savior (Acts 5:31)? Would you as well be ruled by Christ's laws as saved by His blood? Christ is *"a priest upon his throne"* (Zech. 6:13). He will never be a priest to intercede, unless your heart is the throne where He sways His scepter. A true applying of Christ is when we so take Him for a husband that we give up ourselves to Him as a Lord.

The knowledge of a godly man is *transforming*. *"We all, with open face beholding as in a glass the glory of the Lord, are changed into the same image"* (2 Cor. 3:18). As a painter looking upon a face, draws a face like it in the picture; so looking upon Christ in the glass of the Gospel, we are changed into His similitude.[47] We may look upon other objects that are glorious yet not be made glorious by them: a deformed face may look upon beauty and yet not be made beautiful. A wounded man may look upon a surgeon and yet not be healed. But this is the excellency of divine knowledge: it gives us such a sight of Christ as makes us partake of His nature. As Moses, when he had seen God's back parts: his face shined, [for] some of the rays and beams of God's glory fell upon him.

The knowledge of a godly man is growing: *"Increasing in the knowledge of God"* (Col. 1:10). True knowledge is as the light of the morning, which increaseth in the horizon until it comes to the meridian.[48] So sweet is spiritual knowledge, that the more a saint knows, the thirstier he is of knowledge. It is called the riches of knowledge (1 Cor.1:5). The more riches a man hath, the more still he desires. Though Paul knew Christ, yet he would know him more: *"That I may know him, and the power of his resurrection"* (Phil. 3:10).

Question: But how shall we get this saving knowledge?

Answer: Not by the power of nature: some speak of how far well-improved reason will go. Alas, the plumb line of reason is too short to fathom the deep things of God. A man can no more by the power of reason reach the saving knowledge of God than a pigmy can reach the pyramids. The light of nature will no more help us to see Christ, than the light of a candle will help us to understand. *"The natural man receiveth not the things of the Spirit of God...neither can he know them"* (1 Cor. 2:14). What shall we do then to know God in a soul-saving manner? I answer, "Let us implore the help of God's Spirit." Paul never saw himself blind until a light shined from

---

47 **similitude** – likeness; resemblance.
48 **meridian** – mid-day; noon; hence, the highest perfection.

heaven (Acts 9:3). God must anoint our eyes ere[49] we can see. What needed Christ to have bid Laodicea to come to Him for eye-salve, if she could see before (Rev. 3:18)? O let us beg the Spirit, which is a Spirit of revelation (Eph. 1:17). Saving knowledge is not by speculation, but by inspiration (Job 32:8). The inspiration of the Almighty giveth understanding.

We may have excellent notions in divinity,[50] but the Holy Ghost must enable us to know them after a spiritual manner; a man may see the figures upon a dial, but he cannot tell how the day goes unless the sun shines. We may read many truths in the Bible, but we cannot know them savingly until God's Spirit doth shine upon us. *"The Spirit searching all things, yea, the deep things of God"* (1 Cor. 2:10). The Scripture discovers Christ *to* us, but the Spirit reveals Christ *in* us (Gal. 1:16). The Spirit makes known that which all the world cannot do, namely, the sense of God's love.

The godly man is *a man acted by faith*. As gold is the most precious among the metals, so is faith among the graces. Faith cuts us off from the wild olive of nature and innoculates[51] us into Christ. Faith is the vital artery of the soul: *"The just shall live by his faith"* (Hab. 2:4). Such as are destitute of faith though they breathe, yet they [lack] life. Faith is the quickener of the graces; not a grace stirs, until faith sets it a-work. Faith is to the soul, as the animal spirits[52] are to the body: they excite lively operations in the body. Faith excites repentance; it is like the fire to the still that makes it drop. When I believe God's love to me, this makes me weep that I should sin against so good a God. Faith is the mother of hope: first, we believe the promise, then we hope for it. Faith is the oil that feeds the lamp of hope. Faith and hope are two turtle graces; take away one and the other languisheth.[53] If the sinews are cut, the body is lame. If the sinew of faith is cut, hope is lame. Faith is the ground of patience: he who believes God is his God and all providences work for his good, doth patiently yield up himself to the will of God. Thus, faith is a living principle, and the life of a saint is nothing else but a life of faith. His prayer is the breathing of faith (James 5:15). His obedience is the result of faith (Rom. 16:26). A godly man by faith lives in Christ, as the beam lives in the sun: *"I live; yet not I, but Christ liveth in me"* (Gal. 2:20). A Christian by the power of faith sees above reason, treads above the moon (2 Cor. 4:18). By faith his heart is finally quieted (Ps. 12:7). He trusts himself and all his affairs

---

49 **ere** – before.
50 **divinity** – theology.
51 **innoculates** – unites by insertion of a twig into a stock; engrafts.
52 **animal spirits** – the supposed "spirit" or principle of sensation and voluntary motion, answering to nerve fluid, nerve force, nervous action; life, vigor, energy.
53 **languisheth** – to become weak and feeble.

with God: as in a time of war, men get into a garrison and trust themselves and their treasure there; so the name of the Lord is a strong tower (Prov. 18:10). And a believer trusts all that ever he is worth in this garrison: *"For I know whom I have believed, and am persuaded that he is able to keep that which I have committed unto him against that day"* (2 Tim. 1:12). God trusted Paul with His Gospel, and Paul trusted God with his soul. Faith is a catholicon[54] or remedy against all troubles. It is a godly man's sheet-anchor[55] that he casts out into the sea of God's mercy and is kept from sinking in despair.

QUESTION: Wherein do the godly discover their holiness?

ANSWER: 1. In hating the garment spotted by the flesh (Jude 23). The godly do set themselves against evil in both purpose and practice. They are fearful of that which looks like sin (1 Thess. 5:22). The appearance of evil may prejudice a weak Christian: if it doth not defile a man's own conscience, it may offend his brother's conscience; and to sin against him is to sin against Christ (1 Cor. 8:12). A godly man will not go as far as he may, lest he go further than he should.

2. The godly discover their holiness in being advocates for holiness: *"I will speak of thy testimonies also before kings, and will not be ashamed"* (Ps. 119:46). When piety is calumniated[56] in the world, the saints will stand up in the defense of it. They will wipe off the dust of a reproach from the face of religion. Holiness defends the godly, and they will defend holiness. It defends them from danger, and they will defend it from disgrace.

A godly man is very exact and curious about the worship of God. The Greek word for *godly* signifies "a right worshipper of God." A godly man doth reverence divine institutions and is more for the purity of worship than the pomp[57]…The Lord would have Moses make the tabernacle according to the pattern in the mount (Ex. 25:40). If Moses had left out anything in the pattern or added anything to it, it would have been very provoking. The Lord hath always given testimonies of His displeasure against such as have corrupted His worship: Nadab and Abihu *"offered strange fire before the LORD, which he commanded them not. And there went out fire from the LORD, and devoured them, and they died before the LORD"* (Lev. 10:1, 2). Whatsoever is not of God's own appointment in His worship, He looks upon as strange fire. And no wonder He is so highly incensed at it: for as if God were not

---

54 **catholicon** – a universal remedy, which heals all diseases.
55 **sheet-anchor** – an anchor, formerly always a ship's largest anchor, used only in an emergency; hence, that on which one's reliance rests when all else has failed.
56 **calumniated** – falsely and maliciously accused; slandered.
57 **pomp** – splendid display; magnificent show.

wise enough to appoint the manner how He will be served, men will go to prescribe[58] to Him, and as if the rules for His worship were defective, they will attempt to mend the copy and superadd[59] their inventions…A godly man dares not vary from the pattern that God hath shown him in the Scripture. This might not be the least reason why David was called a man after God's own heart—because he kept the springs of God's worship pure and in matters sacred did not superinduce[60] anything of his own devising.

A godly man is a *Christ-prizer*. To illustrate this, I shall show that Jesus Christ is in Himself precious: *"Behold, I lay in Sion a chief corner stone, elect, precious"* (1 Peter 2:6). Christ is compared to things most precious.

[Christ] is precious in His *Person*. He is the picture of His Father's glory (Heb. 1:3).

Christ is precious in His *offices,* which are several rays of the Sun of Righteousness (Mal. 4:2).

1. Christ's prophetical office is precious: He is the great oracle of heaven: He hath a preciousness above all the prophets that went before Him. He teacheth not only the ear, but also the heart; He who hath the key of David in His hand opened the heart of Lydia (Acts 16:14).

2. Christ's priestly office is precious: This is the solid basis of our comfort, *"Now once in the end of the world hath he appeared to put away sin by the sacrifice of himself"* (Heb. 9:26). By virtue of this sacrifice, the soul may go to God with boldness: "Lord, give me heaven; Christ hath purchased it for me. He hung upon the cross that I might sit upon the throne." Christ's blood and incense are the two hinges on which our salvation turns. 3. Christ's regal office is precious: *"And he hath on his vesture and on his thigh a name written, KING OF KINGS, AND LORD OF LORDS"* (Rev. 19:16). Christ hath preeminence[61] above all other kings for majesty. He hath the highest throne, the richest crown, the largest dominions, and the longest possession: *"Thy throne, O God, is forever and ever"* (Heb. 1:8)…Christ sets up His scepter where no other king doth. He rules the will and affections; His power binds the conscience.

If we are prizers of Christ, then we prefer Him in our judgments before other things. We value Christ above honor and riches; the pearl of great price lies nearest our hearts (Matt. 13:46). He who prizeth Christ esteems the gleanings of Christ better than the world's vintage. He counts the worst things of Christ better than the best things of the world: *"Esteeming*

---

58 **prescribe** – to lay down a rule.
59 **superadd** – to add over and above.
60 **superinduce** – to introduce an addition to something already in existence.
61 **preeminence** – to have first place; to be above all else.

the reproach of Christ greater riches than the treasures in Egypt" (Heb. 11:26). Is it thus with us? You shall hear some say, they have honorable thoughts of Christ, but they prize their land and estate above Him. The young man in the Gospel preferred his bags of gold before Christ (Mark 10:17-22); Judas valued thirty pieces of silver above Him (Matt. 26:15). May it not be feared, if an hour of trial come, there are many would rather renounce their baptism and throw off Christ's livery[62] than hazard the loss of their earthly possessions for Him?

If we are prizers of Christ, we cannot live without Him. Things that we value, we know not how to be without: a man may live without music, but not without food. A child of God can want[63] health and friends, but he cannot want Christ. In the absence of Christ, he saith as Job, *"I went mourning without the sun"* (Job 30:28). I have the starlight of creature comforts, but I want the Sun of Righteousness. *"Give me children,"* said Rachel, *"or else I die"* (Gen. 30:1). So saith the soul, "Lord, give me Christ or I die; one drop of the water of life to quench my thirst!"…Do these prize Christ, who can sit down content without Him?

If we are prizers of Christ, then we shall not grudge at any pains to get Him. He who prizeth gold will dig for it in the mine: *"My soul followeth hard after thee"* (Ps. 63:8). Plutarch[64] reports of the Gauls, an ancient people in France, after they had tasted the sweet wine of the Italian grape, they inquired after the country and never rested until they had arrived at it. He in whose eye Christ is precious never rests until he hath gotten Christ: *"I sought him whom my soul loveth…I held him, and would not let him go"* (Song 3:1, 4).

If we are prizers of Christ, then we will part with our dearest lusts for Him. Paul saith of the Galatians, they did so esteem him, that they were ready to have pulled out their own eyes and have given them to him (Gal. 4:15). He, who esteems Christ, will pull out that lust which is his right eye. A wise man will throw away a poison for a cordial;[65] he, who sets a high value upon Christ, will part with his pride, unjust gain, sinful passions. He will set his feet upon the neck of his sins (Josh. 10:24). Try by this: how they can be said to prize Christ, who will not leave a vanity for Him? What a scorn and contempt do they put upon the Lord Jesus, who prefer a damning lust before a saving Christ?

---

62 **livery** – a distinctive uniform worn by the servants of a household.
63 **want** – lack.
64 **Plutarch** (AD 46-120?) – Greek biographer and philosopher, who wrote *Parallel Lives*, a collection of biographies that Shakespeare used in his Roman plays.
65 **cordial** – a tonic that is stimulating, comforting, or invigorating to the heart.

If we are prizers of Christ, we will be willing to help others to a part in Him. That which we esteem excellent, we are desirous our friend should have a share in. If a man hath found a spring of water, he will call others that they may drink and satisfy their thirst. Do we commend Christ to others? Do we take them by the hand and lead them to Christ? This shows how few prize Christ because they strive not more that their relations should have a part in Him. They get land and riches for their posterity, but have no care to leave them the Pearl of Great Price for their portion…O then, let us have endearing thoughts of Christ; let Him be accounted our chief treasure and delight. This is the reason why millions perish: because they do not prize Christ. Christ is the Door by which men are to enter into heaven (John 10:9). If they do not know this Door, or are so proud that they will not stoop to go in at it, how can they be saved?

A Godly Man Is a Lover of the Word

O how love I thy law! —Ps. 119:97

1. A godly man loves the Word written. Chrysostom[66] compares the Scripture to a garden set with knots and flowers. A godly man delights to walk in this garden and sweetly solace himself; he loves every branch and parcel of the Word.

a. He loves the counseling part of the Word, as it is a directory and a rule of life. It contains in it *credenda et facienda*, [meaning] "things to be believed and practiced." A godly man loves the aphorisms[67] of the Word.

b. A godly man loves the minatory[68] part of the Word. The Scripture, like the Garden of Eden, as it hath a tree of life in it, so it hath a flaming sword at the gates of it. This is the threatening of the Word; it flasheth fire in the face of every person that goes on obstinately in wickedness: *"But God shall wound the head of his enemies, and the hairy scalp of such an one as goeth on still in his trespasses"* (Ps. 68:21). The Word gives no indulgence to evil. It will not let a man halt between sin and God: the true mother would not let the child be divided (1 Kings 3:26), and God will not have the heart divided.

c. A godly man loves the menaces of the Word. He knows there is love in every threatening; God would not have us perish, therefore doth mercifully threaten us, that He may scare us from sin. God's threatenings are as the seamark,[69] which shows the rocks in the sea and threateneth death to such as

---

66 **John Chrysostom** (AD 347-407) – early theologian and expositor of the Greek Church, whose name means "golden mouthed."
67 **aphorisms** – a brief and concise statement of truth or opinion.
68 **minatory** – threatening; menacing.
69 **seamark** – a clearly visible object distinguishable at sea that serves as a guide or warning to sailors in navigation.

come near. The threatening is a curbing bit to check us that we may not run in a full career to hell; there is a mercy in every threatening.

d. A godly man loves the consolatory part of the Word, the promises. He goes feeding upon these, as Samson went on his way eating the honeycomb. The promises are all marrow and sweetness; they are our bezoar stone[70] when we are fainting; they are the conduits of the water of life. *"In the multitude of my thoughts within me thy comforts delight my soul"* (Ps. 94:19). The promises were David's harp to drive away sad thoughts; they were the breasts that milked out divine consolation to him.

A Godly Man Shows His Love to the Word Written

1. By diligent reading of it: the noble Bereans did search the Scriptures daily (Acts 17:11). Apollos was mighty in the Scriptures (Acts 18:24). The Word is our Magna Carta[71] for heaven; we should be daily reading over this charter. The Word shows what truth is and what error is. It is the field where the Pearl of price is hid: how should we dig for this Pearl! A godly man's heart is the library to hold the Word of God; it dwells richly in him (Col. 3:16). The Word hath a double work: to *teach* us and to *judge* us. They that will not be taught by the Word shall be judged by the Word. Oh, let us make the Scripture familiar to us! What if it should be as in the time of Diocletian,[72] who commanded by proclamation the Bible to be burned; or as in Queen Mary's days,[73] wherein it was death to have a Bible in English? By diligent conversing with Scripture, we may carry a Bible in our head.

2. By frequent meditating: *"It is my meditation all the day"* (Ps. 119:97). A pious soul meditates on the verity and sanctity of the Word. He hath not only a few transient thoughts, but lays his mind a-steeping[74] in the Scripture: by meditation, he sucks from this sweet flower and concocts holy truth in his mind.

3. By delighting in it. It is his recreation: *"Thy words were found, and I did eat them; and thy word was unto me the joy and rejoicing of mine heart"* (Jer. 15:16). Never did a man take such delight in a dish that he loved, as the prophet did in the Word. Indeed, how can a saint choose but take great complacency in the Word because all that ever he hopes to be worth is contained in it? Doth

---

70 **bezoar stone** – hard, indigestible mass of material found in the stomach or intestines of animals, formerly considered an antidote for poisons.
71 **Magna Carta** – the charter of English political and civil liberties that King John granted at Runnymede, June 1215; hence, a document that guarantees basic rights.
72 **Dioclesian** or **Diocletian** (AD 245-313) – Roman emperor who persecuted Christians.
73 **Queen Mary** (1553-1558) –Catholic "Bloody Mary"; relentlessly persecuted Protestants.
74 **a-steeping** – to soak in water for cleansing.

not a son take pleasure in reading over his father's will and testament, where he makes a conveyance of his estate to him?

4. By hiding it: *"Thy word have I hid in mine heart"* (Ps. 119:11), as one hides a treasure that it should not be stolen away. The Word is the jewel; the heart is the cabinet where it must be locked up. Many hide the Word in their memory but not in their heart. And why would David enclose the Word in his heart? *"That I might not sin against thee."* As one would carry an antidote about him when he comes to an infected place, so a godly man carries the Word in his heart as a spiritual antidote to preserve him from the infection of sin. Why have so many been poisoned with error, others with moral vice, but because they have not hid the Word as a holy antidote in their heart?

5. By preferring it above things most precious: a. Above food: *"I have esteemed the words of his mouth more than my necessary food"* (Job 23:12). b. Above riches: *"The law of thy mouth is better unto me than thousands of gold and silver"* (Ps. 119:72). c. Above *worldly honor*: Memorable is the story of King Edward VI, who upon the day of his coronation, when they presented before him three swords signifying to him that he was monarch of three kingdoms, the king said, "There is yet one sword wanting." Being asked what that was, he answered, "The Holy Bible," which is the sword of the Spirit and is to be preferred before these ensigns of royalty.

6. By conforming to it. The Word is his sundial by which he sets his life, the balance in which he weighs his actions. He copies out the Word in his daily walk.

A godly man loves the Word preached: which is a commentary upon the Word written. The Scriptures are the sovereign oils and balsams;[75] the preaching of the Word is the pouring of them out. The Scriptures are the precious spices; the preaching of the Word is the beating of these spices, which causeth a wonderful fragrancy and delight…The preaching of the Word is called, *"the power of God"* (1 Cor. 1:24). By this, Christ is said to speak to us from heaven (Heb. 12:25). A godly man loves the Word preached partly from the good he hath found by it: he hath felt the dew fall with this manna; and partly because of God's institution: the Lord hath appointed this ordinance to save him.

A godly man is a praying man. This is in the text, *"Every one that is godly [shall] pray unto thee"* (Ps. 32:6). As soon as grace is poured in, prayer is poured out: *"But I give myself unto prayer"* (Ps. 109:4). In the Hebrew it is, "But I prayer." Prayer and I are all one. Prayer is the soul's traffic with heaven: God comes down to us by His Spirit, and we go up to Him by prayer. A godly

---

75 **balsams** – healing or soothing medicinal preparations.

man cannot live without prayer: a man cannot live unless he takes breath, nor can the soul unless it breathes forth its desires to God. As soon as the babe of grace is born, it cries; no sooner was Paul converted but, *"Behold, he prayeth"* (Acts 9:11). No doubt he prayed before, [having been] a Pharisee, but it was either superficially or superstitiously; but when the work of grace had passed upon his soul, behold, now he prays. A godly man is every day upon the mount of prayer; he begins the day with prayer: before he opens his shop, he opens his heart to God. We used to burn sweet perfumes in our houses; a godly man's house is a house of perfume: he airs it with the incense of prayer. He engageth in no business without seeking God. A godly man consults with God in everything.

From "The Godly Man's Picture Drawn with a Scripture-Pencil" in The Sermons of Thomas Watson, Soli Deo Gloria, a division of Reformation Heritage Books: www.heritagebooks.org.

Thomas Watson (c. 1620-1686): Non-Conformist Puritan preacher; prolific author of *A Body of Divinity, The Lord's Prayer, The Ten Commandments, Heaven Taken by Storm*, and numerous others; place and date of birth unknown.

There is no better definition of a true Christian than that he is a godly man, one who walks in the fear of the Lord. That is invariably the biblical description of God's people; clearly, it is the point at which we must start because it is the center and the soul of all truth.
—David Martyn Lloyd-Jones

Husbands, Love Your Wives

WILLIAM GOUGE (1575-1653)

> *Husbands, love your wives, even as Christ also loved the church, and gave himself for it.* —Ephesians 5:25

As the wife is to know her duty, so the husband much more his because he is to be a guide and good example to his wife. He is to dwell with her according to knowledge (1 Peter 3:7). The more eminent[76] his place is, the more knowledge he ought to have to walk worthy thereof. Neglect of duty in him is more dishonorable unto God because, by virtue of his place, he is the image and glory of God (1 Cor. 11:7). [This is] more pernicious,[77] not to his wife only, but also to the whole family because of that power and authority he hath, which he may abuse to the maintenance of his wickedness. [There is in his] house no superior power to restrain his fury, whereas the wife, though never so wicked, may by the power of her husband be kept under and restrained from outrage.

Of that love that husbands owe their wives. This head of all the rest—Love—is expressly set down and alone mentioned in this and in many other places of Scripture, whereby it is evident that all other duties are [included] under it. To omit other places where this duty is urged, *Love* in this place is four times by name expressed. Beside that, it is intimated under many other terms and phrases (Eph. 5:25, 28, 33).

All the branches that grow out of this root of love, as they have respect to husbands' duties, may be drawn to two heads: 1) a wise maintaining of his authority [and] 2) a right managing of the same.

That these two are branches of a husband's love is evident by the place wherein God hath set him, which is a place of authority. For the best good that any can do and the best fruits of love that he can show forth to any are such as are done in his own proper place and by virtue thereof. If then a husband *relinquish* his authority, he disableth himself from doing that good and showing those fruits of love which otherwise he might. If he *abuses* his authority, he turneth the edge and point of his sword amiss: instead of holding it over his wife for her protection, he turneth it into her [heart] to her destruction and so manifesteth thereby more hatred than love. Now then, to handle these two severally and distinctly:

1. Of husbands' wisely maintaining their authority: This is implied under the Apostolical precept: *"Likewise, ye husbands, dwell with them according to*

---

76 **eminent** – exalted; dignified.
77 **pernicious** – having the quality to destroy; tending to injure; ruinous.

knowledge" (1 Peter 3:7), that is, as such as are well able to maintain the honor of that place wherein God hath set you, not as sots[78] and fools without understanding.

The honor and authority of God and of His Son Christ Jesus is maintained in and by the honor and authority of a husband, as the King's authority is maintained by the authority of his Privy Council[79] and other Magistrates under him, yea, as an husband's authority is in the family maintained by the authority of his wife: *"Forasmuch as he is the image and glory of God: but the woman is the glory of the man"* (1 Cor. 11:7).

The good of the wife herself is thus also much promoted, even as the good of the body is helped forward by the head's abiding in his place. Should the head be put under any of the parts of the body, the body and all the parts thereof could not but receive much damage thereby. Even so, the wife and whole family would feel the damage of the husband's loss of his authority.

Question: How may a husband best maintain his authority?

Answer: The direction that the Apostle had given to Timothy to maintain his authority may firstly be applied for this purpose unto an husband: *"Be thou an example of the believers, in word, in conversation, in charity, in spirit, in faith, in purity"* (1 Tim. 4:12). Even thus may husbands best maintain their authority by being an ensample in love, gravity, piety, honesty, etc. The fruits of these and other like graces showed forth by husbands before their wives and family cannot but work a reverent and dutiful respect in their wives and whole house towards them; for by this means they shall more clearly discern the image of God shining forth in their faces.

Of husbands' losing their authority: Contrary is their practice who by their profaneness, riotousness, drunkenness, lewdness, lightness, unthriftiness, and other like base carriage[80] make themselves contemptible and so lose their authority. Though a wife ought not to take these occasions to despise her husband, yet is it a just judgment on him to be despised, seeing he maketh himself contemptible.

Contrary also to the forenamed directions is the stern, rough, and cruel carriage of husbands, who by violence and tyranny go about to maintain their authority. Force may indeed cause fear, but a slavish fear, such a fear as breedeth more hatred than love, more inward contempt than outward respect.

2. Of husbands' rightly managing their authority, through a high account of their wives: As authority must be well maintained, so must it be

---

78 **sots** – foolish, stupid persons; blockheads.
79 **Privy Council** – the body of advisors and counselors for a king.
80 **base carriage** – despicably mean behavior.

well managed: for which purpose two things are needful: 1) that a husband tenderly respect his wife; [and] 2) that providently he care for her.

Her place is indeed a place of inferiority[81] and subjection, yet the nearest to equality that may be. [Hers is] a place of common equity in many respects, wherein man and wife are, after a sort, even fellows and partners. Hence then it followeth that the husband must account his wife a yoke-fellow and companion (1 Peter 3:7). This is one point of giving honor to the wife: and it is implied under that phrase whereby the end of making a wife is noted (Gen. 2:18), which in our English is translated, "meet for him," word for word "as before him," that is, like himself, one in whom he might see himself.

As a wife's acknowledgement of her husband's superiority[82] is the groundwork of all her duties, so a husband's acknowledgement of that fellowship which is between him and his wife will make him carry himself much more amiably,[83] familiarly, lovingly, and every way as beseemeth a good husband towards her.

Of husbands' too mean account of wives: Contrary is the conceit of many who think there is no difference between a wife and servant but in familiarity,[84] and that wives were made to be servants to their husbands because subjection, fear, and obedience are required of them. Whence it cometh to pass that wives are oft used little better than servants are. [This is] conceit and practice savoring too much of heathenish and sottish arrogance. Did God at first take the wife out of man's side that man should tread her under his feet? Or rather that he should set her at his side next to him above all children, servants, or any other in the family, how near or dear unto him soever? For none can be nearer than a wife can, and none ought to be dearer.

Of husbands' entire affection to their wives: A husband's affection to his wife must be answerable to his opinion of her. He ought therefore to delight in his wife entirely, that is, so to delight in her as wholly and only delighting in her. In this respect the Prophet's wife is called *"the desire [delight, pleasure] of thine eyes"* (Ezek. 24:16): that wherein he most of all delighted and therefore by a propriety,[85] so called. Such delight did Isaac take in his wife as it drove out a contrary strong passion, namely the grief which he took for the departure of his mother. For it is noted that he loved her and was comforted after his mother's death (Gen. 24:67).

---

81 **inferiority** – inferiority here means "a role of submission." It does not mean a woman is an inferior creature, but of a different rank in God's order.
82 **superiority** – again, superiority here refers to the husband's *role*, not his created nature.
83 **amiably** – showing a friendly, good-tempered disposition.
84 **familiarity** – behavior due from a familiar friend or family member.
85 **propriety** – fitness; appropriateness.

This kind of affection the wise man doth elegantly set forth in these words, *"Rejoice with the wife of thy youth. Let her be as the loving hind and pleasant roe… and be thou ravished always with her love"* (Prov. 5:18, 19). Here note both the metaphors and the hyperbole[86] that are used to set forth a husband's delight in his wife. In the metaphors, again note both the creatures whereunto a wife is resembled and the attributes given to them. The creatures are two: a hind and a roe, which are the females of a hart and a roebuck. Now it is noted of the hart and roebuck that of all other beasts they are most [passionate] with their mates and even mad again in their heat and desire after them.

These comparisons applied to a wife do lively set forth the delight that a husband ought to take in her…First so far to exceed, as to make a man oversee some such blemishes in his wife, as others would soon espy and mislike, or else to count them no blemishes, delighting in her never a whit the less for them. For example, if a man have a wife, not very beautiful or proper, but having some deformity in her body, some imperfection in her speech, sight, gesture, or any part of her body; yet so to affect[87] her and delight in her, as if she were the fairest and every way most complete woman in the world. Secondly, so highly to esteem, so ardently to affect, so tenderly to respect her as others may think him even to dote[88] on her. A husband's affection to his wife cannot be too great if it is kept within the bonds of honesty, sobriety, and [decency].

Of husbands' forbearing to exact[89] all that they may: as a wife's reverence, so also her obedience must be answered with her husband's courtesy. In testimony whereof, a husband must be ready to accept that wherein his wife showeth herself willing to obey him. He ought to be sparing in exacting too much of her. In this case, he ought so to frame his carriage towards her, as the obedience that she performeth, may rather come from her own voluntary disposition from a free conscience to God-wards, even because God hath placed her in a place of subjection, and from a wife-like love than from any exaction on her husband's part, as it were by force.

Husbands…must observe what is lawful, needful, convenient, expedient, fit for their wives to do, yea, and what they are most willing to do before they be too [obstinate] in exacting it. For example,

1. Though the wife ought to go with her husband and dwell where he

---

86 **hyperbole** – figure of speech used consisting of exaggeration in order to make an impression.
87 **affect** – have affection for; be fond of.
88 **dote** – to bestow excessive fondness; to be foolishly in love.
89 **exact** – to require by force or with authority the performance of some duty.

thinks meet, yet ought not he [unless by virtue of some urgent calling he be forced thereto] remove her from place to place, and carry her from that place where she is well settled without her good liking. Jacob consulted with his wives, and made trial of their willingness, before he carried them from their father's house (Gen. 31:4).

2. Though she ought cheerfully to entertain what guests he bringeth into the house, yet ought not he to be grievous and burdensome therein unto her. The greatest care and pains for entertaining guests lieth on the wife; she ought therefore to be tendered therein.

If he observe her conscionable[90] and wise, well able to manage and order matters about house, yet loath to do anything without his consent, he ought to be ready and free in yielding his consent, and satisfying her desire, as Elkanah (1 Sam. 1:23). And if she be bashful and backward in asking consent, he ought voluntarily of himself to offer it: yea and to give her a general consent to order and dispose matters as in her wisdom she seeth meet, as the said Elkanah did; and the husband of that good housewife which Solomon describeth (Prov. 31:10-31).

A general consent is especially requisite for ordering of household affairs, for it is a charge laid upon wives to guide the house (1 Tim. 5:14): whereby it appeareth that the businesses of the house [pertain] and are most proper to the wife in which respect she is called the housewife. So as therein, husbands ought to refer matters to their ordering and not restrain them in every particular matter from doing anything without a special license and direction. To exemplify this in some particulars, it appertaineth in peculiar to a wife, 1. to order the decking and trimming[91] of the house (Prov. 31:21, 22); 2. to dispose the ordinary provision for the family (Prov. 31:15); 3. to rule and govern maid servants (Gen. 16:6); 4. to bring up children while they are young with the like (1 Tim. 5:10; Titus 2:4).

These therefore ought he with a general consent to refer to her discretion (2 Kings 4:19) with limitation only of these two cautions: 1. That she have in some measure sufficient discretion, wit, and wisdom, and be not too ignorant, foolish, simple, lavish, etc; 2. That he have a general oversight in all, and so interpose his authority as he suffer nothing that is unlawful or unseemly to be done by his wife about house, children, servants, or other things.

Of husbands' too much strictness towards their wives: Contrary is the rigor and austerity of many husbands, who stand upon the uttermost step

---

90 **conscionable** – conscientious; principled.
91 **decking and trimming** – decorating and remodeling.

of their authority, and yield no more to a wife than to any other inferior. Such are they:

1. Who are never contented or satisfied with any duty the wife performeth, but ever are exacting more and more.

2. Who care not how grievous and burdensome they are to their wives—grievous by bringing such guests into the house as they know cannot be welcome to them, burdensome by *too frequent* and *unseasonable* inviting of guests or imposing other like extraordinary businesses over and above the ordinary affairs of the house: *too frequent* imposing of such things cannot but breed much wearisomeness, [and] *unseasonable* cannot but much disquiet her and give her great offence [as when the wife is weak by sickness, childbearing, nursing, or other like means, and so not able to give that contentment which otherwise she would].

3. Who hold their wives under as if they were children or servants, restraining them from doing anything without their knowledge and particular express consent.

Of husbands' ungrateful discouraging their wives: Contrary is an ungrateful, if not envious disposition of such husbands as passing by many good things ordinarily and usually every day done by their wives without any [approval], commendation, or [reward], are ready to dispraise the least slip or neglect in them. [They do this] in such general terms as if they never did anything well, so as their wives may well complain and say as it is in the proverb, "Oft did I well, and that hear I never: Once did I ill, and that hear I ever."

Of a husband's manner of instructing his wife: To instruction, the Apostle expressly annexeth[92] meekness. Instruct [saith he] with meekness *"those that oppose themselves"* (2 Tim. 2:25). If ministers must use meekness when they instruct their people, much more husbands when they instruct their wives: if in case of opposition meekness must not be laid aside, then in no case, at no time.

In this case to manifest meekness, let these rules be observed.

1. Note the understanding and capacity of thy wife and accordingly fit thine instructions. If she is of mean capacity, give precept upon precept, line upon line, here a little and there a little. A little at once oft given [namely every day something] will arise in time to a great measure, and so arise, as, together with knowledge of the thing taught, love of the person that teacheth will increase.

2. Instruct her in private between thyself and her so that her ignorance may not be blazed forth. Private actions passing between man and wife are

---

92 **annexeth** – adds.

tokens of much kindness and familiarity.

3. In the family so instruct children and servants when she is present, as she may learn knowledge thereby. There can be no more meek and gentle manner of instructing, than by one to instruct another.

4. Together with thy precepts mix sweet and pithy persuasions that are testimonies of great love. Contrary is a harsh and rough manner of instructing, when husbands go about to thrust into their wives' heads, as it were by violence, deep mysteries that they are not able to conceive. Yet if they conceive not, they will be angry with them, in anger give them evil language, and proclaim their ignorance before children, servants, and strangers. This harshness is ordinarily so fruitless and withal so exasperateth a woman's spirit, as I think he [would do] better [to] clean omit the duty than do it after such a manner.

Of a husband's providing means of spiritual edification for his wife: For her soul, means of spiritual edification must be provided, and those both private and public. Private means are holy and religious exercises in the house, as reading the word, prayer, catechizing, and such like; which being the spiritual food of the soul are to be every day, as our bodily food, provided and used. A husband as a master of a family must provide these for the good of his whole house; but as a husband, in special for the good of his wife: for to his wife, as well as to the whole house he is a king, a priest, and a prophet.

By himself therefore, for his wife's good, ought he to perform these things or to provide that they may be done by some other. Cornelius himself performed those exercises (Acts 10:2, 30). Micah hired a Levite [though his idolatry were evil, yet his care to have a Levite in his house was commendable] (Judg. 17:10). The Shunammite's husband provided a chamber for the prophet and that especially for his wife's sake, for it was at her request (2 Kings 4:11).

Public means are the holy ordinances of God publicly performed by God's minister. The care of a husband for his wife in this respect is to order his habitation and provide other needful things, as his wife may be made partaker thereof. It is expressly noted of Elkanah that he so provided for his wives, that they went with him every year to the house of God (1 Sam. 1:7; 2:19): the like is intimated of Joseph, the husband of the virgin Mary (Luke 2:41). In those days, there was a public place and house of God, whither all God's people [how far soever they dwelt from it] were to resort every year. The places where Elkanah and Joseph dwelt were far remote from the house of God, yet they so provided, as not only themselves, but their wives also went to the public worship of God. Now there are many houses of God, places for the public worship of God, yet through the corruption of our times, the ministry of the Word [the principal means of spiritual edification] is not everywhere to be enjoyed. Therefore, such ought a husband's care for his wife in this respect to be, as to dwell where she may have the benefit of the Word preached, or else [he should so] provide for her, as she may weekly go where it may be had.

Of neglecting their wives' edification: Contrary is their practice, who having their calling in places where the Word is plentiful, yet upon outward respects of pleasure, delight, ease, and profit, remove their families into remote places where preaching is scarce, if at all. There [they] leave their wives to govern the family, not regarding their want of the Word, for as much as they themselves oft coming to London or other like places by reason of their calling, enjoy the Word themselves. Many citizens, lawyers, and others are guilty of great neglect of their wives in this respect. So also are they, who abandon all religious exercise out of their houses, making their houses rather stews[93] of the devil than churches of God. If for want of means, either public or private, a wife live and die in ignorance, profaneness, infidelity, and impenitency, which cause eternal damnation, assuredly her blood shall be required at his hands, for an husband is God's watchman to his wife (Ezek. 3:18).

Of an husband's care to provide for his wife so long as she shall live: The continuance of an husband's provident care for his wife must be so long as she liveth, yea though she outlive him. Not that he can actually provide for her when he is dead, but that he may before his death so provide for her, as she may have wherewithal to maintain herself, and to live according to that place whereunto by him she is advanced. [He should at least] leave her not only so much as he had with her, but something more also in testimony of his love to her and care for her. Husbands have the example of Christ to press this duty upon them: for when He went away from His Church here on earth, He left His Spirit, which furnished [her] with gifts as plentifully, as if Christ had still remained with her, if not more abundantly (Eph. 4:8). At the time of a man's departure out of this world from his wife will the truest trial of his affection to his wife be given. For many that bear their wives' fare in hand while they live with them, at their death show that there was no soundness of affection in their heart towards them. All was but a mere show for some by-respects.[94]

Of the freeness of husbands' love: The cause of Christ's love was His

---

93 **stews** – brothels; houses of prostitution.
94 **by-respects** – regard to something other than the main object.

love, as Moses noteth, He set His love on you because He loved you (Deut. 7:7-8). His love arose only and wholly from Himself and was every way free: as there was nothing in the Church, before Christ loved her, to move Him to love her, so can there be nothing that He could hope for afterwards, but what He bestowed. Indeed, He delighteth in that righteousness wherewith as with a glorious robe she is clothed and with those heavenly graces, wherewith as with precious jewels she is decked. Yet, that righteousness and those graces are His own and of His free gift. He presents it to Himself a glorious Church (Eph. 5:27).

In imitation hereof, husbands should love their wives, though there were nothing in wives to move them so to do, but only that they are their wives. Yea [they should love their wives] though no future benefit could after be expected from them. True love hath respect to the object that is loved, and the good it may do thereunto, rather than to the subject that loveth, and the good that it may receive. For love seeketh not her own (1 Cor. 13:5)…Christ's love in this branch thereof should further move husbands to do what lieth in their power to make their wives worthy of love. Thus will it be in truth said that they dwell with their wives according to knowledge (1 Peter 3:7), and thus will their love appear to be as Christ's love—free.

Of husbands loving their wives more than themselves: The quantity of Christ's love cannot be expressed: for the measure of it was above measure. He gave Himself for His Church (Eph. 5:25), and in that respect He calleth Himself that Good Shepherd that gave His life for His sheep (John 10:11). *"Greater love hath no man than this"* (John 15:13). What will He not do for His spouse, [who] gave His life for her?

Of husbands' unkindness: Contrary is their unkindness that prefers every trifle of their own before the good of their wives: their profit, their pleasure, their promotion, clean draw away their hearts and affections from their wives. If any extraordinary charge must be laid out or pains taken for their wives' good, little love will then appear.

Of husbands' constancy in love: The continuance of Christ's love was without date: *"Having loved his own which were in the world, he loved them unto the end"* (John 13:1). His love was constant [not by fits, now loving, then hating] and everlasting (Hos. 2:19) [never repenting thereof, never changing or altering His mind]. No provocations, no transgressions could ever make Him forget to love and cease to do that good which He intended for His Church. Note what He said to her even when she revolted from Him, *"Thou hast played the harlot with many lovers; yet return again to me"* (Jer. 3:1); and again, *"My mercy shall not depart away"* (2 Sam. 7:15)…For His love resteth not on the desert of His Church, but on the unchangeableness of His own will. As this manifested Christ's love to be true, sound love, so it made it profitable and beneficial to the Church, which, notwithstanding her many frailties, by virtue hereof is glorified.

Of husbands' loving their wives as themselves: To the example of Christ the Apostle annexeth the pattern of one's self in these words: *"So ought men to love their wives as their own bodies"* (Eph. 5:28)…Christ's example is a full, complete, perfect, and every way sufficient pattern, far more excellent than this of a man's self. This is not annexed to add anything to that or in regard of the excellency hereof, but only in regard of our dullness to make the point somewhat more plain and perspicuous. For this pattern is more sensible and better discerned. Every one knoweth how he loveth his own body, but few or none knows how Christ loveth His Church. Besides, that example of Christ may seem too high and excellent for any to attain unto, even [out of reach]. Therefore, to show that he requireth no more than a man may perform, if he will set himself with care and conscience to do his duty, [the Apostle] addeth the pattern of one's self; that which one doth to his body, if he will, he may do to his wife.

No other man will or can so tenderly handle a man's hand, arm, leg, or any other part of his body as himself: he is very sensible of his own smart. The metaphors that the Apostle useth in these words, *"[He] nourisheth and cherisheth it,"* do lively set forth this tenderness (Eph. 5:29). They are taken from fowls and birds that very [carefully] and tenderly hover over their young ones, covering them all over with their wings and feathers, but so bearing up their bodies as no weight lieth upon them…Thus ought husbands with all tenderness and mildness to deal with their wives, as we have before noted in many particulars. Only this example of a man's self, I thought good to set before husbands, as a lively pattern wherein they might behold a precedent without exception going before them, and whereby they might receive excellent direction for the better performing of the particulars before noted.

Such affection ought husbands to have to their wives: they ought more willingly and cheerfully to do anything for their wives than for parents, children, friends, or any other. Though this cheerfulness is an inward disposition of the heart, yet may it be manifested by a man's forwardness and readiness to do his wife good. When his wife shall no sooner desire a kindness, than he will be ready to grant it: as Boaz saith to Ruth, *"I will do to thee all that thou requirest"* (Ruth 3:11).

Contrary is the disposition of those husbands who so grudgingly, repiningly,⁹⁵ and discontentedly do those things which they do in their wives' behalf, as their wives had rather they were not done at all. The manner of doing them causeth more grief to tenderhearted wives, than the things themselves can do good.

Of Christ's example, a motive to provoke husbands to love their wives: The forenamed examples of Christ and of ourselves as they are patterns for our direction, so general motives to provoke and stir us up the more to perform all the forenamed duties after the manner prescribed…A greater and stronger motive cannot be yielded than the example of Christ. Example in itself is of great force to provoke us to do anything: especially if it be the example of some great one, a man of place and renown. But who greater than Christ? What more worthy pattern? If the example of the Church is of great force to move wives to be subject to their husbands, the example of Christ must needs be of much greater force to move husbands to love their wives. A great honor it is to be like unto Christ: His example is a perfect pattern.

From *Of Domestical Duties*, Puritan Reprints: www.puritanreprints.com.

William Gouge (1575-1653): Puritan minister for 46 years at Blackfriars, London; born in Stratford-Bow, Middlesex County, England.

> *Generally, men are diligent in the exercise of their dominion, but negligent in regard of affection. Hence, their authority degenerateth into tyranny.*
> *—George Swinnock*

---

95 **repiningly** – grumblingly.

The Conversion of Family Members
SAMUEL LEE (1627-1691)

Brethren, my heart's desire and prayer to God for Israel is, that they might be saved. —Romans 10:1

Question: "What course shall we take, what means shall we use, what method will you prescribe, that we may be able to manage this important and weighty duty, [and] that we may be helpful towards the conversion and salvation of our near relations that are in the state of nature[96]?"

I shall draw up directions under [several] heads. Some whereof, though usual and obvious in such as treatment upon [household] duties, yet being further improved, may by no means be here passed by in silence, since they are exceeding useful and no less practical than others. Most men under the Gospel perish for [lack] of practicing known duties. Wherefore let me beg of thee, O Christian, that every prescription may be duly weighed and conscientiously improved; so shalt thou not doubt of admirable success through Divine assistance.

1. Preserve and uphold the honor and preeminence of that station wherein God hath set you by all wise and cautious means. The Prophet bewails those times wherein *"the child shall behave himself proudly against the ancient, and the base against the honourable"* (Isa. 3:5). Distance of years calls for distance of behavior…There is a great deal of reverence to be manifested by adults towards youth, if they would cherish and preserve that due reverence which ought to be in the hearts of young ones towards themselves. Yet notwithstanding, you must not carry yourselves with any proud, haughty, or pretentious behavior. Your countenance, though grave, yet must not be stern. As you need not indent your cheeks with continual smiles, so neither to plough your foreheads with rough and sour wrinkles. Rigid severity in words and actions will produce a slavish, disheartened temper in children.

2. Be frequent, pithy,[97] and clear in family instruction. We are all by nature like barren wildernesses and stony deserts: instruction is the culture and improvement of the soul. It is observed by naturalists, that bees "do carry small gravel in their feet" to poise their little bodies through the stormy winds. Such are instructions to the floating and wavering minds of youth. The keel of their weak judgments would soon capsize without the ballast of discipline…But in all your instructions, have a care of being tediously

---

96 **in the state of nature** – in an unconverted state; not born of God's Spirit, and, therefore, unrepentant and unbelieving.
97 **pithy** – containing much matter in a few words.

long-winded. Make up the shortness of your discourse by frequency. Thou art enjoined to talk of God's precepts *"when thou sittest in thine house, and when thou walkest by the way, and when thou liest down, and when thou risest up"* (Deut. 6:7; 11:19), a little now and a little then. Long orations burden their small memories too much and through such imprudence may occasion the loathing of spiritual manna, considering their being yet in the state of nature. A young plant may quickly be overloaded with manure and rotted with too much watering. Weak eyes, newly opened from sleep, cannot bear the glaring windows: *"For precept must be upon precept...line upon line...here a little, and there a little"*(Isa. 28:10). You must drive the little ones as Jacob did, very gently towards Canaan (Gen. 33:13).

Entertain their tender attentions with discourses of God's infinite greatness and amiable goodness, of the glories of heaven, of the torments of hell. Things that affect the senses must be spiritualized to them: catch their affections by a holy cunning. Deal as much in allegories as thou canst. If you are together in a garden, draw some sweet and heavenly discourse out of the beautiful flowers. If by a riverside, treat of the water of life and the rivers of pleasure that are at God's right hand. If in a field of corn, speak of the nourishing quality of the bread of life. If you see birds flying in the air or hear them singing in the woods, teach them the all-wise providence of God that gives them their meat in due season. If thou lookest up to the sun, moon, and stars, tell them they are but the shining spangles of the outer rooms of heaven. O then what glory is there within! If thou seest a rainbow adorning some waterish cloud, talk of the covenant of God. These and many more may be like so many golden links drawing divine things into their memories. *"I have also spoken by the prophets...and used similitudes,"* saith God (Hos. 12:10). Moreover, let young ones read and learn by heart some portions of the historical books of Holy Scripture. But, above all, the best way of instruction, especially as to the younger sort, may be performed by catechisms[98]—question and answer in a short, concise method—whose terms, being clear and distinct, might be phrased out of Holy Scripture and fitted to their capacities by a plain, though solid style and to their memories by brief expressions.

---

98 **catechisms** – a method for teaching the essential doctrines of the Christian faith, used and proven effective for many centuries. Several are available from CHAPEL LIBRARY: "A Catechism with Proofs," similar to the Westminster Shorter Catechism, but tailored to the London Baptist Confession of 1677/89 by Benjamin Keach and updated by Charles Haddon Spurgeon for his congregation; "A Catechism for Boys and Girls," by Erroll Hulse, which is a simplified version of "A Catechism with Proofs"; and "Gadsby's Catechism" by William Gadsby (1773-1884).

3. Add to thine instructions mandatory requirements. Lay it as a charge upon their souls in the name of God that they hearken to and obey thine household regulations and practices. An instance we have in the case of Solomon, who acquaints us that he was *"my father's son, tender and only beloved in the sight of my mother. He taught me also, and said unto me, Let thine heart retain my words: keep my commandments, and live"* (Prov. 4:3-4)…For this matter, Abraham was commended by God Himself as a pattern to all posterity. *"I know him,"* says God, *"that he will command his children and his household after him, and they shall keep the way of the LORD, to do justice and judgment"* (Gen. 18:19), and therefore God was pleased to reveal secrets to him.

4. Set a narrow guard upon the first sproutings of sin in their behavior. Crush vipers in the egg. Exercise your hazel-rods upon the serpents' heads, when they first creep out of their holes, being chill and feeble in the beginning of the spring. *"I will early destroy all the wicked of the land,"* says David (Ps. 101:8). You must set about this work early in life [and] stop every evil and disagreeable word at the first hearing. Watch the beginnings, the first bubblings of corruption in them. A man may pull off a tender bud with ease; but if he let it grow to a branch, it will cost him some pains.

O that you would then begin to cast water upon the first kindlings of sin in your little ones! Cut off the occasions of sin by prudent interference. It is strange to see what excuses and disguises for sin, what deceitfulness in speech [that] little children will use! Before thou canst teach them to speak plain English, the devil and a corrupt heart will teach them to speak plain lies. While their tongues do yet falter much in pronunciation, they will falter more in double speaking. What great need is there then to put a curb and bridle upon thy child's tongue as well as thine own (Ps.39:1)!

Undermine their fallacies by discerning examinations and shrewd questions. If this work be not set to early in their lives, possibly in process of years they may prove too cunning to be caught, unless thou inspire them quickly with the awe of God's judgments and the danger of sin. Teach their conscience to blush, as well as their cheeks, that they from an inwrought principle may avoid the evil and do the good. If thou suffer a child to go on in sin unregarded, untaught, unrebuked, and think it is too little to give attention to at first, that sinful folly will be thy scourge in the end. God many times whips an aged parent by that child that was unwhipped at first.

5. Preserve them from evil society. David not only hated sin in general, but especially he detested having it become an inmate in his house. *"He that worketh deceit shall not dwell within my house: he that telleth lies shall not tarry in my sight"*

(Ps. 101:7), so that the evil example and spiritually darkened companionship of wicked persons might not cleave to and corrupt his close relations. Imitation is natural to children: associates and companions are the patterns of their imitation. For, according to the proverb, "He that lives with a lame man will learn to limp." [Solomon] tells us that *"with a furious man thou shalt not go: Lest thou learn his ways"* (Prov. 22:24, 25). Children especially may be dangerously infected by lewd and corrupt company. Many children of godly parents have had their manners fouled and extremely corrupted by frequent and familiar consorting with the naughty children of wicked neighbors.

6. Let well-timed and prudent rebukes be administered according to the nature and quality of their offences. Begin gently. Use all persuasive motives to draw and allure them, if possible, to the ways of God. Tell them of the rewards of glory, of the sweet society in heaven; endeavor to satisfy their hearts that God is able to fill their souls with such joys as are not to be found in the creatures. *"Of some have compassion, making a difference"* (Jude 22). But if this will not do, then begin to mix some more severe expressions of thy holy anger against sin. As there is a linking-together in virtues, so in passions. Love and anger are not altogether "incompatible affections." Nay, love may be the principle and foundation of that anger, which shoots its rebuking arrows against the [target] of sin…Thou mayest tell thy child, and that with some grains of severity, that if he continue in sinful courses, God will be angry, and thou wilt be angry. Then let him know what a *"fearful thing [it is] to fall into the hands of the living God"* (Heb. 10:31). This is the way to *"be ye angry, and sin not"* as the apostle commands (Eph. 4:26). Let not your passions, like unruly torrents, overflow the banks that are limited by Scripture and reason. There is a grave and sober anger that will procure reverence and advance reformation. That which is mixed with horrid noise and shouting floweth from the breasts of fools. In vain shalt thou attempt to reclaim others, who art so excessive and frantic thyself. How shall that person in his rebukes speak reason to another that hath lost his own? He that is a slave to his hot-tempered appetite can never manage noble reproofs. A child can never persuade himself that such anger proceedeth from love, when he is made the sink to receive the daily vomitings of a fiery stomach, when the unhappy necessity of his relation ties him to be always in the way where an angry disposition must vent and empty itself…Observe, therefore, a prudent administration of thy rebukes. Gild those bitter pills[99] with the hopes of recovering thy favor upon amendment.[100]

---

99 **gild those bitter pills** – to soften or tone down something unpleasant.
100 **amendment** – reforming; changing for the better.

Consider, likewise, the station and place of thy several relations. A wife ought not to be rebuked before children and servants, lest her subordinate authority be diminished. Contempt cast upon the wife will reflect upon the husband at last. Yea, for smaller offences in children and servants, if they are not committed openly, rebuke them apart and in private. But, above all, take heed thou be not found more severe in reproving faults against thyself, than sins against the great God. If thou hast cause to be angry, yet let not thy storms run all upon the rocks, but endeavor speedily to cool the inflammation, to abate the fever, and slake the fire of anger.

Wink at infirmities: if not such as are immediately sinful, chide them with frowns and not with bitter assaults. Reserve thy public and sharp reprehensions for open and scandalous offences, for reiterated and repeated transgressions that bear a show of great neglect, if not of some contempt and disdain.

7. Keep up a constant and vigorous practice of holy duties in thy family. *"As for me and my house,"* says Joshua, *"we will serve the Lord"* (Josh. 24:15). Moses commanded the Israelites to go over the laws and precepts that he had given them from God in their own families in private among their children (Deut. 6:7). The instructions and exhortations of God's ministers in public should be repeated at home and whetted to and again upon the little ones. Samuel had a feast upon the sacrifice in his own house (1 Sam. 9:12, 22). Job and others had sacrifices in their own families. The Passover lamb was to be eaten in every particular house (Ex. 12:3, 4). God says He will *"pour out [his] fury...upon the families that call not on [his] name"* (Jer. 10:25).

The keeping up of family-duties makes every little house become a sanctuary, a Beth-el, a house of God. Here I would advise that Christians be not over-tedious in their duties of private worship. Take heed of making the ways of God burdensome and unpleasant. If God draw forth thy heart sometimes, do not reject and repress Divine breathings, but usually labor for conciseness and brevity. The spirit is willing many times, when the flesh is weak (Matt. 26:41). And a person may better for a little time keep his thoughts from wandering and disarray, whereas the large expense of expressions gives occasion for too much diversion. *"God is in heaven, and thou upon earth: therefore let thy words be few"* (Eccl. 5:2). It is of good use likewise to vary the duties of religion: sometimes sing and sometimes read, sometimes repeat, sometimes catechize, sometimes exhort. But in two things be principally frequent: the offering up the sacrifice of prayers and the keeping of children to read daily some portion of Holy Scriptures.

8. Endeavor by all good means to draw them to public ordinances. For there God is in a more special manner present. He makes the place of His feet to be glorious. Though it were God's appointment that the males only should at the solemn feasts repair to Shiloh, yet Elkanah carries up all his house to the yearly sacrifice (1 Sam. 1:21). He would have his wife, children, and servants *"to behold the beauty of the LORD, and to enquire in his temple"* (Ps.27:4). Cornelius also, when Peter came to preach at Caesarea upon God's immediate command, calls together all his kindred and acquaintances to hear the sermon (Acts 10:24)…As for such as can be present at ordinances, remember to examine them of what they heard as our blessed Lord, the grand pattern of our imitation, dealt by His beloved disciples, when He had preached that famous sermon by the seaside. Jesus asks them, *"Have ye understood all these things?"* (Matt. 13:51). When they were alone and apart from the multitude, then He expounded and explained all things that He taught more fully to them (Mark 4:34).

9. If all these things forementioned will not prevail, but inferiors will still run on in a course of sin, then oughtest thou to resort to paternal correction. Now chastisements must be suited to their age, the temperament of their natures, [their] dispositions, [and] the various qualities and kinds of their offences. Indulge a pardon sooner to lesser faults upon repentance and sorrow. You must consider whether their faults proceed from imprudence and weakness, upon what ground and occasion, [and] upon what provocation or seduction. Observe whether they appear to be deeply sorrowful and truly humbled…In these and the like cases, you must apply great diligence and prudence. Due punishment is a part of family justice, and there must be care taken, lest by frequent exemption from punishment they and their fellows be hardened in the ways of sin and grow obstinate and rebellious against the commandments of God. *"He that spareth his rod hateth his son: but he that loveth him chasteneth him betimes. Thou shalt beat him with the rod, and shalt deliver his soul from hell"* (Prov. 13:24; 23:14). This is an ordinance and appointment of God."*We have had fathers of our flesh which corrected us, and we gave them reverence"* (Heb. 12:9).

Some cruel parents and masters carry themselves more like raging brutes than men: [they] take pleasure in tyrannical corrections. They can let their children swear, and lie, and steal, and commit any other sin, and yet correct them not. But if they do not what they would have them, then they fall upon them and tear them like wild beasts. Know that God will require such vile acts at your hands in the great Day! O rather let them see that thou art angry for God's sake and not for thine own! There must be a great deal of gracious pity to their souls and holy love mixed with thine anger against sin…Be careful to use both your ears, and hearken to both parties in matters of complaint. But if upon deliberate and mature conviction nothing less will prevail, follow God's command herein and *"thy son…shall give delight unto thy soul"* (Prov. 29:17)…But take heed of all violent and passionate corrections. He that smites when his passion boils, is too, too subject to transcend the limits of moderation…take heed lest thou make thy child to become vile in thine own eyes by too many stripes (Deut. 25:3).

10. If the forementioned means through Divine blessing prove effectual, then praise and encourage them, when they come on, though yet but a little. As magistrates, so parents must be sometimes praisers of them that do well (Rom. 13:3). Our Lord comes in sometimes with, *"Well done, thou good and faithful servant"* (Matt. 25:21). So when they show promise and a sense of duty, you must encourage them by showing your approval…Only take heed of exceeding too much, for little vessels can bear no great sails. Pride and arrogance are many times nursed up by overflowing and lavish expressions, and sometimes inappropriate haughtiness and familiarity appear.

11. Do they flourish and thrive in duty and obedience and begin to take in precepts freely and kindly? Then win them on further by rewards according to their several capacities and the quality of thine own estate. God is pleased most graciously to draw and allure us on in the ways of holiness by the proposal of reward: *"He is a rewarder of them that diligently seek him"* (Heb. 11:6). As to years of further growth, such rewards as become them may be more proper. In some cases, these have proved great spurs and incitations, at least to the outward work of religion in younger ones…You know the father of the prodigal in the parable, when his son returned home to lead a new life—he killed a fatted calf for him, put the best robe upon his back, a ring upon his hand, and shoes upon his feet (Luke 15:22).

From "What Means May Be Used towards the Conversion of Our Carnal Relations?" in *Puritan Sermons 1659-1689, Being the Morning Exercises at Cripplegate, Vol. 1,* Richard Owen Roberts Publishers.

Samuel Lee (1627-1691): Congregational Puritan minister of St. Botolph, Bishopsgate; born in London, England.

My brethren, let me say, be ye like Christ at all times, imitate Him in public. Most of us live in some sort of publicity; many of us are called to work before our fellow men every day. We are watched; our words are caught; our lives are examined—taken to pieces. The eagle-eyed, argue-eyed world observes everything we do; and sharp critics are upon us. Let us live the life of Christ in public. Let us take care that we exhibit our Master and not ourselves, so that we can say, "It is no longer I that live, but Christ that liveth in me." Take heed that you carry this into the church too, you who are church members. Be like Christ in the church. How many there are of you like Diotrephes, seeking preeminence (3 John 1:9). How many are trying to have some dignity and power over their fellow Christians, instead of remembering that it is the fundamental rule of all our churches, that there all men are equal-alike brethren, alike to be received as such.

Carry out the spirit of Christ then, in your churches, wherever ye are. Let your fellow members say of you, "He has been with Jesus"…But most of all take care to have religion in your houses. A religious house is the best proof of true piety. Not my chapel, it is my house—not my minister, it is my home companion who can best judge me. It is the servant, the child, the wife, the friend, that can discern most of my real character. A good man will improve his household. Rowland Hill once said he would not believe a man to be a true Christian, if his wife, his children, his servants, and even the dog and cat, were not the better for it…If your household is not the better for your Christianity, if men cannot say, "This is a better house than others," then be not deceived—ye have nothing of the grace of God…Carry out your godliness in your family. Let everyone say that you have practical religion. Let it be known and read in the house, as well as in the world. Take care of your character there; for what we are there, we really are. —Charles Haddon Spurgeon

A Godly Father's Anger
JOHN GILL (1697-1771)

First, negatively expressed: *"Ye fathers, provoke not your children to wrath"* (Eph. 6:4) which may be done,

1. By words: by laying upon them unjust and unreasonable commands, by frequent, public, and severe [scolding]; by indiscreet and passionate expressions, and by [humiliating] and [abusive] language; such as that of Saul to Jonathan (1 Sam. 20:30).

2. By deeds: as by showing more love to one than to another, as Jacob did to Joseph, which so incensed his brethren that they hated Joseph and could not speak peaceably to him (Gen. 37:4); by not allowing them proper food and a sufficiency of it (Matt. 7:9-10; 1 Tim. 5:8); by not indulging them with innocent recreation, which children should have (Zech. 8:5); and when at a proper age for marriage, of [giving] them to persons not agreeable to their inclinations; and by restraining them from those that would be without any just reason; [or] by squandering away their substance in riotous living, when they should have preserved it and laid it up for the present use or future good of their children; and especially by any cruel and inhuman treatment as that of Saul to Jonathan, when he made an attempt on his life (1 Sam. 20:33-34). Such provocation should be carefully avoided, since it renders all commands, counsel, and corrections ineffectual, alienating the affections of their children from them. The reason to [avoid] it, given by the apostle, is *"lest they be discouraged"* (Col. 3:21); [they may] be overwhelmed with grief and sorrow and thereby their spirits be broken [and] become [cowardly], disheartened, and dispirited. Despairing of pleasing their parents and sharing in their affections, [they may] become careless of duty and [lazy in] business. Parents, no doubt, have a right to rebuke and reprove their children when they do amiss: it was Eli's fault that he was too soft and lenient and his reproofs too easy, when he should have restrained his sons from acting the vile part. [He] should have frowned upon them, put on stern looks, laid his commands on them, and severely threatened them, and punished them if [obstinate and disobedient] (1 Sam. 2:23-24; 3:13). And they may use the rod of correction, which they should do early, and while there is hope; but always with moderation and in love; and should take some pains with their children to convince them that they do love them; and that it is in love to them, and for their good, that they chastise them. "Fathers" are particularly mentioned because they are apt to be most severe, and mothers most indulgent.

Chapter 2—Godly Manhood: A Godly Father's Anger

From *A Body of Divinity*, The Baptist Standard Bearer: www.standardbearer.org.

John Gill (**1697-1771**): Baptist theologian; born in Kettering, England.

Threats to Godliness in Young Men
JOHN ANGELL JAMES (1785-1859)

It is well to know what these are and where they lie, that you may know how to avoid them. Ignorance on such a subject would be itself one of the chief dangers. In many cases, to know our perils is itself one way of avoiding them. Steadily, then, contemplate the following:

1. You are in danger of falling into evil from the removal of parental inspection, admonition, and restraint. It must be admitted, that home itself is sometimes a scene of peril to morals and religion. In some homes, young people see and hear very little but what is calculated to do them harm: parental example is on the side of sin, and almost everything that is said or done is of a nature likely to produce impressions unfavorable to piety and perhaps even to morality. Where this is the state of things, removal is a benefit...Many a young man—who at the time of leaving home wept over the necessity that caused him to quit the scenes of his childhood and to go from beneath the wing of his parents—has lived to consider it the brightest era of his life. [For] it took him away from scenes of moral danger and led him to the means of grace and the path of eternal life...This, however, is not applicable to all families. If there are some parents who take no care about the religious or even moral character of their children, who neither set them good examples, nor deliver to them any instruction, nor impose upon them any restraint, but who allow them the unchecked gratification[101] of their passions and the unreproved commission of sin,[102] there are many others who act a wiser and a better part.

In [many] instances, parents are moral; in many they are pious.[103] While the former are anxious to keep their sons from vice and train them to virtue, the latter go further and endeavor to bring them up in the fear of the Lord... You have been brought up in habits of rigid morality. Your parents have been solicitous[104] to form your character on a right basis. You have been long familiar with the voice of instruction, admonition, and warning. You have been the constant subject of an anxiety that you could neither be ignorant of nor mistake. If you were seen in company with a stranger or with a youth of doubtful character, you were questioned and warned. If you brought home a book, it was examined. If you stayed out at night later than usual, you saw

---

101 **unchecked gratification** – unrestrained self-satisfying.
102 **unreproved commission of sin** – sins committed without disapproval or correction.
103 **pious** – faithfully obedient and reverent to God; devout; godly.
104 **solicitous** – careful; desirous.

a mother's anxious eye turned upon you and heard a father's voice saying, "My son, why so late, where have you been?" In short, you felt yourself within the range of an ever-present inspection and under the pressure of a never-relaxing restraint. The theater and other places of pollution were strictly forbidden; indeed, you felt little inclination to visit those haunts of vice. Morning and evening you heard the Scriptures read, and the voice of prayer ascend to God and ascend for you. With such examples, under such instruction, and amidst such scenes, you had no opportunity and felt no disposition to be vicious.[105] Sometimes you thought, perhaps, that the restraint was too severe and the care too fastidious[106]…

All this is now over: you have left or are leaving home. The moment has arrived or is past and will never be forgotten, when those arms that sustained your infant frame were thrown around your neck and pressed you to the bosom that nourished you, while a mother's faltering voice exclaimed, "Farewell, my boy." And a father, always kind, but kinder then than ever, prolonged the sad [farewell] and said, "My son, I can watch over you no longer. The God whose providence removes you from your father's house be your Protector and preserve you from the evils of this sinful world. Remember, that though my eye cannot see you, His can and ever does. Fear Him." And there, young man, you now are, where your parents' hearts trembled to place you, amidst the snares and perils of this evil world, where your father's inspection cannot reach you or your mother's tearful eyes behold you… Away from home, a viciously inclined youth will find opportunities for the gratification of his evil [inclinations] in situations the most friendly to virtue. His wicked heart, rejoicing in the absence of his parents, will make that absence [a motivation] to sin. Ever and anon[107] the whisper will come from within, "My father is not here to see it; my mother will not know it; I am not under inspection now; restraint is over. I can go where I like, associate with whom I please and fear neither rebuke nor reproach." O young man, think of the unutterable baseness[108] of such conduct as this. Ought you not to despise yourself, if you can thus meanly, as well as wickedly, take advantage of a father's absence to do that which you know would excite his strongest [disapproval] and afflict him with the bitterest grief, if he were present? Yet multitudes are thus base, wicked, and have gone from their parents to

---

105 **vicious** – addicted to vice or immorality; wicked. Throughout this article, the author does not use *vicious* in the modern sense of "savage" or "malicious."
106 **fastidious** – exacting; difficult to please.
107 **ever and anon** – every now and then.
108 **baseness** – contemptible meanness; shameful selfishness.

ruin themselves forever. Act, young man, act as you would do, if you were conscious that your father's eye was upon you.

2. Your danger is increased by the spirit of independence and self-confidence (connected, as of course it must be, with much ignorance and inexperience) that young men are apt to assume, when they leave their father's house and go out into the world. "Paternal rule is now over; my parents are not at hand to be consulted or obeyed; and if they were, it is time for me to think and act for myself. I am my own master now. I am a young man, and no longer a child. I am capable of judging, discriminating, and determining between right and wrong. I have the right, and will exercise it, of forming my own standard of morals, selecting my own models of character, and laying down my own plans of action. Who has authority to interfere with me?"

Such probably are your thoughts, and they are encouraged by many around you, who suggest that you are not always to go in leading strings,[109] but ought now to assert your liberty and act like a man. Yes, and how many have employed and abused this liberty to the most criminal and fatal purposes. It has been a liberty to destroy all the habits of virtue formed at home, to subvert all the principles implanted by their parents' [anxious care] and to rush into all the evil practices against which the voice of warning had been raised from their boyhood. Many young men have no sooner been freed from parental restraint and become their own masters, than they have hurried to every place of amusement, resorted to every species of vicious diversion, initiated themselves into all the mysteries of iniquity, and with prurient[110] curiosity to know what it is bliss to be ignorant of, [and] have entered into fellowship with all the unfruitful works of darkness. Happy, happy had they been, had they considered that an independence that sets them free from parental advice and control is the bane[111] of piety, morality, and happiness and has proved, where it has been assumed, the ruin for both worlds of multitudes of once hopeful youths. Wise is that young man and blessed in all probability he will be, who though he has left his father's house, and it may be has arrived at the age of maturity, feels it his privilege as well as his duty to look up to his parents as his counselors, his comforters, and, in some respects, his rulers. [He] allows the restraints of home to follow him abroad. [He,] amidst the dangerous intricacies of life, is thankful to accept

---

109 **leading strings** – strings with which children used to be guided and supported when learning to walk; to be still a child; to be in a state of dependence.
110 **prurient** – inordinate interest in lewd ideas; inordinate interest in sexual matters.
111 **bane** – a cause of destruction or ruin; deadly poison.

the kind offices of a [wise] father to be the guide of his youth.

3. The numerous incentives to vice with which every place, but especially the [cities] and large provincial towns, abounds, and the opportunities of concealment that are to be found there are a source of great danger. At the head of all these must be placed the theater, which is there to be found in all its most powerful attractions and most destructive fascinations. Nothing can be said too strong or too bad of the injurious tendency of the stage nor too earnest or impassioned in the way of warning young men from venturing within its precincts. It is emphatically and eminently the broad road and wide gate that leads to destruction.

The staple matter of which the ordinary run of dramatic representations are composed is altogether adapted to corrupt the youthful mind by appealing to the most inflammable, powerful, and dangerous of its passions. Tragedy, with whatever fine passages and occasional lofty sentiment it may be adorned, is usually calculated to produce pride, ambition, and revenge; while comedy, such as is most suited to the public taste, and therefore most in demand, is the school for intrigue, amours,[112] and licentiousness.[113]

It is not, however, the subject matter only of the play itself that is corrupting, but the representation of it upon the stage with all the accompaniments of the theater…It is bad sentiment,[114] borrowing every possible aid to render it still worse. It is vice recommended by the charms of music, painting, architecture, oratory, and eloquence with all that is fascinating in female beauty and dazzling in elegant costume…It were easy to enumerate the evils, though they are many and great, to which frequenting the theater will expose you…It raises the passions above their proper tone and thus induces a dislike for those grave and serious subjects of life that have nothing but their simplicity and importance to recommend them. It kindles low and base appetites and creates a constant [craving] after their indulgence. It not only hardens the heart against religion, so that a theater-loving man never becomes religious until he is persuaded to abandon these amusements, but it gradually [numbs] the conscience into an insensibility to good morals.

Bad companions are a source of danger. Perhaps more young men are ruined by this than by any other means that could be mentioned. Many who have left home with a character unsullied and a mind not only comparatively pure, but really ignorant of the crooked ways of vice, who,

---

112 **intrigue, amours** – secret, illicit love affairs.
113 **licentiousness** – lewdness; inclined to lust; preoccupied with lustful desires.
114 **sentiment** – emotional thought conveyed in literature or art.

simple, [inexperienced], and without guile, would have shuddered at the temptation to any of the grosser acts of sin, have at length fallen sacrifices to the powerful influence of evil associates. Man is a social being, and the propensity for company is peculiarly strong in youth, the season when it requires to be watched with greater care than at any other because of the greater force that it exerts in the formation of character. Now and then we meet with a youth who is so engrossed with business, so intent on cultivating his mind, or so reserved in disposition, as to have no desire for companions. But by far the greater number are fond of society and eager to enjoy it; and, if not extremely careful in the selection of their friends, are in imminent peril of choosing such as will do them harm. It is next to impossible, young man, for you to remain virtuous in vicious society…and they will never cease until they have made you as bad as themselves. The more agreeable, amiable, and intelligent they are, the more dangerous and ensnaring is their influence. A youthful profligate[115] of elegant manners, lively humor, amiable temper, and intelligent mind is Satan's most polished instrument for ruining immortal souls.

Vicious women are as much to be dreaded as bad men and far more so… Youthful reader, be upon your guard against this peril to your health, your morals, your soul. Go where you will, this snare is spread for your feet. Watch and pray that you enter not into temptation. Set a strict guard upon your senses, your imagination, and your passions. Once yield to temptation, and you are undone. Purity is then lost. Sunk from self-esteem,[116] you may give yourself up to commit all uncleanness with greediness.

Drinking parties, though not so common as they were or as are some other snares, are still sufficiently prevalent to be pointed out as a source of danger…Still it is an object of ambition with some misguided youths to be able to drink the bumper[117] and the toast with convivial[118] grace as a matter of course. What a low and sensual aim! Young man, as you would not lie down in the grave of a drunkard, worn out by disease, and closing your miserable career in poverty and wretchedness, beware of the filthy, degrading, and destructive habit of drinking. Remember the words of the wisest of men: *"Who hath woe? who hath sorrow? who hath contentions? who hath babbling? who hath wounds without cause? who hath redness of eyes? They that tarry long at the*

---

115 **profligate** – one recklessly given to lewd, sensual pleasures and extravagance.
116 **self-esteem** – favorable opinion of one's self.
117 **bumper** – a glass of wine filled to the brim.
118 **convivial** – sociable; fond of feasting, drinking, and good company.

wine; they that go to seek mixed wine" (Prov. 23:29, 30). Study this inimitable[119] and graphic picture of drinking and its consequences, and begin life with a horror of drunkenness...I again say and *with all possible emphasis*, begin life with a horror of drunkenness.

4. I close this fearful list of perils by mentioning the prevalence of infidelity[120] and the zeal and wily arts of its [instigators] and propagators, as forming another source of danger to youth. There never was an age when infidelity was busier than it is now...The efforts of infidels to diffuse their principles among the common people and middle classes are peculiarly energetic just now...The system [of *socialism*], if system it may be called... announces as its leading dogma that man is entirely the creature of circumstances,[121] is in no sense the author of his opinions and volitions, nor the founder or supporter of his own character...As if it were not enough to shock the public mind by a system so monstrous, the public taste and all our social feelings are outraged by the unblushing avowal of its author,[122] that it is his design and wish to abolish the institution of marriage and reconstruct society upon the basis of the unlegalized association of the sexes and the unrestricted freedom of divorce. Absurd and demoralizing as such a system is, it is popular with many. The reason is obvious: its very immorality proves to them its recommendation. If they can believe it, they feel that, commit what crimes they may, accountability is gone and remorse is extinguished. The blame rests not on them for any sin whatever, but on the circumstances which led to it:[123] a short way to be very wicked and yet very easy.

It must be obvious that between immorality and infidelity there is a close connection and a constant reaction going on in some minds. A young man falls into temptation and commits sin: instead of repenting, as is his duty and his interest, he in many cases attempts to quiet his conscience by persuading himself that religion is all hypocrisy and the Bible untrue. His infidelity now prepares him to go greater lengths in sin. Thus, vice calls in the aid of error, and error strengthens vice, while both together lead their victim to ruin and misery. To guard yourselves against such dangers, study well the evidences of revelation...[Christ] in the heart is the only thing to be relied upon as a defense against the attacks of infidels and the influence of their principles.

---

119 **inimitable** – without compare; defying imitation; having no match or equal.
120 **infidelity** – the attitude of one who has no religious belief, especially of Christianity.
121 **man...the creature of circumstances** – socialism teaches that human action is determined by external forces acting upon man's will; he is therefore not responsible for what he does.
122 **Karl Marx (1818-1883)** – German atheist, revolutionary, founder of socialism.
123 **blame rests...led to it** – this is highly visible in our modern courtrooms.

Chapter 2—Godly Manhood: Threats to Godliness in Young Men

It has been a dark day in the annals of myriads of families, when a son bade adieu to his parents, and commenced his probation and his struggles in the great business of human life. The tears that fell on that occasion were a sad [prediction], though unknown at the time, of others that were to flow in long succession over the follies, vices, and miseries of that unhappy youth. The history of ten thousand prodigal sons, the untimely graves of ten thousand broken-hearted parents, and the deep and heavy woes of ten thousand dishonored families attest the fact of the dangers that await a youth on leaving home: and he is most in danger, who is ignorant of what awaits him or who on being informed treats the subject with indifference, smiles at the fears of his friends and feels no fear for himself.

Young man, there is hope of you if this representation shall awaken alarm, produce self-distrust, and excite vigilance and caution. Inexperienced, [self-confident], and rash with all your appetites sharpening and all your passions strengthening; with an imagination lively, a curiosity prurient, and a heart susceptible; eager to act for yourself, panting to try your scarcely fledged wings on leaving the nest, and perhaps ambitious of distinction, you are in imminent peril of the lusts of the flesh and of the mind. All but yourself are anxious. Pause and consider what you may become—an ornament of the profession you have chosen, a respectable member of society, a holy professor of religion, a useful citizen of your country, a benefactor of your species, and a light of the world. But according to the height to which you may rise is the depth to which you may sink: for as the bottom of the ocean is supposed to be proportioned in measurement to the tops of the mountains, so the dark gulfs of sin and [damnation] into which you may plunge, sustain a similar relation to the summits of excellence and happiness to which you may ascend…Survey for a moment the sphere which you may occupy and fill up with misery, desolation, and ruin. See what opportunities of destruction are within your reach, and to what suicidal and murderous havoc sin may lead you, if you give yourself up to its influence and government.

You can blast your *reputation*. After building up with great care your good name for some years and acquiring respect and esteem from those who knew you, "in one single hour, by yielding to some powerful temptation, you may fix a dark stain upon your character, which no tears can ever wash away or repentance remove, but which will cause you to be read and known of all men, until the grave receives you out of their sight. You may render yourself an object of the universal disgust and abhorrence of the good and be the taunt and scorn of the wicked, so that wherever you turn your eyes, you will find none to bestow upon you a single smile of complacency. How many in this condition, bitterly realizing that, 'without a friend, the world is but a wilderness,' have in a paroxysm[124] of desperation, committed suicide."

Your *intellect*, strong by nature and capable of high cultivation, may, like a fine flower, be suffered to run wild by neglect, be trodden down by brute lusts, or be broken by violence. Your *affections*, given to be your delight by virtuous exercise on right objects, may be all perverted so [that you] become like so many demons, possessing and tormenting your soul because they are set on things forbidden and indulged to excess. Your *conscience*, granted to be your monitor, guide, and friend, may be wounded, benumbed, seared till it is insensible, silent, deaf, and of no use in warning you against sin, in restraining or reproving you for it. In short, you may destroy your immortal soul; and what ruin is like that of the soul, so immense, so horrible, so irretrievable?

You may break the hearts of your parents; make your brothers and sisters ashamed to own you; be a nuisance and pest to society; a bane to your country; the corrupter of youthful morals; the seducer of female virtue; the consumer of the property of your friends; and to reach the climax of your mischief, you may be the Apollyon[125] of the circle of immortal souls in which you move, sending some to perdition before you reach it yourself and causing others to follow you to the bottomless pit, where you will never escape the sight of their torments nor the sound of their [curses]. How great the power, how malignant the virulence[126] of sin that can spread its influence so widely and exert its force with such deadly effect, not only destroying the sinner himself, but involving others in his ruin! No man goes alone to perdition. No one perishes alone in his iniquity, a consideration that every transgressor should regard. He sustains the character not only of a suicide, but also of a murderer, and the worst of all murderers, for he is *the murderer of souls*. What a critical position you now occupy, between the capability of rising to so much excellence or sinking to ruin so deep and misery so intense! Reflect. Oh, that you were wise; that you understood this; that you would consider your end!

From *Addresses to Young Men: A Friend and Guide*, Soli Deo Gloria, a division of Reformation Heritage Books: www.heritagebooks.org.

---

124 **paroxysm** – a violent outburst of emotion.
125 **Apollyon** – the destroyer, a name given to the devil.
126 **virulence** – extreme bitterness of temper or speech; bitterly hostile and hateful.

John Angell James (1785-1859): English Congregationalist preacher and author; born in Blandford Forum, Dorset, England.

The true Christian is to be such a husband as Christ was to His church. The love of a husband is special. The Lord Jesus cherishes for the church a peculiar affection, which is set upon her above the rest of mankind: "I pray for them, I pray not for the world" (John 17:9). The elect church is the favorite of heaven, the treasure of Christ, the crown of His head, the bracelet of His arm, the breastplate of His heart, the very center and core of His love. A husband should love his wife with a constant love, for thus Jesus loves His church…A husband should love his wife with an enduring love, for nothing "shall be able to separate us from the love of God, which is in Christ Jesus our Lord" (Rom 8:39). A true husband loves his wife with a hearty love, fervent and intense. It is not mere lip service. Ah! Beloved, what more could Christ have done in proof of His love than He has done? Jesus has a delighted love towards His spouse: He prizes her affection and delights in her with sweet complacence. Believer, you wonder at Jesus' love; you admire it: are you imitating it? —Charles Haddon Spurgeon

The formation of the woman out of man showeth how great his affection should be to her, nay, to himself. She was not made of his head to be his sovereign, nor of his feet to be his slave; but of a rib in his side to show how near she should lie to his heart. God is so urgent for fervent love to a wife that He slights the husband's love to her when it is but little and counts it no better than hatred. —George Swinnock

God bestows more goodness upon one godly man than upon all the ungodly in the world. Put all their preservations, all their deliverances, all their wealth, all their comforts that have been heaped upon them by providence together— those things are but trifles that God bestows on ungodly men. But they are peculiar blessings that He bestows on the righteous. They are precious things that God has in reserve for His own favorites in comparison of which all earthly treasure is but dirt and dross As for the saints, Christ has died for them, they have all their sins pardoned, they are delivered from a hell of eternal misery, they have a title to eternal life bestowed upon them, they have God's own image conferred on them, they are received into favor and will enjoy God's ever-lasting love. —Jonathan Edwards

How True Manhood Is Restored

CHARLES HADDON SPURGEON (1834-1892)

To help the seeker to a true faith in Jesus, I would remind him of the work of the Lord Jesus in the room and place and stead of sinners. *"For when we were yet without strength, in due time Christ died for the ungodly"* (Rom. 5:6). *"Who his own self bare our sins in his own body on the tree"* (1 Peter 2:24). *"The Lord hath laid on him the iniquity of us all"* (Isa. 53:6). *"For Christ also hath once suffered for sins, the just for the unjust, that he might bring us to God"* (1 Peter 3:18).

Upon one declaration of Scripture let the reader fix his eye. *"With his stripes we are healed"* (Isa. 53:5). God here treats sin as a disease, and He sets before us the costly remedy that He has provided.

I ask you very solemnly to accompany me in your meditations for a few minutes, while I bring before you the stripes of the Lord Jesus. The Lord resolved to restore us, and therefore He sent His only begotten Son, *"very God of very God,"*[127] that He might descend into this world to take upon Himself our nature in order for our redemption. He lived as a man among men. In due time, after thirty years or more of obedience, the time came when He should do us the greatest service of all, namely, stand in our stead and bear *"the chastisement of our peace"* (Isa. 53:5). He went to Gethsemane; and there at the first taste of our bitter cup, He sweat great drops of blood. He went to Pilate's hall and Herod's judgment-seat, and there He drank draughts of pain and scorn in our room and place. Last of all, they took Him to the cross and nailed Him there to die—to die in our stead.

The word *stripes* is used to set forth His sufferings, both of body and of soul. The whole of Christ was made a sacrifice for us. His whole manhood suffered. As to His body, it shared with His mind in a grief that never can be described. In the beginning of His passion, when He emphatically suffered instead of us, He was in an agony; and from His bodily frame, a bloody sweat distilled so copiously[128] as to fall to the ground.

It is a very rare occurrence that a man sweats blood. There have been one or two instances of it, and they have been followed by almost immediate death. But our Savior lived—lived after an agony that to anyone else would have proved fatal. Before He could cleanse His face from this dreadful crimson, they hurried Him to the high priest's hall. In the dead of night,

---

127 **very God of very God** – from the Nicene Creed, originally the theological confession resulting from the Council of Nicaea in A.D. 325. This confession reflects the teaching that the Son is of one substance with the Father.
128 **copiously** – profusely; abundantly.

they bound Him and led Him away. Anon[129] they took Him to Pilate and to Herod. These scourged[130] Him, and their soldiers spat in His face and buffeted[131] Him, and put on His head a crown of thorns.

Scourging is one of the most awful tortures that can be inflicted by malice. It was formerly the disgrace of the British army that the "cat"[132] was used upon the soldier—a brutal infliction of torture. But to the Roman, cruelty was so natural that he made his common punishments worse than brutal. The Roman scourge is said to have been made of the sinews of oxen, twisted into knots, and into these knots were inserted slivers of bone and huckle-bones[133] of sheep. Every time the scourge fell upon the bare back, *"the plowers plowed upon my back: they made long their furrows"*[134] (Ps. 129:3). Our Savior was called upon to endure the fierce pain of the Roman scourge; and this not as the finish of His punishment, but as a preface to crucifixion. To this, His persecutors added buffeting and plucking out the hair. They spared Him no form of pain.

In all His faintness, through bleeding and fasting, they made Him carry His cross until another was forced by the forethought of their cruelty to bear it, lest their victim should die on the road. They stripped Him, threw Him down, and nailed Him to the wood. They pierced His hands and His feet. They lifted up the tree with Him upon it and then dashed it down into its place in the ground, so that all His limbs were dislocated according to the lament of the psalmist, *"I am poured out like water, and all my bones are out of joint"* (Ps. 22:14a).

He hung on the cross in the burning sun until the fever dissolved His strength, and He said, *"My heart is like wax; it is melted in the midst of my bowels. My strength is dried up like a potsherd;*[135] *and my tongue cleaveth to my jaws; and thou hast brought me into the dust of death"* (Ps. 22:14b–15). There He hung, a spectacle to God and men. The weight of His body was first sustained by His feet, until the nails tore through the tender nerves. Then the painful load began to drag upon His hands and rend those sensitive parts of His frame. How small a wound in the hand has brought on lockjaw! How awful must have been the torment caused by that dragging iron tearing through the delicate parts of the hands and feet!

---

129 **anon** – straightway; at once.
130 **scourged** – beaten with a whip; severely flogged.
131 **buffeted** – beaten repeatedly with the fist.
132 **cat** – a whip used to inflict punishment or scourging.
133 **huckle-bones** – small bones or knucklebones of a sheep.
134 **furrows** – long, narrow, shallow trenches; used metaphorically of the cuts made by the whips on Christ's body.
135 **potsherd** – a fragment of broken pottery.

Now were all manner of bodily pains centered in His tortured frame. All the while, His enemies stood around, pointing at Him in scorn, thrusting out their tongues in mockery, jesting at His prayers, and gloating over His sufferings. He cried, *"I thirst"* (John 19:28), and then they gave Him vinegar mingled with gall. After a while He said, *"It is finished"* (John 19:30). He had endured the utmost of appointed grief and had made full vindication to divine justice. Then, and not until then, He gave up the ghost.

Holy men of old have enlarged most lovingly upon the bodily sufferings of our Lord, and I have no hesitation in doing the same, trusting that trembling sinners may see salvation in these painful "stripes" of the Redeemer. To describe the outward sufferings of our Lord is not easy. I acknowledge that I have failed.

Christ's soul-sufferings, which were the soul of His sufferings, who can even conceive, much less express what they were? At the very first, I told you that He sweat great drops of blood. That was His heart driving out its life-floods to the surface through the terrible depression of spirit that was upon Him. He said, *"My soul is exceeding sorrowful, even unto death"* (Matt. 26:38). The betrayal by Judas and the desertion of the twelve grieved our Lord, but the weight of our sin was the real pressure on His heart. Our guilt was the olive-press that forced from Him the moisture of His life. No language can ever tell His agony in prospect of His passion. How little then can we conceive the passion itself?

When nailed to the cross, He endured what no martyr ever suffered. Martyrs, when they have died, have been so sustained of God that they have rejoiced amid their pain. But our Redeemer was forsaken of His Father until He cried, *"My God, my God, why hast thou forsaken me?"* (Matt. 27:46). That was the bitterest cry of all, the utmost depth of His unfathomable grief.

Yet it was necessary that He should be deserted, because God must turn His back on sin and consequently upon Him who was *"made him to be sin for us"* (2 Cor. 5:21). The soul of the great Substitute suffered a horror of misery, instead of that horror of hell into which sinners would have been plunged had He not taken their sin upon Himself and been made a curse for them. It is written, *"Cursed is every one that hangeth on a tree"* (Gal. 3:13). But who knows what that curse means?

The remedy for your sins and mine is found in the substitutionary sufferings of the Lord Jesus and in these only. These "stripes" of the Lord Jesus Christ were on our behalf. Do you ask, "Is there anything for us to do, to remove the guilt of sin?" I answer: "There is nothing whatever for you to do. By the stripes of Jesus, we are healed. All those stripes He has endured and left not one of them for us to bear."

"But must we not believe on Him?" Yes, certainly. If I say of a certain ointment that it heals, I do not deny that you need a bandage with which to apply it to the wound. Faith is the linen that binds the plaster of Christ's reconciliation to the sore of our sin. The linen does not heal; that is the work of the ointment. So faith does not heal; that is the work of the atonement of Christ.

"But we must repent," cries another. Assuredly, we must and shall, for repentance is the first sign of healing. But the stripes of Jesus heal us and not our repentance. These stripes, when applied to the heart, work repentance in us. We hate sin because it made Jesus suffer.

When you intelligently trust in Jesus as having suffered for you, then you discover the fact that God will never punish you for the same offense for which Jesus died. His justice will not permit Him to see the debt paid, first by the Surety, and then again by the debtor. Justice cannot twice demand a recompense. If my bleeding Surety has borne my guilt, then I cannot bear it. Accepting Christ Jesus as suffering for me, I have accepted a complete discharge from judicial liability. I have been condemned in Christ, and there is therefore now no condemnation to me anymore. This is the groundwork of the security of the sinner who believes in Jesus. He lives because Jesus died in his place and stead. He is acceptable before God because Jesus is accepted. The person for whom Jesus is an accepted Substitute must go free. None can touch him. He is clear.

O my hearer, will you have Jesus Christ to be your Substitute? If so, you are free. *"He that believeth on him is not condemned"* (John 3:18). Thus *"with his stripes we are healed"* (Isa. 53:5).

From *Around the Wicket Gate*, available from Chapel Library.

Charles Haddon Spurgeon (1834-1892): English Baptist minister; history's most widely read preacher (apart from those found in Scripture); born at Kelvedon, Essex.

An experienced servant of God has said that, while popularity is a snare that few are not caught by, a more subtle and dangerous snare is to be famed for holiness. The fame of being a godly man is as great a snare as the fame of being learned or eloquent. It is possible to attend with scrupulous anxiety even to secret habits of devotion in order to get a name for holiness. —Andrew Bonar

All men are not godly. Alas! The ungodly are the great majority of the human race. When a man is beginning to be godly, this is the first sign of the change that is being wrought in him: "Behold, he prayeth." Prayer is the mark of godliness in its infancy. Until he has come to pleading and petitioning, we cannot be sure that the divine life is in him at all. There may be desires; but if they never turn to prayers, we may fear that they are as the morning cloud and as the early dew, which soon pass away. But…when he cannot rest without pouring out his heart at the mercy seat, you begin to hope that now he is indeed a godly man…Prayer is the first cry by which it is known that the newborn child truly lives. If he does not pray, you may suspect that he has only a name to live and that he lacks true spiritual life.
—Charles Haddon Spurgeon

Chapter 3
VIRTUOUS WOMANHOOD

This chapter explains the details of biblical womanhood. No higher view of women exists than that displayed in God's infallible Word. This is why no other religion or system of philosophy (including atheism and feminism) exalts women like Christianity does. This chapter explains the lofty heights and the fresh streams of biblical womanhood. There we find that women's worth, security, and prosperity are so highly valued that men are told to sacrifice their very lives for them. Men are commanded to cherish, nourish, provide for, and protect them. Women are to be treated as precious because they are precious, and their contribution to God's eternal purpose and to family life are indispensable. Furthermore, their worth is made even clearer when they embrace their biblical opportunities and limitations. When they do, blessings fall down from heaven.

John Angell James writes, "A community is not likely to be overthrown where woman fulfills her mission, for by the power of her noble heart over the hearts of others, she will raise it from its ruins and restore it again to prosperity and joy."[1] However, the prevailing philosophies, social systems, and movements in the modern world have severely marred the beauty, power, and service of womanhood. These false doctrines assert that a woman can only find fulfillment and happiness by working against the way God has designed and commanded her. As a result, many women have traded the beauties of womanhood for the roles of men, attempting to live men's lives and bear men's burdens. These women view the responsibilities of biblical womanhood as limitations to their personal freedom instead of opportunities to glorify God and build His kingdom. But in reality, by trading away their biblical roles, they have relinquished the peace of obedience for the turmoil of serfdom through an ungodly form of independence.

God promises forgiveness and restoration for those women who will repent and return to His purpose for them. Only God can restore womanhood. Only God can win her heart to His ways, bring her life-giving instruction from His Word, and teach her how to bring glory to her Creator through her womanhood. The following articles are dedicated to such a restoration.

—Scott Brown

---

[1] John Angell James, *Female Piety* (Morgan, PA: Soli Deo Gloria Publications, 1999), 59.

Christianity's Influence on the Condition of Women
JOHN ANGELL JAMES (1785-1859)

> *There is neither Jew nor Greek; there is neither bond nor free; there is neither male nor female; for ye are all one in Christ Jesus. —Galatians 3:28*

Woman was the finishing grace of the creation. Woman was the completeness of man's bliss in Paradise. Woman was the cause of sin and death to our world. The world was redeemed by the Seed of the woman. Woman is the mother of the human race. She is either our companion, counselor, and comforter in the pilgrimage of life; or she is our tempter, scourge, and destroyer. Our sweetest cup of earthly happiness or our bitterest draught of sorrow is mixed and administered by her hand. She not only renders smooth or rough our path to the grave, but helps or hinders our progress to immortality. In heaven we shall bless God for her aid in assisting us to reach that blissful state; or amidst the torments of unutterable woe in another region, we shall deplore the fatality of her influence…

My subject is religion; my object is the soul; my aim is salvation. I view you, my female friends, as destined for another world; and it is my business to aid and stimulate you by patient continuance in well-doing to seek for glory, honor, and immortality and to obtain eternal life. I look beyond the painted and gaudy scene of earth's fading vanities to the everlasting ages through which you must exist in torment or bliss; and, God helping me, it shall not be my fault if you do not live in comfort, die in peace, and inherit salvation.

Our first attention must be directed, of course, to the condition of the sex beyond the boundaries of Christendom…. In some countries, [woman is] not even allowed the rank of a moral and responsible agent; so tenderly alive to her own degradation that she acquiesces[1] in the murder of her female offspring; immured[2] from infancy; without education; married without her consent; in a multitude of instances sold by her parents; refused the confidence of her husband and banished from his table; on his death, doomed to the funeral pyre or to contempt that renders life a burden…. Sometimes worshipped as a goddess, next fondled as a toy, then punished as a victim, she could never attain to dignity, and even with all her brightest charms could rarely appear but as a doll or a puppet.

Let us now consider what there is in Christianity that tends to elevate and improve the condition of woman….From Christianity woman has

---

1 **acquiesces** – consents or complies passively or without protest.
2 **immured** – shut off; excluded.

Chapter 3—Virtuous Womanhood: Christianity's Influence on the Condition of Women

derived her moral and social influence, yea, almost her very existence as a social being. The mind of woman, which many of the philosophers, legislators, and sages[3] of antiquity doomed to inferiority and imbecility, Christianity has developed. The Gospel of Christ in the Person of its divine Founder has descended into this neglected mine, which even wise men had regarded as not worth working, and brought up many a priceless gem, flashing with the light of intelligence and glowing with the lovely hues of Christian graces. Christianity has been the restorer of woman's plundered rights and has furnished the brightest jewels in her present crown of honor. Her previous degradation accounts, in part at least, for the instability of early civilization. It is impossible for society to be permanently elevated where woman is debased and servile.[4] Wherever females are regarded as inferior beings, society contains within itself the elements of dissolution and the obstruction of all solid improvement. It is impossible that institutions and usages, which oppose and stifle the instincts of our nature and violate the revealed Law of God, can be crowned with ultimate success. Society may change in its external aspect; it may exhibit the glitter of wealth, the refinements of taste, the embellishments of art, or the more valuable attainments of science and literature. But if the mind of woman remains undeveloped, her tastes uncultivated, and her person enslaved, the social foundations are insecure and the cement of society is weak. Wherever Christianity is understood and felt, woman is free. The Gospel, like a kind angel, opens her prison doors and bids her walk abroad and enjoy the sunlight of reason and breathe the invigorating air of intellectual freedom. And in proportion as pure Christianity prevails, this will be ever found to be the case…Christianity elevates the condition of woman by its genius[5] as a system of universal equity and benevolence. When it descended from heaven to earth, it was heralded into our world by the angel's song, *"Glory to God in the highest, and on earth peace, good will toward men"* (Luke 2:14). The offspring of infinite love, it partakes of the spirit and reflects the character of its divine Parent. It is essentially and unalterably the enemy of all injustice, cruelty, and oppression, and the friend of all that is just, kind, and courteous. The rough, the brutal, and the ferocious are alien to its spirit, while the tender, the gentle, and the courteous are entirely in unison with its nature. It frowns with indignant countenance upon tyranny, whether in the palace or the parlor, while it is the friend of liberty and the patron of right. The man

---

3 **sages** – men of profound wisdom; wise men.
4 **debased and servile** – lowered in value and thought of as slaves.
5 **genius** – distinctive character and tendency.

who understands its genius and lives under its inspiration, whether he is a monarch, a master, a husband, or a father, must be a man of equity and love. Christianity inspires the purest chivalry,[6] a chivalry shorn of vanity, purified from passion, elevated above frivolity; a chivalry of which the animating principle is love to God, and the scene of its operation the domestic circle and not the public pageant. He who is unjust or unkind to anyone, especially to the weaker sex, betrays a total ignorance of or a manifest repugnance to the practical influence of the Gospel of Christ…

The personal conduct of our Lord during His sojourn upon earth tended to exalt the female sex to a consideration before unknown. Follow Him through the whole of His earthly career, and mark the attention that He most condescendingly paid to and as condescendingly received from the female sex. He admitted them to His presence, conversed familiarly with them, and accepted the tokens of their gratitude, affection, and devotedness. See Him accompanying His mother to the marriage feast of Cana in Galilee. See Him conversing with the woman of Samaria, instructing her ignorance, enduring her petulance,[7] correcting her mistakes, awakening her conscience, converting her soul, and afterwards employing her as a messenger of mercy and salvation to her neighbors…[Christ's] treatment of woman raised her from her degradation without exalting her above her level. He rescued her from oppression without exciting her vanity and invested her with dignity without giving her occasion for pride. While He allowed her not only to come into His presence, but to minister to His comfort; and while He conciliated[8] her grateful and reverent affection, He inspired her with awe. And thus, He taught man how to behave toward woman and what return woman was to make to man.

The conduct of Jesus Christ towards the female sex was one of the most attractive excellences of His beautiful character, though perhaps it is one of the least noticed. To Him they must ever point not only as the Savior of their souls, but as the Advocate of their rights and the Guardian of their peace…. The actual abolition of polygamy by Christianity is a vast improvement in the condition of woman. Wherever polygamy prevails, the female sex must ever be in a state of degradation and misery. Experience has abundantly and painfully proved that polygamy debases and brutalizes both the body and the soul….Here, then, is the glorious excellence of Christianity: it revived and re-established the original institution of marriage and restored to woman

---

6 **chivalry** – brave, honorable, courteous character, especially towards women.
7 **petulance** – rudeness.
8 **conciliated** – gained.

Chapter 3—Virtuous Womanhood: Christianity's Influence on the Condition of Women

her fortune, her person, her rank, and her happiness, all of which she had been cheated by polygamy. It thus raised the female sex to the elevation to which they were destined by their wise and beneficent Creator…the springs of national prosperity rise from beneath the family hearth, and the domestic constitution is the mold where national character is cast. And that mold must of necessity take its form from the unity, sanctity, and inviolability of marriage.

The jealousy with which Christianity guards the sanctity of the marriage tie must ever be regarded as having a most favorable influence upon the condition of woman. Let this be relaxed or impaired, and that moment, woman sinks in dignity, in purity, and in happiness. There have been nations in which the facility of divorce took the place of polygamy and of course was accompanied with some of its vices and many of its miseries too.…With what devout and reverential gratitude should she then turn to that divine Teacher, Who has interposed His authority to strengthen the marriage bond and to guard it from being severed at the demand of illicit passion or the dictates of temperament or caprice. How should she rejoice to hear Him say, *"Whosoever shall put away his wife, except it be for fornication, and shall marry another, committeth adultery: and whoso marrieth her which is put away doth commit adultery"* (Matt. 19:9).

I may surely mention the equal participation in religious blessing to which women are admitted by the Christian religion. How explicitly and how firmly has the Apostle claimed for women all the blessings obtained by Christ for the human race when he says, *"There is neither Jew nor Greek, there is neither bond nor free, there is neither male nor female: for ye are all one in Christ Jesus"* (Gal. 3:28). There is the charter granting to woman all the blessings of salvation.…There is not a blessing necessary to eternal life which she does not receive in the same measure and in the same manner as the other sex.… Christianity places the wife by the side of the husband, the daughter by the side of the father, the sister by the side of the brother, and the maid by the side of the mistress at the altar of the family, in the meeting of the church, at the table of the Lord, and in the congregation of the sanctuary.…Male and female meet together at the cross and will meet in the realms of glory. Can anything more effectually tend to raise and sustain the condition of woman than this? God in all His ordinances, Christ in His glorious undertaking, and the Holy Spirit in His gracious work gave woman her proper place in the world by giving her a proper place in the church. It is for her with peculiar emphasis to say, *"But God, who is rich in mercy, for his great love wherewith he loved us…hath raised us up together, and made us sit together in heavenly places in Christ Jesus"* (Eph. 2:4, 6).

But the finishing stroke which Christianity gives in elevating the condition of women is by inviting and employing their energies and influence in promoting the spread of religion in the world, and by thus carrying out, through them as well as men, the great purposes of God in the redemption of the world by the mission of His Son….Christianity has thus carried out its genius and its precepts in the actual elevation of the female character wherever it has gone….In every view that we can take of Christianity, whether we contemplate it in its aspects towards another world or towards this one, in its relations to God or society, in its sublime doctrines or its pure morality, we see a form of inimitable beauty sufficient to captivate every heart but that which is petrified by false philosophy, avowed infidelity, or gross immorality. But never does it appear more lovely than in its relation to woman. With what equity does it hold the balance between the sexes! With what kindness does it throw its shield over the weaker vessel! With what wisdom does it sustain the rank and claims of those whose influence is so important to society, and yet so limit their claims that they shall not be carried to such a length as to defeat their end!…Woman's virtue, dignity, honor, and happiness are nowhere safe but under the protection of the Word of God. The Bible is the aegis[9] of the female sex. Beneath this protection they are secure in their rights, their dignity, and their peace. It is their vine and fig tree, under which, in calm repose, they may enjoy the shade and relish the fruit. It protects their purity from taint and their peace from disturbance….Woman! Regard your Savior for the next world as your Emancipator for this present one. Love the Bible as the charter of your liberty and the guardian of your bliss. And consider the church of Christ as your asylum from the wrongs of oppression and the arts of seduction.

From *Female Piety* reprinted by Soli Deo Gloria.

John Angell James (1785-1859): English Congregationalist preacher and author; preached and wrote to common people of every age group and station in life; held in high esteem, yet a humble and unpretentious man, who said, "My design is to aid the Christian in the practice of Scriptural truth." Author of *Female Piety*, *A Help to Domestic Happiness*, *An Earnest Ministry*, and many others.

---

9 **aegis** – shield; defensive armor; impregnable defense.

Woman's Mission

JOHN ANGELL JAMES (1785-1859)

And the LORD God said, It is not good that the man should be alone; I will make him an help meet for him. —Genesis 2:18

Woman, as such, has her mission. What is it? What is precisely the rank she is to occupy? What is the purpose she is to fulfill, above which she would be unduly exalted and below which she would be unjustly degraded? This is a subject which should be thoroughly understood in order that she may know what to claim, and man what to concede; that she may know what she has to do, and that he may know what he has a right to expect.

I shall endeavor to answer this question and point out the nature of woman's mission. In doing this, I shall consult the infallible oracle[10] of Scripture and not the speculations of moralists, economists, and philosophers. I hold this to be our rule in the matter before us: God is the Creator of both sexes, the Constructor of society, the Author of social relations, and the Arbiter[11] of social duties, claims, and immunities. And this is admitted by all who believe in the authority of the Bible. You are content, my female friends, to abide by the decisions of this oracle. You have every reason to be so. He Who created you is best qualified to declare the intention of His own acts, and you may safely, as you should humbly, [trust] Him to fix your position and make known your duties. In common with man, woman has a heavenly calling to glorify God as the end of her existence and to perform all the duties and enjoy all the blessings of a religious life. Like man, she is a sinful, rational, and immortal creature, placed under an economy of mercy, and called by repentance towards God and faith in our Lord Jesus Christ to eternal life. Religion is as much her vocation as that of the other sex. In Christ Jesus, there is neither male nor female, but all are on a level as to obligations, duties, and privileges…

To know what [woman's mission] is, we must, as I have said, consult the pages of revelation and ascertain the declared motive of God for her creation. *"And the LORD God said, It is not good that the man should be alone; I will make him an help meet for him"* (Gen. 2:18). This is further expressed, or rather repeated, where it is said, *"And Adam gave names to all cattle, and to the fowl of the air, and to every beast of the field; but for Adam there was not found an help meet for him"* (Gen. 2:20). Nothing can be more clear from this than that woman was made for man. Adam was created as a being with undeveloped

---

10 **oracle** – divine revelation.
11 **arbiter** – one who has power to decide or ordain according to his own absolute pleasure.

social propensities,[12] which indeed seem essential to all creatures. It is the sublime peculiarity of deity to be entirely independent of all other beings for happiness. He, and He only, is the theater of His own glory, the fountain of His own felicity,[13] and a sufficient object of His own contemplation, needing nothing for His bliss but self-communion. An archangel alone in heaven would pine, even there, for some companionship, either divine or angelic.

Adam, surrounded by all the glories of Paradise and by all the various tribes it contained, found himself alone and needing companionship. Without it, his life was but a solitude, Eden itself a desert. Endowed with a nature too communicative to be satisfied from himself alone, he sighed for society, for support, for some complement to his existence, and only half-lived so long as he lived alone. Formed to think, to speak, to love, his thoughts yearned for other thoughts with which to compare and exercise his soaring aspirations. His words were wearisomely wasted upon the wanton air, or at best awoke but an echo, which mocked instead of answering him. His love, as regards an earthly object, knew not where to bestow itself and, returning to his own bosom, threatened to degenerate into a desolating egotism. His entire being longed, in short, for another self, but that other self did not exist; there was no help meet for him. The visible creatures that surrounded him were too much beneath him, and the invisible Being Who gave him life was too much above him to unite their condition with His own. Whereupon God made woman, and the great problem was immediately solved.

It was then the characteristic of unfallen man to want someone to sympathize with him in his joys, as it is of fallen man to want someone to sympathize with him in his sorrows. Whether Adam was so far conscious of his wants as to ask for a companion we are not informed. It would appear from the inspired record as if the design of this precious boon originated with God, and as if Eve, like so many of His other mercies, was the spontaneous bestowment of His own free will. Thus, Adam would have to say, as did one of his most illustrious descendants many ages afterwards, *"For thou preventest*[14] *him with the blessings of goodness"* (Ps. 21:3).

Here, then, is the design of God in creating woman: to be a suitable helpmate to man. Man needed a companion, and God gave him woman. And as there was no other man than Adam at that time in existence, Eve was designed exclusively for Adam's comfort. This teaches us from the beginning that whatever mission woman may have to accomplish in reference to man,

---

12 **propensities** – a tendency to demonstrate particular behavior.
13 **felicity** – intense happiness; bliss.
14 **preventest** – went before and met; welcomed.

in a generic sense, her mission, at least in wedded life, is to be a suitable helpmate for that one man to whom she is united. It was declared from the beginning that every other tie, though not severed by marriage, shall be rendered subordinate, and a man shall *"leave his father and his mother, and shall cleave unto his wife: and they shall be one flesh"* (Gen. 2:24).

If woman's mission in Paradise was to be man's companion and joy, such must be the case still. Her vocation[15] has not been changed by the Fall. By that catastrophe, man needs still more urgently a companion, and God has rendered this mission of hers still more explicit by the declaration, *"Thy desire shall be to thy husband, and he shall rule over thee"* (Gen. 3:16). It has been often shown that by being taken from himself, she was equal to man in nature, while the very part of the body from which she was abstracted indicated the position she was intended to occupy. She was not taken from the head, to show she was not to rule over him; nor from his foot, to teach that she was not to be his slave; nor from his hand, to show that she was not to be his tool; but from his side, to show that she was to be his companion. There may perhaps be more of ingenuity and fancy in this than of God's original design; but if a mere conceit,[16] it is at once both pardonable and instructive.

That woman was intended to occupy a position of subordination and dependence is clear from every part of the Word of God. This is declared in language already quoted: *"Thy desire shall be to thy husband, and he shall rule over thee."* This referred not only to Eve personally, but to Eve representatively. It was the divine law of the relation of the sexes, then promulgated for all time. The preceding language placed woman, as a punishment for her sin, in a state of sorrow; this placed her in a state of subjection. Her husband was to be the center of her earthly desires and to a certain extent the regulator of them also; and she was to be in subjection to him....Man was made to show forth God's glory and praise, to be in subordination to Him and only to Him; woman was created to be, in addition to this, the glory of man by being in subordination to him, as his help and his ornament. She was not only made out of him, but for him. All her loveliness, comeliness, and purity are not only the expressions of her excellence, but of his honor and dignity, since all were not only derived from him, but made for him.

This then is woman's true position; and if anything more need be said to prove it from the records of Christianity, we may refer to Apostolic language in other places, where wives are enjoined to *"be [subject] to their own husbands in everything, [even] as the church is subject unto Christ"* (Eph. 5:24). Nor is the

---

15 **vocation** – action on the part of God, calling a person to exercise a special function.
16 **conceit** – personal opinion.

Apostle Paul alone in this, for Peter writes in the same strain. Let woman then bow to this authority and not feel herself degraded by such submission. It has been said that in domestic life, man shines as the sun, but woman as the moon with a splendor borrowed from the man. It may be said with greater truth and propriety and less invidiously[17] that man shines as the primary planet reflecting the glory of God, Who is the center of the moral universe. And woman, while she equally derives her splendor from the central Luminary[18] and is governed by His attraction, is yet the satellite of man, revolves around him, follows him in his course, and ministers to him.

Behold, then, I say again, woman's position and mission is summed up in love and subjection to her husband. Everything connected with the relationship of man and woman has, however, since the Fall, a more serious character. Her love has become more anxious; her humility more profound. Bashful of her own defects and anxious to reinstate herself in her husband's heart, woman lives to repair the wrong she has inflicted on man and lavishes upon him consolations, which may sweeten the present bitterness of sin, and warnings, which may preserve from the future bitterness of hell.

Woman, then, whatever relation she may bear to society at large, whatever duties in consequence of this relation she may have to discharge, and whatever benefits by the right discharge of these duties she may have in her power to confer upon the community, must consider herself chiefly called to advance the comfort of man in his private relations. [She will] promote her own peace by promoting his; and to receive from him all that respect, protection, and ever assiduous affection to which her equal nature, her companionship, and her devotedness give her so just a claim. She is, in wedded life, to be his constant companion, in whose society he is to find one who meets him hand to hand, eye to eye, lip to lip, and heart to heart; to whom he can unburden the secrets of a heart pressed down with care or wrung with anguish; whose presence shall be to him better than all society; whose voice shall be his sweetest music, whose smiles his brightest sunshine; from whom he shall go forth with regret, and to whose converse he shall return with willing feet when the toils of the day are over; who shall walk near his loving heart, and feel the throbbing of affection as her arm leans on his and presses on his side. In his hours of retired conversation, he shall tell her all the secrets of his heart, find in her all the capabilities and all the promptings of the most tender and endeared fellowship, and in her gentle smiles and unrestrained speech enjoy all to be expected in one who was given by God to be his associate and friend.

---

17 **invidiously** – likely to cause resentment.
18 **Luminary** – a natural light-giving body, i.e., the sun; metaphorically here of God.

In that companionship, which woman was designed to afford to man, must of course be included the sympathetic offices of the comforter. It is her role, in their hours of retirement, to console and cheer him; when he is injured or insulted, to heal the wounds of his troubled spirit; when he is burdened by care, to lighten his load by sharing it; when he is groaning with anguish, to calm by her peace-speaking words the tumult of his heart and to act in all his sorrows the part of a ministering angel.

Nor should she be backward to *offer*, nor he backward to *receive*, the counsels of wisdom which her prudence will suggest, even though she may not be intimately acquainted with all the entanglements of this world's business. Woman's advice, had it been asked for and acted upon, would have saved thousands of men from bankruptcy and ruin. Few men have ever had to regret their taking counsel from a prudent wife, while multitudes have had to reproach themselves for their folly in not asking, and multitudes more for not following, the counsels of such a companion.

If, then, this is woman's mission according to the representation of her Almighty Creator, to be the suitable helpmate of that man to whom she has given herself as the companion of his pilgrimage upon earth, it of course supposes that marriage, contracted with a due regard to prudence and under all proper regulations, is the natural state of both man and woman. And so, I affirm, in truth it is. Providence has willed it and nature prompts it. But as the exceptions are so numerous, is there no mission for those to whom the exception appertains? Is it married women only who have a mission and an important one? *Certainly not*. In these cases, I fall back upon woman's mission to society at large. And is not this momentous? Has it not been admitted in all ages and by all countries that the influence of female character upon social virtue and happiness, and upon national strength and prosperity, is prodigious,[19] whether for good or for evil?…Every woman, whether rich or poor, married or single, has a circle of influence within which, according to her character, she is exerting a certain amount of power for good or harm. Every woman by her virtue or her vice, by her wisdom or her folly, by her dignity or her levity[20] is adding something to our national elevation or degradation. As long as female virtue is prevalent, upheld by one sex and respected by the other, a nation cannot sink very low in the scale of ignominy[21] by plunging into the depths of vice.

To a certain extent, woman is the conservator of her nation's welfare. Her virtue, if firm and uncorrupted, will stand sentinel over that of the

---

19 **prodigious** – impressively great in size or power; enormous.
20 **levity** – undignified behavior.
21 **ignominy** – dishonor; disgrace; shame.

empire. Law, justice, liberty, and the arts all contribute, of course, to the well-being of a nation; beneficial influence flows in from various springs, and innumerable contributors may be at work, each laboring in his vocation for his country's weal.[22] But let the general tone of female morals be low, and all will be rendered nugatory,[23] while on the other hand, the universal prevalence of womanly intelligence and virtue will swell the stream of civilization to its highest level, impregnate it with its richest qualities and spread its fertility over the widest surface. A community is not likely to be overthrown where woman fulfills her mission, for by the power of her noble heart over the hearts of others she will raise it from its ruins and restore it again to prosperity and joy. Here then, beyond the circle of wedded life as well as within it, is no doubt part of woman's mission, and an important one it is. Her field is social life, her object is social happiness, her reward is social gratitude and respect.

If I am right as to the nature of woman's mission, I cannot err as to the proper sphere of it. If she was created for man, and not only for the race of man, but for one man, then the easy and necessary inference is that home is the proper scene of woman's action and influence. There are few terms in the language around which cluster so many blissful associations as that delight of every…heart, the word "home." The Elysium[24] of love, the nursery of virtue, the garden of enjoyment, the temple of concord,[25] the circle of all tender relationships, the playground of childhood, the dwelling of manhood, the retreat of age; where health loves to enjoy its pleasures, wealth revels in its luxuries, and poverty bears its rigors; where sickness can best endure its pains and dissolving nature expire; which throws its spell over those who are within its charmed circle and even sends its attractions across oceans and continents, drawing to itself the thoughts and wishes of the man who wanders from it to the antipodes[26]—this home, sweet home is the sphere of wedded woman's mission.

From *Female Piety* reprinted by Soli Deo Gloria.

John Angell James (1785-1859): English Congregationalist preacher and author; born in Blandford Forum, Dorset, England.

---

22 **weal** – well-being; prosperity.
23 **nugatory** – worthless; of no value or importance.
24 **Elysium** – a place or state of ideal happiness.
25 **concord** – harmony; agreement between persons.
26 **antipodes** – places on the surface of the earth directly opposite to each other.

A Virtuous Woman Described

CHARLES BRIDGES (1794-1869)

Proverbs 31:10-31

So rare is this treasure that the challenge is given: *"Who can find a virtuous woman?"* (Prov. 31:10). Abraham sent to a distant land for this inestimable blessing for his beloved son (Gen. 24:3, 4). Perhaps one reason of the rarity of the gift is that it is so seldom sought. Too often is the search made for accomplishments, not for virtues; for external and adventitious[27] recommendations, rather than for internal godly worth.

The enquiry also implies the value of the gift when found. Even Adam's portion in innocence was not complete, until his bountiful Father made *"an help meet[28] for him"* (Gen. 2:18). Truly, her price is above rubies. No treasure is comparable to her…

Verses 11-12

The price of the virtuous woman has been told; her different features will now be given. The first lines of the portrait describe her character as a wife. Her fidelity, oneness of heart, and affectionate dutifulness make the heart of her husband *safely to trust in her*. He feels his comfort to be regarded, his burdens relieved, and his mind exempted from many teasing vexations.[29] He is at ease in constrained absence from home, having left his interests safe in her keeping, while he is sure that his return will be welcomed with the gladdening smile. A faithful wife and a confiding husband thus mutually bless each other. With such a jewel for his wife, the husband has no misgivings.[30] His home is the home of his heart. He needs not to look into the matters entrusted to her with suspicious eye. He has no reserves or jealousies. Ruling in this sphere without, he encourages her to rule in her sphere within. All is conducted with such prudence and economy that he has *no need of spoil*,[31] no temptation to unjust gain, *no need* to leave his happy home in order to enrich himself with the soldier's *spoils*. The attachment of such a wife is as lasting as the time of their union—constant—consistent. Instead of abusing confidence, she only seeks to make herself daily more worthy of it, not fretful and uncertain, caring *"how she may please her husband"* (1 Cor. 7:34), *doing him good, and not evil, all the days of her life*. Would that it were always so! But look at Eve—the help-meet

---

27 **adventitious** – from outside.
28 **help meet** – Eve was an "help," who was *meet* or suitable for Adam.
29 **teasing vexations** – annoying irritations or distresses.
30 **misgivings** – feelings of mistrust or loss of confidence.
31 **spoil** – goods, property, territory seized by force, often taken from an enemy during war.

becoming a tempter; Solomon's wives drawing away his heart; Jezebel stirring up her husband to abominable wickedness; Job's wife calling upon her husband to *"curse God, and die"* (Job 2:9); the painful cross of the *"brawling woman"* (Prov. 21:9; 25:24)—this is a fearful contrast—evil, not good. Often again is it a mixture of evil with the good….But in this picture it is good, and not evil.

Her husband's comfort is her interest and her rest. To live for him is her highest happiness. Even if her minute attentions to this object are not always noticed, yet never will she harbor the suspicion of indifference or unkindness; nor will she return fancied neglect with sullenness,[32] or by affected or morbid sensibility[33] force on a feverish interchange of expression,[34] which has little substantial foundation.

This course of disinterested regard[35] and devoted affection, when conducted on Christian principles, commends most graciously the holy and honorable estate of matrimony. If it implies subjection, it involves no degradation. Indeed no greater glory could be desired than that which is given to it, that it should illustrate "the great mystery"—*"Christ and the church"* (Eph. 5:32), the identity of interest between them: her trials His; His cause hers.

Verses 13-27

This lovely character is drawn according to the usage of ancient times, though the general principles are of universal application. It describes not only the wife of a man of rank, but a wise, useful, and godly matron in her domestic responsibilities. It is *"[a woman] professing godliness,"* adorned *"with good works"* (1 Tim. 2:10); a Mary no less than a Martha….One thing, however, is most remarkable. The standard of godliness here exhibited is not that of a religious recluse,[36] shut up from active obligations under the pretence of greater sanctity and consecration to God. Here are none of those habits of monastic asceticism[37] that are now extolled as the highest point of Christian perfection. At least one-half of the picture of the virtuous woman is occupied with her personal and domestic industry. What a rebuke also does this convey to a self-indulgent inactivity!...

But let us look more minutely into the features of the portrait drawn before us. Her personal habits are full of energy. Manual labor, even menial[38]

---

32 **fancied…sullenness** – acting moody or gloomy because of imagined neglect.
33 **affected…sensibility** – unreasonable suspicion.
34 **feverish…expression** – excited, agitated reaction; overreaction.
35 **disinterested regard** – unselfish care or concern.
36 **religious recluse** – one secluded or shut off from society for religious reasons.
37 **asceticism** – extreme self-denial characteristic of monks or nuns in monasteries.
38 **menial** – work that requires little skill or training; work of a household servant.

service, in olden times was the employment of females in the highest ranks. Self-denial is here a main principle. *The virtuous woman* goes before her servants in diligence, no less than in dignity, imposing nothing upon them, which she had not first bound upon herself, ruling her household most efficiently by the government of herself. Thus, *she seeks* out her materials for work. Her needle is at the service of her family. Instead of a suppressed murmur at some inconvenient demand, she sets the pattern of working *willingly with her hands*. Instead of loitering[39] herself, while they were laboring, she counts it no shame to be employed at *the spindle and distaff.*[40] She is early and late at her work, *rising in the night*. The fruit of her work she turns to good account. She exchanges it in commerce for *food brought from far. Her merchandize* is good in quality—*tapestry, fine linen, and girdles delivered to the merchant.* Her whole soul is in her work—*girding her loins with strength and strengthening her arms*—ready to do any work befitting her sex and station. The land has also her due share of attention. Ever careful for her husband's interests, *she considers* the value of *a field*; and, if it be a good purchase, she *buys* it and *plants the vineyard* for the best produce.

We now again observe her conduct as a mistress. And here also her praise is not that she spends her time in devotional exercises (though these, as *"a woman that feareth the Lord"* (v. 30), she duly prizes); but that according to the Scriptural canon, *"[she guides her] house"* (1 Tim. 5:14), watching carefully over her charge, distributing both her meat[41] and her work in due proportion and *"in due season."* This is her responsibility. If a *"man goeth forth unto his work and to his labour until the evening"* (Ps. 104:23), the woman finds her work as *"[a keeper*[42]*] at home"* (Titus 2:5). And beautiful indeed is it to see, how by her industry, self-denial, and heartiness she *"buildeth her house"* (Prov. 14:1). *She rises while it is yet night*, not for the sake of being admired and talked of, but to *give meat to her household*. The delicacy also, with which she preserves her own sphere, is remarkable…..So *well does she look to the ways of her household*, such untiring energy does she show in every department, that none can accuse her of *eating the bread of idleness*. In her household, order is the principle of her rule….Nor is her provident[43] care limited to her own dependents. Her *spindle and distaff* are worked, not for herself only, or for her household, but for *the poor and needy*. And, having first drawn out her soul (Isa. 58:10), *she*

---

39 **loitering** – wasting one's time in idleness.
40 **distaff** – a rod on which a fiber, such as wool or flax, is wound for spinning by hand.
41 **meat** – food in general.
42 **keeper** – one who stays at home and oversees the house; homemaker.
43 **provident** – foresight of and making provision for the future; frugal; economical.

stretcheth out her hands (Deut. 15:7, 8), to embrace those at a distance from her with the flow of her love; and thus the blessing of those that were ready to perish cometh upon her (Job 29:13; Acts 9:39). Her spirit and manner also are of the same character, all in full accordance with her professions… the godly matron has not only the law of love in her heart, but *wisdom in her mouth* and *in her tongue the law of kindness*. The same love that binds her heart governs her tongue….Thus indeed *"a virtuous woman is a crown to her husband"* (Prov. 12:4). *He is known in the gates, when he sitteth among the elders of the land*, as blessed with no common treasures of happiness; as indebted perhaps for his promotion to the wealth acquired by her management at home, and, it may be, for the preservation and establishment of his virtue, to the encouragement furnished by her example and conversation.[44] For herself—manifest and manifold blessings rest upon her. *Strength is the clothing* of her inner man. Christian courage and resolution lift her up above appalling difficulties. *The clothing of honor* stamps her with the Lord's acceptance, as His faithful servant, the child of His grace, and the heir of His glory…

Verses 28-31: the virtuous woman is obviously subserving[45] her own interest. For what greater earthly happiness could she know than *her children's* reverence and her husband's *blessing*? We may picture to ourselves her condition—crowned with years, her children grown up, perhaps themselves surrounded with families and endeavoring to train them as [they] had been trained. Their mother is constantly before their eyes. Her tender guidance, her wise counsels, her loving discipline, her holy example, are vividly kept in remembrance. They cease not *to call her blessed* and to bless the Lord for her as His invaluable gift. No less warmly does *her husband praise her*. His attachment to her was grounded, not on the *deceitful and vain charms of beauty*, but on *the fear of the Lord*. She is therefore in his eyes to the end, the stay of his declining years, the soother of his cares, the counselor of his perplexities, the comforter of his sorrows, the sunshine of his earthly joys (Ecclus[46] 36:23, 24). Both children and husband combine in the grateful acknowledgment—*many daughters have done virtuously; but thou excellest them all*.

But why, it may be asked, do external recommendations form no part

---

44 **conversation** – manner of conduct; behavior.
45 **subserving** – furthering; promoting.
46 **Ecclesiasticus** – also known as *The Wisdom of Ben Sira* or simply *Sirach*. Bridges is here quoting from the *Apocrypha*, a collection of books, which Roman Catholicism and Eastern Orthodoxy consider canonical. Though the *Apocrypha* was included as a separate collection between the OT and NT in the original version of the 1611 KJV, neither the Jews nor the Protestant churches believed that the apocryphal writings were inspired, infallible Scripture.

of this portrait? All that is described is solid excellence; and *favor is deceitful*. A graceful form and mien[47] often end in disappointment, more bitter than words can tell. Often do they furnish a cover for the vilest corruptions. And then *beauty*—what a fading *vanity* it is! One fit of sickness sweeps it away (Ps. 39:11). Sorrow and care wither its charms. And even while it remains, it is little connected with happiness. It proves itself the fruitful occasion of trouble, the source of many hurtful temptations and snares; and without substantial principle, to a well-judging mind it becomes an object of disgust rather than of attraction (Prov. 11:22).

The portrait, here penciled by divine inspiration, begins with the touch of a virtuous woman and fills up the sketch with the lineaments[48] of *a woman that feareth the Lord* (31:10, 30). For the lovely features described—her fidelity to her husband, her active personal habits, her good management and diligence in her family, her consideration for the necessities and comforts of others, her watchfulness of conduct, her tenderness for the poor and afflicted, her kind and courteous behavior to all—this completeness of character and grace could only flow from that virtue which is identified with vital godliness. They are the good fruit that prove the tree to be good (Matt. 7:17). They are such fruit, flowing from a right principle, as the natural corrupt stock of man could never produce.

How valuable also is this picture as a directory for the marriage choice. Let *virtue*, not beauty, be the primary object. Set against the *vanity of beauty* the true happiness, [which is] connected with *a woman that feareth the Lord*. Here is the solid basis of happiness. "If," says Bishop Beveridge—"I choose her for her *beauty*, I shall love her no longer than while that continues; and then farewell at once both duty and delight. But if I love her for her virtues; then, though all other sandy foundations fail, yet will my happiness remain entire"…."Thus, and once more," says Matthew Henry, "is shut up this looking-glass for ladies, which they are desired to open and dress themselves by. And if they do so, their adorning will be found to praise, and honor, and glory at the appearing of Jesus Christ."

From *Proverbs* reprinted by The Banner of Truth Trust.

Charles Bridges (1794-1869): A leader of the Evangelical party in the Church of England. Best known for *The Christian Ministry*, *Proverbs*, and *Psalm 119*.

---

47 **mien** – expression; appearance.
48 **lineaments** – distinctive features or characteristics.

Christ's Call to Young Women

THOMAS VINCENT (1634-1678)

> *Hearken, O daughter, and consider, and incline thine ear; forget also thine own people, and thy father's house; So shall the king greatly desire thy beauty: for he is thy Lord; and worship thou him. —Psalm 45:10-11*

This psalm is called a song of loves, the most high, pure, and spiritual, the most dear, sweet, and delightful loves, namely those loves which are between Christ the Beloved and His Church, which is His spouse. Here is set forth, first, the Lord Jesus Christ in His majesty, power, and divinity, His truth, meekness, and equity; and then the spouse is set forth in regard of her ornaments, companions, attendants, and posterity. And both are set forth in regard of their loveliness and beauty. After a description is given of Christ, an invitation is made to His espousals,[49] and that of the children of men, called by the name of "daughter." Therefore, it is particularly applicable unto the daughters of men, yet not so as excluding the sons of men as any more than when God speaks unto the sons of men He excludes the daughters. I shall now speak unto the words, and from hence observe this doctrine, as comprehensive as I can make it…

    1. Christ espouses and betroths people unto Himself in this world. The public solemnization of the marriage is reserved until the last day when His spouse shall be brought to Him in white robes and raiment of perfect righteousness, more rich and curious than any needlework. The marriage feast will be held in His Father's house in heaven, where they shall be received into the nearest and closest embraces of His love. The espousal between them and the marriage knot is tied here.

    2. Christ invites all the children of men, and particularly the daughters of men, to be His spouse. This is that which they are invited to in the text. It is upon this account that Christ sends His ministers to be His ambassadors, to whom He gives commission in His name to call the children of men unto this most near and sweet relationship. They represent His person and are to invite and woo in His name so that people would come and join themselves unto Him. The Apostle Paul tells the Corinthians how successful His embassage[50] was among them in 2 Corinthians 11:2: *"I have espoused you to one husband, that I may present you as a chaste virgin to Christ."* And when any ministers are instrumental in the conversion of any, they espouse them to Christ. In conversion, sinners are divorced from sin and are married unto the Lord Jesus…

---

49 **espousals** – promise to enter into marriage.
50 **embassage** – mission of being sent as an official messenger.

Does the Lord Jesus Christ, the King of glory, [call] all the children of men, and particularly the daughters of men, to be His spouse? And is He so greatly desirous of the beauty of such as are joined to Him? This, then, should put all of you upon inquiry whether you are espoused unto Jesus Christ. You have been called hereunto; have you hearkened?...If you are espoused unto Christ, then:

1. You are disjoined[51] from sin. Is the cursed league broken which naturally exists between sin and your hearts? Before you are espoused to Christ, you are, as it were, espoused and married to sin. Sin is your husband, and you are tied in its bonds. Sin inhabits you and dwells in the embraces of your dearest love and delight. You care for the things of sin, how you may please your flesh and gratify your inordinate[52] desires. And while this Husband and Beloved of your hearts lives, you are not at liberty to be espoused and married to Jesus Christ. Sin lives in the affections while it possesses the most prevailing, liking affections; and as long as you are knit and linked to sin, examine whether or not sin has yet received its death wounds in your hearts; whether the false mask of sin has ever been plucked off, and the odiousness of it has ever been made manifest to you; whether your hearts have been brought to a loathing and detesting of it; whether sin has been killed in your affections, and the knot loosened which has tied your hearts to it. Do you indeed hate sin with the greatest and most implacable hatred? Is sin mortified and subdued as to its reigning power? If sin is dead, you are at liberty to be espoused, and it is a good sign that you are espoused to Jesus Christ.

2. If you are espoused unto Christ, then you have been drawn to Him by the Spirit. *"No man can come to me, except the Father which hath sent me draw him"* (John 6:44). You have had external calls of the Word to come unto Christ; have you been called effectually, and drawn powerfully, irresistibly, and yet most sweetly by the Spirit unto Jesus Christ? Have you had a discovery by the Spirit not only of your necessity of and lost estate without an interest in Christ, but also of His beauty and transcendent loveliness, His excellency and great willingness to entertain[53] you in this relationship? And have you been moved and drawn hereby unto Him?

3. If you are espoused unto Christ, then you have laid hold on Him by faith. The Spirit draws unto Christ by working the grace of faith and enabling persons to believe in Him. By faith Christ is received. *"But as many as received him, to them gave he power to become the sons of God, even to them*

---

51 **disjoined** – separated; parted from.
52 **inordinate** – exceeding reasonable limits; excessive.
53 **entertain** – to receive.

that believe on his name" (John 1:12). By believing on Christ's name, people receive Christ in this relationship. Faith is the hand of the soul which lays hold of Christ; and by this joining of the hand with Christ, the knot is tied and the soul is united to Christ in the relationship of a spouse. Have you this grace of faith wrought in you with power? Have you received and applied Christ to yourselves? Have you received Him upon His own terms? And do you by faith draw quickening and strengthening influences from Him?

4. If you are espoused unto Christ, then you embrace Him in the arms of your dearest love; then you love the Lord Jesus in sincerity, and you love Him with the supremacy of your love. If you love father or mother, houses or lands, riches or honors, delights or pleasures, or anything in the world more than Christ, you have no true love to Christ. Be sure that you are not espoused to Him, if that is the case. But if Christ is chiefly loved, it is an evidence that you are joined in this relationship to Him.

5. If you are espoused unto Christ, you have acquaintance and converse[54] with Christ, and you like His company best. You highly value and diligently attend upon all those ordinances which are the means of bringing you and Christ together. This is the great thing you desire and seek after in hearing and prayer and the Table of the Lord: that you may have a sight of your Beloved and a taste of His love and more intimate communion with Him. And is acquaintance begun with Christ and further intimacy desired by you? Are pure and powerful ordinances of great esteem with you? Do you give all diligence to wait upon and look for your Beloved in them?

6. If you are espoused to Christ, then you endeavor to promote His interest and advance His name in the world. While others seek their own things, you seek the things of Jesus Christ and look upon them as your own. When others labor chiefly to lift themselves up in the esteem of men, you labor above all to lift up Christ in men's esteem. You are commending your Beloved above all others and endeavor to bring others to love Him and into the same relationship with Him.

Exhortation

You who are not as yet espoused unto Christ, I shall direct my speech unto you, and that to both men and women, but particularly to you who are young women, whom I am especially called now to preach to….Come, virgins, will you give me leave to be a suitor[55] unto you, not in my own name, but in the name of my Lord? May I prevail with you for your affections and persuade you

---

54 **converse** – spiritual communion.
55 **suitor** – one who seeks a woman in marriage.

to give them unto Christ? May I be instrumental to join you and Christ together this day? Do not be coy, as some of you possibly are in other loves. Modesty and the virgin blush may very well become you when motions of another kind are made to you; but here coyness is folly, and backwardness to accept this motion is a shame. And you have ten thousand times more reason to blush at your refusal of Christ as your Beloved than at the acceptance, when otherwise the devil and sin would ravish your virgin affections. Never did you have a better motion made to you….Consider Who the Lord Jesus is, to Whom you are invited to espouse yourselves. He is the best husband; none is comparable to Jesus Christ.

1. Do you desire one who is great? He is of the highest dignity; none ever did or could climb into so high a feat or attain to such excellent majesty as that to which Christ is exalted. He is exalted above all the kings of the earth. *"And he hath on his vesture and on his thigh a name written, KING OF KINGS, AND LORD OF LORDS"* (Rev. 19:16). Yea, He is exalted above the angels of heaven, and none have such authority: *"Who is gone into heaven…angels and authorities and powers being made subject unto him"* (1 Peter 3:22). He is the Firstborn of every creature, by Whom and for Whom all things were created. *"He is before all things, and by him all things consist. And he is the head of the body, the church: who is the beginning, the firstborn from the dead; that in all things he might have the preeminence"* (Col. 1:17-18). *"Who being the brightness of his [Father's] glory, and the express image of his person"* (Heb. 1:3). He is the glory of heaven, the darling of eternity, admired by angels, dreaded by devils, and adored by saints. If the meanest[56] beggar should be matched unto the greatest earthly prince who ever lived, it would not be such an advancement unto her as for you to be espoused unto the Lord Jesus Christ, the King of glory, Whose honor and dignity you will partake of in and by this relationship.

2. Do you desire one who is rich? None is comparable unto Christ, Who is the Heir of all things (Heb. 1:2), in Whom all the fullness dwells (Col. 1:19). Not only the fullness of the earth belongs to Him (Ps. 24:1), but also the fullness of heaven is at His disposal, all things being given and delivered unto Him by the Father (John 3:35; Matt. 11:27). The riches of grace and the riches of glory are at His disposal. In Him are hidden all treasures (Col. 2:3). The Apostle speaks of *"the unsearchable riches of Christ"* (Eph. 3:8). The riches of Christ are unsearchable in regard to their worth; they are inestimable; the value of them is past finding out. And they are unsearchable in regard to the abundance of them. They are inexhaustible; none can draw Christ's fountain dry. None can search and find out the bottom of Christ's treasury. If you are espoused unto Christ, you shall share in His unsearchable riches; you shall receive of His fullness grace for grace

---

56 **meanest** – lowliest; poorest.

here and glory for glory hereafter. And He will make all needful provisions for your outward man while your abode is here in this world.

3. Do you desire one who is wise? There is none comparable unto Christ for wisdom. His knowledge is infinite and His wisdom corresponds….Christ is not only wise, but wisdom (Matt. 11:19). He is the wisdom of God (1 Cor. 1:24). Christ is infinitely wise in Himself, and He is the spring of all true, spiritual, and heavenly wisdom, which is derived unto any of the children of men. *"In [Him] are hid all the treasures of wisdom and knowledge"* (Col. 2:3). If you are espoused unto Christ, He will guide and counsel you and make you wise unto salvation.

4. Do you desire one who is potent,[57] who may defend you against your enemies and against any kind of injuries and abuses? There is none equal to Christ in power. Others have some power, but Christ has *all* power (Matt. 28:18). Others may be potent, but Christ is omnipotent. Others have power, but Christ *is* power, the power of God (1 Cor. 1:24). And if you are espoused to Christ, His infinite power is engaged in your defense against your enemies. He will subdue your iniquities (Mic. 7:19) by that power whereby He is able to subdue all things (Phil. 3:21). He will bruise Satan under your feet (Rom. 16:20). He will keep you from the evil of the world (John 17:15). He will make you more than conquerors over all your spiritual enemies, who, without His help, would not only abuse and injure you, but also ruin and destroy you (Rom. 8:37).

5. Do you desire one who is good? There is none like Christ in this regard. Others may have some goodness, but it is imperfect. Christ's goodness is complete and perfect. He is full of goodness, and in Him dwells no evil. He is good and He does good; and if you are espoused unto Christ, however bad you are by nature, He will make you in some measure good like Himself.

6. Do you desire one who is beautiful? Christ is fairer than the children of men (Ps. 45:2). He is white and ruddy, the chiefest among ten thousand (Song 5:10). His mouth is most sweet, yea, He is altogether lovely (Song 5:16). His eyes are most sparkling. His looks and glances of love are most ravishing. His smiles are most delightful and refreshing unto the soul. Christ is the most lovely and amiable person of all others in the world. None are so accomplished in all regards as He is accomplished; and therefore He is most desirable in this relationship. However unlovely you are in yourselves, however deformed and defiled by sin, yet if you are espoused unto Christ, He will put His comeliness[58] upon you. He will wash you from your defilements in a bath made of His own blood and beautify you with His own image, and so you shall become exceedingly fair. And as you may have leave to delight

---

57 **potent** – possessed of great power.
58 **comeliness** – pleasing and wholesome appearance; attractiveness.

yourselves in Christ's beauty, so He will greatly desire and delight in yours…

7. Do you desire one who can love you? None can love you like Christ. His love is incomparable, and His love is incomprehensible. His love passes all other loves, and it passes knowledge too (Eph. 3:19). His love is first, without any beginning. His love is free, without any motive. His love is great, without any measure. His love is constant, without any change. And His love is everlasting, without any end.

It was the love of Christ which brought Him down from heaven, which veiled His divinity in a human soul and body, which put upon Him the form of a servant, which exposed Him to contempt, reproach, and many indignities. It was love which made Him subject to hunger, thirst, sorrow, and many human infirmities, which humbled Him unto death, even the painful and ignominious death of the cross. And when out of love He had finished the work of redemption on earth, as to what was needful by way of satisfaction, it was His love which carried Him back to heaven where He was before, so that He might make application of what He had purchased; that there He might make intercession for those whom He had redeemed and prepare a place for them, even glorious mansions with Himself in the house not made with hands, which is eternal in the heavens. It is out of love that He sends such tokens to His people from heaven to earth, which He conveys through His ordinances by His Spirit unto them. And His love tokens are infinitely beyond all other love tokens in worth and excellence. Sure, then, none is so desirable as the Lord Jesus Christ for you to espouse yourselves unto. If you are espoused to Christ, He is yours—all that He is and all that He has. You shall have His heart and share in the choicest expressions of His dearest love.

And now put all these things together. The Lord Jesus Christ, being incomparable in dignity, in riches, in wisdom, in power, in goodness, in loveliness, and in love, I think you should need no other motive to persuade you to willingness to espouse yourselves to Him.

From "Christ the Best Husband" in *The Good Work Begun* reprinted by Soli Deo Gloria.

Thomas Vincent (1634-1678): English Puritan preacher; beloved and respected author of *The Shorter Catechism Explained from Scripture, True Christian's Love for the Unseen Christ* and others.

Grace for a Wife's Submission
WILLIAM GOUGE (1575-1653)

> *Wives, submit yourselves unto your own husbands, as unto the Lord. For the husband is the head of the wife, even as Christ is the head of the Church: and he is the saviour of the body. Therefore as the Church is subject unto Christ, so let the wives be [subject] to their own husbands in every thing.* —Ephesians 5:22-24

Four graces needful to season a wife's subjection: this general conclusion might be applied to the *matter* of subjection as well as to the *manner*. For the Church acknowledges Christ her superior, fears Him inwardly, reverenceth Him outwardly, obeys Him also both by forbearing to do what He forbids, and also by doing what He commands…there are four virtues which are especially needful hereunto, whereby the Church seasons her subjection to Christ and wives also may and must season their subjection to their husbands…

I. *Humility* is that grace that keeps one from thinking highly of himself above that which is meet[59]…if humility be placed in a wife's heart, it will make her think better of her husband than of herself, and so make her the more willing to yield all subjection unto him. The Apostle requires it of all Christians as a general sauce to season all other duties (Phil. 2:3; Eph. 4:2). But after a peculiar[60] manner is it needful for inferiors:[61] most of all for wives because there are many prerogatives[62] appertaining to their place, which may soon make them think they ought not to be subject, unless they be humbly minded. That the Church does herewith season her subjection is clear by the book of *Song of Solomon*, where often she acknowledges her own meanness[63] and the excellency of her spouse. Therefore, as the Church is humbly subject to Christ, so let wives be to their husbands.

Contrary is pride, which puffeth up wives and makes them think there is no reason they should be subject to husbands. They can rule themselves well enough, yea, and rule their husbands too, as well as their husbands rule them! [There is] no more pestilent[64] vice for an inferior than this. It is the cause of all rebellion, disobedience, and disloyalty: *"Only by pride cometh contention"* (Prov. 13:10).

---

59 **meet** – appropriate.
60 **peculiar** – particular; special.
61 **inferiors** – in our day *inferior* is used primarily in the sense of "low quality"; however, Gouge's sense is *position*: "lower in rank, not quality or nature; subordinate." For example, a private is inferior to a sergeant in rank, but equally human by nature.
62 **prerogatives** – exclusive rights or privileges.
63 **meanness** – humility; lowliness.
64 **pestilent** – morally, socially, or politically harmful.

II. *Sincerity* is that grace that makes one to be within, even in truth, what without he appears to be in show. This is that singleness of heart, which is expressly required of servants and may be applied to wives, for indeed it appertains to all sorts (Eph. 6:5). Because it is only discerned by the Lord, Who is the searcher of all hearts (Acts 1:24), it will move a wife to have an eye to Him in all she does and to endeavor to approve herself to Him above all.... Though there were no other motive in the world to move her to subjection, yet for conscience sake to Christ, she should yield it. Saint Peter testifies of holy women, that they trusted in God and were subject to their husbands (1 Peter 3:5). [This implies] that their conscience to God made them be subject to their husbands. Was not Sarah's subjection seasoned with sincerity, when within herself, in her heart she called her husband *"lord"* (Gen. 18:12)?

Great reason there is that wives should in sincerity subject themselves: 1. In their subjection even to their husbands, they have to do with Christ, in whose room their husbands stand. Though their husbands, who are but men, see only the face and outward behavior, yet Christ sees their heart and inward disposition. Though their husbands see only the things which they do before their faces and can hear only of such things as are done before others, yet Christ sees and knows the things that are done in the most secret places that can be, when no creature beside themselves is privy thereunto. Now let it be granted that in their outward carriage they give very good contentment unto their husbands and please them every way, yet if sincerity have been wanting, with what face can they appear before Christ? He will take another manner account of them. Before Christ, all their outward complement will stand them in no stead at all.

2. Herein lies a main difference between true, Christian, religious wives and mere natural women. [Natural women] may be subject on by-respects,[65] as namely, that their husbands may the more love them or live the more quietly and peaceably with them; or that they may the more readily obtain what they desire at their husbands' hands; or for fear of their husbands' displeasure and wrath, knowing him to be an angry, furious man. So as otherwise it might be worse with them, they might [lack] many needful things or carry away many sore blows if they were not subject.

But [Christian women] have respect to Christ's ordinance, whereby their husbands are made their head, and to His Word and will, whereby they are commanded subjection. Thus, holy women subjected themselves (1 Peter 3:5). They cannot be holy that do not thus subject themselves: for this is a sweet perfume that sends forth a good savor into Christ's nostrils and makes the things we do pleasant and acceptable to Him.

---

65 **onby-respects** – with an ulterior motive.

3. The benefit of this virtue being planted in a wife's heart is very great, and that both to her husband and to herself. To her *husband,* it will make her manifest her respect of him before others, behind his back, as well as before himself in his presence. And [it] will make her faithful to him and careful to do his will wheresoever he be—with her or from her. To *herself*, in that it will minister inward sweet comfort unto her, though her husband should take no notice of her subjection or misinterpret it or ill require it. For she might say as Hezekiah did, *"Remember now, O LORD, I beseech thee, how I have walked before thee in truth and with a perfect heart, and have done that which is good in thy sight"* (Isa. 38:3).

Contrary to sincerity is dissimulation[66] and mere outward, complemental subjection,[67] when a wife does even despise her husband in her heart as Michal did David (2 Sam. 6:16) and yet carry a fair face before him…. Though such a wife should perform all the duties named before, yet would those all be nothing to God, if they were done with a double heart and not in singleness of heart…

III. *Cheerfulness* is more apparent than sincerity and makes subjection the more pleasing not only to God, but also to man, who by the effects thereof may easily discern it. For God, as He does Himself all things willingly and cheerfully, so He expects that His children should therein follow Him, and thereby show themselves His children. *"God loveth a cheerful giver"* (2 Cor. 9:7), not only a cheerful giver of alms, but of all duty to God and man.

For men, it makes them also much better accept any duty when they observe it to be done cheerfully. This did even ravish David with joy, to see his people offer their gifts willingly unto the Lord (1 Chron. 29:9). When an husband sees his wife willingly and cheerfully perform her duty, it cannot but raise up love in him. This cheerfulness is manifested by a ready, quick, and speedy performance of her duty. Sarah's readiness to obey shows that what she did, she did willingly. That thus the Church subjects herself to Christ is evident by that which David says, *"Thy people shall be willing in the day of thy power"* (Ps. 110:3). Therefore, as the Church is cheerfully subject unto Christ, so let wives be to their husbands.

Contrary to this cheerfulness is the sullen disposition of some wives, who will indeed be subject to their husbands and obey, but with such a lowering[68] and sour countenance, with such pouting and muttering, as they

---

66 **dissimulation** – concealment of one's true feelings or intentions; hypocrisy.
67 **complemental subjection** – false submission in which a woman pays compliments to her husband but does not submit in her heart.
68 **lowering** – frowning; scowling; angry-looking.

grieve their husbands more in the manner, than they can be pleased with the thing itself that they do. Herein they show themselves like to a cursed cow, which having given a fair sop[69] of milk, casts all down with her heel....Such subjection is in truth no subjection. It can be neither acceptable to God, nor profitable to their husbands, nor comfortable[70] to their own souls.

IV. *Constancy* is a virtue which makes all the rest perfect and sets the crown upon them, without which they are all nothing. This is in those who, after they have begun well, continue to do well unto the end and thereby reap the fruit of all. It has respect both to continuance without intermission and to perseverance without revolting and giving clean over.[71] So as it is not enough to be subject by starts and fits[72]—one while yielding all good obedience, another while stout[73] and rebellious—neither is it sufficient in former times to have been a good wife and after prove bad. But there must be daily proceeding and holding on from time to time, so long as husband and wife live together. This grace was in her of whom it is said, *"She will do him good and not evil all the days of her life"* (Prov. 31:12). Such were all the holy wives commended in Scripture....This grace does the Church add to all her other virtues, she in all parts of her subjection remains constant and faithful unto the death, whereby it comes to pass that at length she receives the reward of her holy obedience, which is full and perfect communion and fellowship with her spouse Christ Jesus in heaven. In regard of her unmovable constancy, it is said, *"The gates of hell shall not prevail against it"* (Matt. 16:18). Therefore, as the Church is constantly subject unto Christ, so let wives be to their husbands.

Of the extent of a wife's obedience: The extent of a wife's subjection is set down under these general terms "in every thing," which are not so generally to be taken as if they admitted no restraint or limitation. For then would they contradict such cautions as these: *"in the fear of God," "as unto the Lord," "in the Lord"* (Eph. 5:21-22; Col. 3:18). For man is so corrupt by nature and of so perverse a disposition, that often he wills and commands that which is contrary to God's will and commandment: which when he does, that Christian principle laid down as a ruled case by the Apostle must take place, we ought rather to obey God than men (Acts 5:29)....From that extent, I gather these two conclusions: 1. A wife must labor to bring her judgment and will to her husband's. 2. Though in her judgment she cannot

---

69 **fair sop** – abundant quantity.
70 **comfortable** – encouraging; strengthening.
71 **revolting...clean over** – rebelling and entirely giving up.
72 **starts and fits** – in intervals; starting and stopping.
73 **stout** – obstinate; stubborn.

think that most meet which her husband requires, yet she must yield to it in practice. In the former of these, I say not simply that a wife is bound to bring her judgment to the bent of her husband's. For he may be deceived in his judgment, and she may see his error; and then unless her understanding should be blinded, she cannot conceive that to be true which he judges so.... This submission even of her judgment respects not only things necessary, for which her husband has an express determinate warrant out of the Scripture, but also things doubtful and indifferent. For even so far does this clause "in every thing" extend. The subjection of a wife respects not her practice only, but her judgment and opinion also, which if she can bring to the lawfulness and meetness[74] of that which her husband requires, she will much more cheerfully perform it...

Contrary is the presumption of such wives as think themselves wiser than their husbands and able better to judge matters than they can. I deny not but that a wife may have more understanding than her husband: for some men are very ignorant and blockish.[75] And on the other side, some women [are] well-instructed, who thereby have attained to a great measure of knowledge and discretion. But many, though they have husbands of sufficient and good understanding—wise and discrete men—yet think that that which they have once conceived to be a truth, must needs be so. And such is their peremptoriness,[76] that they will not be brought to think that they may err. [They] say they will never be brought to think otherwise than they do, though all the husbands in the world should be of another opinion....The latter conclusion concerning a wife's yielding in practice to that which her husband requires, though she cannot bring her judgment to think as he does about the meetness of it, has respect to indifferent things, namely, to such as are neither in their particulars commanded, nor forbidden by God: as the outward affairs of the house, ordering it, disposing goods, entertaining guests, etc.

QUESTION: May she not reason with her husband about such matters as she thinks unmeet and labor to persuade her husband not to persist in the pressing thereof, yea, endeavor to bring her husband to see the unmeetness (as she thinks) of that which she sees?

ANSWER: With modesty, humility, and reverence she may so do; and he ought to hearken unto her, as the husband of the Shunammite did (2 Kings 4:23-24). If notwithstanding all that she can say, he persist in his resolution

---

74 **meetness** – appropriateness; suitableness.
75 **blockish** – senseless, like a block; extremely dull; stupid.
76 **peremptoriness** – the character of not allowing contradiction; dogmatic; obstinate.

and will have it done, she must yield....If her husband command her to do that which God has expressly forbidden, then ought she by no means to yield unto it. If she do, it may rather be termed a joint conspiracy of husband and wife together against God's will—as Saint Peter said to Sapphira, the wife of Ananias, *"How is it that ye have agreed together to tempt the Spirit of the Lord?"* (Acts 5:9)—than subjection to the image of God in her husband.

Secondly, her yielding in indifferent things tends much to the peace of the family, as subjects yielding to their magistrates in such cases makes much to the peace of the commonwealth. For in differences and dissensions one side must yield or else great mischief is like to follow...

Of the reasons to move wives to do their duties: The main ground of all the reasons which the Apostle here intimates is taken from the place wherein God has set an husband, which is first by consequence implied in these words *as to the Lord*. Then more plainly and directly expressed in these: *the husband is the head of the wife*....Upon an husband's resemblance unto Christ, he infers that a wife should have a resemblance unto the Church, and so concludes, *"Therefore as the church is subject unto Christ, so let the wives be to their own husbands in every thing."*

REASON 1: The place wherein God has set an husband as it serves to direct a wife in the manner of her subjection, whereof I have spoken before, so also it serves to move a wife to yield such subjection as is required, which will evidently appear by these two conclusions following from thence: 1. A wife by subjecting herself to her husband therein is subject unto Christ. 2. A wife by refusing to be subject unto her husband, therein refuses to be subject unto Christ. That these two conclusions are rightly and justly gathered from the forenamed ground I prove by like conclusions, which the Holy Ghost infers upon the like ground. It is evident that Christ Jesus, even incarnate and made flesh, was in the room and stead of His Father, whereupon Christ said to Philip that desired to see the Father, *"He that hath seen me hath seen the Father"* (John 14:9). Now mark what Christ thence infers both on the one side, *"He that receiveth me receiveth him that sent me"* (Matt. 10:40); and on the other side, *"He that honoureth not the Son honoureth not the Father which hath sent him"* (John 5:23). It is also evident that ministers of the Gospel stand in the room and stead of Christ, for thus says the Apostle of himself and other ministers: *"We are ambassadors for Christ, as though God did beseech you by us: we pray you in Christ's stead"* (2 Cor. 5:20).... To apply this reason, I hope such wives as live under the Gospel have so much religion and piety in them as to acknowledge, it becomes them well to be subject unto the Lord Christ Jesus. Here then learn one especial and principal part of subjection unto Christ, which is to be subject unto your husbands. Thus shall you show yourselves to be the wives of the Lord Christ, as the Apostle says of obedient servants, they are the servants of God (1 Peter 2:16).

Again I hope none are so void of all religion and piety as to refuse to be subject unto Christ: here then take notice, that if willfully ye refuse to be subject to your husbands, ye willfully refuse to be subject to Christ. Fitly on this ground may I apply that to wives, which the Apostle speaks of subjects: whosoever resisteth the power and authority of an husband, resisteth the ordinance of God; and they that resist shall receive to themselves judgment (Rom. 13:2).

A strong motive is this first motive. If it were duly considered of wives, they would more readily and cheerfully be subject than many are; they would not so lightly think of their husband's place, nor so reproachfully speak against God's ministers who plainly declare their duty unto them, as many do.

Reason 2: The second reason is like unto this, taken from an husband's office: he is the wife's head (1 Cor. 11:3), which is also urged to this very purpose in other places. This metaphor shows that to his wife, he is as the head of a natural body, both more eminent in place and also more excellent in dignity. By virtue of both, he is a ruler and governor of his wife. Nature teaches us that this is true of the head of a natural body, and the Apostle by entitling an husband an head, teaches us that it is as true of an husband…

Go therefore, O wives, unto the school of nature, look upon the outward parts and members of your bodies. Do they desire to be above the head? Are they loath[77] to be subject unto the head? Let your soul then learn of your body. [Is] it not monstrous for the side to be advanced above the head? If the body should not be subject to the head, would not destruction follow upon head, body, and all the parts thereof? As monstrous and much more monstrous is it for a wife to be above her husband, and as great, yea, and greater disturbance and ruin would fall on that family. The order which God has set therein would be clean overthrown thereby. And they that overthrow it would show themselves oppugners[78] of God's wisdom in establishing order. [Since] this reason drawn from nature is of force to move very pagans and savages to yield subjection, how much more Christian wives, it being also agreeable to God's Word and ratified thereby?

Reason 3: The third reason taken from an husband's resemblance unto Christ herein, adds an edge unto that former reason: in being an head, he is like Christ. There is a kind of fellowship and co-partnership between Christ

---

77 **loath** – unwilling; reluctant.
78 **oppugners** – opponents.

and an husband: they are brothers in office, as two kings of several places.

OBJECTION: There is no equality between Christ the Lord from heaven and an earthly husband. The disparity between them is infinite!

ANSWER: Yet there may be resemblance and fellowship….There may be a resemblance where there is no parity[79] and a likeness where there is no equality. The glorious and bright sun in the firmament and a dim candle in an house have a kind of fellowship and the same office which is to give light. Yet there is no equality between them. So then, an husband resembles not only the head of a natural body but also the glorious image of Christ, and is that to his wife which Christ is to His Church…

REASON 4: The fourth reason taken from the benefit which a wife receives from her husband, does yet further press the point in hand. Though Christ be properly the Savior of the body, yet even herein a husband carries a resemblance of Christ and is after a manner a savior. For by virtue of his place and office, he is on the one side her *protector*, to defend her from hurt and preserve her from danger; and on the other side, a *provider* of all needful and necessary things for her, in which respect she is taken from her parents and friends, and wholly committed to him…she herself and all she has is given to him. And he again communicates whatsoever he has to her good and for her use. David compares a wife to a vine in relation to her husband (Ps. 128:3), intimating thereby, that by him she is raised to that height of honor she has, as a vine by the tree, or frame near unto which it is planted. By his honor is she dignified, by his wealth is she enriched. He is, under God, all in all to her: in the family he is a king to govern and aid her, a priest to pray with her and for her, a prophet to teach and instruct her. As the head is placed in the highest place over the body and understanding placed in it, to govern, direct, protect, and every way seek the good of the body; and as Christ is united to the Church as a spouse and made her Head that she might be saved, maintained, and provided for by Him; so for this end was an husband placed in his place of superiority. His authority was committed to him to be a savior of his wife….As the Church is wisely governed and safely protected by subjecting herself to her Head, Christ Jesus; and as the body partakes of much good and is preserved from much evil by subjecting itself to the Head, so if a wife be subject to her husband, she will fare much the better thereby. All the ease, profit, and benefit thereof will be hers. If therefore she render her own good, this is a way and means ordained of God for this end; let her herein seek it…

REASON 5: The last reason taken from the example of the Church is also of good force to persuade wives unto subjection. Example more prevails

---

79 **parity** – equality.

with many than precept. If any example may be of force, then this most of all. For it is not the example of one only, but of many; not of many ignorant and wicked persons, but of understanding, wise, holy, and righteous persons, even all the saints that ever were, are, or shall be. For the Church comprises all under it, even that whole society of saints, which are chosen of God in His eternal counsel, redeemed of Christ by His precious blood, and effectually called by the Gospel of salvation, God's Spirit working inwardly and powerfully upon them, those very souls of just and perfect men now triumphing in heaven not excepted. Note how this Church is described in the 26th and 27th verses. Let this example therefore be often thought of: it will never repent any to follow it, for it treadeth the only right path to eternal glory, whereunto they shall assuredly come that follow it.

But to show the force of this reason more distinctly, note these two conclusions following from it: 1. Wives are as much bound to be subject to their husbands as the Church to Christ. Else, why should this example be thus pressed upon them? Why are husbands set in Christ's stead and resembled to Him? 2. A wife's subjection to her husband, answerable to the Church's subjection unto Christ, is evidence that she is of the Church, guided by the same Spirit that the Church is. For it cannot be performed by the power of nature; it is a supernatural work and so an evidence of the Spirit.

Wherefore, O Christian wives, as your husbands by their place resemble Christ, so do you by your practice resemble the Church. Of the two, this is the more commendable: for that is a dignity, this a virtue. True virtue is much more glorious than any dignity can be.

These reasons being well poised and the force of them all joined together, they cannot but work on the stoutest stomach[80] that is. Wherefore, if this point of subjection seem to be too bitter a pill to be well digested, let it be sweetened with the syrup of these reasons, and it will much better be swallowed and have the more kindly work.

From *Of Domestical Duties* reprinted by Still Waters Revival Books.

William Gouge (1575-1653): Puritan minister for 46 years at Blackfriars, London; born in Stratford-Bow, Middlesex County, England.

---

80 **stout stomach** – stubborn, rebellious heart or disposition.

For Mothers, Experienced or New
JOHN ANGELL JAMES (1785-1859)

The aged women likewise...that they may teach the young women to be sober, to love their husbands, to love their children, to be discreet, chaste, keepers at home, good, obedient to their own husbands, that the Word of God be not blasphemed. —Titus 2:3-5

What associations with all that is lovely are connected with that blissful word *mother!* To that sound the tenderest emotions of the human heart, whether in the bosom of the savage or the sage, wake up. The beauty of that term is seen and its power felt alike by the prince and the peasant, the rustic and the philosopher. It is one of the words which infant lips are first taught to lisp, and the charm of which the infant heart first feels. It is a note to the music of which it is difficult to say whose soul most responsively vibrates, that of the parent or the child. Humanity, however semi-brutalized by oppression, ignorance, or even vice, has rarely been sunk so low as to have the last spark of maternal love extinguished or the last sensibility of this kind crushed out of it. This strength of woman's love for her child must be turned to good account and be directed in its exercises to the best and most useful purposes…

At a pastoral conference held not long ago, at which about one hundred and twenty American clergymen united in the bonds of a common faith were assembled, each was invited to state the human instrumentality to which, under the divine blessing, he attributed a change of heart. How many of these, do you think, gave the honor of it to their mother? Of one hundred and twenty, over one hundred! Here then are facts, which are only selected from myriads[81] of others, to prove a mother's power, and to demonstrate at the same time her responsibility. But how shall we account for this? What gives her this influence? What is the secret of her power? Several things:

First, there is, no doubt, the ordinance of God. He, Who created us, Who formed the ties of social life, and Who gave all the sweet influences and tender susceptibilities of our various relationships, appointed that a mother's power over the soul of her child should be this mighty. It is God's ordinance, and the woman who forgets or neglects this is disobedient to a divine institution. God has made the child to be peculiarly susceptible to this power over his nature.

Then comes a mother's love, which is stronger, at any rate *more tender*, than a father's. There is more of instinct, if not of reason, in her affection.

---

81 **myriads** – countless numbers.

She has had more to do with the physical being of her child, having borne him in her womb, fed him from her breast, and watched him in his cradle. All this naturally and necessarily generates a feeling which nothing else can produce. Now love is the great motivating power in and for human conduct. *"I drew them,"* said God, *"with cords of a man, with bands of love"* (Hos. 11:4). Here is the true philosophy of both man's natural constitution and evangelical religion. Human nature is made to be moved, governed by love, to be drawn with the cords of affection rather than to be dragged with the chains of severity. *Woman's heart is made to love*; and love is exerted more gently, sweetly, and constrainingly upon her child by her than by the other sex. It makes her more patient, more ingenious,[82] and therefore more influential. Her words are more soft, her smile more winning, and her frown more commanding because they are less terrific and repulsive. The little floweret she has to nurture opens its petals more readily to the mild beams of her countenance…

The mother has most to do with the child's character while yet in the flexible state in which it receives its shape. The earliest exercises of thought, emotion, will, and conscience are all carried on under her eye. She has to do not only with the body in its infancy, but with the soul in its childhood. Both mind and heart are in her hands at that period when they take their first start for good or for evil. The children learn to lisp their first words and to form their first ideas under her teaching. They are almost always in her company and are insensibly to themselves and imperceptibly to her receiving a right or wrong bias from her. She is the first model of character they witness; the first exhibitions of right and wrong in practice are what they see in her. They are the constant observers of the passions, graces, virtues, and faults, which are shown in her words, temper, and actions. She is therefore, unconsciously to herself, educating them not only by designed teaching, but by all she does or says in their presence….It is therefore of immense importance that everyone who sustains this relation should have a high idea of her own power. She should be deeply and duly impressed with the potency of her influence…

Mothers, then, should be thoroughly acquainted with the work that is allotted to them. I speak not of the physical training of the children, nor primarily of their intellectual culture, but of their social, moral, and religious education. A mother's object and duty is the formation of character. She has not merely to communicate knowledge, but habits. Her special department is to cultivate the heart and regulate the life. Her aim must be not only what her children are to know, but what they are to be and do. She is to look at

---

82 **ingenious** – marked by inventive skill or imagination.

them as the future members of society, and heads of families of their own, but above all as probationers[83] for eternity. This, I repeat, must be taken up as the primary idea, the formation of character for *both* worlds....A mother should look upon her offspring with this idea: "That child has to live in two worlds and to act a part in both. It is my duty to begin his education for both and to lay in infancy the foundation of his character and happiness for time and eternity too. What ought to be my qualifications and my diligence for such a task?" Ah, what?

Deep thoughtfulness certainly on the momentous nature of your charge. It is an awful[84] thing to be a parent, especially a mother, and to be responsible for the training of men and women, both for time and for eternity....O woman! Your child's welfare for all time and all eternity too depends much upon your conduct towards him during the period when he is under your influence, in the first years of his being. To you is committed the care of the infant's body, the healthfulness, vigor, and comfort of which for all his future existence upon earth depend much upon you. What would be your feelings of poignant remorse if, by any neglect of yours, whether by a fall or an accident, the result of your carelessness, the poor babe was injured in his spine or distorted in his limbs! Oh! To see that young cripple injured for life in bodily comfort, ever presenting to you the sad reminder of your guilty neglect! Yet what is this to the sadder spectacle of a deformed and crippled *soul*, a character distorted into crooked and frightful shapes, and to have the tormenting reflection that this was the result of your neglect!...

Qualify yourself for maternal duties above all things by sincere and eminent piety. A mother should never forget that those little engaging creatures which sport about the room so gaily and so innocently with all the unconsciousness of childhood are young immortals....One should almost think that solicitude about this matter would be so overpowering as to extinguish parental delight. But a mother cannot look at the babe that is feeding at her breast, and smiling sweetly in her face as if it meant the thanks it had not yet learned to speak—or watch his slumbers in his cradle, breathing as softly as if he lived without breathing at all—and at the same time feel her soul shiver and shudder in the dark shadow cast over her spirit by such a thought as "Oh, should you live to be a profligate[85] in this world, and a fiend in the next!"

---

83 **probationers** – those qualifying for; candidates.
84 **awful** – awesome; awe-inspiring.
85 **profligate** – given over to evil and immorality.

Instead of a reflection so harrowing to every maternal feeling, she exults in the hope that the dear babe will be a holy, useful, happy Christian on earth and then a glorified immortal in heaven. Such reflections ought to be, at some times, in the mind of every parent. All should realize the sublime idea that their houses are the seminaries for eternity, their children the scholars, themselves the teachers, and evangelical religion the lesson. Yes, with every infant born into the family comes the injunction from God, "Take this child and bring it up for Me." It is one of God's own children by creation, sent to be trained up in the way he should go, that is, in the nurture and admonition of the Lord….We shudder at the cruelties of those who sacrificed their babes to Moloch; but how much more dreadful an immolation[86] do they practice who offer up their sons and daughters to Satan by neglecting their religious education and leaving them to grow up in ignorance of God and their eternal destiny.

But can anyone, will anyone, teach or teach effectually that religion which she does not feel and practice herself? Therefore, I say, a mother's heart must be deeply imbued[87] with piety if she would teach it to her children. Without this, can she have the will to teach, the heart to pray, or the right to hope? Mothers, can you conceive of a higher, nobler elevation to which, in your maternal relation, you can rise than when, to the opening mind of your wondering child, *you give the first idea of God?* Or than when you direct him to that divine Babe Who was born at Bethlehem; Who was subject to His parents; Who grew up to be the Savior; Who said, *"Suffer the little children to come unto me"* (Mark 10:14), took them in His arms and blessed them, and then died for their salvation upon the cross? Or than when you talk to them of heaven, the dwelling place of God and of His angels? Oh, to see the first look of holy inquisitiveness and the first tear of infant piety start in the eye; to hear the first question of concern or the first breathing of prayer from infant lips! How has many a woman's heart amidst such scenes swelled with delight until, in an ecstasy of feeling, she sank upon her knees and breathed a mother's prayer over the child of her heart, while he looked wonderingly up and felt a mysterious power come over him which he could neither fully express nor understand!

Your religion, if it is genuine, will teach you at once the greatness of the work, and your own insufficiency to perform it aright in your own strength. Your business is to train mortals for earth and immortal beings for God, heaven, and eternity…Cultivate, then, a trembling consciousness

---

86 **immolation** – sacrificial slaughter of a victim.
87 **imbued** – filled with a particular quality.

of your own insufficiency; and cast yourselves by believing, constant, and fervent prayer upon God. Be, in an eminent sense, praying mothers. Distrust yourselves, and, by believing prayer, secure the aid of Omnipotence.

Do not forget what I have already said, that affection is the golden key fitted by God to the wards of the lock in every human heart, to the application of which the bolts that nothing else could move will fly back and open with ease. Severity is out of place in anyone, but most of all in women. But beware of allowing affection to degenerate into a fond and foolish indulgence...while I enjoin affection, it must not be allowed to impair *authority*. A parent must not be a tyrant, but neither must he be a slave to his children. It is a painful and, to the parents, a disgraceful spectacle to see a family like a state where rebellion reigns rampant, the father deposed, the scepter broken, and the insurgent children possessed of sovereign rule. And a mother as well as a father must be obeyed, and it is her own fault if she is not. A persevering system of government, where the reins are held tightly in the hand of love, will be sure to produce submission at last. But it must be a mixture of kindness, wisdom, and authority. Submission must be felt by a child to be a duty yielded to authority, and not merely a compliance won by affection. Authority must not stiffen into severity, nor love degenerate into coaxing. Commands should be obeyed not only because it is pleasant to obey them, but because it is right that they should be obeyed.

A judicious mother will exercise much discrimination and will adapt her treatment to the disposition of her children. There are as many varieties of temperament in some families as there are children....One is forward and obtrusive, and should be checked and rebuked; another is timid and retiring, and needs to be encouraged and emboldened. One is more easily wrought upon by appeals to her hope, another by reasonings addressed to her fear. One is too close and reserved, and needs to have frankness and communicativeness encouraged; another is too open and ingenuous,[88] and should be taught caution and self-restraint. Every child should be a separate study. Quackery should be banished from education as well as from medicine. One treatment will no more suit all minds than one medicine or kind of food all bodies...

The woman who would fulfill the duties of her relationship must surrender herself to her mission and be content to make some sacrifices and endure some privations.[89] Who can witness the patient submission of the mother bird to her solitude and self-denial during the term of incubation

---

88 **ingenuous** – straightforward; candid.
89 **privations** – losses; instances of being deprived of certain necessities or pleasures.

without admiration at the quiet and willing surrender which instinct teaches her to make of her usual liberty and enjoyments? A woman must be willing, for the sake of her children, to do, under the influence of reason and religion, what the bird does from the unintelligent impulses of nature. Her children are a charge for which she must forego some of the enjoyments of social life, and even some of the social pleasures of religion. She who would have a maternal power over her children must give her company to them….I would not have a mother incarcerated[90] in her own house, so as never to go abroad or enter into company. She who is devoted to her family needs occasional relaxation amidst the pleasures of society, and especially the exhilarating engagements of public worship. Some mothers are such absolute slaves to their children that they scarcely ever stir from home, even to the house of God. This is an error in one extreme, which might be avoided…those run into an opposite extreme who will not, even for the benefit of their children, give up a social party or a public meeting. The woman who is not prepared to make many sacrifices of this kind, for the sake of her children, her home, and her husband should never think of entering into wedded life.

Be ingenious, inventive, and studious as to the best method of gaining the attention and informing the minds of your children while young. There are too many who imagine that education, and especially religious education, consists in just hearing a chapter read, a catechism taught, or a hymn repeated, and that when this is done, all is done. The memory is the only faculty they cultivate; the intellect, affections, and conscience are wholly neglected. A Christian mother should set herself to invent the best mode of gaining attention and keeping it; she should never weary it or keep it so long that it wanders off itself.

Be familiar in your religious instruction. The freedom of incidental conversation, rather than the formality of set and stated lessons; the introduction of religious topics in the common intercourse of life, rather than the grave and forbidding annunciation of a change from secular to sacred subjects; and the habit of referring all things to God and comparing the truths and maxims of the Bible with the events of every hour, rather than merely lighting a Sabbath lamp and forcing all things out of their channel when the season of devotion returns—these are the means of opening the avenues to the youthful heart and rendering religion with its great Author the object not of aversion or terror, nor only of cold and distant homage, but of mingled reverence and love. *"And these words, which I command thee this day, shall be in thine heart: And thou shalt teach them diligently unto thy children,*

---

90 **incarcerated** – shut up as in prison.

and shalt talk of them when thou sittest in thine house, and when thou walkest by the way, and when thou liest down, and when thou risest up" (Deut. 6:6, 7).

Mothers, invested as you are with such an influence, often dwell upon your responsibility. With such a power conferred upon you by God, you are responsible to your children themselves....You are responsible to your husbands. They entrust the education of their children to you....You are responsible to the church of God, for family education is, or ought to be, in the families of the godly, the chief means of conversion. It is a fatal error for Christian parents to look to the ministers of religion for the conversion of their children. And, alas! It is the error of the day. The pulpit is looked to for those benefits, which should flow from the parents' chair...

In all things, it is of importance to begin well. The beginning usually determines the progress and the close. Errors, both in theory and practice, however long and pertinaciously[91] persisted in, may by intelligence, determination, and the blessing of God be corrected. Reformation would otherwise be hopeless. But how much better and easier is it to avoid faults than to amend them! Many mothers have seen their mistakes when it was too late to correct them. Their children have grown up under the influence of a bad system of domestic government and maternal guidance and have acquired a fixedness of bad habit which no subsequent wisdom, firmness, severity, or affection could correct. And the parents have had to pour out bitter but unavailing regrets that they had not begun life with those views of their duties with which they were closing it.

If a mother begins well, she is likely to continue well, and the same is true if she begins ill. Her conduct towards her first child is likely, of course, to determine her conduct with respect to all the following ones. How momentous is it, then, at this stage of her domestic history, to weigh well, and solemnly, and prayerfully her responsible situation! Indeed, it is quite clear that this subject ought not to be driven off by any wife till she becomes a mother. The very prospect ought to lead to a due preparation for the expected new duties...It becomes us to prepare ourselves for any situation into which we have a confident expectation of soon entering. Forethought is given to man for the purpose of meeting with propriety the situation and duties to which we are looking forward. The woman who never *studies* maternal responsibilities and duties till she is called actually to sustain them is not very likely to do herself much credit in that very important relationship....Unhappily, a young wife, in prospect of giving birth to a child, is in some cases so bowed down with an unnecessary solicitude about her

---

91 **pertinaciously** – stubbornly; obstinately.

own safety, and in others so absorbed with the preparations which are made for the physical well-being and the elegant habiliments[92] of her promised baby, as to forget to prepare herself for those more important duties which devolve upon her in relation to the mind, heart, and conscience of the child.

A mother who wishes to fulfill her duties to her children should take special pains to educate herself for those momentous functions. She should read to store her mind with knowledge. She should reflect, observe, and gain useful information from every quarter. Her principles should be fixed, her plans laid, and her purposes formed. She must cultivate all the habits and tempers which will fit her to teach and to govern. She must seek to acquire thoughtfulness, careful vigilance, quick observation, and discretion in various forms. Habits of activity, dispatch, order, and regularity are indispensable for her; so is the exercise of all the good and benevolent feelings. She must unite gentleness with firmness and attain patience and the entire command of her temper. It is of immense importance also that she should have a correct knowledge of human nature and of the way of dealing with the human heart. And, above all things, let her remember that piety is the vivifying[93] spirit of all excellence, and example the most powerful means to enforce it. She should never let the recollection be absent from her mind that children have both eyes and ears for attention to a mother's conduct. Not content with preparing herself for her important functions beforehand, she should carry on the education of herself simultaneously with that of her children. There are few situations which more imperatively require preparation, and yet few that receive less.

Again, we often see in a mother such a solicitude about the health and comfort of her babe; such an engrossing attention to all matters respecting its physical well-being, united with such an exuberant delight in the child, as a child; such a mother's pride and joyousness in her boy, that her mind is diverted by these circumstances from all the serious thoughts and solemn reflections which ought to be awakened by the consideration that a rational, immortal, and fallen creature is committed to her charge, to be trained for both worlds. Thus, her attention is absorbed month after month, while all this while her infant's faculties are developing. Its judgment, will, affection, and conscience, at least in their capabilities, are opening, but neglected, and its natural bias to evil grows unnoticed and unchecked. The very time when judicious care over the formation of character could be most advantageously exerted is suffered to pass by unimproved; passion

---

92 **habiliments** – garments; items of clothing associated with an occasion or office.
93 **vivifying** – life-imparting; animating.

is allowed to strengthen unrestrained, and self-will to attain a resoluteness which stiffens into obstinacy. And the careless mother, who at some time or other intended to begin a system of moral training (always saying there was time enough yet), when she does commence, wonders that the subject of her discipline is so difficult to manage. And then she finds that she has so neglected to prepare herself for her duties that she knows not how to set about them, or what in fact she has to do. An ill-managed child continues growing not only in stature and in strength, but in his wayward disposition and obstinate self-will; the poor mother has no control; and as for the father, he is too much taken up with the cares of business to aid his imperfect helpmate; thus the scene is exhibited, described by Solomon, of *"a child left to himself"* (Prov. 29:15)…

Young mothers, begin well, then. Manage that first child with judgment; put forth all your skill, all your affection, all your diligence and devotedness in training him; and, the habit thus acquired, all will be comparatively easy with the others that follow. It is the novelty of that first child, the new affections which it calls forth, and the new interest it creates that are likely (if you are not careful) to throw you off your guard and divert your attention from the great work of moral training. The first child makes the good or injudicious[94] mother.

And as it is of immense consequence to begin your maternal excellence with the first child, so it is of equal importance to him, and to every one who is added, as I have already said, to begin *early*. Education, as has been observed, does not begin with the alphabet. It begins with a mother's look; with a father's nod of approbation[95] or sign of reproof; with a sister's gentle pressure of the hand, or a brother's noble act of forbearance; with a handful of flowers in green dells, or on hills or in daisy meadows; with creeping ants, and almost imperceptible emmets;[96] with humming bees, and glass beehives; with pleasant walks in shady lanes; and with thoughts directed in affectionate and kindly tones and words to nature, to beauty, to the practice of benevolence, and to the remembrance of Him who is the Fountain of all good. Yes, and before all this can be done, before lessons of instruction can be taught to the child from flowers, insects, and birds, the moral training can commence: a mother's look, her nod of approbation or sign of reproof.

One of the greatest mistakes into which mothers fall is that of supposing that the first two or three years of a child's life are unimportant as regards his training. The truth is that in the formation of character they are the most

---

94 **injudicious** – showing very poor judgment; unwise
95 **approbation** - approval
96 **emmets** – ants.

important of all. It has been truly said that from the impressions made, the principles implanted, and the habits formed, during these years, the child's character for time and eternity may take its complexion. It is perfectly clear that a child, before he can speak, is susceptible of moral training. The conscience, or moral sense, may, by a judicious woman, be developed soon after, if not before, the child has spent his first birthday. So early may he be made to distinguish between what his mother considers right and wrong, between what will please and what will displease her. Why, the brute creatures will do this; and if they can be taught this, may not very young children? It is admitted that there is more of reason in many brutes than in very young children. Still, even very young animals may be trained to know what they may and may not do; and so may very young children. I often hear mothers say that their children are too young to be taught obedience. The mother who acts upon the maxim that children may have their own way for a certain number of years, or even months, will find to her cost that that lesson at least will not speedily be forgotten. Moral training may and should precede that which is intellectual. The cultivation of the affections and conscience should be the commencement and foundation of education, and will facilitate every succeeding effort whether of the child or of those who train or teach him….Fearful, timid, and anxious mothers, be not afraid! Prayer will bring God's help and God's blessing.

Injudicious indulgence is the most common, as it is the most injurious, danger into which a young mother can fall. Be kind; you ought to be. An unloving, hard-hearted mother is a double libel upon her sex and her relationship. Love is her power, her instrument… She can do nothing, worse than nothing, without it. But then her love must be like that of the divine Parent who said, *"As many as I love, I rebuke and chasten"* (Rev. 3:19). Can you say "No" to a child when, with winning smiles, beseeching voice, or weeping eyes, he asks for what it is not good that he should receive? Can you take from him that which is likely to be injurious to him, but which it will give him pain to surrender? Can you correct him for his faults when your heart rises up in opposition to your judgment? Can you put him off from your arms, at a proper season for so doing, when he clings to your neck and cries to remain? Can you exact obedience in what is to him a difficult, but to you a necessary, command? Can you stand out against his tears, resolute in purpose, unyielding in demand, and first conquer your own heart, so stoutly resisting you, in order to conquer his? Or do you allow yourself to be subdued to put an end to the contest, and, by soothing his sufferings, foster the temper which ought to be eradicated at any pains and any cost? She who cannot answer all this in the affirmative is not fit to be a mother. There must be discipline in a family. A parent must be obeyed. Give this up, and you train your children for evil and not for good. Here again I say, begin early. Put on the soft and easy yoke quickly. The horse is broken in while still a colt. Wild beasts are tamed while yet they are young. Both the human species and animals soon grow beyond the power of discipline….Viewing your children as immortal beings destined to eternity and capable of the enjoyments of heaven, you will labor even from infancy to imbue their minds with religious ideas. It is immortality, which rescues from littleness and insignificance all that it appertains to, and hence arises in no inconsiderable degree the exalted honor of a mother.

She has given birth, by the sovereign ordination of the Almighty, not to a being of a mere momentary existence, whose life will perish like that of the beast of the field, but to an immortal! Her sucking infant, feeble and helpless as it may appear, possesses within its bosom a rational soul, an intellectual power, a spirit which all-devouring time cannot destroy, which can never die, but which will outlive the splendors of the glorious sun, and the burning brilliance of all the material part of heaven. Throughout the infinite ages of eternity, when all these shall have served their purpose and answered the beneficent end of their creation, and shall have been blotted out from their position in the immense regions of space, the soul of the humblest child will shine and improve before the eternal throne, being filled with holy delight and divine love, and ever active in the praises of its blessed Creator. Mothers, such is your dignity, such your exalted honor. Feel and value your rich distinction in being called to educate the sons and daughters of the Lord God Almighty, and to prepare the holy family who are to dwell in those many mansions of His Father's house, which the Lord Jesus is gone to prepare. Give yourselves up to this glorious work. But be judicious in all you do, lest you produce prejudice against true religion, instead of prepossession[97] in its favor. Let your warmest affection, your greatest cheerfulness, your most engaging smiles be put on when you teach religion to your children. Approach as nearly as possible to a seraphic[98] form. Represent religion in all its beauty, loveliness, sanctity, and ineffable sweetness. Let them see it in your character as well as hear it from your lips.

From "To Young Mothers" in *Female Piety* reprinted by Soli Deo Gloria.

John Angell James (1785-1859): English Congregationalist preacher and author; born in Blandford Forum, Dorset, England.

---

97 **prepossession** – influencing the mind.
98 **seraphic** – angelic; showing ecstasy of devout contemplation.

Christ's Work and Single Women
W.K. TWEEDIE (1803-1863)

One of the most peculiar chapters in the Bible is the last to the Romans. The insight which it gives into early Christian life—the light which it sheds, in hopes at least, upon the home scenes of the first Christians; the depth of affection which it displays; the unity of aim, of action, and of spirit which it manifests, and the prominence which it gives to female activity and zeal—all combine to render that portion of Scripture one of the fairest sights where all are green and goodly. He who would understand the spirit of apostolic life should often study it with care. It gives prominence, we say, to female exertion for Christ, and as there are many homes where the single reside and devote themselves to His cause, it may be well to glance for a moment at such abodes.

They may be centers of influence for good such as only the religion of Jesus can produce. And it is not too much to say that from those homes, where the Spirit of wisdom dwells, there emanates much of what is fitted to soothe man's sorrows, to restore happiness to the wretched, and promote Christ's glory upon earth. Single women often have a mission of mercy such as is not entrusted to these who have the cares of a home to carry or the duties of a home to discharge. It may be among relatives—it may be in the homes of the poor or the diseased—it may be in the prison to clothe and teach and pray for—or the workhouse[99] to cheer—or the schoolhouse to instruct—or by the deathbed to point to life everlasting. But wherever it is, in all the varied scenes of sorrow or of toil, an unmarried woman, if the Spirit of God be her teacher, has such means and such power of doing good as God has entrusted to no other class.

Nor is this wonderful.[100] The unmarried, if they be also the Spirit-taught, can leisurely cultivate the graces of the divine life, can without distracting cares give themselves calmly to work the work of God; and hence there is probably not a minister, if he be zealously watching for souls, who would not confess how much he is indebted to the aid of this class. Rising by grace above all that is deemed irksome[101] or isolating in their solitary position, they often learn to spend and be spent in work of doing good. Phoebe, *"a servant of the Church"* (Rom. 16:1) and *"a succourer"* of the Church and of Paul (Rom. 16:2); *"Mary, who bestowed much labor"* on the Apostles (Rom. 16:6); *"Tryphena and Tryphosa"* with others who will be held in everlasting

---

99 **workhouse** – workshop; factory.
100 **wonderful** – surprising; astonishing.
101 **irksome** – annoying; tedious.

remembrance have still their sisters and successors in the churches (Rom. 16:12). And if sometimes a feeling of loneliness or insulation do creep over them, it is dispelled, we believe, or it may even be turned into gladness by a more intense devotedness to the service and the glory of our Lord. He is with us always. There need, therefore, be no loneliness—at least, the lonely are as safely guarded as the Prophet was by his chariots and horsemen of fire (2 Kings 6:17). Thus kept in safety, communion with God becomes the secret at once of their happiness and their efforts.

No need then for such devoted souls to flee to nunneries[102] for peace—they find it in the full, free service of their God. In feeding the hungry, in clothing the naked, in drawing out the soul to the poor, they have enough to make the heart and the home perennially happy. The tear of misery dried, the wanderer reclaimed, the fallen raised up, may surely impart a joy with which the world cannot intermeddle.[103] And while the frivolous flutter life away in the pursuit of shadows, delusions, follies, sin, those whom we now describe are walking in the footsteps of Him who *"went about doing good"* (Acts 10:38). With Dorcas, they make garments for the poor (Acts 9:36, 39); with Priscilla, they are helping forward the cause of truth in its death-strife with all that is false (Acts 18:2, 18, 26); and when God gives the means, they are as ready to distribute as to sympathize. Some of them at least know, that an idle day is worse than lost—it will meet us at the Judgment demanding why we lost it. And under that conviction they do good—it may be by stealth, yet resolutely. "Fearful of fame, unwilling to be known," they shrink from public notice, yet are they unwearied in their work of faith. Some are even self-sacrificing in that cause, and, rising above "self, that narrow, miserable sphere," welcoming the work, which their Lord has in His holy providence allotted, they try to cheat pain of its groans and grief of its tears, and by a blessing from on high, they often succeed. In a word, we look in vain for more devoted servants of Christ than may often be found in the homes of unmarried females.

And the tact[104] of such workwomen is often not less remarkable than their zeal. There are no doubt silly women who yield to mere emotion and deem it principle—who give so unwisely, that their gifts are bounties on deception, or idleness, or vice. As there are some whose very charity savors of insult, or whose compassion is like smoke to the eyes or niter[105] to a wound, there are also some so lavish and unwise as to promote the very evils which they

---

102 **nunneries** – residences where nuns live under religious rule and discipline; convents.
103 **intermeddle** – interfere.
104 **tact** – ready and delicate sense of what is fitting and proper in dealing with others.
105 **niter** – a salt, also called saltpeter.

try to cure. But in other cases, a skill in detecting and a firmness in resisting imposture,[106] as well as a tenderness in aiding, are acquired by experience, lend a moral weight to all other actions. The family just sinking silently into want is helped with a delicacy, which saves every feeling. The gentlewoman in decay is treated as a companion and a friend in the act of being relieved. The pale and dying mother is aided in a manner so feminine and kindly, that no poignancy is added to the coming pain of separation. And these are truly Christian sights: they help to reconcile us in some degree to sorrow, or if we still weep, the tears of gratitude are mingled with those of grief.

Now, in all this we are just telling how happy are the hearts and the homes of those single women who are thus employed. The position which they occupy and the work which they do approximate closely to the character of the redeemed, or the "zealous of good works" (Titus 2:14), while by the grace of God, they are brought within the sweep of the beatitude, *"Blessed are the merciful: for they shall obtain mercy"* (Matt. 5:7). They correspond to the standard of the King and Judge, Who says, *"For I was an hungred, and ye gave me meat: I was thirsty, and ye gave me drink: I was a stranger, and ye took me in: Naked, and ye clothed me: I was sick, and ye visited me: I was in prison, and ye came unto me"* (Matt. 25:35-36).

From "Home of the Single" in *Home: A Religious Book for the Family*.

W.K. Tweedie (1803-1863): Free Church minister and author; minister of the Tolbooth Kirk in Edinburgh, leader of the disruption in 1843 when the Free Church broke away from the Established Church in Scotland. Born in Ayr, Scotland.

> *Women, by men's wretched idolizing them, are vainly proud of their beauty and more jealous lest their faces be deformed than their souls. Now what is flesh and blood, but a mixture of earth and water? What is beauty, [but] a superficial appearance, a flower blasted by a thousand accidents? How soon are the colors and charms of the face vanished? How often does it betray them to those sins that are signally punished with the foulest deformity and rottenness? The most beautiful are not less mortal than others: they must shortly be the prey of death and pasture of worms. And can such a fading toy inspire pride into them? —William Bates*

---

106 **imposture** – giving a false appearance.

To a Recent Woman Convert
JONATHAN EDWARDS (1703-1758)

(Some time in 1741, a young lady residing in Smithfield, Connecticut, who had lately made a profession of religion, requested Mr. Edwards to give her some advice as to the best manner of maintaining a religious life. In reply, he addressed to her the following letter...)

Do not leave off seeking, striving, and praying for the very same things that we exhort unconverted persons to strive for, and a degree of which you have already had in conversion. Pray that your eyes may be opened, that you may receive sight, that you may know yourself and be brought to God's footstool, that you may see the glory of God and Christ and be raised from the dead, and have the love of Christ shed abroad in your heart. Those who have most of these things have need to still pray for them; for there is so much blindness and hardness, pride and death remaining that they still need to have that work of God wrought upon them, further to enlighten and enliven them

When you hear a sermon, hear for yourself....let the chief intent of your mind be to consider, "In what respect is this applicable to me? And what application ought I to make of this for my own soul's good?"

When you engage in the duty of prayer, come to the Lord's Supper, or attend any other duty of divine worship, come to Christ, as Mary Magdalene did (Luke 7:37-38). Come and cast yourself at His feet and kiss them, and pour forth upon Him the sweet, perfumed ointment of divine love out of a pure and broken heart, as she poured the precious ointment out of her pure, broken alabaster box.

When the exercise of grace is low and corruption prevails, and by that means, fear prevails, do not desire to have fear cast out by any other way than by the reviving and prevailing of love in the heart. By this, fear will be effectually compelled, as darkness in a room vanishes away when the pleasant beams of the sun are let into it.

In your course, walk with God and follow Christ as a little, poor, helpless child. [Take] hold of Christ's hand, keeping your eye on the marks of the wounds in His hands and side, whence came the blood that cleanses you from sin, and hiding your nakedness under the skirt of the white, shining robes of His righteousness.

From *God's Call to Young People* reprinted by Soli Deo Gloria.

A Grandmother in Glory
JABEZ BURNS (1805-1876)

As I was sitting, says an American writer, at my door, one of the unusually lovely evenings with which we have been favored this spring, watching the playfulness of my two little children, who were running through the walks of the garden, and now and then stopping to gather a sweet-scented purple or white violet with which the whole air was perfumed, I saw at a little distance the carriage of a dear and intimate friend, which quickly drove to the door, and my friend alighted. I noticed nothing peculiar in his demeanor, until he drew my little girl toward him and with a solemn manner said, "Lizzie, your grandmother is dead. You will never see her." "Dead!" I exclaimed, "Have you a letter?" "Yes." And as he turned to hand me the letter, I saw the look of utter despondency and felt that he had lost a mother.

That mother and that son were equally devoted to each other. He was the youngest of six children. They had been for years separated, and he had bright anticipations of seeing her in a few short weeks and presenting his two little cherished ones whom she had so often heard of, but never seen. Alas! Alas! These anticipations are all blighted now, and, "Lizzie, your dear grandmother is dead. You will never see her," still rings in my ears as when I first heard it.

But the aged mother was a Christian. The letter says, "Her reason was clear during her whole sickness; not a murmur did she utter, but was anxious to depart." And doubtless, long ere this, she has beheld *"the king in his beauty"* (Isa. 33:17) and been introduced to scenes of glory, where even the cherubim, so long accustomed to celestial visions, veil their faces. What now to her seems the pilgrimage of threescore years and ten? She has entered eternity. What to her the sorrows and afflictions which once grieved her? *"Not worthy to be compared with the glory which shall be revealed in us"* (Rom. 8:18). With holy rapture, she bows before the throne and adores the Trinity. I think I see her, not as once I saw her, clothed in sable robes[107] and mourning that death had entered her household. No, death has at last proved her friend, separated the mortal from the immortal, and ushered her into the felicities[108] of heaven. There, clothed in a white robe, with a crown upon her brow, a harp in her hand, unfading youth in her countenance, and the fullness of joy in her heart, she looks to the completion of time upon earth, as the perfection of her existence, in eternity, in heaven. Then, at the sound of the Archangel's trumpet, that friend which so long had enshrined

---

107 **sable robes** – black garments, the symbol of mourning.
108 **felicities** – happinesses; blessings.

her spirit and been the servant of her will, that body, purified, ennobled, immortalized, will rush once more to her companionship, and they two being one shall *"ever be with the Lord"* (1 Thess. 4:17).

The resurrection of the body, the immortality of the soul, the divinity, the atonement, the intercession of Christ, the perpetuity of happiness—what elevating—what glorious doctrines are these! A wonderful destiny is ours!—entering the world the most helpless of all earthly beings, progressing, step by step, until we become but *"little lower than the angels"* (Heb. 2:7), reaching an elevation superior to that of any created intelligence.

Does that sainted mother now regret having given her lifetime to her Maker? Does she wish she had lived the life of the moralist[109] and enjoyed some of the pleasures of sin for a season? If a blush of shame can burn upon the countenances of the inhabitants of heaven, it is when they think of the inexhaustible love of God toward them and their unaccountable ingratitude.

The lamp of the moralist may serve to light his steps as far as a sickbed, but we may rest assured, so soon as death appears, even in the distance, its flame will weaken and then expire. There will be naught to direct his path through *"the valley of the shadow of death"* (Ps. 23:4), but the lightnings of Divine wrath, the glarings of the lake that burneth forever and ever.

The Christian's pathway through the dark valley is first cheered by the dawnings of the Sun of Righteousness. The further he advances, the plainer becomes the passage and the more dazzling the brilliancy, until at length he enters heaven, where there is *"no need of the sun...for the glory of God did lighten it"* (Rev. 21:23).

From *Mothers of the Wise and Good*, Solid Ground Christian Books: www.solid-ground-books.com

---

Jabez Burns (1805-1876): English nonconformist theologian and philosopher; born in Oldham, Lancashire, England.

> *A virtuous woman is a crown to her husband: but she that maketh ashamed is as rottenness in his bones.* —Proverbs 12:4

---

109 **moralist** – one who lives by a system of natural moral principles; a merely moral person.

Chapter 4

MARRIAGE

It is difficult to exaggerate the place that the Bible gives to marriage. Jesus said that the kingdom of heaven is like a wedding (Mat. 22:2-14). Yet these words only begin to communicate the importance of marriage. The apostle Paul reveals in Eph. 5:22-33 that God created marriage for a very particular purpose: to visibly declare the glory of the love of Jesus Christ for His Church. This explains why the devil has always waged an unrelenting attack on marriage, seeking to pervert it, steal from it, and destroy it.

Why does the devil hate marriage so much? Is it because he simply desires to cause as much hate, alienation, discord, and disappointment as he can between spouses? Is it because he hates the offspring that comes from marriage? While these may be some of his reasons, consider that the devil hates marriage because he hates the gospel of God's grace in Jesus Christ. God created marriage in order to give the world an earthly illustration of His love for His Church, His sacrifices on behalf of His Church, His union with His Church, His sanctification of the Church, and the glorious purposes that He has in mind for His Church.

Furthermore, a wife's submission to her husband is an evidence that she believes the gospel, as her life pictures the Church submitting to Christ. In this way, a wife's submission pictures a fruit of the power of the gospel. This is true because true belief in the gospel leads to a life of obedience, for *"faith without works is dead"* (James 2:20). Scripture teaches that a wife is to "submit" to her own husband "in everything" and to "respect" him (Eph. 5:22, 24, 33). By a wife's submission she displays how the true Church obeys her Lord. When she does not submit to her husband, she declares a false gospel to the world.

Conversely, a husband who does not love his wife as Christ loves the Church is declaring that Jesus Christ does not love or cherish or nourish His Church and has not given Himself for her. This is how a husband declares a false gospel to the world through his relationship with his wife.

As you enter into this chapter, you will be taken back to the "old paths," the good paths where marriage is properly understood and healed (Jer. 6:16).

—Scott Brown

The Excellence of Marriage
ARTHUR W. PINK (1886-1952)

> *Marriage is honourable in all, and the bed undefiled: but whoremongers and adulterers God will judge.* —Hebrews 13:4

As God hath knit the bones and sinews together for the strengthening of our bodies, so He has ordained the joining of man and woman together in wedlock for the strengthening of their lives, for *"two are better than one"* (Eccl. 4:9). Therefore, when God made the woman for the man, He said, *"I will make him an help meet for him"* (Gen. 2:18), showing that man is advantaged by having a wife. That such does not actually prove to be the case in all instances is, for the most part at least, to be attributed unto departure from the divine precepts thereon. As this is a subject of such vital moment, we deem it expedient to present a fairly comprehensive outline of the teaching of Holy Writ upon it, especially for the benefit of our young readers, though we trust we shall be enabled to include that which will be helpful to older ones too.

It is perhaps a trite[1] remark, yet nonetheless weighty for having been uttered so often, that with the one exception of personal conversion, marriage is the most momentous of all earthly events in the life of a man or woman. It forms a bond of union that binds them until death. It brings them into such intimate relations that they must either sweeten or embitter each other's existence. It entails circumstances and consequences that are not less far-reaching than the endless ages of eternity. How essential it is then that we should have the blessing of heaven upon such a solemn yet precious undertaking; and in order to this, how absolutely necessary it is that we be subject to God and to His Word thereon. Far, far better to remain single unto the end of our days, than to enter into the marriage state without the divine benediction[2] upon it. The records of history and the facts of observation bear abundant testimony to the truth of that remark.

Even those who look no further than the temporal happiness of individuals and the welfare of existing society are not insensible to the great importance of our domestic relations, which the strongest affections of nature secure, and which even our wants and weaknesses cement. We can form no conception of social virtue or felicity,[3] yea, no conception of human society itself, which has not its foundation in the family. No matter

---
1 **trite** – lacking interest because of overuse.
2 **benediction** – blessing.
3 **felicity** – happiness; state of well-being.

how excellent the constitution and laws of a country may be, or how vast its resources and prosperity, there is no sure basis for social order or public as well as private virtue, until it be laid in the wise regulation of its families. After all, a nation is but the aggregate[4] of its families, and unless there be good husbands and wives, fathers and mothers, sons and daughters, there cannot possibly be good citizens. Therefore, the present decay of home life and family discipline threaten the stability of our nation today far more severely than does any foreign hostility.

But the Scriptural view of the relative duties of the members of a Christian household portrays the prevailing effects in a most alarming manner, as being dishonoring to God, disastrous to the spiritual condition of the churches, and as raising up a most serious obstacle in the way of evangelical progress. Sad beyond words is it to see that professing Christians are themselves largely responsible for the lowering of marital standards, the general disregard of domestic relations, and the rapid disappearance of family discipline. As, then, marriage is the basis of the home or family, it is incumbent[5] on the writer to summon his readers to a serious and prayerful consideration of the revealed will of God on this vital theme. Though we can hardly hope to arrest the awful disease that is now eating out the very vitals of our nation, yet if God is pleased to bless this article to a few individuals, our labor will not be in vain.

We will begin by pointing out the excellency of wedlock: *"Marriage is honourable,"* says our text, and it is so first of all because God Himself has placed special honor upon it. All other ordinances or institutions (except the Sabbath) were appointed of God by the medium of men or angels (Acts 7:35), but marriage was ordained immediately by the Lord Himself—no man or angel brought the first wife to her husband (Gen. 2:22). Thus, marriage had more divine honor put upon it than had all the other divine institutions because it was directly solemnized by God Himself. Again, this was the first ordinance God instituted, yea, the first thing He did after man and woman were created, and that, while they were still in their unfallen state. Moreover, the *place* where their marriage occurred shows the honorableness of this institution: whereas all other institutions (save the Sabbath) were instituted outside of paradise, marriage was solemnized in Eden itself!—intimating how happy they are that marry in the Lord.

"God's crowning creative act was the making of woman. At the close of each creative day, it is formally recorded that God saw what He had made,

---

4 **aggregate** – sum total.
5 **incumbent** – necessary as an obligation or duty.

that it was good (Gen. 1:31). But when Adam was made, it is explicitly recorded that God saw it was not good that the man should be alone (Gen. 2:18). As to man, the creative work lacked completeness, until, as all animals and even plants had their mates, there should be found for Adam also a help meet[6] for him—his counterpart and companion. Not until this want[7] was met did God see the work of the last creative day also to be good.

"This is the first great Scripture lesson on family life, and it should be well learned…The divine institution of marriage teaches that the ideal state of both man and woman is not in separation but in union, that each is meant and fitted for the other. God's ideal is such union, based on a pure and holy love, enduring for life, exclusive of all rivalry or other partnership, and incapable of alienation or unfaithfulness because *it is a union in the Lord*—a holy wedlock of soul and spirit in mutual sympathy and affection."[8]

As God the Father honored the institution of marriage, so also did God the Son. *First*, by His being *"made of a woman"* (Gal. 4:4). *Second*, by His miracles, for the first supernatural sign that He wrought was at the marriage of Cana in Galilee (John 2:8), where He turned the water into wine, thereby intimating that if Christ be present at your wedding (i.e., if you "marry in the Lord") your life shall be a joyous or blessed one. *Third*, by His parables, for He compared the kingdom of God unto a marriage (Matt. 22:2) and holiness to a *"wedding garment"* (Matt. 22:11). So also in His teaching: when the Pharisees sought to ensnare Him on the subject of divorce, He set His imprimatur[9] on the original constitution, adding *"What therefore God hath joined together, let not man put asunder"* (Matt. 19:4-6).

The institution of marriage has been still further honored by the Holy Spirit: For He has used it[10] as a figure of the union that exists between Christ and the church: *"For this cause shall a man leave his father and mother, and shall be joined unto his wife, and they two shall be one flesh. This is a great mystery: but I speak concerning Christ and the church"* (Eph. 5:31-32). The relation, which obtains between the Redeemer and the redeemed, is likened again and again unto that which exists between a wedded man and woman: Christ is the *"Husband"* (Isa. 54:5), the church is the *"Wife"* (Rev. 21:9). *"Turn, O backsliding children, saith the Lord; for I am married unto you"* (Jer. 3:14). Thus, each person of the blessed Trinity has set His seal upon the honorableness of the marriage state.

---

6 **meet** – suitable; fitting.
7 **want** – lack; need.
8 Arthur Tappan Pierson (1837-1911) – American pastor and writer.
9 **imprimatur**– official approval.
10 The author here refers to the Spirit's use of the relation of husband and wife as a *type* or figure of Christ and the church in Holy Scripture. In this way He honors marriage.

Chapter 4—Marriage: The Excellence of Marriage

There is no doubt that in true marriage, each party helps the other equally; and in view of what has been pointed out above, any who venture to hold or teach any other doctrine or philosophy join issue with the Most High. This does not lay down a hard and fast rule that every man and woman is obliged to enter into matrimony: there may be good and wise reasons for abiding alone [and] adequate motives for remaining in the single state—physical and moral, domestic and social. Nevertheless, a single life should be regarded as…exceptional, rather than ideal. Any teaching that leads men and women to think of the marriage bond as the sign of bondage and the sacrifice of all independence [or] to construe wifehood and motherhood as drudgery[11] and interference with woman's higher destiny, any public sentiment [that cultivates] celibacy as more desirable and honorable or [that substitutes] anything else for marriage and home not only invades God's ordinance, but opens the door to nameless crimes and threatens the very foundations of society.

Now it is clear that marriage must have particular reasons for the appointment of it. Three are given in Scripture:

First, for the propagation of[12] children: This is its obvious and normal purpose. *"So God created man in his own image, in the image of God created he him; male and female created he them"* (Gen. 1:27)—not both males or both females, but one male and one female. To make the design of this unmistakably plain, God said, *"Be fruitful, and multiply"* (1:28). For this reason, marriage is called "matrimony," which signifies *motherage* because it results in virgins becoming mothers. Therefore, it is desirable that marriage be entered into at an early age, before the prime of life be passed: twice in Scripture we read of *"the wife of thy youth"* (Prov. 5:18; Mal. 2:15). We have pointed out that the propagation of children is the "normal" end of marriage; yet there are special seasons of acute "distress" when 1 Corinthians 7:29 holds good.

Second, marriage is designed as a preventive of immorality: *"Nevertheless, to avoid fornication, let every man have his own wife, and let every woman have her own husband"* (1 Cor. 7:2). If any were exempted, it might be supposed that kings would be given dispensation[13] because of the lack of a successor to the throne should his wife be barren; yet the king is expressly forbidden a plurality of wives (Deut. 17:17), showing that the endangering of a monarchy is not sufficient to countervail[14] the sin of adultery. For this cause, a whore is

---

11 **drudgery** – dull, distasteful work.
12 **propagation of** – act of producing.
13 **dispensation** – exemption from the rule.
14 **countervail** – offset the effect of.

termed a *"strange woman"* (Prov. 2:16), showing that she should be a stranger to us; and children born out of marriage are called "bastards," which under the Law were excluded from the congregation of the Lord (Deut. 23:2).

The third purpose of marriage is for the avoiding of the inconveniences of solitude: [This is] signified in the *"it is not good that the man should be alone"* (Gen. 2:18), as though the Lord had said, "This life would be irksome[15] and miserable for man if no wife be given him for a companion." *"Woe to him that is alone when he falleth; for he hath not another to help him up"* (Eccl. 4:10). Someone has said, "Like a turtle which has lost his mate, like one leg when the other is cut off, like one wing when the other is clipped, so had man been if woman had not been given to him." Therefore, for mutual society and comfort, God united man and woman that the cares and fears of this life might be eased by the cheer and help of each other.

Let us next consider the choice of our mate. First, the one selected for our life's partner must be outside those degrees of near kinship prohibited by the Divine law (Lev. 18:6–17).

Second, the Christian must wed a fellow Christian. From earliest times, God has commanded that *"the people shall dwell alone, and shall not be reckoned among the nations"* (Num. 23:9). His law unto Israel in connection with the Canaanites was, *"Neither shalt thou make marriages with them; thy daughter thou shalt not give unto his son, nor his daughter shalt thou take unto thy son"* (Deut. 7:3 and *cf.* Josh. 23:12). How much more, then, must God require the separation of those who are His people by a spiritual and heavenly tie than those who occupied only a fleshly and earthly relation to Him. *"Be ye not unequally yoked together with unbelievers"* (2 Cor. 6:14)…

There are but two families in this world: the children of God and the children of the devil (1 John 3:10). If then a daughter of God marries a son of the evil one, she becomes a daughter-in-law to Satan! If a son of God marries a daughter of Satan, he becomes a son-in-law to the devil! By such an infamous step, an affinity is formed between one belonging to the most High and one belonging to His arch-enemy. "Strong language!" Yes, but not too strong. O the dishonor done to Christ by such a union! O the bitter reaping from such a sowing! In every case, it is the poor believer who suffers…As well might an athlete attach to himself a heavy weight and then expect to win a race, as for one to progress spiritually after marrying a worldling.[16]

---

15 **irksome** – troublesome; tedious.
16 **worldling** – person more interested in material things rather than spiritual matters.

Should any Christian reader be inclined or expect to become betrothed,[17] the first question for him or her to carefully weigh in the Lord's presence is will this union be with an unbeliever? For if you are really cognizant[18] of and heart and soul be impressed with the tremendous difference which God, in His grace, has put between you and those who are—however attractive in the flesh—yet in their sins, then you should have no difficulty in rejecting every suggestion and proposal of making common cause with such. You are *"the righteousness of God"* in Christ, but unbelievers are *"unrighteous."* You are *"light in the Lord,"* but they are darkness. You have been translated into the kingdom of God's dear Son, but unbelievers are under the power of Belial. You are a son of peace, whereas all unbelievers are *"children of wrath."* Therefore, *"Be ye separate, saith the Lord, and touch not the unclean thing; and I will receive you"* (2 Cor. 6:17).

The danger of forming such an alliance is *before* marriage or even betrothal, neither of which could be seriously entertained by any real Christian unless the sweetness of fellowship with the Lord had been lost. The affections must first be withdrawn from Christ before we can find delight in social intimacy with those who are alienated from God, and whose interests are confined to this world. The child of God who is keeping his heart with all diligence (Prov. 4:23) will not, *cannot* have a joy in intimacies with the unregenerate. Alas, how often is the seeking or the accepting of close friendship with unbelievers the first step to open departure from Christ. The path that the Christian is called upon to tread is indeed a narrow one; but if he attempts to widen it or leave it for a broader road, it must be in contravention[19] of the Word of God and to his or her own irreparable damage and loss.

Third, *"married...only in the Lord"* (1 Cor. 7:39) goes much further than prohibiting an unbeliever for a mate. Even among the children of God there are many who would not be suitable to each other in such a tie. A pretty face is an attraction, but O how vain to be governed in such a serious undertaking by such a trifle. Earthly goods and social position have their value here, yet how base and degrading to suffer them to control such a solemn undertaking. O what watchfulness and prayerfulness is needed in the regulation of our affections! Who fully understands the temperament that will match mine, that will be able to bear patiently with my faults, be a corrective to my tendencies, and a real help in my desire to live for Christ in this world? How many make a fair show at the start, but turn out

---

17 **betrothed** – engaged or pledged to be married.
18 **cognizant** – aware.
19 **contravention** – violation.

wretchedly! Who can shield me from a host of evils that beset the unwary, but God my Father?

"A virtuous woman is a crown to her husband" (Prov. 12:4): a pious and competent wife is the most valuable of all God's temporal blessings; she is the special gift of His grace. *"A prudent wife is from the LORD"* (Prov. 19:14), and He requires to be definitely and diligently sought unto (see Gen. 24:12). It is not sufficient to have the approval of trusted friends and parents, valuable and even needful as that (generally) is for our happiness: for though they are concerned for our welfare, yet their wisdom is not sufficiently far-reaching. The One who appointed the ordinance must needs be given the first place in it if we are to have His blessing on it. Now prayer is never intended to be a substitute for the proper discharge of our responsibilities: we are ever required to use care and discretion and must never act hurriedly and rashly…

"Whoso findeth a wife (a real one) findeth a good thing, and obtaineth favour of the LORD" (Prov. 18:22). *"Findeth"* implies a definite quest. To direct us therein, the Holy Spirit has supplied two rules or qualifications. First, *godliness*, because our partner must be like Christ's spouse, pure and holy. Second, *fitness*, *"an help meet for him"* (Gen. 2:18), showing that a wife cannot be a "help" unless she be "meet," and for that she must have much in common with her mate. If her husband be a laboring man, it would be madness for him to choose a lazy woman; if he be a learned man, a woman with no love of knowledge would be quite unsuited. Marriage is called a "yoke," and two cannot pull together if all the burden is to fall upon one—as it would if one weak and sickly was the partner chosen.

Now for the benefit of our younger readers, let us point out some of the marks by which a godly and fit mate may be identified. First, the reputation: a good man commonly has a good name (Prov. 22:1). None can accuse him of open sins. Second, the countenance: our looks reveal our characters, and therefore Scripture speaks of "proud looks" and "wanton looks"—*"the shew of their countenance doth witness against them"* (Isa. 3:9). Third, the speech: *"For out of the abundance of the heart the mouth speaketh"* (Matt. 12:34). *"The heart of the wise teacheth his mouth, and addeth learning to his lips"* (Prov. 16:23). *"She openeth her mouth with wisdom; and in her tongue is the law of kindness"* (Prov. 31:26). Fourth, the apparel: a modest woman is known by the modesty of her attire. If the clothing be vulgar or showy, the heart is vain. Fifth, *the company kept:* birds of a feather flock together—a person may be known by his or her associates.

A word of warning is, perhaps, not quite needless. No matter how carefully and prayerfully one's partner be selected, he will not find marriage a perfect thing. Not that God did not make it perfect, but man has fallen since, and the fall has marred everything. The apple may still be sweet, but it has a worm inside. The rose has not lost its fragrance, but thorns grow with it. Willingly or unwillingly, everywhere we must read the ruin which sin has brought in. Then let us not dream of those faultless people that a diseased fancy[20] can picture and novelists portray. The most godly men and women have their failings; and though such be easy to bear when there is genuine love, yet they have to be borne.

A few brief remarks now on the home-life of the wedded couple. Light and help will be obtained here if it be borne in mind that marriage pictures forth the relation between Christ and His church. This, then, involves three things.

First, the attitude and actions of husband and wife are to be regulated by love. That is the cementing tie between [the] Lord Jesus and His spouse: a holy love, sacrificial love, an enduring love which naught can sever. There is nothing like love to make the wheels of home life run smoothly. The husband sustains to his mate the same relation as does the Redeemer to the redeemed, and hence the exhortation, *"Husbands, love your wives, even as Christ also loved the church"* (Eph. 5:25): with a hearty and constant love, ever seeking her good, ministering to her needs, protecting and providing for her, bearing with her infirmities, thus *"giving honour unto the wife, as unto the weaker vessel, and as being heirs together of the grace of life; that your prayers be not hindered"* (1 Peter 3:7).

Second, the headship of the husband. *"The head of the woman is the man"* (1 Cor. 11:3). *"For the husband is the head of the wife, even as Christ is the head of the church"* (Eph. 5:23). Unless this Divine appointment be duly heeded, there is sure to be confusion. The household must have a leader, and God has committed its rule unto the husband, holding him responsible for its orderly management. Serious will be the loss if he shirks his duty and turns the reins of government over to his wife. But this does not mean that Scripture gives him license to be a domestic tyrant, treating his wife as a servant: his dominion is to be exercised in love toward the one who is his consort. *"Likewise, ye husbands, dwell with them"* (1 Peter 3:7): seek their society after the day's labor is over…

Third, the subjection of the wife. *"Wives, submit yourselves unto your own husbands, as unto the Lord"* (Eph. 5:22). There is only one exception to be made in the application of this rule, namely when he commands what God forbids or forbids what God commands. *"For after this manner in the old time the holy women also, who trusted in God, adorned themselves, being in subjection unto their*

---

20 **fancy** – imagination.

own husbands" (1 Peter 3:5). Alas, how little of this spiritual "adornment" is evident today! *"Even as Sara obeyed Abraham, calling him lord: whose daughters ye are, as long as ye do well, and are not afraid with any amazement"* (1 Peter 3:6). Willing and loving subjection to the husband out of respect for the authority of God is what characterizes the daughters of Sarah. Where the wife refuses to submit to her husband, the children are sure to defy their parents—sow the wind, reap the whirlwind…

From "Marriage 13:4" in *An Exposition of Hebrews*.

Arthur W. Pink (1886-1952): Pastor, itinerate Bible teacher, author; born in Nottingham, England.

What Are the Duties of Husbands and Wives[21]

RICHARD STEELE (1629-1692)

Nevertheless let every one of you in particular so love his wife even as himself; and the wife see that she reverence her husband. —Ephesians 5:33

Marriage is the foundation of all society, and so this topic is very important. Explaining marital duties to you is much easier than persuading you to do them. Conform your will to Scripture, not vice versa. Take Ephesians 5:33 to heart.

1. The connection: *"Nevertheless"* is a transition from the spiritual reality of Christ's relationship to the Church. It means either that in spite of the unattainable ideal, strive to attain it; or because of the noble example, imitate it in your relationship with your spouse.

2. The direction: in the rest of the verse, *"Let every one of you, etc."* Wherein you see,

a. The universal obligation of it: *"Let every one of you"*—no matter how good you are or how bad your spouse. All husbands are entitled to their wives' respect, whether they are wise or foolish, intelligent or slow, skillful or clumsy. All wives are entitled to their husbands' love, whether beautiful or ugly, rich or poor, submissive or rebellious.

b. The particular application of it: *"In particular"*—each and every husband and wife should apply this to their own particular case.

3. The summary description of each of their duties:

a. Every husband's duty: To love his wife. This is not the only duty, but it includes all others. He should love her as himself. This is both *how* (the Golden Rule, Matt. 7:12) and *why* he is to love her (because they are both really one; loving her will result in blessings to him).

b. Every wife's duty: To *fear*[22] or *reverence*[23] her husband, both for his person and his position. This necessarily includes love because if she loves him, she will try to please him and avoid offending him.

Doctrine: Every husband should love his wife as himself, and every wife should respect her husband. Remember, this is your Creator's counsel, clearly articulated in both the Old and New Testaments, and by both Paul, the apostle to Gentiles (Eph. 5:22ff.; Col. 3:18ff.) and Peter, the apostle to Jews (1 Peter 3:1ff.). These two duties (husband, *love*; wife, *respect*) are not

---

21 Abridgment and paraphrase by D. Scott Meadows, pastor of Calvary Baptist Church, Exeter, New Hampshire; booklet available from CHAPEL LIBRARY
22 In the Greek text φοβῆται
23 In the KJV translation

exhaustive, but are mentioned particularly either because they are the most common failures of each or because they include all other duties. Another explanation is that respect is what husbands need most, and love what wives need most, from their spouses. God counsels not only that we may have eternal life, but comfort here and now. A godly marriage is a bit of heaven on earth. Reviewing these duties should humble us for our past failures and challenge us to future improvement.

The duties belonging to both alike: Let us see what those mutual duties are that are common between husband and wife, in which both of them are equally, at least according to the place and power of each, concerned and obligated.

1. Living with each other. He must *"leave his father and his mother and shall cleave unto his wife"* (Gen. 2:24), and she must *"forget also [her] own people, and [her] father's house"* (Ps. 45:10). He must *"dwell with [his wife]"* (1 Peter 3:7), and she must not *"depart from her husband,"* even if he is an unbeliever (1 Cor. 7:10). The other duties of marriage require living together, as regular sexual relations, which they both owe each other (1 Cor. 7:3-5). The Old Testament prohibits husbands from going to war during their first year of marriage (Deut. 24:5). This shows the importance of living together.

2. Loving each other. This is both the husband's (Col. 3:19) and the wife's duty (Titus 2:4). Love is the great reason and comfort of marriage. This love is not merely romance, but genuine and constant affection and care for each other *"with a pure heart fervently"* (1 Peter 1:22). Marital love cannot be based on beauty or wealth, for these are passing, and not even on piety, for that may decay. It must be based upon God's command, which never changes. The marriage vow obliges "for better or for worse," and married persons ought to consider their own spouses the best in the world for them. Marital love must be durable, lasting even after death has severed the bond (Prov. 31:12). This true-hearted love brings true contentment and comfort in its train. It guards against adultery and jealousy. It prevents or lessens family trouble. Without it, the marriage is like a bone out of joint: there is pain until it is restored.

3. Staying faithful to each other. Every man should have (sexually) his own wife, and every wife her own husband (1 Cor. 7:2), and only their own. Imitate the first Adam, who had but one wife, and the second Adam, Who has but one Church. The marriage covenant binds you to your own spouse as the dearest, sweetest, and best in the world. The slightest infidelity, *even in the heart,* may lead to full-blown adultery. Without repentance,[24] adultery

---

24 **repentance** – Repentance to life is a saving grace, whereby a sinner, out of a true

destroys both earthly happiness and reasonable expectation of heaven. It almost dissolves marriage, and in the OT was a capital crime (Deut. 22:22). Be careful to avoid temptations to this sin. The man who is not satisfied with one woman will never be satisfied with many because this sin has no boundaries. Faithfulness also involves keeping each other's secrets. These must not be disclosed unless there is a greater obligation. Telling your spouse's secrets is bad when accidental, worse when the result of temper, and the worst when it is motivated by hate.

4. Helping each other. The wife should be a helper comparable to her husband (Gen. 2:18), implying they should both help each other. They should carry these things together:

a. Their work. If she works at home and he works outside, both their work shall be easier. For motivation, let him give attention to all of Proverbs, and her to the last chapter especially.

b. Their crosses. Though newlyweds expect only pleasure in marriage, trouble is bound to come (1 Cor. 7:28). You may face loss of worldly goods, harm to your children, afflictions from both friends and enemies. Spouses must be friends to each other through thick and thin.

c. Their commitment to Christ. Live *"as being heirs together of the grace of life"* (1 Peter 3:7). The highest end of marriage is to promote each other's eternal happiness. Co-operation here is very important. His knowledge must aid her ignorance, and her zeal his discouragement. When the husband is home, he must instruct and pray with his family and sanctify the Sabbath, but in his absence, she must look to these things.

5. Being patient with each other. This duty we owe to all, but especially to our spouse (Eph 4:31-32). There are many temptations in marriage to become impatient! Hot tempers ignite civil wars indoors, and no good ever comes of them. Both need a meek and quiet spirit. Learn to hold your peace to keep the peace. Withdraw until the storm is over. You are not two angels married, but two sinful children of Adam. Wink at lesser faults, and be careful in confronting greater ones. Acknowledge your faults to one another and confess them all to God. Yield to one another rather than to the devil (Eph. 4:27).

6. Promoting the salvation of each other. 1 Corinthians 7:16 insinuates that our great duty is to promote the salvation of our spouse. What good is it to enjoy marriage now and then go to hell together? If you [do not care

---

sense of his sins and apprehension of the mercy of God in Christ, does with grief and hatred of his sin turn from it to God, with full purpose to strive after new obedience. (Spurgeon's Catechism Q. 70); See FGB 203, *Repentance*.

that your spouse may be] damned, where is your love? Both should inquire into each other's spiritual state, and use the means appointed to improve it. Chrysostom (c. A.D. 347-407) said, "Let them both go to church and then discuss the sermon together." If both are Christians already, then they should do what they can to help each other to become *thorough* saints. Speak often of God and spiritual things. Be fellow-pilgrims to the Celestial City.[25]

7. Maintaining regular but moderate marital sex. *"Marriage is honorable in all, and the bed undefiled: but whoremongers and adulterers God will judge"* (Heb. 13:4). Marital sex is designed to remedy impure affections, not excite them. You cannot follow every sexual folly you can imagine with your spouse, just because you are married. Owning wine gives you no permission to get drunk. Be moderate and sensible. For example, you might abstain for a time to give yourselves to prayer (1 Cor. 7:5). Even in marital relations, we must show reverence to God and respect for each other. True love does not behave rudely (1 Cor. 13:5).

8. Looking out for each other's interests in all things. Help each other's health, and be sick together, at least in spirit. One should not be rich while the other suffers want.[26] Advance each other's good reputation. A husband naturally and rightly cares for things that are of the world, how he may please his wife, and the wife does the same (1 Cor. 7:33-34). This brings honor to their faith, comfort to their lives, and a blessing on all they have. They should be bosom friends, laughing and weeping together, with nothing but death separating their interests.

9. Praying for each other. Peter warns against their prayers being hindered (1 Peter 3:7), which suggests they should pray for and with each other. "Isaac intreated the LORD for his wife, because she was barren" (Gen. 25:21). We should pray for everyone, but especially our spouse. The purest love is expressed by earnest prayer, and prayer will preserve love. Seek times for prayer together. Mr. Bolton prayed twice privately, twice with his wife, and twice with his family, each day. Prayer elevates Christian marriage above heathen marriages and the co-habitation of animals.

How to accomplish these duties, so that husbands and wives may certainly be blessings to each other:

1. Keep yourself pure before marriage. This will help you in the duties of marriage later. Everyone should "possess his vessel in sanctification and honor" (1 Thess. 4:4). The fornicator before marriage continues his sin in

---

25 **Celestial City** – reference to heaven, the abode of all God's true children, as described in John Bunyan's classic *The Pilgrim's Progress* (1678), available from Chapel Library.

26 **want** – lack; deprivation.

marriage. Beware of lust's first beginning, and flee it like poison. Keep your heart filled with the things of God and your body busy about your duties. The greatest fires begin with a spark. Momentary pleasure that precedes eternal torment is utter folly. If you have sinned in this way, cleanse your hearts and hands with Christ's blood by confession to God, with fasting and prayer for His forgiveness and strength against future temptation. Get a taste of the more ravishing delights of God's favor and promises, pardon of sin, and assurance of life and immortality. Once you have drunk from the pure spring, you will not prefer the muddy stream.

2. Choose your spouse carefully. Now that you know how difficult godly marriage is, you should be praying that He would guide you into it. Do not first love, and then consider. First consider, and then love. Let their soul be your main concern, not their looks or money. Why espouse a perpetual cross for some passing profit or delight?[27] Marry only a Christian—the godlier the better. Consider also their personality. Speak honestly to one another about your faults and liabilities before marrying. If someone sold you a sick animal as a healthy one, you would feel cheated. How much worse is it when someone pretends to be better than they really are to secure marriage to one they profess to love!

3. Study biblical marriage duties before you have them. Being a godly spouse is such a big challenge that you must prepare for it well beforehand. It is no wonder that so many marriages fail! Too often the husband does not know how to rule, [and] the wife does not know how to obey. They are both ignorant, conceited, and miserable. Therefore, parents ought to teach their children about the duties of marriage. Otherwise families, which should be the nurseries of the church, prove to be hotbeds of disorder and immorality. Read not only Scripture, but good books like Gouge's *Of Domestical Duties*...[28]

4. Resolve to obey God without any reservation. Until you are born again and made holy in your heart and conduct, you cannot please God or be a complete blessing to your spouse. You can only live together as civil pagans. The husband that truly fears God cannot remain bitter against his wife. A Bible placed between you will eliminate many differences, comfort many

---

27 **espouse a perpetual cross...delight** – the cross is a symbol of cruelty, torture, and death; here it is used as a figure of speech: "Why take up lifelong trouble, vexation, and misery for a marriage based on the temporary pleasure of beauty that fades or wealth that can disappear?"

28 See *Building a Godly Home*, a quality modernized reprint in three volumes of William Gouge's (1575-1653) classic *Of Domestical Duties*, edited by Joel Beeke and Scott Brown, Reformation Heritage Books, Grand Rapids, Michigan; available from the NCFIC, www.ncfic.org.

distresses, and guide you in many confounding circumstances. Remember, God's commands have the highest reason, and so obedience has the greatest sweetness. Keep the Golden Rule in your marriage. Righteousness abroad will not excuse wickedness at home. When you each focus on your own duties, you will be blessed.

5. Get and maintain true affection for your spouse. Give no place to jealousy. Do not give ear to backbiters and gossips. Jealousy often develops where true affection was lacking from the start.

6. Pray for spiritual graces.

a. Wisdom. A lack of wisdom causes many troubles in marriage. We need much wisdom to rule as husbands and to submit as wives.

b. Humility. This keeps the husband from becoming a tyrant, and the wife in ready subjection to her husband. *"Only by pride cometh contention"* (Prov. 13:10). A proud person could not agree with an angel; the humble will agree with anybody. Humility will also promote contentment. The humble husband and wife will say, "My spouse is far too good for such a sinful person as myself. I don't deserve such a wonderful partner. That was a sharp reproof, but it was nothing compared to hell, which is what I deserve." Truly humble people are easy companions.

c. Uprightness. An upright heart is needed to keep these commandments of God. An upright heart will choose the safest course, even if it is the hardest. It will suffer the worst injury rather than cause the least. It will watch against the beginnings of sin, which produce marriage's worst troubles. The upright husband and wife will strive each to do their own duty, and will be most severe against their own failures.

From "What Are the Mutual Duties of Husbands and Wives Towards Each Other" in *Puritan Sermons 1659-1689*, Vol. 2, Richard Owen Roberts, Publishers.

Richard Steele (1629-1692): Puritan preacher and author; born at Bartholmley, Cheshire, England.

Mutual Duties of Husbands and Wives
JOHN ANGELL JAMES (1785-1859)

See that ye love one another with a pure heart fervently. —1 Peter 1:22

Marriage is the foundation of the domestic constitution.[29] This, says the Apostle, *"is honourable in all"* (Heb. 13:4); and he has condemned as *"doctrines of devils"* the opinions of those by whom it is forbidden (1 Tim. 4:1). It is an institute of God, it was established in Eden, [and it] was honored by the personal attendance of Christ and furnished an occasion for the first of that splendid series of miracles by which He proved Himself to be the Son of God and the Savior of the world…Distinguishing, as it does, man from brutes; providing not only for the *continuance*, but for the *comfort* of our species; containing at once the source of human happiness and of all those virtuous emotions and generous sensibilities that refine and adorn the character of man, it can never as a general subject be guarded with too much solicitous[30] vigilance, nor be contracted, in particular instances, with too much prudence and care…My first object will be to state those duties which are common to both husband and wife:

1. The first that I mention is love—the ground of all the rest: Let this be wanting,[31] and marriage is degraded at once into a brutal or a sordid compact. This duty, which…is especially enjoined on the husband, belongs equally to the wife. It must be mutual, or there can be no happiness. None for the party that does not love: For how dreadful the idea of being chained for life to an individual for whom we have no affection, to be almost ever in the company of a person from whom we are driven back by revulsion, yet driven back upon a bond that prevents all separation and escape. Nor can there be any happiness for the party that does love: Such an unrequited[32] affection must soon expire or live only to consume that wretched heart in which it burns. A married couple without mutual regard is one of the most pitiable spectacles on earth. They cannot, and indeed in ordinary circumstances, ought not to separate; yet they remain united only to be a torment to each other. They serve one important purpose, however, in the history of mankind: that is to be a beacon to all who are yet disengaged, to warn them against the sin and folly of forming this union upon any other basis than that of a pure and mutual attachment, and to admonish all that are united to watch with most

---

29 **domestic constitution** – household arrangement; family structure.
30 **solicitous** – extremely careful or attentive.
31 **wanting** – lacking.
32 **unrequited** – not returned in the same way; one-sided.

assiduous[33] vigilance their mutual regard, that nothing be allowed to damp the sacred flame.

As the union should be formed on the basis of love, so should great care be taken, especially in the early stages of it, that nothing might arise to unsettle or loosen our attachments. Whatever knowledge we may obtain of each other's tastes and habits before marriage, it is neither so accurate, so comprehensive, nor so impressive as that which we acquire by living together. And it is of prodigious[34] consequence, that when little defects are first noticed and trivial faults and oppositions first occur, they should not be allowed to produce an unfavorable impression upon the mind.

If they would preserve love, let them be sure to study most accurately each other's tastes and distastes, and most anxiously abstain from whatever, even in the minutest things, they know to be contrary to [their tastes]… If they would preserve love, let them most carefully avoid all curious and frequently repeated distinctions of mine and thine: for this hath caused all the laws, all the suits, and all the wars in the world…

2. Mutual respect is a duty of married life: For though, as we shall afterwards consider, especial reverence is due from the wife, yet is respect due from the husband also. As it is difficult to respect those who are not entitled to it on any other ground than superior rank or common relationship, it is of immense consequence that we should present to each other that conduct which deserves respect and commands it. Moral esteem is one of the firmest supports and strongest guards of love, and a high degree of excellence cannot fail to produce such esteem. We are more accurately known to each other in this connection than either to the world or even to our own servants and children. The privacies of such a relationship lay open our motives and all the interior of our character, so that we are better known to each other than we are to ourselves. If therefore we would be respected, we should be respectable. Charity covers a multitude of faults, it is true. But we must not presume too far upon the credulity[35] and blindness of affection: there is a point beyond which even love cannot be blind to the crimson coloring of a guilty action. Every piece of real sinful conduct, the impropriety of which cannot be mistaken, tends to sink us in each other's esteem, and thus to remove the safeguards of affection…In all the conduct of the conjugal[36] state then, there should be the most marked and unvarying mutual respect

---

33 **assiduous** – attentive.
34 **prodigious** – enormous.
35 **credulity** – gullibility; disposition of being too ready to believe.
36 **conjugal** – relating to the marriage; marital.

even in little things. There must be no searching after faults, no examining with microscopic scrutiny such as cannot be concealed, no reproachful epithets,[37] no rude contempt, no incivility,[38] no cold neglect. There should be courtesy without ceremony, politeness without formality, attention without slavery. In short, it should be the tenderness of love, supported by esteem, and guided by politeness. Then, we must maintain our mutual respectability before others…It is in the highest degree improper for either party to do an action, to say a word, or [to] assume a look that shall have the remotest tendency to lower the other in public esteem.

3. Mutual attachment to each other's society is a common duty of husband and wife: We are united to be companions—to live together, to walk together, to talk together. The husband is commanded to dwell with the wife according to knowledge (1 Peter 3:7). "This," says Mr. Jay,[39] "intends nothing less than residence, opposed to absence and roving. It is absurd for those who have no prospect of dwelling together to enter this state, and those who are already in it should not be unnecessarily abroad. Circumstances of various kinds will doubtless render occasional excursions unavoidable, but let a man return as soon as the design of his absence is accomplished. Let him always travel with the words of Solomon in his mind, *As a bird that wandereth from her nest, so is a man that wandereth from his place'* (Prov. 27:8). Can a man while from home discharge the duties he owes to his household? Can he discipline his children? Can he maintain the worship of God in his family? I know it is the duty of the wife to lead the devotion in the absence of the husband; and she should take it up as a cross, if not for the time as a privilege. Few, however, are thus disposed, and hence one of the sanctuaries of God for weeks and months together is shut up. I am sorry to say that there are some husbands who seem fonder of *any* society than the company of their wives. It appears in the disposal of their leisure hours. How few of these are appropriated to the wife! The evenings are the most domestic periods of the day. To these the wife is peculiarly entitled: she is now most free from her numerous cares and most at liberty to enjoy reading and conversation. It is a sad reflection upon a man when he is fond of spending his evenings abroad. It implies something bad, and it predicts something worse."

To insure as far as possible the society of her husband at his own fireside, let the wife be a keeper at home (Titus 2:5) and do all in her power to render

---

37 **reproachful epithets** – critical or blameful abusive words or phrases.
38 **incivility** – rudeness; impolite behavior or language.
39 **William Jay (1769-1853)** – English Noncomformist theologian and author.

that fireside as attractive as good temper, neatness, and cheerful, affectionate conversation can make it. Let her strive to make his own home the soft green[40] on which his heart loves to repose in the sunshine of domestic enjoyment…

United to be associates then, let man and wife be as much in each other's society as possible. There must be something wrong in domestic life when they need the aid of balls, routes,[41] plays, card parties to relieve them from the tedium produced by home pursuits. I thank God, I am a stranger to that taste that leads a man to flee from his own comfortable parlor and the society of his wife, from the instruction and recreation contained in a well-stored library, or from the evening rural walk when the business of the day is over, to scenes of public amusement for enjoyment. To my judgment, the pleasures of home and of home society, when home and home society are all that could be desired, are such as never cloy[42] and need no change, but from one kindred scene to another. I am sighing and longing, perhaps in vain, for a period when society shall be so elevated and so purified; when the love of knowledge will be so intense and the habits of life will be so simple; when religion and morality will be so generally diffused that men's homes will be the seat and circle of their pleasures; when in the society of an affectionate and intelligent wife and of well educated children, each will find his greatest earthly delight; and when it will be felt to be no more necessary to happiness to quit their own fireside for the ballroom, the concert, or the theatre, than it is to go from the well-spread table to the public feast to satisfy the cravings of a healthy appetite. *Then* will it be no longer imposed upon us to prove that public amusements are improper, for they will be found to be unnecessary…

4. Mutual forbearance is another duty: This we owe to all, not excepting the stranger or an enemy. And most certainly it must not be denied to our nearest friend. For the charity that *"suffereth long, and is kind; [that] envieth not; [that] vaunteth not itself, is not puffed up, [that] doth not behave itself unseemly, seeketh not her own, is not easily provoked, thinketh no evil; rejoiceth not in iniquity, but rejoiceth in the truth; [that] beareth all things, believeth all things, hopeth all things, endureth all things"* (1 Cor. 13:4-7), for *this* charity there is both need and room in every relation of life. Wherever sin or imperfection exists, there is scope for the forbearance of love. There is no perfection upon earth. Lovers, it is true, often fancy they have found it; but the more sober judgment of husbands and wives generally corrects the mistake. First impressions of this

---

40 **green** – a grassy ground or spot.
41 **routes** – fashionable gatherings; large evening parties.
42 **cloy** – cause disgust by overloading with something that was pleasant at first.

kind usually pass away with first love. We should all enter the married state, remembering that we are about to be united to a fallen creature…Affection does not forbid but actually demands that we should mutually point out our faults. But this should be done in all the meekness of wisdom, united with all the tenderness of love, lest we only increase the evil we intend to remove or substitute a greater one in its place…

5. Mutual assistance is the duty of husbands and wives: This applies to the cares of life…The husband should never undertake anything of importance without communicating the matter to his wife, who, on her part, instead of shrinking from the responsibility of a counsellor and leaving him to struggle alone with his difficulties and perplexities, should invite him to communicate freely all his anxieties. For if she cannot counsel, she can comfort. If she cannot relieve his cares, she can help to bear them. If she cannot direct the course of his trade, she may the current of his feelings. If she cannot open any source of earthly wisdom, she can spread the matter before the Father and Fountain of Lights. Many men, under the idea of delicacy to their wives, keep all their difficulties to themselves, which only prepares them to feel the stroke the heavier when it does come.

And as the wife should be willing to help the husband in matters of business, he should be willing to share with her the burden of domestic anxieties and fatigue. Some go too far and utterly degrade the female head of the family by treating her as if her honesty or ability could not be trusted in the management of the domestic economy. They keep the money and dole it out as if they were parting with their life's blood, grudging every shilling[43] they dispense and requiring an account as rigid as they would from a suspected servant. They take charge of everything, give out everything, interfere in everything. This is to despoil a woman of her authority, to thrust her from her proper place, to insult and degrade her before her children and servants. Some, on the other hand, go to the opposite extreme, and take no share in anything. My heart has ached to see the slavery of some devoted, hardworking, and ill-used wives. After laboring all day amidst the ceaseless toils of a young and numerous family, they have had to pass the hours of evening in solitude, while the husbands, instead of coming home to cheer them by their society or to relieve them of only half an hour of their fatigue, have been either at a party or a sermon. And then have these hapless[44] women had to wake and watch the livelong night over a sick or restless babe, while the men whom they accepted as the partner of their

---

43 **shilling** – an English coin.
44 **hapless** – unfortunate.

sorrows were sleeping by their side, unwilling to give a single hour of their slumber, though it was to allow a little repose to their toil-worn wives. Why, even the irrational creatures shame such men. For it is a well-known fact that the male bird takes his turn upon the nest during the season of incubation to allow the female time to renew her strength by food and rest and with her also goes in diligent quest of food and feeds the young ones when they cry. No man should think of marrying who does not stand prepared to share, as far as he can do it with his wife, the burden of domestic cares.

They should be helpful to each other in the concerns of personal religion. This is clearly implied in the Apostle's language: *"For what knowest thou, O wife, whether thou shalt save thy husband? or how knowest thou, O man, whether thou shalt save thy wife?"* (1 Cor. 7:16). Where both parties are unconverted or only one of them is yet a partaker of true piety, there should be the most anxious, judicious, and affectionate efforts for their salvation. How heathenish a state is it to enjoy together the comforts of marriage and then travel in company to eternal perdition; to be mutual comforters on earth, and then mutual tormentors in Hell; to be companions in felicity in time, and companions in torment through eternity! And where both parties are real Christians, there should be the exercise of a constant reciprocal solicitude,[45] watchfulness, and care in reference to their spiritual and eternal welfare…Do we converse with each other, as we ought, on the high themes of redemption by Christ and eternal salvation? Do we study each other's dispositions, snares, troubles, and decays in piety that we may apply suitable remedies? Do we exhort one another daily, lest we should be hardened through the deceitfulness of sin? Do we practice fidelity without censoriousness[46] and administer praise without flattery? Do we invite one another to the most quickening and edifying means of grace of a public nature and recommend the perusal of such instructive and improving books as we have found beneficial to ourselves? Do we mutually lay open the state of our minds on the subject of personal religion and state our perplexities, our joys, our fears, our sorrows? Alas, alas! Who must not blush at their neglects in these particulars? Yet such neglect is as criminal as it is common. Fleeing from the wrath to come, and yet not doing all we can to aid each other's escape! Contending side by side for the crown of glory, honor, immortality, and eternal life, and yet not doing all we can to ensure each other's success! Is this love? Is this the tenderness of connubial[47] affection?

---

45 **reciprocal solicitude** – mutual concern for the well-being of each other; care given by each side of the couple.
46 **censoriousness** – the character of being harshly critical; finding fault.
47 **connubial** – marital; pertaining to husband and wife.

This mutual help should extend to the maintenance of all the habits of domestic order, discipline, and piety. The husband is to be the prophet, priest, and king of the family to instruct their minds, to lead their devotions, and to govern their tempers. But in all that relates to these important objects, the wife is to be of one mind with him. They are in these matters to be workers together, neither of them leaving the other to labor alone, much less opposing or thwarting what is done…A lovelier scene is not to be found on earth than that of a pious couple, employing their mutual influence and the hours of their retired companionship in stirring up each other's hearts to deeds of mercy and religious benevolence. Not Adam and Eve in Paradise, with the unspotted robes of their innocence about them, engaged in propping the vine or trailing the rose of that holy garden, presented to the eyes of angels a more interesting spectacle than this.

6. Mutual sympathy is required: Sickness may call for this, and females seem both formed and inclined by nature to yield it. "O woman!...A ministering angel thou!"…If we *could* do without her and be happy in health, what are we in sickness without her presence and her tender offices? Can we smooth, as woman can, the pillow on which the sick man lays his head? No. We cannot administer the medicine or the food as she can. There is a softness in her touch, a lightness in her step, a skill in her arrangements, a sympathy looking down upon us from her beaming eye, which ours wants…

Nor is this sympathy exclusively the duty of the wife, but belongs *equally* to the husband. He cannot, it is true, perform the same offices for her that she can discharge for him. But much he *can* do; and all he can, he *should* do…Husbands, I call upon you for all the skill and tenderness of love, on behalf of your wives, if they are weak and sickly. Watch by their couch, talk with them, pray with them, wake with them; in all their afflictions, be you afflicted. Never listen heedlessly to their complaints. And oh, by all that is sacred in conjugal affection, I implore you, never, by your cold neglect, or petulant[48] expressions, or discontented look, to call up in their imaginations, unusually sensitive at such a season, the phantom of a fear that the disease which has destroyed their health has done the same for your affection. Oh! Spare their bosom the agonizing pangs of supposing that they are living to be a burden to your disappointed heart. The cruelty of that man wants a name, and I know of none sufficiently emphatic, who denies his sympathy to a suffering woman…Such a man does the work of a murderer without his punishment, and in some instances, without his reproach, but not always without his design or his remorse.

---

48 **petulant** – foolish, irritated, annoyed.

But sympathy should be exercised by man and wife, not only in reference to their sicknesses, but to all their afflictions, whether personal or relative; all their sorrows should be common: like two strings in unison, the chord of grief should never be struck in the heart of one, without causing a corresponding vibration in the heart of the other. Or like the surface of the lake answering to the heaven, it should be impossible for calmness and sunshine to be upon one, while the other is agitated and cloudy: heart should answer to heart and face to face.

From "What Are the Duties of Husbands and Wives Towards Each Other?" in *Puritan Sermons 1659-1689, Being the Morning Exercises at Cripplegate,* Vol. 1, reprinted by Richard Roberts, Publishers. Available from CL in booklet form.

John Angell James (1785-1859): English Congregationalist preacher and author; author of *Female Piety, A Help to Domestic Happiness, An Earnest Ministry,* and many others. Born at Blandford, Dorsetshire, England.

A Husband's Love for His Wife
RICHARD STEELE (1629-1692)

Nevertheless let every one of you in particular so love his wife even as himself. —Ephesians 5:33a

The great duty of every husband is to love his own wife. This is the foundation of all the rest; this must be mixed with all the rest; this is the epitome of all the rest of his duty…

I. For the first, the nature and property of this love: It is conjugal, true, and genuine, such as is peculiar to this relation. [It is] not that fondness which is proper [towards] children, nor the brutish lust which is peculiar to beasts, but that which is right and true.

1. For the *ground* of it…The ordinance of God hath made her one flesh with me, and the law of nature obligeth me to love my own flesh. Therefore, though her beauty be decayed, her portion spent, her weaknesses great, and her usefulness small, yet she is a piece of myself. Here the wise God hath determined my affection. When all is said, this is the only sure foundation and [it] holds perpetually.

2. This love must be right for the *extent* of it: It reaches the whole person, both soul and body. Every man should choose such an one, whose outward features and proportion he can highly esteem and affect…True conjugal love to a wife reaches her soul, so as to see an amiableness in her mind and disposition, so as to study how to polish her soul more and more with wisdom and piety, and to endeavor that her soul may prosper as her body prospers.

3. Right for the *degree* of it: It must be transcendent, above your love to parents: *"Therefore shall a man leave his father and his mother, and shall cleave unto his wife"* (Gen. 2:24). The husband must honor his parents, but he must love his wife as himself and must (yet with all prudence) prefer her in his respects, whenever they come in competition…He must prefer her in his affection before his children and rather love them for her sake, than her for theirs, and before all others in the world. In short, he must so love her as to delight in her company above all others: *"Be thou ravished always with her love"* (Prov. 5:19).

4. The husband's love must be right for the *duration* of it: And the last named Scripture clears that: "Be thou ravished always with her love," not only kind before other folk and then cold in private, but *always*—not for a week, or month, or the first year, but while life lasts. Yea, as he hath experience of her virtue and sweetness, his love should daily increase…You

have had her beauty and strength; why should you not also have her wrinkles and infirmities, yea, and give the more respect to her tried fidelity?[49]…And if there be less comeliness in the body, yet usually there is more beauty in the mind, more wisdom, humility, and fear of the Lord, so that still there are sufficient arguments in her, or arguments in the Bible, to perpetuate your conjugal affection.

II. Let us trace the husband's love to his wife in its pattern, laid down in the scripture, and particularly in the context and words that i am handling:

1. The husband ought to love his wife, as our Savior Christ loveth His church: *"Husbands, love your wives, even as Christ also loved the church"* (v. 25). He must *"nourisheth and cherisheth[her], even as the Lord the church"* (v. 29). Now these texts direct us to the *quality* of our love, though we cannot reach to an *equality* with Christ herein…His love is represented here to be,

a. Hearty, without dissimulation:[50] He *"loved the church, and gave himself for it"* (v. 25). His love was real, for He died of it. The husband must write after this copy. Not to love his wife in word and tongue only, but in deed and in truth, that if his heart were opened, her name might be found written there…

b. Free, without [expectation of reward]: For He gave Himself that He might cleanse His church (v. 26), which implies that she was in ill plight[51] when He began His motions.[52] She was no beauty. No. We loved Him *because* He loved us first (1 John 4:19). The husband must precede and by his love draw out the love of his wife. For love is the whetstone of love. If she appears weak, as their sex by constitution is—in wisdom, strength, and courage, or prove unlovely and negligent of her duty—yet he must love her, for love*"seeketh not her own"* (1 Cor. 13:5). True love doth more study to better the object beloved, than to advantage the subject that loveth. To love a wife only in hopes of some advantages by her is unworthy the heart of a husband and no way like the example of Christ.

c. Holy, without impurity: For He *"loved the church…that he might sanctify and cleanse it with the washing of water by the word"* (vv. 25, 26)…The husband cannot have a better copy and is taught hereby to endeavor, at any cost and pains whatsoever, to further the sanctification and salvation of his wife.

d. Great, without comparison: For *"greater love hath no man than this, that a man lay down his life for his friends"* (John 15:13), and so did our Savior. He

---

49 **tried fidelity** – tested and proven faithfulness.
50 **dissimulation** – hypocrisy.
51 **ill plight** – a distressing situation or condition.
52 **motions** – activities or movements in pursuing something.

gave Himself for His church (v. 25)…The husband must herein imitate his Lord and Master by preserving a singular and superlative respect for his wife because she is a member "of his body, of his flesh, and of his bones"…

e. His is an active and fruitful love: For He *"nourisheth and cherisheth"* His church (v. 29). His poor church is always wanting; He supplies her. She is in trouble; He protects her. She is ready to sink; but He awakes to save her. Such must be a husband's love. He must spare no cost, no pains, to do his wife good…Thus the husband must love his wife as Christ loveth His church.

2. The husband ought to love his wife as himself: So saith my text. The Apostle had said, *"So ought men to love their wives as their own bodies"* (v. 28) and, lest that should not be sufficient, he goes on in my text and says, *"Let every one of you in particular so love his wife even as himself"*…he that doth not know with what manner of love Christ doth love His church, yet knows with what love he loves himself. And that is,

a. Tenderly: No one can touch or handle a man's sores and griefs so tenderly as himself: *"No man ever yet hated his own flesh,"* how unlovely soever, but nourisheth and cherisheth it (v. 29). Such ought the husband's love to be toward his wife, accompanied with the greatest tenderness. For they are like crystal glasses, soon broken if not tenderly handled…

b. Cheerfully: No man is so ready to help a man as himself. His best friends sometimes falter and are weary at length; but every man [helps] himself. Let the business be never so hard or hazardous, a man will venture when it is for himself. So must the husband most readily and cheerfully assist, comfort, and help his wife. If a cloud arises between them, the husband's love must dissolve it quickly; for no man is long angry with himself…he should have his ear open, his hand, his heart ready to pity, help, and gratify her, even as he is ready to help himself.

III. This brings us to the effects of the husband's love to his wife, which is the third thing to be described. And they are:

1. In word:

a. By diligent instruction of his wife, wherein she is ignorant: He ought to *"dwell with [his wife] according to knowledge"* (1 Peter 3:7). And she ought to *"ask [her] husband[s] at home,"* when she would learn and not *"speak in the church"* (1 Cor. 14:35)…For this the husband hath excellent opportunity, and woe to him if he [lacks] will or skill!…This is certain: if he can do her soul good, he lays an eternal obligation upon her to love and honor him. If he neglects his endeavors, she will be likely to curse him forever in hell!

b. The husband demonstrates his love by gentle reproof of his wife, when she doeth amiss: He must indeed overlook many infirmities, for love *"shall cover the multitude of sins"* (1 Peter 4:8). As he that is always using his sword will make it dull at length, so he that is continually reproving shall have the less regard given to his reproofs. Yet he cannot love her, if he do not, when need is, reprove her. But, let it be with all the wisdom and tenderness imaginable: not before strangers and rarely before the family; not for natural defects, seldom for inadvertencies.[53] When he does it, let him make way for his reproof by commending in her what is good; and when he hath done, back it with a reason. He must be sure to mingle the oil of kindness with the myrrh of reproof. For if he gives her this potion too hot, the operation is hindered and his labor worse than lost…Sooner or later, if she be not brutish, she will be thankful and amend.

c. The husband's love must be demonstrated by ready encouragement of his wife, when she doeth well: *"Her husband also, and he praiseth her"* (Prov. 31:28). He that is discreet and faithful herein perhaps taketh the readiest way to do her good…

2. The effects of a husband's love to his wife must be in deed also:

a. By making provision for her of what is necessary and also of what is convenient for her according to his ability: *"Her food, her raiment, and her duty of marriage, shall he not diminish"* (Ex. 21:10). Not that she hath any privilege to be maintained in idleness or, like a drone, live upon the industry of her husband without adding her helping hand. But the main care hereof must lie upon her husband…As he hath the strongest obligation upon him and the greatest advantages, he must lay about him by all lawful means to support and provide for her. Not only for her maintenance while he lives, but he ought to make provision for her, as far as he is able, after his departure hence. For so did Jesus Christ for His church.

b. This conjugal love is to be showed in the tenderness of the husband towards the wife: And this duty is incumbent on him, as he is the head of the wife: *"The head of the woman is the man"* (1 Cor. 11:3). Hence, the husband is bound to protect his wife from dangers and to sympathize with her in them…Upon this account he must protect her soul from temptation, her body from harm, her name from reproach, and her person from contempt either of children, servants, or others. In short, his whole carriage to her should be full of tenderness and composed of love and pity.

c. The husband's love is showed to his wife in giving her a good example: Namely, of piety, gravity, charity, wisdom, and goodness, which will be the most constant and effectual lecture that he can read unto her…If he be holy, quiet, and industrious, she cannot for shame, be wicked, froward, and

---

53 **inadvertencies** – forgotten or unintentionally ignored responsibilities.

idle. His discourses will direct hers. His prayers will teach her to pray. His justice, temperance, and charity will be a law, a rule, a motive to make her just, and sober, and charitable. If he be an atheist, an epicure, a Pharisee, it undoes her. He is to go before her, and usually she follows him either to hell or to heaven.

    d. The effects of a husband's love to his wife are to be seen in his behavior towards her: that is, in the mild use of his authority…Herein lies an act of the husband's love: (i) *Wisely* to keep, (ii) *Mildly* to use this authority. (i) He must keep it by a religious, grave, and manly carriage…If his behavior be light, she will be apt to set lightly by him. If he be weak and effeminate, it loses him…But then, (ii) Herein shines his love, to use the same with all sweetness…He is not to rule her as a king doth his subjects, but as the head doth the body. Though she was not taken out of Adam's head, so neither out of his foot, but out of his side near his heart. Therefore, his countenance must be friendly, his ordinary language to her mild and sweet, his behavior obliging, his commands sparing and respectful, and his reproofs gentle… He should never imagine that a rude insolency or perpetual bitterness is either the way to keep or use his authority aright…If meekness of wisdom will not prevail with thy wife, thou art undone in this world and she in the world to come.

From "What Are the Duties of Husbands and Wives Towards Each Other?" in *Puritan Sermons 1659-1689, Being the Morning Exercises at Cripplegate,* Vol. 1, reprinted by Richard Roberts, Publishers. Available from CL in booklet form.

Richard Steele (1629-1692): Puritan preacher and author; remembered as "a good scholar, a hard student, and an excellent preacher"; author of *The Character of the Upright Man* and others. Born at Bartholmley, Cheshire, England.

A Wife's Submission

JOHN BUNYAN (1628-1688)

Passing [by] the master of the family, I will speak a word or two to those that are under him, and first to the wife: the wife is bound by the Law to her husband, so long as her husband lives (Rom. 7:2). Therefore, she also has her work and place in the family, as well as the rest. Now there are these things considered in the carriage[54] of a wife toward her husband that she should conscientiously observe:

First, that she look upon him as her head and lord: *"The head of the woman is the man"* (1 Cor. 11:3). And so Sarah called Abraham *"lord"* (1 Peter 3:6).

Second, she should therefore be subject to him, as is fit in the Lord. The apostle says that the wife should submit herself to her husband, as to the Lord (1 Peter 3:1; Col. 3:18; Eph. 5:22). I told you before that if the husband does walk towards his wife as is fitting to him, he will therein be an ordinance of God to her—besides the relation of a husband—that will preach to her the behavior of Christ to His Church. And now I say also that the wife, if she walk with her husband as is fitting to her, she shall preach the obedience of the Church to her husband. *"Therefore as the church is subject unto Christ, so let the wives be to their own husbands in every thing"* (Eph. 5:24). Now, for your performing of this work, you must first shun these evils.

1. The evil of a wandering and a gossiping spirit: this is evil in the church and is evil also in a wife, who is the figure of the Church. Christ loves to have His spouse keep at home; that is, to be with Him in the faith and practice of His things, not ranging and meddling with the things of Satan. No more should wives be given to wander and gossip abroad. You know that Proverbs 7:11 says, *"She is loud and stubborn; her feet abide not in her house."* Wives should be about their own husbands' business at home, as the apostle says, Let them *"be discreet, chaste, keepers at home, good, obedient to their own husbands."* And why? Because otherwise the word of God will be blasphemed (Titus 2:5).

2. Take heed of an idle, talking, or contentious tongue. This also is odious, either in maids or wives, to be like parrots, not bridling their tongues; whereas the wife should know, as I said before, that her husband is her lord and is over her, as Christ is over the Church. Do you think it is seemly for the Church to parrot it against her Husband? Is she not to be silent before Him and to look to His laws rather than her own fictions? Why…should the wife so carry it towards her husband? *"Let the woman,"* says Paul, *"learn in silence with all subjection. But I suffer not a woman to teach, nor to usurp authority over*

---

54 **carriage** – conduct.

the man, but to be in silence" (1 Tim. 2:11-12). It is an unseemly thing to see a woman so much as once in all her lifetime to offer to overtop her husband; she should in everything be in subjection to him, and to do all she does as having her warrant, license, and authority from him. And indeed here is her glory, even to be under him, as the Church is under Christ: Now *"she openeth her mouth with wisdom; and in her tongue is the law of kindness"* (Prov. 31:26).

3. Do not wear immodest apparel or walk in a seductive way.[55] This will be evil both abroad and at home. Abroad it will not only give ill example, but also tend to tempt to lust and lasciviousness;[56] and at home it will give an offence to a godly husband, and be infecting to ungodly children, etc. Therefore, as says the apostle, Let women's apparel be modest, as becomes women professing godliness, with good works, *"not with broidered hair, or gold, or pearls, or costly array"* (1 Tim. 2:9-10). And as it is said again, *"Whose adorning, let it not be that outward adorning of plaiting the hair, and of wearing of gold, or of putting on of apparel; but let it be the hidden man of the heart, in that which is not corruptible, even the ornament of a meek and quiet spirit, which is in the sight of God of great price. For after this manner in the old time the holy women also, who trusted in God, adorned themselves, being in subjection unto their own husbands"* (1 Peter 3:3-5).

But yet, *do not* think that by the subjection I have here mentioned, that I do intend women should be their husbands' slaves. Women are their husbands' yoke-fellows, their flesh and their bones; and he is not a man that hates his own flesh, or that is bitter against it (Eph. 5:29). Wherefore, let every man *"love his wife even as himself; and the wife see that she reverence her husband"* (Eph. 5:33). The wife is master next to her husband and is to rule all in his absence; yes, in his presence she is to guide the house, to bring up the children, provided she does it [so] as the adversary has no occasion to speak reproachfully (1 Tim. 5:10, 13). *"Who can find a virtuous woman? for her price is far above rubies…A gracious woman retaineth honour,"* and guides her affairs with discretion (Prov. 31:10; 11:16; 12:4).

OBJECTION: But my husband is an unbeliever; what shall I do?

ANSWER: If so, then what I have said before lies upon you with an engagement so much the stronger. For, 1. Your husband being in this condition, he will be watchful to take your slips and infirmities, to throw them as dirt in the face of God and your Savior. 2. He will be apt to make the worst of every one of your words, actions, and gestures. 3. And all this does tend to the possessing his heart with more hardness, prejudice, and

---

55 See FGB 216, *Modest Apparel,* available from CHAPEL LIBRARY.
56 **lasciviousness** – inclination to lust or sexual desires.

opposition to his own salvation; therefore, as Peter says, *"ye wives, be in subjection to your own husbands; that, if any obey not the word, they also may without the word be won by the conversation of the wives; while they behold your chaste conversation coupled with fear"* (1 Peter 3:1-2). Your husband's salvation or damnation lies much in[57] your good behavior before him; therefore, if there is in you any fear of God or love to your husband, seek—by behavior full of meekness, modesty, holiness, and a humbleness before him—to win him to the love of his own salvation; and by doing this, how *"knowest thou, O wife, whether thou shalt save thy husband?"* (1 Cor. 7:16).

Objection: But my husband is not only an unbeliever, but one very contentious, peevish,[58] and testy;[59] yes, so contentious, etc., that I know not how to speak to him or behave myself before him.

Answer: Indeed, there are some wives in great slavery by reason of their ungodly husbands, and as such should be pitied and prayed for—so they should be so much the more watchful and circumspect in all their ways.

1. Therefore, be very faithful to him in all the things of this life.

2. Bear with patience his unruly and unconverted behavior. You are alive, he is dead; you are principled with grace, he with sin. Now then, seeing grace is stronger than sin and virtue than vice, be not overcome with his vileness, but overcome that with your virtues (Rom. 12:21). It is a shame for those that are gracious to be as lavishing[60] in their words, as those that are graceless: they that are slow to wrath are of great understanding: but they that are *"hasty of spirit[61] exalteth folly"* (Prov. 14:29).

3. Your wisdom, therefore—if at any time you have a desire to speak to your husband for his conviction concerning anything, either good or evil—is to observe convenient times and seasons. There is *"a time to keep silence, and a time to speak"* (Eccl. 3:7). Now for the right timing of your intentions,

a. Consider his disposition and take him when he is farthest off of those filthy passions that are your afflictions. Abigail would not speak a word to her churlish[62] husband until his wine was gone from him, and he in a sober temper (1 Sam. 25:36-37). Not heeding this observation is the cause why so much is spoken and so little effected.

---

57 **lies much in** – is influenced much by. Salvation is the gift of God, but He is pleased often to use human instruments.
58 **peevish** – easily irritated or annoyed.
59 **testy** – impatient and somewhat bad-tempered.
60 **lavishing** – reckless and unrestrained.
61 **hasty of spirit** – quick-tempered.
62 **churlish** – rude, in a mean-spirited, unfriendly way.

b. Take him at those times when he has his heart taken with you, and when he shows tokens of love and delight in you. Thus did Esther with the king, her husband, and prevailed (Esth. 5:3, 6; 7:1-2).

c. Observe when convictions seize his conscience, and then follow them with sound and grave sayings of the Scriptures. Somewhat like to this dealt Manoah's wife with her husband (Judg. 13:22-23). Yet then,

1) Let your words be few. 2) And none of them savoring of a lording it over[63] him; but speak still as to your head and lord by way of entreaty and beseeching. 3) And that in such a spirit of sympathy and a heart of affection after his good that the manner of your speech and behavior in speaking may be to him an argument that you speak in love, as being sensible of his misery and inflamed in your soul with desire [for] his conversion.[64] 4) And follow your words and behavior with prayers to God for his soul. 5) Still keeping yourself in a holy, chaste, and modest behavior before him.

Objection: But my husband is stupid, a fool, and one that has not wit enough to follow his outward employment in the world.

Answer: 1) Though all this be true, yet you must know he is your head, your lord, and your husband. 2) Therefore, you must take heed of desiring to usurp authority over him. He was not made for you—that is, for you to have dominion over him—but to be your husband and to rule over you (1 Tim. 2:12; 1 Cor. 11:3, 8).

3. Therefore, though in truth you may have more discretion than he, you should know that you and all that is yours are to be used as under your husband—even [in] everything (Eph. 5:24). Take heed, therefore, that what you do goes not in your name, but his; not to your exaltation, but his—doing all things so that by your dexterity and prudence,[65] not one of your husband's weaknesses is discovered to others by you. *"A virtuous woman is a crown to her husband: but she that maketh ashamed is as rottenness in his bones."* For then, as the wise man says, *"She will do him good and not evil all the days of her life"* (Prov. 12:4; 31:12).

4. Therefore act, and do still, as being under the power and authority of your husband.

---

63 **lording it over** – acting like the master or ruler of.
64 **conversion** – repenting of sin (that is, changing one's mind about sin and turning from it to God) andbelieving in the Lord and Savior Jesus Christ, resulting from the regenerating work of the Holy Spirit in the human heart.See FGB 195, *Conversion*.
65 **dexterity and prudence** – mental skill and cleverness, coupled with wisdom and caution.

Now, touching your behavior toward your children and servants: You are a parent[66] and a mistress,[67] and so you should demean[68] yourself. Besides, seeing [that] the believing woman is a figure of the Church, she should, as the Church, nourish and instruct her children and servants as the Church that she may answer in that particular[69] also. Truly, the wife being always at home has great advantage that way; therefore do it, and the Lord prosper your proceeding.[70]

From *Christian Behavior*, available from Chapel Library.

John Bunyan (1628-1688): English minister, preacher, and author; born at Elstow near Bedford, England.

---

66 See FGBs 204, *Biblical Parenthood*, and 229, *Motherhood*.
67 **mistress** – woman who rules.
68 **demean** – conduct; express.
69 **she may answer in that particular also** – her life may picture the church doing this as well.
70 **proceeding** – carrying out your course of action.

A Wife's Respect for Her Husband
RICHARD STEELE (1629-1692)

And the wife see that she reverence her husband. —Ephesians 5:33b
The great duty of every wife is to reverence her own husband. She stands obliged to many other duties, as you have heard, which lie common between them; but she is still signalized[71] by this. This is her peculiar qualification as she is a wife. Let her have never so much wisdom, learning, grace;[72] if she does not reverence her husband, she cannot be a good wife.

Look to her creation: She was made *after* man; he has some honor by his seniority. *"For Adam was first formed, then Eve"* (1 Tim. 2:13). She was made out of man; he was the rock whence she was hewn. *"For the man is not of the woman: but the woman of the man"* (1 Cor. 11:8). She was made *for* man: *"Neither was the man created for the woman; but the woman for the man"* (1 Cor. 11:9). So that it is not man that hath set this order, but God Himself. Look again to the Fall, and there you hear what God saith: *"Thy desire shall be to thy husband, and he shall rule over thee"* (Gen. 3:16). See in the New Testament, lest Christ's being *"made of a woman"* should seem to alter this inviolable law: *"Wives, submit yourselves unto your own husbands, as it is fit in the Lord"* (Col. 3:18). *"Likewise, ye wives, be in subjection to your own husbands"* (1 Peter 3:1). *"Your chaste conversation"* must be *"coupled with fear"* (v. 2)."*In the old time the holy women also...adorned themselves, being in subjection unto their own husbands"* (v. 5). And so in my text. Let her be never so great, never so good, and though her husband be never so mean and never so bad, yet this is her indispensable duty to reverence her husband...it is neither agreeable to nature nor decency to set the head below or no higher than the rib. And when she is resolved in this, then will she with much delight and ease go through her duty. A wise God hath ordered it thus, and therefore it is best.

I. For the first, the nature of this reverence: It is a true, cordial, and conjugal reverence, such as is peculiar to a good woman. And I conceive it is made up of,

1. The wife ought to honor and esteem her husband: *"All the wives shall give to their husbands honour, both to great and small"* (Esth. 1:20). To this end, she ought to contemplate all the excellencies of his person, whether of body or mind; to set a due value upon them and not to think meanly[73] of everything

---
71 **signalized** – characterized; marked conspicuously.
72 **Let...grace** – no matter how much wisdom, learning, and grace she may have.
73 **meanly** – poorly; as having little worth.

in her husband…And if the husband be but meanly accomplished,[74] yet she ought highly to value the excellency of his place, seeing the Holy Ghost hath in this very respect styled him *"the image and glory of God"* (1 Cor. 11:7). Whatever he is in himself or to others, yet to the wife he is a nonesuch.[75] Such you esteemed him when you chose him, and so you ought still to esteem him…The wife ought to consider that her honor and respect among her family and neighbors doth very much rise and fall according to that which she bears to her husband, so that in honoring him she honors herself.

2. This reverence is made up of love: Which though it be most pressed upon the husband, yet is also the duty of the wife: *"Teach the young women to be sober, to love their husbands, to love their children"* (Titus 2:4). Thus Sarah, Rebekah, and Rachel left parents, friends, and country out of their entire love to their husbands…And indeed there is no better means to increase the husband's love than the wife's reverence, and that alone will make this sweet and easy.

3. Fear[76] is the third ingredient into the reverence that the wife owes unto her husband…this is required: A *"chaste conversation[77] coupled with fear"* (1 Peter 3:2). The one is not sufficient without the other. This…is no more than a cautious diligence to please him and care lest she should offend him…

II. Now, let us trace this reverence of the wife to her husband in its pattern, laid before her in the context of these words. Here I affirm these two things:

1. That the wife ought to reverence her husband, as the church doth Jesus Christ: So, verse 22: *"Wives, submit yourselves unto your own husbands, as unto the Lord,"* and verse 24, *"Therefore as the church is subject unto Christ, so let the wives be to their own husbands in every thing."* Examples are prevalent, especially of wise and good people. Here is the example of all the wise and godly people in the world to persuade the wife to reverence her husband. The Apostle seems to say that it is as much a duty in the wife to be subject to the husband, as it is in the church to be subject to Christ…Two things proclaim the reverence that the church bears to Christ:

(1) The matter of her subjection: That is in everything…She doth not yield to him only so far as her interest or appetite permits her, but when he requires it…So saith the Apostle: *"Let the wives be [subject] to their own husbands in every thing"* (v. 24), that is, in everything that is not forbidden by a

---

74 **meanly accomplished** – poorly skilled.
75 **nonesuch** – a person who has no equal; a model of excellence.
76 **fear** – a cautious diligence and care, not a slavish, cowering fear.
77 **chaste conversation** – holy, pure conduct.

higher power, even the Law of God. Indeed, if a thing be only inconvenient, the wife may mildly reason and show the inexpediency[78] of it; but if she cannot convince and satisfy her husband, she must, if there be no sin in the case, submit her reason and her will to his.

(2) The manner of her subjection speaks her reverence: and that is free, willing, and cheerful. Thus, the church yields up herself to the will of her Husband, insomuch as it is made a kind of proverbial pattern: *"With good will doing service, as to the Lord"* (Eph. 6:7), implying that the subjection and service that we perform to the Lord is with a goodwill. Such ought to be the subjection of the wife, most free and willing; so, as if there were but one will in two breasts…Therefore, a contradicting or grudging spirit is very unsuitable to the religious wife and ever leaves a sting in his heart and guilt in hers. For usually it is a sign of unmortified pride and self-conceit and entails the curse of unquietness upon the family…If the husband's government be too heavy, it is better for you to leave him to answer for his severity than for you to answer for your contempt.

2. The wife ought to reverence her husband, as the members do the Head. So, Ephesians 5:23: *"For the husband is the head of the wife."* He is a head for influence and sympathy: that is her privilege. He is a head for eminence and rule: that is his. And how should she expect *benefit* from her head, if she does not *honor* her head? To dishonor a man's head is always ranked among unnatural sins (1 Cor. 11:4)…She must not cross the purposes of her head. It is preposterous for the head to go one way and the rib another. She must readily follow the directions and counsels of her head, for the members must not teach the head which way to go. They support it, but they do not direct it… it will be the wisdom and duty of the wife to be subject to the husband as unto her head (except cases wherein the head is crazed or notoriously distempered[79]).

III. This hath brought us to the third thing, by which the reverence of the wife is described and that is by the effects thereof. And they also are,

1. In word: *"For out of the abundance of the heart the mouth speaketh"* (Matt. 12:34). If there be that inward fear and respect in the heart, which God requires, it will be legible in the words of their mouths. The same law that binds the heart in this case doth also govern the tongue. *"In her tongue is the law of kindness"* (Prov. 31:26). And here certainly *"a wholesome tongue is a tree of life,"* whereas *"perverseness therein is a breach in the spirit"* (Prov. 15:4.)

---

78 **inexpediency** – disadvantages; unprofitableness.
79 **distempered** – mentally disordered.

Now this reverence in the wife is showed,

(1) *In her words of her husband*: Which should always be composed of respect and honor. Thus Sarah is brought in by the Apostle: *"Even as Sara obeyed Abraham, calling him lord: whose daughters ye are, as long as ye do well"* (1 Peter 3:6). And this was the language of her heart, as you heard before out of Genesis 18:12. And no wife is too great or good to imitate her example in the main by giving respectful titles and expressions of her husband…all the reproach and ignominy[80] that they pour out on their husbands doth infallibly redound[81] to their own shame, their honor and respect standing and falling together.

(2) The words of the wife to her husband ought to be full of reverence. She should beware, (i) Of an excess in the quantity, not preposterously interrupting her husband while he is speaking, nor answering ten words for one. For silence doth more commend the wisdom of a woman than speech; and she that is wise spareth her words. Though she seem to be religious, yet if she do not bridle her tongue, her religion is vain. And, (ii)She must beware of a defect in the quality of them, namely, of meekness and respect. For the great study of the wife should be to get a *"meek and quiet spirit, which in the sight of God,"* yea, and of man too, *"is of great price"* (1 Peter 3:4). When the heart is once meekened[82] by the grace of God, then her words will savor[83] of it, and not until then…Hath not God said, *"A soft tongue breaketh the bone"* (Prov. 25:15)? [This] is more than any virulent[84] tongue can do…It will be an unspeakable comfort at death and judgment to reflect upon the victories that their patience hath gotten and how oft their quiet silence and mild answers have kept the peace…This is certain: if meekness and respect will not prevail, anger and passion never can…

2. The effects of a wife's reverence to her husband must be in *deed* also. And that by obedience to his directions and restraints…The wife is bound in conscience to obey her husband in every thing that is not contrary to the will of God. Indeed, if he command her to do any thing that is sinful by the Law of God—if he should bid her tell a lie, bear false witness, or the like—she must modestly and resolvedly refuse it. If he forbid her to do anything, that is by God's command made an undispensable duty unto her—if he should absolutely forbid her to pray, to read the Scripture, to sanctify the Lord's day,

---

80 **ignominy** – dishonor.
81 **redound** – return as a consequence.
82 **meekened** – made submissive; humbled.
83 **savor** – show traces of the presence or influence of.
84 **virulent** – violently bitter; spiteful.

or the like—then she must *"obey God rather than men"* (Acts 5:29). But in all other cases, though she may respectfully persuade with him, yet if he insist upon it, her obedience will be her best sacrifice and her compliance will be the means to make her yoke the more easy…

The house is her proper place: for she is the *beauty* of the house. There her business lies, there she is safe…When sun and moon both disappear, the sky is dark; and when both husband and wife are abroad, many disorders breed at home; and you know whose character it is: *"She is loud and stubborn; her feet abide not in her house"* (Prov. 7:11.)

So also where the husband judges most convenient to dwell, there the wife must cheerfully consent to dwell with him, though it may be, either in respect of her friends or of his, more uncomfortable to her. Thus…He that appoints them to *"love their husbands"* (Titus 2:4) doth in the next verse enjoin them to be *"discreet, chaste, keepers at home, good, obedient to their own husbands, that the word of God be not blasphemed"* (2:5). For though even good women be put to silence, yet good works never can…

Few husbands [are] so bad, but the discretion and respect of a wife would reform them; and few wives [are] so ill-tempered, but the wisdom and affection of a husband would make them better.

From "What Are the Duties of Husbands and Wives Towards Each Other?" in *Puritan Sermons 1659-1689, Being the Morning Exercises at Cripplegate,* Vol. 2, *reprinted by Richard Owen Roberts, Publishers. This sermon is available in an abridged booklet from Chapel Library.*

Richard Steele (1629-1692): Puritan preacher and author; born at Bartholmley, Cheshire, England.

Duties That Preserve Marriage
WILLIAM GOUGE (1575-1653)

The first, highest, chiefest, and most absolutely necessary common mutual duty between man and wife is matrimonial unity, whereby husband and wife do account one another to be one flesh and accordingly preserve the inviolable[85] union whereby they are knit together. This is that duty which the Apostle enjoins to husbands and wives in these words, *"Let not the wife depart from her husband… and letnot the husband put away his wife"* (1 Cor. 7:10-11). He there speaks of renouncing each other and making the matrimonial bond frustrate[86] and of no effect. [This] bond he would have to be kept firm and inviolable and they two who are thereby made one, constantly to remain one and not to make themselves two again. This matrimonial unity is so necessary as it may not be disunited or dissolved though one be a Christian and the other a pagan. *"If any brother,"* says the Apostle, *"hath a wife that believeth not, and she be pleased to dwell with him, let him not put her away. And the woman which hath an husband that believeth not, and if he be pleased to dwell with her, let her not leave him"* (1 Cor. 7:12-13)…

Of Mutual Peace Between Man and Wife
Among other means of maintaining an inward loving affection between man and wife, outward mutual peace, concord,[87] and agreement is one of the principal. Whereupon, the Apostle exhorts to keep the unity of the spirit in the bond of peace (Eph. 4:3); for peace is a bond that tieth one to another and makes them to be as one, even one in spirit. On the contrary side, outward discord disunites men's spirits. We are enjoined to follow peace with all men: how much more of all persons ought husbands to have peace with their wives and wives with their husbands? They are nearer than brothers and sisters. Behold then how good and pleasant a thing it is for them to dwell together in unity (Ps. 133:1)! Dwell together they must: but without peace, there is no dwelling together. It is better to dwell in a corner of the housetop than with a contentious woman in a wide house (Prov. 21:9, 19; 25:24). Persons at variance [would be] far better out of sight and place, than present together. Out of sight and place, man and wife must *not* be; at peace, therefore, they *must* be. Mutual peace between them is a great refreshing to their minds, being beaten with the discords of others. It is said that a wife is in this respect a haven to man: how much more man to his wife?...

---

85 **inviolable** – not to be violated.
86 **frustrate** – useless; fruitless.
87 **concord** – harmony or agreement of interests.

For Maintaining Peace

1. Avoid Offence: All offences, so much as possibly may be, must be avoided. The husband must be watchful over himself that he give no offence to his wife, and so the wife on the other side. Offences cause contentions.

2. Take Not Offence: When an offence is given by the one party, it must not be taken by the other, but rather passed by. Then will not peace be broken. The second blow makes the fray.[88]

3. Offer Reconciliation: If both be incensed together, the fire is likely to be the greater. With the greater speed therefore must they both labor to put it out. Wrath must not lie in bed with two such bedfellows; neither may they part beds for wrath's sake. That this fire may be the sooner quenched, they must both strive first to offer reconciliation. Theirs is the glory, who do first begin, for they are most properly the blessed peacemakers. Not to accept peace when it is offered is more than heathenish; but when wrath is incensed, to seek atonement is the duty of a Christian and a grace that comes from above.

4. Take No Part with Others: Neither children, servants, nor any other in the family must be bolstered up by the one against the other. The man's partaking with any of the house against his wife or the wife against her husband is a usual cause of contention between man and wife.

5. Make Not Comparisons: They must forbear to twit one another in the teeth[89] with the husbands or wives of other persons or with their own former husbands or wives (in case they have had any before). Comparisons in this kind are very odious. They stir up much passion, and cause great contentions.

6. Be Not Jealous: Above all, they must take heed of rash and unjust jealousy, which is the bane[90] of marriage and greatest cause of discontent that can be given between man and wife. Jealous persons are ready to pick quarrels and to seek occasions of discord. They will take every word, look, action, and motion in the worse part and so take offence where none is given. When jealousy is once kindled, it is as a flaming fire that can hardly be put out. It makes the party whom it possesses implacable.[91]

7. Please One Another: In all things that may stand with a good conscience, they must endeavor to please one another and suffer their own will to be crossed rather than discontent to be given to the other. Saint Paul

---

88 **fray** – noisy fight.
89 **twit…in the teeth** – harassing with persistent criticism.
90 **bane** – ruin; fatal injury.
91 **implacable** – impossible to pacify; irreconcilable.

notes this as a common mutual duty belonging to them both and expresses their care thereof under a word that signifies more than ordinary care and implies a dividing of the mind into divers thoughts, casting this way, that way, and every way how to give best content…

Of Husbands' and Wives' Mutual Prayers

The matter whereabout husbands' and wives' mutual providence ought to be conversant is in general the good of one another. Each of them [ought to] do that for the other, which Solomon in particular applies to a wife, viz.,[92] good and not evil all the days of their life. Now the good of man extends to his soul, body, good name, and goods.

Prayer a Mutual Duty

A general duty tending to the good of all these is prayer. Saint Peter requires such a carriage of man and wife one towards another, as their prayers be not hindered. He takes it for grant[ed] that prayer is a mutual duty that one owes to the other, which duty Isaac performed for his wife (Gen. 25:21). Herein may man and wife be helpful each to [the] other in all things needful to either of them. It is the means that God in wisdom has sanctified for the obtaining of every needful blessing for others or ourselves. By many it is counted but a slight duty and of small use; but the truth is that to perform it aright in truth and faith is both difficult in the deed and powerful in the effect. It is the best duty that one can perform for another and the least to be neglected. We heard before that Isaac prayed for his wife: to show the good he did to her thereby, it is noted that the Lord was entreated of him. So she, being barren before, by that means conceived. All the physic[93] in the world could not have done her so much good. Always, therefore, without ceasing is this duty to be performed. Whensoever man and wife make any prayer, therein they must be mindful of one another: yea and often must they of purpose take occasion to make prayers in special one for another, and that both in absence and in presence of one another.

This latter does especially concern the husband, who is as a priest unto his wife and ought to be her mouth to God when they two are together…

Of the Things for Which Husbands and Wives are to Pray Alone: There are sundry needful blessings which husbands and wives are to pray for that appertain only to themselves and are most meet to be mentioned in private prayer between themselves, as—

---

92 **viz.** – from the Latin *videlicet,* that is to say; namely.
93 **physic** – medical treatment; medicine.

1. That as they two are one flesh, so they may be also one spirit: that their hearts may be as one, knit together by a true, spiritual, matrimonial love: always delighting one in another, ever helpful one to another, and ready with all willingness and cheerfulness to perform all those duties which they owe one to another.

2. That their marriage bed may be sanctified: As it is by God's ordinance, so it may remain to them by their well using it, a bed undefiled. There is no other thing for which mutual prayer in private between man and wife is more needful…because of the natural heat of lust which is in most. If it be not by prayer assuaged[94] (the best means for that purpose), it may prove a defilement of the undefiled bed and man and wife [may] become adulterers one to another. As other things, so this also is sanctified by the Word and prayer. The Word gives a warrant and direction for the use of it. Prayer both seasons it and procures a blessing upon it.

3. That they may have children and those such as may be heirs of salvation and live in this world to their own and others' good…

4. That God would give them competency of this world's goods, and other good means to nourish, nurture, and place forth their children well: and a sufficiency for the maintenance of their family and of that estate wherein God sets them.

5. That such needful gifts and graces as are wanting in either of them may be wrought: and such vices and infirmities as they are subject unto may be redressed.[95]

These and many other like things give occasion to man and wife in special manner to pray one *for* another and one *with* another…

Of Husbands' and Wives' Mutual Care for One Another's Salvation

Of the Particular Duty of Husbands in This Respect

From the general duty of prayer which is profitable to all things, I come to the particular branches of man and wife's mutual provident[96] care. [I] will first begin with that which is first to be sought: the good of one another's soul. [This] the Apostle intimates to be a thing to be sought after, where he says, *"For what knowest thou, O wife, whether thou shalt save thy husband? or how knowest thou, O man, whether thou shalt save thy wife?"* (1 Cor. 7:16). Saint Peter enjoins wives to do their endeavor to win their husbands (1 Peter 3:1-5). And Saint Paul sets before husbands the pattern of Christ's love, which had

---

94 **assuaged** – made less intense; diminished.
95 **redressed** – made right; corrected.
96 **provident** – exercising foresight; making provision for the future.

especial respect to the soul and the salvation thereof (Eph. 5:22-32). This is a mutual duty appertaining to them both, which Saint Peter further implies where he styles them coheirs of the grace of life (1 Peter 3:7).

It is the greatest good that one can possibly do for another, to be a means of helping forward his salvation. And there is nothing that can more soundly and firmly knit the heart of one to another than to be a means thereof.

Of Husbands' and Wives' Care to Win One the Other When One of Them Is Not [a Believer]

That the salvation of the soul may be the better effected, respect must be had to the present and particular estate of husband or wife. If one be a believer [and] the other not, the believer must use all the means that may be to draw on the other also to believe. If both be believers, their mutual care must be to edify one another in their most holy faith.

For the first, it is the main drift of Saint Peter's exhortation to believing wives about their conversation[97] to draw on their unbelieving husbands to the true faith…Now if this duty appertain to a wife, much more to a husband, who is appointed a head to his wife and a savior. To this end does Saint Paul advise believing husbands and wives that are married to unbelievers to dwell with them…

Means of Conversion the Best Cause of Love

If it please the Lord to give such a blessing to the endeavour of a husband or wife, as to be a means of the conversion of their bedfellow, then will the party converted both entirely love the other and also heartily bless God… that ever they were so nearly linked together…

Of Husbands and Wives Edifying One Another

The second duty tending to the soul's salvation is that two believers being married together endeavor mutually to build up one another more and more. One Christian owes this duty to another, much more man and wife…A spiritual edifying of one another is the best use that we can make and ought to make of those joints and bonds whereby we are knit one to another. By virtue of them, the body (namely the mystical body of Christ) receiveth increase to the edifying of itself and increaseth with the increase of God (Col. 2:19). Now the bond of marriage being of all other the firmest and that whereby we are nearest knit together, by virtue of what bond should we edify one another, if not by virtue of the marriage bond?…

---

97 **conversation** – conduct.

Man and Wife to Prevent Sin in One Another

That it is a mutual duty for husbands and wives, so much as they can, to prevent sin one in another is evident by that reason that the Apostle uses: to keep them from defrauding[98] one another in these words: *"That Satan tempt you not"* (1 Cor. 7:5). For out of the scope and matter of those words, this general doctrine may be gathered: Husbands and wives ought to be careful to keep one another from the temptations of Satan, that is, from sin, whereunto all his temptations tend…

Direction for Preventing Sin

For the better effecting of this duty, husbands and wives must be watchful over one another and observe what sins either of them are given unto or what occasions are offered to draw either of them into sin…If both should be testy and hasty to wrath, when the one sees the other first moved, the party whose passion is not yet stirred ought the rather to be settled and composed to all meekness and patience, lest, if both together be provoked, the whole household be set on fire…

Of Husbands and Wives Redressing Sin in One Another

When either husband or wife is fallen into any sin, a mutual duty it is for the other to use what redress may be of that sin. As if one of them were wounded, the other must take care for the healing of that wound. Abigail performed her duty in this kind, when after she had heard what churlish entertainment her husband gave to David's servants, she hastened to carry store of provision to David, and humbled herself before him (1 Sam. 25:23). [This] so moved David to assuage his wrath. Yea, she took a seasonable time also to tell her husband his fault and the danger whereinto he brought himself thereby. More directly and with better success did Jacob redress the superstition or rather idolatry of his wife Rachel, as may be gathered by comparing Genesis 31:19, 34 and 35:2, 4. A brother at large must not suffer sin to lie on his brother: much less may husband or wife the one upon the other.

It is a Branch of Hatred to Suffer Sin to Lie on Any

Thou shalt not hate thy brother (says the Law) and suffer sin to lie on him (Lev. 19:17). To do this then is a token and fruit of hatred. If a husband should see his wife or a wife her husband lying in the fire or water, ready to be burnt or drowned, and not afford their best help to pull them out, might they not justly be thought to hate them? But sin is as fire and water,

---

98 **defrauding** – depriving by dishonest means; cheating.

which will burn and drown men in perdition. This duty may be performed by meek instructions, pithy⁹⁹ persuasions, and gentle reproofs, yea, and by the help of some good minister or other discreet and faithful friend…

How Growth in Grace May be Helped Forward

This duty may be the better effected by these means following:

1. By taking notice of the beginning and least measure of grace¹⁰⁰ and approving the same.

2. By frequent conference about such things as concern the same: mutually propounding questions one to another thereabouts and answering the same.

3. By their mutual practice and example: making themselves each to [the] other a pattern of piety.

4. By performing exercises of religion, as praying, singing psalms, reading the Word, and the like together.

5. By maintaining holy and religious exercises in the family: Though this duty especially appertans to the husband, yet the wife must put her husband in mind thereof, if he forget it, and stir him up, if he be backward…No man's persuasion in this kind can so much prevail with a man as his wife's.

6. By stirring up one another to go to the house of God, to hear the Word, partake of [Christ's ordinances], and conscionably perform all the parts of God's public worship.

From *Of Domestical Duties* reprinted by Puritan Reprints and Still Waters Revival Books.

William Gouge (1575-1653): Puritan minister for 46 years at Blackfriars, London; born in Stratford-Bow, Middlesex County, England.

---

99 **pithy** – condensed and forcible in expression or style.
100 **least measure of grace** – a small step forward, a bit of progress.

Thoughts on Finding a Marriage Partner
JOHN ANGELL JAMES (1785-1859)

Marriage is a step of incalculable importance and ought never to be taken without the greatest consideration and the utmost caution. If the duties of this state are so numerous and so weighty, and if the right discharge of these obligations as well the happiness of our whole life…depend, as they necessarily must do, in no small measure upon the choice we make of a husband or wife, then let reason determine with what deliberation we should advance to such a connection.

It is obvious that no decision of our whole earthly existence requires more of the exercise of a calm judgment than this, yet observation proves how rarely the judgment is allowed to give counsel and how generally the imagination and the passions settle the business. A very great portion of the misery and of the crime with which society is depraved and afflicted is the result of ill-formed marriages. If mere passion without prudence or covetousness without love be allowed to guide the choice, no wonder that it is improperly done or that it is highly disastrous in its consequences. How often are passion and covetousness alone consulted…If it were merely the comfort of the married pair themselves that was concerned, it would be a matter of less consequence, a stake of less value. But the well-being of a family, not only for this world, but for the next, and equally so the well-being of their descendants, even to a remote period, depends upon this union. In the ardor of passion, few are disposed to listen to the counsels of prudence. Perhaps there is no advice, generally speaking, more thrown away than that which is offered on the subject of marriage. Most persons, especially if they are already attached to a selected [person], although they have not committed themselves by a promise or even a declaration, will go on in the pursuit, blinded by love to the indiscretion of their choice…Upon such individuals, reasoning is wasted. They must be left to gain wisdom in the only way by which some will acquire it: *painful experience*. To others who may be yet disengaged and disposed to hearken to the language of advice, the following remarks are offered.

In the affair of marriage, be guided by the advice of parents or guardians. Parents have no right to select for you, nor ought you to select for yourself without consulting with them. How far they are vested with authority to prohibit you from marrying a person whom they disapprove is a point of casuistry,[101] very difficult to determine. If you are of age and able to provide

---

101 **casuistry** – the application of rules and principles to questions of what is right and wrong.

for yourselves or are likely to be well provided for by those to whom you are about to be united, it is a question whether they can do anything more than advise and persuade. But until you are of age, they have positive authority to forbid. It is an undutiful[102] act in you to form connections without their knowledge and to carry them on against their prohibitions. Their objections ought always, I admit, to be founded on reason and not on caprice,[103] pride, or cupidity.[104] For where this is the case and children are of full age and are guided in their choice by prudence, piety, and affection, they certainly may and must be left to decide for themselves.

Where, however, parents rest their objections on sufficient grounds and show plain and palpable[105] reasons for prohibiting a connection, there it is the manifest duty of sons and especially of daughters to give it up. A union formed in opposition to the reasonable objection of a discreet father or mother is very rarely a happy one. The bitter cup is rendered additionally bitter, in such a case, by the wormwood and gall of self-reproach. What miseries of this kind have we all seen! How many beacons are set up, if young people would but look at them, to warn them against the folly of giving themselves up to the impulse of an imprudent attachment and following it to a close against the advice, remonstrance,[106] and prohibition of their parents! Very seldom does that connection prove otherwise than a source of wretchedness, on which the frown of an affectionate and wise father and mother fell from the beginning. God seems to rise up in judgment and to support the parents' authority by confirming their displeasure with His own.

Marriage should in every case be formed upon the basis of mutual attachment.[107] If there be no love before marriage, it cannot be expected there should be any after it.[108] Lovers, as all are supposed to be who are looking forward to this union, without love,[109] have no right to expect happiness. The coldness of indifference is soon likely, in their case, to be changed into aversion.[110] There ought to be personal attachment. If there be

---

102 **undutiful** – lacking respect.
103 **caprice** – unpredictable change of mind; whim.
104 **cupidity** – greed for material wealth.
105 **palpable** – obvious.
106 **remonstrance** – earnest opposition or protest.
107 **mutual attachment** – affection between both parties.
108 Many couples have entered marriage without in-depth knowledge, let alone love. God can bless with growing love even when this occurs.
109 **love** – Biblical *agape* love can be defined as the act of the will to give oneself unconditionally to another. This love gives birth to the best of feelings.
110 **aversion** – feeling of intense dislike.

anything, even in the exterior, that excites disgust, the banns[111] are forbidden by the voice of nature. I do not say that beauty of countenance or elegance of form is necessary—by no means. A pure and strong attachment has often existed in the absence of these. I will not take upon me to determine that it is absolutely impossible to love deformity. But we certainly ought not to unite ourselves with it unless we can love it or at least are so enamored with the fascination of mental qualities that may be united with it, as to lose sight of the body in the charms of the mind, the heart, and the manners. All I contend for is that to proceed to marriage against absolute dislike and revulsion is irrational, base, and sinful.

But love should respect the mind, as well as the body. For to be attached to an individual simply on the ground of beauty is to fall in love with a doll, or a statue, or a picture. Such an attachment is lust or fancy, but certainly not a rational affection. If we love the body, but do not love the mind, the heart, and the manners, our regard is placed upon the inferior part of the person, and therefore, only upon that which by disease may be next year a very different thing to what it is now. Nothing fades so soon as beauty. It is like the delicate bloom of an attractive fruit and, if there be nothing agreeable underneath, will be thrown away in disgust when that is brushed off and thrown away too, by the very hand of him that plucks it. It is so commonly remarked as to be proverbial, that the charms of mind increase by acquaintance, while those of the exterior diminish. While the former easily reconciles us to a plain countenance, the latter excites, by the power of contrast, a distaste for the insipidity,[112] ignorance, and heartlessness with which they are united, like gaudy,[113] scentless flowers, growing in a desert. Instead of determining to stake our happiness upon the act of gathering these blooming weeds, to place them in our bosom, let us ask how they will look a few years hence or how they will adorn and bless our habitation. Let us ask, will the understanding, united with that countenance, render its subject fit to be my companion and the instructor of my children? Will that temper patiently bear with my weaknesses, kindly consult my tastes, affectionately study my comfort? Will those manners please me in solitude, as well as in society? Will those habits render my dwelling pleasant to me and to my friends? We must try these matters, and hold our passions back, that we may take counsel with our judgment, and suffer reason to come down and talk with us in the cool of the evening.

---

111 **banns** – public announcements of a proposed marriage.
112 **insipidity** – dullness; lacking character.
113 **gaudy** – brightly colored.

Chapter 4—Marriage: Thoughts on Finding a Marriage Partner

Such then is the love on which marriage should be contracted: love to the whole person; love to the mind, heart, and manners, as well as to the countenance and form; love tempered with respect. This only is the attachment that is likely to survive the charms of novelty, the spoliation[114] of disease, and the influence of time. [This only] is likely to support the tender sympathies and exquisite sensibilities of the conjugal state and render man and wife to the verge of extreme old age, what it was the intention of Him Who instituted the marriage union they should be—the help and the comfort of each other.

By what language then, sufficiently strong and indignant, can we reprobate[115] those compacts, so disgraceful and yet so common, by which marriage is converted into a money speculation, a trading enterprise, a mere business of pounds, shillings, and pence?[116]…Young people themselves should be extremely careful on their own part to let no persuasions of others, no impulse of their own covetousness, no anxiety to be their own masters and mistresses, no ambition for secular splendor induce them to enter into a connection to which they are not drawn by the solicitations[117] of a pure and virtuous love. What will a large house, splendid furniture, a gay equipage,[118] and fashionable entertainments do for their possessor in the absence of connubial love? "Is it for these baubles, these toys," exclaims the wretched heart as it awakens, alas! too late, in some sad scene of domestic woe, "Is it for this I have bartered away myself, my happiness, my honor?"

O there is a sweetness, a charm, a power to please in pure and mutual affection, though it be cherished in the humblest abode, maintained amidst the plainest circumstances, and has to contend with many difficulties! Compared with [this], the elegance and brilliance of worldly grandeur are but as the splendor of an eastern palace to one of the bowers[119] of the Garden of Eden…

Marriage should ever be contracted with the strictest regard to the rules of prudence[120]…Imprudent marriages, as we have already considered, spread far and wide their bad consequences and also send these consequences down to posterity. Understanding is given to us to control the passions and the imagination. They, who in an affair of such consequence as choosing a

---

114 **spoliation** – damage; injury.
115 **reprobate** – reject as invalid.
116 **pounds, shillings, and pence** – terms for English money and coins.
117 **solicitations** – attraction.
118 **gay equipage** – small articles of domestic furniture, such as fine china or glass.
119 **bowers** – places closed in or overarched with branches of trees, shrubs, or other plants.
120 **prudence** – the ability to discern with caution the most suitable course of action.

companion for life, set aside the testimony of the former and listen only to the voice of the latter, have, in that instance at least, forfeited the character of a rational being and sunk to the level of those creatures who are wholly governed by appetite unchecked by reason. Prudence would prevent, if it were allowed to guide the conduct of mankind, a very large portion of human misery.

In the business before us, it would allow none to marry until they had a prospect of support. It is perfectly obvious to me that the present generation of young people are not distinguished by a discretion of this kind. Many are too much in haste to enter the conjugal state and place themselves at the heads of families before they have any rational hope of being able to support them. As soon almost as they arrive at the age of manhood, whether they are in business or not, before they have ascertained whether their business will succeed or not, they look round for a wife and make a hasty, perhaps an injudicious, selection. A family comes on before they have adequate means of maintaining it…Let young people exercise their reason and their foresight. If they will not, but are determined to rush into the expenses of housekeeping before they have opened sources to meet them, let them hear, in spite of the syren song of their imagination, the voice of faithful warning and prepare to eat the bitter herbs of useless regrets…

"It has been said that no class of men err so much in this article as *ministers*. But surely, this cannot be admitted. It cannot be supposed that those whose office it is to inculcate prudence should themselves be proverbial for indiscretion?…A minister is to recommend neatness and all the decencies of life, and would he marry a slattern?[121] A minister is to shew that the ornament of a meek and quiet spirit is in the sight of God of great price, and would he marry a scold?[122] A minister is to stand in the same relation to all his people who demand his love and service, and would he marry a female who would fondly attach herself to a few cronies, listen to all their secrets and divulge her own, and form cabals[123] and schisms, which will render his residence unpleasant or occasion his removal?"

To my brethren in the ministry I do recommend, and recommend with an earnestness that I have no language sufficiently emphatic to express, the greatest caution in this most delicate and important affair. In their case, the effects of an imprudent marriage are felt in the church of the living God…How can he exhibit in his domestic constitution the beautiful order

---

121 **slattern** – a dirty, untidy woman.
122 **scold** – a woman who persistently nags or criticizes.
123 **cabals** – small, exclusive groups of people.

and harmony that should prevail in every Christian family, especially in every minister's house, without the intelligent and industrious cooperation of his wife? How can this be expected of one who has no intelligence or industry? Not only much of the comfort, but of the character of a minister depends upon his wife, and what is of still greater consequence, much of his usefulness…Considering, therefore, how much mischief may be done by their indiscretion, ministers should raise imprudence in marriage to the rank of a great sin…

Marriage should always be formed with a due regard to the dictates of religion. A pious person should not marry anyone who is not also pious. It is not desirable to be united to an individual, even of a different denomination, who as a point of conscience attends her own place of worship. It is not pleasant on a Sabbath morning to separate and go one to one place of worship and the other to another. The most delightful walk that a holy couple can take is to the house of God in company and when, in reference to the high themes of redemption and the invisible realities of eternity, they take sweet counsel together. No one would willingly lose this…If however, the comfort of the parties only were concerned, it would be a matter of less consequence. But it is a matter of conscience and an affair in which we have no option. *"She is at liberty to married to whom she will,"* says the Apostle, speaking to the case of a widow, but *"only in the Lord"* (1 Cor. 7:39).

Now though this was said in reference to a female, all the reasons of the Law belong with equal force to the other sex. This appears to me to be not only advice, but also law. [It] is as binding upon the conscience as any other law that we find in the Word of God. The incidental manner in which this injunction occurs is…the strongest confirmation of the rule in all cases, where marriage is in prospect and where there has been no engagement previous to conversion. As to the other passage, where the Apostle commands us not to be *"unequally yoked together with unbelievers"* (2 Cor. 6:14), it does not apply to marriage except by inference, but to church fellowship or rather to association and conduct in general, in reference to which professing Christians are not to symbolize[124] with unbelievers. But if this be improper in regard to other matters, how much more so in that connection which has so powerful an influence over our character as well as our happiness? For a Christian, then, to marry an individual who is not decidedly and evidently a pious person is a direct opposition to the Word of God…A difference of taste in *minor* matters is an impediment in the way of domestic comfort. But to be opposed to each other on the all-important

---

124 **symbolize** – enter into union with.

subject of religion is a risk, even as it respects our comfort, which no prudent person should be induced on any considerations to incur. How can the higher ends of domestic constitution be answered, where one of the parents has not the spiritual qualifications necessary for accomplishing them? How can the work of religious education be conducted and the children be trained in the nurture and admonition of the Lord? As it respects individual and personal assistance in religious matters, do we not all want helps instead of hindrances? A Christian should make everything bend to religion, but allow religion to bend to nothing. This is the one thing needful, to which *everything* should be subordinate…The neglect of this plain and reasonable rule is becoming, I am afraid, more and more prevalent…In the excellent treatise that Mr. Jay published…he makes the following just and important remarks. "I am persuaded that it is very much owing to the prevalence of these indiscriminate and unhallowed connections, that we have fallen so far short of those men of God who are gone before us in our seclusion from the world, in the simplicity of our manners, in the uniformity of our profession, in the discharge of family worship, and in the training up of our households in the nurture and admonition of the Lord" (William Jay, 1769-1853).

No one should contemplate the prospect of such a connection as marriage without the greatest and most serious deliberation, nor without the most earnest prayer to God for direction. Prayer, however, to be acceptable to the Almighty, should be sincere and should be presented with a real desire to know and do His will. Many, I believe, act towards the Deity as they do towards their friends: they make up their minds and then ask to be directed. They have some doubts, and very often strong ones, of the propriety of the step they are about to take, which are gradually dissipated by their supplications until they have prayed themselves into a conviction that they are quite right in the decision, which they have in fact already made. To pray for direction in an affair that we know to be in opposition to God's Word and on which we have already resolved to act is adding hypocrisy to rebellion. If there be reason to believe that the individual who solicits a Christian to unite herself with him in marriage is not truly pious, what need has she of praying to be directed? This seems like asking the Almighty to be permitted to do that which He has forbidden to be done.

It cannot be sufficiently deplored that all suitable preparation for the marriage state is usually put aside for the busy activities of vanity, which in fact are but as dust in the balance of the conjugal destiny. Every thought, anticipation, and anxiety is too often absorbed in the selection of a house and furniture and in matters still more insignificant and frivolous. How common is it for a female to spend those hours, day after day and week after week, in communion with her milliner,[125] debating and discussing the subject of the color, form, and material, in which she is to shine forth in nuptial splendor, which ought to be employed in meditating the eventful step that is to fix for life her destiny, and that of her intended husband; as if the great object were to appear a gay and fashionable bride, rather than to be a good and happy wife…

"Study," says an old author, "the duties of marriage before you enter into it. There are crosses to be borne, there are snares to be avoided, and manifold obligations to be discharged, as well as great felicity to be enjoyed. And should no provision be made? [Lack of this results in] the frequent disappointments of that honorable estate. Hence that repentance which is at once too soon and too late. The husband knows not how to rule, and the wife knows not how to obey. Both are ignorant, both conceited, and both miserable."

In all thy ways acknowledge him, and he shall direct thy paths. —Proverbs 3:6

From *A Help to Domestic Happiness* reprinted by Soli Deo Gloria.

Richard Steele (1629-1692): Puritan preacher and author; born at Bartholmley, Cheshire, England.

---

125 **milliner** – one that makes, trims, designs, or sells hats.

The Marriage of the Lamb
CHARLES HADDON SPURGEON (1834-1892)

> *Let us be glad and rejoice, and give honour to him: for the marriage of the Lamb is , and his wife hath made herself ready. And to her was granted that she should be arrayed in fine linen, clean and white: for the fine linen is the righteousness of saints. —Revelation 19:7-8*

The marriage of the lamb is the result of the eternal gift of the father. Our Lord says, *"Thine they were, and thou gavest them me"* (John 17:6). His prayer was, *"Father, I will that they also, whom thou hast given me, be with me where I am; that they may behold my glory, which thou hast given me: for thou lovedst me before the foundation of the world"* (John 17:24). The Father made a choice, and the chosen He gave to His Son to be His portion. For them He entered into a covenant of redemption,[126] whereby He was pledged in due time to take upon Himself their nature, pay the penalty of their offenses, and set them free to be His own. Beloved, that which was arranged in the councils of eternity and settled there between the high contracting parties is brought to its ultimate end in that day when the Lamb takes unto Himself in everlasting union the whole of those whom His Father gave Him from of old.

This is the completion of the betrothal, which took place with each of them in time. I shall not attempt elaborate distinctions; but as far as you and I were concerned, the Lord Jesus betrothed each one of us unto Himself in righteousness, when first we believed on Him. Then He took us to be His and gave Himself to be ours, so that we could sing, *"My beloved is mine, and I am his"* (Song 2:16). This was the essence of the marriage. Paul, in the Epistle to the Ephesians, represents our Lord as already married to the church. This may be illustrated by the Oriental custom, by which, when the bride is betrothed, all the sanctities of marriage are involved in those espousals. Yet there may be a considerable interval before the bride is taken to her husband's house. She dwells with her former household, and has not yet forgotten her kindred and her father's house, though still she is espoused in truth and righteousness. Afterwards, she is brought home on an appointed day, the day that we should call the actual marriage. Yet the betrothal is to Orientals of the very essence of the marriage. Well, then, you and I are betrothed to our Lord *today*, and He is joined to us by inseparable

---

126 **covenant of redemption** – the term used to describe the agreement between the members of the Godhead, especially between the Father and the Son, regarding the plan of redemption: God the Father purposed 1. the accomplishment of salvation through the Person and work of God the Son and 2. the application of salvation through the regenerating power of the Spirit.

bonds. He does not wish to part with us, nor could we part from Him. He is the delight of our souls, and He rejoices over us with singing. Rejoice that He has chosen you and called you, and through the betrothal look forward to the marriage! Feel even now, that though in the world, you are not of it: your destiny does not lie here among these frivolous sons of men. Our home is henceforth on high!

The marriage day indicates the perfecting of the body of the church. I have already told you that the church will then be completed, and it is not so now. Adam lay asleep, and the Lord took out of his side a rib and fashioned thereof a helpmeet for him. Adam saw her not when she was in the forming; but he opened his eyes, and before him was the perfect form of his helpmeet. Beloved, the true church is now in the forming…The church which is affianced[127] unto the heavenly Bridegroom is not visible as yet, for she is in the process of formation. The Lord will not allow such simpletons as we are to see His half-finished work. But the day will come when He shall have completed His new creation, and then will He bring her forth whom He has made for the second Adam, to be His delight to all eternity. The church is not perfected yet. We read of that part of it which is in heaven, that *"they without us should not be made perfect"* (Heb. 11:40). Unless you and I get there, if we are true believers, there cannot be a perfect church in glory! The music of the heavenly harmonies yet lacks certain voices. Some of its needful notes are too bass for those already, and others are too high for them, until the singers come who are ordained to give the choir its fullest range…Beloved, in the day of the marriage of the Lamb, the chosen shall all be there—the great and the small—even all the believers who are wrestling hard this day with sins and doubts and fears. Every living member of the living church shall be there to be married to the Lamb!

By this marriage is meant more than I have told you: There is the home-bringing. You are not to live here forever in these tents of Kedar, among a people of a strange tongue. The blessed Bridegroom cometh to take you to the happy country, where you shall no longer say, "My soul is among lions." All the faithful shall soon be away to thy land, O Emmanuel! We shall dwell in the land that floweth with milk and honey, the land of the unclouded and unsetting sun, the home of the blessed of the Lord! Happy indeed will be the home-bringing of the perfect church!

The marriage is the coronal-avowal. The church is the bride of the great King, and He will set the crown upon her head and make her to be known as His true spouse forever! Oh, what a day that will be, when every member

---

127 **affianced** – bound in a pledge to marry; betrothed.

of Christ shall be crowned in Him, and with Him, and every member of the mystical body shall be glorified in the glory of the Bridegroom! Oh, may I be there in that day! Brethren, we must be with our Lord in the fight if we would be with Him in the victory. We must be with Him in wearing the crown of thorns, if we are to be with Him in wearing the crown of glory. We must be faithful by His grace, even unto death, if we are to share the glory of His endless life.

I cannot tell you all it means, but certainly this marriage signifies that all who have believed in Him shall then enter into a bliss that shall never end, a bliss that no fear approacheth or doubt becloudeth. They shall be forever with the Lord, forever glorified with Him! Expect not lips of clay fitly to speak on such a theme. Tongues of fire are needed and words that fall like fire-flakes on the soul.

A day will come, the Day of days, time's crown and glory, when, all conflict, risk, and judgment ended for ever, the saints, arrayed in the righteousness of Christ, shall be eternally one with Him in living, loving, lasting union, partaking together of the same glory, the glory of the Most High! What must it be to be there! My dear hearers, will you be there? Make your calling and election sure. If you are not trusting in the Lamb on earth, you will not reign with the Lamb in His glory. He that doth not love the Lamb as the atoning sacrifice shall never be the bride of the Lamb. How can you hope to be glorified with Him if you neglect Him in the day of His scorning? O Lamb of God, my sacrifice, I must be one with Thee, for this is my very life! I could not live apart from Thee. If, my hearer, thou canst thus speak, there is good hope that thou shalt be a participator in the marriage of the Lamb.

The character under which the bridegroom appears is that of the lamb: *"The marriage of the Lamb is come."* It must be so because first of all our Savior was the Lamb in the eternal covenant, when this whole matter was planned, arranged, and settled by the foresight and decree of eternity. He is *"the Lamb slain from the foundation of the world"* (Rev. 13:8), and the covenant was with Him, as one who was to be the Surety, the Substitute, the Sacrifice for guilty men. So, and not otherwise, was it of old.

It was next as the Lamb that He loved us and proved His love. Beloved, He did not give us words of love merely when He came from heaven to earth and dwelt among us "a lowly man before his foes," but He proceeded to deeds of truest affection. The supreme proof of His love was that He was led as a lamb to the slaughter. When He poured out His blood as a sacrifice, it might have been said, "Behold, how he loved them!" If you would prove the love of Jesus, you would not mention the transfiguration, but the crucifixion. Gethsemane and Golgotha would rise to your lips. Here to demonstration, beyond all possibility of doubt by any true heart, the Well-beloved proved His love to us. See how it runs: "He loved me, and gave himself for me," as if that giving of Himself for me was the clear proof that He loved me. Read again: *"Christ also loved the church, and gave himself for it"* (Eph. 5:25). The proof of His love to the church was the giving up of Himself for it. *"And being found in fashion as a man, he humbled himself, and became obedient unto death, even the death of the cross"* (Phil. 2:8). *"Herein is love, not that we loved God, but that he loved us"* (1 John 4:10). So you see, as a Lamb He proved His love, and as a Lamb He celebrated His marriage with us.

Go a step further. Love in marriage must be on both sides, and it is as the Lamb that we first came to love Him. I had no love to Christ. How could I have, until I saw His wounds and blood? *"We love him, because he first loved us"* (1 John 4:19). His perfect life was a condemnation to me, much as I was compelled to admire it. But the love that drew me to Him was shown in His substitutionary character, when He bore my sins in His own body on the tree. Is it not so with you, beloved? I have heard a great deal about conversions through admiration of the character of Christ, but I have never met with one: all I have ever met with have been conversions through a sense of need of salvation and a consciousness of guilt, which could never be satisfied save by His agony and death, through which sin is justly pardoned and evil is subdued. *This is the great heart-winning doctrine.* Christ loves us as the Lamb, and we love Him as the Lamb.

Further, marriage is the most perfect union. Surely, it is as the Lamb that Jesus is most closely joined to His people. Our Lord came very close to us when He took our nature, for thus He became bone of our bone, and flesh of our flesh. He came very near to us when, for this cause, He left His Father and became one flesh with His church. He could not be sinful as she was; but He did take her sins upon Himself and bear them all away. As it is written, *"The Lord hath laid on him the iniquity of us all"* (Isa. 53:6). When "he was numbered with the transgressors," and when the sword of vengeance smote Him in our stead, then He came nearer to us than ever He could do in the perfection of His Incarnation. I cannot conceive of closer union than that of Christ and souls redeemed by blood. As I look at Him in death, I feel forced to cry, "Surely a husband by blood art thou to me, O Jesus! Thou art joined to me by something closer than the one fact that thou art of my nature; for that nature of Thine has borne my sin and suffered the penalty of wrath on my behalf. Now art Thou one with me in all things by a union like to that which links Thee with the Father." A wonderful union is thus effected by our Lord's wearing the character of the Lamb…

If I had my choice today, while abiding in this present state, to see my Lord in His glory or on His cross, I should choose the latter. Of course, I would prefer to see His glory and be away with Him; but, while dwelling here surrounded with sin and sorrow, a sight of His griefs has the most effect upon me. "O sacred head once wounded," I long to behold Thee! I never feel so close to my Lord as when I survey His wondrous cross, and see Him pouring out His blood for me…I have almost felt myself in His arms, and like John, I have leaned on His bosom, when I have beheld His passion. I do not wonder, therefore, that since He comes closest to us as the Lamb, and since we come closest to Him when we behold Him in that character, He is pleased to call His highest eternal union with His church, "the marriage of the Lamb."

And O beloved, when you come to think of it, to be married to Him, to be one with Him, to have no thought, no object, no desire, no glory but that which dwells in Him that liveth and was dead—will not this be heaven indeed, where the Lamb is the light thereof? Forever to contemplate and adore Him, Who offered up Himself without spot unto God, as our sacrifice and propitiation—this shall be an endless feast of grateful love! We shall *never* weary of this subject! If you see the Lord coming from Edom, with dyed garments from Bozrah, from the winepress wherein He has trampled on His foes, you are overawed and overcome by the terror of that dread display of justice. But when you see Him clad in a vesture dipped in no blood but His own, you will sing aloud evermore, "Thou wast slain, and hast redeemed us to God by thy blood; to thee be glory for ever and ever." I could go on singing, "Worthy is the Lamb that was slain," throughout all eternity! The theme has an inexhaustible interest about it: there is everything in it: justice, mercy, power, patience, love, condescension, grace, and glory. All over glorious is my Lord when I behold Him as a Lamb. This shall make heaven seven times heaven to me to think that even then I shall be joined to Him in everlasting bonds as the Lamb! [Here a voice from the gallery cried, "Praise the Lord!"] Yes, my friend, we will praise the Lord! "Praise ye the Lord" is the command which was heard coming out of the throne—"Praise our God, all ye his servants, and ye that fear him, both small and great: for the marriage of the Lamb is come, and his wife hath made herself ready."

I am done when I have again put this question: Do you trust the Lamb? I warn you, if you have a religion that has no blood of Christ in it, it is not worth a thought: you had better be rid of it. It will be of no use to you. I warn you also that unless you *love* the Lamb, you cannot be *married* to the Lamb. He will never be married to those who have no love to Him. You must take Jesus as a sacrifice or not at all. It is useless to say, "I will follow Christ's example." You will not do anything of the sort. It is idle to say, "He shall be my teacher." He will not own you for a disciple unless you will own Him as a sacrifice. You must take Him as the Lamb or have done with Him. If you do despite to the blood of Christ, you do despite to the whole person of Christ. Christ is nothing to you if He is not your atonement. As many of you as hope to be saved by the works of the Law or by anything else apart from His blood and righteousness, you have un-Christianized yourselves; you have no part in Jesus here, and you shall have no part in Him hereafter, when He shall take to Himself His own redeemed church, to be His spouse for ever and ever. God bless you, for Christ's sake. Amen.

Delivered on Lord's Day morning, July 21, 1889, at the Metropolitan Tabernacle, Newington.

Charles Haddon Spurgeon (1834-1892): Influential English Baptist minister. The collected sermons of Spurgeon during his ministry fill 63 volumes. The sermons' 20–25 million words are equivalent to the 27 volumes of the ninth edition of the *Encyclopedia Britannica* and stand as the largest set of books by a single author in the history of Christianity. Born at Kelvedon, Essex, England.

Chapter 5
BRINGING UP CHILDREN

God is a culture maker. This is very clear in the commands He has issued for bringing up children. He has instructed parents to create a culture of honor and obedience in the home. We see this "original culture" in the functional relationships of the Godhead, the three Persons of the Holy Trinity. The holy communion and eternal love among the Father, Son, and Holy Spirit formed the original culture that serves as the paradigm for all other cultures.

Some of the simplest elements of the culture of the family are honor and obedience. There is a relational paradigm of honor and obedience in the relationships of the Trinity that becomes the pattern for relationships in the family on earth. In the co-equal, co-eternal, undivided, unified relationships in the Godhead (1 John 5:7), the Father exercises authority over the Son (1 Cor. 11:3); the Son submits to the Father (John 6:38); the Holy Spirit glorifies the Father and the Son (John 16:13-14); the Father delights in the Son, and the Son delights to do the will of His Father (John 14:31; John 15:10). It is a communion of love characterized by honor, obedience, delight, and submission. It is a wonderful family of unmatched beauty, grace, and harmony. God ordained this heavenly culture, and, by His grace and power, we may experience something of it's love and beauty in our earthly families. God desires to bring the culture of heaven to earth (Matt. 6:10).

One of the ways God does this is to establish homes on the earth and then teaches them to reflect the culture of heaven on the earth. As parents train their children from God's Word they build a biblical culture of righteousness and love after the pattern of the Father, the Son, and the Holy Spirit. This builds a powerful culture. Honor and obedience are foundational to every relationship God has ordained. Therefore, God has designed that this culture be built from the heart and in the family.

What would it be like to experience a culture like that? In this chapter you will see the beautiful, multifaceted program that God has designed for bringing up children.

—Scott Brown

Bringing Up Children for God
EDWARD PAYSON (1783-1827)

Take this child away, and nurse it for me, and I will give thee thy wages.
—Exodus 2:9

These words were addressed by Pharaoh's daughter to the mother of Moses. Of the circumstances that occasioned them, it can scarcely be necessary to inform you. You need not be told that soon after the birth of this future leader of Israel his parents were compelled by the cruelty of the Egyptian king to expose him in an ark of bulrushes on the banks of the Nile. In this situation, he was found by the daughter of Pharaoh. So powerfully did his infantile cries excite her compassion that she determined not only to rescue him from a watery grave, but to adopt and educate him as her own. His sister Miriam, who at a distance had watched his fate unseen, now came forward like a person entirely unacquainted with the circumstances of his exposure and, on hearing of the princess' determination, offered to procure a Hebrew woman to take the care of him until he should be of sufficient age to appear at her father's court. This offer being accepted, she immediately went and called the child's mother to whose care he was committed by the princess in the words of our text—*"Take this child away and nurse it for me, and I will give thee thy wages."*

In similar language, my friends, does God address parents. To everyone on whom He bestows the blessing of children, He says in His Word and by the voice of His Providence, "Take this child and educate it for Me, and I will give thee thy wages." From this passage, therefore, we may take occasion to show what is implied in educating children for God.

The first thing implied in educating children for God[1] is a realizing, heartfelt conviction that they are His property, His children, rather than ours. He commits them for a time to our care, merely for the purpose of education, as we place children under the care of human instructors for the same purpose. However carefully we may educate children, yet we cannot be said to educate them for God unless we [believe] that they are His; for if we [believe] that they are ours exclusively, we shalt and must educate them for ourselves and not for Him. To know that they are His is to feel a cordial, operative conviction[2] that He has a sovereign right to dispose of them as He pleases and to take them from us whenever He thinks fit. That they are His

---

1 **educating…God** – by this the author means bringing our children up in the knowledge of God, especially employing the practice of daily family worship.
2 **cordial, operative conviction** – heartfelt, significant persuasion.

and that He possesses this right is evident from innumerable passages in the inspired writings. We are there told that God is the former of our bodies and the Father of our spirits, that we are all His offspring, and that consequently we are not our own but His. We are also assured that as the soul of the parent, so also the souls of the children are His. God once and again severely reproves and threatens the Jews because they sacrificed *His* children in the fire to Moloch (Ezek. 16:20-21). Yet plain and explicit as these passages are, how few parents appear to feel their force. How few appear to feel and act as if conscious that they and theirs were the absolute property of God, that they were merely the foster parents of their children, and that, in all which they do for them, they are or ought to be acting for God. But it is evident that they must feel this before they can bring up their children for Him; for how can they educate their children for a being whose existence they do not realize, whose right to them they do not acknowledge, and whose character they do not love?

Nearly connected with this is a second thing implied in educating children for God—namely, a cordial and solemn dedication or surrender of them to Him to be His forever. We have already shown that they are His property and not ours. By dedicating them to Him, we mean nothing more than an explicit acknowledgment of this truth or an acknowledgment that we consider them as entirely His and that we unreservedly surrender them to Him for time and eternity…If we refuse to give them to God, how can we be said to educate them for Him?

In the third place, if we would educate children for God, we must do all that we do for them from right motives. Almost the only motive that the Scriptures allow to be right is a regard for the glory of God and a disinterested[3] desire to promote it; and they consider nothing as really done for God that does not flow from this source. Without this, however exemplary we may be, we do but bring forth fruit to ourselves and are no better than empty vines. We must be governed therefore by this motive in the education of our children if we would educate them for God and not for ourselves. In all our cares, labors, and sufferings for them, a regard to the divine glory must be the main spring that moves us. If we act merely from parental affection, we act from no higher principle than the irrational animals around us; many of them evidently appear to love their offspring no less ardently and to be no less ready to encounter dangers, toils, and sufferings to promote their happiness than we are to promote the welfare of ours. But if parental affection can be sanctified by the grace of God and parental duties hallowed by a wish

---

3 **disinterested** – free from self-interest.

to promote His glory, then we rise above the irrational world to our proper station and may be said to educate our children for God. Here, my friends, we may observe that true religion, when it prevails in the heart, sanctifies *everything*. [It] renders even the most common actions of life acceptable to God and gives them a dignity and importance, which of themselves they by no means deserve…Thus, the care and education of children, however trifling it may be thought by some, ought to be attended to from a regard to the divine glory. When this is done, it becomes an important part of true religion.

In the fourth place, if we would educate our children for God, we must educate them for His service. The three preceding particulars that we have mentioned refer principally to ourselves and our motives. But this has more immediate relation to our children themselves…In order to qualify yourselves for instructing and preparing your children for God's service, you [must] diligently study His Word to ascertain what He requires of them and frequently pray for the assistance of His Spirit, both for them and yourselves…You will carefully guard against saying or doing anything which may, either directly or indirectly, lead them to consider religion as an object of secondary importance. On the contrary, you will constantly labor to impress upon their minds a conviction that you consider religion as the great business of life, the favor of God as the only proper object of pursuit, and the enjoyment of Him hereafter as the only happiness, while everything else is comparatively of no consequence, however important it may otherwise be.

From "Children to Be Educated for God" in *The Complete Works of Edward Payson*, Vol. III, reprinted by Sprinkle Publications.

Edward Payson (1783-1827): American Congregational preacher; pastor of the Congregational Church of Portland, ME; born in Rindge, NH, USA.

Nurture and Admonition

DAVID MARTYN LLOYD-JONES (1899-1981)

And, ye fathers, provoke not your children to wrath: but bring them up in the nurture and admonition of the Lord. —Ephesians 6:4

If we are to carry out the Apostle's injunction...we must sit back for a moment and consider what we have to do. When the child comes, we must say to ourselves, "We are the guardians and the custodians of this soul." What a dread responsibility! In business and in professions, men are well aware of the great responsibility that rests upon them in the decisions they have to take. But are they aware of the infinitely *greater* responsibility they bear with respect to their own children? Do they give even the same amount of thought and attention and time to it, not to say more? Does it weigh as heavily upon them as the responsibility that they feel in these other realms? The Apostle urges us to regard this as the greatest business in life, the greatest matter that we ever have to handle and transact.

The Apostle does not stop at that: *"Bring them up,"* he says, *"in the nurture and admonition of the Lord."* The two words he uses are full of interest. The difference between them is that the first, *nurture*, is more general than the second. It is the totality of nurturing, rearing, bringing up the child. It includes, therefore, general discipline. And, as all the authorities are agreed in pointing out, its emphasis is upon actions. The second word, *admonition*, has reference rather to words that are spoken. *Nurture* is the more general term and includes everything that we do for the children. It includes the whole process in general of the cultivation of the mind and the spirit, the morals and the moral behavior, the whole personality of the child. That is our task. It is to look upon the child, care for it, and guard it...

The word *admonition* carries much the same meaning, except that it puts greater emphasis upon speech. Thus, there are two aspects of this matter. First, we have to deal with general conduct and behavior, the things we have to do by actions. Then, in addition, there are certain admonitions that should be addressed to the child: words of exhortation, words of encouragement, words of reproof, words of blame. Paul's term includes all these, indeed everything we say to the children in actual words when we are defining positions and indicating what is right or wrong, encouraging, exhorting, and so on. Such is the meaning of the word *admonition*.

Children are to be reared in *"the nurture and admonition"*—and then the most important addition of all—*"of the Lord."* This is where Christian parents, engaged in their duty towards their children, are in an entirely

Chapter 5—Bringing Up Children: Nurture and Admonition

different category from all other parents. In other words, this appeal to Christian parents is not simply to exhort them to bring up their children in terms of general morality or good manners or commendable behavior in general. That, of course, is included. Everyone should be doing it; non-Christian parents should be doing it. They should be concerned about good manners, good general behavior, an avoidance of evil. They should teach their children to be honest, dutiful, respectful, and all these various things. That is but common morality, and Christianity has not started at that point. Even pagan writers interested in the good ordering of society have always exhorted their fellow men to teach such principles. Society cannot continue without a modicum[4] of discipline and of law and order at every level and at every age. But the Apostle is not referring to that only. He says that the children of Christians are to be brought up *"in the nurture and admonition of the Lord."*

It is at this point that the peculiar and specific Christian thinking and teaching enter. In the forefront of the minds of Christian parents must ever be the thought that the children are to be brought up in the knowledge of the Lord Jesus Christ as Savior and as Lord. That is the peculiar task to which Christian parents alone are called. This is not only their supreme task: their greatest desire and ambition for their children should be that they should come to know the Lord Jesus Christ as their Savior and as their Lord. Is that our main ambition for our children? Does that come first?—that they may come to "know Him Whom to know is life eternal," that they may know Him as their Savior and that they may follow Him as their Lord? *"In the nurture and admonition of the Lord!"* These, then, are the terms the Apostle uses.

…In the Bible itself there is a great deal of emphasis laid upon child training. Take, for instance, words found in the sixth chapter of Deuteronomy. Moses has reached the end of his life, and the children of Israel are shortly to enter the Promised Land. He reminds them of the Law of God and tells them how they are to live when they enter into the land of their inheritance. And among other things, he is very careful to tell them that they have to teach their children the Law. It is not enough that they know it and observe it themselves; they must pass on their knowledge. The children must be taught it and must never forget it…

It is very interesting to observe in the long history of the Christian church how this particular matter always reappears and receives great prominence

---

4 **modicum** – small amount.

at every period of revival and re-awakening. The Protestant Reformers[5] were concerned about it, and the instruction of children in moral and spiritual matters was given great prominence. The Puritans[6] gave it still greater prominence, and the leaders of the Evangelical Awakening[7] of two hundred years ago also did the same. Books have been written about this matter and many sermons preached about it.

This happens, of course, because when people become Christian it affects the whole of their lives. It is not merely something individual and personal; it affects the marriage relationship, and so there are far fewer divorces among Christian people than among non-Christian people. It also affects the life of the family, it affects the children, it affects the home, it affects every department of human life. The greatest epochs in the history of this country, and of other countries, have always been the years that have followed a religious awakening, a revival of true religion. The moral tone of the whole of society has been raised; even those who have not become Christian have been influenced and affected by it.

In other words, there is no hope of dealing with the moral problems of society except in terms of the Gospel of Christ. Right will never be established apart from godliness; but when people become godly they proceed to apply their principles all along the line, and righteousness is seen in the nation at large. But, unfortunately, we have to face the fact that for some reason this aspect of the matter has been sadly neglected in this present century…For one reason or another, the family does not count as it used to do. It is not the center and the unit that it was formerly. The whole idea of family life has somehow been declining; and this, alas, is partly true in Christian circles also. The family's central importance that is found in the Bible and in all the great periods to which we have referred seems to have disappeared. It is no longer being given the attention and the prominence that it once received. That makes it all the more important for us to discover the principles that should govern us in this respect.

---

5 **Protestant Reformers** – 16th century Christians who sought to reform the abuses of Roman Catholicism, such as Martin Luther (1483-1546), John Calvin (1509-1564), and Huldrych Zwingli (1484-1531).

6 **Puritans** – name applied to English Protestants of the 16th century who sought to "purify," i.e., to further reform the Church of England under Elizabeth I. This included groups such as Presbyterians, Congregationalists, Baptists, and others who embraced Reformed Theology and had great theological and practical impact on 16th and 17th century England and America.

7 **Evangelical Awakening** – loosely connected series of English revivals that spread to the American colonies as the Great Awakening (app. 1739-1743), which included leaders such as George Whitefield (1714-1770), Jonathan Edwards (1703-1758), and others.

Chapter 5—Bringing Up Children: Nurture and Admonition

First and foremost, the bringing up of children *"in the nurture and admonition of the Lord"* is something that is to be done in the home and by the parents. This is the emphasis throughout the Bible. It is not something that is to be handed over to the school, however good the school may be. It is the duty of *parents*—their primary and most essential duty. It is their responsibility, and they are not to hand over this responsibility to another. I emphasize this because we are all well aware of what has been happening increasingly during this present century. More and more, parents have been transferring their responsibilities and their duties to the schools.

I regard this as a most serious matter. There is no more important influence in the life of a child than the influence of the home. The home is the fundamental unit of society; and children are born into a home, into a family. There you have the circle that is to be the chief influence in their lives. There is no question about that. It is the biblical teaching everywhere, and it is always in so-called civilizations where ideas concerning the home begin to deteriorate that society ultimately disintegrates…

In the Old Testament, it is quite clear that the father was a kind of priest in his household and family; he represented God. He was responsible not only for the morals and the behavior but for the instruction of his children. The Bible's emphasis everywhere is that this is the primary duty and task of the parents. And it remains so to this day. If we are Christians at all, we must realize that this great emphasis is based upon those fundamental units ordained by God—marriage, family, and home. You cannot play fast and loose with them…

What are parents to do? They are to supplement the teaching of the church, and they are to apply the teaching of the church. So little can be done in a sermon. It has to be applied, to be explained, to be extended, to be supplemented. That is where the parents play their part. And if this has been always right and important, how much more so today than ever before! I ask Christian parents, Have you ever given serious thought to this matter? You face a greater task, perhaps, than parents have ever done, and for the following reason. Consider what is now being taught the children in the schools. The theory and hypothesis of organic evolution is being taught them as a fact. They are not being presented with it as a mere theory that has not been proved; they are given the impression that it is an absolute fact, and that all people of scientific knowledge and learning believe it. And they are regarded as odd if they do not accept it. We have to meet that situation…Children are being taught perverse things in the schools. They hear them on the wireless and see them on the television. The whole emphasis is anti-God, anti-Bible, anti-true Christianity, anti-miraculous, and anti-supernatural. Who is going to counter these trends? That is precisely the business of parents—"Bring them up in the nurture and admonition of the Lord." It demands great effort by the parents at the present time because the forces against us are so great. Christian parents today have this unusually difficult task of protecting their children against these powerful adverse forces that are trying to indoctrinate them. There, then, is the setting!

To be practical, I wish, in the second place, to show how this is not to be done. There is a way of trying to deal with this situation that is quite disastrous and does much more harm than good. How is this not to be done?

It is never to be done in a mechanical, abstract manner, almost "by numbers," as if it were some sort of drill. I remember an experience of my own in this connection some ten years or so ago. I went to stay with some friends while I was preaching in a certain place; and I found the wife, the mother of the family, in a state of acute distress. In conversation, I discovered the cause of her distress. A certain lady had been there lecturing that very week, her theme being "How to bring up all the children in your family as good Christians." It was wonderful! She had five or six children, and she had so organized her home and her life that she finished all her domestic work by nine o'clock in the morning, and then gave herself to various Christian activities. All her children were fine Christians; and it was all so easy, so wonderful. The mother talking to me, who had two children, was in a state of real distress feeling that she was a complete and utter failure. What had I to say to her? This: I said, "Wait a moment; how old are the children of this lady?" I happened to know the answer, and my friend knew also. Not one of them at that time was above the age of sixteen, or thereabouts. I went on: "Wait and see. This lady tells you that they are all Christians, and that all you need is a scheme that you carry out regularly. Wait a while; the story may be different in a few years." And, alas, it turned out to be very different. It is doubtful whether more than one of those children is a Christian. Several of them are openly anti-Christian and have turned their backs upon it all. You cannot bring up children to be Christians in that way. It is not a mechanical process, and in any case, it was all so cold and clinical…A child is not a machine, and so you cannot do this work mechanically.

Nor must the work ever be done in an entirely negative or repressive manner. If you give children the impression that to be religious is to be miserable and that it consists of prohibitions and constant repression, you may well drive them into the arms of the devil and into the world. Never be entirely negative and repressive…

My last negative at this point is that we must never force a child to a decision. What trouble and havoc has been wrought by this! "Isn't it marvelous?" say the parents, "my little So-and-So, a mere youngster, decided for Christ." Pressure had been brought to bear in the meeting. But that should never be done. You are violating the personality of the child. In addition, of course, you are displaying a profound ignorance of the way of salvation. You can make a little child decide anything. You have the power and the ability to do so; but it is wrong, it is unchristian, it is not spiritual… Do not force them to a decision…

What then is the true way?…The important point is that the impression should always be given that Christ is the Head of the house or the home. How is that impression given? Chiefly by your general conduct and example! The parents should be living in such a way that the children should always have a feeling that they themselves are under Christ, that Christ is their Head. The fact should be obvious in their conduct and behavior. Above all, there should be an atmosphere of love…The fruit of the Spirit is love, and if the home is filled with an atmosphere of the love produced by the Spirit, most of its problems are solved. That is what does the work, not the direct pressures and appeals, but an atmosphere of love….

From *Life in the Spirit in Marriage, Home & Work: An Exposition of Ephesians 5:18 to 6:9,* published by The Banner of Truth Trust: www.banneroftruth.org.

David Martyn Lloyd-Jones (1899-1981): Perhaps the greatest expository preacher of the 20th century; Westminster Chapel, London, 1938-68; born in Wales.

Primary Obligations of Parents

J.C. RYLE (1816-1900)

> *Train up a child in the way he should go: and when he is old, he will not depart from it.* —Proverbs 22:6

I suppose that most professing Christians are acquainted with the text at the head of this page. The sound of it is probably familiar to your ears, like an old tune. It is likely you have heard it, read it, talked of it, or quoted it many a time. Is it not so? But after all, how little is the substance of this text regarded! The doctrine it contains appears scarcely known, the duty it puts before us seems fearfully seldom practiced. Reader, do I not speak the truth?

It cannot be said that the subject is a new one. The world is old, and we have the experience of nearly six thousand years to help us. We live in days when there is a mighty zeal for education in every quarter. We hear of new schools rising on all sides. We are told of new systems and new books for the young of every sort and description. Still for all this, the vast majority of children are manifestly not trained in the way they *should* go; for when they grow up to man's estate, they do not walk with God.

Now how shall we account for this state of things? The plain truth is the Lord's commandment in our text is not regarded. Therefore, the Lord's promise[8] in our text is not fulfilled.

Reader, these things may well give rise to great searching of heart. Suffer then a word of exhortation from a minister about the right training of children. Believe me, the subject is one that should come home to every conscience and make every one ask himself the question, "Am I in this matter doing what I can?"

It is a subject that concerns almost all. There is hardly a household that it does not touch. Parents, nurses, teachers, godfathers, godmothers, uncles, aunts, brothers, sisters—all have an interest in it. Few can be found, I think, who might not influence some parent in the management of his family or affect the training of some child by suggestion or advice. All of us, I suspect, can do something here, either directly or indirectly; and I wish to stir up all to bear this in remembrance…

First, then, if you would train your children rightly, train them in the way they *should* go, and not in the way that they would. Remember children are born with a decided bias towards evil. Therefore, if you let them choose for themselves, they are certain to choose wrong.

---

[8] Not all Christian commentators, pastors, and theologians understand this to be a promise that the children of Christians will infallibly be saved.

The mother cannot tell what her tender infant may grow up to be—tall or short, weak or strong, wise or foolish. He may be any of these things or not—it is all uncertain. But one thing the mother *can* say with certainty: he will have a corrupt and sinful heart. It is natural to us to do wrong. "Foolishness," says Solomon, *"is bound in the heart of a child"* (Prov. 22:15). *"A child left to himself bringeth his mother to shame"* (Prov. 29:15). Our hearts are like the earth on which we tread: let it alone, and it is sure to bear weeds.

If, then, you would deal wisely with your child, you must not leave him to the guidance of his own will. Think for him, judge for him, act for him, just as you would for one weak and blind. But for pity's sake, give him not up to his own wayward tastes and inclinations. It must not be his likings and wishes that are consulted. He knows not yet what is good for his mind and soul any more than what is good for his body. You do not let him decide what he shall eat, what he shall drink, and how he shall be clothed. Be consistent, and deal with his mind in like manner. Train him in the way that is Scriptural and right and not in the way that he fancies.

If you cannot make up your mind to this first principle of Christian training, it is useless for you to read any further. Self-will is almost the first thing that appears in a child's mind. It must be your first step to resist it.

Train up your child with all tenderness, affection, and patience. I do not mean that you are to spoil him, but I do mean that you should let him see that you love him. Love should be the silver thread that runs through all your conduct. Kindness, gentleness, long-suffering, forbearance, patience, sympathy, a willingness to enter into childish troubles, a readiness to take part in childish joys—these are the cords by which a child may be led most easily—these are the clues you must follow if you would find the way to his heart…

Now children's minds are cast in much the same mold as our own. Sternness and severity of manner chill them and throw them back. It shuts up their hearts, and you will weary yourself to find the door. But let them only see that you have an affectionate feeling towards them—that you are really desirous to make them happy and do them good—that if you punish them, it is intended for their profit, and that, like the pelican, you would give your heart's blood to nourish their souls. Let them see this, I say, and they will soon be all your own. But they must be wooed with kindness if their attention is ever to be won…Love is one grand secret of successful training. Anger and harshness may frighten, but they will not persuade the child that you are right. If he sees you often out of temper, you will soon cease to have his respect. A father who speaks to his son as Saul did to Jonathan (1 Sam. 20:30) need not expect to retain his influence over that son's mind.

Try hard to keep up a hold on your child's affections. It is a dangerous thing to make your children afraid of you. Anything is almost better than reserve and constraint between your child and yourself; and this will come in with fear. Fear puts an end to openness of manner. Fear leads to concealment—fear sows the seed of much hypocrisy and leads to many a lie. There is a mine of truth in the Apostle's words to the Colossians: *"Fathers, provoke not your children to anger, lest they be discouraged"* (Col. 3:21). Let not the advice it contains be overlooked.

Train with this thought continually before your eyes—that the soul of your child is the first thing to be considered. Precious, no doubt, are these little ones in your eyes; but if you love them, think often of their souls. No interest should weigh with you so much as their eternal interests. No part of them should be so dear to you as that part that will never die. The world with all its glory shall pass away; the hills shall melt; the heavens shall be wrapped together as a scroll; the sun shall cease to shine. But the spirit that dwells in those little creatures, whom you love so well, shall outlive them all, and whether in happiness or misery (to speak as a man) will depend on you.[9]

This is the thought that should be uppermost on your mind in all you do for your children. In every step you take about them, in every plan and scheme and arrangement that concerns them, do not leave out that mighty question, "How will this affect their souls?"

Soul love is the soul of all love. To pet, pamper, and indulge your child, as if this world was all he had to look to and this life the only season for happiness—to do this is not true love, but *cruelty*. It is treating him like some beast of the earth that has but one world to look to and nothing after death. It is hiding from him that grand truth that he ought to be made to learn from his very infancy—that the chief end of his life is the salvation of his soul.

A true Christian must be no slave to fashion if he would train his child for heaven. He must not be content to do things merely because they are the custom of the world; to teach them and instruct them in certain ways, merely because it is usual; to allow them to read books of a questionable sort, merely because everybody else reads them; to let them form habits of a doubtful tendency, merely because they are the habits of the day. He must train with an eye to his children's souls. He must not be ashamed to hear his training called *singular*[10] and *strange*. What if it is? The time is short—

---

9 Scripture reveals both the sovereignty of God in salvation and the responsibility of man. The author is not denying God's role in salvation here. He is speaking in terms of parental responsibility, hence his comment, "to speak as a man."

10 **singular** – different from that which is customary; peculiar.

the fashion of this world passeth away. He that has trained his children for heaven rather than for earth—for God, rather than for man—is the parent that will be called wise at last.

Train your child to a knowledge of the Bible. You cannot make your children love the Bible, I allow. None but the Holy Ghost can give us a heart to delight in the Word. But you can make your children acquainted with the Bible. Be sure they cannot be acquainted with that blessed book too soon or too well.

A thorough knowledge of the Bible is the foundation of all clear views of religion. He that is well-grounded in it will not generally be found a waverer[11] and carried about by every wind of new doctrine. Any system of training that does not make knowledge of Scripture the first thing is unsafe and unsound.

You have need to be careful on this point just now, for the devil is abroad and error abounds. Some are to be found amongst us who give the Church the honor due to Jesus Christ. Some are to be found who make the sacraments saviors and passports to eternal life. And some are to be found in like manner who honor a catechism more than the Bible or fill the minds of their children with miserable little storybooks instead of the Scripture of truth. But if you love your children, let the simple Bible be everything in the training of their souls; and let all other books go down and take the second place.

Care not so much for their being mighty in the catechism as for their being mighty in the Scriptures. This is the training, believe me, that God will honor. The Psalmist says of Him, *"For thou hast magnified thy word above all thy name"* (Ps. 138:2). I think that He gives an especial blessing to all who try to magnify it among men.

See that your children read the Bible reverently. Train them to look on it not as the word of men, but as it is in truth, the Word of God, written by the Holy Ghost Himself—all true, all profitable, and able to make us wise unto salvation through faith that is in Christ Jesus.

See that they read it regularly. Train them to regard it as their soul's daily food—as a thing essential to their soul's daily health. I know well you cannot make this anything more than a form; but there is no telling the amount of sin that a mere form may indirectly restrain.

See that they read it all. You need not shrink from bringing any doctrine before them. You need not fancy that the leading doctrines of Christianity are things that children cannot understand. Children understand far more of the Bible than we are apt to suppose.

---

11 **waverer** – one who is undecided in opinion or choice.

Tell them of sin—its guilt, its consequences, its power, its vileness. You will find they can comprehend something of this.

Tell them of the Lord Jesus Christ and His work for our salvation—the atonement, the cross, the blood, the sacrifice, the intercession. You will discover there is something not beyond them in all this.

Tell them of the work of the Holy Spirit in man's heart, how He changes, renews, sanctifies, and purifies. You will soon see they can go along with you in some measure in this. In short, I suspect we have no idea how much a little child can take in of the length and breadth of the glorious Gospel. They see far more of these things than we suppose.

Fill their minds with Scripture. Let the Word dwell in them richly. Give them the Bible, the whole Bible, even while they are young.

Train them to a habit of prayer. Prayer is the very life-breath of true religion. It is one of the first evidences that a man is born again. *"Behold,"* said the Lord of Saul in the day He sent Ananias to him, *"Behold, he prayeth"* (Acts 9:11). He had begun to pray, and that was proof enough.

Prayer was the distinguishing mark of the Lord's people in the day that there began to be a separation between them and the world. *"Then began men to call upon the name of the LORD"* (Gen. 4:26).

Prayer is the peculiarity of all real Christians now. They pray—for they tell God their wants, their feelings, their desires, their fears, and mean what they say. The nominal Christian[12] may repeat prayers and good prayers too, but he goes no further.

Prayer is the turning point in a man's soul. Our ministry is unprofitable, and our labor is vain until you are brought to your knees. Until then, we have no hope about you.

Prayer is one great secret of spiritual prosperity. When there is much private communion with God, your soul will grow like the grass after rain. When there is little, all will be at a standstill; you will barely keep your soul alive. Show me a growing Christian, a going forward Christian, a strong Christian, a flourishing Christian, and sure am I, he is one that speaks often with his Lord. He asks much, and he has much. He tells Jesus everything, and so he always knows how to act.

Prayer is the mightiest engine God has placed in our hands. It is the best weapon to use in every difficulty and the surest remedy in every trouble. It is the key that unlocks the treasury of promises and the hand that draws forth grace and help in time of need. It is the silver trumpet God commands us to

---

12 **nominal Christian** – one who is Christian in name only and gives no evidence of true conversion.

sound in all our necessity, and it is the cry He has promised always to attend to, even as a loving mother to the voice of her child.

Prayer is the simplest means that man can use in coming to God. It is within reach of all—the sick, the aged, the infirm, the paralytic, the blind, the poor, the unlearned—all can pray. It avails you nothing to plead want[13] of memory, want of learning, want of books, and want of scholarship in this matter. So long as you have a tongue to tell your soul's state, you may and ought to pray. Those words, *"Ye have not, because ye ask not"* (James 4:2), will be a fearful condemnation to many in the Day of Judgment.

Parents, if you love your children, do all that lies in your power to train them up to a habit of prayer. Show them how to begin. Tell them what to say. Encourage them to persevere. Remind them if they become careless and slack about it. Let it not be your fault, at any rate, if they never call on the name of the Lord.

This, remember, is the first step in religion which a child is able to take. Long before he can read, you can teach him to kneel by his mother's side and repeat the simple words of prayer and praise that she puts in his mouth. And as the first steps in any undertaking are always the most important, so is the manner in which your children's prayers are prayed—a point that deserves your closest attention. Few seem to know how much depends on this. You must beware lest they get into a way of saying them in a hasty, careless, and irreverent manner. You must beware…of trusting too much to your children doing it when left to themselves. I cannot praise that mother who never looks after this most important part of her child's daily life herself. Surely if there be any habit which your own hand and eye should help in forming, it is the habit of prayer. Believe me; if you never hear your children pray yourself, *you* are much to blame…

Prayer is of all habits the one that we recollect the longest. Many a grey-headed man could tell you how his mother used to make him pray in the days of his childhood. Other things have passed away from his mind perhaps. The church where he was taken to worship, the minister whom he heard preach, the companions who used to play with him—all these, it may be, have passed from his memory and left no mark behind. But you will often find it is far different with his first prayers. He will often be able to tell you where he knelt, what he was taught to say, and even how his mother looked all the while. It will come up as fresh before his mind's eye as if it was but yesterday.

---

13 **want** – lack.

Reader, if you love your children, I charge you, do not let the seedtime of a prayerful habit pass away unimproved. If you train your children to do anything, train them at least to a habit of prayer.

From *The Duties of Parents*, reprinted and available from Chapel Library.

J.C. Ryle (1816-1900): Anglican bishop; born at Macclesfield, Cheshire County, England.

Ours is peculiarly an age of irreverence, and as the consequence, the spirit of lawlessness, which brooks no restraint and which is desirous of casting off everything that interferes with the free course of self-will, is rapidly engulfing the earth like some giant tidal wave. The members of the rising generation are the most flagrant offenders, and in the decay and disappearing of parental authority, we have the certain precursor of the abolition of civic authority. Therefore, in view of the growing disrespect for human law and the refusal to "render honor to whom honor is due," we need not be surprised that the recognition of the majesty, the authority, the sovereignty of the Almighty Law-giver should recede more and more into the background, and that the masses have less and less patience with those who insist upon them. —Arthur W. Pink

General Duties of Parents to Children
JOHN BUNYAN (1628-1688)

If you are a parent—a father or a mother—then you are to consider your calling under this relation. Your children have souls; and they must be born of God as well as of you, or they perish. And know also that unless you be very circumspect in your behavior to and before them, they may perish through you—the thoughts of which should provoke you both to *instruct* and also to *correct* them.

First, to instruct them as the Scripture says: *to "bring them up in the nurture and admonition of the Lord"* (Eph. 6:4), and to do this diligently, *"when thou sittest in thine house…when thou liest down, and when thou risest up"* (Deut. 6:7).

Now to do this to purpose:

1. Do it in terms and words easy to be understood: do not use high expressions; they will drown your children. Thus God spoke to His children (Hos. 12:10), and Paul to his (1 Cor. 3:2).

2. Take heed of filling their heads with whimsies[14] and unprofitable notions. This will sooner teach them to be bold[15] and proud, than sober and humble. Open, therefore, to them the state of man by nature; discourse with them of sin, death, and hell; of a crucified Savior, and the promise of life through faith: *"Train up a child in the way he should go: and when he is old, he will not depart from it"* (Prov. 22:6).

3. There must be much gentleness and patience in all your instructions, *"lest they be discouraged"* (Col. 3:21). And,

4. Labor to convince them by a conversation answerable, that the things of which you instruct them are not fables but realities—yes, and realities so far above what can be enjoyed here, that all things, were they a thousand times better than they are, are not worthy to be compared with the glory and worthiness of these things.

Isaac was so holy before his children that, when Jacob remembered God, he remembered that He was *"the fear of his father Isaac"* (Gen. 31:53).

Ah! when children can think of their parents, and bless God for that instruction and good they have received from them, this is not only profitable for children, but honorable and comfortable to parents: *"The father of the righteous shall greatly rejoice: and he that begetteth a wise child shall have joy of him. Thy father and thy mother shall be glad, and she that bare thee shall rejoice"* (Prov. 23:24-25).

---

14 **whimsies** – ways of thinking that are not serious.
15 **bold** – showing lack of respect.

Second, the duty of *correction*:

1. See if fair words will win them from evil. This is God's way with His children (Jer. 25:4-5).

2. Let those words you speak to them in your reproof be both sober, few, and pertinent,[16] adding always some suitable sentence of the Scripture therewith. If they lie, then such as Revelation 21:8, 27. If they refuse to hear the Word, such as 2 Chronicles 25:14-16.

3. Look to them that they be not companions with those that are rude and ungodly. Show with soberness a continual dislike of their naughtiness, often crying out to them as God did of old unto His, *"Oh, do not this abominable thing that I hate"* (Jer. 44:4).

4. Let all this be mixed with such love, pity, and compunction[17] of spirit that, if possible, they may be convinced you dislike not their persons, but their sins. This is God's way (Ps. 99:8).

5. Be often endeavoring to fasten on their consciences the day of their death and judgment to come. Thus also God deals with His (Deut. 32:29).

6. If you are driven to the rod, then strike advisedly in cool blood[18] and soberly show them: a) their fault; b) how much it is against your heart to deal with them in this way; c) that what you do, you do in conscience to God and love to their souls; d) and tell them that if fair means would have done,[19] none of this severity should have been. This, I have proved it, will be a means to afflict their hearts as well as their bodies; and it being the way that God deals with His, it is the most likely to accomplish its end.

7. Follow all this with prayer to God for them, and leave the issue to Him. *"Foolishness is bound in the heart of a child; but the rod of correction shall drive it far from him"* (Prov. 22:15).

Lastly, observe these *cautions*.

1. Take heed that the misdeeds for which you correct your children be not learned by them from you. Many children learn that wickedness of their parents for which they beat and chastise them.

2. Take heed that you smile not upon them to encourage them in small faults, for your behavior toward them will be an encouragement to them to commit greater.

---

16 **pertinent** – pertaining to the matter at hand.
17 **compunction** – feeling of deep regret.
18 **cool blood** – calm frame of mind.
19 **if fair means...done** – if they had done the right thing.

3. Take heed that you use not unsavory and unseemly[20] words in your chastising of them, as insulting, name-calling, and the like. This is devilish.

4. Take heed that you do not accustom them to many chiding[21] words and threatenings, mixed with lightness and laughter. This will harden [them]. Speak not much, nor often, but pertinent to them with all sobriety.

From *Christian Behavior*, available from Chapel Library.

John Bunyan (1628-1688): English minister, preacher, and author; born at Elstow near Bedford, England.

---

20 **unsavory and unseemly** – offensive and inappropriate.
21 **chiding** – scolding; harshly rebuking.

Teaching Children about God
PHILIP DODDRIDGE (1702-1751)

I very readily allow that no human endeavors, either of ministers or of parents, can ever be effectual to bring one soul to the saving knowledge of God in Christ without the cooperating and transforming influences of the blessed Spirit. Yet you well know, and I hope you seriously consider, that this does not in the least weaken our obligation to the most diligent use of proper means. The great God has stated rules of operation in the world of grace as well as of nature. Though He is not limited to them, it is arrogant and may be destructive to expect that He should deviate from them in favor of us or ours.

We live not by bread alone, *"but by every word that proceedeth out of the mouth of God"* (Matt. 4:4). Were He determined to continue your lives or the lives of your children, He could no doubt feed or support you by miracles. Yet you think yourselves obligated to a prudent care for your daily bread. [You] justly conclude that, were you to neglect to administer it to your infant offspring, you would be chargeable with their murder before God and man; nor could you think of pleading it as any excuse that you referred them to a miraculous divine care while you left them destitute of any human supplies. Such a plea would only add impiety[22] to cruelty and greatly aggravate the crime it attempted to palliate.[23] As absurd would it be for us to flatter ourselves with a hope that our children should be taught of God, and regenerated and sanctified by the influences of His grace, if we neglect that prudent and religious care in their education which it is my business this day to describe and recommend...

1. Children should undoubtedly be trained up in the way of piety and devotion towards God. This, as you well know, is the sum and foundation of everything truly good. *"The fear of the LORD is the beginning of wisdom"* (Ps. 111:10). The Psalmist therefore invites children to him with the promise of instructing them in it: *"Come, ye children, hearken unto me: I will teach you the fear of the LORD"* (Ps. 34:11). And, it is certain, some right notions of the Supreme Being must be implanted in the minds of children before there can be a reasonable foundation for teaching them those doctrines that peculiarly relate to Christ under the character of the Mediator. *"For he that cometh to God must believe that he is, and that he is a rewarder of them that diligently seek him"* (Heb. 11:6).

---

22 **impiety** – lacking reverence for God.
23 **palliate** – partially excuse.

The proof of the being of God and some of those attributes of the divine nature in which we are most concerned depends on such easy principles that I cannot but think the weakest mind might enter into it. A child will easily apprehend that as every house is built by some man and there can be no work without an author, so He that built all things is God. From this obvious idea of God as the Maker of all, we may naturally represent Him as very great and very good, that they may be taught at once to reverence and love Him.

It is of great importance that children early imbibe[24] an awe of God and a humble veneration for His perfections and glories. He ought, therefore, to be represented to them as the great Lord of all. And, when we take occasion to mention to them other invisible agents, whether angels or devils, we should…always represent them as entirely under the government and control of God…

There should be a peculiar caution that when we teach these infant tongues to pronounce that great and terrible name, The Lord our God, they may not learn to take it in vain, but may use it with a becoming solemnity, remembering that we and they are but dust and ashes before Him. When I hear the little creatures speaking of "the *great* God, the *blessed* God, the *glorious* God," as I sometimes do, it gives me a sensible pleasure. I consider it as a probable proof of great wisdom and piety in those who have the charge of their education.

Yet, great care should be taken not to confine our discourses to these awful views lest the dread of God should so fall upon them that His excellencies should make them afraid to approach Him. We should describe Him as not only the greatest, but the *best* of beings. We should teach them to know Him by the most encouraging name of:*"The LORD, The LORD God, merciful and gracious, longsuffering, and abundant in goodness and truth, keeping mercy for thousands, forgiving iniquity and transgression and sin"* (Ex. 34:6-7). We should represent Him as the universal, kind, indulgent[25] parent, Who loves His creatures and by all proper methods provides for their happiness. And we should particularly represent His *goodness* to them: with what more than paternal tenderness He watched round their cradles, with what compassion He heard their feeble cries before their infant thoughts could form themselves into prayer. We should tell them that they live every moment on God and that all our affection for them is no more than He puts

---

24 **imbibe** – receive into the mind and retain.
25 The author does not mean *sinful* indulgence as is mentioned in other articles, but rather "ready to show favor."

into our hearts and [that] all our power to help them is no more than He lodges in our hands.

We should also solemnly remind them that in a very little while their spirits are to return to this God. As He is now always with them and knows everything they do, speak, or think, so He will bring every work into judgment and make them forever happy or miserable, as they, on the whole, are found obedient or rebellious. Here the most lively and pathetic[26] descriptions that the Scriptures give us of heaven and hell should be laid before them and urged on their consideration.

When such a foundation is laid in the belief of the being and providence of God and of a future state both of rewards and punishments, children should be instructed in the duty they owe to God. [They] should be particularly taught to pray to Him and to praise Him. It would be best of all if, from a deep sense of His perfections and their own necessities, they could be engaged to breathe out their souls before Him in words of their own, were they ever so weak and broken. Yet you will readily allow that, until this can be expected, it may be very proper to teach them some forms of prayer and thanksgiving, consisting of such plain Scriptures or other familiar expressions as may best suit their circumstances and understandings…

2. Children must be trained up in the way of faith in the Lord Jesus Christ. You know, my friends, and I hope many of you know it to the daily joy of your souls, that Christ is *"the way, the truth, and the life"* (John 14:6). It is by Him we have boldness and access with confidence to a God, Who might otherwise appear as a *"consuming fire"* (Heb. 12:29). It is, therefore, of great importance to lead children quickly into the knowledge of Christ, which is no doubt a considerable part of the *"nurture and admonition of the Lord,"* which the Apostle recommends and was perhaps what he principally intended by those words (Eph. 6:4).

We should, therefore, teach them quickly that the first parents of the human race most ungratefully rebelled against God and subjected themselves and all their offspring to His wrath and curse (Gen. 1-3). The awful consequences of this should be opened at large, and we should labor to convince them that they have made themselves liable to the divine displeasure—that dreadful thing!—by their own personal guilt. Thus, by the knowledge of the Law, should we make way for the Gospel—the joyful news of deliverance by Christ.

---

26 **lively and pathetic** – vivid and moving.

In unfolding this, great care ought to be taken that we do not fill their minds with an aversion[27] to one sacred person while we endeavor to attract their regards to another. The Father is not to be represented as severe and almost inexorable,[28] hardly prevailed upon by the intercession of His compassionate Son to entertain thoughts of mercy and forgiveness. Far from that, we should speak of Him as the overflowing fountain of goodness, Whose eye pitied us in our helpless distress, Whose almighty arm was stretched out for our rescue, Whose eternal counsels of wisdom and love formed that important scheme to which we owe all our hopes. I have had occasion to show you at large that this is the Scripture doctrine. Our children should be early taught it and taught what that scheme was, as far as their understanding can receive it and ours can explain it. We should often repeat to them that God is so holy, and yet so gracious that, rather than He would on the one hand destroy man or on the other leave sin unpunished, He made His own Son a sacrifice for it, appointing Him to be humbled that we might be exalted, to die that we might live.

We should also represent to them—with holy wonder and joy!—how readily the Lord Jesus Christ consented to procure our deliverance in so *expensive* a way. How cheerfully He said, *"Lo, I come to do thy will, O God"* (Heb. 10:7, 9)! To enhance the value of this amazing love, we should endeavor, according to our weak capacities, to teach them Who this compassionate Redeemer is, to represent something of His glories as the eternal Son of God and the great Lord of angels and men. We should instruct them in His amazing condescension in laying aside these glories that He might become a little, weak, helpless child, and afterwards an afflicted, sorrowful man. We should lead them into the knowledge of those circumstances of the history of Jesus that may have the greatest tendency to strike their minds and to impress them with an early sense of gratitude and love to Him. We should tell them how poor He made Himself that He might enrich us, how diligently He went about doing good, how willingly He preached the Gospel to the lowest of the people. We should *especially* tell them how kind He was to little children and how He chided[29] His disciples when they would have hindered them from being brought to Him. It is expressly said that Jesus was much displeased and said, *"Suffer little children to come unto me, and forbid them not: for of such is the kingdom of God"* (Luke 18:16)—a tender circumstance that perhaps was recorded, in part at least, for this very reason: that children

---

27 **aversion** – feeling of intense dislike.
28 **inexorable** – unmoved by persuasion or pleading.
29 **chided** – expressed disapproval.

in succeeding ages might be impressed and affected with it.

Through these scenes of His life, we should lead them on to His death. We should show how easily He could have delivered Himself—of which He gave so sensible an evidence in striking down by one word those who came to apprehend Him (John 18:6)—and yet how patiently He submitted to the most cruel injuries: to be scourged and spit upon, to be crowned with thorns, and to bear His cross. We should show them how this innocent, holy, and divine Person was brought as a lamb to the slaughter; and, while they were piercing Him with nails, instead of loading them with curses, He prayed for them, saying, *"Father, forgive them; for they know not what they do"* (Luke 23:34). And when their little hearts are awed and melted with so strange a story, we should tell them it was thus He groaned, bled, and died for us, and often remind them of their own concern in what was then transacted.

We should lead on their thoughts to the glorious views of Christ's resurrection and ascension and tell them with what adorable goodness He still remembers His people in the midst of His exaltation, pleading the cause of sinful creatures, and employing His interest in the court of heaven to procure life and glory for all that believe in Him and love Him.

We should then go on to instruct them in those particulars of obedience by which the sincerity of our faith and our love is to be approved. At the same time, [we must remind] them of their own weakness and [tell] them how God helps us by sending His Holy Spirit to dwell in our hearts to furnish us for every good word and work. An important lesson without attending to which our instruction will be vain and their hearing will likewise be vain!

From *The Godly Family*, reprinted by Soli Deo Gloria, a division of Reformation Heritage Books: www.heritagebooks.org.

Philip Doddridge (1702-1751): English Nonconformist minister; prolific author and hymn writer; born in London, England.

Parents should polish the rude natures of their children with good manners.
—Thomas Boston

The Art of Balanced Discipline
DAVID MARTYN LLOYD-JONES (1899-1981)

> *And, ye fathers, provoke not your children to wrath: but bring them up in the nurture and admonition of the Lord. —Ephesians 6:4*

Notice that [Paul] mentions the fathers only. He has just quoted the words of the Law—*"Honour thy father and mother"*—but now he singles out the fathers because the whole of his teaching has been, as we have seen, that the father is the one who is in the position of authority. That is what we always find in the Old Testament; that is how God has always taught people to behave; so he naturally addresses this particular injunction to the fathers. But the injunction is not to be confined to the fathers; it includes the mothers also; and at a time like the present, we have reached a position in which the order almost has to be reversed! We are living in a kind of matriarchal society where fathers, alas, and husbands, have so abdicated their position in the home that almost everything is being left to the mothers. We have to realize therefore that what is said here to the fathers applies equally to the mothers. It applies to the one who is in the position of having to exercise discipline. In other words, what we are introduced to here in this fourth verse, and it is involved in the previous verse, is the whole problem of discipline.

We must examine this subject carefully, and it is of course a very extensive one. There is no subject, I would say once more, that is of such urgent importance in this country,[30] and in every other country,[31] as this whole problem of discipline. We are witnessing a breakdown in society, and it is mainly in connection with this matter of *discipline*. We have it in the home, we have it in the schools, we have it in industry; it is everywhere. The problem confronting society today in every walk of life is ultimately the problem of discipline. Responsibility, relationships, how life is to be conducted, how life is to proceed! The whole future of civilization, it seems to me, rests upon this...I venture on this assertion, this prophecy: If the West goes down and is defeated, it will be for one reason only: *internal rot*...If we continue to spend our lives in jollification,[32] doing less and less work, demanding more and more money, more and more pleasure and so-called happiness, more and more indulgence of the lusts of the flesh, with a refusal to accept our responsibilities, there is but one inevitable result—complete and abject failure. Why did the Goths and the Vandals and other

---

30 England.
31 Especially in the United States of America—*Editor*.
32 **jollification** – merrymaking; boisterous celebrations.

barbarians conquer the ancient Roman Empire? Was it by superior military power? Of course not! Historians know that there is only one answer: the fall of Rome came because of the spirit of indulgence that had invaded the Roman world—the games, the pleasures, the baths. The moral rot that had entered into the heart of the Roman Empire was the cause of Rome's "decline and fall." It was not superior power from the outside, but internal rot that was Rome's ruination. And the really alarming fact today is that we are witnessing a similar declension in this and most other Western countries. This slackness, this indiscipline, the whole outlook and spirit is characteristic of a period of decadence. The pleasure mania, the sports mania, the drink and drug mania have gripped the masses. This is the essential problem, this sheer *absence* of discipline and of order and of true notions of government!

These matters, it seems to me, are raised very clearly by what the Apostle tells us here. I shall proceed to present these further to view and to show how the Scripture enlightens us in regard to them. But before doing so, let me mention something that will assist and stimulate your whole process of thinking. One of our problems today is that we no longer do our own thinking. Newspapers do it for us, the people interviewed on radio and television do it for us, and we sit back and listen. That is one of the manifestations of the breakdown of self-discipline. We must learn to discipline our minds! So I will give two quotations of Scripture, one on the one side, and one on the other side of this whole position. The problem of discipline lies between the two. Here is the limit on one side: *"He that spareth his rod hateth his son"* (Prov. 13:24). The other is, *"Fathers, provoke not your children to wrath."* The whole problem of discipline lies between those two limits, and they are both found in the Scriptures. Work the problem out in the Scriptures, try to get at the great Scriptural principles that govern this vital; this urgent matter, this great problem confronting all the Western nations, if not also others, at this hour. All our problems result from our going to one extreme or the other. That is never found in Scripture. What characterizes the teaching of the Scriptures always and everywhere is their perfect balance, a fairness that never fails, the extraordinary way in which grace and law are divinely blended…

We come now to the question of the administration of discipline… Discipline is essential and must be enforced. But the Apostle exhorts us to be very careful as to how we exercise it because we can do more harm than good if we do not do it in the right way…

The Apostle divides his teaching into two sections, the *negative* and the *positive*. This problem he says is not confined to the children: the fathers, the parents, also have to be careful. *Negatively*, he tells them, *"Provoke not your children to wrath." Positively*, he says, *"But bring them up in the nurture and admonition of the Lord."* As long as we remember both aspects all will be well.

We start with the negative: *"Provoke not your children to wrath."* These words can be translated, "Do not exasperate[33] your children, do not irritate your children, do not provoke your children to become resentful." That is always a very real danger when we exercise discipline. And if we become guilty of it we shall do much more harm than good…As we have seen, both extremes are altogether wrong. In other words, we must exercise this discipline in such a manner that we do not irritate our children or provoke them to a sinful resentment. We are required to keep the balance.

How is this to be done? How is such discipline to be exercised by parents?… Once more we must go back to chapter 5, verse 18 [of Ephesians]: *"Be not drunk with wine wherein is excess, but be filled with the Spirit."* That is always the *key*. We saw when we were dealing with that verse that the life lived in the Spirit, the life of a man who is filled with the Spirit, is characterized always by two main things—*power* and *control*. It is a *disciplined* power. Remember how Paul puts it in writing to Timothy. *"For God,"* he says, *"hath not given us the spirit of fear; but of power, and of love, and of a sound mind (discipline)"* (2 Tim. 1:7). Not uncontrolled power, but power controlled by love and a sound mind—*discipline!* That is always the characteristic of the life of a man who is *"filled with the Spirit"*…

How, then, am I to exercise this discipline? *"Provoke not your children to wrath."* This is to be the first principle governing our action. We are incapable of exercising true discipline unless we are first able to exercise self-control and discipline our own tempers…People who are filled with the Spirit are always characterized by *control*. When you are disciplining a child, you should have first controlled yourself. If you try to discipline your child when you are in a temper, it is certain that you will do more harm than good. What right have you to say to your child that he needs discipline when you obviously need it yourself? Self-control, control of temper is an essential pre-requisite in the control of others…So the very first principle is that we must start with ourselves. We must be certain that we are in control of ourselves, that we are cool…There must be this personal discipline, this self-control that enables a man to look at the situation objectively and to deal with it in a balanced and controlled manner. How important this is!…

---

33 **exasperate** – enrage.

The second principle arises, in a sense, out of the first. If a parent is to exercise this discipline in the right way, he must never be capricious.[34] There is nothing more irritating to the one who is undergoing discipline than a feeling that the person who is administering it is capricious and uncertain. There is nothing more annoying to a child than the kind of parent whose moods and actions you can never predict, who is changeable, whose condition is always uncertain. There is no worse type of parent than he who one day, in a kindly mood, is indulgent and allows the child to do almost anything it likes, but who the next day flares up in a rage if the child does scarcely anything at all. That makes life impossible for the child…Such a parent, I say again, fails to exercise a true and helpful discipline, and the position of the child becomes impossible. He is provoked and irritated to wrath and has no respect for such a parent.

I am referring not only to temperamental reactions, but to conduct also. The parent who is not *consistent* in his conduct cannot truly exercise discipline in the case of the child. A parent who does one thing today and the contrary thing tomorrow is not capable of sound discipline. There must be *consistency*, not only in the reaction but also in the conduct and the behavior of the parent. There must be a pattern about the life of the parent, for the child is always observing and watching. But if he observes that the parent is erratic[35] and himself does the very thing that he forbids the child to do, again you cannot expect the child to benefit from any discipline administered by such a parent…

Another most important principle is that the parents must never be unreasonable or unwilling to hear the child's case. There is nothing that so annoys the one who is being disciplined as the feeling that the whole procedure is utterly unreasonable. In other words, it is a thoroughly bad parent who will not take any circumstances into consideration at all or who will not listen to any conceivable explanation. Some fathers and mothers, in the desire to exercise discipline, are liable to become utterly unreasonable; and they themselves may be very much at fault. The report they have received concerning the child may be wrong, or there may have been peculiar circumstances of which they are ignorant; but the child is not even allowed to state the position or to give any kind of explanation. Of course, one realizes that advantage can be taken of this by the child. All I am saying is that *we* must never be unreasonable. Let the explanation be given by the child, and if it is not a true reason, then you can chastise for that also as well as for the particular act that constitutes the offence. But to refuse to

---

34 **capricious** – guided by whim or fancy, not settled judgment; given to sudden changes.
35 **erratic** – given to sudden unpredictable change.

listen, to prohibit any kind of reply, is inexcusable…Such conduct is always wrong; that is to provoke our children to wrath. It is certain to exasperate and irritate them into a condition of rebellion and of antagonism…

That leads inevitably to [another] principle: Discipline must never be too severe. Here is perhaps the danger that confronts many good parents at the present time as they see the utter lawlessness about them, and as they rightly bemoan it and condemn it. Their danger is to be so deeply influenced by their revulsions as to go right over to this other extreme and to become much too severe. The opposite of no discipline at all is not cruelty; it is balanced discipline, it is controlled discipline…

Let me summarize my argument. Discipline must always be exercised in love; and if you cannot exercise it in love, do not attempt it at all. In that case, you need to deal with yourself first. The Apostle has already told us to speak the truth in love in a more general sense; but exactly the same applies here. Speak the truth, but in love. It is precisely the same with discipline: it must be governed and controlled by love. *"Be not drunk with wine, wherein is excess; but be filled with the Spirit"* (Eph. 5:18). What is *"the fruit of the Spirit"? "Love, joy, peace, longsuffering, gentleness, goodness, faith, meekness, temperance"* (Gal. 5:22-23). If, as parents, we are *"filled with the Spirit,"* and produce such fruit, discipline will be a very small problem as far as we are concerned…You must have a right view of parenthood and regard the child as a life given to you by God. What for? To keep to yourself, and to mould to your pattern, to impose your personality upon it? Not at all! But put into your care and charged by God that his soul may ultimately come to know Him and to know the Lord Jesus Christ…

From *Life in the Spirit in Marriage, Home & Work: An Exposition of Ephesians 5:18 to 6:9*, published by The Banner of Truth Trust: www.banneroftruth.org.

David Martyn Lloyd-Jones (1899-1981): Perhaps the greatest expository preacher of the 20th century; Westminster Chapel, London, 1938-68; born in Wales.

Children to Be Educated for Christ
EDWARD W. HOOKER (1794-1875)

The Church of the Lord Jesus Christ was instituted in this sinful world to seek its conversion. It was said to her eighteen hundred years ago, *"Preach the gospel to every creature"* (Mark 16:15). Her time, talents, and resources have all been justly owed to her Lord for this purpose. Yet, *"the whole world lieth in wickedness"* (1 John 5:19). Few, comparatively, have heard *"the name of the Lord Jesus,"* that *"there be any Holy Ghost"* (Acts 19:5, 2), or that there is a God that ruleth in the earth (Rev. 19:6).

In this affecting[36] moral condition of the world, the questions are to be solemnly considered by the friends of Christ: "Have we not something more to do? Is there not some great duty that we have overlooked, some covenant that we have made with our Lord yet unfulfilled?" And an answer will be found if we look upon the children of Christian parents, who have professed to dedicate their all to God, but to a great extent have neglected to educate their offspring for the express purpose of serving Christian the advancement of His kingdom. Said a Christian mother whose heart is deeply interested in this subject, "I fear that many of us think that parental duty is limited to labors for the salvation of our children: that we have prayed for them only that they may be saved, instructed them only that they may be saved." Infinitely important, indeed it is, that they should be saved. But if ardent desires for the glory of our Redeemer and the salvation of souls glowed in our hearts like an inextinguishable flame, our most earnest prayers from their very birth would be that they might not only be saved themselves, but be instrumental in saving others.

So far as the service of Christ has been contemplated, it appears to have been regarded as consisting of becoming a Christian, professing religion, taking care of one's own soul, maintaining a reputable standing in the church, wishing well to the cause of Christ, giving as much as is convenient for its advancement, and, finally, taking a pious[37] leave of the world to go and be happy in heaven. Thus, *"one generation passeth away, and another generation cometh,"* to live and die in the same manner (Eccl. 1:4). And truly the earth might abide forever, [yet] the mass of its population still lie in ruin, should all Christians continue to live thus.

There is need then of an appeal to Christian parents in view of the present condition of the world. You give your prayers and a portion of your money.

---
36 **affecting** – moving; influencing; inclining toward some result.
37 **pious** – godly.

But, as said the Christian already quoted, "What affectionate parent does not love his children more than his money? And why should not these living treasures be given to Christ?" This seeking our *"own, not the things which are Jesus Christ's"* (Phil. 2:21) must cease, if the world is ever to be converted. We must act, and teach our children to act, more faithfully according to that Scripture: *"He died for all, that they which live should not henceforth live unto themselves, but unto him which died for them, and rose again"* (2 Cor. 5:15).

Let us be understood. We do not say to dedicate your children to the cause of missions exclusively, or to any field of benevolence. You must leave their assignment to *"the Lord of the harvest"* (Matt. 9:38). He will appoint them to stations, public or private; to spheres of extended or limited influence as shall seem *"good in [his] sight"* (Matt. 11:26). Your duty is to do all that is comprehended in the injunction,[38] *"Bring them up in the nurture and admonition of the Lord"* (Eph. 6:4), assured that the time will come when it will be said to you by the voice of Providence,[39] respecting each, *"the Lord hath need of him"* (Mark 11:3)—and he will be led to that station in which the Lord will be pleased to bless him. And whether it prove retired and lowly[40] or public and eminent,[41] be assured of this: he will find work enough assigned him and responsibilities enough laid upon him to keep him at the footstool seeking grace to strengthen him, and to require the anxious and diligent employment of all his powers while life shall last.

It is, then, an interesting inquiry for Christian parents: "What qualifications will best prepare our children to be efficient servants of Christ?" There are many pertaining to the *heart*, the *mind*, and the *physical constitution*.

1. First of all, piety: They must fervently love Christ and His kingdom, heartily consecrate themselves to His service, and be ready for any self-denial, sacrifice, or work to which He may call. Eminent[42] piety it must be, counting *"all things but loss for…Christ"* (Phil. 3:8).

Said one, now the wife of an American missionary, "To make and receive visits, exchange friendly salutations, attend to one's wardrobe, cultivate a garden, read good and entertaining books, and even attend religious meetings for one's own enjoyment—all this does not satisfy me. I want to

---

38 **injunction** – command.
39 **Providence** – What are God's works of providence? A: God's works of providence are His most holy, wise, and powerful preserving and governing all His creatures and all their actions. (Spurgeon's Catechism, Q. 11, available from Chapel Library)
40 **retired and lowly** – quiet and humble.
41 **eminent** – famous and respected.
42 **eminent** – present in a notable degree.

be where every arrangement will have unreserved and constant reference to eternity. On missionary ground, I expect to find new and unlooked for trials and hindrances; still, it is my choice to be there; and so far from looking upon it as a difficult task to sacrifice my home and country, I feel as if I should *'flee as a bird to[her] mountain'* (Ps. 11:1)."

A piety that thus glows and prays to live, labor, and suffer for Christ is the first and grand qualification to be sought in your child. It is necessary to act efficiently for Christ anywhere—at home or abroad, in an elevated or a lowly sphere. The Lord Jesus has no work adapted to Christians who live at the poor dying rate with which so many are content. It is all work for them that are *"strong in the grace that is in Christ Jesus"* and willing and determined to be *"faithful unto death"* (2 Tim. 2:1; Rev. 2:10).

2. Intellectual qualifications: It is a great mistake of some that moderate qualifications will suffice for "the work of Christ." Shall Christians be satisfied with these in the business of the Redeemer's kingdom, when the men of the world are not in their concerns? Be cautious of perverting dependence upon divine aid, by trusting to warmth of heart to compensate for lack of knowledge. The injunction, "Thou shalt love the Lord thy God with all thy mind," applies to the service as well as love of Him. Your child will need a well-balanced and cultivated mind as much as a pious heart. Let his desires to do good never be frustrated through your neglect of his intellectual education. We are not saying [to] send all your sons to college and your daughters to female seminaries; but prepare them to deal with minds under the dominion of sin anywhere, having intellectual qualifications not to be despised.

3. Qualifications pertaining to the physical constitution:[43] The interests of religion have suffered enough through the breaking down of constitutions and the premature deaths of promising young men. Do not dedicate a feeble, sickly son to the ministry because he is not sufficiently robust for some secular employment or profession. No men more need iron constitutions than ministers and missionaries. *"If ye offer the blind for sacrifice, is it not evil? and if ye offer the lame and sick, is it not evil? offer it now unto thy governor; will he be pleased with thee, or accept thy person?"* (Mal. 1:8). You have a daughter whom Providence may call to the self-denials of missionary life. Do not nurse her in the lap of enervating indulgence, or allow her to follow habits and fashions injurious to health, to become a *"tender and delicate woman…which would not adventure to set the sole of her foot upon the ground for delicateness and tenderness"* (Deut. 28:56), and who will be at the sport of a morbid sensibility, or a disordered nervous temperament. Will you be satisfied with such an

---

43 **constitution** – condition of the body regarding vitality, health, and strength.

offering to the King of Sion?[44] Will it be kindness to her who may be called to suffer much, and will want all the capacity for endurance, as well as action, which can be acquired in a most thorough physical education? No, dedicate to Christ and the Church your *"young men [that] are strong"* (1 John 2:14), and your daughters prepared to be companions for such in labors and sufferings for Christ.

Thus far[45] of qualifications. We come now to speak more particularly of the duties of parents in training sons and daughters for the service of Christ.

1. Pray much respecting your great work. "Who is sufficient for these things?" (2 Cor. 2:16), well may you say. But says God, *"My grace is sufficient for thee"* (2 Cor. 12:9). Keep near the throne of grace with this great subject weighing upon your spirit. Half your work is to be done in your closet. If you fail there, you will fail in all you do out of it. You must have wisdom from above in training servants for the Most High. Commune with God respecting the particular case of each of your children. While you do this you will obtain views of duty that human wisdom never can attain and feel motives that will be nowhere else rightly appreciated. In the final day, there doubtless will be disclosures of transactions of Christian parents with God respecting their children that will delightfully explain the secret of their devotedness and usefulness. There will then be known more than can be now, respecting the prayers of mothers especially. The mother of Mills had some peculiar exercises in her closet respecting him that help to account for his remarkable usefulness. The interesting fact is stated in one of our religious journals, that "of one hundred and twenty students in one of our theological seminaries, more than one hundred had been borne by a mother's prayers, and directed by a mother's counsels, to the Savior." See what prayer can do. Be *"instant in prayer"* (Rom. 12:12).

2. Cultivate a tender sense of parental accountability. God holds you accountable for the character of your children, so far as fidelity in the use of means is concerned. You are to "give account in the day of judgment for what you do, or neglect to do, for the right formation of your children's characters. You may so educate them that, by the sanctifying grace of God, they will be the instruments of salvation to hundreds, yea, thousands— and through your neglect of them, hundreds, thousands, may be lost, and their blood be required at your hands.[46] You cannot divest yourself of this

---

44 **Sion** – heavenly Jerusalem (Heb. 12:22-29).
45 **thus far** – to this point (and therefore concluding).
46 **their blood be required at your hands** – Parents must take their duties to their children's souls very seriously, but they must not understand the author's words to imply that their

responsibility. You must act under it, and meet it in the Judgment. Remember this with godly fear, and yet "encourage yourself in the Lord." If faithful in the closet and in doing what you there acknowledge your duty, you will find sustaining grace. And the thought will be delightful, as well as solemn: "I am permitted to train these immortals to glorify God in the salvation of souls."

3. Have a devoted spirit yourself. Your soul must be in health and prosper; must burn with love to Christ and His kingdom; and all your instructions be enforced by a godly example, if you would lead your children to live devotedly. The father of a large family, most of them pious, was asked, "What means have you employed with your children?" "I have endeavored so to live," said he, "as to show them that it was my own grand purpose to go to heaven, and to take them along with me."

4. Give religious instruction early. Watch [for] opportunities for this in every stage of childhood. Early impressions will last through life, when later ones fade away. Said an American missionary, "I recollect particularly that once my mother came and stood by me as I sat in the door, and tenderly talked to me of God and my soul's concerns; and her tears dropped upon my head. That made me a missionary." Cecil[47] says, "I had a pious mother, who dropped things in my way. I could never rid myself of them. I was a professed infidel, but then I liked to be an infidel in company rather than alone. I was wretched by myself. Parental influence thus cleaves to a man; it harasses him; it throws itself continually in his way." John Newton[48] never could divest himself of the impressions of his mother's instructions.

5. Seek the early conversion of your children. Regard every day of their continuance out of Christ as an increase of their danger and guilt. "A mother," says a missionary, "who had brought up a large family, all of whom had become hopefully pious, was asked what means she had used for their conversion. She replied, 'I have felt that if not converted before seven or eight years of age, they would probably be lost; and when they have approached that age, have been in agony lest they should pass it impenitent; and have gone to the Lord with my anguish. He has not turned away my prayers nor His mercy from me.'"

---

children's salvation will of necessity follow from parental training. Scripture makes clear that God is sovereign and salvation is of the Lord (Jonah 2:9). Faithful parents must pursue the salvation of their children diligently and faithfully, entrusting them into God's hands. God's glory must be our focus, not the results.

47 **Richard Cecil** (1748-1810) – English Anglican minister and author.
48 **John Newton** (1725-1807) – English Anglican minister, author, and hymnwriter; formerly a rebellious infidel in his youth and early adulthood, eventually a slave trader; miraculously saved at 23; ordained a pastor in the Church of England; author of *Amazing Grace*.

Pray for this: *"Arise, cry out in the night: in the beginning of the watches pour out thine heart like water before the face of the Lord: lift up thy hands toward him for the life of thy young children"* (Lam. 2:19). Hope for the early bestowment of divine grace from such promises as this: *"I will pour water upon him that is thirsty, and floods upon the dry ground: I will pour my spirit upon thy seed, and my blessing upon thine offspring: And they shall spring up as among the grass, as willows by the water courses. One shall say, I am the LORD'S; and another shall call himself by the name of Jacob; and another shall subscribe with his hand unto the LORD, and surname himself by the name of Israel"* (Isa. 44:3-5). The history of some families is a delightful fulfillment of this promise. Young hearts are the best in which to lay, deep and broad, the foundations of usefulness. There is no hope that your child will do anything for Christ until you can see him at the foot of the cross, repenting, believing, devoting himself.

It seems that some suppose that religion cannot enter a child's mind: that it demands maturity of years to *"repent...and believe the gospel"* (Mark 1:15). A Christian child, therefore, seems often regarded as a prodigy;[49] and grace in a young soul is a dispensation of divine mercy too unusual to be expected in the use of common means. "Parents," said a mother, "labor and pray prospectively for the conversion of their children." We have seen parents weeping over deceased children of four, five, six, seven years, who seemed to feel no solicitude whether they had died in a safe spiritual state, nor self-reproach for neglect to labor for their conversion. It is an interesting fact, and a serious one in its bearing upon parental neglect, that children under the age of four years have been known to feel deep convictions of sin against God and of their ruined state; and to sorrow for sin, believe on Christ, fix their affections on God and to exhibit all the evidences of grace seen in persons of adult years.

The late Mrs. Huntington,[50] writing to her son, says her biographer, "speaks of having a distinct remembrance of a solemn consultation in her mind, when about three years old, whether it was best to be a Christian then or not, and of having come to the decision that it was not." The biographies of Janeway[51] and numerous others forbid the idea that religion in a young heart is a miracle, and show that parents have reason to be anxious lest their young children die without hope, as well as to be encouraged to seek their early conversion.

---

49 **prodigy** – something out the ordinary course of nature.
50 **Susan Huntington** (1791-1823) – American pastor's wife, known for her godliness and the spiritual advice contained in her memoirs, letters, journal, and poetry.
51 **James Janeway** (1636-1674) – English Puritan minister and author who, after John Bunyan, had the widest and longest popularity as the author of works read by English-speaking children.

We should be cautious of unreasonable distrust of apparent conversions of children. Watch over the little disciple affectionately, faithfully. His tender years plead for more careful and tender protection. Give him not occasion to say, "I have been neglected because supposed too young to be a Christian." True, parents and pastors have been often disappointed in children seemingly converted. But the Day of Judgment[52] may reveal that there have been more cases of undetected deception and hypocrisy in adults than disappointments respecting children supposed pious. Childhood is more guileless[53] than manhood: it sooner, perhaps always, throws off the mask, if it be but the mask of religion—and is again open to conviction, and perhaps becomes converted. Manhood—more cautious, deceitful, adventurous in false profession—wears the mask, shuts out conviction, cries *"peace and safety"* (1 Thess. 5:3), and goes on decently, solemnly, formally, down to hell.

Desire the early conversion of your children that they may have the longest possible time in this world to serve Christ. If "the dew of our youth" be devoted to God, advancing years are sure to be marked with proportionate maturity of Christian character and fitness for more efficient labors for Christ.

6. Maintain familiar Christian [communication] with your children. Converse with them as freely and affectionately on religious subjects as on others. If you are a warmhearted and prosperous Christian, you will do this naturally and easily. Let religious intimacy be interwoven with your whole family habits. You will thus know how to counsel, caution, reprove, and encourage what advances they make; what the *"reason of the hope that is in"* them (1 Peter 3:15); and for what particular department of service for Christ they are fitted. And if they die early, or before you, then you will have the consolation of having watched and known the progress of their preparation to *"depart, and to be with Christ"* (Phil. 1:23).

7. Place and keep before the mind of your child, as the great object for which he should live, the glory of God and the salvation of men. We do much to give direction to the mind and form the character of the man by placing an object for life before him. Men of the world know and act on this principle. So should the Christian. The object above-named is the only one worthy of an immortal and renewed soul, and prepares the way for the noblest elevation of character: it will raise him above living to himself and constrain him to fidelity in his Lord's service. Teach him to lay at the foot of the cross attainments, eminence, influence, honor, wealth—all things; and to live in the desire, *"Father, glorify thy name"* (John 12:28).

---

52 See FGB 210, *Day of Judgment*.
53 **guileless** – free of deceit.

Chapter 5—Bringing Up Children: Children to Be Educated for Christ

8. Choose instructors for your children with great care. Know to whose influence you commit the son or daughter of your vows. You have a great and sacred object to accomplish. The teachers of your children must be such as will aid you in that object. Correct moral character in a teacher is not enough. This is often allied with most dangerous religious opinions.[54] Your child should be placed under the care of a self-dedicated teacher, who will feel in relation to his charge, "I am to aid this parent in training a servant for Christ." In your choice of a school or seminary of learning, never be governed merely by its reputation as literary, fashionable, popular—irrespective of the possibility that its atmosphere may have no vitality from decided religious influence, or may even be poisoned by erroneous religious views in the instructors…Christian parent, your prayers, your best efforts, may all be frustrated by the influence of a teacher who has no religion.

9. Be cautious of defeating your own efforts for the spiritual welfare of your children. Neglect of some essential duty, though you may perform many others, will do this. Prayer without instruction will not do; nor instruction without a right example; nor prayer in the family without earnest wrestlings in the closet; nor all these together without watching over them to keep them out of temptation.

Be afraid of indulging them in vain amusements. A mother once went to a meeting of her female friends and asked their supplications for her daughter, whom it appeared she had permitted, at that very time, to attend a dancing party. She justified herself in the rashness and inconsistency of the permission by reference to her own early habits of seeking amusements. If parents will permit their children to run directly into "the snare of the devil," let them, at least, not mock God by entreating Christians to pray that He will take care of them there! If they do, let them not wonder if their children live *"the servants of sin"* and die the *"vessels of wrath"* (Rom. 6:17; 9:22).

Guard yourself against setting them the example of fitfulness in religion: now, all fervor and bustle; then, languid,[55] having scarce the breath of spiritual life. A considerate son or daughter will say, "My father's religion is one of fits and starts, of times and seasons. It is everything now, but it will soon be nothing, as before." If you would have your children serve Christ in uniform activity, do so yourself. Be afraid of that periodical religion, which all at once breaks out from the midst of worldliness and unfaithfulness, and in which feeling shows itself *"deceitfully as a brook"* (Job 6:15). Or, as some author has

---

54 For this reason and numerous others, many parents have chosen to educate their children at home.

55 **languid** – exhibiting only faint interest.

expressed it, "like a mountain torrent, swollen by spring floods, foaming, roaring, dashing along; seeming a mighty and permanent river; but which, after a few days, sinks away, becomes a mere rivulet, or comes to nothing; leaving a channel dry, rocky, silent as death." The deepest piety is like the deep, full river: noiseless, fed by living springs, never disappointing, always flowing, fertilizing, beautifying. Be of that humble, steadfast, heartfelt, industrious, active cast of Christian character, by which your children shall see that the service of Christ is the great business of life, and be constrained to enter into it *"with all thine heart"* (Deut. 6:5).

10. Be cautious of countenancing[56] your children in living *"after the manner of this world"*—in seeking its honors, entering into its ambitious strifes, its secularizing habits and fashions. The children of pious parents must not be found among the votaries of fashion, emulating their display and useless accomplishments. "How is Christ thus robbed of His own?" said a Christian parent. "I have observed many instances of parents, exemplary, faithful, and judicious with their children, until perhaps fifteen years old; and then the desire to have them associate with distinguished people, and the dread of having them singular would cause them to turn right about and dress them like worldly people, and even court their intimacy for them." And parents have smarted severely under the rod of divine chastisement—been mortified, yea, had their hearts broken for such sins, in their disastrous consequences to the character of their children.

11. Be cautious what views and feelings you foster in your children respecting property. The love of property, in families called Christian, is one of the greatest hindrances to the spread of the gospel. The systems of Christian benevolence are all embarrassed, every year, from this cause. Parents set their children the example of making *"haste to be rich"* (Prov. 28:20), as though this were all for which God made them. They give a pittance[57] to the cause of Christ. And sons and daughters follow in the same course, even after having professed to know the way of holy boldness and said, we *"are not [our] own"* (1 Cor. 6:19). Facts might be mentioned that would make any true-hearted Christian blush for the Church of God.

Teach your children to remember what God has said: *"The silver is mine, and the gold is mine"* (Hag. 2:8). Remind them that you and they are stewards who are going to give account. Treat the acquirement of property as of importance only that you may do good and honor Christ. Let not your children expect you to make them heirs to large possessions. Let them see

---

56 **countenancing** – permitting.
57 **pittance** – very small, inadequate amount of money.

you annually giving, *"as God hath prospered"* you to all the great objects of Christian benevolence (1 Cor. 16:2). They will follow your example when you have gone to your reward. To leave your children the inheritance of your own devoted spirit and benevolent habits will be infinitely more desirable than to bequeath to them *"thousands of gold and silver"* (Ps. 119:72). Such examples we have seen.

As an aid to this, every parent should teach his family economy as a matter of religious principle. [Seek to have] early gain over their consciences to the side of a benevolent, spirited economy. Teach them that *"it is more blessed to give than to receive"* (Acts 20:35); to write "holiness to the Lord" upon their pocket money instead of spending it for useless or hurtful indulgences; to study simplicity and economy in dress, furniture, style of living; and to regard all useless expenditure of money as sin against God.

12. Be cautious of frustrating your efforts for the spiritual good of your children by wrong habits in your family. [Some examples are] levity[58] in conversation, dull and hasty formality in family worship, and worldly conversation on the Sabbath. Censorious remarks, we fear, keep whole families of children in the neglect of religion. Guard also against gloom, sanctimoniousness,[59] moroseness.[60] Some professing parents seem to have just religion enough to make them unhappy and to have all the unloveliness in religious temperament and habits that naturally comes of having consciences irritated by their unfaithful "manner of life." There is a heavenly cheerfulness and sweetness in some Christians, which declares to their families that religion is a blessing as well as serious reality, and gives them an inestimable influence and power to win them to the service of Christ. Cultivate this. Let *"the love of God…shed abroad in [your] hearts by the Holy Ghost"* (Rom. 5:5) continually prove to your children that religion is the source of the truest enjoyment, of the richest blessings.

13. If you would have your children obedient servants of Christ, you must govern them well. Subordination[61] is one grand law of His kingdom. Implicit obedience to your authority will well accord with the submission your child must render to Christ. How must the habit of insubordination and self-will increase the sorrows of his Christian conflict; render him often unamiable and uncomfortable in his social and domestic relations; and in

---

58 **levity** – treating serious matters with humor or lack of due respect.
59 **sanctimoniousness** – making a show of being morally superior to other people; self-righteous.
60 **moroseness** – being bad-tempered, moody, resentful.
61 **subordination** – submission to authority.

the church an unmanageable member, or an unlovely minister—or, if in the missionary work, an occasion of trials, frequent and bitter, to all his associates. Said a minister, respecting a departed member of his church, for whom he hoped the best he could, "He was one of the stubbornest oaks that ever grew upon Mount Zion."

A child well-governed, when he becomes a Christian, is ready to serve the Lord Jesus Christ *"with all humility of mind"* (Acts 20:19) in any work to which he is called, and will work kindly, harmoniously, and efficiently with others. He enters his Lord's field saying, *"Lo, I come to do thy will, O God"* (Heb. 10:9). He will have that heavenly spirit, *"the meekness and gentleness of Christ"* (2 Cor. 10:1), and as he goes forward from duty to duty, will be able to say with David, *"my soul is even as a weaned child"* (Ps. 131:2). *"I delight to do thy will, O my God"* (Ps. 40:8)! And with such a spirit he will find precious satisfaction in a life of successful labor for his Lord on earth, and *"in hope of the glory of God"* (Rom. 5:2).

So that your children may be fitted to serve Christ by a right government, study the manner in which a holy God governs. His is the government of a Father: persuasive without weakness; in love and mercy, and yet in accordance with justice; patient and forbearing, yet strict in the rebuke and punishment of offences. He loves His children, but chastens them for their profit. He employs encouragements to obedience, but in His determination to be obeyed He is as firm as His own everlasting throne. He gives His children every reason to fear offending Him; still, He assures them that to love and serve Him shall be to them the beginning of heaven on earth!

We have incidentally spoken of the interest of *mothers* in this subject. Maternal duty and influence, in truth, lie at the foundation of the whole work of educating children for the service of Christ. A Christian mother may more richly bless the world through her children, than many who have sat on thrones. Mothers, divine providence places your children under your peculiar care just at that period of life when first and eternal impressions will be made.

Let your influence be *"sanctified by the word of God and prayer"* (1 Tim. 4:5), and be consecrated to the high object of educating sons and daughters for *"the work of Christ"* (Phil. 2:30).

Brethren in the sacred office of the ministry: Have we done what we could, or estimated our responsibilities relative to this subject as we ought? Have our labors been conducted with sufficient reference to our younger hearers, and their preparations to serve "*the Lord of the harvest*"? A minister should acquaint himself with the children of his charge, and know what their parents are doing for their good and their preparation to serve the Lord

Jesus Christ. We must act steadily and efficiently on the minds of parents: preach to them, converse with them, prompt their consciences respecting their duties. We should sit down with them in the retirement of their homes and ask them such questions as these: What are your views of your duty to God respecting your children? What are your expectations relative to their future usefulness to the kingdom of God on earth? Are you fulfilling your duty with your eyes on the Judgment Seat of Christ? What means do you employ that you may realize your expectations? Do you wish to see the glory of God, and the conversion of this lost world, aided by the children God has graciously given you?

Such inquiries, made in the affectionate seriousness of watchmen for souls, will come home to hearts in which there is grace; [they] will awaken to thoughtfulness and quicken to activity. We shall assist parents to see how they and their families stand related to God and to this revolted world. And if we would promote their personal prosperity in the divine life, there is no way better than this [to] stimulate them to their high and solemn duties.

Christian parents: Our children have too long been educated without that direct and single reference to the glory of Christ, and the good of this fallen world, that becomes us. Their dedication to the work of Christ, too, has been exceedingly imperfect. For this reason, among others, the work of evangelizing the world has gone on slowly. To address you in the language of a Christian parent whose feelings are deeply interested in this subject, "There is much justly said of the duty of Christians to hold their property consecrated to Christ; and it is often remarked that until they act upon higher principles, the world cannot be converted." It is true, but our delinquency here is not the basis of our unfaithfulness. It is to be feared that many who feel their obligations respecting their property, forget that they are answerable to Christ, to the Church, and to the heathen, for their children. Thousands [in] gold and silver are wanted to carry on the work of evangelizing the world, but a thousand sanctified minds will do more than millions of money. When the children of pious parents, with the spirit of true Christians, shall give themselves for the saving of the world, there will be no more any *"dark places...full of the habitations of cruelty"* (Ps. 74:20).

Has a greater duty ever rested on men than that which binds them to educate their children for the benefit of the world? Were this our constant, prominent desire, it would give definiteness to our instructions and prayers; we should watch against every habit or influence that would hinder the accomplishment of our wishes. Our children would be taught self-government, self-denial, industry, and effort. We should not be guilty of such a miserable wavering between Christ and the world. Every parent would know for what he was training his children. Every child would know for what he was living. His conscience would feel the pressure of duty. He could not be faithless to the object set before him without violating his conscience. Would not such education be owned and blessed of the Spirit of God, and our children be converted early? Then their powers would all be given to God.

Christian parents, *whatsoever our hand findeth to do, let us do it with our might* (Eccl. 9:10). The pupilage[62] of our children is passing away on the swift wings of time. Let us enter into the spirit of the first propagators of Christianity and take our children along with us in the labors of love. Let our aim be at higher attainments in piety. The "feeble" should become as "David," and David as the Son of God (Zech. 12:8). It must cease to be that a few men and women only, in a century, shall appear with the spirit of Taylor,[63] Brainerd,[64] Martyn,[65] and Livingston.[66] There ought to be Christians of their standard in every church. Yea, why should not every church be composed of such, so that the places of their abode should become *"too strait"* for them (2 Kings 6:1); and they, with *"the love of Christ constrain[ing]"* them (2 Cor. 5:14), go forth in the untiring spirit of Christian enterprise over the whole face of the earth. With such pillars and polished stones (Ps. 144:12), the temple of the Lord would indeed be beautiful. Blessed with such supporters of the cause of Christ at home, the Church will be strong for her Lord's work. Blessed with such messengers of salvation to the heathen, the work of evangelizing the nations will go rapidly on. As they go forth and proclaim the Savior's love, there will break forth from all "the dark places" the cry, *"How beautiful upon the mountains are the feet of him that bringeth good tidings, that publisheth peace; that bringeth good tidings of good, that publisheth salvation; that saith unto Zion, Thy God reigneth!"* (Isa. 52:7).

---

62 **pupilage** – period during which one is a student.
63 **James Hudson Taylor** (1832-1905) – English missionary to China for 51 years; brought more than 800 missionaries that began 125 schools and established 300 mission stations in all 18 provinces.
64 **David Brainerd** (1718-1747) -- American missionary to Native Americans in New Jersey; suffered numerous trials and difficulties, dying at a young age; became a great inspiration for other missionaries and Christians.
65 **Henry Martyn** (1781-1812) – Anglican missionary to India and Persia; translated the entire New Testament into Urdu, Persian, and Judaeo-Persic.
66 **David Livingstone** (1813-1873) – Scottish Congregationalist and pioneer medical missionary to Africa for the London Missionary Society; one of the most popular national heroes of late 19th century Britain through his pioneering exploration of the interior of Africa.

From *Children to be educated for Christ: in Reference to the Heart, the Mind, and the Physical Constitution,* American Tract Society, in the public domain.

Edward W. Hooker (1794-1875): American Congregational minister, author, professor of rhetoric and church history; born in Goshen, Connecticut.

Teaching Children Character
PHILIP DODDRIDGE (1702-1751)

Children should be trained up in the way of obedience to their parents. This is a command that God [ordained] from Mount Sinai by annexing to it a peculiar promise of long life, a blessing that young persons greatly desire (Ex. 20:12). The Apostle, therefore, observed that it is the first commandment with promise, namely, a command eminently remarkable for the manner in which the promise is adjoined. And it is certainly a wise constitution of Providence that gives so much to parental authority, especially while children are in their younger years, their minds being then incapable of judging and acting for themselves in matters of importance. Children should, therefore, be early taught and convinced by Scripture that God has committed them into the hands of their parents. Consequently, [they should be taught] that reverence and obedience to their parents is a part of the duty they owe to God and disobedience to them is rebellion against Him. Parents should by no means indulge their children in a direct and resolute opposition to their will in matters of greater or smaller moment, remembering, *"A child left to himself bringeth his mother to shame"* and himself to ruin (Prov. 29:15). And with regard to subjection, as well as affection, *"It is good for a man that he bear the yoke in his youth"* (Lam. 3:27).

Children should be trained in the way of benevolence and kindness to all. The great Apostle tells us that *"love is the fulfilling of the law"* (Rom. 13:10), and that all those branches of it that relate to our neighbor are comprehended in that one word: *love*. This love, therefore, we should endeavor to teach them. We shall find that in many instances it will be a law to itself and guide them right in many particular actions, the obligations to which may depend on principles of equity[67] that lie far beyond the reach of their feeble understandings. There is hardly an instruction relating to our duty more happily adapted to the capacity of children than that Golden Law (so important to all of the maturest age): *"Therefore all things whatsoever ye would that men should do to you, do ye even so to them"* (Matt. 7:12). This rule we should teach them and by this should examine their actions. From their cradles we should often inculcate[68] it upon them that a great deal of religion consists in doing good, that the wisdom from above is full of mercy and good fruits, and that every Christian should do good unto all as he has opportunity.

---

67 **equity** – what is fair and right.
68 **inculcate** – teach and impress by frequent repetition.

That such instructions may be welcome to them, we should endeavor by all prudent methods to soften their hearts to sentiments of humanity and tenderness, and guard against everything that would have a contrary tendency. We should remove from them, as much as possible, all kinds of cruel and bloody spectacles, and should carefully discourage any thing barbarous in their treatment of brute creatures. By no means [should we allow] them to sport themselves in the death or pain of domestic animals, but rather [teach] them to treat the poor creatures kindly and take care of them, the contrary to which is a most detestable sign of a savage and malignant disposition. *"A righteous man regardeth the life of his beast: but the tender mercies of the wicked are cruel"* (Prov. 12:10).

We should, likewise, take care to teach them the odiousness and folly of a selfish temper and encourage them in a willingness to impart to others what is agreeable and entertaining to themselves. Especially we should endeavor to form them to sentiments of compassion for the poor. We should show them where God has said, *"Blessed is he that considereth the poor: the LORD will deliver him in time of trouble"*(Ps. 41:1).He that has pity upon the poor lends to the Lord, and that which he has given will He pay him again. And we should show them, by our own practice, that we verily believe these promises to be true and important. It might not be improper, sometimes, to make our children the messengers by which we send some small supply to the indigent and distressed; and, if they discover a disposition to give something out of the little stock we allow them to call their own, we should joyfully encourage it and should take care that they never lose by their charity, but that in a prudent manner we abundantly repay it. It is hardly to be imagined that children thus brought up should, in the advance of life, prove injurious and oppressive; they will rather be the ornaments of religion and blessings to the world and probably will be in the number of the last whom Providence will suffer to want.

Children should be trained up in the way of diligence. This should undoubtedly be our care if we have any regard to the welfare either of their bodies or their souls. In whatever station of life they may at length be fixed, it is certain there is little prospect of their acquitting themselves with usefulness, honor, and advantage without a close and resolute application; whereas the wisest of princes and of men has said, *"Seest thou a man diligent in his business? he shall stand before kings; he shall not stand before mean men"* (Prov. 22:29). And it is evident that a diligent prosecution of business keeps one out of the way of a thousand temptations that idleness seems to invite, leading a man into numberless instances of vice and folly because he has nothing else to do.

A prudent and religious parent will therefore be concerned that his children may not early contract so pernicious a habit, nor enter upon life like persons that have no business in it but to crowd the stage and stand in the way of those who are better employed. Instead of suffering them to saunter about from place to place (as abundance of young people do to no imaginable purpose of usefulness or even of entertainment), he will quickly assign them some employment for their time: an employment so moderated and so diversified as not to overwhelm and fatigue their tender spirits, yet sufficient to keep them wakeful and active. Nor is this so difficult as some may imagine; for children are a busy kind of creatures, naturally fond of learning new things and trying and showing what they can do. So that, I am persuaded, were perfect inactivity to be imposed upon them as a penance but for one hour, they would be heartily weary of it and would be glad to seek their refuge from it in almost any business you would think fit to employ them about…

Children should be trained up in the way of integrity. Simplicity and godly sincerity is not only a very amiable, but an essential, part of the Christian character…It is very melancholy to observe how soon the artifices[69] and deceits of corrupt nature begin to reveal themselves. In this respect, we are transgressors from the womb and go astray almost as soon as we are born, speaking lies (Ps. 58:3). Great care, therefore, should be taken to form the minds of children to a love for truth and candor and a sense of the meanness as well as the guilt of a lie. We should be cautious that we do not expose them to any temptations of this kind, either by unreasonable severities on account of little faults or by hasty surprises when inquiring into any matter of fact, which it may seem their interest to disguise by a falsehood. When we find them guilty of a known and deliberate lie, we should express our horror of it not only by an immediate reproof or correction, but by such a conduct towards them for some time afterwards as may plainly show them how greatly we are amazed, grieved, and displeased. When so solemn a business is made of the first faults of this kind, it may be a means of preventing many more.

I will further add that we ought not only thus severely to critically remark upon a direct lie, but likewise, in a proper degree, to discourage all kinds of equivocations[70] and double meanings and those little tricks and artifices by which they may endeavor to impose on each other or on those that are older than themselves. We should often inculcate upon them that excellent Scripture, *"He that walketh uprightly walketh surely: but he that perverteth his*

---

69 **artifices** – deceptions of people using cleverness or subtlety.
70 **equivocations** – statements that are vague and often deliberately misleading.

ways (that twists and distorts it with the perplexities of artifices and deceit) shall be known" (Prov. 10:9). Be showing them every day how easy, how pleasant, how honorable, and how advantageous it is to maintain a fair, open, and honest temper; and, on the other hand, what folly there is in cunning and dishonesty in all its forms; and how certain it is that by studying and practicing it, they take the readiest way to make themselves noxious[71] and useless, infamous and odious.[72] Above all, should we remind them that the righteous Lord loves righteousness, and His favorable countenance beholds the upright; but lying lips are such an abomination to Him that He expressly declared, *"All liars, shall have their part in the lake which burneth with fire and brimstone"* (Rev. 21:8).

Children should be trained up in the way of humility. This is a grace that our Lord particularly invites us to learn of Him and most frequently recommends to us, well knowing that without it so humbling a scheme as He came to introduce would never meet with a welcome reception. And, with regard to the present life, it is a most lovely ornament which engages universal esteem and affection, so that before honor is humility (Prov. 15:33). On the whole, we find he that exalts himself is abased, and he that humbles himself is exalted, both by God and by man.

A regard, therefore, to the ease, honor, and happiness of our children should engage us to an early endeavor of checking that pride which was the first sin and the ruin of our natures and diffuses itself so wide and sinks so deep into all that draw their original from de-generate Adam. We should teach them to express humility and modesty in their converse[73] with all.

They should be taught to treat their superiors with peculiar respect and should at proper seasons be accustomed to silence and reserve before them. Hence, they will learn in some degree the government of the tongue, a branch of wisdom that, in the advance of life, will be of great importance to the quiet of others and to their own comfort and reputation.

Nor should they be allowed to assume airs of insolence towards their equals, but rather be taught to yield, to oblige, and to give up their right for the sake of peace. To this purpose, I cannot but think it desirable that they should be generally accustomed to treat each other with those forms of civility and complaisance[74] that are usual among well-bred people in their rank of life. I know those things are mere trifles in themselves, yet they are

---

71 **noxious** – harmful to minds and morals.
72 **odious** – arousing hatred or disgust; detestable.
73 **converse** – manner of life.
74 **complaisance** – the desire and care to please.

the outguards[75] of humanity and friendship, and effectually prevent many a rude attack which, taking its rise from some little circumstance, may nevertheless be attended with fatal consequences...

Last, children should be trained up in the way of self-denial. As without something of this temper, we can never follow Christ or expect to be owned by Him as His disciples, so neither indeed can we pass comfortably through the world. For, whatever inexperienced youth may dream, a great many distasteful and mortifying circumstances will occur in life that will unhinge our minds almost every hour if we cannot manage and, in many instances, deny our appetites, our passions, and our humors. We should, therefore, endeavor to teach our children this important lesson quickly; and, if we succeed in our care, we shall leave them abundantly richer and happier in this rule and possession of their own spirits than the most plentiful estates or the most unlimited power over others could make them.

When a rational creature becomes the slave of appetite, he sinks beneath the dignity of the human nature as well as the sanctity of the Christian profession. It is therefore observable that when the Apostle mentions the three grand branches of practical religion, he puts sobriety in the front, perhaps to intimate that where that is neglected, the other cannot be suitably regarded. The grace of God, namely the Gospel, teaches us to live soberly, righteously, and godly. Children therefore, as well as young men, should be exhorted to be sober-minded; and they should be taught it by early self-denial. It is certain that if their own appetite and taste were to determine the kind and quantity of their food, many of them would quickly destroy their constitution and perhaps their lives, since they have often the greatest desire for those things that are the most improper. And it seems justly observed by a very wise man (who was himself a melancholy instance of it), that the fondness of mothers for their children, in letting them eat and drink what they will, lays a foundation for most of those calamities in human life which proceed from bodily indisposition. Nay, I will add that it is the part of wisdom and love not only to deny what would be unwholesome, but to guard against indulging them in too great a nicety,[76] either of food or of dress. People of sense cannot but see, if they would please to consider it, that to know how to fare plainly, and sometimes a little hardly, carries a man with ease and pleasure through many circumstances of life that to luxury and delicacy would be almost intolerable.

---

75 **outguards** – guards placed at a distance outside the main body of an army.
76 **nicety** – excessive refinement or elegance in dress or manner of living.

The government of the passions is another branch of self-denial to which children should early be habituated; and so much the rather because, in an age when reason is so weak, the passions are apt to appear with peculiar force and violence. A prudent care should, therefore, be taken to repress the exorbitances of them. For which purpose it is of great importance that they never be suffered to carry any point by obstinacy, noise, and clamor, which is indeed to bestow a reward on a fault that deserves a severe reprimand. Nay, I will venture to add that, though it is very inhuman to take pleasure in making them uneasy by needless mortifications, yet when they are eagerly and intemperately desirous of a trifle, they ought, for that very reason, sometimes to be denied it to teach them more moderation for the future. And if, by such methods, they gradually learn to conquer their little humors and fancies, they learn no inconsiderable branch of true fortitude and wisdom…

From *The Godly Family*, reprinted by Soli Deo Gloria, a division of Reformation Heritage Books: www.heritagebooks.org.

Philip Doddridge (1702-1751): English Nonconformist minister; prolific author and hymn writer; born in London, England.

Wicked parents are the most notable servants of the devil in all the world and the bloodiest enemies to their children's souls. More souls are damned [by God through the influence of] ungodly parents—and next [to] them… ungodly ministers and magistrates—than by any instruments in the world besides. —Richard Baxter

Principle Obstacles in Bringing Up Children for Christ
JOHN ANGELL JAMES (1785-1859)

That, in many cases, the means employed by Christian parents for their children's spiritual welfare are unsuccessful is a melancholy fact established by abundant and, I fear, accumulating evidence. I am not now speaking of those families—and are there indeed such?—where scarcely the semblance of domestic piety[77] or instruction is to be found, where no family altar[78] is seen, no family prayer[79] is heard, no parental admonition is delivered! What! This cruel, wicked, ruinous neglect of their children's immortal interests in the families of *professors!*[80] Monstrous inconsistency! Shocking dereliction of principle! No wonder that their children go astray. This is easily accounted for. Some of the most profligate[81] young people that I know have issued from such households. Their prejudices against religion and their enmity to its forms are greater than those of the children of avowed worldlings. Inconsistent, hypocritical, negligent professors of religion frequently excite in their sons and daughters an unconquerable aversion and disgust against piety, which seems to produce in them a determination to place themselves at the furthest possible remove from its influence.

But I am now speaking of the failure of a religious education where it has been in some measure carried on, instances of which are by no means infrequent...Too often do we see the child of many prayers and many hopes forgetting the instructions he has received and running with the multitude to do evil. Far be it from me to add affliction to affliction by saying that this is to be traced in every case to parental neglect. I would not thus, as it were, pour niter and vinegar[82] upon the bleeding wounds with which filial[83] impiety has lacerated many a father's mind. I would not thus cause the wretched parent to exclaim, "Reproach hath broken my heart, already half-broken by my child's misconduct." I know that in many cases no blame whatever could be thrown on the parent. It was the depravity of the child alone, which nothing could subdue but the power of the Holy Ghost, that led to the melancholy

---

77 **domestic piety** – reverence and obedience to God in the home.
78 **family altar** – the place or scene of family worship.
79 **family prayer** – many older writers used this as another term for family worship. For encouragement and help with this important practice, see FGB 188, *Family Worship*.
80 **professors** – those who profess to be Christians.
81 **profligate** – recklessly immoral.
82 **niter...wounds** – pouring sodium carbonate and vinegar on an open wound would be extremely painful.
83 **filial** – relationship of a child to his parents.

Chapter 5—Bringing Up Children: Principle Obstacles in Bringing Up Children for Christ

result. The best possible scheme of Christian education, most judiciously directed and most perseveringly maintained, has in some cases totally failed. God is a sovereign, and He hath mercy on whom He will have mercy (Rom. 9:15). Still, however, there is in the order of means a tendency in a religious education to secure the desired result. God usually does bless with His saving influence such efforts. *"Train up a child in the way he should go: and when he is old, he will not depart from it"* (Prov. 22:6). This is certainly true, as a general rule, though there are many exceptions to it.

I shall now lay before you the principal obstacles to the success of religious education as they strike my mind.

FIRST: It is frequently too negligently and capriciously[84] maintained, even where it is not totally omitted. It is obvious that, if at all attended to, it should be attended to with anxious earnestness, systematic order, and perpetual regularity. It should not be maintained as a dull form, an unpleasant drudgery, but as a matter of deep and delightful interest. The heart of the parent should be *entirely* and *obviously* engaged. A part of every returning Sabbath should be spent by him in the instruction of his filial charge. His concern should be embodied, more or less, with the whole habit of parental conduct. The father may lead the usual devotions at the family altar. The mother may join with him in teaching their children catechism, hymns, and Scripture. But, if this be unattended by serious admonition, visible anxiety, and strenuous effort to lead their children to think seriously on religion as a matter of *infinite* importance, little good can be expected. A cold, formal, capricious system of religious instruction is rather likely to create prejudice against religion than prepossession[85] in its favor.

Then again, a religious education should be *consistent*. It should extend to everything that is likely to assist in the formation of character…It should select the schools,[86] the companions, the amusements, the books of youth. For if it do nothing more than merely teach a form of sound words to the understanding and to the memory, while the impression of the heart and the formation of the character are neglected, very little is to be expected from such efforts. A handful of seed, scattered now and then upon the ground without order or perseverance, might as rationally be expected to produce a good crop as that a mere lukewarm, capricious, religious education should be followed by true piety. If the parent be not visibly in earnest, it cannot be expected that the child will be so. Religion, by every Christian parent, is

---

84 **capriciously** – unpredictably.
85 **prepossession** – favorable inclination toward.
86 For this reason, many in our day have chosen to educate their children at home.

theoretically acknowledged to be the most important thing in the world. But if in practice the father appears a thousand times more anxious for the son to be a good scholar than a real Christian, and the mother more solicitous for the daughter to be a good dancer or musician than a child of God, they may teach what they like in the way of good doctrine, but they are not to look for genuine piety as the result. This can only be expected where it is really taught and inculcated as the one thing needful.

SECONDLY: The relaxation of domestic discipline is another obstacle in the way of a successful religious education. A parent is invested by God with a degree of authority over his children, which he cannot neglect to use without being guilty of trampling underfoot the institutions of heaven. Every family is a community, the government of which is strictly despotic,[87] though not tyrannical. Every father is a sovereign, though not an oppressor. He is a legislator, not merely a counselor. His will should be law, not merely advice. He is to command, to restrain, to punish; and children are required to obey. He is, if necessary, to threaten, to rebuke, to chastise; and they are to submit with reverence. He is to decide what books shall be read, what companions invited, what engagements formed, and how time is to be spent. If he sees anything wrong, he is not to interpose merely with the timid, feeble, ineffectual protest of Eli—*"Why do ye such things?"* (1 Sam. 2:23)—but with the firm though mild prohibition. He must rule his own house and by the whole of his conduct make his children feel that obedience is his due and his demand.

The want of discipline, wherever it exists, is supplied by confusion and domestic anarchy. Everything goes wrong in the absence of this. A gardener may sow the choicest seeds; but if he neglect to pluck up weeds and prune wild luxuriances,[88] he must not expect to see his flowers grow or his garden flourish. So a parent may deliver the best instructions. But if he does not by discipline eradicate evil tempers, correct bad habits, repress rank corruptions, nothing excellent can be looked for. He may be a good prophet and a good priest; but if he be not also a good *king*, all else is vain. When once a man breaks his scepter or lends it to his children as a plaything, he may give up his hopes of success from a religious education…The misfortune in many families is that discipline is unsteady and capricious, sometimes carried even to tyranny itself, at [other times] relaxed into a total suspension of law, so that the children are at one time trembling like slaves, at others revolting like rebels; at one time groaning beneath an iron yoke, at others rioting in a

---

87 **despotic** – having an absolute ruler, in this case the father.
88 **luxuriances** – excessive growths.

state of lawless liberty. This is a most mischievous system, and its effects are generally just what might be expected.

In some cases, discipline commences too late. In others, it ceases too early. A father's magisterial[89] office is nearly coeval[90] with his parental relation. A child, as soon as he can reason, should be made to feel that obedience is due to parents. For if he grow up to boyhood before he is subject to the mild rule of paternal authority, he will very probably, like an untamed bullock, resist the yoke. On the other hand, as long as children continue beneath the parental roof, they are to be subject to the rules of domestic discipline. Many parents greatly err in abdicating the throne in favor of a son or daughter because the child is becoming a man or a woman. It is truly pitiable to see a boy or girl of fifteen…allowed to sow the seeds of revolt in the domestic community and to act in opposition to parental authority until the too compliant father gives the reins of government into filial hands or else by his conduct declares his children to be in a state of independence. There need not be any contest for power. For where a child has been accustomed to obey, even from an infant, the yoke of obedience will generally be light and easy. If not, and a rebellious temper should begin to show itself early, a judicious father should be on his guard and suffer no encroachments[91] on his prerogative.[92] At the same time, the increased power of his authority, like the increased pressure of the atmosphere, should be felt without being seen. This will make it irresistible.

THIRDLY: Undue severity, in the other extreme, is as injurious as unlimited indulgence. If injudicious fondness has slain its tens of thousands, unnecessary harshness has destroyed its thousands. By an authority that cannot err, we are told that the cords of love are the bands of a man. There is a plastic[93] power in love. The human mind is so constituted as to yield readily to the influence of kindness. Men are more easily led to their duty than driven to it…Love seems so essential an element of parental character that there is something shockingly revolting not only in a cruel, not only in an unkind or severe, but even in a coldhearted father. Study the parental character as it is exhibited in that most exquisitely touching moral picture, the Parable of the Prodigal Son. When a father governs entirely by cold, bare, uncovered authority; by mere commands, prohibitions, and threats; by

---

89 **magisterial** – authoritative.
90 **coeval** – equal in duration.
91 **encroachments** – gradual intrusions.
92 **prerogative** – exclusive right.
93 **plastic** – formative; creative.

Chapter 5—Bringing Up Children: Principle Obstacles in Bringing Up Children for Christ

frowns, untempered with smiles; when the friend is never blended with the legislator, nor authority modified with love; when his conduct produces only a servile[94] fear in the hearts of his children instead of a generous affection; when he is served from a dread of the effects of disobedience rather than from a sense of the pleasure of obedience. When he is rather dreaded in the family circle as a frowning specter than hailed as the guardian angel of its joys; when even accidents raise a storm or faults produce a hurricane of passion in his bosom; when offenders are driven to equivocation or lying with the hope of averting by concealment those severe corrections which disclosure always entails; when unnecessary interruptions are made to innocent enjoyments; when in fact nothing of the father, but everything of the tyrant is seen: can we expect religion to grow in such a soil as this? Yes, as rationally as we may look for the tenderest hothouse plant to thrive amidst the rigors of eternal frost.

It is useless for such a father to teach religion. He chills the soul of his pupils. He hardens their hearts against impression. He prepares them to rush with eager haste to their ruin as soon as they have thrown off the yoke of their bondage and to employ their liberty as affording the means of unbridled gratification.

Let parents then in all their conduct blend the lawgiver and the friend, temper authority with kindness…Let them so act that their children shall be convinced that their law is holy and their commandment is holy, and just, and good and that to be so governed is to be blessed.

Fourthly: The inconsistent conduct of parents themselves is a frequent and powerful obstacle to success in religious education…What then must be the influence of parental example? Now, as I am speaking of religious parents, it is of course assumed that they do exhibit in some measure the reality of religion…Religion may be seen in dim outline by the children in their parents' conduct. But it is attended with so many minor inconsistencies, such a mist of imperfections, that it presents little to conciliate their regard or raise their esteem. There is so much worldly-mindedness, so much conformity to fashionable follies, so much irregularity of domestic piety, such frequent sallies[95] of unchristian temper, such inconsolable grief and querulous[96] complaint under the trials of life, such frequent animosities towards their fellow Christians observable in the conduct of some Christians that their children see religion to the greatest possible disadvantage. The

---

94 **servile** – slave-like submission.
95 **sallies** – outbursts.
96 **querulous** – whiney.

consequence is that it either lowers their standard of piety or inspires disgust towards it altogether.

Parents, as you would wish your instructions and admonitions to your family to be successful, enforce them by the power of a holy example. It is not enough for you to be pious on the whole, but you should be wholly pious; not only to be real disciples, but *eminent* ones; not only sincere Christians, but *consistent* ones. Your standard of religion should be very high. To some parents I would give this advice: *Say less* about religion to your children, or else *manifest more* of its influence. Leave off family *prayer,* or else leave off family *sins.* Beware how you act, for all your actions are seen at home. Never talk of religion but with reverence. Be not forward to speak of the faults of your fellow Christians. When the subject is introduced, let it be in a spirit of charity towards the offender and of decided abhorrence of the fault. Many parents have done irreparable injury to their children's minds by a proneness to find out, to talk of, and almost to rejoice over the inconsistencies of professing Christians. Never cavil[97] at nor find fault with the religious exercises of the minister you attend. Rather, commend his discourses in order that your children may listen to them with greater attention. Direct their views to the most eminent Christians. Point out to them the loveliness of exemplary piety. In short, seeing that your example may be expected so much to aid or to frustrate your efforts for the conversion of your children, consider *"what manner of persons ought ye to be in all holy conversation and godliness"* (2 Peter 3:11).

FIFTHLY: Another obstacle to the success of religious instruction is sometimes found in the wild conduct of an elder branch of the family, especially in the case of a dissipated[98] son. The elder branches of a family are found, in general, to have considerable influence over the rest and often times to give the tone of morals to the others. They are looked up to by their younger brothers and sisters. They bring companions, books, amusements into the house and thus form the character of their juniors. It is of great consequence therefore that parents should pay particular attention to their elder children. If unhappily the habits of these should be decidedly unfriendly to the religious improvement of the rest, they should be removed, if possible, from the family. One profligate son may lead all his brothers astray. I have seen this, in some cases, most painfully verified. A parent may feel unwilling to send from home an unpromising child under the apprehension that he will grow worse and worse. But kindness to him in

---

97 **cavil** – raise trivial objections.
98 **dissipated** – excessive in the pursuit of pleasure.

Chapter 5—Bringing Up Children: Principle Obstacles in Bringing Up Children for Christ

this way is cruelty to the others. Wickedness is contagious, especially when the diseased person is a brother.

SIXTHLY: Bad companions out of the house counteract all the influence of religious instruction delivered at home. A Christian parent should ever be on the alert to watch the associations that his children are inclined to form. On this subject, I have said much to the young themselves in the following work. But it is a subject that equally concerns the parent. One ill-chosen friend of your children's may undo all the good you are the means of doing at home. It is impossible for you to be sufficiently vigilant on this point. From their very infancy, encourage them to look up to you as the selectors of their companions. Impress them with the necessity of this and form in them a habit of consulting you at all times. Never encourage an association that is not likely to have a decidedly friendly influence on their religious character. This caution was never more necessary than in the present age. Young people are brought very much together by the religious institutions that are now formed…Yet it is too much even for charity to believe that all the active young friends of Sunday Schools, Juvenile Missionary Societies, etc., are fit companions for our sons and our daughters.

SEVENTHLY: The schisms that sometimes arise in our churches and embitter the minds of Christians against each other have a very unfriendly influence upon the minds of the young. They see so much that is opposite to the spirit and genius[99] of Christianity in both parties and enter so deeply into the views and feelings of one of them that either their attention is drawn off from the essentials of religion, or their prejudices raised against them. I look upon this as one of the most painful and mischievous consequences of ecclesiastical contentions…

[LASTLY]: The spirit of filial independence, which is sanctioned by the habits if not by the opinions of the age, is another hindrance and the last that I shall mention to the good effect contemplated and desired by a religious education. The disposition, which is but too apparent in this age to enlarge the privileges of the children by diminishing the prerogative of their parents, is neither for the comfort of the latter, nor for the wellbeing of the former. Rebellion against a justly constituted authority can never be in any case a blessing; all wise parents, together with all wise youth, will unite in supporting that just parental authority, which, however the precocious[100] manhood of some might feel it to be oppression, the more natural and slowly approaching maturity of others will acknowledge to be a blessing.

---

99 **genius** – distinctive character.
100 **precocious** – early developed.

Children who find the parental yoke a burden are not very likely to look upon that of Christ as a benefit.

Such, my dear friends, as they appear to my mind, are the principal obstacles to the success of those efforts that are carried on by many for the religious education of their children. Seriously consider them and, having looked at them, endeavor to avoid them…and while you neglect not any one means that can promote their comfort, reputation, and usefulness in this world, concentrate your chief solicitude[101] and employ your noblest energies in a scriptural, judicious, persevering scheme of *religious* education.

From *The Christian Father's Present to His Children,* reprinted by Soli Deo Gloria, a division of Reformation Heritage Books: www.heritagebooks.org.

John Angell James (1785-1859): English Congregationalist preacher and author; born at Blandford, Dorsetshire, England.

---

101 **solicitude** – concern for the well-being of another.

The Calamity of Ungodly Children
EDWARD LAWRENCE (1623-1695)

> *A foolish son is a grief to his father, and bitterness to her that bare him.*
> —Proverbs 17:25

It is a very great calamity to godly parents to have wicked and ungodly children. "A foolish son (says the Proverbs text) *is a grief to his father, and bitterness to her that bare him.*" To the same purpose is Proverbs 17:21: *"He that begetteth a fool doeth it to his sorrow: and the father of a fool hath no joy."* A foolish son dampens all his joy. And Proverbs 19:13: *"A foolish son is the calamity of his father"*…

The greatness of this calamity appears by the passions in the parents that are moved and affected hereby. I shall only give you three: fear, anger, and sorrow.

Fear: This is a troublesome passion, and godly parents are never void of fear of their wicked children. They are afraid that everyone who knocks at the door, and that every post,[102] and every friend who comes to visit them brings them some sad tidings of their disobedient children. I shall amplify this by giving three great evils that such parents are greatly perplexed with the fear of.

They are afraid lest their children are in the practice of some great sins. This was Job's fear when his children were feasting together (Job 1:5). Job said, "It may be my sons have sinned and cursed God in their hearts." Their children are seldom out of their sight, but the good parents are in fear of this. They know their children are always exposed to the devil's temptations, to the snares of the world, to the allurements of evil company, that their corrupt hearts are set to comply with all of those, and that they have provoked God to give them up to their own lusts. And therefore, they are in continual fear lest these poor children are lying, swearing, cursing, whoring, or are drunk, defiling, debauching,[103] and destroying themselves and others.

They are in fear lest some heavy judgment of God will befall them in this life. Thus David, when his son Absalom was in the head of a high rebellion against his father and the battle was to be fought with the rebels, was fearful lest his son should then perish in his sins. These parents know that their poor children are out of God's way, and are, as birds wandering from the nest (Prov. 27:8), exposed to all manner of danger. They know what the Word threatens against them and what fearful instances there are of the vengeance

---

102 **post** – one who bears a letter or message.
103 **debauching** – indulging in excess sensual pleasures.

of God upon disobedient children. And therefore, they are in fear lest their sins should bring them to some untimely and shameful death.

They are in fear of their eternal damnation. They are sensible that their children are children of wrath and live in those sins for which the wrath of God comes on the children of disobedience. And these parents believe what hell is. For as faith in the promises is the substance of things hoped for, so faith as it believes the threatenings is the substance of things feared. Therefore, they cannot but tremble to think that their dear lambs, whom they so tenderly nourished and cherished, are in danger every moment of being cast into the fire that is prepared for devils.

Anger: Anger is another passion that is moved in godly parents because of the wickedness of their children. And this is troublesome, for a man is never out of trouble while he is in anger. And the more the wills of these parents are bent to have their children godly, the more are they displeased and provoked to anger by their sins. They are angry to see them provoke that God Whom they themselves are so careful to please, to see them destroying their precious souls that they are laboring to save, and to see them waste those estates on their filthy lusts that they have gotten by their care and labor and prayers. They cannot but think of them with anger, speak of them with anger, and look at them with anger. And thus, their children, who should be their delight and pleasure, are a continual cross and vexation to them.

Sorrow: They are deeply affected with grief and sorrow for the wickedness of their children. The parents' graces cause them to mourn for their children's sins. Their saving knowledge makes their hearts bleed to see their children scorn and despise that glory which they see in God and Christ. And while they by faith are feeding on Christ, it grieves them to see their children feeding themselves with the dirty pleasures of sin. Their love to God makes them groan that their children love sin, the worst evil, and hate God, the chief good.

The greatness of this affliction appears by these eight aggravations of it:

First, it aggravates their grief to remember what pleasure and delight these children were to them in their childhood. It torments them now to see their sweet and pleasant smiles turned into scornful and disdainful looks at their parents and their pretty, broken words turned into oaths and lies and other rotten speeches. It torments them to think that these who were so forward to clasp their arms around their necks, to kiss them, and to run at their commands, now lift up the heel against them.

Second, it aggravates their sorrow to see themselves so miserably disappointed in their former hopes of these children. *"Hope deferred* (said Solomon) *maketh the heart sick"* (Prov. 13:12), but to be crossed and disappointed in hopes of such great mercy even breaks the heart. When these parents remember how pleasant it was to them to hear these children lisp out their catechisms and to hear their good words of God and Christ, it cannot but be very grievous to them that the same children whom with Hannah they lent to the Lord should sell themselves to the devil.

Third, it aggravates their sorrow that their children are so void of love to their parents and to see that the company of liars, drunkards, whoremongers, and thieves is more delightful to them than the company of their parents.

Fourth, it aggravates their sorrow to look upon the holy children of others and say, "Yonder are children that make a glad father and mother, when the children of our bodies and counsels and prayers and vows and tears live as if their father was an Amorite and their mother an Hittite!" (Ezek. 16:3).

Fifth, it aggravates the parents' sorrow when they have but one child, and that one proves to be foolish and disobedient. Of this, there are many instances. The Scripture, to set forth the saddest kind of mourning, compares it to mourning for an only son. Jeremiah 6:26: *"Make thee mourning, as for an only son, most bitter lamentation."* Zechariah 12:10: *"They shall mourn for him, as one mourneth for his only son."* I know that these Scriptures speak of parents mourning for the death of an only son, but it is not so sad to follow an only son to the grave as to see an only child live to the dishonor of God, to be a curse to his generation, and to be continually destroying his precious soul. It is a very bitter case when as much love, kindness, care, cost, pains, prayers, and fastings are bestowed upon one child as other parents bestow upon many children. And, notwithstanding all this, one child still proves to be such a monster of wickedness, as if the sins of many ungodly children met in him.

Sixth, it is an aggravation when God's holy ministers are the fathers of fools, which…often happens. And this is a most dreadful case for such who have the keys of the kingdom of heaven, and yet must bind over their own children to the wrath of God. Such know the terrors of the Lord and the torments of hell more than others know, and therefore must be more affected to believe that this at present is the portion of their own children.

Seventh, it is an aggravation when such children, whom their parents designed to serve God in the ministry of the Gospel, prove to be ungodly. This is a matter of great lamentation, for the parents intend them for the highest office in the church, give them education for that end, and then these children make themselves as salt without savor, which is good for nothing but to be cast out and trodden under foot of men.

EIGHTH, it is an aggravation when children are a grief to their parents in their old age, and do, as it were, throw dirt upon their hoary heads, which is their crown of glory. It is the command of God in Proverbs 23:22: *"Despise not thy mother when she is old."* Solomon tells us that the days of old age are evil days (Eccl. 12); their very age is a troublesome and incurable disease. They are like the grasshopper: every light thing is a burden to them. Therefore it must be more troublesome to them to be tormented with wicked children when the strong men (as divines think) Solomon calls "the legs" bow themselves, and their children, who should be a staff and support to them, break their hearts and cause their gray hairs to go with sorrow to the grave.

From *Parents' Concerns for Their Unsaved Children*, reprinted by Soli Deo Gloria, a division of Reformation Heritage Books: www.heritagebooks.org.

Edward Lawrence (1623-1695): Nonconformist English minister; born in Moston, Shropshire, England.

> *Unless we are careful over the young, there may be none to bear the Lord's banner when we sleep among the clods. In matters of doctrine, you will find orthodox congregations frequently change to heterodoxy in the course of thirty or forty years, and that is because too often there has been no catechizing of the children in the essential doctrines of the Gospel.* —Charles Haddon Spurgeon

> *Learn to say "No" to your children. Show them that you are able to refuse whatever you think is not fit for them. Show them that you are ready to punish disobedience, and that when you speak of punishment, you are not only ready to threaten, but also to perform.* —J.C. Ryle

Directions for Grieving over Ungodly Children
EDWARD LAWRENCE (1623-1695)

Direction 1
Abhor it as a great sin to faint under this affliction, that is, either to be disabled for your duty or to sink in your comforts. For it is a sign that you placed too much of your happiness in your children if their wickedness makes you faint under this calamity. I shall only plead with you as Joab did with David when he made that bitter lamentation for his son Absalom in 2 Samuel 19:6: *"For thou hast declared this day, that thou regardest neither princes nor servants."* So I say to you, you hereby declare that you do not regard God and Christ if your soul faints under the burden of a disobedient child.

Direction 2
Consider…that this is an affliction that ordinarily befalls God's dearest children. You must not think of this as if you were the first godly parents of ungodly children, or as if herein some strange thing happened unto you. I confess where a calamity seems singular or extraordinary, it is more apt to overwhelm the afflicted because they will be then apt to think that there is some extraordinary displeasure in God against them and to say with the church, *"Behold, and see if there be any sorrow like unto my sorrow, which is done unto me, wherewith the LORD hath afflicted me in the day of his fierce anger"* (Lam. 1:12). But this affliction is ordinary and is consistent with the saving and distinguishing grace of God to them and is a rod that is usually lain on the lot of the righteous.

Direction 3
Consider that there might have befallen you greater miseries than this. I will give you three greater evils that would have made you more miserable. First, you might have been a wicked, ungodly wretch yourself. And for the great Jehovah to have cursed and damned you forever would have made you unspeakably more miserable than to be tormented a while with a wicked child. Second, you might have had an ungodly spouse to be as rottenness in your bones. Solomon seems to speak of a troublesome spouse as being more grievous than a wicked child is. Proverbs 19:13: *"A foolish son is the calamity of his father: and the contentions of a wife are a continual dropping."* This is like the constant dropping of rain into a house, which rots the building, spoils the goods, and ruins both house and inhabitants. To the extent that your spouse is nearer and ought to be dearer to you than your child, to be

afflicted therein is a greater calamity. Third, God might have left all your children to perish in their sins. But if you have even one godly child, your joy in that should greatly abate your sorrow for your other wicked children…

Direction 4

Let your sorrow be guided by Scripture and reason, so that you may not provoke God, defile your souls, and wound your consciences by sinful groans and tears. For this end, observe two rules: First, mourn more for their sins whereby they provoke and dishonor God and defile and destroy themselves and others, than for any shame or loss in worldly things that befall you hereby. In this way, it may appear that the love of God and your children's souls, and not the love of the world, has the greatest influence on your sorrow. For I fear that there is usually in good parents too much of carnal sorrow and too little of godly sorrow in their mourning under this great calamity. Second, do not let your sorrow disease your body and impair your health. God does not require us to mourn more for our children's sins than our own, and He never makes it our duty by sorrow for either to destroy our bodies, which are the temples of the Holy Ghost. The truth is that godly sorrow is the health of the soul and never hurts the body. For grace is always a friend and never an enemy to nature. Therefore, do not deprive yourself of all opportunities to honor God and serve His Church. Do not make your spouse desolate or your children orphans by such sorrow that will neither please God, ease yourself, nor do any good to your wicked and miserable children.

Direction 5

Labor to get your graces strengthened under this great affliction; for you have need of more knowledge, wisdom, faith, hope, love, meekness, and patience to enable and fit you to bear this than most other affections. And you must see and enjoy more of God and Christ to keep your hearts up under this than under most other troubles. Yet by the strength of Christ, you may be enabled not only to bear this tribulation, but to glory in it. And the greater the trouble is, the more good you may gain by it.

Direction 6

Comfort yourself in that the greatest and best things that you have most prayed for, trusted unto, expected, and chiefly loved and desired are all safe and sure. God is and will be blessed and glorious forever, whatever becomes of your child. All His infinite perfections are working for His glory. Christ Himself is God's and does the whole work of a Mediator as His servant and for His glory. All the blessed angels and saints will forever honor, admire, love, and praise Him.

God the Father, Son, and Holy Ghost are forever your own and will to all eternity be glorified in making you blessed and glorious. You have a bad child, but a good God. All your work will be done, your sins pardoned and killed, your graces perfected, and your body and soul glorified—and shall an ungodly child make all your consolations herein small to you?

Direction 7

Last, consider this trouble will last but a little while. I confess I do not know or can upon search find anything that can lift up the heart above this trouble but the knowledge and sense of the infinite love of God in Christ to a man's self and of that holy and glorious eternity which this love will shortly bring him unto. To tell you that this is and has been the case of other godly parents may allay something of your grief. But what is this but to tell you that others are and have been as miserable as you, or to tell you that children as wicked as yours have been sanctified and saved yields some hopes? But it can amount to nothing more than to think that they may be saved or they may be damned, and there is as much reason to fear the one as to hope for the other. But for a man to see a gainful death, ready to loose him into that world where there is none of this sorrow and to know that at the Day of Judgment…he himself shall sit with Christ to judge them; and that he shall love and delight in the holiness and justice of the Judge of all the world in passing that sentence upon them, *"Depart from me, ye cursed, into everlasting fire, prepared for the devil and his angels"* (Matt. 25:41)—this is sufficient to overcome all immoderate grief for his ungodly children.

From *Parents' Concerns for Their Unsaved Children*, reprinted by Soli Deo Gloria, a ministry of Reformation Heritage Books: www.heritagebooks.org.

Edward Lawrence (1623-1695): Nonconformist English minister; born in Moston, Shropshire, England.

> *The willow grows fast, and so do young Christians. If you want the eminent men in God's Church, look for them amongst those converted in youth… our Samuels and Timothys must come from those who knew the Scriptures from their youth. O Lord! Send us many such whose growth and advance shall as much astonish us as the growth of the willows by the watercourses.*
> *—Charles Haddon Spurgeon*

The Lord teach you all how precious Christ is and what a mighty and complete work He path done for our salvation. Then, I feel confident you will use every means to bring your children to Jesus that they may live through Him. The Lord teach you all your need of the Holy Spirit to renew, sanctify, and quicken your souls. Then, I feel sure you will urge your children to pray for Him without ceasing and never rest until He has come down into their hearts with power and made them new creatures. The Lord grant this, and then I have a good hope that you will indeed train up your children well—train well for this life and train well for the life to come; train well for earth and train well for heaven; train them for God, for Christ, and for eternity.
—*J.C. Ryle*

A Unique Opportunity of Witnessing to the World
DAVID MARTYN LLOYD-JONES (1899-1981)

The Apostle reminds us that at a time of apostasy, at a time of gross godlessness and irreligion, when the very foundations are shaking, one of the most striking manifestations of the lawlessness is *"[disobedience] to parents"* (2 Tim. 3:2)...When will the civil authorities learn and realize that there is an indissoluble connection between godlessness and a lack of morality and decent behavior?...The tragedy is that the civil authorities—irrespective of which political party is in power—all seem to be governed by modern psychology rather than by the Scriptures. They all are convinced that they can deal with unrighteousness directly, in and by itself. But that is impossible. Unrighteousness is always the result of ungodliness, and the only hope of getting back any measure of righteousness into life is to have a *revival of godliness*. That is precisely what the Apostle is saying to the Ephesians and to ourselves (Eph. 6:1-4). The best and the most moral periods in the history of this country, and every other country, have always been those periods that have followed mighty religious awakenings. This problem of lawlessness and lack of discipline, the problem of children and of youth, was just not present fifty years ago as it is today. Why? Because the great tradition of the Evangelical Awakening of the 18th century was still operating. But as that has gone, these terrible moral and social problems are coming back, as the Apostle teaches us, and as they have always come back throughout the running centuries.

Present conditions therefore *demand* that we should look at the Apostle's statement. I believe that Christian parents and children, Christian families, have a unique opportunity of witnessing to the world at this present time by just being different. We can be true evangelists by showing this discipline, this law and order, this true relationship between parents and children. We may be the means under God's hand of bringing many to a knowledge of the Truth. Let us therefore think of it in that way.

From *Life in the Spirit in Marriage, Home & Work: An Exposition of Ephesians 5:18 to 6:9.*

David Martyn Lloyd-Jones (1899-1981): Perhaps the greatest expository preacher of the 20th century; Westminster Chapel, London, 1938-68; born in Wales.

Chapter 6
FATHERHOOD

One of the great tragedies of modern culture is the obliteration of biblical fatherhood. Fatherlessness is a significant cause of poverty, homosexuality, juvenile delinquency, out-of-wedlock births, drug abuse, depression, and a host of other social and spiritual maladies. Thankfully, God has given us, in His Word, all we need to recover His beautiful design for fathers. He has given us both commands and patterns in order to conform us to His vision of fatherhood. He has given us Jesus Christ His Son, Who is *"the express image of His person"* (Heb. 1:3), to teach us what fatherhood should look like in everyday life. God's design for fatherhood is communicated by godly pattern or command in nearly every book of the Bible.

God is a father, and He has ordained that earthly fathers reflect His faithful fatherhood. The chapter before you attempts to explain many facets of the diamond that is fatherhood. Yet this testimony is summed up in one single English word: love. And so it is helpful to recognize that the first mention of the word "love" in the Bible is the love of a father for his son. God said to Abraham, *"Take now thy son, thine only son Isaac, whom thou lovest, and get thee into the land of Moriah; and offer him there for a burnt offering upon one of the mountains which I will tell thee of"* (Gen. 22:2). When we turn to the New Testament, the first words spoken by a father are also words of love for a son. At Jesus' baptism a voice was heard from heaven, saying, *"This is my beloved Son, in whom I am well pleased"* (Matt. 3:17). This is the backdrop of the doctrine of fatherhood.

God the Father loves His sons. He walks with them and instructs them. His mission is to bring many sons to glory. This is the grand design for fatherhood. Simply put, God created fatherhood as an earthly means to lead children to the Redeemer. In this scheme, God stands as the example for every father; and every good principle of fatherhood comes from Him as you will see in this chapter. The articles here explain the many roles and responsibilities of fathers who desire to bring many sons to glory.

—Scott Brown

Father as Prophet, King, Priest

WILLIAM GURNALL (1617-1679)

Every father hath the care of souls upon him. He is prophet, king, and priest in his own house, and from these will appear his duty.

First, he is a *prophet* to teach and instruct his family. Wives are bid to learn at home of their husbands (1 Cor. 14:35); then surely they are to teach them at home. Parents are commanded to instruct their children: *"Ye shall teach them…when thou sittest in thine house"* (Deut. 11:19). *"Bring them up in the nurture and admonition of the Lord"* (Eph. 6:4). Now, there is a teaching and admonition by prayer to God and praising of God, as well as in catechizing of them: *"Teaching and admonishing one another in psalms and hymns"* (Col. 3:16). The father's praying with his family will teach them how to pray when by themselves. The confessions he makes, petitions he puts up, and mercies he acknowledges in his family duty are an excellent means to furnish them with matter for their devotion. How comes it to pass that many…children, when they come to be themselves heads of families, are so unable to be their relations' mouth to God in prayer, but because they have in their [childhood] lived in prayerless families and were kept in ignorance of this duty…?

Again, he is a *king* in his house to rule his family in the fear of God…He is to say with Joshua, *"As for me and my house, we will serve the LORD"* (Josh. 24:15). Would it be a sin in a prince not to set up the public worship of God in his kingdom, although he served God himself in his palace? Surely, then, it is a sin in the father not to set it up in his house, though he prays himself in his closet.

Lastly, he is a *priest* in his own house; and where there is a priest, there must be a sacrifice. What sacrifice [is there] among Christians, but the spiritual sacrifices of prayer and thanksgiving? Thus, David went from public ordinances to perform private duty with his family: *"[Then] David returned to bless his house"* (1 Chron. 16:43), that is, saith one upon the place, he returned to worship God in private with them and to crave a blessing from God upon them.

From *The Christian in Complete Armor,* The Banner of Truth Trust: www.banneroftruth.org.

William Gurnall (1616-1679): Anglican Puritan minister and author; born in St. Margaret's parish, King's Lynn, Norfolk, England.

Fatherhood: Responsibility and Privilege

ARTHUR W. PINK (1886-1952)

One of the saddest and most tragic features of our twentieth-century[1] "civilization" is the awful prevalence of disobedience on the part of children to their parents during the days of childhood and their lack of reverence and respect when they grow up. This is evidenced in many ways and is general, alas, even in the families of professing Christians. In his extensive travels during the past thirty years, the writer has sojourned in a great many homes. The piety and beauty of some of them remain as sacred and fragrant memories, but others of them have left the most painful impressions. Children who are self-willed or spoiled not only bring themselves into perpetual unhappiness but also inflict discomfort upon all who come into contact with them. [They] augur,[2] by their conduct, evil things for the days to come.

In the vast majority of cases, the children are not nearly so much to be blamed as the parents. Failure to honor father[3] and mother, wherever it is found, is in large measure due to parental departure from the scriptural pattern. Nowadays the father thinks that he has fulfilled his obligations by providing food and raiment for his children, and by acting occasionally as a kind of moral policeman. Too often, the mother is content to be a domestic drudge,[4] making herself the slave of her children instead of training them to be useful. She performs many a task that her daughters should do in order to allow them freedom for the frivolities of a giddy set.[5] The consequence has been that the home, which ought to be—for its orderliness, its sanctity,[6] and its reign of love—a miniature heaven on earth, has degenerated into "a filling station for the day and a parking place for the night," as someone has tersely expressed it.

Before outlining the duties of *fathers* toward their children, let it be pointed out that they cannot properly discipline their children unless they have first learned to govern themselves. How can they expect to subdue self-will in their little ones and check the rise of an angry temper if their own passions are allowed free reign? The character of *fathers* is to a very large

---

1 The same sadly applies to our 21st century.
2 **augur** – predict; become a sign that something is about to happen.
3 **Editor's note:** Several articles in this chapter are addressed to both parents—fathers and mothers. To emphasize the father's role, *parent* is sometimes replaced with *father* in italics.
4 **drudge** – person made to do hard, dull work; slave.
5 **frivolities…giddyset** – silly behaviors of foolish people, incapable of serious thought.
6 **sanctity** – holiness.

degree reproduced in their offspring: *"And Adam lived an hundred and thirty years, and begat a son in his own likeness, and after his image"* (Gen. 5:3). The *father*...must be in subjection to God if he would lawfully expect obedience from his little ones. This principle is enforced in Scripture again and again: *"Thou therefore which teachest another, teachest thou not thyself?"* (Rom. 2:21).

Of the bishop, that is, elder or pastor, it is written that he must be *"One that ruleth well his own house, having his children in subjection with all gravity; (For if a man know not how to rule his own house, how shall he take care of the church of God?)"* (1 Tim. 3:4-5). And if a *father* knows not how to rule his own spirit (Prov. 25:28), how shall he care for his offspring?

God has entrusted to *fathers* a most solemn charge, and yet a most precious privilege. It is not too much to say that in their hands are deposited the hope and blessing, or else the curse and plague, of the next generation. Their families are the nurseries of both Church and State, and according to the cultivating of them *now* will be their fruitfulness hereafter. Oh, how prayerfully and carefully should you who are parents discharge your trust!

Most assuredly, God will require an account of the children from your hands; for they are His and only lent to your care and keeping. The task assigned you is no easy one, especially in these superlatively[7] evil days. Nevertheless, if trustfully and earnestly sought, the grace of God will be found sufficient in this responsibility as in others. The Scriptures supply us with rules to go by, with promises to lay hold of, and, we may add, with fearful warnings lest we treat the matter lightly.

Instruct Your Children

We have space to mention but four of the principal duties devolving[8] on *fathers*. First, it is your duty to instruct your children. *"And these words, which I command thee this day, shall be in thine heart: And thou shalt teach them diligently unto thy children, and shalt talk of them when thou sittest in thine house, and when thou walkest by the way, and when thou liest down, and when thou risest up"* (Deut. 6:6-7). This work is far too important to allocate to others: parents, and not Sabbath School[9] teachers, are divinely required to educate their little ones. Nor is this to be an occasional or sporadic[10] thing, but one that is to have constant attention. The glorious character of God, the requirements of His holy Law, the exceeding sinfulness of sin, the wondrous gift of His

---

7 **superlatively** – in the highest degree.
8 **devolving** – passing down.
9 **Sabbath School** – Sunday School.
10 **sporadic** – happening only occasionally.

Son, and the fearful doom that is the certain portion of all who despise and reject Him are to be brought repeatedly before the minds of your little ones. "They are too young to understand such things" is the devil's argument to deter you from discharging your duty.

"And, ye fathers, provoke not your children to wrath: but bring them up in the nurture and admonition of the Lord" (Eph. 6:4). It is to be noted that the *"fathers"* are here specifically addressed, and this for two reasons: (1) because they are the heads of their families and their government is especially committed to them; and (2) because they are prone to transfer this duty to their wives. This instruction is to be given by reading to them the Holy Scriptures and enlarging upon those things most agreeable to their age. This should be followed by catechizing[11] them. A continued discourse to the young is not nearly as effective as when it is diversified by questions and answers. If they know they will be questioned on what you read, they will listen more closely; and the formulating of answers teaches them to think for themselves. Such a method is also found to make the memory more retentive,[12] for answering definite questions fixes more specific ideas in the mind. Observe how often Christ asked His disciples questions.

Be a Good Example

Second, good instruction is to be accompanied by good example. The teaching that issues only from the lips is not at all likely to sink any deeper than the ears. Children are particularly quick to detect inconsistencies and to despise hypocrisy.[13] It is at this point that parents need to be most on their faces before God, *daily* seeking from Him that grace that they so sorely need and that He alone can supply. What care you need to take, lest you say or do anything before your children that would tend to corrupt their minds or be of evil consequence for them to follow! How you need to be constantly on your guard against anything that might render you mean and contemptible in the eyes of those who should respect and revere you! The *father* is not only to instruct his children in the ways of holiness, but is himself to walk before them in those ways and show by his practice and demeanor[14] what a pleasant and profitable thing it is to be regulated by the Divine Law.

In a Christian home, the supreme aim should be household piety—the honoring of God at all times. Everything else must be subordinated to this

---

11 **catechizing** – instructing in the Christian faith by means of question and answer.
12 **retentive** – able to store facts and remember things easily.
13 See FGB 193, *Hypocrisy*, available from Chapel Library.
14 **demeanor** – way a person looks or behaves toward other people.

high purpose. In the matter of family life, neither husband nor wife can throw on the other all the responsibility for the religious character of the home. The mother is most certainly required to supplement the efforts of the father, for the children enjoy far more of her company than they do of his. If there is a tendency in fathers to be too strict and severe, mothers are prone to be too lax and lenient; and they need to be much on their guard against anything that would weaken their husband's authority. When he has forbidden a thing, she must not give her consent to it. It is striking to note that the exhortation of Ephesians 6:4 is preceded by instruction to *"be filled with the Spirit"* (5:18), while the parallel exhortation in Colossians 3:21 is preceded by the exhortation to *"let the Word of Christ dwell in you richly"* (3:16), showing that parents cannot possibly discharge their duties unless they are filled with the Spirit and the Word.

Discipline Your Children

Third, instruction and example is to be enforced by correction and discipline. This means, first of all, the exercise of authority—the proper reign of Law. Of "the father of the faithful," God said, *"For I know him, that he will command his children and his household after him, and they shall keep the way of the LORD, to do justice and judgment; that the LORD may bring upon Abraham that which he hath spoken of him"* (Gen. 18:19). Ponder this carefully, Christian fathers. Abraham did more than proffer[15] good advice: he enforced law and order in his household. The rules he administered had for their design the keeping of *"the way of the Lord"*—that which was right in His sight. And this duty was performed by the patriarch in order that the blessing of God might rest on his family. No family can be properly brought up without household laws, which include reward and punishment; and these are especially important in early childhood, when as yet moral character is unformed and moral motives are not understood or appreciated.

Rules should be simple, clear, reasonable, and inflexible like the Ten Commandments—a few great moral rules, instead of a multitude of petty restrictions. One way of needlessly provoking children to wrath is to hamper them with a thousand trifling restrictions and minute regulations that are capricious[16] and are due to a fastidious[17] temper in the parent.

It is of vital importance for the child's future good that he or she should be brought into subjection at an early age. An untrained child means a

---

15 **proffer** – offer for acceptance.
16 **capricious** – guided by whim or fancy, not settled judgment.
17 **fastidious** – difficult to please.

lawless adult. Our prisons are crowded with those who were allowed to have their own way during their minority. The least offense of a child against the rulers of the home ought not to pass without due correction; for if he finds leniency in one direction or toward one offense, he will expect the same toward others. And then disobedience will become more frequent until the parent has no control save that of brute force.

The teaching of Scripture is crystal clear on this point. *"Foolishness is bound in the heart of a child; but the rod of correction shall drive it far from him"* (Prov. 22:15; *cf.* 23:13-14). Therefore, God has said, *"He that spareth his rod hateth his son: but he that loveth him chasteneth him betimes[18]"* (Prov. 13:24). And again, *"Chasten thy son while there is hope, and let not thy soul spare for his crying"* (Prov. 19:18). Let not a foolish fondness stay thee. Certainly God loves His children with a much deeper parental affection than you can love yours, yet He tells us, *"As many as I love, I rebuke and chasten"* (Rev. 3:19; *cf.* Heb. 12:6). *"The rod and reproof give wisdom: but a child left to himself bringeth his mother to shame"* (Prov. 29:15). Such severity must be used in his early years, before age and obstinacy[19] have hardened the child against the fear and smart of correction. Spare the rod, and you spoil the child; use it not on him, and you lay up one for your own back.

It should hardly need pointing out that the above Scriptures are by no means teaching that a reign of terror is to mark the home life. Children can be governed and chastened in such a way that they lose not their respect and affection for their father. Beware of souring their temper by unreasonable demands or provoking their wrath by striking them to vent your own rage. The father is to punish a disobedient child not because he is angry, but because it is right—because God requires it, and the welfare of the child demands it. Never make a threat that you have no intention of executing nor a promise you do not mean to perform. Remember that for your children to be well informed is good, but for them to be well controlled is better.

Pay close attention to the unconscious influences of a child's surroundings. Study how to make your home attractive, not by introducing carnal and worldly things, but by noble ideals, by inculcating[20] a spirit of unselfishness, by genial[21] and happy fellowship. Separate the little ones from evil associates. Watch carefully the periodicals and books that come into your home, the occasional guests that sit at your table, and the companionships that your

---

18 **betimes** – speedily; diligently.
19 **obstinacy** – stubbornness.
20 **inculcating** – teaching or impressing upon the mind by frequent instruction or repetition.
21 **genial** – friendly; cheerful.

children form. Parents often carelessly let others have free access to their children who undermine parental authority, overturn parental ideals, and sow seeds of frivolity and iniquity before they are aware. Never let your child spend a night among strangers. So train your children that your girls will be useful and helpful members of their generation and your boys industrious and self-supporting.

Pray for Your Children

Fourth, the last and most important duty, respecting both the temporal and spiritual good of your children, is fervent supplication to God for them. Without this, all the rest will be ineffectual. Means are unavailing unless the Lord blesses them. The *"throne of grace"* (Heb. 4:16) is to be earnestly implored that your efforts to bring up your children for God may be crowned with success. True, there must be a humble submission to His sovereign will, a bowing before the truth of election. On the other hand, it is the privilege of faith to lay hold of the divine promises and to remember that *"the effectual fervent prayer of a righteous man availeth much"* (James 5:16). Of holy Job, it is recorded concerning his sons and daughters that he *"rose up early in the morning, and offered burnt offerings according to the number of them all"* (Job 1:5). A prayerful atmosphere should pervade the home and be breathed by all who share it.

From *Studies in the Scriptures*, available from Chapel Library.

Arthur W. Pink (1886-1952): Pastor, itinerate Bible teacher, author; born in Nottingham, England.

A Father's Main Responsibility
JOHN CALVIN (1509-1564)

For I know him, that he will command his children and his household after him, and they shall keep the way of the LORD, to do justice and judgment; that the LORD may bring upon Abraham that which he hath spoken of him. —Genesis 18:19

Let us...note that we are told here that God knows Abraham will instruct his children to walk in his way after him. First, there is instruction, and then what kind [of instruction] is noted. In other words, we are told the nature of that instruction and then how it extends beyond death. So in the person of Abraham, we see what the responsibility of all believers is, principally the responsibility of the fathers of family whom God set up as heads of household and to whom He gave life, children, and servants so they would be diligent in teaching them. For when a father has children, his responsibility is not only to feed and clothe them, but his *principal* responsibility is to guide them so that their lives will be well regulated, and he will dedicate his full attention to that...

God values His servant Abraham's piety,[22] which is shown in the effort he will make to serve and honor Him and to guide his family and those entrusted to his charge, for it is particularly stated that he will teach them to walk in the way of the Lord. Consequently, we see the nature of the right kind of instruction. For someone could be rather careful to give many rules and many laws without providing stability. There can be no foundation to build on unless God dominates and people obey Him and conform to His Word. That, then, is what we have to remember.

When fathers of family and those of some preeminence get ready to teach, they must not be presumptuous and say, "This seems good to *me*," and then try to subject everybody to their opinion and their concepts. "What? Shall I teach what I learned from God in His school?" What we have to remember from this passage is, briefly, that no one will ever be a good teacher unless he is God's pupil. So let there be no teaching authority that advances what we invent and what our minds come up with, but let us learn from God so that He will dominate and alone have all preeminence; and may great and small bring themselves into conformity with Him and obey Him. That much for that instruction.

At that time, there was no written law and even less gospel; but Abraham still knew God's will to the extent necessary. So Abraham is without Scripture,

---

22 **piety** – godliness.

but even so, he does not presume to or attempt to set up laws to his own liking. But he asks God alone to govern and show the way to everybody else and lead them, for he does not wish to say, "Let us go the way I say," but, "I am teaching you what I have learned from God. And may He alone have all mastery,[23] and may I be a teacher only if I speak as by His mouth." That is the second point we have to remember here.

So what is to be noted here is that heads of family must go to the trouble of being instructed in God's Word if they are to do their duty. If they are stupid, if they do not know the basic principles of religion or of their faith and do not know God's commandments or how prayer is to be offered to Him or what the road to salvation is, how will they instruct their families? All the more, then, must those who are husbands and have a family, a household to govern, think, "I must establish my lesson in His Word so that I will not only try to govern myself in accordance with His will, but that I will also bring to it at the same time those who are under my authority and guidance."

Now in the third place, Abraham will teach his family to walk in the fear of the Lord after his death, just as if it were said that the faithful man is not only to get honor for God and live tomorrow, but that he leaves good seed after his death. For God's Word is the incorruptible seed of life: it endures forever. And even though heaven and earth tend to corruption and will pass away, the Word of God must *always* retain its power (*cf.* Matt. 24:35; Isa. 40:8; 55:11). Therefore, it is not without reason that it dies with us, is extinguished when God withdraws us from this world, and we carry everything off with us. But let us work, though we are weak and mortal and must depart this world, to leave the Word of God with a root here. And when we are dead and have turned to dust, may God be honored and may His memory endure forever. That, then, is what we have to remember…

Now since God spoke that way, He is saying that Abraham's children, whom he will teach, will do *justice* and *judgment*. With those two words, Scripture comprises what concerns the second table of the Law. Moses says they will do justice and judgment. That shows us what the way of God is and how we will show we are obeying Him. For those two words… involve uprightness and equity[24] so that we may be kind, give ourselves to charity,[25] help one another, protect everyone's right and not defraud, abstain from doing wrong and violence to one another, and even help those who need our help.

---

23 **mastery** – the condition of being ruler; authority.
24 **equity** – fairness.
25 **charity** – benevolence to one's neighbors; provision for relief of the poor.

Now, it is certain that in God's Law there is nothing but justice and judgment. In the first table, we see how we are to worship God, how we are to revere His name, and how we are to practice calling upon Him and trusting in Him so that we will devote ourselves this way to His service and dedicate ourselves to it. All of that is properly called justice and judgment.

Now as I said, that commonly involves our neighbors and the rule of living right with men in uprightness and equity; but that is an ordinary way of speaking in Scripture, and the prophets are filled with it (*cf.* Isa. 1:27; 5:16; 28:17). When they deal with God's Law, they sometimes depart from the first table and speak of uprightness and equity. They cry out against fraud, violence, robbery, and such like. Those things, in brief, mention a part while signifying the whole. In this way, although there is here only a type and a portion of God's way, God, in general, nonetheless wanted to declare that Abraham would teach his family to govern itself in all equity and uprightness so that no one would rise up against his neighbor, that no one would commit fraud or do any wrong. That is what we have to remember.

John Calvin, *Sermons on Genesis chapters 11-20* (Edinburgh: The Banner of Truth Trust, 2012) © 2012, used by permission. www.banneroftruth.org

---

John Calvin (1509-1564): French theologian, pastor, and important leader during the Protestant Reformation; born in Noyon, Picardie, France.

In the Old Testament, it is quite clear that the father was a kind of priest in his household and family: he represented God. He was responsible not only for the morals and the behavior but for the instruction of his children. The Bible's emphasis everywhere is that this is the primary duty and task of the parents. And it remains so to this day. If we are Christians at all, we must realize that this great emphasis is based upon those fundamental units ordained by God—marriage, family, and home. You cannot play fast and loose with them. —D. M. Lloyd-Jones

A Father's Oversight

JOHN BUNYAN (1628-1688)

A father's duty to the family in general: He that is the master of a family has, under that relation, a work to do for God: the right governing of his own family. And his work is twofold: *first*, touching the spiritual state of it; *second*, touching the outward state of it.

First, as touching the spiritual state of his family, he should be very diligent and circumspect, doing his utmost endeavor both to increase faith where it is begun, and to begin it where it is not.[26] For this reason, he should diligently and frequently lay before his household such things of God out of His Word as are suitable for each particular. And let no man question his rule in the Word of God for such a practice. If the thing itself were but of good report and a thing tending to civil honesty, it is within the compass and bounds even of nature itself and should be done; much more [so,] things of a higher nature. Besides, the apostle exhorts us to whatsoever things are honest, whatsoever things are just, pure, lovely, and of good report, to think of them, that is, to be mindful to do them (Phil. 4:8). But to be conversant in this godly exercise in our family is very worthy of praise and is very fitting to all Christians. This is one of the things for which God so highly commended His servant Abraham, and that with which His heart was so much affected by. "I know Abraham," says God, "I know him to be a good man indeed," for *"he will command his children, and his household after him, and they shall keep the way of the LORD"* (Gen. 18:19). This was a thing also that good Joshua designed should be his practice as long as he had a breathing time in this world. *"As for me,"* says he, *"and my house, we will serve the LORD"* (Josh. 24:15).

Further, we find also in the New Testament that they are looked upon as Christians of an inferior rank [who] have not a due regard to this duty; yes, so inferior as not fit to be chosen to any office in the church of God. A [bishop or] pastor must be *"One that ruleth well his own house, having his children in subjection with all gravity"* (1 Tim. 3:4); *"For if a man know not how to rule his own house, how shall he take care of the church of God?"* (1 Tim. 3:5). The deacons also, says Paul, must *"be the husbands of one wife, ruling their children and their own houses well"* (1 Tim. 3:12). Notice, the apostle seems to lay down this much, that a man that governs his family well has one

---

26 **to begin it where it is not** – Bunyan is not here suggesting that a father can *create* faith in his child, for faith is a gift from God (Eph. 2:8; Phil. 1:29); rather, in God's grace and by faith in Christ, the father must teach his child God's Word and to model living faith before him, trusting God's Spirit to work savingly in his child's heart.

qualification belonging to a pastor or deacon in the house of God, for he that knows not how to rule his own house, how will he take care of the church of God? This, considered, gives us light into the work of the master of a family, touching the governing of his house.

1. A pastor must be sound and incorrupt in his doctrine; and, indeed, so must the master of a family (Titus 1:9; Eph. 6:4).

2. A pastor should be apt to teach, to reprove, and to exhort; and so should the master of a family (1 Tim. 3:2; Deut. 6:7).

3. A pastor must himself be exemplary in faith and holiness; and so also should the master of a family (1 Tim. 3:2-4; 4:12). *"I,"* says David, *"will behave myself in a perfect way...I will walk within [or before] my house with a perfect heart"* (Ps. 101:2).

4. The pastor is for getting the church together; and when they are so come together, then to pray among them, and to preach unto them. This is also commendable in Christian masters of families.

OBJECTION: But my family is ungodly and unruly touching all that is good. What should I do?

ANSWER: 1. Though this be true, yet you must rule them and not them you! You are set over them of God, and you are to use the authority which God has given you both to rebuke their vice and to show them the evil of their rebelling against the Lord. Eli did this, though not enough; and so did David (1 Sam. 2:24-25; 1 Chron. 28:9). Also, you must tell them how sad your state was when you were in their condition, and so labor to recover them out of the snare of the devil (Mark 5:19).

2. You should also labor to draw them out to God's public worship, if perhaps God may convert their souls. Said Jacob to his household and to all that were about him, *"Let us arise, and go up to Bethel; and I will make there an altar unto God, who answered me in the day of my distress"* (Gen. 35:3). Hannah would carry Samuel to Shiloh that he might abide with God forever (1 Sam. 1:22). Indeed, a soul rightly touched will labor to draw not only their families, but a whole city, after Jesus Christ (John 4:28-30).

3. If they are obstinate and will not go with you, then bring godly and sound men to your house, and there let the Word of God be preached when you have, as Cornelius, gathered your family and friends together (Acts 10).

You know that the jailor, Lydia, Crispus, Gaius, Stephanas, and others, had not only themselves, but their families made gracious by the word preached, and that some of them, if not all, by the word preached in their houses (Acts 16:14-34; 18:7-8; 1 Cor. 1:14-16). And this, for all I know, might be one reason among many why the apostles taught in their day not only publicly but from house to house; I say, that they might, if possible, bring in those in some family, which yet remained unconverted and in their sins (Acts 10:24; 20:20-21). For some, you know how usual it was in the day of Christ to invite Him to their houses if they had any afflicted, that either would not or could not come unto Him (Luke 7:2-3; 8:41). If this be the way with those that have outward diseases in their families, how much more then where there are souls that have need of Christ to save them from death and eternal damnation!

4. Take heed that you do not neglect family duties among them yourself—as reading the Word and prayer. If you have one in your family that is gracious,[27] take encouragement. If you are alone, yet know that you have both liberty to go to God through Christ, and also are at that time in a capacity of having the universal Church join with you for the whole number of those that shall be saved.

5. Do not allow any ungodly, profane, or heretical books or discourse in your house. *"Evil communications corrupt good manners"* (1 Cor. 15:33). I mean such profane or heretical books, etc., that either tend to provoke looseness of life or such as do oppose the fundamentals of the gospel. I know that Christians must be allowed their liberty as to things indifferent; but for those things that strike either at faith or holiness, they should be abandoned by all Christians, and especially by the pastors of churches and masters of families. This practice was shown by Jacob's commanding his house and all that were with him to put away the strange gods from among them and to change their garments (Gen. 35:2). All those in the [book of] Acts set a good example for this, who took their curious books and burned them before all men, though they were worth fifty thousand pieces of silver (Acts 19:18-19). The neglect of this fourth particular has occasioned ruin in many families, both among children and servants. It is easier for vain talkers and their deceivable works to subvert whole households than many are aware of (Titus 1:10-11).

We have touched the spiritual state of your household. And now to its outward state:

Second, touching the outward state of your family, you are to consider these three things.

1. That it lies upon you to care for them that they have a convenient livelihood. *"If any provide not for his own, and specially for those of his own house, he hath denied the faith, and is worse than an infidel"* (1 Tim. 5:8). But notice, when the Word says you are to provide for your house, it gives you no license to distracting carefulness;[28] neither does it allow you to strive to

---

27 **one in your family that is gracious** – one who knows Christ as Savior.
28 **distracting carefulness** – bewildered anxiety.

grasp the world in your heart or bank account, nor to take care for years or days to come, but so to provide for them that they may have food and raiment—and if either they or you are not content with that, you launch out beyond the rule of God (1 Tim. 6:8; Matt. 6:34). This is to labor that you may have the means *"to maintain good works for necessary uses"* (Titus 3:14). And never object that unless you reach farther, it will never do—for that is but unbelief. The Word says that God feeds ravens, cares for sparrows, and clothes the grass; in which three [things]—to feed, clothe, and care for—is as much as heart can wish (Luke 12:22-28).

2. Therefore, though you should provide for your family, yet let all your labor be mixed with moderation: *"Let your moderation be known unto all men"* (Phil. 4:5). Take heed of driving so hard after this world as to hinder yourself and family from those duties towards God that you are by grace obliged to—as private prayer, reading the Scriptures, and Christian conference.[29] It is a base[30] thing for men so to spend themselves and families after this world, [because by this] they disengage their heart to God's worship.

Christians, *"The time is short: it remaineth, that both they that have wives be as though they had none; and they that weep, as though they wept not; and they that rejoice, as though they rejoiced not...and they that use this world, as not abusing it: for the fashion of this world passeth away"* (1 Cor. 7:29-31). Many Christians live and do in this world as if religion were but a by-business,[31] and this world the one thing necessary—when, indeed, all the things of this world are but things by-the-by,[32] and religion only the one thing needful (Luke 10:40-42).

3. If you would be such a master of a family as is fitting for you, you must see that there is that Christian harmony among those under you, as is fitting for a house where one rules that fears God.

a. You must see that your children and servants are under subjection to the Word of God; for though it is only of God to rule the heart, yet He expects that you should rule their outward man; which if you do not, He may in a short time cut off all your stock [even every male] (1 Sam. 3:11-14). See therefore that you keep them temperate in all things—in apparel, in language, that they be not gluttons nor drunkards—not suffering either your children vainly to domineer over your servants, or they again to carry themselves foolishly towards each other.

---

29 **conference** – fellowship.
30 **base** – vile; worthless.
31 **by-business** – secondary activity of little importance relative to the primary focus.
32 **by-the-by** – of secondary importance.

b. Learn to distinguish between that injury in your family that is done to you, and that which is done to God. And though you should be very zealous for the Lord, and bear nothing that is open transgression to Him, yet here will be your wisdom: to pass by personal injuries and to bury them in oblivion, for love *"shall cover the multitude of sins"* (1 Peter 4:8). Be not, then, like those that will rage and stare like madmen when *they* are injured, but either laugh, or at least not soberly rebuke and warn, when *God* is dishonored.

Rule thy own house well, having thy children—with others in thy family—in subjection with all gravity (1 Tim. 3:4). Solomon was so excellent sometimes this way that he made the eyes of his beholders to dazzle (2 Chron. 9:3-4).

But to break off from this general and to come to particulars: Do you have a wife? You must consider how you should behave yourself in that relation. To do this right, you must consider the condition of your wife, whether she is one that indeed believes or not.

First, if she believes, then,

1. You are engaged to bless God for her, *"For her price is far above rubies"* (Prov. 31:10), and she is the gift of God unto thee, and is for thy adorning and glory (Prov. 12:4; 1 Cor. 11:7). *"Favor is deceitful, and beauty is vain: but a woman that feareth the Lord, she shall be praised"* (Prov. 31:30).

2. You should love her under a double consideration:

a. As she is your flesh and your bone, *"For no man ever yet hated his own flesh"* (Eph. 5:29).

b. As she is together with you an heir of the grace of life (1 Peter 3:7). This, I say, should engage you to love her with Christian love—to love her as believing you both are dearly beloved of God and the Lord Jesus Christ, and as those that must be together with Him in eternal happiness.

3. You should carry yourself to and before her as does Christ to and before His Church; as says the apostle: So should men love their wives, *"even as Christ also loved the church, and gave himself for it"* (Eph. 5:25). When husbands behave themselves like husbands indeed, then will they be not only husbands, but such an ordinance of God to the wife as will preach to her the carriage of Christ to His spouse. There is a sweet scent wrapped up in the relations of husbands and wives that believe (Eph. 4:32); the wife, I say, signifying the Church, and the husband the head and Savior thereof, *"For the husband is the head of the wife, even as Christ is the head of the church: and he is the saviour of the body"* (Eph. 5:23).

This is one of God's chief ends in instituting marriage, that Christ and His Church, under a figure, might be wherever there is a couple that believe through grace. Therefore, that husband who carries himself indiscreetly towards his wife, he does not only behave himself contrary to the rule, but also makes his wife lose the benefit of such an ordinance, and crosses the mystery of his relation.

Therefore, I say, *"So ought men to love their wives as their own bodies. He that loveth his wife loveth himself. For no man ever yet hated his own flesh; but nourisheth and cherisheth it, even as the Lord the church"* (Eph. 5:28-29). Christ laid out His life for His Church, covers her infirmities, communicates to her His wisdom, protects her, and helps her in her employments in this world; and so should men do for their wives. Solomon and Pharaoh's daughter had the art of thus doing, as you may see in the book of The Song of Solomon. Therefore bear with their weaknesses, help their infirmities, and honor them as the weaker vessels, and as being of a frailer constitution (1 Peter 3:7).

In a word, be such a husband to your believing wife that she may say, God has not only given me a husband, but such a husband as preaches to me every day the behavior of Christ to His Church!

Second, if your wife be unbelieving or carnal, then you have also a duty lying before you that you are engaged to perform under a double engagement: 1. She lies liable every moment to eternal damnation. 2. That she is your wife that is in this evil case.

Oh! how little sense of the worth of souls is there in the heart of some husbands, as is manifest by their unchristian behavior toward and before their wives! Now, to qualify you for a behavior suitable,

1. Labor seriously after a sense of her miserable state, [so] that your heart may yearn towards her soul.

2. Beware that she take no occasion from any unseemly behavior of yours to proceed in evil. And here you have need to double your diligence, for she lies in your bosom, and therefore is capable of espying the least miscarriage in you.

3. If she behaves herself unseemly and unruly, as she is subject to do being Christless and graceless, then labor to overcome her evil with your goodness, her adversity with your patience and meekness. It is a shame for you, who has another principle, to do as she.

4. Take fit opportunities to convince her. Observe her disposition, and when she is most likely to bear, then speak to her very heart.

5. When you speak, speak to purpose. It is not necessary for many words, provided they be pertinent. Job in a few words answers his wife, and takes her off from her foolish talking: *"Thou speakest,"* saith he, *"as one of the foolish women speaketh. What? shall we receive good at the hand of God, and shall we not receive evil?"* (Job 2:10).

6. Let all be done without bitterness or the least appearance of anger: *"In meekness instructing those that oppose themselves; if God peradventure will give them repentance…that they may recover themselves out of the snare of the devil, who are taken captive by him at his will"* (2 Tim. 2:25-26). *"How knowest thou, O man, whether thou shalt save thy wife?"* (1 Cor. 7:16).

From *Christian Behavior*, available from Chapel Library.

John Bunyan (1628-1688): English minister, preacher, and author; born at Elstow near Bedford, England.

Leading a Family for Christ
RICHARD BAXTER (1615-1691)

The principal thing requisite to the right governing of families is the fitness of the governors and the governed thereto…But if persons unfit for their relations have joined themselves together in a family, their first duty is to repent of their former sin and rashness and presently to turn to God, [seeking] after that fitness that is necessary to the right discharge of the duties of their several places. In *fathers*, these three things are of greatest necessity hereunto: 1. authority, 2. skill, 3. holiness and readiness of will.

1. General Directions

Let fathers maintain their authority in their families. For if once that is lost and you are despised by those you should rule, your word will be of no effect with them. You do but ride without a bridle: your power of governing is gone when your authority is lost. And here you must first understand the nature, use, and extent of your authority: for as your relations are different to your wife [and] your children…so is your authority. Your authority over your wife is but such as is necessary to the order of your family, the safe and prudent management of your affairs, and your comfortable cohabitation. The power of love and complicated interest must do more than magisterial[33] commands. Your authority over your children is much greater; but only such as conjunct[34] with love is needful to their good education and felicity… For the maintaining of this your authority, observe these following sub-directions:

Direction 1

Let your family understand that your authority is of God, Who is the God of order, and that in obedience to Him they are obliged to obey you. *"There is no power but of God"* (Rom. 13:1), and there is none that the intelligent creature can so much reverence as that which is of God. All bonds are easily broken and cast away—by the soul at least, if not by the body—which are not perceived to be divine. An enlightened conscience will say to ambitious usurpers, "God I know, and His Son Jesus I know, but who are ye?"

Direction 2

The more of God [that] appeareth upon you in your knowledge, holiness, and unblamableness of life, the greater will your authority be in the eyes of

---

33 **magisterial** – authoritative.
34 **conjunct** – combined.

all your [household] that fear God. Sin will make you contemptible and vile; holiness, being the image of God, will make you honorable. In the eyes of the faithful, *"a vile person is contemned*[35]*"*; but they honor *"them that fear the LORD"* (Ps. 15:4). *"Righteousness exalteth a nation"*—and a person—*"but sin is a reproach*[36] *to any people"* (Prov. 14:34). Those that honor God He will honor, and those that despise Him shall be lightly esteemed (1 Sam. 2:30). They that give up themselves to vile affections and conversations[37] (Rom. 1:26) will seem vile when they have made themselves so. Eli's sons made themselves vile by their sin (1 Sam. 3:13). I know men should discern and honor a person placed in authority by God, though they are morally and naturally vile; but this is so hard that it is seldom well done. And God is so severe against proud offenders that He usually punisheth them by making them vile in the eyes of others. At least when they are dead and men dare freely speak of them, their names will rot (Prov. 10:7). The instances of the greatest emperors in the world—Persian, Roman, and Turkish—do tell us that if (by whoredom, drunkenness, gluttony, pride, and especially persecution) they will make themselves vile, God will permit them to become the shame and scorn of men by uncovering their nakedness. And shall a wicked *father* think to maintain his authority over others while he rebelleth against the authority of God?

Direction 3

Show not your natural weakness by passions or imprudent words or deeds. For if they think contemptuously of your person, a little thing will draw them further to despise your words. There is naturally in man so high an esteem of reason that men are hardly persuaded that they should rebel against reason to be governed (for order's sake) by folly. They are very apt to think that rightest reason should bear rule. Therefore, any silly, weak expressions, any inordinate passions, or any imprudent actions are very apt to make you *contemptible* in your [household's] eyes.

Direction 4

Lose not your authority by a neglect of using it. If you suffer children… to have the head[38] but a little while and to have, say, and do what they will, your government will be but a name or image. A moderate course between a lordly rigor and a soft subjection…will best preserve you from your [household's] contempt.

---

35 **contemned** – treated with contempt; despised.
36 **reproach** – disgrace.
37 **vile affections and conversations** – disgraceful lusts and lifestyles.
38 **head** – leadership.

Direction 5

Lose not your authority by too much familiarity. If you make your children… your playfellows or equals and talk to them and suffer them to talk to you as your companions, they will quickly grow upon you and hold their custom.[39] Though another may govern them, they will scarce ever endure to be governed by you, but will scorn to be subject where they have once been as equal.

2. General Directions

Labor for prudence and skillfulness in governing. He that undertaketh to be a *father* undertaketh to be their governor; and it is no small sin or folly to undertake such a place [that] you are utterly unfit for, when it is a matter of so great importance. You could discern this in a case that is not your own, as if a man undertake to be a schoolmaster that cannot read or write; or to be a physician, who knoweth neither diseases nor their remedies; or to be a pilot that cannot tell how to do a pilot's work; why can you not much more discern it in your own case?

Direction 1

To get the skill of holy governing, it is needful that you be well studied in the Word of God. Therefore, God commandeth kings themselves that they read in the Law all the days of their lives (Deut. 17:18-19) and that it depart not out of their mouths, but that they meditate in it day and night (Josh. 1:8). And all *fathers* must be able to teach it [to] their children and talk of it both at home and abroad, lying down and rising up (Deut. 6:6-7; 11:8-9). All government of men is but subservient to the government of God to promote obedience to His laws…

Direction 2

Understand well the different tempers of your [household] and deal with them as they are and as they can bear, not with all alike. Some are more intelligent and some more dull. Some are of tender and some of hardened dispositions. Some will be best wrought upon by love and gentleness, and some have need of sharpness and severity. Prudence must fit your dealings to their dispositions.

Direction 3

You must put much difference between their different faults and accordingly suit your reprehensions. Those that have [the] most willfulness must be most

---

[39] **grow…custom** – get used to being treated as equals and eventually lose respect for your authority.

severely rebuked, [along with] those that are faulty in matters of greatest weight. Some faults are so much through mere disability and unavoidable frailty of the flesh that there is but little of the will appearing in them. These must be more gently handled as deserving more compassion than reproof. Some are habitual vices, and the whole nature is more desperately depraved than in others. These must have more than a particular correction. They must be held to such a course of life as may be most effectual to destroy and change those habits. And some there are upright at the heart, and in the main and most momentous things are guilty but of some actual faults; and of these, some [are] more seldom and some more frequent. If you do not prudently diversify your rebukes according to their faults, you will but harden them and miss of your ends.[40] For there is a family justice that must not be overthrown unless you will overthrow your families, [just] as there is a more public justice necessary to the public good.

Direction 4

Be a good husband to your wife, a good father to your children, and let love have dominion in all your government that your [household] may easily find that it is [in] their interest to obey you. For interest and self-love are the natural rulers of the world. And it is the most effectual way to procure obedience or any good, to make men perceive that it is for their own good and to engage self-love for you that they may see that the benefit is like to be their own. If you do them no good, but are sour, uncourteous, and close-handed[41] to them, few will be ruled by you.

Direction 5

If you would be skillful in governing others, learn first exactly to command yourselves. Can you ever expect to have others more at your will and government than yourselves? Is he fit to rule his family in the fear of God and a holy life, who is unholy and feareth not God himself? Or is he fit to keep them from passion, drunkenness, gluttony, lust, or any way of sensuality that cannot keep himself from it? Will not [your household] despise such reproofs that are by yourselves contradicted in your lives? You know this [is] true of wicked preachers: is it not as true of other governors?

3. General Directions

You must be holy persons if you would be holy governors of your families. Men's actions follow the bent of their dispositions. They will do as they are.

---

40 **miss of your ends** – fail to accomplish your purpose in discipline.
41 **close-handed** – stingy.

An enemy *of* God will not govern a family *for* God, nor [will] an enemy of holiness (nor a stranger to it) set up a holy order in his house and in a holy manner manage his affairs. I know it is cheaper and easier to the flesh to call *others* to mortification[42] and holiness of life than to bring ourselves to it, but when it is not a bare command or wish that is necessary, but a course of holy and industrious government, unholy persons—though some of them may go far—have not the ends and principles that such a work requireth.

Direction 1

To this end, be sure that your own souls be entirely subjected to God and that you more accurately obey His laws than you expect any [household member to] obey your commands. If you dare disobey God, why should they fear disobeying you? Can you more severely revenge disobedience or more bountifully reward obedience than God can? Are you greater and better than God Himself is?

Direction 2

Be sure that you lay up your treasure in heaven and make the enjoyment of God in glory to be the ultimate commanding end, both of the affairs and government of your family and all things else with which you are entrusted. Devote yourselves and all to God, and do all for Him…If thus *you* are separated unto God, you are sanctified; then you will separate all that you have to His use and service…

Direction 3

Maintain God's authority in your family more carefully than your own. Your own is but for His. More sharply rebuke or correct them that wrong and dishonor God than those that wrong and dishonor you. Remember Eli's sad example: make not a small matter of any of the sins, especially the great sins, of your children…God's honor must be greatest in your family, and His service must have the preeminence of yours. Sin against Him must be the most intolerable offence.

Direction 4

Let spiritual love to your family be predominant, let your care be greatest for the saving of their souls, and [let] your compassion [be] greatest in their spiritual miseries. Be first careful to provide them a portion in heaven and to save them from whatsoever would deprive them of it. Never prefer

---

42 See FGB 201, *Mortification*

the transitory pelf[43] of earth before their everlasting riches. Never be so cumbered about many things as to forget that one thing is necessary, but choose for yourselves and them the better part (Luke 10:42).

From "A Christian Directory" in *The Practical Works of Richard Baxter*, Vol. 4, Soli Deo Gloria, a division of Reformation Heritage Books: www.heritagebooks.org.

Richard Baxter (1615-1691): Anglican Puritan preacher and theologian; born in Rowton, Shropshire, England.

Many are careful to educate their children in the favor of great men, but, alas! who brings up his children in the fear of the great God?
—George Swinnock

---

43 **transitory pelf** – temporary wealth and possessions.

A Father Must Be Godly

NICHOLAS BYFIELD (1579–1622)

The signs of the true Christian that has true grace in this world and shall be saved in heaven when he dies may be cast into two catalogs[44]—the one more brief and the other more large. The one catalog of signs describes him by such marks as, for the most part, outwardly distinguish him among men. The large catalog I intend especially as a more infallible and effectual way of trial, containing such signs as, for the most part, are not observed by other men, or not fully, but are known to himself and can be found in no one who is a reprobate.[45]

For the FIRST catalog: The true Christian usually discovers himself by these marks. *First*, he will not *"have...fellowship with the unfruitful works of darkness"* (Eph. 5:11). He will not walk *"in the counsel of the ungodly,"* nor stand *"in the way of sinners"* (Ps. 1:1). He will not sort himself with workers of iniquity (2 Cor. 6:14-18).

SECOND, he will afflict and humble his soul for his sins, mourning and weeping for them...He accounts his sins to be his greatest burden. He cannot make a mockery of sin.

THIRD, he labors to be holy in all parts of his conversation, watching over his own ways at all times and in all companies (Ps. 50:23; 2 Peter 3:11).

FOURTH, he makes conscience of the least commandments as well as the greatest, avoiding filthy speaking, vain jesting, and lasciviousness[46] (Eph. 5:4), as well as whoredom; lesser oaths as well as greater; reproachful speeches as well as violent actions.

FIFTH, he loves, esteems, and labors for the powerful preaching of the Word above all earthly treasures.

SIXTH, he honors and highly accounts of the godly and delights in the company of such as truly fear God above all others (Ps. 15).

SEVENTH, he is careful of the sanctification of the [Lord's Day], neither daring to violate that holy rest by labor nor to neglect the holy duties belonging to God's service—public or private (Isa. 56, 58).

EIGHTH, he does not love the world, neither the things of it (1 John 2:15), but is more heartily affected in things that concern a better life. So [he] does in some degree love the appearing of Christ (2 Tim. 4:8).

---

44 **catalogs** – complete lists of things, usually arranged systematically.
45 **reprobate** – one rejected by God.
46 **lasciviousness** – inclined to lust or sexual desires.

NINTH, he is *"easy to be intreated"* (James 3:17). He forgives his enemies, desires peace, and does good even to those that persecute him if it lies in his power (Matt. 5:44-45).

TENTH, he goes on in the profession of the sincerity of the gospel and does such duties as he knows God requires of him in the business of his soul, notwithstanding the oppositions of profane persons or the dislike of carnal friends.

ELEVENTH, he sets up a daily course of serving God and that with his family too, if he has any. [He] exercises himself in the Word of God as the chief joy of his heart and the daily refuge of his life, calling on God continually. So much of the shorter catalog of signs.

[Second catalog:]…I will now by God's assistance, for the helping of the weakest Christians…endeavor to express myself in this doctrine of the trial of a true Christian's estate in a more plain and easy course of examination. [I will] leave…this new catalog to the blessing of God and the free choice of the godly reader to use, which he finds most agreeable to his own taste, being both such as are warranted and founded on the infallible evidence of God's unchangeable truth…

There are three sorts of places in Scripture (as I conceive) that point out the grounds of infallible assurance in those that can attain to them. As FIRST, such places as expressly affirm that such and such things are signs. For example, *"We know that we have passed from death unto life, because we love the brethren"* (1 John 3:14). Here the Holy Spirit shows us expressly that the love of the brethren is a sign by which a Christian may know that he is translated from death to life. And so the Apostle Paul gives signs to know whether their sorrow was *"after a godly sort"* or not (2 Cor. 7:11). So does the Prophet David (Ps. 15) give diverse signs by which the man that shall dwell in God's holy hill may be known. So the Apostle James tells us how he may know the wisdom from above: by reckoning the fruits and effects of it (James 3:17). So does the Apostle Paul tell us how we may know whether we have the Spirit of Christ in us or not (Rom. 8:9, 15; Gal. 5:22, 4:6-7).

SECOND, I find out signs by marking what graces in man the promises of God are made to. For in this way I reason: Whatsoever gifts of God in man bring him within the compass of God's promises of eternal mercy, that gift must be an infallible sign of salvation…Therefore, the man that can find those gifts in himself shall be certainly saved. For example, the Kingdom of heaven is promised to such as are *"poor in spirit"* (Matt. 5:3). From there, I gather that poverty of spirit is an infallible sign. The like I may say of the love of the Word, of uprightness of heart, of the love of God, and the love of the appearing of Christ.

THIRD, I find out other signs by observing what godly men in Scripture have said for themselves when they have pleaded their own evidence for their interest in God's love or their hope of a better life. Look how godly men in Scripture have proved that they were not hypocrites. Even so may any Christian prove that he is not a hypocrite either. For example, Job, being charged to be a hypocrite and lying under the heavy hand of God, pleads his cause and proves that he was not a hypocrite by his constancy in God's ways and by his constant estimation of God's Word: *"I have esteemed the words of his mouth more than my necessary food"* (Job 23:10-12).

Now, whereas some signs are *general* and thou mightest doubt the exposition,[47] namely, how that sign is infallible in such and such senses… you may observe that I expound the sign as it is expounded in several other Scriptures. For example, the love of the brethren is a general sign. Now how shall I know that I have the right love of the brethren? This I explain by flying to diverse other Scriptures in which the particular explications[48] of this sign are pleaded.

The first way, then, by which a Christian may try himself is to examine himself about his humiliation for sin, whether it is right or not. For under this head is comprehended the explication of the doctrine of poverty of spirit and godly sorrow—and so in general of repentance of sins.

Now the true Christian in this matter of humiliation shows himself to have attained that which no reprobate could ever attain, and that in diverse particulars, such as, FIRST, he has a true sight and sense of his sins. He discerns his sinfulness of life both past and present and is affected and pained under the burden of his daily wants[49] and corruptions. [He] sees his misery in respect of his sins (Matt. 11:29; 5:4).

SECOND, he trembles at God's Word and fears His displeasure, while it yet hangs in the threatenings (Isa. 66:1-2).

THIRD, he renounceth his own merits and disclaims all opinion of true happiness in himself or in anything under the sun. [He is] fully persuaded that he cannot be saved by any works of his own or be happy in enjoying any worldly things.[50] Therefore, [he] is fully resolved to seek for the chief good in God's favor in Jesus Christ only.

FOURTH, he mourns heartily and secretly for his sins; and so he [mourns] 1. for all sorts of sins, for secret sins as well as known sins; for lesser sins as

---

47 **thou…exposition** – you might doubt the author's interpretation.
48 **explications** – explanations.
49 **wants** – inadequacies.
50 The author is referring to sinful, worldly pursuits, not the enjoyment of God's creation.

well as greater; for the present evils of his nature and life, as well as the sins he has loved or [that] have been gainful and pleasing to him. Yes, he grieves for the evil that cleaves to his best works as well as for evil works (Isa. 6:5, 1:16; Rom. 7:24; Matt. 5:6). 2. For sin as it is sin and not as it does or might bring him shame or punishments in this life or in hell. 3. He is as much troubled for his sins as he was accustomed, or now should be, for crosses in his estate.[51] He mourns as heartily for the sorrows that fell on God's Son for his sin, as if *he* had lost his one and only son (Zech. 12:10-11); or at least he strives for this and judges himself if worldly afflictions trouble him more than his sins (Ps. 38:5).

Fifth, he is truly grieved and vexed in soul for the abominations that are done by others to the dishonor of God, [to the] slander of true religion, or [to] the ruin of the souls of men—thus, Lot (2 Peter 2:7), David (Ps. 119:136), and the mourners marked for God's own people (Ezek. 9:4).

Sixth, he is heartily affected, troubled, and grieved for spiritual judgments that reach to the souls of men, as well as wicked men are wont[52] to be troubled for temporal crosses. So he is grieved and perplexed for hardness of heart (when he cannot mourn as he would), for the famine of the Word, for the absence of God, for the blasphemies of the wicked, or the like (Ps. 44:2-3, 13; Neh. 1:3-4; Isa. 63:17).

Seventh, he is most stirred up to abase[53] himself and mourn for his sins when he feels God to be most merciful. The goodness of God makes him fear God and hate his sins rather than [God's] justice (Hos. 3:5).

Eighth, his griefs are such as can be assuaged[54] only by spiritual means. It is not sport or merry company that eases him. His comfort is only from the Lord in some of His ordinances. As it was the Lord that wounded him with the sight of his sins, so to the Lord only he goes to be healed of his wounds (Hos. 6:1-2; Ps. 119:24, 50).

Ninth, in his grief, he is inquisitive:[55] he will ask the way and desires to know how he may be saved. He cannot smother and put off his doubts in so great a business. He does not dare now any longer to be ignorant of the way to heaven. He is not careless, as he was accustomed to be, but is seriously bent to get directions from the Word of God about his reconciliation, sanctification,[56] and salvation (Jer. 50:4-5; Acts 2:37).

---

51 **crosses in his estate** – afflictions in one's moral, bodily, or mental condition.
52 **wont** – accustomed.
53 **abase** – humble.
54 **assuaged** – relieved.
55 **inquisitive** – given to questioning; eager for knowledge.
56 See FGB 215, *Sanctification*

Tenth, he is fearful of being deceived and therefore is not slightly satisfied. He will not rest on a common hope, nor is he carried with probabilities. Nor does it content him that other men have a good opinion of him. Nor is he pleased that he has mended some faults or begun to repent; but, repenting, he repents still, that is, he takes a sound course to be sure his repentance is effectually performed (Jer. 31:19).

Eleventh, he is vehemently carried with the desires of the sound reformation of his life…Godly sorrow [for sin] always tendeth to reformation and sound amendment.

Twelfth, in all his sorrows, he is supported by a secret trust in the mercy and acceptance of God, so as no misery can beat him from the consideration, inward assurance, and hope in the mercy of God. In the very disquietness[57] of his heart, the desire of his soul is to the Lord and before His presence. Though he is never so much cast down, yet he waits upon God for the help of His countenance and, in some measure, condemns the unbelief of his own heart. [He] trusts in the name of God and His never-failing compassions (Ps. 38:9, 42:5, 11; Lam. 3:21; Zeph. 3:12).

Thirteenth, he is wonderfully inflamed with love to God, if He at any time lets him know that He heareth his prayers.[58] In the midst of his most desperate sorrows, his heart is eased if he speeds well[59] in prayer (Ps. 116:1, 3).

Fourteenth, he daily keeps a watch upon his own soul. He judgeth himself for his sins before God, arresting, accusing, and condemning his sins. He confesseth his sins particularly to God, without hiding any sin, that is, without forbearing to pray against any sin he knows by himself, out of any desire he still has to continue in it. By this sign, he may be sure he has the Spirit of God and that his sins are forgiven him (1 John 1:7; 1 Cor. 11:32).

Fifteenth, his requests are daily poured to God. He cries to God with affection and confidence, though it is with much weakness and many defects, as the little child does to the father. Thereby he discovers the Spirit of adoption in him (Rom. 8:15; Eph. 3:12).

Sixteenth, he is unfeignedly desirous to be rid of all sins as well as one. There is no sin he knows [to be in] himself, but he doth desire as heartily that he might never commit it, as he doth that God should never impute it.[60] This is a never-failing sign, a fundamental one (2 Tim. 2:19).

---

57 **disquietness** – restlessness; uneasiness.
58 God "hearing" a believer's prayer, in this context, appears to mean granting the thing prayed for.
59 **speeds well** – meets with success; attains his desire.
60 In other words, when a believer finds any sin in himself, he is as earnest about not wanting to commit that sin as much as he earnestly fears God charging him guilty for it.

SEVENTEENTH, he is content to receive evil[61] at the hand of God, as well as good, without murmuring or letting go his integrity, as being sensible of his own deserts[62] and desirous to approve himself to God, without respect of reward. This proved that Job was a holy and upright man (Job 1:1, 2:3, 10).

[FINALLY], he has a spirit without guile[63] (Ps. 32:2). He is more desirous to be good, than to be thought to be so. [He] seeks the power of godliness [rather] than the show of it (Job 1:1; Prov. 20:6-7). His praise is of God, not of men (Rom. 2:29). And in this way, we see much of the trial of his humiliation.

From *The Signs of a Wicked Man and the Signs of a Godly Man*, Puritan Publications: www.puritanpublications.com.

Nicholas Byfield (1579-1622): Anglican Puritan preacher and author; born in Warwickshire, England.

A father may deliver the best instructions. But if he does not by discipline eradicate evil tempers, correct bad habits, repress rank corruptions, nothing excellent can be looked for. He may be a good prophet and a good priest; but if he be not also a good king, all else is vain.
—John Angell James

Fathers…must go before their households in the things of God. They must be as prophets, priests, and kings in their own families; and, as such, they must keep up family doctrine, family worship, and family discipline.
—Matthew Henry

---

61 **receive evil** – to receive difficulties, trials, or afflictions.
62 **his own deserts** – what he deserves.
63 **guile** – deceit; treachery.

Fathers Must Teach God's Word and Pray
THOMAS DOOLITTLE (1632-1707)

As for me and my house, we will serve the LORD. —Joshua 24:15

FATHERS ought to read the Scripture to their families [and] teach and instruct their children…in the matters and doctrines of salvation. Therefore, they are to pray *in* and *with* their families.

No man that will not deny the Scripture can deny the unquestionable duty of reading the Scripture in our houses, governors of families teaching and instructing them out of the Word of God. Amongst a multitude of express Scriptures, look into these: *"And it shall come to pass, when your children shall say unto you, What mean ye by this service?* ^{27} *That ye shall say, It is the sacrifice of the LORD'S passover, who passed over the houses of the children of Israel in Egypt, when he smote the Egyptians, and delivered our houses"* (Ex. 12:26-27). There is as much reason that Christian parents should explain to their children the [ordinances] of the New Testament to instruct them in the nature, use, and ends of baptism and the Lord's Supper: *"And these words, which I command thee this day, shall be in thine heart: And thou shalt teach*[64] *(whet or sharpen) them diligently unto thy children, and shalt talk of them when thou sittest in thine house, and when thou walkest by the way, and when thou liest down, and when thou risest up,"* that is, morning and evening (Deut. 6:6-7; 11:18-19). *"And, ye fathers, provoke not your children to wrath: but bring them up in the nurture and admonition of the Lord"* (Eph. 6:4). And God was pleased with this in Abraham: *"For I know him, that he will command his children and his household after him, and they shall keep the way of the LORD"* (Gen. 18:19). This, then, is undeniable if the Word is to be believed, received as our rule, and obedience to be yielded thereunto. And the heathens taught a necessity of instructing youth betimes.[65]

The reason of this consequence—from family reading and instructions to family praying—is evident (we need to beg of God the illumination of His Spirit, the opening of the eyes of everyone in the family, the blessing of God upon our endeavors, without which it will be to no saving benefit) and will be more manifest if we consider and lay together these things following:

FIRST, whose word it is that is to be read in the family together—the Word of the eternal, blessed, glorious God. And doth this call for and require preceding prayer, no more than if you were to read the book of some mortal man? The Word of God is that *out of which* God speaketh to

---

64 **teach** – Hebrew = וְשִׁנַּנְתָּם

65 **betimes** – in good time; before it is too late.

us. It is that *by which* He doth instruct and inform us in the highest and weightiest concernments of our souls. It is that *from which* we must fetch remedies for the cure of our spiritual maladies. It is that *from whence* we must have weapons of defense against our spiritual enemies that do assault our souls and be directed in the paths of life.

And is not prayer together needful, then, that God would prepare all their hearts to receive and obey what shall be read to them of the mind of God? Is all the family so serious and so sensible of the glory, holiness, and majesty of that God that speaketh to them in His Word that prayer is not needful that they may be so? And if it is needful, should it not first be done? And when it hath been read and the threatenings, commands, and promises of the glorious God been heard, your sins and God's wrath against them discovered, duties enjoined, precious privileges opened, and promises of a faithful God—both "great and precious promises" made to such as do repent, believe, and turn to God with all their hearts unfeignedly[66]—have you not all need together to fall down upon your knees; to beg, cry, and call to God for pardon of those sins that by this Word you are convinced you are guilty of and to lament them before the Lord? And that when your duty is discovered, you might all have hearts to practice and obey? That you might unfeignedly repent and turn to God so that you may apply those promises to yourselves and be partaker of those privileges? From this, then, there is great reason, when you read together, [that] you should also pray together.

SECONDLY, consider what great and deep mysterious things are contained in the Word of God that you are to read together, and there will appear a necessity of praying together also. Is there not in this Word the doctrine concerning God—how He might be known, loved, obeyed, worshipped, and delighted in? Concerning Christ, the God-man, a mystery that the angels wonder at and no man fully understands or can express and fully unfold? Concerning the offices of Christ—Prophet, Priest, and King,[67] the example and the life of Christ, the miracles of Christ, the temptations of Christ, the sufferings of Christ, His death, the victories of Christ, the resurrection, ascension, and intercession of Christ, and His coming to judgment? Is there not in the Scripture the doctrine of the Trinity, of the misery of man by sin, and of his remedy by Christ? Of the covenant of grace, the conditions of this covenant, and the seals thereof? The many precious, glorious privileges that

---

66 **unfeignedly** – with sincerity.
67 See FGBs 183, *Christ the Mediator,* and 225, *The Work of Christ*

we have by Christ—reconciliation with God, justification,[68] sanctification,[69] and adoption? The several graces to be got, duties to be done, and of men's everlasting state in heaven or hell[70]? Are these and such like contained in the Word of God that you ought to read daily in your houses? And yet do you not see the need of prayer before and after your reading of it? Weigh them well, and you will.

THIRDLY, consider how much all the family are concerned to know and understand these things so necessary to salvation. If they are ignorant of them, they are undone. If they know not God, how shall they love Him? "Things *unseen* may be loved, but things *unknown* cannot." We might love an *unseen* God and an *unseen* Christ (1 Peter 1:8), but not an *unknown* God. If they in your family know not Christ, how shall they believe on Him? And yet they must perish and be damned if they do not. They must forever lose God, Christ, heaven, and their souls, if they do not repent, believe, and be converted. Yet when that Book is read by which they should understand the nature of true saving grace, is not prayer needful? Especially when many have the Bible and read it, yet do not understand the things that do concern their peace?

FOURTHLY, consider further the blindness of their minds and their inability without the teachings of God's Spirit to know and understand these things. And yet is not prayer needful?

FIFTHLY, consider yet further: the backwardness of their hearts to hearken to these weighty, necessary truths of God and their natural unwillingness to learn show prayer to be necessary that God would make them able and willing to receive them.

SIXTHLY, once more, consider that prayer is a special means to obtain knowledge from God and a blessing upon the teachings and instructions of the *father*. David prayed that God would open his eyes that he might behold wondrous things out of God's Law (Ps. 119:18). There are "wondrous things" in the Word of God. That fallen man should be recovered is a wondrous thing. That a holy God should be reconciled to sinful man is a wondrous thing. That the Son of God should take upon Him the nature of man, [that] God be manifested in the flesh, and [that] a believer [is] justified by the righteousness of another—these are wondrous things! But there is darkness upon our minds, a veil over our eyes, and the Scripture is a clasped, closed book that we cannot savingly understand these great, wonderful things, to

---

68 See FGB 187, *Justification*.
69 See FGB 215, *Sanctification*.
70 See FGB 211, *Hell*.

have our love chiefly upon them and our delight in them, except the Spirit of God take away the veil, remove our ignorance, and enlighten our minds. This wisdom is to be sought from God by fervent prayer. You that are *fathers*—would you have your children… know these things and be affected with them? Would you have impressions made upon their minds and hearts of the great concernments of their souls? Therefore do you instruct them. But can *you* reach their hearts? Can *you* awaken their consciences? Can you not? Doth it not become you to pray to God with them that He would do it? While you are praying jointly with them, God may be secretly disposing and powerfully preparing their hearts to receive His Word and your instructions from it.

From all this I argue thus for family prayer: If it be the duty of families, as such, to read and hear the Word of God together read, then it is the duty of families, as such, to pray together (this is shown by the six things last mentioned). It is the duty of families, as such, to read the Word of God and to hear it together read (this was proved from Scripture before). Therefore, it is the duty of families, as such, to pray together.

From "How May the Duty of Daily Family Prayer Be Best Managed for the Spiritual Benefit of Everyone in the Family?" in *Puritan Sermons*, Vol. 2, Richard Owen Roberts, Publishers.

Thomas Doolittle (1632-1707): English Nonconformist minister; born at Kidderminster, Worcestershire, England.

Fathers and Discipline

WILLIAM GOUGE (1575-1653)

And, ye fathers, provoke not your children to wrath: but bring them up in the nurture and admonition of the Lord. —Ephesians 6:4

The fountain of a father's duties is love…Great reason there is why this affection should be fast fixed in the heart of fathers towards their children. For great is that pain, pains, cost, and care that fathers must undergo for their children. But if love is in them, no pain, pains, cost, or care will seem too much. Herein appeareth the wise providence of God, Who by nature hath so fast fixed love in the hearts of fathers—if there be any in whom it aboundeth not, he is counted unnatural. If love did not abound in fathers, many children would be neglected and lost…They are not able to help themselves. As God by nature hath planted love in all parents, so Christians, for conscience sake, ought to nourish, increase, and blow up this fire of love. [By this,] they may thereby be made more forward to do every duty with cheerfulness. The more fervent love is, the more readily will every duty be performed…In my text, the apostle nameth *fathers*. Solomon saith that his father taught him even while he was tender (Prov. 4:3-4); and David felt the smart of neglecting his other children…Fathers therefore must do their best endeavor and see that mothers do theirs also because he is governor over child, mother, and all…

Of adding admonition to instruction: The means of helping forward the good work of nurture are especially two: 1. frequent admonition, 2. due correction. Both of them are implied in this text: one in the word translated *admonition*, which [according to the notation of the Greek word] is a putting of a thing into the mind—an urging and pressing of it. The other [is] in the word translated *nurture*.

Now both these are to be joined together as being very helpful to each other. For admonition without correction is likely to prove but mere vanity, and correction without admonition will be too much austerity.[71] The duty that the first of these setteth forth is this:

Fathers must often whet[72] instruction upon their children. They may not think it enough to tell their children what they ought to do, but to instruction, they must add admonition and, as it were, beat into their children's heads[73] the lessons that they teach them, so that they may make a deeper impression

---

71 **austerity** – harshness to the feelings; severity of discipline.
72 **whet** – urge.
73 **beat into…heads** – this is an obsolete way of saying "to insist on with repetition."

in their hearts. Thus shall their instructions be like the words of the wise that are as nails fastened (Eccl. 12:11) or fast knocked in. They remain firm where they are once fastened and cannot easily be plucked out. For as many blows do knock a nail up to the head [as we speak], so many admonitions do settle good instructions in a child's heart and cause that the heart be established in that which is taught. [This] is a thing to be labored after (Heb. 13:9)…The direction that is in particular given to fathers of whetting God's words upon their children (Deut. 6:7)…may be applied to this purpose.

To this purpose it is that Solomon useth to double his instructions and urge them again and again, as *"Hear the instruction…forsake not the law"* (Prov. 1:8); *"receive my words, and hide my commandments with thee…incline thine ear…apply thine heart"* (Prov. 2:1-2). Yea, often he repeateth the very same precepts.

The apprehension of children is fickle[74] and their memory weak: if they be but once, seldom, or slightly instructed, that which is taught will soon slip away and do little or no good.

For the better performing of this duty, fathers must think of the best means they can to fasten their instructions upon their children, observe their inclination and disposition, and see with what they are most moved. Constant exhortations and powerful persuasions are comprised under admonition, which in their kinds, as occasion requireth, are to be used…

Of fathers *reproving* their children: The other means of helping nurture is correction, which is of two sorts: *verbal* by words, *real* by [the use of the rod]. The former is *reprehension*;[75] and it must always go before the latter, which is most usually and properly called *correction*.

Reprehension is a kind of middle thing betwixt admonition and correction: it is a sharp admonition, but a mild correction. It is rather to be used because it may be a means to prevent [spanking], especially in ingenuous[76] and good-natured children [*A reproof entereth more into a wise man than an hundred stripes into a fool* (Prov. 17:10)] and because it may be used, when it is not so meet[77] to use [spanking], as when children are grown to man-age.

The many good fruits that the Holy Ghost noteth to proceed from due reproof do show that it is a duty whereof fathers ought to make conscience as they desire to promote the good of their children, and so much the rather

---

74 **fickle** – unreliable.
75 **reprehension** – an act of reproving or finding fault with.
76 **ingenuous** – honest.
77 **meet** – proper for the occasion.

because many good fruits redound[78] to the fathers that reprove, as well as to the children reproved. In regard of their good who are reproved, it is said, *"Reproofs of instruction are the way of life"* (Prov. 6:23). They cause understanding (Prov. 15:32) and make prudent[79] (Prov. 15:5). In regard of their good who reprove, it is said, *"To them that rebuke...shall be delight* [that is, much comfort and matter of rejoicing, so as they shall not need to repent what they have done],*and a good blessing shall come upon them"* (Prov. 24:25). That is, either a blessing of good men, who will bless, praise, and commend them, or a blessing of good things and that from the Lord Who will reward them for this conscionable[80] performance of their duty.

Upon these grounds, holy men have not spared to rebuke their children as there was occasion (Gen. 9:25; 34:30; 49:4). Though Eli did somewhat in this duty, yet because he was not more severe therein, he brought destruction both upon himself and his children (1 Sam. 2:23)…

Of correcting children: The latter and more proper kind of correction, that is, by [the rod,] is also a means appointed by God to help the good nurture and education of children. It is the *last* remedy that a father can use—a remedy that may do good when nothing else can.

It is by the Holy Ghost both expressly commanded and also very often pressed under these and such like phrases: *"chasten thy son"* (Prov. 19:18); *"correct thy son"* (Prov. 29:17); *"withhold not correction from the child"* (Prov. 23:13); *"thou shalt beat him with the rod"* (Prov. 23:14). Were there no other motive, this is sufficient. God's charge was such a motive to Abraham [that] he would have sacrificed his son (Gen. 22:2-3). Wilt thou not correct thy child at God's command?

It is further commended by God's own example, which is not only set forth in some particular instances, but by His general constant dealing with all, and that as an especial token and fruit of His love. *"For whom the Lord loveth he chasteneth, and scourgeth every son whom he receiveth…But if ye be without chastisement, whereof all are partakers, then are ye bastards, and not sons"* (Heb. 12:6, 8). Let this example of God be well weighed, for it is of great weight. Who can better tell what kind of dealing is fittest for children than God? Who can better nurture children than God? Who doth more truly aim at and procure the good of children than God? Yea, who doth more tender[81] children than God? If God, the Father of spirits in wisdom and love, thus

---

78 **redound** – result.
79 **prudent** – wise with a sense of caution.
80 **conscionable** – conscientiously observant; showing a regard for conscience.
81 **tender** – act tenderly toward; treat with tenderness.

deals with His children, fathers of the flesh may not think by the contrary to show wisdom or love. Their wisdom will be folly, their love, hatred. Upon these grounds, it is taken for a thing granted that fathers [who tender the good of their children as they should] do chastise their children as need requireth; for it is said, *"For whom the LORD loveth he correcteth; even as a father the son in whom he delighteth"* (Prov. 3:12)…As a thing without controversy, it is said, *"We have had fathers of our flesh which corrected us"* (Heb. 12:9).

The grounds of the equity of this duty respect partly the children corrected and partly the fathers that correct. Regarding children, it freeth them from much evil and worketh in them much good.

Correction is as physic[82] to purge out much corruption that lurketh in children and as a salve to heal many wounds and sores made by their folly. In which respect Solomon saith, *"Foolishness is bound in the heart of a child; but the rod of correction shall drive it far from him"* (Prov. 22:15)…In regard to the inward operation of this physic, correction is further said to preserve a child from death, [*if thou beatest him…he shall not die* (Prov. 23:13)] and that not only from temporal death [as many children are thus preserved from the Magistrate's sword] but also from external death [*thou…shalt deliver his soul from hell* (Prov. 23:14)]. Note this, ye cockering[83] fathers, whose over-much lenity[84] is very great cruelty. For may we not justly count him a cruel father who should suffer diseases, boils, sores, and wounds to remain, increase, and fester in his child, and give him no physic, nor apply any plasters or medicines to him? Nay, rather, who seeth his son running into a flaming fire or deep water and would not hold him back? Even so cruel and crueler are they who suffer their children to run on in evil, rather than correct them.

OBJECTION: Who can endure to make his own child smart[85] and to put him to pain?

ANSWER: The future fruit is more to be considered than the present pain. Potions, pills, and corrosives are fulsome,[86] bitter, and painful; but because there is a necessity of using them, and great mischief is prevented by the use of them, wise fathers will not forbear them for the sensible bitterness and pain. Fitly doth the Apostle thus answer that objection: *"No chastening for the present seemeth to be joyous, but grievous: nevertheless, afterward it yieldeth the peaceable fruit of righteousness"* (Heb. 12:11). This may be applied to

---

82 **physic** – medicine.
83 **cockering** – pampering; treating with excessive indulgence.
84 **over-much lenity** – excessive mildness.
85 **make…smart** – cause to feel pain or stinging.
86 **fulsome** – nauseating.

fathers' corrections as well as to God's. The good that correction bringeth to children is by Solomon noted in this and such like phrases [as,] *"The rod... [giveth] wisdom"* (Prov. 29:15); for it maketh children observe what is good, evil, commendable, and blameworthy. And, accordingly, [it teacheth them] to do the good and leave the evil, which is a great point of wisdom…

In regard of fathers, due correcting of their children both freeth them of many inconveniences and bringeth to them much quiet. 1. It spareth them many pains. For many admonitions oft repeated and inculcated again and again will not make many children so much to heed wholesome and good advice as a little correction. They are much more sensible of smart than of words. 2. It preventeth much grief, shame, and vexation. For *"a foolish son is a grief to his father, and bitterness to her that bare him"* (Prov. 17:25). But it is the rod of correction that driveth away foolishness (Prov. 22:15) and so preventeth that grief and bitterness. 3. It freeth them from the guilt of their children's sin, so [that] they are not accessory thereto as Eli was (1 Sam. 3:13). For correction is the last remedy that a father can use: if by that he can do no good, it is presupposed that he hath done his uttermost endeavor. In [this] respect, though the child die in his sin, yet the father hath delivered his own soul.

The quiet that is brought to fathers by correcting their children is thus noted out by Solomon: *"Correct thy son, and he shall give thee rest; yea, he shall give delight unto thy soul"* (Prov. 29:17). For children well-nurtured, and by correction kept in a filial awe, will so carry themselves as their fathers may rest somewhat secure and not disquiet themselves [as they do with children set at liberty]. Yea, as trees well pruned and ground well tilled, they will bring forth pleasant and abundant fruit; and their fathers will have just cause to rejoice in them.

A direction to fathers in correcting their children: For well using this biting corrosive[87] of correction, fathers must have respect to the *matter* for which they do correct and to their *manner* of correcting.

In regard of the *matter*, these three things must be noted: 1. That they are sure there is a fault committed, so that there is just cause for correcting. [Otherwise,] more hurt than good will proceed from thence. If corrosive is laid where there is no sore, it will make one. If correction is unjustly given, it may provoke to wrath, but will do little good. This is it wherein earthly fathers are taxed[88] and made unlike to God, for that many times they correct

---

87 **corrosive** – medically speaking, a remedy or drug that eats away or consumes by chemical action like an acid.
88 **taxed** – called into question.

after their own pleasure (Heb. 12:10), which is a point of great injustice. 2. That the fault be made known to the child corrected and he apparently convinced thereof. Correction must be for instruction, which cannot be except the child knows *why* he is corrected. For it is all one to him, as if he were corrected for no fault, if he know not his fault. God thus at first proceeded with the serpent, with Eve, and with Adam (Gen. 3:11). Thus judges proceed in punishing malefactors. Yea, thus will men deal with a dog. Should they not much more with a child? 3. That the faults be such especially as the fathers can show to their children [if at least they be of so much discretion] to be against God's Word, [such as] swearing, lying, pilfering,[89] and the like. For (1) these are most dangerous faults and therefore more carefully to be purged out. (2) The child corrected will thus be the better evicted[90] of his fault, will the more condemn himself, and will more contentedly bear the correction.

In regard of the *manner* of correcting, four *general* and four *particular* rules are to be observed. The *general* rules are these: 1. An eye must be had to God's manner of correcting His children and, in particular, of God's correcting the father himself. No better general direction can be given, for God's pattern is a perfect rule. 2. Prayer must be made by fathers for themselves and for their children: for themselves to be directed in doing it [and] for their children to be bettered by it. Thus will good physicians in ministering physic. In all duties is prayer to be used, especially in this: for a father is ready, partly through his own intemperate passion and partly through the child's impatience, to fall into one extreme or other. This is not to impose upon all, whenever they take up the rod, to go and make a solemn prayer, but to lift up the heart for direction and blessing. 3. Correction must be given in love. All things must be done in love (1 Cor. 16:14)—much more this that carries a show of anger and hatred…God correcteth His children in love: so must fathers. Love will make them do it with tenderness and compassion. 4. Correction must be given in a mild mood, when the affections are well ordered and not distempered[91] with choler,[92] rage, fury, and other like passions. Disturbed passions cast a mist before the understanding, so [that] a man cannot discern what is enough [or] what [is] too much. When passion is moved, correction must be deferred. God correcteth in measure.

---

89 **pilfering** – stealing in small quantities or things of little value.
90 **evicted** – convinced.
91 **distempered** – disordered; disturbed.
92 **choler** – anger.

The *particulars* are these: 1. Due order must be kept. Correction by word must go before correction by the rod. *"I rebuke and chasten,"* saith the Lord (Rev. 3:19). Thus, a father will show that he taketh no delight in smiting his child; it is *necessity* that forceth him thereunto. Thus, a father showeth himself like God, Who doth not punish willingly (Lam. 3:33). Physicians, when they minister strong physic, will give preparative; rebuke may be as a preparative. Good and pitiful surgeons will try all other means before they come to lance and sear. 2. Due respect must be had to the party corrected. If he is young and tender, the lighter correction must be used. Solomon oft mentioneth a rod as [appropriate] oft for a child, for that is the lightest correction. So if the child is of a flexible and ingenuous disposition, soon snapped, the correction must accordingly be moderated. If he is well grown and withal be stout and stubborn, the correction may be more severe. 3. Due respect must be had to the fault. Sins directly against God, open, notorious, scandalous sins, known sins, sins often committed, in which they are grown up and whereof they have [become] a habit are with greater severity to be corrected. 4. A father must behold his own faults in correcting his child's, so more compassion will be wrought in him.

From *Of Domestical Duties*, Puritan Reprints: www.puritanreprints.com.

William Gouge (1575-1653): English Puritan pastor, theologian, and author; born in Stratford-Bow, Middlesex County, England.

How Fathers Can Provoke Their Children to Wrath
THOMAS WATSON (C. 1620-1686)

Ye fathers, provoke not your children to wrath. —Ephesians 6:4

Act prudently towards your children. It is a great point of prudence in father not to provoke his children to wrath. *"Fathers, provoke not your children to anger, lest they be discouraged"* (Col. 3:21). How may a *father* provoke his children to wrath?

1. By giving them abusive terms. *"Thou son of the perverse rebellious woman,"* said Saul to his son Jonathan (1 Sam. 20:30). Some parents use imprecations[93] and curses to their children, which provoke them to wrath. Would you have God bless your children, and do you curse them?

2. *Fathers* provoke children to wrath when they strike them without a cause or when the correction exceeds the fault. This is to be a tyrant rather than a father. Saul cast a javelin at his son to smite him, and his son was provoked to anger. *"So Jonathan arose from the table in fierce anger"* (1 Sam. 20:33-34). "A father exercises a kingly power over his son, not that of a tyrant."[94]

3. When parents deny their children what is absolutely needful. Some have thus provoked their children: they have stinted them and kept them so short [of necessities] that they have forced them upon indirect courses and made them put forth their hands to iniquity.

4. When parents act partially towards their children, showing more kindness to one than to another. Though a parent may have a greater love to one child, yet discretion should lead him not to show more love to one than to another. Jacob showed more love to Joseph than to all his other children, which provoked the envy of his brethren. *"Now Israel loved Joseph more than all his children, because he was the son of his old age: and he made him a coat of many colours. And when his brethren saw that their father loved him more than all his brethren, they hated him, and could not speak peaceably unto him"* (Gen. 37:3-4).

5. When a parent does anything that is sordid and unworthy, which casts disgrace upon himself and his family, as to defraud or take a false oath, it provokes the child to wrath. As the child should honor his father, so the father should not dishonor the child.

6. Parents provoke children when they lay commands upon them that they cannot perform without wronging their consciences. Saul commanded

---

93 **imprecations** – acts of calling down evil, calamity, or divine vengeance on someone.
94 Latin = *In filium pater obtinet non tyrannicum imperium, set basilicum.* "Among children, a father holds not a tyrannical, but a kingly rule." From John Davenant (1572-1641), *An Exposition of St. Paul to the Colossians*, 191.

his son Jonathan to bring David to him. *"Fetch him unto me, for he shall surely die"* (1 Sam. 20:31). Jonathan could not do this with a good conscience, but was provoked to anger. *"Jonathan arose from the table in fierce anger"* (1 Sam. 20:34). The reason why parents should show their prudence in not provoking their children to wrath is this: *"Lest they be discouraged"* (Col. 3:21). This word *discouraged* implies three things. Grief: The *father's* provoking the child, the child so takes it to heart that it causes premature death. Despondency: The *father's* austerity dispirits the child and makes it unfit for service, like members of the body stupefied,[95] which are unfit for work. Contumacy and refractoriness:[96] The child being provoked by the cruel and unnatural carriage of the parent grows desperate and often studies to irritate and vex his parents, which, though it be evil in the child, yet the parent is accessory to it as being the occasion of it.

7. If you would have honor from your children, pray much for them. Not only lay up a portion for them, but also lay up a stock of prayer for them. Monica prayed much for her son Augustine;[97] and it was said [that] it was impossible that a son of so many prayers and tears should perish. Pray that your children may be preserved from the contagion[98] of the times. Pray that as your children bear your images in their faces, they may bear God's image in their hearts. Pray that they may be instruments and vessels of glory. One fruit of prayer may be that the child will honor a praying parent.

8. Encourage that which you see good and commendable in your children. "Goodness increases when praised."[99] Commending that which is good in your children makes them more in love with virtuous actions and is like the watering of plants, which makes them grow more. Some parents discourage the good they see in their children and so nip virtue in the bud and help to damn their children's souls. They have their children's curses.

9. If you would have honor from your children, set them a good example. It makes children despise fathers when [they] live in contradiction to their own precepts; when they bid their children be sober, and yet they themselves get drunk; or bid their children fear God, and [they] are themselves loose in their lives. O if you would have your children honor you, teach them by a

---

95 **stupefied** – deprived of feeling; deadened.
96 **contumacy and refractoriness** – rebellious stubbornness and disobedience to authority.
97 **Aurelius Augustine (A.D. 354-430)**– Bishop of Hippo in Northern Africa and leader in the early Christian Church; converted as a young man from a life of immorality to become wise and godly.
98 **contagion** – hurtful, defiling, or corrupting contact; infecting influence.
99 Latin = *Virtus laudata crescit*. This was the original motto of Berkhamsted School, founded 1541, in Berkhamsted, Hertfordshire, England.

holy example. A father is a looking glass that the child often dresses himself by. Let the glass be clear and not spotted. Fathers should observe great decorum[100] in their whole conduct, lest they give occasion to their children to say to them as Plato's servant, "My master has made a book against rash anger, but he himself is passionate"; or, as a son once said to his father, "If I have done evil, I have learned it of you."

From *The Ten Commandments,* The Banner of Truth Trust: www.banneroftruth.org.

Thomas Watson (c. 1620-1686): English Nonconformist Puritan preacher and author; possibly born in Yorkshire, England.

The very inquisitiveness of little ones affords their elders an opportunity to make known unto them the wonderful works of God that their minds may be informed and their hearts awed by His perfections. But note well, it is the father (the "head" of the home) upon whom the main responsibility devolves, to see to it that his children are taught by him the things of God (Eph. 6:4). Let him not pass on this task to his wife, still less to Sunday School teachers. —Arthur W. Pink

*Let no Christian parents fall into the delusion that the Sunday School is intended to ease them of their personal duties. The first and most natural condition of things is for Christian parents to train up their own children in the nurture and admonition of the Lord. —Charles Haddon Spurgeon
Holy Jacob, the famous patriarch, was a prophet to instruct his family in true religion and a king to govern them for God; so a priest to set up an altar [and] offer sacrifices and perform religious worship for and with his family. Even the poorest man that has a family is to be a prophet, priest, and king in his own home. —Oliver Heywood*

---

100 **decorum** – that which is proper to the character, position, rank, or dignity of a person.

Counsel to Reforming Fathers

RICHARD BAXTER (1615-1691)

PAUL:[101] Welcome, Neighbor! How do you like the new life that you have begun? You have taken home instructions already… but what do you find in the practicing of them?

SAUL: I find that I have foolishly long neglected a necessary, noble, joyful life, and thereby lost my time and made myself both unskillful and undisposed to the practice of it. I find that the things that you have prescribed me are high, excellent, and doubtless must be very sweet to them that have a suitable skill and disposition. And some pleasure I find in my weak beginnings; but the greatness of the work and the great untowardness and strangeness of my mind doth much abate the sweetness of it by many doubts, fears, and difficulties. When I fail, I find it hard both to repent aright and, by faith, to fly to Christ for pardon…

PAUL: Where is your great difficulty that requireth counsel?

SAUL: I find a great deal of work to do in my family: to govern them in the fear of God, to do my duty to them all, especially to educate my children and daily to worship God among them. And I am so unable for it that I am ready to omit all! I pray you help me with your advice.

PAUL: My first advice to you is that you resolve by God's help to perform your duty as well as you can. Devote your family to God, and take Him for the Lord and Master of it. Use it as a society sanctified to Him. And I pray you let these reasons fix your resolution:

1. If God is not master of your family, the devil will be. And if God is not first served in it, the flesh and the world will be. I hope I need not tell you how bad a master, work, and wages they will then have.

2. If you devote your family to God, God will be the Protector of it. He will take care of it for safety and provision as His own. Do you not need such a Protector? And can you have a better [One] or [can you] better take care for the welfare and safety of you and yours? And if your family is not God's, they are His enemies and under His curse as rebels…

3. A holy family is a place of comfort, a church[102] of God. What a joy will it be to you to live together daily in this hope that you shall meet and live together in heaven—to think that wife, children, and servants shall shortly be

---

101 EDITOR'S NOTE: The author wrote the following in the form of a dialogue between "Paul," a teacher, and "Saul," a learner.
102 The author does not mean that a family is the equivalent of a local church, performing the ordinances of baptism and the Lord's Supper, but like a church gathered for worship in singing, praying, and reading the Word.

fellow citizens with you of the heavenly Jerusalem! How pleasant is it to join with one heart and mind in the service of God and in His cheerful praises! How lovely will you be to one another when each one beareth the image of God! What abundance of jars[103] and miseries will be prevented, which sin would bring among you daily. And when any of you die, how comfortably may the rest be about their bed and attend their corpse unto the grave, when they have good hopes that the soul is received to glory by Christ. But if your family is ungodly, it will be like a nest of wasps or like a jail, full of discord and vexation.[104] It will be grievous to you to look your wife or children in the face and think that they are likely to lie in hell. Their sickness and death will be tenfold heavier to you to think of their woeful and unseen end.

4. Your family hath such constant need of God, as commandeth you constantly to serve Him. As every man hath his personal necessities, so families have family necessities that God must supply or they are miserable. Therefore, family duty must be your work.

5. Holy families[105] are the seminaries of Christ's Church on earth, and it is very much that lieth upon them to keep up the interest of religion in the world. Hence come holy magistrates, when great men's children have a holy education. And, oh, what a blessing is one such to the countries where they are! Hence spring holy pastors and teachers to the churches, who, as Timothy, receive holy instructions from their parents and grace from the Spirit of Christ in their tender age. Many a congregation that is happily fed with the bread of life may thank God for the endeavors of a poor man or woman that trained up a child in the fear of God (2 Tim. 3:15) to become their holy, faithful teacher. Though learning is found in schools, godliness is more often received from the education of careful parents. When children and servants come to the church with understanding, godly, prepared minds, the labors of the pastor will do them good; they will receive what they hear with faith, love, and obedience. It will be a joy to the minister to have such a flock; and it will be joyful to the people that are such to meet together in the sacred assemblies [and] to worship God with cheerful hearts. Such worshippers will be acceptable to God. But when families come together in gross ignorance with unsanctified hearts, there they sit like images, understanding little of what is said. [They] go home little the better for all the labors of the minister. The motions of their tongue and bodies are most of the worship that they give to God, but their hearts are not offered in faith

---

103 **jars** – quarrels.
104 **discord and vexation** – disagreement and aggravation.
105 1 Tim. 3:12; Deut. 6:7; 30:2; Ps. 147:13; Acts 2:39; Eph. 6:4-6; Prov. 22:6, 15; 29:15, 23:13.

and love as a sacrifice to Him; nor do they feel the power and sweetness of the Word and worship Him in spirit and truth (John 4:24).

6. In times when the churches are corrupted and good ministers are [in short supply], and bad ones either deceive the people or are insufficient for their work, there is no better supply to keep up religion than godly families. If parents and masters will teach their children…faithfully, worship God with them holily and constantly, and govern them carefully and orderly, it will much make up the [lack] of public teaching, worship, and discipline. Oh, that God would stir up the hearts of people thus to make their families as little churches that it might not be in the power of rulers or pastors that are bad to extinguish religion or banish godliness from any land! For,

7. Family teaching, worship, and discipline hath many advantages that churches have not. 1. You have but a few to teach and rule, and the pastor hath many. 2. They are always with you, and you may speak to them as seasonably and as often as you will, either together or one by one; [he] cannot. 3. They are tied to you by relation, affection, and covenant and by their own necessities and interest, otherwise than they are to him. Wife and children are more confident of your love to them than of the minister's, and love doth open the ear to counsel. Children dare not reject your words because you can correct them or make their worldly state less comfortable. But the minister doth all by bare exhortation; and if he cast them out of the church for their impenitence, they lose nothing by it in the world. And unless it is in a very hot persecution, families are not so restrained from holy doctrine, worship, and discipline, as churches and ministers often are. Who silenceth you or forbiddeth you to catechize and teach your family? Who forbiddeth you to pray or praise God with them as well and as often as you can? It is self-condemning hypocrisy in many fathers, who now cry out against them as cruel persecutors, who forbid us ministers to preach the Gospel, while they neglect to teach their own children…when no man forbiddeth them (so hard is it to see our own sins and duty in comparison of other men's).

8. You have greater and nearer obligations to your family than pastors have to all the people. Your wife is as your own flesh; your children are, as it were, parts of yourself. Nature bindeth you to the dearest affection and therefore to the greatest duty to them. Who should more care for your children's souls than their own parents? If you will not provide for them, but famish them, who will feed them? Therefore, as ever you have the [hearts] of parents, as ever you care what becometh of your children's souls forever, devote them to God, teach them His Word, educate them in holiness, restrain them from sin, and prepare them for salvation.

SAUL: I must confess that natural affection telleth me that there is great reason for what you say, and my own experience convinceth me. For if my parents had better instructed and governed me in my childhood, I had not been likely to have lived so ignorantly and ungodly as I have. But, alas! Few parents do their duty. Many take more pains about their horses and cattle than they do about their children's souls.

PAUL: O that I could speak what is deeply upon my heart to all the *fathers* of the land! I would be bold to tell them that multitudes are crueler than bears and lions to their own children. God hath committed their souls as much to their trust and care as He hath done their bodies. It is they…that are to teach them (Deut. 6:6-8; 11:19-20). [It is they that are] to catechize them and to remind them of the state of their souls, their need of Christ, the mercy of redemption, the excellence of holiness, and of everlasting life. It is they that are to watch over them with wisdom, love, and diligence, to save them from temptation, Satan, and sin, and to lead them by the example of a holy life.

But, alas! If they teach [their child] to say the Creed,[106] the Lord's Prayer, and the Ten Commandments, they never teach him to understand them. They never seriously remind him of his natural corruptions, of the need and use of a Savior and a Sanctifier, of the danger of sin and hell, of the way of a holy life, or of the joyful state of saints in glory. They teach him his trade and business in the world, but never how to serve God and be saved. They chide him for those faults that are against themselves or against his prosperity in the world, but those that are against God and his soul only, they regard not! If by their own example they do not teach him to be prayerless and neglect God's Word, to curse, to swear, to speak filthily, and to deride a holy life… yet they will bear with him in all this wickedness. They are content that he spend the Lord's Day in idleness and sports, instead of learning the Word of God and practicing His holy worship, so that he may be more willing to do *their* work the week following. In a word, they treacherously teach their children to serve the flesh, the world, and the devil…and to neglect, if not despise, God, the Creator, Redeemer, and Sanctifier of souls…So that their education is but a teaching or permitting them…under the name of Christians, to rebel against God and Jesus Christ.

And is this not greater treachery and cruelty than if they famished their bodies or turned them naked into the world? Yea, or if they murdered them and ate their flesh? If an enemy did this, it were not as bad as for a parent to do it. Nay, consider whether the devil himself be not less cruel in seeking

---

106 **Creed** – the Apostles' Creed: a statement of faith from around the end of the 2nd century.

to damn them than these parents are? The devil is not their parent: he hath no relation to them, no charge of them to educate and save them. He is a known, renounced enemy, and what better could be expected from him? But for father and mother thus to neglect, betray, and undo their children's souls forever! For them to do it that should love them as themselves and have the most tender care of them! O worse than devilish, perfidious[107] cruelty!

Repent, repent, O you forsworn, unmerciful murderers of your children's souls! Repent for your own sakes! Repent for their sakes! Teach them…and tell them what Christianity is! You have conveyed a sinful nature to them; help yet to instruct them in the way of grace. But how can we hope that you should have mercy upon your children's souls that have no mercy on your own? Or that you should help them to that heaven that you despise yourselves? Or save them from sin, which is your own delight and trade?

SAUL: Your complaint is sad and just. But I find that men think that the teaching of their children belongeth to the schoolmaster and the minister only and not to them.

PAUL: Parents, schoolmasters, and pastors have all their several parts to do, and no one's work goeth on well without the rest. But the parents' [work] is the first and greatest of all…A minister should find all his hearers catechized and holily educated that the church may be a church indeed; but if a hundred or many hundred parents…cast their work upon one minister, is it likely, think you, to be well done? Or is it any wonder if we have ungodly churches of [professing] Christians [who] are not Christians, who hate the minister, his doctrine, and a holy life…

I know that all this will not excuse ministers from doing what they can for such. If you will send your children…ignorant and ungodly to him, he must do his best. But O how much more good might he do and how comfortable would his calling be, if parents would but do their parts!

We talk much of the badness of the world, and there are no men (except bad rulers and pastors) that do more to make it bad than bad fathers. The truth is, they are the devil's instruments (as if he had hired them) to betray the souls of their families into his power and to lead them to hell with a greater advantage than a stranger could do or than the devil in his own name and shape could do! Many call for church reformation and state reformation, who yet are the plagues of the times themselves and will not reform one little family. If fathers would reform their families and agree in a holy education of their children, church and state would be soon reformed, when they were made up of such reformed families.

---

107 **perfidious** – deceitful and untrustworthy.

Chapter 6—Fatherhood: Counsel to Reforming Fathers

SAUL: I pray you set me down such instructions together, as you think best, concerning all my duty to my children that I may do my part. And if any of them perish, their damnation may not be along of me.

PAUL: …Let your teaching of them to this end be jointly of the words, the sense, the due affections, and the practice. That is, (1) Teach them the words of…the Creed,[108] the Lord's Prayer, the Ten Commandments, and of a catechism and the words of such texts of Scripture as have the same sense. (2) Teach them the *meaning* of all these words. (3) Join still some familiar, earnest persuasions and motives to stir up holy affections in them. (4) And show them the way of *practicing* all.

No one or two of these will serve without all the rest. (1) If you teach not the forms of wholesome or sound words, you will deprive them of one of the greatest helps for knowledge and soundness in the faith. (2) If you teach them not the meaning, the words will be of no use. (3) If you excite not their affections, all will be but dead opinion and tend to a dreaming and prating[109] kind of religion, separated from the love of God. (4) And if you lead them not on to the practice of all, they will make themselves a religion of zealous affections corrupted by a common life or quickly starved for want of fuel. Therefore, be sure you join all…When you teach them the words of Scripture and catechism, make them *plain*, and often mix familiar questions and discourse about death, judgment, eternity, and their preparations. Many professors teach their children to go in a road of hearing, reading, repeating sermons, and joining in constant prayer, when all proveth but customary formality, for [lack] of some familiar, serious, wakening speech or conference interposed[110] now and then.

To this end, (1) Labor to possess them with the greatest reverence of God and the Holy Scriptures. Then show them the Word of God for all that you would teach them to know or do; for until their consciences come under the fear and government of God, they will be nothing. (2) Never speak of God and holy things to them but with the greatest gravity and reverence that the *manner*, as well as the *matter*, may affect them. For if they [become used] to slight, jest, or play with holy things, they are hardened and undone. (3) Therefore, avoid such kind of frequencies and formality in lifeless duties as tendeth to harden them into a customary deadness and contempt. (4) Often take an account of what they know, how they are affected and resolved, and of what they do, both in their open and their secret practice. Leave them not carelessly to themselves, but narrowly watch over them.

---

108 The reader may choose to substitute his or her church's confession.
109 **prating** – idly chatting.
110 **interposed** – placed at intervals.

Use all your skill and diligence by word and deed to make a holy life appear to them as the most honorable, profitable, safe, and pleasant life in the world that it may be their constant delight. All your work lieth in making good things pleasant to them. Keep them from feeling [the Christian faith] as a burden or taking it for a disgraceful, needless, or unpleasant thing. To which end, (1) Begin with and intermix the easiest parts, such as the Scripture history.[111] Nature is pleased sooner with history than with precept, and it sweetly insinuateth[112] a love of goodness into children's minds…(2) Speak much of the praise of ancient and later holy men, for the due praise of a person allureth to the same cause and way. And speak of the just disgrace that belongs to those sots[113] and beasts who are the despisers, deriders, and enemies of godliness. (3) Overwhelm them not with that which for quality or quantity they cannot bear. (4) Be much in opening to them the riches of grace and the joys of glory. (5) Exercise them much in psalms and praise.

Let your conference and carriage[114] tend to the just disgrace of sensuality, voluptuousness,[115] pride, and worldliness. When fools commend fineness[116] to their children, you tell them how pride is the devil's sin; teach them to desire the lowest room and to give place to others. When others tell them of riches, fine houses, and preferments,[117] tell them that these are the devil's baits by which he stealeth men's hearts from God that they may be damned. When others pamper them and please their appetites, tell them often how base and swinish a thing it is to eat and drink more by appetite than by reason. And labor thus to make pride, sensuality, and worldliness odious[118] to them. Make them often read Luke 12:16, 18, James 4 and 5, Romans 8:1-2; and Matthew 5:1-21, and 6.

Wisely break them from their own wills, and let them know that they must obey and like God's will and yours. Men's own wills are the grand idols of the world, and to be given up to them is next to hell. Tell them how odious and dangerous self-willedness is. In their diet, let them not have what they have a mind to nor yet do not force them to what they loathe…And let them have that in temperance what is wholesome…A corrupted appetite, strengthened by [habit], is hardly overcome by all the teaching and counsel

---

111 **Scripture history** – the portions of the Scriptures that are narratives or stories.
112 **insinuateth** – introduces by gradual degrees.
113 **sots** – foolish persons.
114 **conference and carriage** – conversation and conduct.
115 **voluptuousness** – addiction to sensual pleasures.
116 **fineness** – showy dress; striking appearance.
117 **preferments** – advancements in status or position in life.
118 **odious** – deserving of hatred.

in the world! Especially [do not let them grow accustomed] to strong drink, for it is one of the greatest snares to youth. I know that some "wise" parents (wise to further the everlasting ruin of the children's souls!) do still say that the more they are restrained, the more greedily they will seek it when they are at liberty. Unhappy children that have such parents! As if the experience of all the world had not told us long ago that custom increaseth the rage of appetite and temperance by custom [becomes] a habit…They that will teach them sobriety with the cup at their noses or temperance at a constant feast or full table of delicious food—and this in their injudicious[119] youth—deserve rather to be numbered with the devil's teachers than with God's.

So if their fancies be eagerly set upon any vanity, deny it them and tell them why. [Do not accustom them] to have their wills; let them know that it is the chief thing that the devil himself desireth for them that they may have all their own carnal will fulfilled. But they must pray to God, "Thy will be done," and deny their own.

As you love their souls, keep them as far from temptations as you can. Children are unfit persons to struggle against strong temptations. Their salvation or damnation lieth very much on this. Therefore, my heart melteth to think of the misery of two sorts: (1) the children of heathens, infidels, heretics, and malignants,[120] who are taught the principles of sin and wickedness from their infancy and hear truth and godliness scorned and reproached; (2) the children of most great men and gentlemen, whose condition maketh it seem necessary to them to live in that continual fullness…which is so strong a temptation daily to their children to the sins of Sodom—pride, fullness of bread, and idleness (Ezek. 16:49). It is as hard for them to be godly, sober persons, as for those that are [brought] up in [theaters], alehouses, and taverns. Alas, poor children, that must have your salvation made as hard as a camel's passage through a needle's eye! No wonder if the world is no better than it is, when the rich must be the rulers of it, of whom Christ and James have said what they have done (Luke 12:19; 16:1-31; James 5:1-6).

Be sure, therefore, (1) to [bring up] your children to a temperate[121] and healthful diet; and keep tempting [foods], but specially drinks, from before them. (2) [Bring] them up to constant labor, which may never leave mind or body idle but at the hours of necessary recreation that you allow them. (3) Let their recreations be such as tend more to the health of their bodies than

---

119 **injudicious** – showing very poor judgment; unwise.
120 **malignants** – those who are inclined to rebel against God or any constituted authority.
121 **temperate** – moderate; not excessive.

the humoring of a corrupted fancy[122]; keep them from gaming for money… love-books,[123] and foolish wanton tales and ballads.[124] Let their time be stinted[125] by you; and let it be no more than what is needful to their health and labor…(4) Let their apparel be plain, decent, and warm, but not gaudy [or worn] to signify pride or to tempt people to it.[126] (5) Be sure when they grow towards ripeness that you keep them from opportunity, nearness, or familiarity with tempting persons of another sex…

Be sure that you engage your children in good company and keep them as much as possible out of bad. Wicked children, before you are aware, will infect them with their wicked tongues and practices: they will quickly teach them to drink, to game, to talk filthily, to swear, to mock at godliness and sobriety, and, oh, what tinder is in corrupted nature! But the company of sober, pious children and servants will use them to a sober, pious language, and will further them in knowledge and the fear of God, or at least will keep them from great temptations.

Do all that you do with them in love and wisdom: make them not so familiar with you as shall breed contempt, and be not so strange to them as shall tempt them to have no love to you or pleasure in your company. But let them perceive the tender [heart] of a father, that, indeed, they are dear to you, and that all your counsel and government are for their good, and not for any ends or passions of your own…

Keep a special watch upon their tongues, especially against ribaldry[127] and lying. For dangerous corruptions do quickly this way obtain dominion.

Teach them highly to value time. Tell them the preciousness of it because of the shortness of man's life, of the greatness of his work, and of how eternity dependeth on these uncertain moments. Labor to make time-wasting odious to them. Set death before their eyes, and ask them oft whether they are ready to die.

Let correction be wisely used, as they need it—neither so severely as to disaffect them to you nor so little as to leave them in a course of sin and disobedience. Let it be always in love and more for sin against God than any worldly matters. And show them Scripture against the sin and for the correction…

---

122 **corrupted fancy** – sinful imagination.
123 **love-books** – romance novels.
124 **wanton tales and ballads** – lawless, violent, and/or sexually immoral stories and songs.
125 **stinted** – limited.
126 See FGB 216, *Modest Apparel*, and *Christian Modesty and the Public Undressing of America*
127 **ribaldry** – obscene or humorously vulgar language.

Pray earnestly for them, and commit them by faith to Christ…Go before them by a holy and sober example, and let your practice tell them what you would have them be, especially in representing godliness [as] delightful and living in the joyful hopes of heaven.

These are the counsels that I earnestly recommend to you in this important work. But you must know that your children's souls are so precious and the difference between the good and bad so great that all this must not seem too much ado to you. But as you would have ministers hold on in the labor of their places, so must you in yours, as knowing that a dumb and idle parent is no more excusable than an unfaithful, dumb, and idle minister. The Lord give you skill, will, and diligence to practice all: for I take the due education of children as one of the most needful and most excellent works in the world.

From "The Poor Man's Family Book" in *The Practical Works of the Rev. Richard Baxter,* Vol. 19 (London: James Duncan, 1830).

Richard Baxter (1615-1691): Anglican Puritan preacher and theologian; born in Rowton, Shropshire, England.

A Father's Prayer

GEORGE SWINNOCK (1627–1673)

I [pray] that the Word of Christ may dwell richly in my heart and house that my whole family may have their set meals every day of this spiritual food. How can I expect that children…who know not the God of their fathers, should serve Him with perfect hearts? (1 Chron. 28:9). Alas! How often are their ignorant hearts (like dark cellars abounding in vermin) full of sin! O that I might so talk of the Word of God in my house, when I lie down and when I rise up, that it may be written upon the posts of my house and on my gates (Deut. 6:7-8), that I may so often water the young plants in it that their first acquaintance may be acquaintance with God, and [that] from their childhood they may know the Holy Scriptures and be wise *"unto salvation through faith which is in Christ Jesus"* (2 Tim. 3:15)…Though others labor to leave their children rich, let my endeavor be to leave mine [godly]. Lord, enable me so to teach them Thy trade in their youth that they may not depart from it when they are old (Prov. 22:6), that their young years well led may be like the sweetness of a rose, whose smell remaineth in the dried leaves.

I [pray] that all the voices in my house may [harmoniously] sing God's praises, yet that they may not, like trumpets and pipes, make a sound being filled only with wind, but have hearts fixed and prepared when they sing and give praise…Drunkards have their songs in derision of them that are good; atheists have their sonnets in dishonor of the blessed God; why should not the voice of joy and rejoicing be in the tabernacle of the righteous? (Ps. 118:15). Though my house is a tabernacle and all the inhabitants in it travelers, yet our work is pleasant. O let us go merrily on and make God's statutes our songs in this house of our pilgrimage.

Because my pattern of evil will do more hurt to my family than my precepts can do good—children being apt to be led more by the eye than the ear—I wish that I may take heed to myself, weigh and watch over all my words and works, not only for my own, but also for the sake of them that are committed to my charge…O that I might therefore be wary in all my ways and be so serious in *spiritual* [actions], so sober in *natural* actions, so righteous towards men, so [devout] towards my God, so faithful in every relation, and so holy and heavenly in every condition that I may have cause to say to my children and servants as Gideon to his soldiers, *"Look on me, and do likewise"* (Judg. 7:17).

I [pray] that my house may not only spend some part of every weekday, but also the whole [Lord's Day], in the service of my God. It is a special privilege granted me by the Lord for my family's profit, wherein I may be singularly helpful to my own and my household's everlasting happiness. O that not the least part of it may be lost or profaned by any within my gate, either by worldly labor, pastimes, or idleness, but that I may be so mindful of my charge as to take care that my children…do forbear what my God forbiddeth and spend that sacred day altogether in sacred duties. To which purpose I desire that all my household, both males and females, (if of capacity) may appear before the Lord in public and in His temple give Him praise and that in private I may whet the Word on them (as the mower doth his scythe) by going over it again and again, according to the precept (Deut. 6:6-7). Lord, let my house on Thy day be like Thy house, employed wholly in Thy worship. And let Thy gracious presence so assist us in every ordinance that the glory of the Lord may fill the house.

I [pray] that I may manifest my love to the souls in my family by manifesting my anger against their sins. My God hath told me, *"Thou shalt not hate thy brother in thine heart: thou shalt in any wise rebuke thy neighbour, and not suffer sin upon him"* (Lev. 19:17)…Should I suffer [my children] in unholiness, I should bring them up for hell. Those deepest purple sins many times are those that are dyed in the wool of youth. O the sad aches that many have when they are old by falls that they received when they were young! Let me never, like Eli, honor my sons…above my God, lest my God judge my house forever…because my children make themselves vile, and I restrain them not. Lord, let me never be so fond and foolish as to kill any in my family with soul-damning kindness; but let my house be as thine ark, wherein there may be not only the golden pot of manna, seasonable and profitable instructions, but also Aaron's rod, suitable and proper reprehension and correction.

I [pray] that I may never expose my family to the suggestions of Satan by allowing any in laziness, but may be busy myself in my particular vocation and see that others be diligent in their distinct stations. The lazy drone is quickly caught in the honeyed glass and killed, when the busy bee avoideth that snare and danger. O that I and mine might always be so employed in the work of our God that we may have no leisure to hearken to the wicked one!...Lord, since Thou hast entrusted everyone in my house with one talent or other wherewith he must trade, cause me and mine to labor and work in this and to look after rest in the other world.

I [pray] for the furthering of holiness and purity in my house that I may be careful to keep it in peace. Our bodies will thrive as much in fevers as our souls in the flames of strife. Satan, by the [grenades] of contention, will hope in time to take the garrison. *"Where…strife is, there is confusion; and every evil work"* (James 3:16). O that love (which is the new commandment, the old commandment, and indeed all the commandments) might be the [uniform] of all in my family...Because marriage is a fellowship of the nearest union and dearest communion in this world and because the fruits of religion will thrive much the better if cherished by the sweet breath and warm gale of love in this relation, Lord, let my wife be to me as the loving hind and pleasant roe. Let me be ravished always with her love (Prov. 5:19). Let there be no provocation but to love and to good works. Let our only strife be who shall be most [active in service] to Thy majesty in furthering one another's eternal felicity. Enable us to bear one another's burdens, and so fulfill the law of Christ (Gal. 6:2), and to dwell together as fellow heirs of the grace of life that our prayers be not hindered.

In a word, I [pray] that I may, like Cornelius, fear the Lord with all my house (Acts 10:1-2) [and] so govern it according to God's Law that all in it may be under the influence of His love and heirs of everlasting life. Lord, be Thou pleased so to assist and prosper me in the management of this great and weighty trust that my house may be Thy house...my children Thy children, and my wife belong to the spouse of Thy dear Son, so that when death shall give a bill of divorce and break up our family, we may change our place, but not our company. [May we] be all [promoted] from thy lower house of prayer to thine upper house of praise, where is neither marrying nor giving in marriage, but all are as the angels (Matt. 22:30), ever pleasing, worshipping, and enjoying Thy blessed Self, *"of whom the whole family in heaven and earth is named"* (Eph. 3:15), to Whom be glory, hearty and universal obedience, forever and ever. Amen.

From "The Christian Man's Calling" in *The Works of George Swinnock*, Vol. 1, The Banner of Truth Trust: www.banneroftruth.com.

George Swinnock (1627-1673): Puritan preacher and author; born in Maidstone, Kent, England.

Chapter 7
MOTHERHOOD

All over the world, the number of women who are fully dedicated to the biblical duties of motherhood is dropping at an alarming rate. While modernity has given us many technological advantages and career opportunities, it also has given us fewer and fewer mothers who dedicate their entire lives to the task. J.R. Miller understood the value of a mother: "A true mother is one of the holiest secrets of home happiness. God sends many beautiful things to this world, many noble gifts; but no blessing is richer than that which He bestows in a mother who has learned love's lessons well, and has realized something of the meaning of her sacred calling."[1]

The Bible makes it clear that this sacred calling is dedicated to laying a biblical foundation at the earliest stages and then building upon it throughout each phase of life. This is why the hand that rocks the cradle rules (and blesses) the world. But that is not how things have worked out in the modern world. The hand that once rocked the cradle now taps the keys in a cubicle. This is a terrible loss. Who is taking care of the rising generation? Fewer and fewer mothers!

God reserves the most fundamental role of the preservation of young lives for mothers. Without mothers, babies languish. Without mothers, babies are deprived of twenty-four hour a day care and tenderness. Thus, it is the mother who stands in the gap to ensure the blessing of children. But the ripple effect of her efforts keeps on working either positively or negatively, for the health of families, churches, and nations.

What does biblical motherhood look like? The following chapter offers a clear vision for the teachable heart. Do not look to this world for instruction in motherhood. Do not follow the trends of motherhood that are so popular today. "Do not go down to Egypt" for advice and help (Isaiah 31-32). Instead, learn from these wise ones who have so beautifully captured the essence of motherhood. Look carefully. Read prayerfully so that we might revive the wonderful vision of motherhood you will discover in the coming pages.

—Scott Brown

---

1 J.R. Miller, *Secrets of Happy Home Life: What Have You to Do With It?* (New York: Thomas Y. Crowell & Co., 1894), 19.

The Dignity of Motherhood

JABEZ BURNS (1805-1876)

Mother! The name that is associated in every virtuous mind with all that is amiable and delightful. Mother! Most tender, endearing, and expressive of all human appellations![1] A title employed equally by the royal prince, the sage[2] philosopher, and the untutored[3] peasant—by the savage and the civilized in all nations and through all generations. A relation mercifully founded in the constitution of our nature—universally felt and uniformly acknowledged. And who among all the children of men, except those who in early infancy were bereaved[4] of their anxious parents, has not happily experienced the inexpressible influence of its charming and delightful power? Who of all the great and the mighty upon the earth does not recognize the unnumbered blessings that he has enjoyed through this endeared relation?

His own infinite wisdom and boundless goodness prompted the almighty Creator to ordain this beneficent[5] relation, with all its sweet attractions and happy endearments. Must He not, therefore, have made it honorable, noble, and dignified? And [should] its elevation and importance be forgotten and neglected? Surely it demands our most intelligent consideration and devout acknowledgment. But what mind has ever possessed a capacity enlarged and matured to comprehend fully the true dignity of a mother?

Woman was formed by the glorious Creator as a *"help meet"*[6] for man (Gen. 2:18; *cf.* 1 Tim. 2:12-14; 1 Cor. 11:8-10). Whatever dignity, therefore, attaches to him as a rational being and the representative on earth of his Maker is shared by the partner of his life—his other self. Woman is the equal participator of all the honors that pertain to human nature. But woman's highest dignity and her greatest honors are found in contributing to the perfection of the divine purpose of her Creator in her peculiar[7] character of mother.

A mother's dignity, however, will but imperfectly appear unless she is considered as bringing into the world a rational[8] offspring, whose existence will affect others and will continue through eternal ages. Adam, by intuitive

---

1 **appellations** – names; titles.
2 **sage** – profoundly wise.
3 **untutored** – uneducated; untaught.
4 **bereaved** – deprived of a loved one by death.
5 **beneficent** – characterized by doing good.
6 **helpmeet** – helper suitable.
7 **peculiar** – special.
8 **rational** – endowed with the capacity to reason.

wisdom imparted from God, perceived this surpassing excellence when *"[he] called his wife's name Eve; because she was the mother of all living"* (Gen. 3:20).

Woman must be contemplated as giving birth to those whose principles, characters, and labors will deeply and permanently influence individuals in the domestic circle, which will be felt by large communities and, in some instances at least, by the whole population of the world. Our blessed Lord acknowledges this sentiment,[9] expressed by the woman respecting Him: when having seen His mighty works and heard His wise discourses, she exclaimed, *"Blessed is the womb that bare thee, and the paps*[10] *which thou hast sucked"* (Luke 11:27). On this rational[11] principle, we cannot separate the greatness that distinguished the worthies of ancient and modern times from the characters of their favored mothers. Isaac Watts,[12] Philip Doddridge[13]…and many others have immortalized their names by their personal virtues and by their imperishable works to benefit their country. But while we contemplate and enjoy the fruits of their extraordinary labors, we cannot fail to reflect upon the influence of their excellent mothers. We cannot refrain from tendering[14] to them the honor that is their due [because of] their noble endeavor to discharge their maternal obligations, rendering them public blessings.

Divine inspiration has directly sanctioned this principle in the case of the Virgin Mary. Congratulated by her venerable[15] relative Elizabeth, mother by miracle of the herald[16] prophet of Messiah, and filled with the Holy Spirit, Who directed [Mary] to look forward to the future greatness of her mysterious Son, her enlightened and pious[17] mind burst forth in devout admiration at the honor that would be ascribed to her [because of] His unspeakable blessings to mankind. She gave expression to her elevated thoughts and said, *"My soul doth magnify the Lord, and my spirit hath rejoiced in God my Saviour. For he hath regarded the low estate of his handmaiden: for, behold, from henceforth all generations shall call me blessed"* (Luke 1:46-48).

Mothers in our time, though not dignified in the manner of the Blessed Virgin and not warranted to anticipate a similar honor to that which

---

9 **sentiment** – opinion or view.
10 **paps** – nipples or breasts of a woman.
11 **rational** – logical.
12 **Isaac Watts** (1674-1748) – English hymnwriter and theologian; recognized as the "Father of English Hymnody."
13 **Philip Doddridge** (1702–1751) – English Nonconformist leader, author, and hymnwriter.
14 **tendering** – paying; offering.
15 **venerable** – worthy of being highly respected because of personal character.
16 **herald** – messenger proclaiming the approach of someone, i.e., John the Baptist.
17 **pious** – characterized by showing reverence and obedience to God.

attached to her name, may yet contemplate the influence that their children will have upon society; and their own honor will be secured and promoted by laboring to form their infant minds to religion,[18] to virtue, and to love of their country.

Immortality especially gives dignity to its subjects; [from this] arises, in no inconceivable degree, the exalted honor of a mother. By the sovereign ordination of the Almighty, she gives birth, not to a being of a mere momentary existence and whose life will perish as that of the beasts of the field, but to an immortal! Her sucking infant, feeble and helpless as it may appear, possesses within its bosom a rational soul, an intellectual power, a spirit that all-devouring time cannot destroy—which can *never* die—but which will outlive the splendors of the glorious sun and the burning brilliancy of all the material host of heaven! Throughout the infinite ages of eternity, when all these shall have answered the beneficent[19] end of their creation and shall have been blotted out from their positions in the immense regions of space, the soul of the humblest child will shine and improve before the eternal throne, being filled with holy delight and divine love and ever active in the praises of its blessed Creator.

Likeness to the infinitely glorious Creator constitutes the chief dignity of our nature. And the intelligent, pious mother looks upon her infant offspring[20] with adoring gratitude to God, as possessing that likeness. Originally, *"the LORD God formed man of the dust of the ground, and breathed into his nostrils the breath of life; and man became a living soul"* (Gen. 2:7). By the same omnipotent[21] and gracious will, God has given being to human souls through all generations as at the first creation; but the mother is honored as the medium of this mysterious creation in the case of every child. And though the moral likeness of its blessed Maker is defaced by the fall of our first parents, still, in thousands of instances, by means of early tuition[22] and the prayers of the faithful mother, the child is created in Christ Jesus in righteousness and true holiness (Eph. 2:10; 4:24).[23]

What, then, can be the greatness, dignity, and honor of her who is the appointed medium of such amazing powers and blessings! Must not mothers feel their high distinctions? Should they not frequently be invited to contemplate them? In this, the security, the prosperity, and the happiness

---

18 **religion** – biblical Christianity.
19 **beneficent** – resulting in good.
20 See FGB 224, *Babies*, available from CHAPEL LIBRARY.
21 **omnipotent** – all powerful.
22 **tuition** – instruction.
23 See FGB 202, *The New Birth*

of our country, and even the welfare, the regeneration of the world, are involved. He, therefore, who is most successful in leading their minds to a proper, a rational, and scriptural view of this greatest of earthly relations will most effectually engage, as he will most worthily merit, the gratitude and esteem of dignified, happy, and Christian mothers.

From *Mothers of the Great and Good*, Solid Ground Christian Books: www.solid-ground-books.com.

Jabez Burns (1805-1876): English nonconformist theologian and philosopher; born in Oldham, Lancashire, England.

> *Woman is the mother of all human beings. She carries human beings in her womb, brings them forth into this world, nourishes them with milk, and takes care of them by bathing them and performing other services. What would kings, princes, prophets, and all the saints be if there had been no Eve? For God does not make human beings from stones: He makes them from man and woman. —Martin Luther*

> *Think on this particularly, you that are mothers of children, when you find the fruit of the womb quickened within you: you bear a creature within you of more value than all this visible world—a creature upon whom, from that very moment, an eternity of happiness or misery is entailed. Therefore, it concerns you to travail as in pain for their souls before you feel the sorrows and pangs of travail for their bodies…O let your cries and prayers for them anticipate your kisses and embraces of them. If you be faithful and successful herein, then happy is the womb that bears them. —John Flavel*

> *Any teaching that leads men and women to think of the marriage bond as the sign of bondage and the sacrifice of all independence, to construe wifehood and motherhood as drudgery and interference with woman's higher destiny, any public sentiment to cultivate celibacy as more desirable and honorable or to substitute anything else for marriage and home, not only invades God's ordinance, but opens the door to nameless crimes and threatens the very foundations of society. —Arthur W. Pink*

A Mother's Main Responsibility

THOMAS BOSTON (1676-1732)

If parents provide not for their children, they are worse than beasts to their young. If they give them not civil education, they are worse than heathens. But if they add not religious education, what do they more than civilized heathens? When God gives thee a child, He says, as Pharaoh's daughter to Moses' mother, *"Take this child…and nurse it for me"* (Ex. 2:9). Though we are but parents of their flesh, we must be careful of their souls, otherwise we ruin them.

Mothers[24] ought to instruct their children in the principles of religion and to sow the seeds of godliness in their hearts as soon as they are able to speak and have the use of reason (Deut. 6:6-7). Such early religious education is a blessed means of grace (1 Kings 18:12; compare verse 3). Not only is this the duty of fathers, who should teach their children (Prov. 4:3-4), but of mothers, who, while the children are young about their hand, should be dropping something to them for their soul's good. Solomon had not only his father's lesson, but the prophecy his mother taught him (Prov. 31:1; 1:8).

They should labor for that end to acquaint them with the Scriptures to cause them to read them (2 Tim. 3:15). Let the reading of their chapters be a piece of their daily task, and cause them to read the Scriptures in order that they may be acquainted both with the precepts and histories of the Bible. Let them be obliged to learn their catechism; and catechize them yourselves, according to your ability. For teaching by way of question and answer is most easy for them.

If they ask you any questions concerning these things, do not discourage them; but take pains to answer all their questions, however weakly they may be proposed (Deut. 6:20-21). Children are often found to have very misshapen notions of divine things; but if they were duly encouraged to speak, they might vent their thoughts, which *mothers* thus get occasion to rectify.

Labor to deter them from sin. The neglect of this was Eli's sin, for which God judged his house (1 Sam. 3:13). Endeavor to possess their hearts with an abhorrence of sinful practices and a dread of them. Carefully [put a stop to] their lying, swearing, cursing, and Sabbath-breaking. If they learn these while young, they will be fair to accompany them to gray hairs…

Stir them up to the duties of holiness and the practice of religion. Often inculcate on them the doctrine of their sinful, miserable state by nature,

---

24 **EDITOR'S NOTE**: This article was originally addressed to parents—fathers and mothers. To emphasize the mother's role, *parent* is sometimes replaced with *mother* in italics.

and the remedy provided in Christ. Shew them the necessity of holiness, pointing out Christ to them as the fountain of sanctification. Commend [Christianity] to them, and press them to the study of it as the main thing they have to do in the world (Prov. 4:4).

Pray with them and teach them to pray. For this cause, let not the worship of God be neglected in your families;[25] but for your children's sake maintain it. No wonder that those children seek not God who never see their *mothers* bow a knee. Ye should take them alone and pray with them and teach them to pray, laying the materials of prayer often before them. Let them learn the Lord's Prayer, and use it as a form until such time as they can conceive a prayer by that directory.[26] For though we do not think the Lord has bound us to that form…yet I know none that do affirm that it may not be used as a prayer or as a form, though it is plain it is principally intended for a directory in prayer (Matt. 6:9).

Correct [them] (Eph. 6:4): The Greek word there signifies both correction and instruction, and so does the English word *nurture*. They must go together, for instruction without correction will hardly succeed. *Mothers* must keep their children in subjection: if they lose their authority over them, the children will be children of Belial indeed, without a yoke, the end of which will be sad (Prov. 29:15). They must not only be corrected by reproof, but, when need is, with [the rod] (Prov. 19:18). Begin early, as soon as they are capable to be bettered by it; and let your love to them engage you to it and not restrain you (Prov. 13:24). As ever ye would keep them out of hell, correct them (Prov. 23:13-14).

From "An Illustration of the Doctrines of the Christian Religion, Part 2" in *The Whole Works of Thomas Boston*, Vol. 2, Tentmaker Publications: www.tentmakerpublications.com.

Thomas Boston (1676-1732): Scottish Presbyterian minister and theologian; born in Duns, Berwickshire.

---

25 See FGB 188, *Family Worship*
26 **directory** – guide.

Keepers of the Springs

PETER MARSHALL (1902-1949)

Once upon a time, a certain town grew up at the foot of a mountain range. It was sheltered in the lee of the protecting heights, so that the wind that shuddered at the doors and flung handfuls of sleet against the window panes was a wind whose fury was spent. High up in the hills, a strange and quiet forest dweller took it upon himself to be the Keeper of the Springs. He patrolled the hills and wherever he found a spring, he cleaned its brown pool of silt and fallen leaves, of mud and mold, and took away from the spring all foreign matter, so that the water that bubbled up through the sand ran down clean and cold and pure. It leaped sparkling over rocks and dropped joyously in crystal cascades until, swollen by other streams, it became a river of life to the busy town. Millwheels were whirled by its rush. Gardens were refreshed by its waters. Fountains threw it like diamonds into the air. Swans sailed on its limpid surface, and children laughed as they played on its banks in the sunshine.

But the City Council was a group of hard-headed, hard-boiled businessmen. They scanned the civic budget and found in it the salary of a Keeper of the Springs. Said the Keeper of the Purse: "Why should we pay this romance ranger? We never see him; he is not necessary to our town's work life. If we build a reservoir just above the town, we can dispense with his services and save his salary." Therefore, the City Council voted to dispense with the unnecessary cost of a Keeper of the Springs and to build a cement reservoir.

So the Keeper of the Springs no longer visited the brown pools but watched from the heights while they built the reservoir. When it was finished, it soon filled up with water, to be sure; but the water did not seem to be the same. It did not seem to be as clean, and a green scum soon befouled its stagnant surface. There were constant troubles with the delicate machinery of the mills, for it was often clogged with slime, and the swans found another home above the town. At last, an epidemic raged, and the clammy, yellow fingers of sickness reached into every home in every street and lane.

The City Council met again. Sorrowfully, it faced the city's plight; and, frankly, it acknowledged the mistake of the dismissal of the Keeper of the Springs. They sought him out of his hermit hut, high in the hills, and begged him to return to his former joyous labor. Gladly he agreed, and began once more to make his rounds. It was not long until pure water came lilting down under tunnels of ferns and mosses and to sparkle in the cleansed reservoir.

Millwheels turned again as of old. Stenches disappeared. Sickness waned and convalescent children playing in the sun laughed again because the swans had come back.

Do not think me fanciful, too imaginative, or too extravagant in my language when I say that I think of women, and particularly of our mothers, as Keepers of the Springs. The phrase, while poetic, is true and descriptive. We feel its warmth, its softening influence, and however forgetful we have been, however much we have taken for granted life's precious gifts, we are conscious of wistful[27] memories that surge out of the past—the sweet, tender, poignant fragrances of love. Nothing that has been said, nothing that could be said, or that ever will be said would be eloquent enough, expressive enough, or adequate to make articulate[28] that peculiar emotion we feel to our mothers. So I shall make my tribute a plea for Keepers of the Springs, who will be faithful to their tasks.

There never has been a time when there was a greater need for Keepers of the Springs, or when there were more polluted springs to be cleansed. If the home fails, the country is doomed. The breakdown of home life and influence will mark the breakdown of the nation. If the Keepers of the Springs desert their posts or are unfaithful to their responsibilities, the future outlook of this country is black indeed. This generation needs Keepers of the Springs who will be courageous enough to cleanse the springs that have been polluted. It is not an easy task—nor is it a popular one; but it must be done for the sake of the children, and the young women of today must do it.

The emancipation[29] of womanhood began with Christianity, and it ends with Christianity. It had its beginning one night nineteen hundred years ago when there came to a woman named Mary a vision and a message from heaven (Luke 1:26-38). She saw the rifted clouds of glory and the hidden battlements of heaven. She heard an angelic annunciation of the almost incredible news that she, of all the women on earth—of all the Mary's in history—was to be the only one who should ever wear entwined the red rose of maternity and the white rose of virginity. It was told her…that she should be the mother of the Savior of the world.

It was nineteen hundred years ago "when Jesus Himself a baby deigned[30] to be and bathed in baby tears His deity," and on that night, when that tiny Child lay in the straw of Bethlehem, began the emancipation of womanhood.

---

27 **wistful** – thinking sadly about something in the past that you can no longer have.
28 **make articulate** – express one's thoughts clearly.
29 **emancipation** – set free from social restrictions; liberation.
30 **deigned** – thought it fit to do something.

When He grew up and began to teach the way of life, He ushered woman into a new place in human relations. He accorded her a new dignity and crowned her with a new glory, so that wherever the Christian evangel[31] has gone for nineteen centuries, the daughters of Mary have been respected, revered, remembered, and loved; for men have recognized that womanhood is a sacred and a noble thing, that women are of finer clay…It remained for the twentieth century, in the name of progress, in the name of tolerance, in the name of broadmindedness, in the name of freedom, to pull her down from her throne and try to make her like a man. She wanted equality…and so it is, that in the name of broadminded tolerance, a man's vices have now become a woman's.

Twentieth-century tolerance has won for woman the right to become intoxicated, the right to have an alcoholic breath, the right to smoke, to work like a man, to act like a man—for is she not man's equal? Today they call it "progress"…but tomorrow, oh, you Keepers of the Springs, they must be made to see that it is not progress. No nation has ever made any progress in a downward direction. No people ever became great by lowering their standards. No people ever became good by adopting a looser morality. It is not progress when the moral tone is lower than it was. It is not progress when purity is not as sweet. It is not progress when womanhood has lost its fragrance. Whatever else it is, it is not progress!

We need Keepers of the Springs who will realize *that* what is *socially correct* may not be *morally right*…This generation has seen an entirely new type of womanhood emerge from the bewildering confusion of our time. We have in the United States today a higher standard of living than in any other country or at any other time in the world's history. We have more automobiles, more picture shows, more telephones, more money, more swing bands, more radios, more television sets, more nightclubs, more crime, and more divorce than any other nation in the world. Modern mothers want their children to enjoy the advantages of this new day. They want them, if possible, to have a college diploma to hang on their bedroom wall, and what many of them regard as equally important—a bid to a fraternity or a sorority. They are desperately anxious that their daughters will be popular, although the price of this popularity may not be considered until it is too late. In short, they want their children to succeed, but the usual definition of success, in keeping with the trend of our day, is largely materialistic.

---

31 **evangel** – Christian gospel; the good news of the pardon of sin and the gift of eternal life through repentance of sin, coupled with faith in the Person and work of Jesus Christ; see *God's Gospel of Grace* available from CHAPEL LIBRARY.

The result of all this is that the modern child is brought up in a decent, cultured, comfortable, but thoroughly irreligious home. All around us, living in the very shadow of our large churches and beautiful cathedrals, children are growing up without a particle of [Christian] training or influence. The parents of such children have usually completely given up the search for religious moorings. At first, they probably had some sort of vague idealism as to what their children should be taught. They recall something of the religious instruction received when they were children, and they feel that something like that ought to be passed on to the children today; but they can't do it because the simple truth is that they have nothing to give. Our modern broadmindedness has taken religious education out of the day schools. Our modern way of living and our modern irreligion have taken it out of the homes.

As you think of your own mother, remembering her with love and gratitude—in wishful yearning or lonely longing, I am quite sure that the memories that warm and soften your heart are not at all like the memories the children of today will have…For you are, no doubt, remembering the smell of fresh starch in your mother's apron or the smell of a newly ironed blouse, the smell of newly baked bread, the fragrance of the violets she had pinned on her breast. It would be such a pity if all that one could remember would be the aroma of toasted tobacco or nicotine and the odor of beer on the breath!

The challenge of [modern day] motherhood is as old as motherhood itself. Although the average American mother has advantages that pioneer women never knew—material advantages: education, culture, advances made by science and medicine; although the modern mother knows a great deal more about sterilization, diets, health, calories, germs, drugs, medicines, and vitamins than her mother did, there is one subject about which she does not know as much—and that is God.

The modern challenge to motherhood is the eternal challenge—that of being a godly woman. The very phrase sounds strange in our ears. We never hear it now. We hear about every other kind of women—beautiful women, smart women, sophisticated women, career women, talented women, divorced women, but so seldom do we hear of a *godly* woman[32] or of a godly man either, for that matter.

I believe women come nearer fulfilling their God-given function in the home than anywhere else (Titus 2:3-5; 1 Tim. 5:14; Prov. 7:10-11). It is a much nobler thing to be a good wife than to be Miss America. It is a greater

---

32 See FGB 196, *Virtuous Womanhood*

achievement to establish a Christian home than it is to produce a second-rate novel filled with filth…The world has enough women who know how to hold their cocktails, who have lost all their illusions and their faith. The world has enough women who know how to be smart. It needs women who are willing to be simple. The world has enough women who know how to be brilliant. It needs some who will be brave. The world has enough women who are popular. It needs more who are *pure*. We need women, and men, too, who would rather be [biblically] right than socially correct.

Let us not fool ourselves—without Christianity, without Christian education, without the principles of Christ inculcated into young life, we are simply rearing pagans.[33] Physically, they will be perfect. Intellectually, they will be brilliant. But spiritually, they will be pagan. Let us not fool ourselves. The school is making no attempt to teach the principles of Christ. The Church alone cannot do it. They can never be taught to a child unless the mother[34] herself knows them and practices them every day. If you have no prayer life yourself, it is rather a useless gesture to make your child say his prayers every night. If you never enter a church it is rather futile to send your child to Sunday School. If you make a practice of telling social lies, it will be difficult to teach your child to be truthful. If you say cutting things about your neighbors and about fellow members in the church, it will be hard for your child to learn the meaning of kindness…

A minister tells of going to a hospital to visit a mother whose first child had been born. She was a distinctly modern girl. Her home was about average for young married people. "When I came into the room she was propped up in bed writing. 'Come in,' she said, smiling. 'I'm in the midst of housecleaning, and I want your help.' I had never heard of a woman housecleaning while in a hospital bed. Her smile was contagious—she seemed to have found a new and jolly idea. 'I've had a wonderful chance to think here,' she began, 'and it may help me to get things straightened out in my mind if I can talk to you.' She put down her pencil and pad and folded her hands. Then she took a long breath and started: 'Ever since I was a little girl, I hated any sort of restraint. I always wanted to be free. When I finished high school, I took a business course and got a job—not because I needed the money—but because I wanted to be on my own. Before Joe and I were married, we used to say that we would not be slaves to each other. And after we married, our apartment became headquarters for a crowd just like us. We weren't really bad—but we did just what we pleased.' She

---

33 See FGB 204, *Biblical Parenthood,* and FGB 208, *Duties of Children.*
34 See FGB 188, *Family Worship,* and FGB 228, *Fatherhood.*

stopped for a minute and smiled ruefully. 'God didn't mean much to us—we ignored Him. None of us wanted children—or we thought we didn't. And when I knew I was going to have a baby, I was afraid.' She stopped again and looked puzzled. 'Isn't it funny, the things you used to think?' She had almost forgotten I was there—she was speaking to the old girl she had been before her great adventure. Then remembering me suddenly, she went on: 'Where was I? Oh, yes, well, things are different now. I'm not free anymore, and I don't want to be. And the first thing I must do is to clean house.' Here she picked up the sheet of paper lying on the counterpane. 'That's my housecleaning list. You see, when I take Betty home from the hospital with me, our apartment will be *her* home—not just mine and Joe's. And it isn't fit for her now. Certain things will have to go—for Betty's sake. And I've got to houseclean my heart and mind. I'm not just myself: I'm Betty's mother. And that means I need God. I can't do my job without Him. Won't you pray for Betty and me and Joe, and for our new home?'

"And I saw in her all the mothers of today—mothers in tiny apartments and on lonely farms. Mothers in great houses and in suburban cottages, who are meeting the age-old challenge: that of bringing up their children to the love and knowledge of God. And I seemed to see our Savior with His arms full of children in far-away Judea saying to that mother and to all mothers the old invitation so much needed in these times: *'Suffer the little children to come unto me, and forbid them not: for of such is the kingdom of God'* (Mark 10:14)."

From *Keepers of the Springs*, widely available on the Internet.

Peter Marshall (1902-1949): Scottish-American Presbyterian preacher; twice appointed Chaplain of the U. S. Senate; born in Coatbridge, Scotland.

Biblically Training Children, I

JAMES CAMERON (1809-1873)

Train up a child in the way he should go. —Proverbs 22:6

These are the words of the wise man, who spoke as he was moved by the Holy Ghost (2 Peter 1:21). They are to be viewed, therefore, not as the admonition of a fellow-creature, but as the authoritative injunction of the God of heaven—the Governor of the universe. Christian mothers! This injunction is addressed to you…Suffer me now to address you respecting your duty:

If you would train up your children in the way they should go, it is necessary that you cultivate a deep and abiding sense of your own insufficiency. I need say nothing, I am persuaded, to convince you of the fact of your insufficiency. If you have seriously reflected on the *magnitude* of your responsibility, you are ready to ask, *"Who is sufficient for these things?"* (2 Cor. 2:16). Your work is to train immortal beings for God—the same work, in substance, as that for which the Christian ministry has been instituted. And in reference to this work, even the apostle of the Gentiles said, *"Not that we are sufficient of ourselves to think any thing as of ourselves"* (2 Cor. 3:5). You are partakers of the same sinful nature with those whom you have to train, encompassed with all the weakness of fallen humanity, and subject to all its temptations. You have to contend against your own sinful propensities;[35] to watch over your own spirits; to strive with your own waywardness; and in the midst of all this, to set before your children such an example of patience, forbearance, and holy living, as shall be a true and faithful comment on the sacred truths you teach them. If ever you become self-sufficient, be assured you will labor in vain; *"God resisteth the proud, but giveth grace unto the humble"* (James 4:6).

But why do I urge upon you the consideration of your insufficiency? Is it to sink you into despair? Nay, verily; that would be a profitless, as well as a cheerless undertaking. It is to induce you, in utter hopelessness of accomplishing the desired result by your own wisdom or strength, to cast yourselves on the God of all wisdom and of all strength, for it is written, *"Cast thy burden upon the LORD, and he shall sustain thee"* (Ps. 55:22); and, *"He giveth power to the faint; and to them that have no might he increaseth strength. Even the youths shall faint and be weary, and the young men shall utterly fall: But they that wait upon the LORD shall renew their strength; they shall mount up with wings as eagles; they shall run, and not be weary; and they shall walk,*

---

35 **propensities** – tendencies or inclinations to certain kinds of behavior.

and not faint" (Isa. 40:29-31). You can have no fitness *for* your work and no success *in* your work, but what comes from God. You cannot expect that God will grant this fitness and this success, unless you look to Him alone for them. But such is the natural unwillingness of the human heart to turn to God and to trust only in Him that it is not until we are driven from every other refuge and deprived of every other stay[36] that we cling to Him with the simple childlike dependence of those who have truly learned that there is no other God besides Jehovah; that all power, all wisdom, and all blessings are from Him; and that without Him, every effort must be vain and every undertaking abortive. The [doctrine of the] absolute helplessness and moral impotency of fallen man is one of the most important lessons we can be taught. But alas! It is one of the most difficult for proud human nature to learn. The Spirit of God can teach it; and blessed are they who, being taught by the divine Spirit their own utter helplessness, are taught at the same time that they have a God to go to Who can furnish them richly with all they need.

Again, then, I repeat, cultivate a sense of your insufficiency for the great work to which God has called you; and let this be so thoroughly interwoven in the very texture of your minds—let it so thoroughly pervade your whole habits of thinking and feeling—that you shall be kept in the very lowest depths of self-distrust, feeling that your only safety is in clinging, as with a death-grasp, to the soul-sustaining declaration, *"My grace is sufficient for thee: for my strength is made perfect in weakness"* (2 Cor. 12:9). It is only when a deep sense of insufficiency and a strong confidence in God are combined that you are at all likely to be successful in your arduous[37] work. Your sense of insufficiency will make you cautious, tender, watchful, prayerful; and your confidence in God will nerve your soul and strengthen you to grapple with the difficulties you have to encounter.

If you would train up your children in the way they should go, it is necessary that you diligently cultivate your own minds, imbuing[38] them with sound principles and storing them with useful knowledge. It may be said that this ought to have been done before you occupied the position you do—and it is true. But it will be acknowledged, we think, by almost all who are capable of forming a judgment on the subject, that generally speaking, it is not done before and that in nine-tenths, perhaps, of those cases in which the mind has been fitted for the efficient discharge of a mother's duties, its

---

36 **stay** – support; something upon which someone relies.
37 **arduous** – difficult to accomplish; difficult and tiring.
38 **imbuing** – filling.

cultivation has been chiefly, if not entirely, effected at a period subsequent to that allotted to what is termed *education*.

The education that females generally receive in youth is but ill-fitted for enabling them rightly "to mold the mass of human mind." Education properly so called is the training of the intellect, the conscience, and the affections. But is this a description of female education as it actually is, even with all the boasted improvements of modern times? Is that education in any prominent degree, the education of the mind or heart at all—*in any form*? Alas! It is too frequently the cultivation of *manner* only. The useful is sacrificed to the ornamental. The casket is embellished with all kinds of tinsel-work, which may attract the admiration of the beholder, while the invaluable jewel it contains is left to comparative neglect. Let it not be supposed that we undervalue accomplishments. We believe them to be highly valuable—much more valuable than many who eagerly pursue them seem to be aware…And assuredly they are too dearly purchased whenever they so engross the time and attention as to leave little or no opportunity for the cultivation of the mind itself.

It is distressing to think that while so much depends on the training of the female mind, so little provision is made for that training being effective. Napoleon[39] once asked Madame Campan[40] what the French nation most needed in order that her youth might be properly educated. Her reply was comprised in one word: that word was—"Mothers!" And it was a wise reply. Not the French nation only—*the world* needs mothers—Christian, intelligent, well-trained mothers to whom the destinies of the rising generation may safely be entrusted.

A distinguished philosopher has remarked that all the world is but the pupil and disciple of female influence! How important, then, that females should be fitted for their work! And is the education they generally receive in youth such as is likely to fit them for that work? No one acquainted with the subject will reply in the affirmative. The end desired seems rather that they should be qualified for securing admiration and applause, than for molding the minds and forming the characters of those who are to be the future defenders of the faith—the ministers of the Gospel, the philosophers, the legislators of the next generation. I [think] that I cannot do better than present you with the remarks of one of your own sex on this subject—one who is well-entitled to an attentive hearing—I mean the author of *Woman's Mission*:[41]

---

39 **Napoleon Bonaparte** (1769-1820) – French general who became emperor of France.
40 **Madame Jeanne Louise Henriette Genet Campan** (1752-1822) – a French educator and a lady-in-waiting for Marie Antoinette.
41 Sarah Lewis, *Woman's Mission* (London: John W. Parker, West Strand; 1839).

"What, then, is the true object of female education? The best answer to this question is a statement of future duties; for it must never be forgotten that if education is not training for future duties, it is nothing. The ordinary lot of woman is to marry. Has anything in these educations prepared her to make a wise choice in marriage? To be a mother? Have the duties of maternity—the nature of moral influence—been pointed out to her? Has she ever been enlightened as to the consequent unspeakable importance of personal character *as* the source of influence? In a word, have any means, direct or indirect, prepared her for her duties? No! But she is a linguist, a pianist—graceful, admired. What is *that* to the purpose?...The time when young women enter upon life is the one point to which all plans of education tend and at which they all terminate; and to prepare them for that point is the object of their training. Is it not cruel to lay up for them a store of future wretchedness by an education that has no period in view but one—a very short one, and the most unimportant and irresponsible of the whole life? Who that had the power of choice would choose to buy the admiration of the world for a few short years with the happiness of a whole life?..."[42]

I have a double object in view in directing your attention so prominently to this point: that you may bring these sentiments to bear on the education of your *daughters* and that you may feel the necessity, whatever may have been the nature and extent of your own previous education, of continuing diligently to educate yourselves and add to your resources. You will find that there is need of all, for you have a great work given you to do. Especially, let the sacred truths of God's Word be the subject of your constant study. Be not content with a superficial knowledge of the great things of God's Law, but seek to know them in all their depth and fullness, tracing their bearings and connections, studying their harmonies and proportions that thus, by having the Word of Christ dwelling in you richly in all wisdom (Col. 3:16), you may be *"throughly furnished unto all good works"* (2 Tim. 3:17)... But though the Word of God must be your *chief* study, beware of supposing it must be your *only* study. All truth is *from* God, and all truth may be made subservient to the great work of training your children *for* God...

In all your conduct, manifest the most undeviating[43] consistency... Children, even at a very early age, are eagle-eyed to observe the inconsistencies of a parent. And the slightest inconsistency, though it is manifested only in a word or a look, lowers your influence over them in an inconceivable degree. When a child learns to distrust its mother, all her warnings, admonitions, and

---

42 Lewis, *Mission*, 66-68.
43 **undeviating** – steady; not turning or changing.

remonstrances[44]—however earnest and unremitting—fall powerless. This is the chief reason, it is to be feared, why we so frequently see the children of pious parents grow up impenitent.[45] The example of their parents has not been uniformly consistent with their instructions and therefore have these instructions been useless…Mothers! Watch your conduct. Your children watch it. Every expression of your countenance—every word you utter—every action they see you perform is scanned and scrutinized by them. If they perceive that you act inconsistently, they will in their hearts despise you. And you cannot long deceive a child with regard to character; the only sure way to appear consistent is to be so.

Be firm and unbending in the exercise of your authority, requiring on all occasions implicit, unresisting obedience. Implicit submission to the authority of God is *essential* to true [Christianity]. And God has given you absolute authority over your child, so that by being habituated[46] to the exercise of implicit submission[47] to your will, he may be trained to the exercise of implicit submission to His. Until your child is able in some measure to judge for himself, you are to him in the place of God; and if you allow your will to be disputed—if you shrink from the exercise of absolute, uncompromising authority—you train your child to be a rebel against God. A mother's indulgence lays the foundation for disobedience and insubordination toward God; which, unless divine grace in future years prevents, must issue in the child's eternal ruin…Let it not be said that the principle we inculcate is severe. It is not so. The most unbending authority may be blended with the most unwearied love. And the two ought ever to be blended. These are the two great principles of God's government, and your family government should resemble His. The unwearied exercise of love will prevent your authority from degenerating into harshness—the unbending exercise of authority will prevent your love from degenerating into foolish indulgence.

If you would train up your children in the way they should go, you must restrain and curb their wayward propensities. Never forget that they possess a depraved nature, prone to all evil, averse from all good. Beware, therefore, of allowing them to have their own way. That is the way that leadeth to death (Prov. 14:12; 16:25). Accustom them by times to submit to restraint. Subject them to wholesome discipline; and do this in such a manner as shall prove

---

44 **remonstrances** – protests.
45 **impenitent** – not feeling shame or regret about one's actions or attitudes; not repentant.
46 **habituated** – accustomed to; used to.
47 **implicit submission** – submitting to without question.

even to them that it is done not for the gratification of your passion, but for their profit. A child left to his own way will bring ruin on himself and sorrow and disgrace on his parents. Remember the case of Adonijah. *"His father had not displeased him at any time in saying, Why hast thou done so?"* (1 Kings 1:6). In other words, he was a spoiled child. And what was the consequence? His father's dying bed was disturbed by his treasonable machinations;[48] and in order to secure the peace of the kingdom, his own brother was obliged to issue an order for his death.

If you would train your children in the way they should go, you must make all their training bear, directly or indirectly, on their spiritual and eternal well-being. By this, I do not mean that you should be always speaking to them *about* religion, for there is such a thing as forming in the mind of a child a permanent association between religious truth and the feeling of weariness or disgust; and against this evil, parents should especially guard. I mean that you should yourself always keep in view their eternal interests. It is not merely for the employment of the few fleeting years of the present life that you are training them: it is for the service and enjoyment of God forever. Oh! What a noble work is yours! Contemplate it in the light of eternity, and you will feel that it is the most dignified—the most glorious employment in which an immortal being can engage. The thought that it is for eternity will sustain you amidst every difficulty and cheer you on in your noble career. Yes, it is a noble career! For when all the honor, pomp, and glare of mere temporal pursuits have passed away, the effects of your work shall remain; and ceaseless ages shall record the triumph of your faith, fortitude, and patience…You train your children for eternity. Ought you not, then, to exercise unceasing care and vigilance?

It is surely scarcely necessary for me to add, as my last observation, that if you would train up your children in the way they should go, you must abound in prayer—fervent, wrestling, believing prayer.[49] Without this, you can do nothing as it ought to be done. Great and arduous are your duties, and great is the preparation you need for the discharge of them. You need wisdom; you need firmness; you need decision; you need patience; you need self-control; you need perseverance; and whither can you go for these but to the mercy-seat of Him *"that giveth to all men liberally, and upbraideth not"* (James 1:5). *"Every good gift and every perfect gift is from above, and cometh down from the Father of lights"* (James 1:17). Continual prayer will fit you for your duties and make these duties pleasant. By prayer, you will lay hold on

---

48 **treasonable machinations** – secret and complicated plans of betrayal.
49 See FGB 221, *Vital Prayer*

the strength of God and be able to say with the apostle, *"I can do all things through Christ which strengtheneth me"* (Phil. 4:13).

I close these remarks by reminding you once more of the magnitude of your responsibility. To you (under God) are entrusted the destinies of the rising generation, and through it, the destinies of the generations following. The world looks to you; the Church of God looks to you; the spirits of departed saints look to you; the angelic hosts look to you; God Himself looks to you, as those whose influence shall tell forever on thousands yet unborn. Let a sense of the importance of your high calling animate you to run with patience the race that is set before you; and when you have finished your course, and are called to give in your account, yours will be the unspeakable happiness of being welcomed to the realms of glory by the approving voice of your Savior God: *"Well done, thou good and faithful servant…enter thou into the joy of thy lord"* (Matt. 25:21). And with all your loved ones around you, you will stand on the Mount Zion when earth and seas have fled, and with a heart overflowing with gratitude, will cast your crowns at Jesus' feet, saying, *"Not unto us, O LORD, not unto us, but unto thy name give glory"* (Ps. 115:1).

From *Three Lectures to Christian Mothers*, in the public domain.

James Cameron (1809-1873): Scottish Congregational minister; born in Gourock, Firth of Clyde, Scotland.

Biblically Training Children, II
JOHN ANGELL JAMES (1785-1859)

One of the greatest mistakes into which mothers fall is that of supposing that the first two or three years of a child's life are unimportant as regards his training. The truth is that in the formation of character they are the most important of all. It has been truly said that from the impressions made, the principles implanted, and the habits formed during these years, the child's character for time and eternity may take its complexion.[50]

It is perfectly clear that a child, before he can speak, is susceptible of [51]moral training. The conscience, or moral sense, may by a judicious woman be developed soon after, if not before, the child has spent his first birthday. So early may he be made to distinguish between what his mother considers right and wrong, between what will please and what will displease her. Why, the brute creatures will do this; and if they can be taught this, may not very young children? It is admitted that there is more of reason in many brutes than in very young children. Still, even very young animals may be trained to know what they may and may not do; and so may very young children. I often hear mothers say that their children are too young to be taught obedience. The mother who acts upon the maxim that children may have their own way for a certain number of years, or even months, will find to her cost that that lesson at least will not speedily be forgotten. Moral training may and should precede that which is intellectual. The cultivation of the affections and conscience should be the commencement and foundation of education and will facilitate every succeeding effort whether of the child or of those who train or teach him.

There is in some women a timidity and a distrust of their own capacity, which paralyze or prevent the endeavors that they could make, if they would only believe in their own power. Every woman of good, plain understanding can do more than she imagines for the formation of her children's character. What she is deficient in, let her supply by reading; and no mother, however qualified, should neglect this. Everyone may learn something from others. Fearful, timid, and anxious mothers, be not afraid! Prayer will bring God's help and God's blessing.

Injudicious indulgence[52] is the most common (as it is the most injurious) danger into which a young mother can fall. Be kind; you ought to be. An

---

50 **complexion** – habit of mind; temperament.
51 **susceptible of** – capable of receiving.
52 **injudicious indulgence** – unwise leniency and pampering.

unloving, hard-hearted mother is a double [slander] upon her sex and her relationship. Love is her power, her instrument, and…she can do nothing—*worse than nothing*—without it. But then her love must be like that of the divine Parent Who said, *"As many as I love, I rebuke and chasten"* (Rev. 3:19). Can you say "No" to a child when, with winning smiles, beseeching voice, or weeping eyes, he asks for what it is not good that he should receive? Can you take from him that which is likely to be injurious to him, but which it will give him pain to surrender? Can you correct him for his faults when your heart rises up in opposition to your judgment? Can you put him off from your arms at a proper season for so doing, when he clings to your neck and cries to remain? Can you exact obedience in what is to him a difficult, but to you a necessary, command? Can you stand out against his tears, resolute in purpose, unyielding in demand, and first conquer your own heart, so stoutly resisting you, in order to conquer his? Or do you allow yourself to be subdued to put an end to the contest, and by soothing his sufferings foster the temper that ought to be eradicated at any pains and any cost? She who cannot answer all this in the affirmative is not fit to be a mother. There must be discipline in a family. A parent must be obeyed. Give this up, and you train your children for evil and not for good. Here again I say, *begin early*. Put on the soft and easy yoke quickly…Both the human species and animals soon grow beyond the power of discipline…

Need I say to you that all you do in training up your children in the way they should go will bear directly or indirectly on their eternal welfare?…You will not overlook, as I have already remarked, the intellectual training of your children's minds; but their moral and religious education will, I hope, be your chief object of solicitude.[53] Viewing your children as immortal beings destined to eternity and capable of the enjoyments of heaven, you will labor even from infancy to imbue[54] their minds with [biblically Christian] ideas. It is immortality that rescues from littleness and insignificance all that it appertains to and hence arises in no inconsiderable degree the exalted honor of a mother.

She has given birth, by the sovereign ordination of the Almighty, not to a being of a mere momentary existence, whose life will perish like that of the beast of the field, but to an immortal!…Mothers, *such is your dignity, such* your exalted honor. Feel and value your rich distinction in being called to educate the sons and daughters of the Lord God Almighty and to prepare the holy family who are to dwell in those many mansions of His Father's house that the Lord Jesus is gone to prepare (John 14:2). Give yourselves

---

53 **solicitude** – care and concern.
54 **imbue** – fill, in the sense of saturate; inspire.

up to this glorious work. But be judicious in all you do, lest you produce prejudice against true [Christian faith], instead of prepossession[55] in its favor. Let your warmest affection, your greatest cheerfulness, your most engaging smiles be put on when you teach [the faith] to your children. Approach as nearly as possible to a seraphic[56] form. Represent [following Christ] in all its beauty, loveliness, sanctity, and ineffable[57] sweetness. Let them see it in your character as well as hear it from your lips.

Especially be careful not to enforce as a task what should be proposed as an object of hope and a source of delight. Let them see in you that piety,[58] if in one respect it is a strait[59] and narrow path, is in another a way of pleasantness and a path of peace. Do not inflict learning Scripture or hymns upon them as a *punishment* for offenses, and thus convert religion, which is the foretaste of heaven, into a penance that shall be to them like being tormented before their time. Especially do not make the Sabbath a day of gloom instead of gladness by such an accumulation of services as shall cause the day of rest to be physically more irksome[60] than the common labors of the week…

And now, to sum up all: Consider a mother's *charge*: an immortal creature; a mother's *duty*: to train him up for God, heaven, and eternity; a mother's *dignity*: to educate the family of the Almighty Creator of the universe; a mother's *difficulty*: to raise a fallen, sinful creature to holiness and virtue; a mother's *encouragement*: the promise of divine grace to assist her in her momentous duties; a mother's *relief*: to bear the burden of her cares to God in prayer; and a mother's *hope*: to meet her child in glory everlasting and spend eternal ages of delight with him before the throne of God and the Lamb.

But are mothers only to engage in this work of educating their children for God? No. Fathers, I speak to you, for the Bible speaks to you.[61] "*And, ye fathers, provoke not your children to wrath: but bring them up in the nurture and admonition of the Lord*" (Eph. 6:4)…Are you exercising your authority, giving your instructions, pouring out your prayers, and affording your example, all for the salvation of your children? Is it your wish, your ambition, your endeavor, and your supplication that they may be [godly Christian] men or only rich ones? Are you pouring your influence into the same channel as your holy wife? Are you helping or hindering her in her pious solicitude for the spiritual and eternal

---

55 **prepossession** – influencing the mind.
56 **seraphic** – resembling the beauty, purity, devotion of an angelic being.
57 **ineffable** – too great to be expressed in words.
58 **piety** – godliness.
59 **strait and narrow** – narrow and difficult.
60 **irksome** – wearisome; burdensome.
61 See FGB 228, *Fatherhood*

welfare of your joint offspring? Happy, happy couple, where there is a sympathy of feeling and similarity of sentiment in the most momentous concern that can engage the attention of man, of angels, or of God—religion; where the husband and the wife are of one mind and one heart, not only in reference to themselves, but in regard also to their children, and where both are engaged in training them up for everlasting glory! I can compare such a couple, in their benevolent efforts for their children's welfare, only to the two angels who were sent down from heaven to rescue Lot and who, with holy and benevolent violence, took him by the hand to pluck him from the burning city and conducted him to the place of safety prepared by the mercy of Almighty God.

From *Female Piety*, in the public domain.

John Angell James (1785-1859): English Congregationalist preacher and author; born at Blandford, Dorsetshire, England.

> *Never give a command that you do not intend to be obeyed. There is no more effectual way of teaching a child disobedience than by giving commands that you have no intention of enforcing. A child is thus habituated to disregard its mother; and, in a short time, the habit becomes so strong and the child's contempt for the mother so confirmed that entreaties and threats are alike unheeded. —J. S. C. Abbot*

> *A mother's power lies in the fact that she prays for her child.*
> *—Abraham Kuyper*

> *The mother who is still present with children when they are young [should] be very diligent in teaching them and minding them of good things. When the fathers are abroad, the mothers have more frequent opportunities to instruct them, speaking to them of that which is most necessary and watching over them. This is the greatest service that most women can do for God in the world! Many a church that hath been blessed with a good minister may thank the pious education of mothers. And many a thousand souls in heaven may thank the holy care and diligence of mothers as the first effectual means. Good women this way (by the good education of their children) are ordinarily great blessings both to church and state. —Richard Baxter*

The Mother's Legacy to Her Unborn Child
ELIZABETH JOSCELIN (C. 1595-1622)[62]

Having long, often, and earnestly desired of God that I might be a mother to one of His children and the time now drawing on that I hope He hath appointed to give thee unto me, it drew me into a consideration both wherefore I so earnestly desired thee and (having found that the true cause was to make thee happy) how I might attain this happiness for thee.

I knew it consisted not in honor, wealth, strength of body, or friends, though all these are great blessings. Therefore, it would be a weak request to desire thee only for an heir to my fortune. No, I never aimed at so poor an inheritance as the whole world for thee. Neither would I have begged of God so much pain, as I know I must endure, to have only possessed thee with earthly riches, of which today thou mayest be a great man, tomorrow a poor beggar. Nor did a hope to dandle[63] thy infancy move me to desire thee. For I know all the delight a parent can take in a child is honey mingled with gall.[64]

But the true reason that I have so often kneeled to God for thee is that thou mightest be an inheritor of the kingdom of heaven. To which end I humbly beseech Almighty God thou mayest bend all thy actions and, if it be His blessed will, give thee so plentiful a measure of His grace that thou mayest serve Him as His minister, if He make thee a man.

It is true that this age holds the ministry a most contemptible office, fit only for poor men's children, younger brothers, and such as have no other means to live. But for God's sake, be not discouraged with these vain speeches: fortify yourself with remembering what great worth the winning of one soul is in God's sight, and you shall quickly find how great a place it is to be a minister unto the living God. If it will please Him to move your heart with His Holy Spirit, it will glow and burn with zeal to do Him service. The Lord open thy lips that thy mouth may show forth His praise (Ps. 51:15).

---

62 **Editor's note:** This is an edited version of Elizabeth Joscelin's *The Mother's Legacie to Her Unborn Childe*. It represents a distinctly female literary genre that appeared in 17th century England known as an "advice book." Advice books were a form of Renaissance literature in which a mother wrote instructions, predominantly spiritual, as a legacy to her children. Joscelin's legacy is unique because, concerned about dying in childbirth, she wrote to her *unborn* child. Poignantly, Elizabeth bore a daughter, Theodora, on October 12, 1622, and died nine days later. [This article required more editing than usual for modern readers, so numerous editorial marks have been removed for easier reading.]

63 **dandle** – play with or bounce a child.

64 **gall** – bile, stored in the gall bladder, is known for its bitterness. Used here metaphorically, the author contrasts bitterness with sweetness—the grief and joys of parenthood.

If I had skill to write, I would write all I apprehend of the happy estate of true, laboring ministers. But I may plainly say that of all men, they by their calling are the most truly happy. They are familiar with God, they labor in His vineyard, and they are so beloved of Him that He gives them abundance of knowledge. O be one of them! Let not the scorn of evil men hinder thee. Look how God hath provided for thee sufficient means. Thou needest not hinder thy study to look for a living, as the Israelites hindered their work to look for straw (Ex. 5:6-23). If thou art not content with this, thou wilt not be with more. God deliver thee from covetousness!

I desire thee that, though thou takest a spiritual calling, thou wilt not seek after the livings of the church,[65] nor promotions, though I honor them as I have great cause; but I would have thee so truly an humble and zealous minister that thy only end should be to do God service without desire of anything for thyself, except the kingdom of heaven. Yet as I would not have thee seek these things, so I would have thee as careful not to neglect God's blessings, but with all thankfulness to receive what He bestows and to be a careful steward, distributing it to those that have need.

I could not but choose to manifest this desire in writing, lest it should please God to deprive me of time to speak.[66]

And if thou art a daughter…read on, and thou shalt see my love and care of thee and thy salvation is as great as if thou wert a son and my fear greater.

It may perhaps, when thou comest to some discretion,[67] appear strange to thee to receive these lines from a mother that died when thou wert born. But when thou seest men purchase land and store up treasure for their unborn babes, wonder not at me that I am careful for thy salvation, being such an eternal portion. And not knowing whether I shall live to instruct thee when thou art born, let me not be blamed though I write to thee before. Who would not condemn me if I should be careless of thy body while it is within me? Surely, a far greater care belongs to thy soul. To both these cares I will endeavor myself so long as I live.

Again, I may perhaps be wondered at for writing in this way, considering there are so many excellent books whose least note is worth all my meditations. I confess it and thus excuse myself. I write not to the world, but to mine own child, who, it may be, will more profit by a few weak

---

65 **livings…church** – benefices, that is, permanent church appointments for which property and income are provided in respect of pastoral duties.

66 **I could not…time to speak** – I had no choice but to write my desires to you, for fear that God's will for me is to perish without having time to speak to you.

67 **comest…discretion** – when you are able to exercise discernment.

Chapter 7—Motherhood: The Mother's Legacy to Her Unborn Child

instructions coming from a dead mother (who cannot every day praise or reprove it as it deserves) than by far better from much more learned. These things considered, neither the true knowledge of mine own weakness nor the fear that this may come to the world's eye and bring scorn upon my grave can keep my hand from expressing how much I covet thy salvation.

Therefore, dear child, read here my love. And if God take me from thee, be obedient to these instructions as thou oughtest to be unto me. I have learned them out of God's Word; I beseech Him that they may be profitable to thee.

1. The first charge I give thee, I learned from Solomon in Ecclesiastes 12:1: *"Remember now thy Creator in the days of thy youth."* It is an excellent beginning and a fit lesson for a child…To move thy heart to remember thy Creator betimes,[68] meditate upon the benefits thou continually receivest. First, how He hath created thee when thou were nothing; redeemed thee by the death of His only Son, being worse than nothing; and now by mere grace, He hath given thee His Holy Spirit, sanctifying thee to an eternal kingdom.[69] Thou canst not possibly understand how great these mercies are, but straight thy soul must cry, "What shall I do for so gracious a God? All the powers of my soul and body will I give to His service. My first thoughts will I dedicate to Him. Like Abel's sacrifice (Gen. 4:4), I will present to Him the first fruits of my youth. In the strength of my age will I fall down before Him; and, if I live to old age, [I pray] that weakness will not let my knees bow nor my hands be lifted up. Yet shall my heart meditate on His goodness night and day, and my tongue shall be always telling of His marvelous works."

When thou hast thus remembered the infinite mercies of God, it is appropriate for thee to settle thyself to a constant service of Him; to order thy thoughts, words, and actions to His glory; and to covenant with thyself that thou wilt not break thy promises to God…Mark, I pray thee, these following rules for ordering thy life; and God will bless thee and all thy good endeavors.

2. At thy first waking in the morning, be careful of thyself that thou harbor in thy brain no vain, unprofitable, and, most of all, no ungodly thoughts to hinder thy morning sacrifice.[70] But immediately frame thyself[71] to meditate on the mercies of God, the maliciousness of the devil, and thine own weakness. The devil's malice is as easily perceived [as your weakness is]; for even now he lies lurking ready to catch every good motion from thy

---

68 **betimes** – before it is too late.
69 Joscelin, an Anglican, assumes the conversion of her child.
70 **morning sacrifice** – prayer of thanksgiving.
71 **frame thyself** – direct your thoughts.

heart, suggesting things more delightful to thy fancy and persuading thee to put off thy service of God though but for a little while.

But be warned and armed against his temptations. Be assured if thou once yield to neglect praying to God, but one half hour, when that time comes, thou shalt find thyself far more unfit and thy heart more dull to pray than before. Whereas, if thou preparest thyself to pray, even though thou art heavy and uncheerful in it, yet God, Who searches the heart and sees thy desire to pray—though thou canst not—will enlighten thee and prepare thy heart in anticipation of the next time, so that thou shalt find comfort. Therefore, take heed that the devil deceives you not, for you see his malice is not small in that he seeks to cheat you of all happiness presently and to come. For be assured you can take no true joy in earthly pleasures, no longer than you seek after heavenly.

Having thus discerned the infinite malice of the devil and your own exceeding weakness, how do you think you were preserved from his snares while you slept? Or do you think he only besets you when you are awake? No, be not deceived: he is not so fair an enemy. His hate to you is such that, if he could, he would tear your body and drag your soul to hell while you slept. Alas, all this he might have done because your strength is small to resist him. Now you must necessarily confess who only is able to preserve you: it is God and His mercy—not your desert[72]—by which you are preserved. Gather to yourself a strong resolution with all your force to serve Him all the day and to resist all the temptations of the devil.

Then, being thoroughly awake (for surely, God likes not sleeping prayer), begin to give God thanks and to desire the continuance of His mercy towards thee in these words, until thou canst find such as may better express thine own soul: "O eternal God, gracious from the beginning and merciful to the latter ending of the world, I give Thee humble thanks that according to Thine abundant goodness, Thou hast graciously defended me this night from all dangers that might have happened unto me. I beseech Thee to continue this Thy favorable goodness toward me, and so grant me Thy grace that in all my thoughts, words, and actions I may seek Thy glory and evermore so live in Thy fear that I may die in Thy favor, for Thy Son my only Savior's sake. Amen."

3. Having thus invited God into your soul, take heed you offend not against so great and glorious a Guest…O think, sinful soul, what care oughtest thou to have when the living God graciously grants to dwell in thee: O watch, O be wary. Do not, my dear child, O do not willfully offend

---

72 **your desert** – what you deserve.

Him…But if out of weakness thou offend against Him, run straight before He can be gone, for He is merciful and will stay a while after thou hast sinned to expect thy repentance. Run quickly! Esteem no sin small! Learn to be ashamed to commit sin; but, being committed, hope not to hide it from God by any other means than by hearty repentance.[73] In His Son's passion,[74] He will bury thine offences so as He will hide them from Himself. The Lord will not despise a contrite heart; and though He let thee kneel long, He will have mercy at the last. Learn of Jacob to wrestle with God and to cry with a fervent spirit, *"I will not let thee go, except thou bless me"* (Gen. 32:26). Our Savior saith, *"The kingdom of heaven suffered violence, and the violent take it by force"* (Matt. 11:12).

4. Thus you see, it must be an eager, not a slothful course that must bring you to heaven. Take heed, therefore, that you avoid all the kinds of this sin. Whatsoever you go about, do it with cheerfulness. Be ashamed of idleness, as thou art a man; but tremble at it, as thou art a Christian. For be sure the devil never is so happy in his temptations as when he employs them on a slothful man who cannot endure to take so much pains as to resist him. What more wretched estate can there be in the world? First, to be hated of God as an idle drone,[75] not fit for His service; then through extreme poverty to be despised by all the world. Oh, then by no means yield thy youth to sloth! But as soon as thou hast made thy prayer to God, prepare to rise; and rising, use this prayer: "In Thy name, O blessed Savior, I arise, Who, with the Father and the Holy Spirit, created me and with Thine own most precious blood hast redeemed me. I beseech Thee this day to govern, keep, and bless me. Lead me forth in every good way. Therein direct and continue me; and after this frail and miserable life, bring me to that blessed life that hath no end, for Thy great merit and mercies sake. Amen."

5. Thou art no sooner broken out of the arms of sloth, but pride steps in diligently, waiting to furnish thee with any vain toy[76] in thy attire.[77] And though I believe there are divers sorts of pride more pestilent to the soul than this of apparel, yet this is dangerous enough. And I am sure [it] betrays a man's folly more than any other. Is it not a monstrous thing to see a man, whom God hath created of an excellent form, each part answering the due

---

73 See FGB 203, *Repentance*
74 **passion** – suffering and death; See FGBs 207, *Substitution*, 225, *The Work of Christ*, 226, *Christ upon the Cross*, and 227, *Atonement*.
75 **idle drone** – lazy person.
76 **toy** – something of little essential value, but valued as an ornament.
77 See FGB 216, *Modest Apparel*

proportion of another, who by a fantastical habit[78] make himself so ugly that one cannot find amongst all God's creatures anything like him? One man, though not resembling another in shape or face, yet for his rational soul is like another; but these fashionists[79] have (I fear) exchanged their reasonable souls for proud souls without reason. Could they else deform and transform themselves by these newfangled fashions and apish[80] behavior: crindging,[81] shrugging, starting,[82] and playing the fantastiques[83] every way, so that they may truly say when they are fashionable that they are not like other men? For who wants to be like them? I desire thee for God's sake—shun this vanity, whether thou art a son or daughter. If a daughter, I confess thy task is harder because thou art weaker and thy temptations to this vice greater. For thou shalt see those whom perhaps thou shalt think less able, exalted far above thee in this kind; and it may be thou wilt desire to be like them, if not to out-go[84] them. But believe and remember what I tell thee: the end of all these vanities is bitter as gall. Oh, the remembrance of misspent time, when thou shalt grow in years and have attained no other knowledge than to dress thyself! When thou shalt see half, perhaps all, thy time spent and that of all thou hast sowed thou hast nothing to reap but repentance—*late repentance*—how wilt thou grieve! How wilt thou accuse one folly for bringing in another and in thy memory cast over the cause of each misfortune that hath befallen thee, until passing from one to another, at last thou findest *thy corrupt will* to be the first cause. Then thou wilt with grief enough perceive that if thou hadst served God when thou servedst thy fond desires, thou wouldst now have peace of heart. The God of mercy give thee grace to remember Him in the days of thy youth.

Mistake me not nor give yourself leave to take too much liberty with saying, "My mother was too strict." No, I am not: for I give you leave to follow *modest* fashions, but not to be a *beginner* of fashions…In one word, this is all I desire: that you will not set your heart on such foolish things. You shall see that this modest carriage[85] will win you reputation and love with the wise and virtuous sort.

---

78 **fantastical habit** – clothing that shows the person to be foolishly attentive to and vain in his appearance.
79 **fashionists** – followers of fashion, who conform to the prevailing style of dress.
80 **apish** – ape-like in imitation.
81 **crindging** – behaving in a servile way.
82 **starting** – making sudden movements.
83 **fantastiques** – those who wear extravagant clothing.
84 **out-go** – surpass.
85 **modest carriage** – humble behavior.

If you will desire praise, follow the example of those spiritual women, whose virtuous fame time hath not power to raze out,[86] such as devout Anna, who served the Lord with fasting and prayer (Luke 2:36-38); just Elizabeth, who served God without reproof (Luke 1:6); and religious Esther, who taught her maids to fast and pray (Esth. 4:16).

I am so fearful that thou couldest fall into this sin that I could spend my little time of life in exhorting thee from it. I know it is the most dangerous, subtle sin that can steal the heart of man. It will alter shapes as often as the chameleon doth colors. Shun it for thy soul's sake! For if thou entertain pride, it is such a shameless flatterer that it will make thee believe thou art greater, wiser, more learned than all the company, when indeed, thou wilt prove thyself the greatest fool of them, wearying them all with thy vain talk.

Solomon saith, *"Pride goeth before destruction, and an haughty spirit before a fall"* (Prov. 16:18). And our blessed Savior, the true pattern of humility, exhorts us to learn of Him that was lowly and meek in heart (Matt. 11:29). And if we do so, He promises we shall find rest unto our souls. Neither lack there curses, threatening where persuasions will not serve:

"For whosoever exalteth himself shall be abased" (Luke 14:11). Read the Holy Scriptures often and diligently, and thou shalt find continual threatenings against pride, punishment of pride, and warnings from pride. Thou shalt find no sin so heavily punished as this: it made devils of angels, a beast of great Nebuchadnezzar (Dan. 5:21), and dogs' meat of Jezebel (2 Kings 9:10, 36; 1 Kings 21:23). I will conclude with a good man's saying: "If all the sins reigning in the world were burnt to ashes, even the ashes of pride would be able to produce them all again."

6. Therefore, avoiding all manner of pride, make thyself decently ready, which being done, retire to a place alone, where humbling thyself upon thy knees, again renew thy prayers, humbly confessing and earnestly desiring forgiveness for all thy sins. And use Doctor Smith's morning prayer;[87] I know not a better one, nor ever did I find more comfort in any. In advising you to a set form of prayer, I do not prohibit conceived prayer, but humbly beg of God to give you grace to pray often out of your own meditations according to His will.

7. When you have finished your private prayer, be sure that you absent not yourself from public prayer, if it be used in the house where you live. [When you have finished,] go and use any lawful recreation, either for thy

---

86 **raze out** – erase.
87 Henry Smith, "A Morning Prayer" in *The Works of Henry Smith*, Vol. 2, Tentmaker Publications, 460; Joscelin also commends Smith's "An Evening Prayer" in the same volume.

profit or pleasure. And from all these exercises, reserve a time to sit down to some good study, but use that most that may make thee greatest—*theology*. It will make thee greater, richer, happier than the greatest kingdom of the earth, even if thou couldest possess it. *"If any man serve me,"* saith Christ, *"him will my Father honour"* (John 12:26). Therefore, if thou desirest *honor*, serve the Lord and thou art sure of it. If thy aim be *riches*, Saint Paul assures thee that *"godliness with contentment is great gain"* (1 Tim. 6:6). If thou covet *pleasure*, set David's delight before thine eyes: *"I have rejoiced in the way of thy testimonies, as much as in all riches"* (Ps. 119:14). And in the 92nd Psalm, he saith, *"For thou, LORD, hast made me glad through thy work"* (92:4). In the 4th Psalm, *"Thou hast put gladness in my heart"* (4:7); and reading the 91st Psalm, thou shalt see what manner of blessings they are with which God makes His children merry. And when thou hast once fixed thy heart to this study, it will be so sweet that the more thou learnest, the more thou wilt desire; and the more thou desirest, the more God will show thee His love. Thou wilt study so well in private and practice it in all thy actions publicly; thou wilt weigh thy thoughts so evenly that thy words shall not be light. Now, a few lines I will use to persuade thee to be advised in thy words.

8. Though it is as much to say, "Remember thy Creator when thou speakest," as if I could use all the exhortations and tell thee all the perils that belong to speech. Yet so apt are we to forget God in our foolish talk that sometimes we by our discourse would make gods of ourselves. Therefore, it will not be amiss to receive a few instructions, though weak, from me for ordering thy speech. The morning I have dedicated to meditation, prayer, good studies, and honest recreation. The noon time is most used for discourse, it being all a man can do while he eats. And it is a time wherein a man ought to be careful of his speech, having before him God's good blessings to refresh his body and honest company to recreate his mind. Therefore, he ought to be no way offensive in his speech, either to God or good men. But most especially take heed that neither heedlessness nor earnestness in thy discourse cause thee to take God's holy name in vain, but always speak of Him with reverence and understanding. And I pray thee, as thou wouldest have blessings multiplied upon thee, let no speech pass from thee that may grieve chaste ears. How hateful is obscene speech in rude people! But it makes one of gentle birth offensive to all honest company. Solomon says, *"A prudent man concealeth knowledge: but the heart of fools proclaimeth foolishness"* (Prov. 12:23); and *"He that keepeth his mouth keepeth his life"* (Prov. 13:3); and, *"The lips of the wise shall preserve them"* (Prov. 14:3).

9. If thou keep thy thoughts holy and thy words pure, I shall not need to fear, but all thy actions will be honest. But my fear that thou shouldest know the way and yet go aside will not suffer my counsel to leave thee alone until thou come to thy journey's end.

First, then, be careful when thou art alone that thou do nothing that thou wouldest not do if men saw thee. Remember that God's eye is always open, and thine own conscience will be witness enough against thee. Next, be sure that no action of thine may be a scandal to thy profession, I mean to the profession of the true religion. This indeed is as much as to say to thee, *"Eschew[88] evil"* (1 Peter 3:11). For there is not the least sin thou canst do, but the enemies of truth will be glad to say, "Lo, this is one of them that professes God in his mouth, but see what his life is!" Therefore a great care ought a Christian to have, especially those whom God hath set as lights in His Church.

Whatsoever thou art about to do, examine it by God's commandments: if it be agreeable to them, go on cheerfully. And though the end answer not thy hopes, never grieve nor grudge, but be glad that God's will is performed. Let thy trust in Him assure thee that all things work together for the best to them that love God (Rom. 8:28).

The next vice too, too common in this age is drunkenness, which is the highway to hell. A man may travel in it from sin to sin until the devil shew him he can go no further—as a traveler from inn to inn until he comes to his journey's end. Oh, think how filthy is that sin that makes a man a beast all his life and a devil at his death! Solomon asks, *"Who hath woe? who hath sorrow? who hath contentions? who hath babbling? who hath wounds without cause? who hath redness of eyes?"* (Prov. 23:29). And in the next verse he answers, *"They that tarry long at the wine"* (Prov. 23:30). And to the end of the chapter, he sets forth the miseries occasioned by this vice.

That thou mayest avoid this sin, be careful in the choice of thy friends; for it is they that will betray thee to this sin. Never make choice of a drunkard as thy companion, much less thy friend. To be a drunkard is to be a man unfit for God's service or good men's company. I beseech God give thee grace to detest it.

Next, I must exhort thee from a sin that I cannot name: thou must search thine own heart for it. It is *thy darling sin*: to enjoy it, thou couldest resist all others—at least thou thinkest so. But do not harbor it: search diligently for it in thine own nature; and when thou hast found it, cast it headlong from thee. It is thy soul's subtle betrayer, and all thy other sins depend upon it.

---

88 **eschew** – avoid; keep clear of.

There is not so much danger in all the rest that thou contendest with, as in this one that thou art unwilling to call a sin.

10. When thou hast spent the day in religious and honest exercises, in the evening return again to some good meditation or study. Conclude with prayer, commending thyself to God; so shalt thou joyfully go to thy supper. When this is done and the time of rest comes, as thou beganest in the morning, so close the day with humble thanksgiving for all the benefits that day received and hearty repentance for all thy sins committed, naming and bewailing them. The oftener thou dost settle thy accounts with God, thy sleep will be sounder; and thou shalt awake with a heart full of joy, ready to serve the Lord.

Last, commit thyself and all that is thine to God in zealous prayer, using Doctor Smith's evening prayer, as his morning. Though both be for a family, yet are they easily reduced to a private man's prayer. So going to bed, take thy rest, beginning and ending in Him Who is both First and Last (Isa. 44:6; 48:12; Rev. 1:11, 17; 22:13). Thus spend the six days thou hast to labor in that thou mayest be ready to celebrate the Sabbath, to which there belongs another "Remember" (Ex. 20:8).

11. Remember that thou keep holy the Sabbath day. This duty so often and earnestly commanded by God Himself in the Old Testament, so confirmed to us in the New by the resurrection of our Savior, in memory whereof it is called the Lord's Day and perpetually celebrated by the Church, yet in these days, too many keep no Sabbath (or at the most but a shadow of a Sabbath), as if we neither had part in the creation nor redemption of the world. Where can we find someone that will lose a good bargain rather than make it on the Lord's Day? Or that will bridle his own desires to sanctify that day?

Seeing therefore this danger, in which thou mayest easily be entrapped by the devil's subtlety and following the multitude, I cannot but with all my power exhort thee, carefully to keep the Lord's Day. To which end I pray thee, mark well the Fourth Commandment: *"Remember the sabbath day, to keep it holy. Six days shalt thou labour, and do all thy work: But the seventh day is the sabbath of the LORD thy God: in it thou shalt not do any work, thou, nor thy son, nor thy daughter, thy manservant, nor thy maidservant, nor thy cattle, nor thy stranger that is within thy gates: For in six days the LORD made heaven and earth, the sea, and all that in them is, and rested the seventh day: wherefore the LORD blessed the sabbath day, and hallowed it"* (Ex. 20:8-11). If thou wilt learn how to serve Him as a good scholar, He teaches thee an admirable way, both by rule and example. First, by *rule*: Thou shalt do no manner of work in it. Then by *example*: He made the whole world in six days, and He rested the seventh; wherefore, He blessed it.

Seeing God thus commands thee by His power, persuades thee in His mercy, and teaches thee both by rule and His own most gracious example, how canst thou be so devoid of grace, nay of reason, as not to obey so just a *Master*? So merciful a *Father*? So gracious a *Teacher*? If thou make not a conscience[89] of keeping this day, howsoever a dull security may possess thee to flatter thyself, thou indeed makest conscience of nothing. For I am persuaded, if thou canst dispense with thyself to profane this day, either for thy profit or pleasure, thou wilt not stick upon[90] the like occasion to break all the rest of the Commandments, one after another.

Therefore, for Christ's sake, be watchful that the devil deceives you not; neither let his agents draw thee away from this day's duty. He is *always* busy and ready at hand to draw thee away from God, but this day, without doubt, he doubles all his forces. He will provoke thine eyes to sleep; he will send heaviness and dullness to thy heart and, perhaps, pain to thy body, if he can so much prevail. He will surely use any sleight, any trick to keep thee from God's house and from the congregation of His people. It behooves thee by how much greater his practices are against thee that day, so much the more to fortify thyself against him. By no means, let him stay thee from the church! There, God hath promised to be present, and *there He is*. Darest thou then, silly wretch, to absent thyself from Him? I know thou darest not. Go then with a heart prepared to pray by prayer; and going, meditate on God's great mercies in the creation of the world, His greater mercy in redeeming it, and mingle with thy meditation prayers that may apply these great blessings to thyself.

So approach and enter with reverent and fervent zeal the house of God! And throwing away all thoughts, except those that may further the good work thou art about, bend thy knees and heart to God, desiring of Him His Holy Spirit that thou mayest join with the congregation in zealous prayer and earnest attention to His Word preached. Though perhaps thou hearest a minister preach weakly, as thou thinkest, yet give him thine attention; and thou shalt find that he will deliver something profitable to thy soul, either something thou hast not heard before or not marked or forgotten or well put in practice. It is fit thou shouldest be often put in mind of those things concerning thy salvation…Learn then to prepare thy heart early for this day, which if thou observest well, God will bless thee and thy labors all the week. Thus far I have endeavored to exhort thee to thy duty towards God.

---

89 **make not a conscience** – make it not a matter of conscience.
90 **stick upon** – hesitate.

12. Of which the honor due to thy parents is such a part as cannot be separated, for God commands it: *"Honour thy father and thy mother"* (Ex. 20:12). It is the first commandment of the Second Table, as *"Thou shalt have no other gods before me"* (Ex. 20:3) is of the First. Idolatry being the greatest sin against God and disobedience to parents being the ringleader in sins against man, we are first warned of them, as if in case we should fall into them, it were too late to avoid the other. For if we once become idolaters in heart, it will be no hard matter to bow down to an image, to abuse God's holy name, or to profane His Sabbath. So if we dare disobey good parents, at that breaking of God's Law, theft, murder, adultery, falseness, covetousness easily enter.

(13) The next duty equal to this is one thou must perform to all the world in general: *"All things whatsoever ye would that men should do to you, do ye even so to them"* (Matt. 7:12). This is the commandment our Savior gives us: *"Love one another."* By this we shall be known to be His, if we love one another as He hath loved us (John 13:34-35). Yet of all that is commanded us, there is *nothing* more contrary to our wicked nature than this loving our neighbor as ourselves. We can with ease envy him, if he be rich, or scorn him, if he be poor—*but love him?* Nay, the devil hath more craft than so. It is hard for him if men should once begin to love one another; therefore he useth all art to stir dissension among as many as he can and to mix love with dissimulation.[91]

To avoid this, consider well that God is the author of peace and love and that strife and contention proceed of the devil. Then if thou art the child of God, do the works of God: love thy neighbor as He hath commanded, lest thou provoke our blessed Savior when He shall see that mark of the devil—*malice*—in thee and say as He once did to the unbelieving Jews, *"Ye are of your father the devil, and the lusts of your father ye will do"* (John 8:44).

Oh, take heed thou offend not God thus grievously that He shall disclaim thee as none of His because thou dost not love those that are His. This, if well weighed, is enough to make every man charitable, if it were only for fear to hate whom God loved. But to believe or judge that God should hate where thou doest is such an impious uncharitableness[92] as a good Christian must needs tremble at. God hath given thee no authority to judge any man, but He hath commanded thee to love thine enemy: *"Love your enemies, bless them that curse you, do good to them that hate you, and pray for them which despitefully use you, and persecute you; that ye may be the children of your Father which is in heaven"* (Matt. 5:44-45). *Sine fine finis.*[93]

---

91 **dissimulation** – hypocrisy.
92 **impious uncharitableness** – ungodly lack of Christian love.
93 ***Sine fine finis*** – *Latin* = end without end.

Chapter 7—Motherhood: The Mother's Legacy to Her Unborn Child

From *The Mother's Legacy to Her Unborn Child*, in the public domain.

Elizabeth Brooke Joscelin (c. 1595-1622): Granddaughter of Anglican theologian and bishop, William Chaderton (1540?-1608); born in Cheshire, England.

What is a child but a piece of yourself wrapt up in another skin?
—John Flavel

Loving, Wise Chastening

RICHARD ADAMS (C. 1626-1698)

Fathers, provoke not your children to anger, lest they be discouraged.
—Colossians 3:21

Correction in a due manner and suitable rewards for well-doing are necessary to check[94] rudeness and encourage an ingenuous deportment.[95] As good documents do put in wisdom, so due corrections do drive out folly. A child is not to be left to himself, lest he bring the parent to shame: a rod and reproof may give wisdom to prevent it (Prov. 29:15). Therefore, God bids, *"Correct thy son, and he shall give thee rest; yea, he shall give delight unto thy soul"* (Prov. 29:17). Elsewhere: *"Withhold not correction from the child: for if thou beatest*[96] *him with the rod, he shall not die. Thou shalt beat him with the rod, and shalt deliver his soul from hell"* (Prov. 23:13-14). Here is not only a [general command], but a promise of good fruit upon discharge of the duty in a right manner; but it should be sued-out[97] by prayer because the neglect of this duty is very dangerous to root and branch, parent and child (2 Sam. 7:27-28; 1 Sam. 3:13; 1 Kings 1:6). Yea, and the greater need there is of parents' prayer here, lest they should fall into the extreme that my text emphatically forbids. Christian parents, whose children are to *"obey them in the Lord,"* are concerned to chastise in the fear of God and therefore to seek that this appointment of His may be sanctified, being joined with instruction; that it may be [effective] by the blessing of God in Christ (1 Tim. 4:5; Mic. 6:9)…And here, further, parents are concerned to use much Christian prudence that their children may understand,

First: That they are, from *a principle of love* for their children's amendment and welfare, necessitated to this sharp work that God hath enjoined them in just circumstances, as He Himself chasteneth whom he loveth (Rev. 3:19; Heb. 12:6–8; Deut. 8:5). Therefore, if they should spare the rod through fondness,[98] God, Who knows the heart and affections best, might censure[99] them for hating their children (Prov. 13:24; 3:12)… Hence,

---

94 **check** – stop.
95 **ingenuous deportment** – honorable manners.
96 **beatest** – the idea here is not savage or brutal beating with fists or clubs, but rather the strokes of a rod: "The sage is not talking about a rigorous beating, but rather something equivalent to a spanking. This may be surmised from the matter-of-fact statement 'They will not die' as well as this book's general emphasis on moderation, kindness, and gentleness." (Tremper Longman III, *Proverbs,* Baker Academic, 426)
97 **sued-out** – to make application before a court for the grant of a legal process; therefore, to cry out to the Judge of heaven and earth in prayer that discipline would be effective.
98 **fondness** – foolish affection; unreasoning tenderness.
99 **censure** – to find fault with and condemn as wrong.

SECONDLY: That it is their children's folly, *not their own passion*, which hath engaged them in this smarting exercise. Overmuch heat would be like an over-hot medicine that scalds rather than cures. Some parents are apt to go beyond just measures and to chastise for their own pleasure; but they must learn of God to aim at their children's profit and not correct them *but upon good reason* (Heb. 12:10)…Parents should not take the rod to vent their own anger, but to subdue their children's sin, which a man may not suffer upon his neighbor without rebuke, lest he be guilty of hating him in his heart (Lev. 19:17). Certainly then, [he should not suffer sin] upon his child, whom he is obliged, not only to admonish verbally, but to chastise really.

THIRDLY: But first he should do as God did with our first parents: convict him of his nakedness (Gen. 3:11–13), that is, show him the evil of his lying, railing, idleness, or other faults [that] he is chargeable with, as opposite to the Word of God and prejudicial to his own soul (Prov. 12:22; 8:36) and that he is made to smart for the cure of this evil. Parents may let their children know they dare not suffer [this evil] to remain longer uncorrected, since delays may prove dangerous to the patient if the rod be withheld. The festering wound may rankle[100] and come to a gangrene, if not lanced in due time. A *mother's* love is seen in chastening *"betimes,"*[101] both in respect of the age of the child and of its fault (Prov. 23:13; 13:24). If it is not too soon for children to sin, it should not be thought too soon for parents to correct [promptly], before the sin grows strong, gets head, and sprouts forth. The child should be taken *"while there is hope"* (Prov. 19:18). The twig may be bent whilst it is young, and the sin mortified if nipped in the bud. God, we find, hath been very severe in [pointing out] the first violations of His statutes, as for gathering sticks on the Sabbath Day and Aaron's sons' offering strange fire (Num. 15:25; Lev. 10:2). So parents should timely curb the first exorbitances[102] of their children. Hence,

FOURTHLY: They should let them see they are resolved, after serious deliberation, not to be diverted by the [whining] and [bad temper] of their unhumbled children from inflicting due punishment, since the wise man chargeth, *"Let not thy soul spare for his crying"* (Prov. 19:18), so that they may not remain fearless. Yet it must then be in compassion that they may conceive, as the Father of heaven is afflicted in the affliction of His, so are they in the affliction of their children. And as the Lord doth it *"in measure,"* though He will not suffer them to go unpunished, so do they (Isa. 63:9; Jer. 30:11).

---

100 **rankle…gangrene** – infect surrounding parts causing the death and rotting of body tissue.
101 **betimes** – early.
102 **exorbitances** – misconduct; departures from the right path.

My text [limits] the correction so that it may not exceed a just proportion to the discouraging of children, whose different tempers, as well as different faults, are to be considered, so as no more be laid upon them than they are able to bear (1 Cor. 10:13). There should therefore be a special care taken that the chastisement be no other than what is [appropriate]. Physicians endeavor to apportion the dose [that] they give to the strength of the patient and the peccant humor[103] they would correct. There must be a rational consideration of the age, sex, and disposition of the child, the nature and circumstances of the fault, and what satisfaction is offered by the delinquent upon ingenuous confession, or possibly some interposition of another; so that the offended parent may keep-up his authority, be victorious in his chastisements, and come off with honor and good hopes of the child's amendment. For a parent should be ever ready to forgive and to connive[104] often at smaller failings—wherein there is no manifest sin against God—in confidence of gaining the child's affections, by tenderness and kind forbearance, toward the things that are most desirable…Be sure, our apostle, both in my text, and to the Ephesians, is altogether against any discouraging chastisement and requires moderation.

From "What Are the Duties of Parents and Children; and How Are They to Be Managed According to Scripture?" in *Puritan Sermons,* Vol. 2, (Wheaton, IL: Richard Owen Roberts, Publishers, 1981), 303-304.

Richard Adams (c. 1626-1698): English Presbyterian minister; born at Worrall, England.

"The greatest moral power in the world is that which a mother exercises over her young child." —Adolphe Monod

---

103 **peccant humor** – diseased conditions.
104 **connive** – shut one's eyes to an action that ought to be opposed, but that one sympathizes with.

A Mother's Encouragement

JAMES CAMERON (1809-1873)

Perhaps in no department of Christian exertion are influences of a depressing kind more numerous than in that which you, as mothers, occupy. But, blessed be God, there is an exhaustless fund of all you need for your encouragement and support. Permit me to direct your attention, first of all, to the encouraging fact, that

The work in which you are engaged is directly and pre-eminently the work of God. The great end for which the created universe was called into being and for which it is upheld from age to age is the *manifestation of the divine glory*. In all that God does or permits to be done, He is actuated by a regard to this. All agencies—angelic and human, rational and irrational, animate and inanimate—are made to subserve[105] in all their actions this great design. The tendency of all the apparently involved working of the whole machinery of the universe, whether moral or physical, is to produce motion in this one direction. In the salvation of fallen man by the remedial provisions of the gospel, this great end is especially promoted—for *"by the Church"* is made known, even *"unto the principalities and powers in heavenly places...the manifold wisdom of God"* (Eph. 3:10).

And by what instrumentality is a redeemed Church to be raised up from amongst the sinful children of men? By the instrumentality of those who have themselves, by the grace of God, been delivered from the guilt and the power of sin and made *"[vessels] unto honour, sanctified, and meet for the master's use"* (2 Tim. 2:21). By means of human agency, the multitude that no man can number is to be gathered home to the Redeemer's fold. And you are they whom God has appointed to train up those who are to embark in this glorious enterprise! To you is committed the task of molding and fashioning the human agencies by which God's great purpose of glorifying Himself forever in the sight of all intelligent beings is to be accomplished! In your hands are the leaders of the public sentiment of the next generation—the Luthers, the Knoxes,...the Whitefields, the Wilberforces of a future age. They are in your hands; and through them, you wield the destinies of millions yet unborn. I have already spoken of the awful responsibility of such a situation; but there is another light in which, likewise, I would have you view it.

Consider how honorable a situation it is to have the most important part of the work of God committed to you! Consider how near it brings you to

---

105 **subserve** – serve as a means of furthering.

God: to have the training, not merely of his soldiers, but of those who are to officer his armies and lead them on to glorious, yet bloodless victory. You occupy the highest, the noblest, and the most honorable position in which a human being can be placed. Murmur not that you are excluded from camps, cabinets, and senates; yours is a higher vocation. You are directly engaged in that work that has employed the tongues, the pens, the labors, the hearts, of the world's best and wisest in every age—the work for which the goodly fellowship of the prophets lived, for which the glorious company of the apostles labored, for which the noble army of martyrs died. To witness the progress of this work, angels stoop from their exalted thrones and watch with intensest interest the unfolding of every plan, the development of every principle, and the accomplishment of every event that bears upon it.

For the furtherance of this work, the Son of the Highest left the throne of heaven and became a wanderer on earth,[106] submitting to the reproach and scorn of men, to the anguish and ignominy[107] of the cross. For this, also, the divine Spirit is sent forth from the Father and the Son. In short, this is the work, for the furtherance of which the noblest energies in heaven and earth have been and are continually put forth. Compared with it, the fleeting interests of time dwindle into a speck. But how is it that we derive from such considerations matter of encouragement? Very obviously, as for instance, thus: If you are engaged in a work that God has more at heart (if we may so speak) than aught else in the universe because thereby His own glory is most abundantly manifested, can you for a moment suppose that He will leave you to toil in that work unnoticed and uncared for? Such a supposition is alike impious[108] and absurd. To admit it would be to impeach the divine wisdom, as well as the divine goodness. In immediate connection, then, with the consideration that it is the work of God in which you are engaged, consider in the second place

That God is always willing to grant you the strength and wisdom you need for the successful discharge of your important duties. On the throne of grace He ever sits, ready to dispense blessings, countless and rich, to all who ask. Never is His ear turned away from the cry of the needy suppliant.[109] What an inexhaustible fund of encouragement does this truth present! At what time your heart is overwhelmed, look to the Rock that is

---

106 See FGB 219, *The Person of Christ*
107 **ignominy** – public disgrace; dishonor.
108 **impious** – disrespectful; irreverent toward God.
109 **suppliant** – one who humbly prays.

higher than you (Ps. 61:2). In the confidence of filial[110] love, cast your burden upon the Lord, assured that He will sustain you. He cannot disappoint the expectations that His own Word teaches you to cherish. He will be your Instructor, your Counsellor, your Guide, your Comforter, your Refuge, your Fortress, your Sun, and your Shield. Do you feel that you lack[111] strength? *Go to God.* He is the Almighty One in Whom all strength dwells. Do you feel that you lack wisdom? *Go to God.* He is *"the only wise God"* (1 Tim. 1:17); and of His wisdom, *"[He] giveth to all men liberally, and upbraideth not"* (James 1:5). Do you feel that you lack patience? *Go to God.* He is *"the God of patience"* (Rom. 15:5). Do you feel that you are in danger of fainting by the way? *Go to God.* *"He giveth power to the faint; and to them that have no might he increaseth strength"* (Isa. 40:29). In short, do you feel bowed down under a sense of insufficiency and unworthiness? *Go to God.* Your sufficiency is of Him (2 Cor. 3:5). *"God is able to make all grace abound toward you; that ye, always having all sufficiency in all things, may abound to every good work"* (2 Cor. 9:8). In all generations, He has been the dwelling-place of His people, a refuge in the day of distress, a stay and support in the time of trouble.

Listen to the sweet strains of the sweet singer of Israel, who had often tried God's faithfulness to His promises: *"O magnify the LORD with me, and let us exalt his name together. I sought the LORD, and he heard me, and delivered me from all my fears. They looked unto him, and were lightened: and their faces were not ashamed. This poor man cried, and the LORD heard him, and saved him out of all his troubles. The angel of the LORD encampeth round about them that fear him, and delivereth them. O taste and see that the LORD is good: blessed is the man that trusteth in him"* (Ps. 34:3-8). You may derive much encouragement from the fact that thousands of Christian mothers have tried the faithfulness of God to His promise and have had the happiness of witnessing the success of their labors in the conversion of their offspring. The history of the Church of God is full of instances in point. Let us look at one or two.

The case of Augustine[112]…is a striking one. He was one of the brightest ornaments of Christianity in the latter part of the fourth and the beginning of the fifth century. But up to his twenty-eighth year, he lived in sin. From his remarkable *Confessions*,[113] written by him after his conversion, we learn that he broke loose from every restraint and gave himself up *"to work all*

---

110 **filial**– having the relationship of a child to a parent.
111 The original word *want* has been replaced with *lack*.
112 **Aurelius Augustine** (354-430) – Bishop of Hippo Regius in North Africa and theologian.
113 **Confessions** – in the modern sense of the term, Augustine's *Confessions*, written between 397 and 401 A.D., was the first autobiography ever written. It's most famous line is "Our hearts are restless until they find their rest in You."

uncleanness with greediness" (Eph. 4:19). He had, however, a pious mother; and amidst all his wanderings, her tears and prayers came up for a memorial before God. At length, her cry was heard and the answer came. From her son's own lips, she one day received the glad tidings of his conversion to God; and the voice of lamentation was changed into the song of praise. Not long after, as they were journeying together, she said, "My son, what have I to do here any longer? The only thing for which I wished to live was your conversion, and that the Lord has now granted me in an abundant manner." Five days after, she was seized with a fever, which, in a few days more, wafted her spirit into that blissful region where all tears are forever wiped away. And the son, for whom she had shed so many tears and breathed so many prayers, lived to be the admiration of his age and the means of the conversion of thousands of his fellowmen.

That eminent servant of Christ, John Newton,[114] was the son of a praying mother! Even at the worst period of his life, profane and dissolute[115] as he was, the influence of the pious counsels that he received in childhood was never obliterated. He has himself left it on record that in the midst of the most daring wickedness, the remembrance of his mother's prayers haunted him continually. At times, these impressions were so vivid that "he could almost feel his mother's soft hand resting on his head, as when she used to kneel beside him in early boyhood and plead for God's blessing on his soul." There is no reason to doubt that these impressions, received in childhood and retaining their hold of the spirit in [later] life, were among the principal means by which he was arrested in his career of sin and made a zealous and successful propagator of the gospel that he had so long despised…

A faithful and zealous minister of Christ gives the following account of himself in writing to a friend: "…Ah! Sir, you know but little of my obligations to almighty grace and redeeming love. I look back with dismay and horror to the time when I led the van[116] in wickedness…Even now my heart bleeds at the thought of the nights when, mad with intoxication, I have returned to my tender mother between two and three o'clock, burst open the window, poured out a torrent of abuse, and sunk upon the bed, a monster of iniquity. Next morning, I have been aroused by a mournful voice, smothered with heavy sobs and tears. I have listened; and to my inexpressible astonishment, found it was my mother pouring out her soul in

---

114 **John Newton** (1725-1807) – Anglican minister, author of *Amazing Grace* and numerous other hymns.
115 **dissolute** – overindulging in sensual pleasures.
116 **van** – the foremost position of a company of persons moving forward.

this language: 'O Lord, Oh mercy, mercy, mercy, mercy upon my poor child. Lord, I will not, cannot give him up—he is still my child. Surely he is not yet out of the reach of mercy. O Lord, hear, hear, I beseech thee, a mother's prayers. Spare, oh spare, for Christ's sake, the son of her old age. *"O my son Absalom, O Absalom, my son, my son!"* (2 Sam. 19:4). Yes! Precious mother, thy prayers are now answered; and thy child—thy worthless, guilty child—still lives a monument of boundless grace and incomprehensible mercy"…Let one more fact suffice. It is one that speaks volumes in proof of our position. An inquiry was instituted in the United States in six theological seminaries, belonging to three different denominations of Christians, by which it was ascertained that of 507 students who were being educated for the ministry, no fewer than 428 were children of praying mothers.

Christian mothers! Be of good courage! You are surrounded with a great cloud of witnesses—witnesses to the faithfulness of God's promise, witnesses to the power of believing prayer, witnesses to the efficacy of sound religious instruction. Go forward in your work with holy confidence. Great and many, indeed, are your difficulties, but greater is He that is for you than all that can be against you! *"Trust ye in the LORD for ever: for in the LORD JEHOVAH is everlasting strength"* (Isa. 26:4). In due time you shall reap if you faint not (Gal. 6:9). May the Lord grant you grace to be faithful, and may you at last have the unspeakable happiness of entering, along with all who have been committed to your care, into the heavenly holy place, there to celebrate forever the praise of redeeming love and to serve God day and night without ceasing.

From *Three Lectures to Christian Mothers*.

James Cameron (1809-1873): Scottish Congregational minister; born in Gourock, Firth of Clyde, Scotland.

A Gospel Call to Mothers

JAMES CAMERON (1809-1873)

> *Look unto me, and be ye saved, all the ends of the earth: for I am God, and there is none else.* —Isaiah 45:22

I have addressed these [articles] to Christian mothers; but as they may possibly be perused by some who are not Christians, I feel that I cannot allow them to go to press without adding a few words to all who may read them and who have not the Spirit of God witnessing with their spirits that they are the children of God (Rom. 8:16). Reader! *Are you a child of God?* Do not answer the question hastily. Thousands imagine they are, who will find at last that they have been mistaken. The Word of God teaches us that men may not only live deceived, but die deceived—flattering themselves that all is well and never discovering their mistake until they open their eyes in the place of woe.[117] Oh! Think it not strange, therefore, that we urge upon you the inquiry, "Are you a child of God?" Ponder the solemn question. Keep it before you. And remember that you are not a child of God unless you have been changed in heart and life by the belief of the truth as it is in Jesus (Eph. 4:21).

What, then, is the state of your heart? Is it supremely set on the trifles, the vanities, the pursuits of the present life? Or is it set on *"those things which are above, where Christ sitteth on the right hand of God"* (Col. 3:1)? Is it the abode of unholy passions? Or is it a temple of the Holy Ghost, filled with peace, love, and holy joy? What is the state of your life?

Are you living after the sight of your own eyes, *"according to the course of this world"* (Eph. 2:2)? Or are you adorning the doctrines of God the Savior by a conversation becoming the gospel—bringing forth the fruit of righteousness and keeping yourself unspotted from the world (James 1:27)? Oh! *Be not deceived!* If you have not been changed in heart and life, you are *not* a child of God. And until you are thus changed by [believing] the truth, you are in *"the gall of bitterness, and in the bond of iniquity"* (Acts 8:23). Your external observance of the forms of religion cannot save you. Your amiable dispositions[118] cannot save you. Your worldly morality cannot save you. Your deeds of beneficence cannot save you. With all these, you may find heaven's gate shut against you and *"the gall of bitterness, and in the bond of iniquity"* (Acts 8:23). Do you hesitate to believe this? Do you say, "This is a hard saying!"?Ah! Reader! If it were my saying merely, it would be a small

---

117 See FGB 211, *Hell*
118 **amiable dispositions** – friendly, pleasant qualities.

matter; but it is the saying of Him by Whom you are to be judged: *"Except a man be born again, he cannot see the kingdom of God"* (John 3:3).

These are the words of *"the faithful and true witness"* (Rev. 3:14), and sooner shall heaven and earth pass away than one word of His fall to the ground. Oh! Put not away from you the solemn impression that these words are fitted to produce by saying that God is merciful, and perhaps after all He may allow you to escape. I know, and rejoice to know, that God is merciful—*infinitely merciful*. Were He not so, you and I had, long ere now, been shut up in the prison house of despair, without one ray of hope to enlighten the blackness of darkness. But I know, likewise, that God is true, as well as merciful, and that His mercy can never be exercised in such a manner as to destroy His truth. His mercy, infinite though it be, cannot be exercised towards those who put away from them *"the word of the truth of the gospel"* (Col. 1:5); for this would be to falsify His own express declaration. His mercy is now exhibited to you in His Word. His mercy has provided an atonement[119] for sin, by which you may *now* be saved! His mercy is setting before you this atonement as the ground of hope. But if you *"neglect so great salvation"* (Heb. 2:3), then when the axe is laid to the root of the tree and you are cut down, His mercy—so far as you are concerned—will forever cease. You will be left to experience the fearful effect of mercy despised and justice executed. Do you inquire, *"What must I do to be saved?"* (Acts 16:30). Blessed be God, the answer is at hand: *"Believe on the Lord Jesus Christ, and thou shalt be saved"* (Acts 16:31)...The Lord hath Himself provided a Lamb for an offering. He *"hath laid on him the iniquity of us all"* (Isa. 53:6). *"He was wounded for our transgressions, he was bruised for our iniquities"* (Isa. 53:5). *"Behold,"* therefore, *"the Lamb of God, which taketh away the sin of the world"* (John 1:29). Come unto the Father, through the Son, and you will in no wise be cast out (John 6:37).

The [only] work by which you can be saved has been already accomplished! Jesus hath finished transgression, made an end of sins, and brought in everlasting righteousness (Dan. 9:24)! He hath opened up the way of access for you to the mercy seat of God; and now you may behold the God Whom you have offended sitting on that mercy seat, dispensing pardon and life. You may hear His gracious voice [calling]—yea, beseeching and entreating you to come unto Him that your soul may live (Matt. 11:28-30).

Cast your soul, all guilty as it is, on the finished work of Immanuel (Isa. 7:14), and you will not be rejected. Think not that you have something to do in order to commend yourself to His favor, before you can believe on *"him*

---

119 See FGB 227, *Atonement*

that justifieth[120] *the ungodly"* (Rom. 4:5). Make no attempt to render yourself worthy of acceptance. Bring no price in your hand. God will not make merchandise of the blessings of salvation. He will give eternal life freely, as God; or He will not give it at all. And you must receive it freely, as a sinner guilty and condemned, having no claim upon God; or you will not receive it at all. Are not these His own gracious words? *"Ho, every one that thirsteth, come ye to the waters, and he that hath no money; come ye, buy, and eat; yea, come, buy wine and milk without money and without price"* (Isa. 55:1). Inquire no longer, then, *"Wherewith shall I come before the LORD"* (Mic. 6:6), for *"The word is nigh thee, even in thy mouth, and in thy heart: that is, the word of faith, which we preach; that if thou shalt confess with thy mouth the Lord Jesus, and shalt believe in thine heart that God hath raised him from the dead, thou shalt be saved. For with the heart man believeth unto righteousness; and with the mouth confession is made unto salvation"* (Rom. 10:8-10).

From *Three Lectures to Christian Mothers*.

James Cameron (1809-1873): Scottish Congregational minister; born in Gourock, Firth of Clyde, Scotland.

> *The mother of Jesus had a very firm and practical faith in her Son, concerning whom angels and prophets had borne witness to her. She had seen Him in His infancy and watched Him as a child; and it could not have been easy to believe in the divinity of one whom you have held as an infant to be nourished at your breast. From His marvelous birth, she believed in Him.* —Charles Haddon Spurgeon

> *I remember [Augustine] writes of his mother Monica that she planted the precepts of life in his mind by her words, watered them with her tears, and nourished them with her example. A precious pattern for all mothers.* —John Flavel

---

120 **justifieth** – declares righteous; "Justification is an act of God's free grace, wherein he pardons all our sins and accepts us as righteous in His sight only for the righteousness of Christ imputed to us and received by faith alone." (*Spurgeon's Catechism*, Q. 32) See FGB 187, *Justification*, and FGB 191, *Imputed Righteousness*.

Church and Motherhood

CHARLES HADDON SPURGEON (1834-1892)

The Church of God in Scripture is called a mother. What is a mother's business? What is a mother's duty? A mother's duty is to feed her own child from her own bosom. She loses a joy herself and inflicts a serious injury upon her offspring when, if having the ability, she lacks the affection that would constrain her to support her own child from the fountains that God Himself hath opened. And as the Church of Christ is a mother, she shall lack the greatest joy and lose the sweetest privilege, unless she herself trains her own children and gives them the unadulterated milk of the Word.[121] She has no right to put her children out to nurse. How shall they love her? What affection shall they bear towards her?...It is a mother's business as that child grows up to train and teach it. Let her teach it the first letters of the alphabet; let it gather its first knowledge of Christ from a mother's lips. Who so fit to teach as she that brought it forth? None can teach so sweetly and none so effectually as she. Let her not give up the training of her child to another. And why should we, the Church of Christ, give up our children when we first taught them to speak in Christ's name, to be trained and to be taught by others? No, by every motherly feeling that remains within the bosom of Christ's Church, let us see her children brought up at her own knees, dandled there in her own lap, and not give up the work of training her sons and daughters to others. And who so fit as the mother of the family to inspire her son with holy ardor, when at last he goes forward to the battle of life? Who shall give him the affectionate advice? Who shall give him the cheering word that shall sustain him in the hour of difficulty, so well as a mother whom he loves? And let the Church of God, when her young men go forth to her battles, put her hand upon their shoulders and say, "Be strong, young man, be strong; dishonor not the mother that bare you; but go forth and, like the son of a Spartan mother, return not but in glory…Come back on your shield or with it—a hero or a martyr." Who can speak the words so well and sing at home so powerfully, as the mother to her son or the Church to her child? The Church, then, has no right to delegate to another her own work. Let her bring forth her own children; let her give them nourishment; let her train them up; let her send them forth to do the Master's work.

Charles Haddon Spurgeon (1834-1892): English Baptist minister; history's most widely read preacher (apart from those found in Scripture); born at Kelvedon, Essex.

---

121 Spurgeon is primarily speaking of the local church training its men for gospel ministry; but he also includes general principles that apply to all the members of a church as well.

Chapter 8
CHILDBEARING

What does the Bible teach about childbearing? Are there commands or godly practices that are displayed in the Bible? How does the God of the Bible speak about them? The answers to these questions are critical for our times, since the Bible does have a perspective on babies. We may debate whether men and women have the freedom before God to restrain fertility, but one can hardly debate the fact that the Bible presents one single, consistent, and unqualified message which is summed up in the words, *"be fruitful and multiply"* (Gen. 1:28). It is obvious that it pleases God to convey His image in mankind through men and women bearing children. Children are blessings as Thomas Manton pointed out in his article forthcoming: "They are a great blessing in themselves, and the more of them, the greater blessing." These words may sound strange to modern ears, but they faithfully convey a biblical worldview.

On the other hand, what do people in our culture think of babies? Most people think that although babies are cute, it is necessary for us to minimize their number and control their impact. Indeed, some people have such a low view of the life of a baby that they see no problem killing it in its mother's womb, all in the name of expediency or sexual freedom. This is one reason why, birthrates are plunging and nations all over the world are struggling to sustain their societies. Why is this? The rationale varies—overpopulation, expense, stress, limitation, fear of pain, or even the loss of a shapely figure. Many people love their serenity, time, money, vanity and pleasure more than they love babies. As a result of this shift in thinking, our world culture has mainstreamed a number of ways to marginalize and even destroy them. We abort millions worldwide each year. We avoid them through birth control. We legitimize their removal from the care of their mothers and send them into day care centers. Why do we do this? Primarily because we have turned our back on what God says about childbearing. This chapter calls us back to biblical thinking.

—Scott Brown

God's Image and God's Blessing

JOHN CALVIN (1509-1564)

> *"And God said, Let us make man in our image, after our likeness: and let them have dominion over the fish of the sea, and over the fowl of the air, and over the cattle, and over all the earth, and over every creeping thing that creepeth upon the earth. So God created man in his own image, in the image of God created he him; male and female created he them. And God blessed them, and God said unto them, Be fruitful, and multiply, and replenish the earth, and subdue it: and have dominion over the fish of the sea, and over the fowl of the air, and over every living thing that moveth upon the earth."*
> —Genesis 1:26-28

Man is a creature noble above all others and has in himself worth that exceeds all visible creatures. That is why God deliberates when He prepares to create him. It is true that the angels are above us because they enjoy the presence of God. And their position is more honorable than we can imagine because they are God's messengers. They are even ministers of His power and the governance that He exercises in this world. But of all things above and below, nothing approaches man.

That is why the philosophers have also called him "a little world." If you wish to ponder what is in men, you will find so many wondrous things that it would be like taking a tour of the whole world. It is noteworthy, then, that God begins to consult at this point; not that He encounters problems, but He does so in order to express better the infinite kindness He wanted to extend to us. Therefore, if Moses had simply stated that God finally created man, we would not be so moved or touched by knowing His grace, such as He has revealed it in His nature. But when God compares man to an excellent and singular work and engages counsel as if He were thinking about a matter of great importance, we must be touched even more deeply by knowing that *man* is where God wanted His glory to shine. Otherwise, why is it important that we differ from brute beasts? Is it a part of our substance? We have been taken from the ground. Like oxen, asses, and dogs, our origin is all the same. How is it that we come by a status so high that we approach our God, that we have the capacity to reason and understand, and then have lordship over all? Where does that come from, except that it pleased God to set us apart? Now that difference is pointed out to us when God declares [that] He wishes to make a major work that is greater than everything else He had done. Although the sun and the moon are such noble creatures that they appear to be divine, although the heavens also have an appearance that astonishes and delights men, although the great diversity of fruits and other things that we see here on earth are designed to declare unto us a divine majesty, the fact remains that if we compare all of that with man, we will find in man much grander and more exquisite[1] features…

At this point, we could ask, "With whom does God consult?"…The Father was the sovereign cause and source of all things, and He here enters into consultation with His wisdom and His power…Our Lord Jesus Christ is the everlasting Wisdom that resides in God and has always had His essence in Him. He is one of the Trinity! The Holy Spirit is God's Power. Things will flow very well if we say that the Person of the Father is introduced here because we have the starting point for talking about God when He says, "Let us make man in our image and likeness"…When it is said here that man is to be created in the image of God, after His likeness, it is to declare that there are to be in him such powers and gifts that they serve as signs and imprints to show that the human race is like God's lineage,[2] as Paul proves with the Gentile poet's saying in the seventeenth chapter of Acts: *"For we are also his offspring"* (Acts 17:28)…

We must now understand wherein lie that image and that resemblance or that likeness and conformity with God. Is it in the body or in the soul, or is it in this lordship that has been given to men? Many are they who relate this to the body. In truth, there is such creative skill manifested in the form of the human body that one can say it is *an* image of God, for if His majesty appears in every part of the world, greater is the reason that it should appear in what is much more exquisite. But the fact is that we will not find such perfection in the human body as the image and conformity Moses speaks of. Far from it!

Consequently, neither the hair nor the eyes, the feet nor the hands will lead us to where Moses is guiding us. As for the superiority and the pre-eminence that have been given to man above all creatures, those human features do not convey the image of God, for those are external features that will not lead us very high. Yet for all that, we must come to the *soul*, which is the most worthy and precious part of man. Although God has displayed the great treasures of His power, goodness, and wisdom in forming us, yet the soul, as I have said, has reason, understanding, and will, which is much more than anything to be found in this external body.

---

1 **exquisite** – extremely beautiful, so as to excite delight or admiration; brought to a high degree of perfection.
2 **lineage** – descendant of a specified ancestor.

Now, since the point that the image of God is principally in the soul and extends to the body as an accessory has been exhausted and resolved, we must now consider what the image of God consists of and in what respect we conform to it and are like it…

Our father Adam, being alienated from his Creator, was given over to shame and ignominy,[3] and God stripped him of the excellent gifts with which He had previously adorned him…But because God repairs His image in us through our Lord Jesus Christ, that image which had been effaced in Adam, we can better understand the import of that conformity and likeness that man had in the beginning with God. For when Paul says in Colossians 3 that we must be renewed according to the image of the One Who created us (Col. 3:10), and then in Ephesians 4, when he mentions righteousness and true holiness as the characteristics to which we must be conformed (Eph. 4:24), he shows that the image of God is important: that our souls as well as our bodies must be guided by a certain uprightness and that there is nothing in us that approaches the righteousness of God. It is true that Paul does not give a complete enumeration[4] there, and then he does not speak in general terms either, in order to include everything that testifies to the image of God. But when speaking of the principal characteristics, he tells us what the accessory characteristics are.

In short, the soul must be cleansed of all vanity and all falsehood and God's clarity must shine in it so that there will be a capacity for judgment, discretion, and prudence. That is why God repairs His image in us when He conforms us to His righteousness and renews us by His Holy Spirit so that we can walk in a holy manner. Because that is true, we see at what point we must begin if we want to determine what the image of God is. Such is the beginning of God's image in us, but that is not all there is…When mention is made of the image of God in man and we are blind to the cause of the confusion caused by sin, we must note those passages of Paul and at the same time find in Jesus Christ that which is no longer in us because we have been deprived of it through the ingratitude of our father Adam. Then we will see that man was created in such purity and integrity of nature that his soul possessed a wondrous prudence and was not shrouded in falsehood, hypocrisy, and ignorance, as we see now that there is in us only vanity and darkness. Consequently, there was a sincere longing to obey God and take pleasure in everything good, wherein were no unwholesome desires that urge us to evil, for all our affections are acts of rebellion against God. Then

---

3 **ignominy** – disgrace.
4 **enumeration** – numbered list.

the body was so well and appropriately balanced that every small segment was ready and prompt to serve and honor Him. Such was man, disposed to walk in holiness and in all righteousness. In him was such an array of divine gifts that God's glory would shine everywhere, within and without. That, then, characterizes that image...

Moses adds, *"So God created man in his own image, in the image of God created he him."* That repetition is not superfluous, for if we assembled all the fine words in the world to adorn that excellent work of God, it would be impossible to come close...Moses had good reason to want to give us an opportunity to consider more attentively the fact that we were created in the image of God. If we consider our bodies, they are formed from the earth... with the intention of making [them] a dwelling place for His good favor and the gifts of His Holy Spirit so that we would bear His image. That then is the intention of Moses' repetition. It is so we will be able to glorify our God often for being generous with us and ranking us among His creatures and even giving us superiority over them, but also for imprinting His marks on us and wanting us to be His children...

Now it is said that male and female were created. And Moses sometimes speaks here using the plural number and sometimes using the singular to refer to both sexes, as when he says, *"Let us make man in our image,"* then adds, *"Let them have dominion."* Now we could say that the men who come from Adam will have dominion, but so as not to exclude women, he adds "male and female," and that they were so created. At this point, we could contrast Paul's passage where he says that man alone, not woman, is the image of God (1 Cor. 11:7) and think that there was some contradiction. But the answer is very easy to come by because Moses is speaking here of the gifts that were communicated to both sexes. Now there is reason and understanding in the man as well as in the woman. There is *will*; there is the ability to discriminate between good and evil. In brief, everything that belongs to the image of God...It is noteworthy that it is said in other passages that there is in our Lord Jesus Christ neither male nor female (Gal. 3:28). That means that His grace extends to the man and the woman so that we all become sharers in that grace. Since we have resolved that point beyond contradiction, we can see that man was created not as male only, but also as female, and that both have borne the image of God...

Then the text speaks of the *blessing* God gave Adam. He first says to him and his wife, *"Be fruitful, and multiply, and replenish the earth,"* and then adds, secondly, *"Have dominion over the fish of the sea, and over the fowl of the air, and over every living thing that moveth upon the earth."* The first blessing is the same for humans, animals, fish, and birds. They are to multiply by generation.[5] Now we have already stated that man is not to attribute his origin to some inferior cause of nature, but he must have a Creator. Why so? *Because we are all the products of His blessing!* That is why Scripture often tells us that the fruit of the womb is a compensation from God, that is, *a special gift* (cf. Ps. 127:3) so that we will not be so brutish[6] as to think that the man begets by his power and the woman conceives and that God is not the author of their lineage.

So we must take note of God's blessing here spoken of, for [we see in Gen. 30:2] that Jacob said to his wife Rachel, when she was importuning[7] him to give her a child, *"Am I in God's stead?"* herein he shows that men are not to speak this way, but that God must be glorified since He grants them the grace to be *fathers* and the women to be *mothers*…This, then, is the result of that blessing: that we will know that God declared at the beginning that He wanted the human race to multiply and that, in our day and time, when He provides a lineage and children, it is a special blessing He bestows on fathers and mothers and a treasure they must acknowledge as being from Him and for which they must pay Him homage.

In addition, let us understand that sin produces the inequality we see in the fact that all men will not always father children, that all children emerging from a mother's womb will not always be alike, that there will be some who are already feeble and headed for the grave, and that some will even be bent, one-eyed, blind, hunchbacked, and crippled. God shows in all that is disfigured and deformed that His blessing is diminished, even though it is not completely extinguished. We will even see women often abort.[8] What is the reason? Adam's sin is given as the reason so that we will lower our eyes in the realization that we are rejected and cast far from the grace that was conferred upon us by God at the first creation. With regard to God's blessing, this is what we are to observe: by virtue of that word that He spoke once and for all, children are born now, the world is sustained in this way, and generations succeed one another from age to age.

In addition, this blessing carries with it a much greater privilege than the beasts have; for the oxen, asses, and dogs will beget young, as will the wolves and all the rest. But do their offspring enjoy the same dignity as man's? Therefore, when God gives men and women offspring, He establishes

---

5 **generation** – producing children; begetting offspring.
6 **brutish** – stupid.
7 **importuning** – harassing with troublesome insistence.
8 **abort** – suffer miscarriage.

Chapter 8—Childbearing: God's Image and God's Blessing

them as His lieutenants;[9] for a man cannot be a father unless he is there as one representing the Person of God. There is only one Father, properly speaking, as our Lord Jesus Christ said (Matt. 23:9). And that is understood to mean Father of both souls and bodies. That very honorable title, therefore, belongs only to our Creator. That is, He is our Father, yet we are permitted to say "my father" and "my mother" in this world, though that results from God's gift whereby He is pleased to share His title with creatures as frail as we. Therefore, let us know that the privilege God gives those who produce a posterity[10] is that He wanted to make them His lieutenants, as it were. Therefore, we ought to prize and magnify His grace all the more…

Now, that being the case, Moses rightly proposes the second blessing, which had previously been given by God to the world, I mean, among creatures. Until man was brought forth, there were plants and pasturage; there were lights in the heaven. But even though the sun is called the guide by day and the moon the guide by night, they are not said to *rule*, properly speaking. In fact, it is impossible for them to do so. For what good would it have done the earth with the many good things provided on it if there had not been someone to possess them? So Adam had to be created to live on it, and he had to have God's grace to produce a lineage and in this way be multiplied.

John Calvin, *Sermons on Genesis chapters 1-11* (Edinburgh: The Banner of Truth Trust, 2009) © 2009, used by permission. www.banneroftruth.org

---

John Calvin (1509-1564): French theologian, pastor, and important leader during the Protestant Reformation; born in Noyon, Picardie, France.

---

9 **lieutenants** – persons representing or performing the work of a superior.
10 **posterity** – descendants.

Be Fruitful and Multiply

MARTIN LUTHER (1483-1546)

> *And God blessed them, and God said unto them, Be fruitful, and multiply, and replenish the earth, and subdue it.* —Genesis 1:28

This is a command of God added for the creature. But, good God, what has been lost for us here through sin! How blessed was that state of man in which the begetting of offspring was linked with the highest respect and wisdom, indeed with the knowledge of God! Now the flesh is so overwhelmed by the leprosy of lust that in the act of procreation[11] the body becomes downright brutish and cannot beget in the knowledge of God.

Thus, the power of procreation remained in the human race, but very much debased[12] and even completely overwhelmed by the leprosy of lust, so that procreation is only slightly more moderate than that of the brutes. Added to this are the perils of pregnancy and of birth, the difficulty of feeding the offspring, and other endless evils, all of which point out to us the enormity of original sin.[13] Therefore, the blessing, which remains until now in nature, is, as it were, a cursed and debased blessing if you compare it with that first one. Nevertheless, God established it and preserves it.

So let us gratefully acknowledge this "marred blessing." And let us keep in mind that the unavoidable leprosy of the flesh,[14] which is nothing but disobedience and loathsomeness attached to bodies and minds, is the punishment of sin. Moreover, let us wait in hope for the death of this flesh that we may be set free from these loathsome conditions and may be restored even beyond the point of that first creation of Adam…

Although Adam had fallen because of his sin, he had the promise…that

---

11 **procreation** – the activity of conceiving and bearing children.
12 **debased** – ruined in character.
13 **originalsin** – Original sin, in its full extent, is the guilt of Adam's first sin, the want [*lack*] of original righteousness, and the corruption of the whole nature. All and every one of Adam's natural raceare born or conceived in it: Rom. 5:12, "By one man sin entered into the world, and death by sin; and so death passed upon all men, for that all have sinned." Ps. 51:5, "Behold, I was shapen in iniquity; and in sin did my mother conceive me." It is derived to us from Adam, the original of mankind, Rom. 5:12 forecited. And it is conveyed to us by natural generation: Job 14:4, "Who can bring a clean thing out of an unclean? not one." Ps. 51:5 forecited. Even holy parents convey it to their children because they procreate their children after their own natural image: Gen. 5:3, "And Adam begat a son in his own likeness, after his image; and called his name Seth." Now, our natural state is a sinful state, in respect of original sin; inasmuch as original sin, being a fountain of sin, remains entire in its guilt, filth, and power on every man as long as he is in that state. (Thomas Boston, *Works*, Vol. 7, 9)
14 **leprosy of the flesh** – the destructive power of lust.

from his flesh, which had become subject to death, there should be born for him a shoot of life. So he understood that he was to produce offspring, especially since the blessing, *"Be fruitful, and multiply"* (Gen. 1:28), had not been withdrawn, but had been reaffirmed in the promise of the Seed, Who would crush the serpent's head (Gen. 3:15). Accordingly, in our judgment, Adam did not know his Eve simply because of the passion of his flesh; but the need of achieving salvation through the blessed Seed impelled him too.

Therefore, no one should take offense at the mention of the fact that Adam knew his wife Eve. Although original sin has made this work of procreation, which owes its origin to God, something shameful at which we see pure ears taking offense, nevertheless, spiritually-minded men should make a distinction between original sin and the product of creation. The work of procreation is something *good* and *holy* that God has created; for it comes from God, Who bestows His blessing on it.[15] Moreover, if man had not fallen, it would have been a very pure and very honorable work. Just as no one has misgivings about conversing, eating, or drinking with his wife—for all these are honorable actions—so also the act of begetting would have been something most highly regarded.

So, then, procreation remained in nature when it had become depraved; but there was added to it that poison of the devil, namely, the prurience[16] of the flesh and the execrable[17] lust that is also the cause of sundry adversities and sins, all of which nature in its unimpaired state would have been spared. We know from experience the excessive desire of the flesh; and, for many, not even marriage is an adequate remedy. If it were, there would not be the occurrences of adultery and fornication that, alas, are only too frequent. Even among married people themselves, how manifold are the ways in which the weakness of the flesh displays itself! All this stems, not from what was created or from the blessing, which is from God, but from sin and the curse, which is the outgrowth of sin. Therefore, they must be kept separate from God's creation, which is good; and we see that the Holy Spirit has no misgivings about speaking of it.

---

15 This blessing of God may be regarded as the source from which the human race has flowed. And we must so consider it not only with reference to the whole, but also, as they say, in every particular instance. For we are fruitful or barren in respect of offspring, as God imparts His power to some and withholds it from others. But here Moses would simply declare that Adam with his wife was formed for the production of offspring, in order that men might replenish the earth. (John Calvin, *Commentary on the First Book of Moses Called Genesis*, 97-98)
16 **prurience** – having an excessive interest in sexual matters.
17 **execrable** – detestable; deserving to be cursed.

Not only is there no disgrace in what Moses is saying here about God's creation and His blessing, but it was also necessary for him to impart this teaching and to write it down because of future heresies, such as those of the Nicolaitans,[18] Tatian,[19] etc., but especially because of the papacy. We see that the papists are in no way impressed by what is written above (Gen. 1:27): *"In the image of God created he him; male and female created he them."* The way they live and the way they bind and obligate themselves by vows, it seems that they regard themselves as neither male nor female. It makes no impression on them that it is written above: The Lord brought Eve to Adam, and Adam said, *"This is now bone from my bones"* (cf. Gen. 2:22–23). The promise and the blessing make no impression: *"Be fruitful, and multiply"* (Gen. 1:28). The Ten Commandments make no impression on them: *"Honour thy father and thy mother"* (Ex. 20:12). Their own origin makes no impression on them, namely, that they were born as the result of the union of a man and a woman! Passing over, disregarding, and casting aside all these considerations, they force their priests, monks, and nuns into perpetual celibacy,[20] as if the life of married people, of which Moses is speaking here, were detestable and reprehensible.

But the Holy Spirit has a purer mouth and purer eyes than the pope does. For this reason, He has no misgivings about referring to the…union of husband and wife, which those [Catholic scholars] condemn as execrable and unclean. Nor does the Holy Spirit do this in only one passage. All Scripture is full of such accounts, so that on this score, too, some have restrained young monks and nuns from reading the holy books. What need is there of saying more? Such was the devil's raging against holy matrimony, God's creation, that the papists compelled men to forswear married life…One should, therefore, guard against those doctrines of demons (1 Tim. 4:1) and learn to hold matrimony in honor and to speak with respect of this way of life. For we see that God instituted it, and we hear it praised in the Ten Commandments, where it is stated: *"Honour thy father and thy mother"* (Ex. 20:12). And to this is added the blessing, *"Be fruitful, and multiply"* (Gen. 1:28). About this, we hear the Holy Spirit speaking here, and His mouth is chaste. But the vices and the ignominy,[21] which through sin became attached to what God had created, we should not ridicule or laugh at; but we should cover them, just as we

---

18 **Nicolaitans** – followers of a deviant form of Christianity in Asia Minor, who were sharply condemned by John in his letters to Ephesus (Rev. 2:6) and Pergamum (2:15) and who apparently practiced immorality and eating food sacrificed to idols.
19 **Tatian** – founder of the Encratites, a group who practiced an ascetic mode of life, including permanent abstinence from eating meat, drinking wine, and marriage.
20 **celibacy** – singleness; unmarried life.
21 **ignominy** – disgrace; shame.

see God cover naked Adam and Eve with garments after their sin. Marriage should be treated with honor; from it, we all originate because it is a nursery not only for the state but also for the church and the kingdom of Christ until the end of the world.

The heathen and other godless men do not understand this glory of marriage. They merely compile the weaknesses that exist both in the life of married people and in the female sex. They separate the unclean from the clean in such a manner that they retain the unclean, but what is clean they do not see. In this manner also, some godless jurists[22] pass a wicked judgment on this very book of Genesis and say that it contains nothing but the lewd activities of the Jews. If, in addition to this, there is contempt of marriage and an impure celibacy, are not these men worthy of being exposed to the crimes and punishments of the people of Sodom? But let us disregard these men, and let us hear Moses.

It is not enough for the Holy Spirit to state, *"Adam knew Eve"*; but He also adds, *"his wife"* (Gen. 4:1). For He does not approve of dissolute licentiousness[23] and promiscuous cohabitation.[24] He wants each one to live content with his *own* wife. Although the intimate relationship of married people is in no respect as pure as it would have been in the state of innocence, nevertheless, in the midst of that weakness brought on by lust and of all the rest of our misery, God's blessing persists. This is written here, not because of Adam and Eve (for they had long since been reduced to ashes when these words were written by Moses), but because of ourselves, so that those who cannot contain themselves might live content with their own Eve and might not touch other women.

The expression "he knew his wife" is unique to Hebrew, for Latin and Greek do not express themselves in this way. However, it is a very apt expression, not only because of its chasteness and modesty, but also because of its specific meaning; for the [Hebrew verb] has a wider scope than "to know" has among us. It denotes not only abstract knowledge but, so to speak, feeling and experience. For example, when Job says of the ungodly, "They will know what it is to act contrary to God," he wants to say, "They will experience and feel it."[25] So also Psalm 51:3: *"For I [know] my transgressions."* that is, "I feel and experience it." Likewise Genesis 22:12: *"Now I know that thou fearest God,"* that is, "I have learned the fact and have experienced it."

---

22 **jurists** – experts in or writers on law.
23 **dissolute licentiousness** – unrestrained indulgence in sensual pleasure.
24 **promiscuous cohabitation** – living unmarried with various sexual partners.
25 Apparently either Job 9:5 or Job 19:29 is meant here.

So also Luke 1:34: *"Seeing I know not a man."* Mary indeed knew many men, but she had experienced and felt no man. In this manner, Adam, in this passage, knew Eve, his wife—not objectively or speculatively, but he actually experienced his Eve as a woman.

The addition *"and she conceived, and bare Cain"* (Gen. 4:1) is a sure indication of a better physical condition than there is today. For at that time there were not so many ineffective cohabitations as there are in this declining world; but when Eve was known only once by Adam, she immediately became pregnant.

Here the question arises why Moses says, "She bore Cain," and not rather, as below, *"She bare a son, and called his name Seth."* Yet Cain and Abel were also sons. Why, then, are they not called sons? The answer is that this happens because of their descendants. Abel, who was slain by his brother, perished physically; but Cain perished spiritually through his sin, and he did not propagate that nursery of the Church and of the kingdom of Christ. All his posterity perished in the Flood. Therefore, neither blessed Abel nor cursed Cain has the name of son; but it was Seth from whose descendants Christ, the promised Seed, would be born.

Luther's Works Vol. 1 © 1958, 1986 Concordia Publishing House. Used with permission. www.cph.org.

Martin Luther (1483-1546): German monk, former Roman Catholic priest, theologian, and influential leader of the sixteenth century Protestant Reformation; born in Eisleben, Saxony.

> *In the propagation of the human race, [God's] special benediction is conspicuous; and, therefore, the birth of every child is rightly deemed the effect of divine visitation. —Martin Luther*

The Heritage of the Lord
THOMAS MANTON (1620-1677)

> *Lo, children are an heritage of the LORD: and the fruit of the womb is his reward.* —Psalm 127:3

IN the words [above], children are represented as a *blessing*, in which are two things: (1) The author from whom children come: the Lord. (2) The quality in which we receive this blessing, set forth by a double notion: (1) as *"an heritage"*; (2) as *"his reward."*

The word *heritage* is often, by a Hebraism, put for "a man's portion," be it good or bad. It is used in a bad sense, as in Job 20:29: *"This is the portion of a wicked man from God, and the heritage appointed unto him by God."* In the good sense, Isaiah 54:17: *"This is the heritage of the servants of the LORD."* Reward is put for any gift that cometh by promise or with respect unto obedience because in a promise there is a contract implied: if we will do so and so, God will do so and so for us.

DOCTRINE: It is a blessing that we have from God—and so it should be accounted—that we have children born of our loins. It is not only a bare gift: so it is to the wicked; but [it is] a *blessing*, one of the temporal[26] mercies of the covenant: *"Blessed is every one that feareth the LORD; that walketh in his ways"* (Ps. 128:1). One of the blessings is verse 3: *"Thy wife shall be as a fruitful vine by the sides of thine house: thy children like olive plants round about thy table."* This is a part of our portion and heritage. The saints have so acknowledged it: *"Who are those with thee? And he said, The children which God hath graciously given thy servant"* (Gen. 33:5). Jacob speaketh like a father, and like a godly father. Not only given, but *graciously* given. As a father, he acknowledged it a gift—as a godly father, coming from mere grace.

This may be gathered from the story of Job. Compare 1:2-3 with 1:18-19. Observe, when his blessings are reckoned up, first his numerous issue[27] is mentioned before his great estate. The chief part of a man's wealth and prosperity *is his children*—the choicest of outward blessings…But observe again, in the 18th and 19th verses, the loss of children is mentioned as the *greatest* affliction…

1. There is much of God's providence exercised in and about children.

a. In giving strength to conceive. It is not everyone's mercy. Sarah obtained it by faith: *"Through faith also Sara herself received strength to conceive seed"* (Heb. 11:11). Though bringing forth children be according to

---

26 **temporal** – pertaining to the present life as distinguished from a future existence.
27 **issue** – offspring; children.

the course of nature, yet God hath a great hand in it. Many godly [couples] have been denied the benefit of children and need other promises to make up that want: *"For thus saith the LORD unto the eunuchs that keep my sabbaths, and choose the things that please me, and take hold of my covenant; even unto them will I give in mine house and within my walls a place and a name better than of sons and of daughters: I will give them an everlasting name, that shall not be cut off"* (Isa. 56:4-5).

b. In framing the child in the womb. It is not the parents, but God. The parents cannot tell whether it be male or female, beautiful or deformed.[28] They know not the number of the veins and arteries, bones and muscles. *"For thou hast possessed my reins: thou hast covered me in my mother's womb. I will praise thee; for I am fearfully and wonderfully made: marvellous are thy works; and that my soul knoweth right well. My substance was not hid from thee, when I was made in secret, and curiously wrought in the lowest parts of the earth. Thine eyes did see my substance, yet being unperfect; and in thy book all my members were written, which in continuance were fashioned, when as yet there was none of them"* (Ps. 139:13-16)…

c. In giving strength to bring forth. The heathens had a goddess that presided over this work. [Yet, God's] providence reacheth to the beasts. It is by the Lord that hinds do calve: *"The voice of the LORD maketh the hinds to calve"* (Ps. 29:9). And there is a promise to them that fear Him: *"She shall be saved in child-bearing, if they continue in faith and charity and holiness with sobriety"* (1 Tim. 2:15). It must be understood, as all temporal promises are, with the exception of His will. But thus much we gather: it is a blessing that falleth under the care of His providence, and that by promise, so far as God seeth fit to make it good. Rachel died in this case; every godly woman hath not this deliverance. So did Phinehas' wife (1 Sam. 4:20). God might have taken this advantage against you, to have cut you off. If deliverance were not so ordinary, it would be accounted miraculous. The sorrows and pains of travail are a monument of God's displeasure: *"Unto the woman he said, I will greatly multiply thy sorrow and thy conception; in sorrow thou shalt bring forth children; and thy desire shall be to thy husband, and he shall rule over thee"* (Gen. 3:16). To preserve a weak vessel in great danger, women's pains are more grievous than the females of any kind. And for the child, a sentence of death waylaid it as it was coming into the world.

d. The circumstances of deliverance. In every birth, there are some new circumstances to awaken our stupid thoughts to consider the work of God.

---

28 Modern science now permits us to know the sex or health of our babies before birth.

For God doth all His works with some variety, lest we should be cloyed[29] with the commonness of them.

2. They are a great blessing in themselves, and the more of them the greater blessing. Therefore, they should be acknowledged and improved as *blessings*. Certainly, there is a more special favor showed us in our relations than in our possessions: *"House and riches are the inheritance of fathers: and a prudent wife is from the LORD"* (Prov. 19:14). So for children. By them, the parent is continued and multiplied: they are a part of himself; and in them, he liveth when he is dead and gone. It is a shadow of eternity; therefore, the outward appurtenances[30] of life are not as valuable as children are. Besides, they are capable of the image of God. By them the world is replenished, the Church multiplied, a people continued, [in order] to know, love, and serve God, when we are dead and gone. We read of [Wisdom] *"rejoicing in the habitable part of his earth; and my delights were with the sons of men"* (Prov. 8:31). In the habitable parts of the world, there are great whales; but men were Christ's delight. Especially to God's confederates—*parents in covenant with God*—are children a greater mercy. David was such a one. [We read of] *"thy sons and thy daughters, whom thou hast borne unto me"* (Ezek. 16:20). These are…in a most proper sense, a heritage from the Lord. It is said, *"The sons of God saw the daughters of men that they were fair; and they took them wives of all which they chose"* (Gen. 6:2). [Shem] begat sons and daughters to God: "Unto Shem also, the father of all the children of Eber, the brother of Japheth the elder, even to him were children born" (Gen. 10:21)…

God hath implanted affection in parents to their children: He hath a Son Himself, and He knoweth how He loveth Him, and He loveth Him for His holiness. "Thou hast loved righteousness, and hated iniquity; therefore God, even thy God, hath anointed thee with the oil of gladness above thy fellows" (Heb. 1:9). So many times, in a condescension to good parents, He bestoweth [the privilege of having] godly children. To a minister, those whom he converts to God are his glory, his joy, and his crown of rejoicing at the day of the Lord (cf. 1 Thess. 2:19-20). To those whom we have been a means to bring into the world: if they are in the covenant of grace, it is a greater blessing than to see them monarchs of the world…

USE 1: To reprove those who are not thankful for children, but do grudge and look upon it as a burden, when God blesseth them with a numerous issue. These murmur at that which is in itself a *mercy*. When we [lack] them, we value them; when we are full of children, we are full of distrust and murmuring. It

---

29 **cloyed** – filled to excess.
30 **appurtenances** – belongings.

was counted an *honor* to be a father in Israel. Surely, those that fear God should not count a happiness to be a burden! *"Thy wife shall be as a fruitful vine by the sides of thine house: thy children like olive plants round about thy table. Behold, that thus shall the man be blessed that feareth the LORD"* (Ps. 128:3-4)…

USE 2: Reproof to those who do not acknowledge and improve this mercy. Surely, parents should acknowledge God in *every* child given to them. Much of His providence is seen in giving and withholding children. We have songs of thanksgiving very frequent in Scripture upon this occasion. It is a thing wherein God will have His bounty taken notice of by solemn praises; and for *every* child, God should have a new honor from you!…Oh! It will be a great happiness to be parents to such as shall be heirs of glory! As children ought to be looked upon as a great mercy, so also as a great trust, which as it is managed may occasion much joy or much grief. If parents dote[31] upon them, they make them idols, not servants of the Lord. If they neglect education, they will surely prove crosses and curses to them, or if they taint them by their example.

USE 3: To exhort parents to bring up their children for God. For if they be a heritage *from* the Lord, they must be a heritage *to* the Lord. Give them up to Him again, as you had them from Him at first; for whatever is from Him must be improved for Him. Dedicate them to God, educate them for God,[32] and He will take possession of them in due time…Now, if the dedication be sound, it will engage you to a serious education. God dealeth with us as Pharaoh's daughter did with Moses' mother: *"Take this child away, and nurse it for me"* (Ex. 2:9).

MOTIVE 1: The express charge of God, Who hath made it your duty. *"Fathers…bring them up in the nurture and admonition of the Lord"* (Eph. 6:4). *"Thou shalt teach them diligently unto thy children, and shalt talk of them when thou sittest in thine house, and when thou walkest by the way, and when thou liest down, and when thou risest up"* (Deut. 6:7)…Now we should make conscience of these commands, as we will answer it to God [in the Day of Judgment].

MOTIVE 2: The example of the saints, who have been careful to discharge this trust. God presumeth it of Abraham: *"For I know him, that he will command his children and his household after him, and they shall keep the way of the LORD, to do justice and judgment; that the LORD may bring upon Abraham that which he hath spoken of him"* (Gen. 18:19)…Surely they are unworthy to have children that do not take care that Christ may have an interest in them.

---

31 **dote** – to bestow excessive love or fondness on.
32 This means instructing them in the faith, especially in family worship. *See* FGBs 188, *Family Worship* and 204, *Biblical Parenthood,* available from Chapel Library.

MOTIVE 3: The importance of this duty. Next to the preaching of the Word, the education of children is one of the greatest duties in the world; for the service of Christ, of the church, and state dependeth upon it. Families are the seminaries of church and commonwealth. Religion dwelt first in families; and as they grew into numerous societies, they grew into churches. As religion was first hatched there, so there the devil seeketh to crush it…

MOTIVE 4: To countermine Satan, who hath ever envied the succession of churches, and the growth and progress of Christ's kingdom. [He] therefore seeketh to crush it in the egg by seeking to pervert persons while they are young and, like wax, capable of any form and impression. As Pharaoh would destroy the Israelites by killing their young ones, so Satan, who hath a great spite at the kingdom of Christ, knoweth there is no such [comprehensive] way to subvert and overcome it as by perverting youth and supplanting family duties. He knoweth that this is a blow at the root. Therefore, what care should parents take to season children with holy principles that they may overcome the wicked one by the Word of God abiding in them!

From "Sermon upon Psalm cxxvii.3" in *The Works of Thomas Manton*, Vol. 18, Solid Ground Christian Books, used by permission: www.solid-ground-books.com.

Thomas Manton (1620-1677): Nonconformist Puritan preacher; born in Lawrence-Lydiat, county of Somerset, England.

Loving and Caring for Babies

J. R. MILLER (1840-1912)

God has so constituted us that in loving and caring for our own children the richest and best things in our natures are drawn out. Many of the deepest and most valuable lessons ever learned are read from the pages of unfolding child-life. We best understand the feelings and affections of God toward us when we bend over our own child and see in our human parenthood a faint image of the divine Fatherhood. Then in the culture of character there is no influence more potent than that which touches us when our children are laid in our arms. Their helplessness appeals to every principle of nobleness in our hearts. Their innocence exerts over us a purifying power. The thought of our responsibility for them exalts every faulty of our souls. In the very car which they exact they bring blessing to us. When old age comes very lonely is the home which has neither son nor daughter to return with grateful ministries, to bring solace[33] and comfort to the declining years!

It is a new marriage when the first-born enters the home. It draws the wedded lives together in a closeness they have never known before. It touches chords in their hearts that have lain silent until now. It calls out powers that have never been exercised before. Hitherto unsuspected beauties of character appear. The laughing, heedless girl of a year ago is transformed into a thoughtful woman. The careless, unsettled youth leaps into manly strength and into fixedness of character when he looks into the face of his own child and takes it in his bosom. New aims rise up before the young parents, new impulses begin to stir in their hearts. Life takes on at once a new and deeper meaning. The glimpse they have had into its solemn mystery sobers them. The laying in their hands of a new and sacred burden, an immortal life, to be guided and trained by them, brings to them a sense of responsibility that makes them thoughtful. Self is no longer the centre. There is a new object to live for, an object great enough to fill all their life and engross their highest powers. It is only when the children come that life becomes real, and that parents begin to learn to live. We talk about training our children, but they train us first, teaching us many a sacred lesson, stirring up in us many a slumbering gift and possibility, calling out many a hidden grace an disciplining our wayward powers into strong and harmonious character…

Our homes would be very cold and dreary without the children. Sometimes we weary of their noise. They certainly bring us a great deal of

---

33 **solace** – pleasure; enjoyment.

care and solicitude.³⁴ They cost us no end of toil. When they are very young they break our rest many a weary night with their colics³⁵ and teethings, and when they grow older they wellnigh break our hearts many a time with their waywardness. After they come to us we may as well bid farewell to living for self and to personal ease and independence, if we mean to do faithful duty as parents. There are some who therefore look upon the coming of children as a misfortune. They talk about them lightly as "responsibilities." They regard them as in the way of their pleasure. They see no blessing in them. But it is cold, selfishness that looks upon children in this way. Instead of being hindrances to true and noble living, they are helps. They bring benedictions³⁶ from heaven when they come, and while they stay they are perpetual benedictions…

When the children come what shall we do with them? What duties do we owe to them? How may we discharge our responsibility? What is the parents' part in making the home and the home-life? It is impossible to overstate the importance of these questions…It is a great thing to take these young and tender lives, rich with so many possibilities of beauty, of joy, of power, all of which may be wrecked, and to become responsible for their shaping and training and for the upbuilding³⁷ of their character. This is what must be thought of in the making of a home. It must be a home in which children will grow up for true and noble life, for God and for heaven. Upon the parents the chief responsibility rests. They are the builders of the home. From them it receives its character, whether good or evil. It will be just what they make it. If it be happy, they must be the authors of the happiness; if it be unhappy, the blame must rest with them. Its tone, its atmosphere, its spirit, its influence, it will take from them. They have the making of the home in their own hands, and God holds them responsible for it.

The responsibility rests upon both the parents. There are some fathers who seem to forget that any share of the burden and duty of making the home-life belongs to them. They leave it all to the mothers. They come and go as if they were scarcely more than boarders in their own house, with no active interest in the welfare of their children. They plead the demands of business as the excuse for their neglect. But where is the business that is so important as to justify a man's evasion of the sacred duties which he owes to his own family? There cannot be any other work in this world which

---

34 **solicitude** – feeling excessive concern.
35 **colics** – acute abdominal pain.
36 **benedictions** – blessings; favor.
37 **upbuilding** – development.

a man can do that will excuse him at God's bar for having neglected the care of his own home and the training of his own children. No success in any department of the world's work can possibly atone for failure here. No piling up of this world's treasures can compensate a man for the loss of those incomparable jewels of his own children.

In the prophet's parable he said to the king, "As thy servant was busy here and there he was gone" (1 Kings 20:40). May not this be the only plea that some fathers will have to offer when they stand before God without their children: "As I was busy here and there they were gone"? Men are busy in their worldly affairs, busy pressing their plans and ambitions to fulfillment, busy gathering money to lay up a fortune, busy chasing the world's honors and building up a name, busy in the quest for knowledge; and while they are busy their children grow up, and when they turn to see if they are getting on well they are gone. Then they try most earnestly to get them back again, but their intensest efforts avail not. It is too late then to do that blessed work for them and upon their lives which could so easily have been done in their tender years. Dr. Geikie's book, entitled *Life*,[38] opens with these words: "Some things God gives often: some he only gives once. The seasons return again and again, and the flowers change with the mouths, but youth comes twice to none." Childhood comes but once with its opportunities. Whatever is done to stamp it with beauty must be done quickly.

Then it matters not how capable, how wise, how devoted the mother may be; the fact that she does her part well does not free the father in any degree from his share of the responsibility. Duties cannot be transferred. No other one's faithfulness can excuse or atone for my unfaithfulness. Besides, it is a wrong and an unmanly thing for a strong, capable man, who claims to be the stronger vessel to seek to put off on a woman, whom he calls the weaker vessel, duties and responsibilities which clearly belong to himself. There is a certain sense in which the mother is the real home-maker. It is in her hands that the tender life is laid for its first impressions. In all its education and culture she comes the closer to it. Her spirit makes the home atmosphere. Yet from the end to end of the Scriptures the law of God makes the father the head of the household, and devolves[39] upon him as such the responsibility for the upbuilding of his home, the training of his children, the care of all the sacred interests of his family.

The fathers should awake to the fact that they have something to do in making the life of their own homes besides providing food and clothing and

---

38 Cunningham Geikie, *Life: A Book for Young Men*.
39 **devolves** – transfers.

paying taxes and bills. They owe to their homes the best influences of their lives. Whatever other duties press upon them, they should always find time to plan for the good of their own households. The very centre of every man's life should be his home. Instead of being to him a mere boarding-house where he eats and sleeps, and from which he start out in the mornings to his work, it ought to be the place where his heart is anchored, where his hopes gather, to which his thoughts turn a thousand times a day, for which he toils and struggles, and into which he brings always the richest and best things of his life. He should realize the he is responsible for the character and the influence of his home-life, and that if it should fail to be what it ought to be, the blame and guilt must lie upon his soul…Yet even in these Christian days men are found, men professing to be followers of Christ and to believe in the superiority of life itself to all things else, who give infinitely more thought and pains to the raising of cattle, the growing of crops, the building up of business, than to the training of their children. Something must be crowded out of every earnest, busy life. No one can do everything that comes to his hand. But it will be a fatal mistake if any father allows his duties to his home to be crowded out. They should rather have the first place. Anything else had better be neglected than his children. Even religious work in the kingdom of Christ at large must not interfere with one's religious work in the kingdom of Christ in his home. No man is required by the vows and the spirit of his consecration to keep other men's vineyards to faithfully that he cannot keep his own. That a man has been a devoted pastor or a diligent church officer…will not atone for the fact that he was an unfaithful father…

Something must be said concerning the training of children. It is to be kept in mind that the object of the home is to build up manhood and womanhood. This work of training belongs to the parents and cannot be transferred. It is a most delicate and responsible duty, one from which a thoughtful soul would shrink with awe and fear were it not for the assurance of divine help. Yet there are many parents who do not stop to think of the responsibility which is laid upon them when a little child enters their home.

Look at it a moment. What is so feeble, so helpless, so dependent, as a new-born babe? Yet look onward and see what a stretch of life lies before this feeble infant, away into the eternities. Think of the powers folded up in this helpless form, and what the possible outcome may be. Who can tell what skill there may be lying unconscious yet in these tiny fingers, what eloquence or song in these little lips, what intellectual faculties in this brain, what power of love or sympathy in this heart? The parents are to take this infant and nurse it into manhood and womanhood, to draw out these slumbering powers and teach it to use them. That is, God wants a man trained for a great mission in the world, and he puts into the hands of a young father and mother a little babe, and bids them nurse it and train it for him until the man is ready for his mission; or at least to have sole charge of his earliest years when the first impressions must be made, which shall mould and shape his whole career.

When we look at a little child and remember all this, what a dignity surrounds the work of caring for it! Does God give to angels any work grander than this?

Women sigh for fame. They would be sculptors, and chisel out of the cold stone forms of beauty to fill the world with admiration of their skill. Or they would be poets, to write songs to thrill a nation and to be sung around the world. But is any work in marble so great as hers who has an immortal life laid in her hands to shape for its destiny? Is the writing of any poem in musical lines so noble a work as the training of the powers of a human soul into harmony? Yet there are women who regard the duties and cares of womanhood as too obscure and commonplace tasks for their hands. So when a baby comes a nurse is hired, who for a weekly compensation agrees to take charge of the little one, that the mother may be free from such drudgery to devote herself to the nobler and worthier things that she finds to do.

Is the following indictment too strong?—"A mother will secure from the nearest intelligence-office a girl who undertakes to relieve her of the charge of her little one, and will hand over to this mere hireling, this ignorant stranger, the soul-mothering which God has entrusted to her. She has mothered the body—any one will do to mother the soul. So the little one is left in the hands of the hireling, placed under her constant influence, subjected to the subtle impress of her spirit, to draw into its inner being the life, be it what it may, of this uncultured soul. She wakens its first thoughts, rouses its earliest emotions, brings the delicate action of motivities to bear upon the will—generally in such hands a compound force of bullying and bribing, mean fear and mean desire—tends it, plays with it, lives with it; and thus the young mother is free to dress and drive, to visit and receive, to enjoy balls and operas, discharging her trust for an immortal life by proxy! Is there any malfeasance[40] in office, in these days of dishonor, like unto this? Our women crowd the churches to draw the inspiration of religion for their daily duties, and then prove recreant[41] to the first of all fidelities, the most solemn of all responsibilities…"[42]

---

40 **malfeasance** – wrongdoing; evil doing.
41 **recreant** – unfaithful to duties.
42 Richard H. Newton, *Motherhood: Lectures on Woman's Work in the World* (New York: G.P.

Oh that God would give every mother a vision of the glory and splendor of the work that is given to her when a babe is placed in her bosom to be nursed and trained! Could she have but one glimpse into the future of that life as it reaches on into eternity; could she look into its to see its possibilities; could she be made to understand her own personal responsibility for the training of this child, for the development of its life, and for its destiny, — she would see that in all God's world there is no other work so noble and so worthy of her best powers, and she would commit to no other hands the sacred and holy trust given to her…

What we want to do with our children is not merely control them and keep them in order, but to implant true principles deep in their hearts which shall rule their lives; to shape their character from within into Christlike beauty, and to make of them noble men and women, strong for battle and for duty. They are to be trained rather than governed. Growth of character, nor merely good behavior, is the object of all home governing and teaching…

But when a little child in a mother's bosom is loved, nursed, caressed, held close to her heart, prayed over, wept over, talked with, for days, weeks, months, years, it is no mere fancy to say that the mother's life has indeed passed into the child's soul. What it becomes is determined by what the mother is. The early years settle what its character will be, and these are the mother's years.

O mothers of young children, I bow before you in reverence. Your work is most holy. You are fashioning the destinies of immortal souls. The powers folded up in the little ones that you hushed to sleep in your bosoms last night are powers that shall exist for ever. You are preparing them for their immortal destiny and influence. Be faithful. Take up your sacred burden reverently. Be sure that your heart is pure and that your life is sweet and clean. The Persian apologue says that the lump of clay was fragrant because it had lain on a rose. Let your life be as the rose, and then your child as it lies upon your bosom will absorb the fragrance. If there is no sweetness in the rose the clay will not be perfumed.

History is full of illustrations of the power of parental influence. It either brightens or darkens the child's life to the close. It is either a benediction which makes every day better and happier, or it is a curse which leaves blight and sorrow on every hour. Thousands have been saved from drifting away by the holy memories of happy, godly homes, or, when they have drifted away, have been drawn back by the same charm of power. There are no chains so strong as the cords that a true home throws about the heart…

Putnam's Sons, 1894), 140-141.

When I think of the sacredness and the responsibility of parents, I do not see how any father and mother can look upon the little child that has been given to them and consider their duty to it, and not be driven to God by the very weight of the burden that rests upon them, to cry to him for help and wisdom. When an impenitent man bends over the cradle of his first-born, when he begins to realize that here is a soul which he must train, teach, fashion and guide through this world to God's bar, how can he longer stay away from God? Let him, as he bends over his child's crib to kiss its sweet lips, ask himself: "Am I true to my child while I shut God out of my own life? Am I able to meet this solemn responsibility of parenthood all alone, in my unaided human weakness, without divine help?" I know not how any father can honestly meet these questions as he looks upon his innocent, helpless child, given to him to shelter, to keep, to guide, and not fall instantly upon his knees and give himself to God.

J.R. Miller, *Homemaking* (Philadelphia: Presbyterian Board of Publication, 1882), 93-127.

J. R. Miller (1840-1912): Presbyterian pastor and gifted writer; Superintendent of the Presbyterian Board of Publication; born at Frankfort Springs, PA, USA.

God determines the numbers and names of every man's children.
—*Thomas Boston*

Saved in Childbearing

STEPHEN CHARNOCK (1628-1680)

> *Notwithstanding she shall be saved in child-bearing, if they continue in faith and charity and holiness with sobriety.* —1 Timothy 2:15

The fall of man was the fruit of the woman's first doctrine, and therefore she is not suffered to teach anymore (1 Tim. 2:12). The woman was deceived by the serpent, and so drew her husband and whole posterity into ruin (1 Tim. 2:13-14)…And because, upon this declaration of the apostle, some might be dejected by the consideration of the deep hand the woman had in the first fall [and] in the punishment inflicted upon them for it, the apostle in the text brings in a "notwithstanding" for their comfort.

Notwithstanding [Eve's] guilt in defection[43] [and] her punishment in childbearing, she hath as good a right to salvation as the man. So, by way of anticipation, the apostle here answers an objection that might be made: whether the guilt contracted by the woman and the punishment inflicted might not hinder her eternal salvation. The apostle answers, "No." Though [Eve] was first in the transgression and the pain of childbearing was the punishment of that first sin, yet the woman may arrive to everlasting salvation notwithstanding that pain, *if* she is adorned with those graces that are necessary for all Christians. Though the punishment remains, yet the believing woman is in the covenant of grace[44] [and] under the wings of the Mediator[45] of that covenant, if she has faith (*the condition of the covenant*), which works by love and charity and is attended with holiness and renewal of the heart.

Observe: God hath gracious cordials[46] to cheer up the hearts of believers in their distress, in the midst of those cases that are sufficient of themselves to cast them down. The apostle here alludes to that curse upon the woman: *"Unto the woman he said, I will greatly multiply thy sorrow and thy conception; in sorrow thou shalt bring forth children"* (Gen. 3:16). The punishment is peculiar to the married woman, besides that punishment that was common to her with the man.

---

43 **defection** – falling away from faith, i.e., eating the forbidden fruit (Gen 3:6).

44 **Covenant of Grace** – the outworking in time of God's eternal purpose of redemption in Christ, in which God promises life eternal to His elect, on the ground of Christ's merits, by faith in Him.

45 **Mediator** – a go-between; "It pleased God in His eternal purpose, to choose and ordain the Lord Jesus His only begotten Son, according to the Covenant made between them both, to be the Mediator between God and Man; the Prophet, Priest and King; Head and Savior of His Church, the heir of all things, and judge of the world: Unto whom He did from all Eternity give a people to be His seed, and to be by Him in time redeemed, called, justified, sanctified, and glorified." (1689 London Baptist Confession 8.1)

46 **cordials** – foods or medicines that comfort, gladden, or cheer the heart.

Thy sorrow and thy conception: Hendiadys,[47] say some: "the sorrow *of* thy conception." The word *conception* (Gen. 3:14) signifies the whole time of the woman's bearing in the womb. [It] includes not only those pains in the very time of labor, but also all those precursory indispositions,[48] [such as] the weakness of the stomach,[49] heaviness of the head, irregular longings, and those other symptoms that accompany conceptions. Though this pain seems to be natural from the constitution of the body, yet since some other creatures do bring forth with little or no pain,[50] it would not have been so with the woman in innocence because all pain, which is a punishment of sin, had not been incident[51] to a sinless and immortal body.

We will consider the words [individually]:

Saved: It may note either the salvation of the soul or the preservation of the woman in childbearing. The first, I suppose, is principally intended. For the apostle here would signify some special comfort to women under that curse.

But the preservation of women in childbearing was a common thing, testified by daily experience in the worst as well as in the best women. Christianity did not bring the professors of it into a worse estate in those things that immediately depended upon God…yet a temporal preservation may be included. For when an eternal salvation is promised, temporal salvation is also promised, according to the methods of God's wisdom and goodness in the course of His providence. There [is] in all such promises a tacit reserve,[52] viz.,[53] if God sees it good for us and the manner of their preservation also, wherein the preservation of a believer differs from that of an unregenerate person. Others are preserved by God, as a merciful Creator and Governor in a way of common providence for the keeping up of the world. But believers are preserved in the way of promise and covenant, in the exercise of faith and by the special love of God as a tender Father, and their God in covenant with them through Christ.

In childbearing: *diateknagonias*,[54] "through childbearing." The preposition *through* is often taken for *in*, as Romans 4:11: *"that he might be the*

---

47 **hendiadys** – a figure of speech in which two words, joined by *and*, express a single idea; for example "nice and warm," instead of a noun and a modifier, "nicely warm."
48 **precursory indispositions** – the bodily conditions and ailments that precede giving birth.
49 **weakness of the stomach** – nausea.
50 Aristotle (384-322 BC), *The History of Animals*, I.vii.c.ix.
51 **incident** – likely to happen.
52 **tacit reserve** – unspoken exception.
53 **viz.** – abbreviation for Latin *videlicet*: that is; namely.
54 Διὰτεκνογονίας

father of all them that believe, though they be [dia] not circumcised"—"believing in uncircumcision," where it notes the state wherein they shall be saved. So it notes here, not the *cause* of the salvation of the woman, but the *state* wherein she shall be saved. [It] amounts to this much: the punishment inflicted upon the woman for her first sin shall not be removed in this life; yet notwithstanding this, there is a certain way of salvation by faith, [even] though she passes through this punishment. For by "childbearing" is not meant a simple childbearing, but a childbearing in such a manner as God hath threatened [in Gen. 3:16] with sorrow and grief.

If they continue: By *they* is not meant the children, as some imagine, because of the change of the singular to the plural. The sense then [would] run thus: she shall be saved, if the children remain in faith, etc. That would be absurd to think that the salvation of the mother should depend upon the faith and grace of the children, when it is sometimes seen that the children of a godly mother may prove as wicked as hell itself! But by *they* is meant the woman: the name *woman* is taken collectively for all women, and therefore the plural number is added. The apostle passes from the singular number to the plural, as he had done from the plural to the singular, verse 9: *"In like manner also, that women adorn themselves"* in modesty, where he uses the plural. But verse 11 reassumes the other number again in his discourse. The graces that are here put as the conditions are *faith, charity, sanctification, sobriety*, where the apostle seems to oppose those to the first causes or ingredients of the defection: (1) *Faith* opposed to unbelief of the precept of God and the threatening annexed (Gen. 2:16-17). (2) *Charity* opposed to disaffection to God; as though God were an enemy to their happiness and commanded a thing that did prejudice their happiness, whereupon must arise ill surmises[55] of God and aversion[56] from Him. (3) *Sanctification*.[57] In opposition to this filthiness and pollution brought upon the soul by that first defection, there must therefore be in them an aim and endeavor to attain that primitive integrity and purity they then lost. (4) *Sobriety*, temperance, because giving the reins to sense[58] and obeying the longings thereof was the cause of the fall (Gen. 3:6). She saw that it was pleasant to the eye. Original sin is called concupiscence[59] and lusting; and to this is opposed sobriety.[60]

---

55 **ill surmises** – evil suspicions.
56 **aversion** – turning away morally.
57 *See* FGB 215, *Sanctification*
58 **giving the reins to sense** – giving up self-control to be guided by one's emotions.
59 **concupiscence** – eager desire for the things of the world.
60 **sobriety** – moderation; self-control.

Chapter 8—Childbearing: Saved in Childbearing

1. Faith: This is put first, because it is a fundamental grace. It is the employer of charity, for it works by it; the root of sanctification, for by faith the heart is purified. By faith is chiefly meant the grace of faith: (1) faith in the habit, (2) faith in the exercise.

2. Charity: The first sin was an enmity against God, therefore there is now necessary a love to God. The first sin was virtually an enmity to all the posterity of man, which were to come out of his loins; therefore, love to mankind is necessary; and faith always infers love to God and man.

3. Sanctification is here added because, by that, both the truth of faith and love appears to ourselves and others; and justification by faith is thereby ratified (James 2:24). By sanctification is not here meant a particular holiness or chastity due to the marriage bed, as some of the papists assert, but a universal sanctity of heart and life.

4. Sobriety: This is a natural means for preservation. Intemperance makes bodily [diseases] more dangerous in their assaults. True faith is accompanied with temperance and sobriety in the use of lawful comforts…

Observations: (1) The *punishment* of the woman: *"in childbearing."* (2) The *comfort* of the woman: *"she shall be saved."* (3) The *condition* of the salvation: *"if they continue,"* wherein is implied an exhortation to continue in faith, etc.

Doctrine: Many observations might be raised. (1) The pain in childbearing is a punishment inflicted upon the woman for the first sin. (2) The continuance of this punishment after redemption by Christ doth not hinder the salvation of the woman, if there be the gospel-conditions requisite. (3) The exercise of faith, with other Christian graces, is a peculiar means for the preservation of believers under God's afflicting hand.

I shall sum them up into this one: [61]"The continuance of the punishment inflicted upon the woman for the first sin doth not prejudice her eternal salvation, nor her preservation in childbearing, where there are the conditions of faith and other graces…This very Scripture is a letter of comfort, written only to women in the state of childbearing.[62] Claim it as

---

61 For detailed studies of this passage, see Richard Adams, "How May Child-Bearing Women Be Most Encouraged and Supported against, in, and under the Hazard of Their Travail?" in *Puritan Sermons*, Volume III, xi (Wheaton, IL: Richard Owen Roberts, Publishers, 1981); Thomas Schreiner, "An Interpretation of 1 Timothy 2:9-15" in Andreas J. Kostenberger and Thomas R. Schreiner, eds., *Women in the Church* (Grand Rapids, MI: Baker Academics, 2005), 85-120.

62 Referring to childbearing is also appropriate because it represents the fulfillment of the woman's domestic role as a mother in distinction from the man…To select childbearing is another indication that the argument is transcultural, for childbearing is not limited to

your right by faith! What comfort is here to appeal from the threatening to the promise, from God as a *judge* to God as a *father*, from God *angry* to God *pacified* in Christ!...You can never be under the curse if you have faith, as long as God is sensible of His own credit in the promise. In the material part of the punishment, there is no difference between a believer and an unbeliever. Jacob [was] pinched with famine as well as the Canaanite; but Jacob [was] in covenant and [had] a God in heaven and a Joseph in Egypt to preserve him. God directs every pain in all by His providence, in believers by a particular love; every gripe in all the [remedies] He gives us. He orders even His contendings with His creature in such a measure as the spirit may not fail before Him (Isa. 57:16).

From "A Discourse for the Comfort of Child-Bearing Women" in *The Complete Works of Stephen Charnock, Volume 5*, The Banner of Truth Trust: www.banneroftruth.org.

Stephen Charnock (1628-1680): English Puritan Presbyterian pastor, theologian, and author; born in St. Katherine Cree, London, England.

---

a particular culture but is a permanent and ongoing difference between men and women. The fact that God has ordained that women and only women bear children indicates that the differences in roles between men and women are in the created order...One indication that women are in the proper role is if they do not reject bearing children as evil but bear children in accord with their proper role...Paul is not asserting in 1 Timothy 2:15 that women *merit* salvation by bearing children and doing good works. He has already clarified that salvation is by God's mercy and grace...I think it is fair to understand the virtues described here as evidence that the salvation already received is genuine. Any good works of the Christian, of course, are not the ultimate basis of salvation, for the ultimate basis of salvation is the righteousness of Christ granted to us. (Thomas Schreiner, *Women in the Church*, 118-119)

Four Necessary Graces

RICHARD ADAMS (C. 1626-1698)

> *Notwithstanding she shall be saved in childbearing, if they continue in faith and charity and holiness with sobriety.* —1 Timothy 2:15

THOSE necessary and eminent graces to perseverance or continuance wherein the promise of salvation is made by the apostle unto childbearing women, on which they live for support *against* and *in* their travail, are these four: namely, "faith, charity, holiness, sobriety."[63]

"FAITH"—which we may distinctly conceive of as comprehending both that which is divine and moral, or Christian and conjugal.[64]

1. A divine faith, which is precious and saving (2 Peter 1:1; Heb. 10:39), [is] a grace of the Holy Spirit, whereby the enlightened heart, being united to Christ, doth receive Him and resigns up itself to Him as Mediator and so is *"espoused to one husband"* (2 Cor. 11:2), depending entirely upon Him. By this faith, receiving the Son of God, Who is also the Son of man, born of a woman, is the good wife to live in subjection to Christ, her spiritual Head. Then, though her pains be never so many, her throes never so quick and sharp, she may be confident that all shall go well with her, either in being safely delivered of the fruit of her womb, as the Lord's reward, out of His free love (Ps. 127:3); or having her soul eternally saved, being taken into covenant with the Almighty God (Gen. 17:1–7).

It was this faith that the pious childbearing[65] women, mentioned in the story of our Savior's genealogy (Matt. 1:1-17), did exercise. Continuance [in this faith] is required of every just, Christian woman that she may live by it in the pains that threaten death.[66] For by this principle, she may be the best supported and derive virtue from her Savior for the sweetening of the bitterest cup and strength for staying her up, when *"the anguish as of her that bringing forth her first child"* is upon her (Jer. 4:31), as Sarah, the notable pattern of pious women, in this case did. Concerning [her,] it is recorded, *"Through faith also Sara herself received strength to conceive seed, and was delivered of a child when she was past age, because she judged him faithful who had promised"* (Heb. 11:11). A staying[67] and living by faith upon God's

---

63 **EDITOR'S NOTE:** Due to its original length and verbosity, this article has been edited more than usual. Edits are purposefully visible in other articles, but due to the large number of edits, they have been omitted for readability.
64 **conjugal** – having to do with marriage.
65 **childing** – pregnant.
66 Death in childbirth was common during the time this was written.
67 **staying** – continuing in.

providence and promise will revive the drooping spirits of otherwise weak and fearful women in their good work of childbearing. Though impending danger to mother and child may make even good women to quail[68] when their pangs are upon them, yet "by faith" they can fetch relief out of the faithfulness of the Promiser, as Sarah did or out of this good word [that] He hath recorded in my text.

Hereupon the upright woman, though frail, can resign up herself to God, *"being fully persuaded"* with [Abraham,] the father of the faithful, that *"what he had promised, he was able also to perform"* (Rom. 4:21) in His own time and way, which is ever the best. Hence, in her low estate, the pious wife who lives by faith above nature, when *"[she] spreadeth her hands"* and utters her doleful[69] groans before the Almighty (Jer. 4:31) concludes, *"It is the Lord: let him do what seemeth him good"* (1 Sam. 3:18; 2 Sam. 15:26; Luke 22:42). If it seems good unto Him to call for her life and the life of her babe, she can say, "Lord, here am I, and the child which thou hast given me," as the prophet speaks upon another account (Isa. 8:18). She trusts to that good and great promise that the Seed of the woman shall break the serpent's head (Gen. 3:15). [She] therefore comforts herself that the serpent's sting is taken away by Him that is born of a woman. If she hath been in such a condition before, she can say, *"Tribulation worketh patience; and patience, experience; and experience, hope"* (Rom. 5:3-4). So by faith, [she may] conclude, *"Because thou hast been my help, therefore in the shadow of thy wings will I rejoice"* (Ps. 63:7). This saving faith, I might further show, doth presuppose and imply repentance[70] and expresses itself in meditation and prayer.

a. It doth presuppose and imply repentance. Which, from a true sense of sin and an apprehension of the mercy of God in Christ, doth cause a loathing of ourselves for our iniquities (Ezek. 20:43; 36:31). [This] is a very proper exercise for a childbearing woman, who is eminently concerned antecedently to *"bring forth...fruits meet for repentance"* (Matt. 3:8) that God may receive her graciously, upon her hearty turning from sin and returning to and trusting in Him.

b. This saving faith doth usually express itself—in those women who are really espoused unto Christ and in whom He dwells—*by meditation and prayer*. [These] are also very requisite for the support of childbearing ones at the approaches of their appointed sorrows. (i) Faith doth express itself in meditation. Bringing the soul to contemplate upon God doth (as wax

---

68 **quail** – lose heart; give way through fear.
69 **doleful** – full of pain, grief, or suffering.
70 *See* FGB 203, *Repentance*

is softened and prepared for the seal) make the heart soft for any sacred characters or signatures to be imprinted upon it. Further, (ii) Faith doth exercise itself in prayer to God, [it] being the mouth of faith in God through Christ, in Whose prevailing name Christians are concerned to lift up their hearts unto Him for relief in all their straits. [When] her heart is sore pained within her and the terrors of death are fallen upon her (cf. Ps. 55:4), her precious faith should fervently utter her most necessary and affectionate requests unto Him, Who hath freely given by His apostle the good word of support in my text. [Christ] is able to save to the uttermost, deliver effectually, and keep in perfect peace all that fly to Him and stay themselves upon Him in that good work [that] He hath appointed them. The next grace required here in my text is "CHARITY" OR "LOVE." This, in a good wife, I take, as I did faith, for that which is *Christian* and *conjugal*, [that is], respecting *Christ* and *her husband*.

1. [To] be sure, every Christian wife should love the Lord Jesus Christ. She should sincerely love Christ *in Himself*, [and] her faith toward Him should *"worketh by love"* (Gal. 5:6). It behoves[71] her to give the primacy of her affection unto Christ Himself. She is obliged, above all, most entirely and heartily to love the Lord Jesus Christ, her spiritual Husband. Let this be the chief care of the Christian wife, and she may conclude upon good grounds [that] Christ is hers, and she is His (Song 2:16). Now, if the good wife hath Christ present with her in her travail—as they who love Him with a prevailing love certainly have in all their affliction—she hath *all*, having Him Who will *"command deliverances for [her]"* (Ps. 44:4) and a *"blessing upon [her]"* (Lev. 25:21).

2. Next to Christ, the good wife is, above all others, dearly and constantly to love her own husband, and that *"with a pure heart fervently"* (1 Cor. 7:2; Titus 2:4; 1 Peter 1:22). Yea, and she should never entertain low thoughts of him, in that relation, whom she could once think worthy of embracing for her husband. Where this *conjugal* love is consequent upon the foregoing *Christian* love, all will become easy. So did Mrs. Wilkinson, "a most loving wife, whose patience was remarkable in the midst of very sore pains, which frequented her in the [conception] and bearing of children. Yet then her speech was, 'I fear not pains. I fear myself, lest through impatience I should let fall any unbefitting word.'" "It is a blessed frame," said that grave divine who recorded it, "when pain seems light and sin heavy."

"HOLINESS"—which I take, as the former, for that which is *Christian* and *conjugal*, more *general* and *special*.

---

71 **behoves** – is appropriate for.

1. There is holiness that is considered more generally, being a universal grace, agreeing to a Christian as such, wrought by the Spirit in the new creature from the peace made by Christ. [By this]—the soul being changed into His likeness—there is an abiding in a state of gracious acceptation with God and a striving in some measure to be holy as He is holy, in every particle of our [behavior], both toward God and man, publicly and privately, in some degrees. As all Christians are to mind their salvation in the holiness of the Spirit (2 Thess. 2:13; 1 Peter 1:2) and to follow after it by Christ (Heb. 12:14; 13:12), so Christian wives in a childbearing state are highly concerned for that good work to *"have [their] fruit unto holiness"* (Rom. 6:22), [so that] they may comfortably bring forth the fruit of their wombs.

2. Holiness may be considered more specially as it is conjugal and more peculiarly appropriated to the marriage state, this being a more particular exercise of Christian holiness in the matrimonial band. [Although] everyone (both husband and wife) in that relation is concerned, so the childbearing woman is obliged to be singularly careful to *"possess [her] vessel in sanctification,"* or sanctimony, *"and honour,"* (1 Thess. 4:4) in a special kind of conjugal cleanness and chasteness, which is opposite to all turpitude[72] and "lust of concupiscence" in the very appearance of it. [Then] there may be, as much as possible, no show or tincture of uncleanness in the marriage bed; but that there may be a holy seed, and she may keep herself pure from any taint of lasciviousness.

"SOBRIETY"—so we render it. Others [render it] "temperance"; others, "modesty," as in our old translation; others, "chastity." And, taking it largely, "the word seems to speak that gracious habit that may best become a prudent, grave, temperate, moderate, or modest mother of a family,"[73] for that seems to reach the apostle's sense…I might consider this, like the former graces, more *generally* and *specially*.

1. More generally, as Christian—*"Every one that nameth the name of Christ,"* being under an obligation thereby to "depart from iniquity" (2 Tim. 2:19). Certainly, then, a Christian wife, and that in a child-bearing condition, is concerned to seek that she may be endued with sobriety, which purgeth the mind from [disturbances] and putteth the affections into an orderly frame acceptable to God.

2. More particularly, the special conjugal grace of temperance and modesty is to be exercised by the childbearing woman in sobriety, chastity, and [graciousness,] with reference both to her affections and senses,

---

72 **turpitude** – depravity; wickedness.
73 Apparently a quote from Theodore Beza, source unknown.

a. With modesty—she is to govern her passions and affections.

b. With temperance—she should moderate her senses; especially take care to govern well those of taste and touch. (i) *Sobriety*—which more strictly respects the moderation of the appetite and sense of tasting, for the desiring of that which is convenient, and the avoiding of riot…The [pregnant] woman is highly concerned to take special care for her own and the child's safety…childbearing wives, who have *"put…on the Lord Jesus Christ"* (Rom. 13:14) are to eat and drink for health, and not for pampering of the flesh. (ii) *Chastity*—it much concerns the Christian wife to give check to any suggestion, much more to any [conversation], which is in a tendency to violate her matrimonial contract; or to bring her into any [act] unbecoming that *"honourable"* state she is brought into, or the undue use of the undefiled bed (Heb. 13:4).

In the exercise of this, with the precedent graces, the good wife, having well learned the lesson of self-denial,[74] can bear her burden in humble confidence of aids from above, in the hour of her childbed sorrow, and a safe deliverance in the best way. For, being thus qualified, she hath, from the precious promise in my text, a sure ground of a comfortable exemption from the curse in childbearing and of the removal of that original guilt that otherwise greatens the sorrows of women in such a case.

From "How May Child-Bearing Women Be Most Encouraged and Supported against, in, and under the Hazard of Their Travail?" in *Puritan Sermons*, Vol. 2, Richard Owen Roberts, Publishers: www.rorbooks.com.

Richard Adams (c. 1626-1698): English Presbyterian minister; born at Worrall, England.

---

[74] *See* FGB 218, *Self-denial*.

Sarah Gave Birth by Faith
ARTHUR W. PINK (1886-1952)

> *Through faith also Sara herself received strength to conceive seed, and was delivered of a child when she was past age, because she judged him faithful who had promised.* —Hebrews 11:11

It was *"through faith"* that Sarah *"received strength,"* and it was also *"through faith"* that she was now *"delivered of a child."* It is the constancy and perseverance of her faith that is here intimated. There was no abortion, no miscarriage; she trusted God right through unto the end. This brings before us a subject upon which very little is written these days: the duty and privilege of Christian women counting upon God for a safe issue in the most trying and critical season in their lives. Faith is to be exercised not only in acts of worship, but also in the ordinary offices of our daily affairs. We are to eat and drink in faith, work and sleep in faith; and the Christian wife should be delivered of her child by faith. The danger is great, and if in any extremity there is need of faith, much more so where life itself is involved. Let us seek to condense from the helpful comments of the Puritan Manton.[75]

First, we must be sensible what *need* we have to exercise faith in this case, that we may not run upon danger blindfolded; and if we escape, then to think our deliverance a mere chance. Rachel died in this case; so also did the wife of Phineas (1 Sam. 4:19-20): a great hazard is run, and therefore you must be sensible of it. The more difficulty and danger be apprehended, the better the opportunity for the exercise of faith (cf. 2 Chron. 20:12; 2 Cor. 1:9). *Second*, because the sorrows of travail are a monument of God's displeasure against sin (Gen. 3:16), therefore this must put you the more earnestly to seek an interest in Christ that you may have remedy against sin. *Third*, meditate upon the promise of 1 Timothy 2:15, which is made good eternally or temporally as God sees fit. *Fourth*, the faith you exercise must be the glorifying of His power and submitting to His will. This expresses the kind of faith that is proper to all temporal mercies: "Lord, if Thou wilt, Thou canst save me"—it is sufficient to ease the heart of a great deal of trouble and perplexing fear.

"And was delivered of a child." As we have pointed out in the last paragraph, this clause is added to show the continuance of Sarah's faith and the blessing of God upon her. True faith not only appropriates His promise, but continues resting on the same until that which is believed be actually accomplished. The principle of this is enunciated in Hebrews 3:14 and

---

[75] **Thomas Manton** (1620-1677) – Nonconformist Puritan preacher.

Hebrews 10:35. *"For we are made partakers of Christ, if we hold the beginning of our confidence steadfast unto the end"*; *"Cast not away therefore your confidence."* It is at this point so many fail. They endeavor to lay hold of a divine promise, but in the interval of testing let go of it. This is why Christ said, *"If ye have faith, and doubt not, ye shall not only do this,"* etc. Matthew 21:21—*"doubt not,"* not only at the moment of pleading the promise, but during the time you are awaiting its fulfillment. Hence also, unto *"Trust in the LORD with all thine heart"* is added *"and lean not unto thine own understanding"* (Prov. 3:5).

"When she was past age." This clause is added so as to heighten the miracle that God so graciously wrought in response to Sarah's faith. It magnifies the glory of His power. It is recorded for our encouragement. It shows us that no difficulty or hindrance should cause a disbelief of the promise. God is not tied down to the order of nature, nor limited by any secondary causes. He will turn nature upside down rather than not be as good as His word. He has brought water out of a rock, made iron to float (2 Kings 6:6), sustained two million people in a howling wilderness. These things should arouse the Christian to wait upon God with full confidence in the face of the utmost emergency. Yea, the greater the impediments that confront us, faith should be increased. The trustful heart says, "Here is a fit occasion for faith; now that all creature-streams have run dry is a grand opportunity for counting on God to show Himself strong on my behalf. What cannot He do! He made a woman of ninety to bear a child—a thing quite contrary to nature—so I may surely expect Him to work wonders for me too."

"Because she judged him faithful who had promised." Here is the secret of the whole thing! Here was the ground of Sarah's confidence, the foundation on which faith rested. She did not look at God's promises through the mist of interposing obstacles, but she viewed the difficulties and hindrances through the clear light of God's promises. The act that is here ascribed unto Sarah is that she *"judged"* or reckoned, reputed and esteemed, God to be faithful. She was assured that He would make good His word on which He had caused her to hope. God had spoken; Sarah had heard. In spite of all that seemed to make it impossible that the promise should be fulfilled in her case, she steadfastly believed. Rightly did Luther[76] say, "If you would trust God, you must learn to crucify the question 'How?' " *"Faithful is he that calleth you, who also will do it"* (1 Thess. 5:24): this is sufficient for the heart to rest upon; faith will cheerfully leave it with Omniscience as to *how* the promise will be made good to us.

---

76 **Martin Luther** (1483-1546) – German leader of the Protestant Reformation.

"Because she judged him faithful who had promised." Let it be carefully noted that Sarah's faith went beyond the promise. While her mind dwelt upon *the thing* promised, it seemed unto her altogether incredible; but when she took her thoughts off all secondary causes and fixed them on God Himself, then the difficulties no longer disturbed her: her heart was at rest in God. She knew that God could be depended upon: He is *"faithful"*—able, willing, sure to perform His word! Sarah looked beyond the promise to the Promiser; and as she did so, all doubting was stilled. She rested with full confidence on the immutability[77] of Him that cannot lie, knowing that where divine veracity[78] is engaged, omnipotence will make it good. It is by believing meditations upon the character of God that faith is fed and strengthened to expect the blessing, despite all apparent difficulties and supposed impossibilities. It is the heart's contemplation of the perfections of God that causes faith to prevail. As this is of such vital practical importance, let us devote another paragraph to enlarging thereon.

To fix our minds on the *things* promised, to have an assured expectation of the enjoyment of them, without the heart first resting upon the veracity, immutability, and omnipotence of God, is but a deceiving imagination. Rightly did John Owen[79] point out, "The formal object of faith in the divine promises is not the things promised in the first place, *but God Himself* in His essential excellencies of truth or faithfulness and power." Nevertheless, the divine perfections do not, of themselves, work faith in us; it is only as the heart believingly ponders the divine attributes that we shall "judge" or conclude Him faithful that has promised. It is the man whose mind is stayed upon God Himself, who is kept in *"perfect peace"* (Isa. 26:3): that is, he who joyfully contemplates Who and what God is that will be preserved from doubting and wavering while waiting the fulfillment of the promise. As it was with Sarah, so it is with us: every promise of God has tacitly annexed to it this consideration, *"Is any thing too hard for the Lord?"* (Gen. 18:14)…

But let our final thought be upon the rich recompense whereby God rewarded the faith of Sarah. The opening *"Therefore"* of verse 12 points the blessed consequence of her relying upon the faithfulness of God in the face of the utmost natural discouragements. From her faith there issued Isaac, and from him, ultimately, Christ Himself. And this is recorded for our

---

77 **immutability** – "The attribute of God whereby He cannot change or be changed in His es-sence or perfections." (Alan Cairns, *Dictionary of Theological Terms*, rev. ed., 224)

78 **veracity** – truthfulness.

79 **John Owen** (1616-1683), *An Exposition of the Epistle to the Hebrews*, Vol. 7, ed. W. H. Goold (Edinburgh: The Banner of Truth Trust), 79.

instruction. Who can estimate the fruits of faith? Who can tell how many lives may be affected for good, even in generations yet to come, through your faith and my faith today! Oh, how the thought of this should stir us up to cry more earnestly, "Lord, increase our faith" to the praise of the glory of Thy grace. Amen.

From *Studies in the Scriptures*, available from Chapel Library.

Arthur W. Pink (1886-1952): Pastor, itinerate Bible teacher, author; born in Nottingham, England.

Most merciful Father, Who hast justly sentenced woman that was first in the transgression to great and multiplied sorrows, and particularly in sorrow to bring forth children: yet grantest preservation and relief, for the propagation of mankind. Be merciful to this thy servant; be near her with thy present help in the needful time of trouble; and though in travail she hath sorrow, give her strength to bring forth. Being delivered, let her remember no more the anguish, for joy that a child is born into the world. Bless her in the fruit of her body; and being safely delivered, let her return Thee hearty thanks, and devote it and the rest of her life to Thy service, through Jesus Christ our Savior. Amen. —Richard Baxter

In our age, marriage has been deprived of its prestige and due honor, and true knowledge of the Word and ordinance of God has become extinct. Among the fathers, this knowledge was pure and proper. For this reason they had a very high regard for the begetting of children. —Martin Luther

It is inhuman and godless to have a loathing for offspring. The saintly fathers acknowledged a fruitful wife as a special blessing of God and, on the other hand, regarded sterility as a curse. This judgment flowed from the Word of God in Genesis 1:28, where He said, "Be fruitful, and multiply." From this, they understood that children are a gift of God —Martin Luther

The Best Support in Childbearing
RICHARD ADAMS (C. 1626-1698)

The application of this…observation—namely, that perseverance in Christian and conjugal graces and duties is the best support to childbearing women against, in, and under their travail—may briefly serve to teach care and administer comfort.

They who have wives already should take special care upon this account, to discharge the duties of good husbands toward their childbearing wives with all good fidelity; namely,

FIRST: To *"dwell with them according to knowledge, giving honour unto the wife as unto the weaker vessel, and as being heirs together of the grace of life; that your prayers be not hindered"* (1 Peter 3:7). Yea, and to labor daily with them, both by their Christian advice and holy conversation,[80] to engage their fruitful wives more and more to the constant exercise of these graces and duties that their sorrows may be sanctified to them and [that] they may see the salvation of God in their conception and bearing of children. And if the great and holy God should, in His wise government, think it best to take them hence from a childbed, they may learn to submit to His disposing will and rest the better satisfied, as having good evidence of their souls' eternal welfare.

SECONDLY: To endeavor, as much as may be, to discharge the parts of good, Christian, and tender husbands toward their dearest yoke-fellows in such a travailing condition. Laying much to heart those antecedent, concomitant, and consequent[81] pains [that] a state of pregnancy involves them in, which these husbands themselves, in such a kind, cannot have experience of. As it becomes them for the sake of their good and godly wives, they may, as is sometimes said of some sympathizing ones, in a sort, [conceive] with them and for them, by *"[putting on], as the elect of God, holy and beloved, bowels of mercies, kindness, humbleness of mind, meekness, long-suffering, etc."* (Col. 3:12). [They should] fulfill all the duties of the relation they are in, readily and timely providing for them, not only necessaries, but conveniences, as they can. [Husbands should provide] for their [wives'] longing appetites and for the heartening of their dear and suffering wives, apt to be cast down under apprehensions of their approaching sorrows; and call in aid of faithful praying ministers and pious friends to make requests known unto God for them. And if God hears prayers,

---

80 **conversation** – behavior; conduct.
81 **antecedent, concomitant, and consequent** – before, during, and after.

THIRDLY: To be heartily thankful to God upon His giving safe deliverance to their gracious wives from the pains and perils of childbearing. When the kind husband hath been really apprehensive of the sicknesses, pains, throes, and groans of his dear wife in her [pregnancy] and bearing a child to him by aids from above, nothing can be more necessarily incumbent[82] on him than to adore and be thankful to God, Who hath made a comfortable separation between her and the fruit of her womb, as [an answer] to prayer and hearkening unto her groaning…The Christian husband—having seen his loving wife in the exercise of the graces I have been discoursing of, pass through the peril of childbearing and admirably preserved therein by God's power and goodness—is greatly obliged to return his hearty thanks to God, Who hath made good His word wherein He caused them to hope, in granting so signal a mercy…Thus briefly, I have touched upon the care of married men with reference to their childbearing wives in the aforementioned particulars. Again, this doctrine teacheth,

A lesson of care to women. Consider…If you are already married, and that *"in the Lord,"* Who hath opened your wombs and given you power to conceive, it behoves you as righteous handmaids of the Lord,

FIRST: To continue in the constant exercise of these graces. Certainly, you who are blessed in being instruments for the propagation of mankind—when you find you have conceived and grow pregnant—are highly concerned to put on and use these ornaments. A great work you are usually busy about in preparing your childbed linen;[83] and I shall not discourage, but rather encourage, you to make necessary provision for your tender selves and babes… You ought to be somewhat indulged to make ready and feather your nests wherein to lay yourselves and your young (Luke 9:58). But the modesty and moderation you have heard of will not allow you, above your rank, to be costly in superfluous[84] fine feathers, when Christ's poor ministers and members, up and down, do expect your charity. O, I beseech you, good Christian women, let your chief care be…to be arrayed in that truly spiritual *"fine linen, clean and white,"* which *"is the righteousness of the saints,"* wherewith the Lamb's *"wife hath made herself ready"* (Rev. 19:7-8). This, this is the principal thing: the graces of *"faith, charity, holiness, and sobriety"* speak true Christian prudence…And if God hath given any of you real proof already of performing His promise in my text by vouchsafing temporal salvation to you, it behooves you to take care,

---

82 **incumbent** – necessary as a duty.
83 **childbed linen** – the covering that was prepared for the bed in which the baby would be birthed.
84 **superfluous** – extravagant.

SECONDLY: To record the [experiences] He hath given you of making good His word to you in particular. Hath God vanquished your fears, wiped away your tears, and heard your prayers? Engrave the memorials of His goodness and faithfulness upon the tables of your hearts. You have the great example of our dear Lord and Master, Jesus Christ, Who, when He had been greatly troubled for Lazarus, whom he loved, *"groaned in the spirit,"* and *"wept,"* making His request known to His Father on his behalf. [This] was graciously answered. He, with great devotion of heart, *"lifted up his eyes, and said, Father, I thank thee that thou hast heard me"* (John 11:3, 33, 35, 38, 41). Let every ingenuous[85] and grateful mother, whom God hath safely delivered from her childbearing pains and peril, imprint a grateful remembrance of so signal a mercy with indelible characters in her mind: "Lord, thou hast regarded the low estate of thine hand-maiden. When I was in an agony and well-nigh spent with repeated pains, Thou didst stand by my baby and me. Yea, thou didst admirably help us, making way for it to pass the bars into this world safely, keeping us both alive. Yea, and it may be, when our friends verily thought with sadness, that my child could not have seen the light, and I should shortly have shut mine eyes upon it, being ready to despair in bringing it forth, then didst Thou find a way for us both to escape" (cf. 1 Cor. 10:13)…As Paul, when he was made sensible of great mercy in his deliverance, by superadded favors, *"he thanked God, and took courage"* (Acts 28:15), so should every joyful mother thank God and be of good courage for the time to come…She should communicate her rare [experience] to encourage others…For well said the Greek tragedian, "It becomes one woman to be at hand to help another in her labor."[86]

Thus, we briefly see, this doctrine teacheth care to men and women. It doth also administer *comfort*, as to the good wives themselves, so likewise to the husbands of such good wives.

1. To good wives themselves, who are qualified as you have heard, yet in an hour of temptation are apt to walk very heavily from pre-apprehensions of grievous pains, yea, and, it may be, from great fear of death in their appointed sorrows that are coming upon them, grown weary with their heavy burdens. Whereas a constant abiding in the aforementioned graces and duties is a sure ground of good hope that you shall pass well through your childbed sorrows; which, be sure, shall be no obstacle at all to your eternal welfare…The apostle certainly brings in my text as an antidote against discouragement, and to cheer up suspicious and fearful women.

---

85 **ingenuous** – noble.
86 **Euripides** (480-c.406 B.C.).

They are heart-reviving words to every drooping woman and should lead her, with Sarah, to judge *"him faithful who had promised"* (Heb. 11:11)…God will lay no more upon her than He will enable her to bear. [He will] find a way for her escape, either by a comfortable, sanctified deliverance here, or a blessed translation to heaven to reap in joy what was sown in tears; and those [are] but temporary, when the joys are eternal. Further, it doth administer comfort,

2. To the husbands of such good wives, that is, such as continue in the graces and duties before and in their pregnancy…When they cannot but sympathize with their wives in their sorrows, they may cheer up in humble confidence that—the sting being taken out of the punishment—their wives' joys shall be increased by the pains [that] they undergo. God will deliver them and hear their prayers, and they shall glorify Him (John 16:21; Ps. 50:15). And if, after prayers and tears, their dearest consorts should decease and depart from them out of their childbearing pains; though this be a most cutting and heavy cross in itself, yet comfort may be gathered from it in the issue. For indeed that is the comfort of comforts, which affords life in death…Let pious husbands and gracious childbearing wives in their mutual offices wait upon God with submission for a sanctified support, when they stand in most need of divine aids. Then such handmaids of the Lord may humbly hope they shall receive help in and under their childbearing travail, and, in due time, even a temporal deliverance (supposing that to be best for them) from those pains and perils. [Let them take] comfort from that gracious word of the Lord by the prophet…*"Fear thou not; for I am with thee: be not dismayed; for I am thy God: I will strengthen thee; yea, I will help thee; yea, I will uphold thee with the right hand of my righteousness"* (Isa. 41:10).

From "How May Child-Bearing Women Be Most Encouraged and Supported against, in, and under the Hazard of Their Travail?"

Richard Adams (c. 1626-1698): English Presbyterian minister; born at Worrall, England.

> *When you were born, it was no secret event, nor was it a human invention. Your birth was a work of God.* —Martin Luther

When God Withholds Babies
THOMAS JACOMB (1622-1687)

> *For I have learned, in whatsoever state I am, therewith to be content.*
> —Philippians 4:11

What daily inquietudes[87] of spirit are there in some because of the want of [children]! They have many other comforts, but the not having of this embitters all. Abraham himself was much troubled about it: *"LORD God, what wilt thou give me, seeing I go childless, and the steward of my house is this Eliezer of Damascus?...Behold, to me thou hast given no seed: and, lo, one born in my house is mine heir"* (Gen. 15:2-3). But Rachel's passion rose very high: *"Give me children,"* saith she to her husband, *"or else I die"* (Gen. 30:1). Children are very great blessings; they are promised as such [in] Psalm 128:3-4, and in other places. Indeed, they are one of the sweetest flowers that grow in the garden of earthly comforts. Hence, it is hard for persons contentedly to bear the want of them. But whoever you are upon whom this affliction lies, [I pray you] labor after a contented mind under it. And in order thereunto, consider:

1. It is the Lord Who withholds this mercy. For He gives it or withholds it as seems good to Him. Providence is not more seen in any of the affairs and concerns of men than in this of children; that there shall be many or few, some or none, all falls under the good pleasure and disposal of God. When Rachel was so passionate under the want of these, Jacob rebuked her sharply: *"Am I in God's stead, who hath withheld from thee the fruit of the womb?"* (Gen. 30:2). *"Lo, children are an heritage of the LORD: and the fruit of the womb is his reward"* (Ps. 127:3). *"He maketh the barren woman to keep house, and to be a joyful mother of children"* (Ps. 113:9). Now if this was duly thought of, would it not quiet the heart? When God orders the thing, shall we dislike and fret at what He doeth? May not He dispense His blessings where He pleaseth? O, if He will give, we should be thankful in the owning of His goodness; if He will deny, we must be patient in the owning of His sovereignty.

2. Sometimes this mercy is denied, but better are bestowed. God doth not give children, but He gives Himself; is not He *"better to thee than ten sons?"* as Elkanah said of himself to Hannah (1 Sam. 1:8). There is *"a name better than of sons and of daughters"* (Isa. 56:5) promised. They who have that "better name" have no reason to murmur because they have not that which is worse. They who have God for their Father in heaven may well be content to go childless here on earth. If God will not give me the lesser, yet if He gives me the greater good, have I cause to be angry?...

---

87 **inquietudes** – anxieties.

3. Children sometimes are withheld a long time, but they are given at last. Of which we have many instances. The case is never desperate, so long as we can submit and wait. It is to be hoped [that] God designs to give us that comfort, under the want of which we can be contented.

4. If children are given after froward and irregular desires of them, it is to be questioned whether it be done in mercy. And it is to be feared [that] this frame will very much spoil the mercy! What we get by discontent, we seldom enjoy with comfort. How many parents have experienced the truth of this! They were not quiet until they had children and less quiet after they had them; they proved so undutiful, stubborn, and naughty, that there was much more of vexation in the having than there was in the wanting of them.

5. Children are great comforts, but they are but mixed comforts. The rose hath its sweetness, but it hath its pricks too; so it is with children. O the cares, fears, distractions, that parents are filled with about them! They are certain cares, uncertain comforts, as we usually express it. We eye the sweet only of this relation, and that makes us fretful: did we eye the bitter also, we should be more still and calm.

6. Had we this mercy in the height of it filled up in all respects according to our desires and expectations, it is a thousand to one but our hearts would be too much set upon it. And that would be of fatal consequence to us upon many accounts! Therefore, God foreseeing this, it is out of kindness and love that He withholds it from us.

These things being considered as to this affliction, [I think] they should very much dispose the heart to [contentment] under it.

From "How Christians May Learn in Every State to be Content" in *Puritan Sermons*, Vol. 2, Richard Owen Roberts, Publishers.

Thomas Jacomb (1622-1687): English Presbyterian minister; a man of exemplary life and great learning; born in Melton Mowbray, Leicestershire, UK.

A Child Is Born

THOMAS BOSTON (1676-1732)

For unto us a child is born, unto us a son is given: and the government shall be upon his shoulder: and his name shall be called Wonderful, Counsellor, The mighty God, The everlasting Father, The Prince of Peace. —Isaiah 9:6

The world waited long for Christ's coming into it, and here the prophet gives the news: that long-looked-for [One] is come at last. The *"child is born."* The word rendered *child* is a name of the sex—"a man-child"—and is just a lad, a lad-child. Such was our Lord Jesus Christ. It is a name common to the young of the male sex, competent to them whenever they are born and continuing with them during their younger years until they be grown men. The word rendered *born* doth signify more, even to be shown or presented born. It is a custom so natural that it has ever been in the world: when a child is born and dressed, it is presented or shown to its relations for their comfort. So Machir's children were presented to Joseph, their great grandfather, and on that occasion given him on his knees (Gen. 50:23); and Ruth's son to Naomi (Ruth 4:17).

So says the prophet, "This wonderful child is presented," viz., to his relations. And who are these? He has relations in heaven: the Father is His Father, the Holy Ghost His Spirit, the angels His servants; but it is not these who are here meant. It is to *us*, the sons and daughters of Adam! *We* are His poor relations; and to us as His poor relations on earth, sons of Adam's family, whereof He is the top branch, this Child is presented born for our comfort in our low state.

The birth of Christ was expected and looked for. The Church, His mother (Song 3:11), had an early promise of it (Gen. 3:15). It was in virtue of that promise He was conceived and born. All mankind besides [was] by another word, viz., *"Be fruitful, and multiply, and replenish the earth"* (Gen. 1:28).

Though Mary, His mother in a proper sense, [was pregnant with him for nine months], yet the Church, His mother in a figure, [was "pregnant" with Him] from that time (Gen. 3:15) for about four thousand years. Many a time the delivery was looked for, and she was in hazard of thinking it a false conception [because] it was so long coming forward. Kings and prophets looked and longed for the day: *"For I tell you, that many prophets and kings have desired to see those things which ye see, and have not seen them; and to hear those things which ye hear, and have not heard them"* (Luke 10:24). The whole Church of the Old Testament also longed for Christ's day: *"Make haste, my beloved, and be thou like to a roe or to a young hart upon the mountains of spices"* (Song 8:14).

2. Christ is now born. The happy hour of the long-looked-for birth is come, and the Child is come into the world. Angels proclaim it; *"And the angel said unto them, Fear not: for, behold, I bring you good tidings of great joy, which shall be to all people. For unto you is born this day in the city of David a Saviour, which is Christ the Lord"* (Luke 2:10-11). The fathers, kings, and prophets were in their graves: [they] died in the faith [that] He would be born; and now it is come to pass! He was really born—a little Child, though the Mighty God; an Infant, not one day old, though the Everlasting Father! Wonderful birth—such as the world never saw before, nor ever shall see again!

3. Some have been employed to present this Child to friends and relations, and they are still about the work. O honorable employment! More honorable than the office of presenting a newborn prince of the earth to a king, his father. Joseph and Mary had the office of presenting Him to the Lord (Luke 2:22). But who has the honor of presenting Him to us? Why,

a. The Holy Spirit has the office of presenting Him internally to us. *"For I determined,"* says Paul, *"not to know any thing among you, save Jesus Christ, and him crucified…And my speech and my preaching was not with enticing words of man's wisdom, but in demonstration of the Spirit and of power"* (1 Cor. 2:2, 4). And by [the Spirit,] His Father presents Him to us; *"And Simon Peter answered and said, Thou art the Christ, the Son of the living God. And Jesus answered and said unto him, Blessed art thou, Simon Barjona: for flesh and blood hath not revealed it unto thee, but my Father which is in heaven"* (Matt. 16:16-17). Thus, sinners have presented to them in His heavenly glory, so as they get a broad sight of Him, such as is to be had on earth by faith: *"And the Word was made flesh, and dwelt among us, (and we beheld his glory, the glory as of the only begotten of the Father,) full of grace and truth"* (John 1:14).

b. Ministers of the gospel have the office of presenting Him to us externally, in the swaddling clothes of Word and [ordinances]. They are employed to present believing sinners to Christ, *"For I have espoused you to one husband, that I may present you as a chaste virgin to Christ"* (2 Cor. 11:2), and to present Christ to sinners to be believed on. They come with old Simeon, with the holy child Jesus in their arms in gospel-ordinances (Rom. 10:6-8), and say with John the Baptist, *"Behold the Lamb of God, which taketh away the sin of the world"* (John 1:29).

To whom is Christ presented?

1. Negatively, He is not presented to the fallen angels. He was not born for them; they are none of His relations, *"For verily he took not on him the nature of angels; but he took on him the seed of Abraham"* (Heb. 2:16). Their

house was originally more honorable than the house of Adam; but Christ has put an honor on the house of Adam above the house of angels. The holy angels are His *servants*; the evil angels His *executioners*; but holy men are His *brethren*.

2. Positively, He is presented to mankind sinners—those of the house of His father Adam. To them is the voice directed, *"Behold the Lamb of God"* (John 1:29), etc. to us a child is born (Luke 2:10-11). He was first presented to the Jews, [and shown] to Israel (John 1:31); but then to all the world indifferently, of whatsoever nation (Mark 16:15). Hence, from the uttermost parts of the earth, songs are heard upon occasion of showing Him born to them, His glory appearing unparalleled. Particularly,

a. He is presented to the visible church—even to all and every one of them. There are indeed many in the world to whom He is not presented. They have neither His voice or fame, nor seen His shape represented in the Word. But wheresoever the gospel comes, there Christ is presented to every person as born to them…He is now bodily in heaven indeed; yet really, though spiritually in the Word and ordinances, presented to sinners, and seen by faith; though the most part will not behold Him.

b. He is presented effectually to all the elect. Christ is revealed in them (Gal. 1:15-16). Hence, they believe on Him, and so it is with all them, however others entertain Him. *"As many as were ordained to eternal life believed"* (Acts 13:48). They are all as Paul was, in a sense, chosen to see the Just One; and their seeing Him with a spiritual eye makes them willing to part with all and purchase the field and treasure and the one pearl…

How is Christ presented? He is presented,

1. In the preaching of the gospel. *"O foolish Galatians, who hath bewitched you, that ye should not obey the truth, before whose eyes Jesus Christ hath been evidently set forth, crucified among you?"* (Gal. 3:1). To whomsoever the gospel comes, Christ is presented to them, as being in the word of the gospel, to be discerned by faith. *"The word is nigh thee, even in thy mouth, and in thy heart: that is the word of faith, which we preach"* (Rom. 10:8)…

2. In the administration of the [ordinances]. As in the Word He is presented to the ears, in the [ordinances] He is presented to the eyes. In them, there is a lively representation of Christ, bleeding and dying on the cross for sinners. *"This is my body"* (Matt. 26:26). Though He is not corporeally present in the [ordinances], yet He is really and spiritually so to the faith of believers, which realizeth invisible things: *"Faith is…the evidence of things not seen"* (Heb. 11:1)…

3. In the internal work of saving illumination. The Spirit of the Lord not only gives light, but sight, to the elect. [He] not only opens the Scriptures to them, but opens their eyes and reveals Christ in them (Gal. 1:15-16). This is that demonstration of the Spirit [that] Paul speaks of, which is the immediate antecedent of faith, without which no man will believe.

[Why] is Christ presented to us on his birth?

1. That we may see the faithfulness of God in the fulfilling of His promise. The promise of Christ was an ancient promise, the accomplishment whereof was long delayed; but now we see it is performed in its time and thence may conclude that all the rest of the promises depending thereon shall be fulfilled in their season.

2. That we may rejoice in Him. The very birth of His forerunner was to be a joy to many (Luke 1:14); how much more His own? The angels sang for joy at the birth of Christ (Luke 2:13-14). And He is presented to us that we may join them in their song; for it is a matter of great joy (Luke 2:10-11). And whoever see their danger by sin will rejoice on Christ's being presented to them, as a condemned man [does] on the sight of the Prince by whom he is to obtain a pardon.

3. That we may look on Him, see His glory, and be taken with Him. For this cause sinners are often invited to look unto Him: *"Look unto me, and be ye saved, all the ends of the earth"* (Isa. 45:22). *"Go forth, O ye daughters of Zion, and behold King Solomon with the crown wherewith his mother crowned him in the day of his espousals, and in the day of the gladness of his heart"* (Song 3:11). The looking on the forbidden fruit has so [corrupted] the eyes of mankind that the things of the world appear as in a magnifying glass; and there is no getting a right view of them until we behold Jesus in His glory.

4. Lastly, that we may acknowledge Him in the character in which He appears, as the Savior of the world and *our* Savior. For He is presented as a young prince to be acknowledged heir to the crown. The Father has made choice of Him to be the Savior of the world by office, [has] given Him to us for our Savior, and presents Him accordingly for our acknowledgement.

Use: I exhort you then to *believe* that Christ is on His birth presented to you as His relations. If ye enquire what your duty is on that occasion, I answer,

a. Embrace Him cordially. *"Lift up your heads, O ye gates; and be ye lift up, ye everlasting doors; and the King of glory shall come in"* (Ps. 24:7). Old Simeon, when [Jesus] was presented in the temple, took Him in his arms with full satisfaction of soul (Luke 2:28-29). He is now in heaven as to His bodily presence; but He is presented to you in the gospel: embrace Him by faith with the heart, believing on Him for all His salvation, renouncing all other saviors for Him, betaking yourselves to Him for all, for a rest to your consciences and your hearts!

b. Kiss Him—with a kiss of love (Ps. 2:12), giving Him your hearts: *"My son, give me thine heart"* (Prov. 23:26), with a kiss of *honor*, honoring him in your hearts, lips, and lives; and with a kiss of *subjection*, receiving Him as your Lord, King, Head, and Husband.

c. Bless Him—*"Bless his name"* (Ps. 96:2). He is God blessed forever! But we are to bless Him, as we bless God—declaratively, proclaiming Him blessed (Ps. 72:17); praying from the heart that His kingdom may come (Ps. 72:15).

d. Worship Him. So did the wise men of the east (Matt. 2:11). He is the everlasting God and therefore to be adored: *"For he is thy Lord; and worship thou him"* (Ps. 45:11)—thy Husband, thy King, thy God. Worship Him with *internal* worship, consecrating your whole souls to Him; and worship Him with *external* worship.

e. Lastly, present unto Him gifts. So did the wise men (Matt. 2:11). Make a gift of your hearts to Him (Prov. 23:26). [Give] of yourselves wholly (2 Cor. 8:5) to glorify Him in your souls and bodies, your substance, your all!

From "Christ Presented to Mankind-Sinners" in *The Whole Works of Thomas Boston*, Vol. 10, Tentmaker Publications: www.tentmakerpublications.com.

Thomas Boston (1676-1732): Scottish Presbyterian minister and theologian; born in Duns, Berwickshire, Scotland.

Chapter 9
ABORTION

While the word "abortion" is not found in the Bible, we should not conclude that the Bible is therefore silent on the matter. It is not silent—for there are many biblical arguments against the practice of abortion. First, Genesis 1:26-27 declares that man is made in the image of God and therefore babies are valuable and worthy of respect. Second, Exodus 20:13 and Genesis 9:6 declare that murder is a crime against God. Third, Psalm 139:13-16 explains that God Himself forms human beings in the womb. Fourth, Jeremiah 1:5 affirms that God knew Jeremiah while he was in his mother's womb. Fifth, Luke 1:35,41 reveals that John the Baptist was filled with the Spirit while in his mother's womb, long before he was separated from his mother at birth. Sixth, Proverbs 24:11 teaches us to come to the aid of the defenseless. Scripture leads us to believe that there should be equal protection under the law for life in the womb. It is a matter of upholding the Word of God and preserving the love of God for mankind.

This chapter makes it clear that abortion is an act of murder. Yet, in America every day, there are murders performed behind the closed doors of the abortion clinics. While the particular methods of abortion may be relatively recent innovations, many people in many cultures—ancient Canaan, Rome, Greece, and others—have cruelly killed their own children, both before and after birth. Thus, abortion is not a new practice about which the Word of God has nothing to say. In the Law, the Prophets, the Poetic books, the Pauline Epistles, and the Gospels, we find evidence of the sacredness of life in the womb and the sovereignty of God in conception.

People kill their own babies everyday for the most trivial of reasons: convenience, lifestyle, unwillingness for future plans to be disrupted, and so on. They go to clinics where doctors are willing to assist them in killing their babies for money. Knowing this, and what the Bible says about it, should send shockwaves down our spines. At the same time, we need to train up a new generation that understands the value of life in the womb. What follows in this chapter fills out the story of the realities of abortion.

—Scott Brown

Thou Shalt Not Kill

EZEKIEL HOPKINS (1634-1690)

Thou shalt not kill. —Exodus 20:13

This [commandment] forbids that barbarous and inhuman sin of murder,[1] the first-born of the devil, who was a murderer from the beginning (John 8:44). [It forbids] the first branded[2] crime that we read of, wherein natural corruption, contracted by the Fall, vented its rancor and virulence:[3] the sin of Cain—that great instance of perdition[4]—who slew his brother Abel *"because his own works were evil, and his brother's righteous"* (1 John 3:12).[5]

The murdering of another is a most heinous[6] and black sin, a sin that God doth detect and bring to punishment, usually by some wonderful[7] method of His providence.[8] [Murder] dogs the consciences of those who are guilty of it with horrid affrights[9] and terrors and hath sometimes extorted from them a confession of it when there hath been no other proof or evidence.

The two greatest sinners that the Scripture hath set the blackest brand upon were both murderers: Cain and Judas. The one [was] the murderer of his brother; the other, first of his Lord and Master and then of himself.

God so infinitely hates and detests it that, although the altar was a refuge for other offenders, He would not have a murderer sheltered there. He was to be dragged from that inviolable[10] sanctuary unto execution according to that law: *"But if a man come presumptuously upon his neighbour, to slay him with guile; thou shalt take him from mine altar, that he may die"* (Ex. 21:14). Accordingly,

---

1 The scope of this command is the preservation of that life which God hath given unto man, which is man's greatest concern. No man is lord of his own or his neighbor's life; it belongs to Him alone Who gave it, to take it away. (Thomas Boston, *The Complete Works of Thomas Boston*, Vol. 2, 260)
2 **branded** – marked with evil fame.
3 **rancor and virulence** – deep, bitter anger and extreme hostility.
4 **perdition** – destruction.
5 The purport [*intended meaning*] of this commandment is that since the Lord has bound the whole human race by a kind of unity, the safety of all ought to be considered as entrusted to each. In general, therefore, all violence and injustice, and every kind of harm from which our neighbor's body suffers, is prohibited. (John Calvin, *Institutes of the Christian Religion*, II, viii, 39)
6 **heinous** – hateful; highly wicked.
7 **wonderful** – causing astonishment.
8 **providence** – What are God's works of providence? God's works of providence are His most holy, wise, and powerful preserving and governing all His creatures, and all their actions. (Spurgeon's Catechism, Q. 11, available from CHAPEL LIBRARY)
9 **affrights** – sudden and great fears.
10 **inviolable** – to be kept sacred.

we read that when Joab had fled and taken hold on the horns of the altar, so that the messengers who were sent to put him to death durst not violate that holy place by shedding his blood, Solomon gave command to have him slain even there, as if the blood of a willful murderer were a very acceptable sacrifice offered up unto God (1 Kings 2:28-31).

Indeed, in the first prohibition of murder that we meet withal,[11] God subjoins[12] a very weighty reason why it should be so odious[13] unto Him: *"Whoso sheddeth man's blood, by man shall his blood be shed: for in the image of God made he man"* (Gen. 9:6). So that *Homicidium est Decidium*: "To slaughter a man is to stab God in effigy.[14]" Though the image of God's holiness and purity be totally defaced in us since the Fall, yet every man—even the most wicked and impious[15] that lives—bears some strictures[16] of the image of God in his [mind], the freedom of his will, and his dominion over the creatures. God will have every part of His image so revered by us that He esteems him that assaults man as one who attempts to assassinate God Himself.[17]

Murder is a *crying* sin. Blood is loud and clamorous. That first [blood] that ever was shed was heard as far as from earth to heaven: *"The voice of thy brother's blood crieth unto me from the ground"* (Gen. 4:10). God will certainly hear its cry and avenge it.

But, not only he whose hands are embrued[18] in the blood of others, but those also who are accessory[19] are guilty of murder. As,

1. Those who command or counsel it to be done. Thus, David became guilty of the murder of innocent Uriah; and God, in drawing up his charge, accuseth him with it: *"Thou...hast slain him with the sword of the children of Ammon"* (2 Sam. 12:9).

2. Those who consent to murder are guilty of it. Thus Pilate, for yielding to the clamorous outcries of the Jews, *"Crucify him, crucify him"* (Luke 23:21), though he washed his hands and disavowed the fact, was as much guilty as those who nailed Him to the cross.

---

11 **withal** – therewith.
12 **subjoins** – to add at the end of a speech or writing.
13 **odious** – repulsive; causing hatred.
14 **in effigy** – to inflict violence upon the image or figure that represents a person.
15 **impious** – not showing deep respect for God and His ways; wicked.
16 **strictures** – slight traces.
17 Scripture notes a twofold equity on which this commandment is founded. Man is both the image of God and our flesh. Wherefore, if we would not violate the image of God, we must hold the person of man sacred—if we would not divest ourselves of humanity, we must cherish our own flesh. (Calvin, *Institutes*, II, viii, 39)
18 **embrued (imbrued)** – stained.
19 **accessory** – aiding and encouraging a crime.

3. He that concealeth a murder is guilty of it. Therefore, we read that in case a man were found slain and the murderer unknown, the elders of that city were to assemble, wash their hands, and protest *"Our hands have not shed this blood, neither have our eyes seen it"* (Deut. 21:6-7), intimating that if they had seen and concealed it, they had thereby become guilty of the murder.

4. Those who are in authority and do not punish a murder, when committed and known, are themselves guilty of it. Thus, when Naboth was condemned to die by the wicked artifice of Jezebel—although Ahab knew nothing of the contrivance until after the execution—yet, because he did not vindicate that innocent blood when he came to the knowledge of it, the prophet chargeth it upon him. *"Hast thou killed, and also taken possession?"* (1 Kings 21:19). The guilt lay upon him, and the punishment due to it overtook him, although we do not read that he was any otherwise guilty of it than in not punishing those who had committed it.

And those magistrates who, upon any respect whatsoever, suffer a murder to escape unpunished are said to pollute the land with blood: *"Moreover ye shall take no satisfaction for the life of a murderer, which is guilty of death: but he shall be surely put to death…So ye shall not pollute the land wherein ye are: for blood it defileth the land: and the land cannot be cleansed of the blood that is shed therein, but by the blood of him that shed it"* (Num. 35:31, 33).

From "A Practical Exposition of the Ten Commandments" in *The Works of Ezekiel Hopkins*, Vol. 1, Soli Deo Gloria, a division of Reformation Heritage Books: www.heritagebooks.org.

Ezekiel Hopkins (1634-1690): Anglican minister and author; born in Sandford, Crediton, Devonshire, England.

> *Violations of the sixth commandment are manifestly on the increase all over the land by suicides, murders, homicides, parricides, fratricides, infanticides, feticides (abortion); and these awful crimes are often perpetrated with such circumstances of horrid cruelty as to cry to heaven for vengeance.*
> —Original Covenanter Magazine (Vol. 3:1-3:16, 1881)

The Silent Holocaust

PETER BARNES

John Powell[20] has referred to the widespread practice of abortion in our own day as "the Silent Holocaust." This description is tragically apt, as the treatment of unborn children in the Western democracies can indeed be compared with the treatment of Jews in Nazi Germany. Most significantly, Dietrich Bonhoeffer,[21] the Lutheran pastor whom Hitler sent to the scaffold in 1945, spoke as strongly against abortion as ever he did against Nazism.[22] His views are worthy of quotation: "Destruction of the embryo[23] in the mother's womb is a violation of the right to live which God has bestowed upon this nascent[24] life. To raise the question whether we are here concerned already with a human being or not is merely to confuse the issue. The simple fact is that God certainly intended to create a human being and that this nascent human being has been deliberately deprived of his life. And that is nothing but murder."[25] As early as 1933, as Nazi persecution of the Jews gathered momentum, Bonhoeffer saw clearly the duty of the Christian. He turned to the Word of God, and Proverbs 31:8 was often on his lips: *"Open thy mouth for the dumb."* This same duty rests upon the Christian in our own day as increasingly abortion is practiced and accepted.

An age of slogans and deadened moral sensibilities inevitably has many depressing features, but two of the more serious are the lack of clear thinking and the debasement[26] of language. In many places, girls as young as eleven have had abortions; and fourteen-year-olds have returned for their second operation. Yet they would not be allowed to buy liquor and usually would require parental consent before having their ears pierced (this consent is not always required in abortion cases). There are government-sponsored campaigns against smoking by pregnant women because the practice could harm the infant. And unborn children involved in automobile accidents have even secured compensation through the law courts. Yet no action has been taken against the practice of killing the unborn child. In fact, there has been a subtle and pervasive assumption that pro-abortionists are sensitive,

---

20 **John Joseph Powell** (1925-2009) – author of *Abortion: The Silent Holocaust*.
21 **Dietrich Bonhoeffer**(1906-1945) – German Lutheran theologian and pastor.
22 **Nazism** – the political doctrines implemented by Adolph Hitler and his followers.
23 **embryo** – an unborn baby less than 8 weeks old.
24 **nascent** – beginning to develop.
25 Dietrich Bonhoeffer, *Ethics*, 175-76.
26 **debasement** – reducing in quality.

liberal, and humane[27] people who are articulate, intelligent, and in touch with the needs of modern living, while the pro-life side has been often portrayed as a group of dogmatic hard-liners who may even have leanings towards fascism.[28]

In addition, the unborn child has been labeled a "protoplasmic[29] mass" or "fetal tissue," while abortion itself has been called "a method of post-conceptive fertility control" or, more simply but just as deceptively, "the termination of pregnancy." This demeaning of words has had profound effects: language is to be treasured, and it was not for nothing that Augustine of Hippo[30] referred to words as "precious cups of meaning." In the present situation, however, words have been used to disguise reality rather than to reveal it. Therefore, before proceeding any further, we should be very clear as to what exactly takes place during every abortion.

Three main methods are used to end the life of an unborn child. First, for early pregnancies, there is the *dilation and curettage* technique (D&C). The cervix is first dilated, and a tube is inserted into the mother's uterus. This tube is attached to a suction apparatus that tears the little baby apart and deposits him in a jar. A curette[31] is then used to scrape the wall of the uterus to remove any parts of the baby's body that might still be present. Often the suction tube is not used at all, and the curette is simply used to cut the baby's body to pieces and scrape out the placenta.

After about the third month of pregnancy, this technique becomes too dangerous for the mother, so a *saline abortion* is employed. This might be called *salt poisoning*. A solution of concentrated salt is injected into the amniotic[32] fluid in the sac around the growing baby. The salt is absorbed by the baby who is poisoned to death after about an hour. The outer layer of his skin is burned off by the salt; and about a day later, the mother goes into labor and delivers a discolored and shriveled-up baby. A few such babies have been delivered alive, although they rarely survive long. Prostaglandins[33] can also be used after the third month of pregnancy. Prostaglandin chemicals are injected into the uterus, causing the mother to go into premature labor

---

27 **humane** – showing compassion or sympathy for others.
28 **fascism** – extreme right wing, authoritarian, or intolerant views or practice.
29 **protoplasmic** – the colorless liquid of a living cell, composed of proteins, fats, and other organic substances in water, including the nucleus.
30 **Aurelius Augustine** (354-430) – Bishop of Hippo Regius in North Africa and theologian.
31 **curette** – surgical instrument shaped like a scoop to remove tissue from a bodily cavity.
32 **amniotic** – having to do with the amnion, the innermost membrane enveloping an embryo.
33 **prostaglandins** – potent substance that acts like a hormone; found in many bodily tissues; has varying hormone-like effects, notably the promotion of uterine contractions.

and deliver a dead baby. However, prostaglandin babies have been born alive, much to the embarrassment of some in the pro-abortion camp.

The third method, which is used for more developed pregnancies, is the *hysterotomy*.[34] This is like a Caesarean operation, except that in the hysterotomy, the object is not to *save* the child but to kill him. In this case, the baby has to be either killed outright or allowed to die…

It is sometimes said that we cannot know when the fetus becomes a human being. In fact, the Supreme Court of the United States maintained just this view in its momentous and tragic decision of 1973,[35] when it virtually allowed abortion on demand. The Court stated, "We need not resolve the difficult question of when life begins."[36] It then went on to imply that issues of theological, philosophical, and biological speculation have *no place in a court of law*. Such a statement gives the appearance of humility, but it flies in the face of biological reality. Even if it were true, the Court's cavalier[37] attitude to life gives grave cause for alarm. If there is any uncertainty as to when life begins, the duty of the Court is surely to protect what, on the Court's own admission, might be human life…

Abortion has…become so much accepted in places like Britain, the United States, and Australia, that one child out of every three or four conceived is deliberately put to death in the womb. The statistics have indeed become horrifying. In the United States, for example, perhaps as many as fifteen million died in the ten years following 1973. Based on these figures, it is calculated that the number of babies killed through abortion in four months is approximately equal to the number of Americans killed during the whole of World War II. The womb has become more deadly than the battlefield.

Yet all this has taken place in the name of care and compassion, complete with the touching catch-cry, "Every child a wanted child."[38]…Modern

---

34 **hysterotomy** – surgical incision into the uterus.
35 *Roe v. Wade* 410 U.S. 113 (1973): Decision by the U.S. Supreme Court that held unduly restrictive state regulation of abortion to be unconstitutional. In a 7–2 vote the Supreme Court upheld the lower court's decision that a Texas statute criminalizing abortion in most instances violated a woman's constitutional right of privacy, which the court found implicit in the liberty guarantee of the Due Process Clause of the Fourteenth Amendment. ("Roe v. Wade,"*Encyclopedia Britannica Ultimate Reference Suite*, 2011)
36 **Harold Andrew Blackmun** (1908-1999): Associate Justice of the Supreme Court of the United States from 1970 until 1994, author of *Roe v. Wade*.
37 **cavalier** – haughty, careless lack of concern.
38 This phrase appears on the Planned Parenthood web site. Christian apologist Greg Koukl replies to this kind of thinking: "Life might not be beautiful for an unwanted child—I'll grant that—but why isn't it?…The initial answer is, 'The unwanted child's life is not beautiful because she's not wanted.' But it goes deeper than that, doesn't it? No child's life is miserable simply by the bare fact that she is unwanted. Being unwanted doesn't

humanists no longer deviate from an accepted standard; it has become increasingly true that there is no longer any standard from which to deviate… The Prophet Amos had a plumb line by which he could judge Israel (Amos 7:7-9), but modern secular man has been left without any plumb line. As a result, in the abortion debate, he has not simply come up with the wrong answers, he has been unable even to frame the right questions…

Abortion in the Light of God's Word: It is frequently contended that the Bible says next to nothing on the subject of abortion…It is true that the Bible says nothing directly on the subject of abortion, but we do well to remember the important principle laid down by the Westminster Confession of Faith: "The whole counsel of God concerning all things necessary for His glory, man's salvation, faith and life, is either expressly set down in Scripture, or by good and necessary consequence may be deduced from Scripture" (I.vi).[39] On these premises, it is certainly possible to derive the biblical attitude to abortion.

The starting point for any study must be Exodus 21:22-25. This text is not without ambiguities and can be interpreted in two possible ways. The first interpretation can be found in the New American Standard Bible:[40] *"If men struggle with each other and strike a woman with child so that she gives birth prematurely, yet there is no injury, he shall surely be fined as the woman's husband may demand of him; and he shall pay as the judges decide. But if there is any further injury, then you shall appoint as a penalty life for life, eye for eye, tooth for tooth, hand for hand, foot for foot, burn for burn, wound for wound, bruise for bruise."*

If this is the correct translation, it would appear to justify the view that the mother's life is of greater value than that of the unborn child. The unborn child would then be viewed as nascent life rather than as a full human being. However, even this translation does not open the door to abortion

---

make her life miserable. In this case, it isn't a *what* that makes the child's life miserable (being unwanted), but rather a *who* that makes the child's life miserable (the people, the adults, the parents who don't want the child). You see, people are miserable not because of the conditions of their conception, but rather because of the way others treat them afterwards…Yes, many unwanted children lead miserable lives. But whose fault is that? It is not the baby's fault. It's the fault of parents who would rather kill their children than be obliged to love and care for them." (Greg Koukl, *Every Child a Wanted Child*, http://www.str.org/site/News2?page=NewsArticle&id=5238)

39 The same declaration appears with a slight variation in the Second London Baptist Confession of 1677/89: "The whole counsel of God concerning all things necessary for His own glory, man's salvation, faith and life, is either expressly set down or necessarily contained in the Holy Scripture" (I.vi).

40 The use of modern translations by the author does not mean that CHAPEL LIBRARY endorses or agrees with these translations. See *English Bible Translations: By What Standard?*, William Einwechter, available from CHAPEL LIBRARY.

but precludes[41] it. Here, an accidental abortion leads to a fine. "Good and necessary" deduction would entail that deliberate abortion warrants a much heavier punishment. At most, this view of Exodus 21:22-25 might justify abortion in the now extremely rare case in which the pregnancy seriously threatens the physical life of the mother. The point of the passage would then be the extraordinary protection given to the expectant mother, for manslaughter was not usually a capital offence (Josh. 20)—not the lesser protection given to the baby.

The second interpretation, namely that Exodus 21 refers to the death of either mother or child, gains support from the translation of the Authorized Version[42]...This says, *"If men strive, and hurt a woman with child, so that her fruit depart from her,*[43] *and yet no mischief follow:*[44] *he shall be surely punished, according as the woman's husband will lay upon him; and he shall pay as the judges determine. And if any mischief follow, then thou shalt give life for life."*

On this translation, it is possible that the verses do not refer to a miscarriage, but to a premature birth. If the young infant survives, the guilty men are fined; but if he dies, it is life for life. In fact, the passage has been understood in this way by the learned Puritan exegete, Matthew Poole, and by Keil and Delitzsch, whose commentaries on the Old Testament have long been regarded as standard works of reference. Calvin's comments are also most instructive. The great Genevan Reformer wrote, "The fetus, though enclosed in the womb of its mother, is already a human being." Hence, he concluded that the passage referred to the possible death of either mother or child. He therefore protested vigorously against the murder of the unborn: "If it seems more horrible to kill a man in his own house than in a field, because a man's house is his place of most secure refuge, it ought surely to be deemed more atrocious to destroy a fetus in the womb before it has come to light."

This second interpretation of Exodus 21:22-25 has not found widespread support today, but there is much to be said in its favor. In the first place, the Hebrew word for *miscarriage* is not used in the passage, although it can be found in other parts of the Old Testament (e.g. Gen. 31:38; Hos. 9:14). Instead, Exodus 21:22 uses a word that simply means "to depart" or "to go out." It is used, for example, to describe Abram's departure from Haran in Genesis 12:4. It is also used to describe live births (e.g. Gen. 25:26; 38:28-30).

---

41 **precludes** – rules out; prevents.
42 The NIV follows the AV's translation here.
43 "she gives birth prematurely" (NIV)
44 "serious injury" (NIV)

Admittedly, it is used of a stillborn infant in Numbers 12:12, but it still needs to be said that the modern translations that insert the word *miscarriage* into the text are interpreting rather than translating.

The second reason for accepting that Exodus 21 refers to the death of either mother or child is more compelling. The Scriptures, as the Word of God, consistently refer to the unborn child as a human being. Every child in the womb is fearfully and wonderfully made by God (Job 31:15; Ps. 139:13-16; Isa. 44:2, 24; Jer. 1:5) in a way that we can never completely understand (Eccl. 11:5). There is continuity in life from conception to death; so naturally, when David refers to his origins in the womb, he uses the first-person personal pronoun (Ps. 139:13). Even sin is traced back, not to the newborn baby, but to the unborn infant (Ps. 51:5; 58:3). As a result, the unborn are always treated in Scripture as human—they can move, even leap (Gen. 25:22, Luke 1:41, 44), be consecrated in God's service (Jer. 1:5; Gal. 1:15), filled with the Holy Spirit (Luke 1:15), and blessed (Luke 1:42). Furthermore, the same Greek word is used to describe the unborn John the Baptist (Luke 1:41, 44), the newborn baby Jesus (Luke 2:12, 16), and the young children who were brought to Jesus (Luke 18:15). If the unborn child is not a human being, it is difficult to see how these statements could have any meaning. And it is surely significant that when the eternal Son of God became man, He entered Mary's womb. The incarnation,[45] the union of the divine with the human, must be dated from the conception, not the birth, of our Lord.

Since the unborn child is a live human being, it is therefore possible for him to die in the womb (*cf.* Job 10:18). The Apostle Paul could even refer to himself as an abortion—an abortion who lived (1 Cor. 15:8). When the prophet Jeremiah broke out into that remarkable cry of despondency[46] in Jeremiah 20, he cursed the day of his birth and went on to curse the man who could have killed him in his mother's womb, but did not (Jer. 20:14-18). Had the prophet lived in twentieth-century Europe, he might have had his wish fulfilled! The unnamed recipient of Jeremiah's curse was guilty in Jeremiah's jaundiced[47] eyes *"because he slew me not from the womb"* (Jer. 20:17). The word that is used here to describe the killing of a child in the womb is the same word that is used to describe David's slaying of Goliath in 1 Samuel 17:50-51. Apparently, Jeremiah knew of no euphemism[48] such as "termination of pregnancy."

---

45 *See* FGB 219, *The Person of Christ*, available from Chapel Library.
46 **despondency** – feeling downcast, disheartened, and hopeless.
47 **jaundiced** – pessimistic; state of taking an unfavorable view.
48 **euphemism** – a word or phrase used in place of a term that might be considered too direct, harsh, unpleasant, or offensive.

Throughout Scripture, God's judgment always falls on those who slay the unborn. The prophet Elisha wept when he thought of the crimes that Hazael, the king of Syria, would commit against Israel. In Elisha's words, *"[thou] wilt dash their children, and rip up their women with child"* (2 Kings 8:12). Later, the same evil was perpetuated by Menahem, one of Israel's last kings (2 Kings 15:16). When the heathen Ammonites ripped open the pregnant women of Gilead, the prophet Amos declared that God's judgment lay close at hand (Amos 1:13). All this indicates that, contrary to some claims, God's Word does give clear-cut guidelines on the subject of abortion.

The Biblical injunctions[49] against child sacrifice are also not without relevance for the abortion debate. God did not allow the Israelites to enter Canaan until the iniquity of the Amorites was complete (Gen. 15:16). As Canaanite culture became more debased, God prepared the Israelites to take possession of the Promised Land. Repeatedly, God warned the Israelites not to imitate their heathen neighbors (e.g., Lev. 18:24-30; 20:23). One of the things that God especially warned against was the sacrificial offering of children through fire to the Ammonite god Molech (Lev. 18:21; 20:2-5; Deut. 12:31; 18:10). However, as early as Solomon's reign, the worship of Molech was taking place in Israel (1 Kings 11:7). The practice of child sacrifice soon spread to Moab (2 Kings 3:27) and even to Judah, where Ahaz in the eighth century B.C. (2 Kings 16:3; 2 Chron. 28:3) and Manasseh in the seventh century B.C. (2 Kings 21:6; 2 Chron. 33:6) were guilty of the crime. In 722 B.C., the northern kingdom of Israel was destroyed by the Assyrians, partly because of Israel's participation in this brutal and idolatrous practice (2 Kings 17:17; *cf.* Ps. 106:34-39).

These child sacrifices prompted the prophets to declare God's judgment upon His people and to command repentance. Isaiah and later Jeremiah and Ezekiel were particularly moved to denounce the worship of Molech (cf. Isa. 57:5; Jer. 7:31; 19:4-5; 32:35; Ezek. 16:20-21; 20:31; 23:37, 39). When God said that He would not hear the prayers of the Judeans because their hands were full of blood, it is likely that the child sacrifices were at least partly in mind (Isa. 1:15). Much later, as Jerusalem edged closer to disaster, the godly king Josiah tried to reform Judah according to God's Law. Part of this reformation consisted of trying to abolish these sacrifices of children to Molech (2 Kings 23:10). It is indeed a sobering thought that the valley of Hinnom, to the south of Jerusalem, which was the site for these child sacrifices (2 Chron. 33:6; Jer. 7:31), was later used by Jesus as a picture of hell (e.g., Luke 12:5).

---

49 **injunctions** – formal commands.

The word *hell* or *Gehenna* comes from the Greek word *geenna*, which in turn comes from the Hebrew *gê* (valley of) *hinnöm* (Hinnom).

God's Word thus has much to say to us on the issue of abortion. Today, we see again Rachel, the woman of faith, weeping for her children because they are not (Matt. 2:18). Arguments in favor of abortion will also prove to be arguments in favor of euthanasia and infanticide—and hence a return to the practices of Pharaoh (Ex. 1) and Herod (Matt. 2:16-18). Those who hate God invariably love death (Prov. 8:36). Unborn life is indeed human life, and so embraced by God's commandment that forbids murder (Ex. 20:13). The cause of the unborn child is thus God's cause: *"When my father and my mother forsake me, then the* LORD *will take me up"* (Ps. 27:10).

P Barnes, *Abortion* (Edinburgh: The Banner of Truth Trust, 2010) © 2010, used by permission. www.banneroftruth.org.

Peter Barnes: Minister of the Presbyterian Church of Australia; now serving in the parish of Macksville after ministering in Vanuatu (formerly New Hebrides).

The Bible and Sanctity of Life

R. C. SPROUL

In biblical terms, the sanctity[50] of human life is rooted and grounded in creation. Mankind is not viewed as a cosmic accident but as the product of a carefully executed creation by an eternal God. Human dignity is derived from God. Man as a finite, dependent, contingent creature is assigned a high value by his Creator.

The creation account in Genesis provides the framework for human dignity: *"And God said, Let us make man in our image, after our likeness: and let them have dominion over the fish of the sea, and over the fowl of the air, and over the cattle, and over all the earth, and over every creeping thing that creepeth upon the earth. So God created man in his own image, in the image of God created he him; male and female created he them"* (Gen. 1:26-27). Creation in the image of God is what sets humans apart from all other creatures. The stamp of the image and likeness of God connects God and mankind uniquely. Though there is no biblical warrant for seeing man as godlike, there is a high dignity associated with this unique relationship to the Creator. It has often been suggested that whatever dignity was given mankind through creation was erased or canceled through the Fall. Since evil mars the countenance of human beings, is the original image still intact? Because of the Fall, something profound has stained the greatness of humanity. Therefore, we now must distinguish between the image of God in its wide and narrow senses.

The image of God in the *narrow* sense concerns mankind's ethical capacity and behavior. In creation, man was given the ability and the responsibility to mirror and reflect the holy character of God. Since the Fall, the mirror has been splotched[51] by the grime of sin. We have lost our capacity for moral perfection, but we have not lost our humanity with this ethical loss. Man may no longer be pure, but he is still human. Insofar as we are still human, we retain the image of God in the wider sense. We are still valuable creatures. We may no longer be worthy, but we still have worth. This is the resounding biblical message of redemption. The creatures God created are the same creatures He is moved to redeem.

Because Christians speak so tirelessly about human sin, do they have a low view of humanity? Indeed, they have a low view of human *virtue*, but not a corresponding low view of human worth or importance. It is precisely because the Bible has such a high view of human dignity that Christians take

---

50 **sanctity** – the quality of being sacred or holy.
51 **splotched** – marked with heavy splashes, spots, or stains.

human sin so seriously. If one rat steals another rat's food, we do not get morally outraged. But if one human steals another human's food, we rightly become concerned. The biblical view indicates that human theft is more serious than rat theft because humans are a higher order of being. As the psalmist indicated, we are created *"a little lower than the angels"* (Ps. 8:5). This ranking of value is deeply rooted within our own humanity. For instance, when the president of the United States is killed, we do not refer to the deed merely as homicide or murder. We have a special word for it: *assassination*.

During the news reports that followed the announcement of the assassination of President Kennedy,[52] the reporters seemed to have difficulty finding words powerful enough to express their outrage. They called the assassination "diabolical," "fiendish," "inhuman," and other such terms. I wondered at the time what made it difficult to describe Kennedy's murder simply as one human being killing another human being. Not only a devil or a fiend can commit murder. A person is not instantly shorn of humanity when he kills another human. Lee Harvey Oswald[53] was a human being when he pulled the trigger in Dallas. Does this mean, then, that in the hierarchy of value President Kennedy had more human dignity than Officer Tippet,[54] who was killed the same day in the same city by the same man? By no means! The murder of Officer Tippet was just as much an assault on his dignity as the murder of Kennedy was on his. Each was a human person. Each had personal worth and dignity. Kennedy's person was no more laden with dignity than Tippet's. What made the outrage over Kennedy's death greater than that over Tippet's death was the office Kennedy held. He was the president of the United States. He was the supreme *publica persona*[55] of our land. It is by similar reason that an offense against a human is more outrageous than an offense against a rat. Both the rat and the human are creatures created by God. But the "office" of a person is considerably higher than the "office" of the rat. It is mankind—not the rat—who is made in the image of God. The human is given a role of dominion over the earth. Man, not the rat, is God's vice-regent over creation. Does capital punishment violate the sanctity of life? The principle of the special dignity of mankind is echoed later in Genesis in the institution of capital punishment: *"Whoso sheddeth man's blood, by man shall his blood be shed: for in the image of God made he man"* (Gen. 9:6).

---

52 **John Fitzgerald Kennedy** (1917-1963) – 35th President of the US, assassinated in Dallas, Texas.

53 **Lee Harvey Oswald** (1939-1963) – alleged assassin of President John F. Kennedy.

54 **J. D. Tippit** (1924-1963) – Dallas police officer shot and killed by Lee H. Oswald.

55 **publica persona** – public person.

This text is not a prophecy. It is not saying simply that those who live by the sword will die by the sword. Rather, the passage is a divine mandate for capital punishment in the case of murder. The significant point is that the moral basis for capital punishment in Genesis is *the sanctity of life*.

The biblical ethic is [this]: because man is endowed with the image of God, his life is so sacred that any malicious destruction of it must be punished by execution. Note that this verse implies that God considers an assault against human life an assault against *Himself*. To murder a person is to attack one who is the image-bearer of God. God regards homicide as an implicit attempt to murder God. The sanctity of life is reinforced and reaffirmed in the Ten Commandments. We read, *"Thou shalt not kill"* (Ex. 20:13). The biblical prohibition against murder is widely known in our society. It is frequently appealed to as a moral ground against capital punishment. When the state of Pennsylvania voted to reinstate the death penalty for murder, the legislation was vetoed by then-Governor Milton Shapp. Shapp explained to the news media that the ground for his veto was that the Ten Commandments said, "Thou shalt not kill." Governor Shapp should have read on. If we turn just a single page in Exodus, we see what the Law of God required if someone broke the command prohibiting murder: *"He that smiteth a man, so that he die, shall be surely put to death"* (Ex. 21:12). The punitive measures against murder underscore the gravity of the crime precisely because of the value of the victim. Life is regarded as so sacred that it must never be destroyed without just cause. Many Old Testament statements speak of the dignity of human life as it rests in divine creation, including the following:

The spirit of God hath made me, and the breath of the Almighty hath given me life. —Job 33:4

Know ye that the LORD he is God: it is he that hath made us, and not we ourselves; we are his people, and the sheep of his pasture. —Ps. 100:3

Woe unto him that striveth with his Maker! Let the potsherd strive with the potsherds of the earth. Shall the clay say to him that fashioneth it, What makest thou? or thy work, He hath no hands? Woe unto him that saith unto his father, What begettest thou? or to the woman, What hast thou brought forth? Thus saith the LORD, the Holy One of Israel, and his Maker, Ask me of things to come concerning my sons, and concerning the work of my hands command ye me. I have made the earth, and created man upon it: I, even my hands, have stretched out the heavens, and all their host have I commanded. —Isa. 45:9-12

But now, O LORD, thou art our father; we are the clay, and thou our potter; and we all are the work of thy hand. —Isa. 64:8

Interestingly, Jesus Christ gave the most important explanation of the Old Testament view of the sanctity of life: *"Ye have heard that it was said by them of old time, Thou shalt not kill; and whosoever shall kill shall be in danger of the judgment: But I say unto you, That whosoever is angry with his brother without a cause shall be in danger of the judgment: and whosoever shall say to his brother, Raca, shall be in danger of the council: but whosoever shall say, Thou fool, shall be in danger of hell fire"* (Matt. 5:21-22). The words of Jesus have vital significance for our understanding of the sanctity of life. Here Jesus broadened the implications of the Old Testament law. He was speaking to religious leaders who had a narrow and simplistic grasp of the Ten Commandments. The legalists of His day were confident that if they obeyed the explicitly stated aspects of the Law, they could applaud themselves for their great virtue. They failed, however, to grasp the wider implications.

In Jesus' view, what the Law did not spell out in detail was clearly implied by its broader meaning. This quality of the Law is seen in Jesus' expansion of the prohibition against adultery: *"Ye have heard that it was said by them of old time, Thou shalt not commit adultery: But I say unto you, That whosoever looketh on a woman to lust after her hath committed adultery with her already in his heart"* (Matt. 5:27-28). Here Jesus explained that a person who refrains from the physical act of adultery has not necessarily been obedient to the whole Law.

The law on adultery is a complex one, including not only actual illicit intercourse but also everything that falls between lust and adultery. Jesus described lust as adultery of the heart. The Law not only prohibits certain negative behaviors and attitudes, but by implication, it requires certain positive behaviors and attitudes. That is, if adultery is prohibited, chastity and purity are required. When we apply these patterns set forth by Jesus to the prohibition against murder, we understand clearly that, on the one hand, we are to refrain from all things contained in the broad definition of murder; but on the other hand, we are positively commanded to work to save, improve, and care for life.[56] We are to avoid murder in all of its ramifications[57] and, at the same time, do all that we can to promote life.[58]

---

56 As every positive command implies a negative, so every negative implies a positive. Therefore, in so far as God says, *"Thou shalt not kill,"* viz. thyself or others, He thereby obliges men to preserve their own life and that of others. (Thomas Boston, *The Complete Works of Thomas Boston*, Vol. 2, 260)

57 **ramifications** – consequences of actions, especially when complex or unwelcome.

58 To be clear of the crime of murder, it is not enough to refrain from shedding man's blood.

Just as Jesus considered lust a part of adultery, so He viewed unjustifiable anger and slander as parts of murder. As lust is adultery of the heart, so anger and slander are murder of the heart. By expanding the scope of the Ten Commandments to include such matters as lust and slander, Jesus did not mean that it is just as evil to lust after a person as it is to have unlawful physical intercourse. Likewise, Jesus did not say that slander is just as evil as murder. What He did say is that the law against murder includes a law against anything that involves injuring a fellow human unjustly.

How does all of this apply to the abortion issue? In Jesus' teaching, we see another strong reinforcement of the sanctity of life. Murder of the heart, such as slander, may be described as "potential" murder. It is potential murder because, as an example, anger and slander have the potential to lead to the full act of physical murder. Of course, they do not always lead to that outcome. Anger and slander are prohibited, not so much because of what else they may lead to, but because of the actual harm they do to the quality of life.

When we link the discussion of the sanctity of life to abortion, we make a subtle but relevant connection. Even if it cannot be proven that a fetus is an actual living human person, there is no doubt that it is a potential living human person. In other words, a fetus is a *developing* person. It is not in a frozen state of potentiality. The fetus is in dynamic process—without interference or unforeseen calamity, it surely will become a fully actualized living human person. Jesus Christ sees the law against murder as including not only the act of actual murder, but also actions of potential murder. Jesus taught that it is unlawful to commit the potential murder of an actual life.

What, then, are the implications of committing the actual destruction of potential life? The actual destruction of potential life is not the same thing as the potential destruction of actual life. These are not identical cases, but they are close enough to make us pause to consider carefully the possible consequences before we destroy a potential life. If this aspect of the law does not fully and finally capture abortion within the broad and complex prohibition against murder, a second aspect clearly does. As I stated earlier, the negative prohibitions of the law imply positive attitudes and actions. For instance, the biblical law against adultery also requires chastity and purity. Likewise, when a law is stated in a positive form, its negative opposite is implicitly forbidden. For example, if God commands

---

If in act you perpetrate, if in endeavor you plot, if in wish and design you conceive what is adverse to another's safety, you have the guilt of murder. On the other hand, if you do not according to your means and opportunity study to defend his safety, by that inhumanity you violate the law. (Calvin, *Institutes*, II, viii, 39)

us to be good stewards of our money, clearly we ought not to be wild spenders. A positive command to diligent labor carries an implicit negative prohibition against being lazy on the job. A negative prohibition against actual and potential murder implicitly involves a positive mandate to work for the protection and sustenance of life.

To oppose murder is to promote life. Whatever else abortion does, it does not promote the life of the unborn child. Although some people will argue that abortion promotes the quality of life of those who do not desire offspring, it does not promote the life of the subject in question—the developing unborn child. The Bible is consistently strong in its support for the exceedingly great value of all human life. The poor, the oppressed, the widowed, the orphaned, and the handicapped—all are highly valued in the Bible. Thus, any discussion of the abortion issue ultimately must wrestle with this key theme of Scripture. When the destruction or the disposal of even potential human life is done cheaply and easily, a shadow darkens the whole landscape of the sanctity of life and human dignity.

From *Abortion: A Rational Look at an Emotional Issue,* copyright 1990, 2010; used by permission of Reformation Trust Publishing: www.ligonier.org/reformation-trust.

R. C. Sproul: Presbyterian theologian and teaching elder; president of Ligonier Academy of Biblical and Theological Studies; founder and chairman of Ligonier Ministries.

> *The more unnatural any act is the more horrid. It is unnatural for a man to be cruel to his own flesh; for a woman to go about to kill the child in her womb—O how your ears tingle at such a flagitious [shockingly brutal] act!*
> *—William Gurnall*

Mankind and the Death Factor
GEORGE GRANT

All they that hate me love death. —Proverbs 8:36

Sadly, because all men without exception are sinners, the most fundamental factor in understanding anthropology[59] is the Thanatos factor. With entirely non-Freudian implications,[60] the Thanatos Syndrome is simply *the natural sinful inclination to death and defilement*. All men have morbidly embraced death (Rom. 5:12).

At the Fall, mankind was suddenly destined for death (Jer. 15:2). We were all at that moment bound into a covenant with death (Isa. 28:15). Scripture tells us, *"There is a way which seemeth right unto a man, but the end thereof are the ways of death"* (Prov. 14:12; 16:25).

Whether we know it or not, we have chosen death (Jer. 8:3). It has become our shepherd (Ps. 49:14). Our minds are fixed on it (Rom. 8:6), our hearts pursue it (Prov. 21:6), and our flesh is ruled by it (Rom. 8:2). We dance to its cadences[61] (Prov. 2:18) and descend to its chambers (Prov. 7:27).

The fact is *"the wages of sin is death"* (Rom. 6:23) and *"all have sinned"* (Rom. 3:23). *"There is none righteous, no, not one: There is none that understandeth, there is none that seeketh after God. They are all gone out of the way, they are together become unprofitable; there is none that doeth good, no, not one. Their throat is an open sepulchre; with their tongues they have used deceit; the poison of asps is under their lips: Whose mouth is full of cursing and bitterness: Their feet are swift to shed blood: Destruction and misery are in their ways: And the way of peace have they not known: There is no fear of God before their eyes"* (Rom. 3:10-18). And, all those who hate God love death (Prov. 8:36).

It is no wonder then that abortion, infanticide, exposure, and abandonment have always been a normal and natural part of human relations. Since the dawning of time, men have contrived ingenious diversions to satisfy their fallen passions. And child killing has always been chief among them.

Virtually every culture in antiquity was stained with the blood of innocent children. Unwanted infants in ancient Rome were abandoned outside the city walls to die from exposure to the elements or from the

---

59 **anthropology** – the study of men.
60 **non-Freudian implications** – *thanatos* in the theories of Sigmund Freud (1856-1939) was mankind's urge for self-destruction. The author's point is that the Thanatos Syndrome to which he refers is not Freud's, but the revelation of man's radical depravity set forth in God's infallible Word.
61 **cadences** – rhythms.

attacks of wild foraging[62] beasts. Greeks often gave their pregnant women harsh doses of herbal or medicinal abortifacients.[63] Persians developed highly sophisticated surgical curette procedures. Chinese women tied heavy ropes around their waists so excruciatingly tight that they either aborted or passed into unconsciousness. Ancient Hindus and Arabs concocted chemical [contraceptives] …Primitive Canaanites threw their children onto great flaming pyres as a sacrifice to their god Molech. Polynesians subjected their pregnant women to onerous[64] tortures—their abdomens beaten with large stones or hot coals heaped upon their bodies. Japanese women [stood over] boiling cauldrons of parricidal brews.[65] Egyptians disposed of their unwanted children by disemboweling and dismembering them shortly after birth. Their collagen[66] was then ritually harvested for the manufacture of cosmetic creams.

None of the great minds of the ancient world—from Plato and Aristotle to Seneca and Quintilian, from Pythagoras and Aristophanes to Livy and Cicero, from Herodotus and Thucydides to Plutarch and Euripides—disparaged child killing in any way. In fact, most of them actually *recommended* it. They callously discussed its various methods and procedures. They casually debated its sundry legal ramifications. They blithely[67] tossed lives like dice.

Abortion, infanticide, exposure, and abandonment were so much a part of human societies that they provided the primary *leitmotif*[68] in popular traditions, stories, myths, fables, and legends.

The founding of Rome was, for instance, presumed to be the happy result of the abandonment of children, [Romulus and Remus]…Oedipus was presumed to be an abandoned child who was also found by a shepherd and later rose to greatness. Ion, the eponymous[69] monarch in ancient Greece, miraculously lived through an abortion, according to tradition. Cyrus, the founder of the Persian empire, was supposedly a fortunate survivor of infanticide. According to Homer's legend, Paris, whose amorous

---

62 **foraging** – searching for food.
63 **abortifacients** – drugs or other means that cause abortion.
64 **onerous** – oppressive.
65 **parricidal brews** – boiling mixtures used to kill a near relative, in this case, one's baby.
66 **collagen** – protein that is present in the form of fibers that make up bone, tendons, and other connective tissue in the human body, which yields gelatin when boiled.
67 **blithely** – carelessly.
68 **leitmotif** – recurring theme.
69 **eponymous** – of a person who gives his or her name to something, e.g., Ion founded the Ionians, a primary tribe of Greece.

indiscretions started the Trojan War, was also a victim of abandonment. Telephus, the king of Mysia in Greece, and Habius, ruler of the Cunetes in Spain, had both been exposed as children according to various folk tales. Jupiter, chief god of the Olympian pantheon, himself had been abandoned as a child. He in turn exposed his twin sons, Zethus and Amphion. Similarly, other myths related that Poseidon, Aesculapius, Hephaistos, Attis, and Cybele had all been abandoned to die.

Because they had been mired[70] by the minions[71] of sin and death, it was as natural as the spring rains for the men and women of antiquity to kill their children. It was as instinctive as the autumn harvest for them summarily to sabotage their own heritage. They saw nothing particularly cruel about despoiling the fruit of their wombs. It was woven into the very fabric of their culture. They believed that it was completely justifiable. They believed that it was just, good, and right.

But they were wrong. Dreadfully wrong.

Life is God's gift. It is His gracious endowment upon the created order. It flows forth in generative fruitfulness. The earth is literally teeming with life (Gen. 1:20; Lev. 11:10; 22:5; Deut. 14:9). And the crowning glory of this sacred teeming is man himself (Gen. 1:26-30; Ps. 8:1-9). To violate the sanctity of this magnificent endowment is to fly in the face of all that is holy, just, and true (Jer. 8:1-17; Rom. 8:6). To violate the sanctity of life is to invite judgment, retribution, and anathema (Deut. 30:19-20). It is to solicit devastation, imprecation,[72] and destruction (Jer. 21:8-10). The Apostle Paul tells us, *"Be not deceived; God is not mocked: for whatsoever a man soweth, that shall he also reap"* (Gal. 6:7).

But the Lord God, Who is the giver of life (Acts 17:25), the fountain of life (Ps. 36:9), the defender of life (Ps. 27:1), the Prince of life (Acts 3:15), and the restorer of life (Ruth 4:15), did not leave men to languish hopelessly in the clutches of sin and death. He not only sent us the message of life (Acts 5:20) and the words of life (John 6:68), He sent us the light of life as well (John 8:12). He sent us His only begotten Son, the life of the world (John 6:51), to break the bonds of death (1 Cor. 15:54-56)…*"For God so loved the world, that he gave his only begotten Son, that whosoever believeth in him should not perish, but have everlasting life"* (John 3:16)…In Christ, God has afforded us the opportunity…to choose between fruitful and teeming life on the one hand, and barren and impoverished death on the other (Deut. 30:19).

---

70 **mired** – sunk down in swampy mud; held fast.
71 **minions** – servants.
72 **imprecation** – curses.

Apart from Christ it is not possible to escape the snares of sin and death (Col. 2:13). On the other hand, *"If any man be in Christ, he is a new creature: old things are passed away; behold, all things are become new"* (2 Cor. 5:17). All those who hate Christ *"love death"* (Prov. 8:36), while all those who receive Christ are made the sweet savor of life (2 Cor. 2:16).

The implication is clear: The pro-life movement and the Christian faith are synonymous.[73] Where there is one, there will be the other: for one cannot be had without the other. Further, the primary conflict in temporal history always has been and always will be the struggle for life by the Church against the natural inclinations of all men everywhere.

Conclusion: Death has cast its dark shadow across the whole of human relations. Because of sin, all men flirt and flaunt shamelessly in the face of its specter. Sadly, such impudence has led to the most grotesque concupiscence[74] imaginable: the slaughter of innocent children. Blinded by the glare from the nefarious[75] and insidious angel of light (2 Cor. 11:14), we stand by, paralyzed and mesmerized. Thanks be to God, there is a way of escape from these bonds of destruction. In Christ, there is hope. In Him, there is life, both temporal and eternal. In Him, there is liberty and justice. In Him, there is an antidote to the Thanatos factor. In Him, and in Him alone, there is an answer to the age-long dilemma of the dominion of death.

George Grant, *The Light of Life: How the Gospel Shaped a Pro-Life Culture in the West*, (Franklin, TN: Standfast Press, 2015).

George Grant: Pastor of Parish Presbyterian Church, church planter, author, president of King's Meadow Study Center, founder of Franklin Classical School, and chancellor of New College Franklin.

---

73 This does not mean, however, that everyone who is pro-life is in fact a Christian.
74 **concupiscence** – eager desire; lust.
75 **nefarious** – extremely wicked.

Answers to Abortion Arguments

JOEL BEEKE

What is the justification for legal abortion? Let us examine the arguments used by those who promote abortion to determine on how strong of a foundation this practice is based.

Argument 1

The fetus is not a human life, therefore it may be killed. While the fetus will eventually become a human child, this argument says it is not yet so. But science indicates otherwise. First, the words *embryo* and *fetus* are Greek and Latin words that simply mean "young one." When scientists speak of a human embryo or fetus, they are not putting it in the category of another species, but are simply using technical terminology for a stage of development, like the words *infant*, *child*, *adolescent*, and *adult*. A human fetus is a young human person in the womb. It is natural and correct for mothers to speak of the fetus as "my baby" or for pregnancy books to say "your child."

Second, from conception, the child has its own genetic code that clearly identifies it as *homo sapiens*—part of the human race. The child's DNA also has a distinct code from the mother, showing that he or she is not a part of her body, but a distinct individual living temporarily within her.

Third, ultrasound[76] imaging shows that very early in the process of development the embryo grows into a recognizable human form. The child is not a blob of tissue, but a highly complex, though tiny, baby. At three weeks after conception, a baby's heart begins beating and pumping blood through the body. At six weeks, a baby's brain waves are traceable. Virtually all surgical abortions silence a beating heart and a functioning brain. At eight weeks, the arms, hands, legs, and feet are well developed and the child's fingerprints are starting to form. At eleven weeks after conception, all of the baby's internal organs are present and functioning. By the end of the first trimester, the baby kicks, spins, somersaults, opens and closes hands, and makes facial expressions.

By any reasonable standard, a human fetus is a young human being. To kill an innocent baby is murder. That is why the products of abortion are so ugly: severed hands, feet, and heads, wrapped up in bags and discarded. On an intuitive level, we know this. People can shrug off the image of a side of beef or a chicken drumstick, but images of abortion horrify and grieve us

---

76 **ultrasound** – using the reflections of high-frequency sound waves to construct an image of a body organ, commonly used to observe fetal growth.

because they are images of a dismembered human body. Unborn children are precious human beings and must be protected.

Argument 2

The fetus is not fully human because it is dependent on another. Is a baby kangaroo not a kangaroo because it lives in its mother's pouch? Of course not. The location and situation of a human being does not make him or her any less human. Arguments for abortion based on dependence tread on dangerous ground. If dependency makes a person less human, then on that ground we would have the right to kill infants outside the womb, people on dialysis, handicapped people, and the elderly. May we kill all dependent people?

Consider two mothers several months into their pregnancies. One child is born prematurely, and the other remains in the womb. The first is utterly dependent on medical intervention to survive, and the other on her mother's body. Is it right to kill the prematurely born baby? How would the hospital staff react if the mother entered the neonatal[77] ward with a knife to attack her child? If it is not right to kill the premature child, then why is it right to kill the child in the womb? Both are dependent. Both are children. Both must have legal protection.

Argument 3

A woman has a right to do with her body as she desires. We affirm a woman's authority over her body. But there are limits to what we can *rightfully* do with our bodies, including causing harm to another human being. Abortion involves the death of her child. To argue that the living fetus is part of the mother's body defies reason: which organ of her body is it? When the unborn child's heart beats, whose heart is it? When the fetus's brain waves can be traced, whose brain is it? Every pregnancy involves two people: a mother and a child; the rights of both must be considered.

Whenever we speak of the rights of two human beings, we must guard against the more powerful person taking advantage of the weaker person. It is the responsibility of the powerful to protect the weak. It is especially the responsibility of a mother to protect her child. Does any mother have the right to do whatever she pleases with her children? On the contrary, she has the responsibility of caring for them or seeing that someone else cares for them. Certainly, motherhood calls for sacrifice. We should expect adults to make sacrifices of their resources and freedoms when necessary to preserve the lives of children.

---

77 **neonatal** – relating to newborn children.

Argument 4

Sex and reproduction are private matters into which we must not intrude. We believe that human sexuality is a very private matter: it expresses the deep intimacy that a husband and wife share. But sex has very public consequences. How we exercise our sexuality contributes to the restraint or spread of disease, the treatment of women with honor or rape, the nurture or sexual abuse of children, and the strengthening or dissolution of families that are the foundation of society. Society therefore has a compelling interest to guard the dignity of marriage, women, and children with respect to sex and reproduction.

People sometimes argue that the U.S. Constitution guarantees the right to privacy in sexual and reproductive matters. Read the Constitution, and you will not find any such right there. In reality, the Fourth Amendment acknowledges the right of security against "unreasonable searches and seizures" without a "warrant," but says nothing about sexuality, children, or abortion.

Someone might sarcastically say, "I thought what I did in my bedroom was my own business." But if there is reasonable cause to believe that you are murdering a child in your bedroom, then it becomes a matter of public intervention by the authorities. Privacy is not an absolute moral right. But killing a child is an absolute moral wrong.

Argument 5

Making abortion illegal would force women into dangerous, back-alley abortions. The idea of the crudely done abortion resulting in a bleeding, dying mother (and a dead child) has been widely used by abortion advocates. But in reality, 90 percent of abortions performed before they became legal were done by physicians in their offices. The idea of thousands of women dying yearly until abortion was legalized is a myth. In 1972, thirty-nine mothers died in the United States from abortions. The *American Journal of Obstetrics*[78] *and Gynecology*[79] (March 26, 2010) admits that the legalization of abortion has had "no major impact on the number of women dying from abortion in the U.S....legal abortion is now the leading cause of abortion-related maternal deaths in the U.S."

Every woman who dies from a botched abortion is a tragic loss. But so is every child who dies from a successful abortion. We should not make it legal to kill babies in order to make the killing safer for the adults involved.

---

[78] **obstetrics** – the branch of medicine dealing with childbirth and care of the mother.
[79] **gynecology** – the branch of medicine that deals with the diseases and hygiene of women.

Furthermore, abortion has medical and psychological risks; making it illegal would actually protect the lives and health of millions of women.

Argument 6

Better to die before birth than to live as an unwanted child. First, to give a human being the power to determine the future life of another individual based on whether he is "wanted" or "unwanted" is most dangerous. Do we have the right to kill people based on whether or not we want them? Such a viewpoint leads highly cultured societies to commit genocide[80] against the mentally challenged and "inferior" races.

Second, is the child never wanted by anyone? Many mothers did not want the pregnancy but cherish the child, especially after birth. There are also many parents who want to adopt a child. To say that the child is not wanted now by its mother does not mean it will never be loved.

Third, this argument has horrifying implications for "unwanted" children already born. If it is better to kill the baby than to let it be unwanted, then what does that imply about homeless children? Children with abusive parents? Would it be loving to kill these children? Of course not; love calls us to teach their parents to care for them or to find parents for them. In the same way, if unborn children are truly "unwanted," we should try to help their mothers to see them differently or help the children to find adoptive parents. Did you know that Steve Jobs[81] was unwanted by his birth mother and the adoptive parents the government initially chose?

Fourth, what gives us the right to decide whether it is better for a person to live or to die? Are we the owner of that person's life? Do we know with certainty the child's future? Do not many "unwanted" children overcome severe physical or emotional handicaps in their youth and function as useful adult citizens? Do not many people in painful situations nevertheless wisely choose to live rather than to kill themselves?

In the end, the seemingly compassionate argument for the "wanted" child makes no sense at all. At best, it is an emotional, illogical appeal; at worst, it is a mask for deadly selfishness.

Argument 7

Pro-life advocates are trying to force their beliefs on other people. In reality, all who participate in an abortion force their views on another, namely on

---

80 **genocide** – the systematic killing of people based on ethnicity, religion, etc.
81 **Steven Paul Jobs** (1955-2011) – American inventor, computer entrepreneur, and founder of Apple, Inc.

the unborn child—so strongly, in fact, that it results in his or her death. If the unborn child is a human being, then how can one be accused of trying to force his own belief on another when trying to protect the life of the child from his or her killer? If the unborn child is a human being, then abortion is *murder*. If abortion is murder, we must do all in our power to stop it.

The Declaration of Independence says, "We hold these truths to be self-evident, that all men are created equal, that they are endowed by their Creator with certain unalienable rights, that among these are life, liberty and the pursuit of happiness—that to secure these rights, governments are instituted among men, deriving their just powers from the consent of the governed." Currently the rights of some people are more "equal" than others are because their "liberty and the pursuit of happiness" apparently justifies taking the "life" of others. This seriously undermines the political foundation of our nation. But if people exercise their popular power of voting to direct the government to protect all people's right to life, they simply do what the Declaration of Independence says they should.

After critically examining seven basic arguments for abortion upon demand, can we honestly conclude on a rational and ethical basis that abortion should be legal? These arguments are flimsy reasons for murdering more than a million babies each year. This is especially evident when we consider that less than 5% of all abortions are for reason of rape, incest, or a danger to the mother's life. More than 95% of abortions take place for the sake of finances, career, personal convenience, or other selfish reasons. Are these compelling reasons for killing human beings?

From *Is Abortion Really So Bad?*, available from Chapel Library.

Joel R. Beeke: Pastor of Heritage Netherlands Reformed Congregation in Grand Rapids, MI; theologian, author, and president of Puritan Reformed Theological Seminary, where he is Professor of Systematic Theology and Homiletics.

When Does Life Begin?

R. C. SPROUL

The question of when life begins is tightly linked to the secret of life itself... Concepts such as *human*, *living*, and *person* have been the subject of much discussion and analysis. Plato sought desperately for a description that would clearly distinguish humans from all other species of animals. He finally chose "featherless biped[82]" as his working definition. This lasted only until one of Plato's students threw a plucked chicken over the academy wall with an attached note that read, "Plato's man."

When we turn to the Bible, we discover that it offers no explicit statement that life begins at a certain point or that there is human life before birth. However, Scripture assumes a continuity of life from before the time of birth to after the time of birth. The same language and the same personal pronouns are used indiscriminately for both stages. Further, God's involvement in the life of the person extends back to conception (and even before conception). This passage supports the point: *"For thou hast possessed my reins:[83] thou hast covered me in my mother's womb. I will praise thee; for I am fearfully and wonderfully made: marvellous are thy works; and that my soul knoweth right well. My substance was not hid from thee, when I was made in secret, and curiously wrought in the lowest parts of the earth. Thine eyes did see my substance, yet being unperfect; and in thy book all my members were written, which in continuance were fashioned, when as yet there was none of them"* (Ps. 139:13-16).

The psalmist credits God for fashioning him in the womb. He also uses the term *me* to refer to himself before he was born. It is noteworthy that the Hebrew word translated as "unformed substance" is the Hebrew word for "embryo," and this is the only instance of that word in the Bible.

Another passage relevant to God's involvement in life within the womb occurs in Isaiah: *"Listen, O isles, unto me; and hearken, ye people, from far; The LORD hath called me from the womb; from the bowels of my mother hath he made mention of my name. And he hath made my mouth like a sharp sword; in the shadow of his hand hath he hid me, and made me a polished shaft; in his quiver hath he hid me; and said unto me, Thou art my servant, O Israel, in whom I will be glorified. Then I said, I have laboured in vain, I have spent my strength for nought, and in vain: yet surely my judgment is with the LORD, and my work with my God. And now, saith the LORD that formed me from the womb to be his servant, to bring Jacob*

---

82 **biped** – an animal that uses two legs for walking.
83 **reins** – the seat of human feelings or affections; representative of the heart.

again to him, Though Israel be not gathered, yet shall I be glorious in the eyes of the LORD, and my God shall be my strength" (Isa. 49:1-5).

This passage indicates not only that the unborn baby was distinct from the mother and was treated with a unique personal identity, but that his formation in the womb was the activity of God.

A similar treatment concerns the Prophet Jeremiah: *"Then the word of the LORD came unto me, saying, Before I formed thee in the belly I knew thee; and before thou camest forth out of the womb I sanctified thee, and I ordained thee a prophet unto the nations"* (Jer. 1:4-5). Jeremiah is told that God knew him before he was born. God had personal knowledge of the person of Jeremiah before the person Jeremiah was born. This indicates that God treated Jeremiah in a personal manner and as a personal being before birth. It is also significant that God "set apart" or sanctified Jeremiah before birth. Clearly, God extends the sanctity principle to life in the womb. Even those who do not agree that life begins before birth grant that there is continuity between a child that is conceived and a child that is born.

Every child has a past before birth. The issue is this: Was that past personal or impersonal, with personhood beginning only at birth? It is clear that Scripture regards personhood as beginning prior to birth. As David says, *"Behold, I was shapen[84] in iniquity; and in sin did my mother conceive me"* (Ps. 51:5). Professor John Frame, in *Medical Ethics*, made the following observation on Psalm 51:5: "Personal continuity extends back in time to the point of conception. Psalm 51:5 clearly and strikingly presses this continuity back to the point of conception. In this passage, David is reflecting on the sin in his heart that had recently taken the form of adultery and murder. He recognizes that the sin of his heart is not itself a recent phenomenon but goes back to the point of his conception in the womb of his mother…The personal continuity between David's fetal life and his adult life goes back as far as conception and extends even to this ethical relation to God."[85]

In Psalm 51, David recounts his personal moral history to the point of conception. An impersonal being, a "blob of protoplasm," cannot be a moral agent. If David's moral history extends back to conception, then his personal history also must extend to the same point. Not merely David's biological substance dates back to conception, but his moral disposition as well.

The New Testament provides a fascinating text that has bearing on the question of life before birth: *"[Mary] entered into the house of Zacharias, and saluted Elisabeth. And it came to pass, that, when Elisabeth heard the salutation of*

---

84 **shapen** – fashioned.
85 John M. Frame, *Medical Ethics* (Philipsburg, NJ: P&R, 1988), 94.

Mary, the babe leaped in her womb; and Elisabeth was filled with the Holy Ghost: And she spake out with a loud voice, and said, Blessed art thou among women, and blessed is the fruit of thy womb. And whence is this to me, that the mother of my Lord should come to me? For, lo, as soon as the voice of thy salutation sounded in mine ears, the babe leaped in my womb for joy" (Luke 1:40-44).

This passage describes the meeting between Mary, the mother of Jesus Christ, and her cousin Elizabeth, who was pregnant with John the Baptist. Upon their meeting, John, while still in the womb of his mother, leaped for joy. This behavior was consistent with the designated prophetic role of John, who was commissioned by God to "announce" the Messiah. In this instance, John performed his prophetic duty before either he or Jesus was born. These verses show that before John was born, he exhibited cognition[86] and emotion. He leaped because he was in a state of joy. The joy was prompted by his recognition of the presence of the Messiah.

Some people may dismiss the relevance of this passage because (1) the writer is speaking poetically or hyperbolically;[87] (2) the passage says nothing about life from conception, only about life prior to birth; or (3) the occasion represents a special miracle and does not prove that other babies could have such prenatal[88] ability. To answer the first objection, it is erroneous to dismiss the passage because it is poetic or hyperbolic. The literary form of this portion of Luke's Gospel is unambiguously[89] historical narrative, not poetry. Also, hyperbole is an exaggerated statement of reality. If this incident is presented with hyperbole, that simply means John did not leap as high or recognize as much as the text implies. The second objection, that the passage says nothing of conception as the beginning point of life, is correct. The passage clearly indicates, however, that John had human powers of cognition and emotion (signs of personality) prior to birth. The third objection, that this incident was a special miracle, is more weighty. Unless we claim that a normal fetus has the ability to recognize the near presence of another fetus in another woman's womb, we must concede that there is something extraordinary or miraculous about this occurrence. It is possible that God miraculously enabled the prenatal John to have extraordinary cognitive powers that do not belong to average unborn children.

---

86 **cognition** – perception; mental action of acquiring knowledge and understanding by thought, experience, and the senses.
87 **hyperbolically** – exaggerated statements not meant to be taken literally.
88 **prenatal** – before birth.
89 **unambiguously** – clearly defined with only one meaning.

However, if we grant the miracle, we are still left with a difficult question: Was the miracle an act of extending normal powers beyond the normal limits or an act of creating the powers? Did the unborn John the Baptist have the natural abilities of cognition and emotion, abilities that were extended by a miracle, or were the very powers of cognition and emotion created by God? There is no way to answer that question absolutely. However, before we dismiss the passage in Luke, two observations must be made. In many other biblical miracles, we see God extending powers or abilities that already exist. For example, in 2 Kings 6:15-17, God opened the eyes of the servant of Elisha so that he could see an angelic host. God did not first miraculously have to give the servant the power to see. Rather, the limit of his natural ability to see was extended. Likewise, for John to recognize Jesus Christ while each was still in his mother's womb, God did not necessarily have to create the powers of cognition and emotion. The second observation is that, however we evaluate this incident, one thing is certain: John the Baptist was an unborn child who manifested cognition and joy…The Bible clearly indicates that unborn babies are considered living human beings before they are born. The weight of the biblical evidence is that life begins at conception.

The development of a human being is a process that begins at conception and continues until death. No one would argue that human development begins at birth. The moment of conception combines forty-six genes—twenty-three from the mother and twenty-three from the father—so that a unique individual begins the process of personal human development. After two weeks, there is a discernible heartbeat. The heart circulates blood within the embryo that is not the mother's blood, but blood the unborn baby has produced. After about six weeks, the embryo is still less than an inch long but has undergone considerable development. Fingers have formed on the hands. At forty-three days, the unborn baby has detectable brain waves. After six and a half weeks, the embryo is moving; however, because of the tiny size of the unborn baby and the thickness of the mother's abdominal wall, she does not sense "quickening" or movement until several weeks later. By the end of nine weeks, the fetus has developed a unique set of fingerprints. By this time, the [reproductive] organs of the male have already appeared so that the gender of the unborn baby can be distinguished. The kidneys also have formed and are functioning. By the end of the tenth week, the gallbladder is functioning. All the organs of the body are functional by the end of the twelfth week, and the baby can cry. All of this is accomplished during the first three months of pregnancy.

Chapter 9—Abortion: When Does Life Begin?

In adults, heartbeat and brain waves are commonly referred to as "vital" signs. When both brain waves and the heartbeat cease for a period of time, a patient may be declared legally dead. Vital signs are a demonstration of life. When such signs are clearly present in the developing embryo, why are people so reluctant to speak of prenatal life? The embryo or fetus is not yet an independent living human person, but that does not mean he or she is not a living human person. If independence is the critical criterion for distinguishing living people from living non-people, then we must admit (as some readily do) that even birth does not yield a living person. At birth, the baby is disconnected physically from the mother—and in that sense is independent—but a newborn is still desperately dependent on outside help for survival. The newborn can breathe by himself in most cases, but he cannot feed himself.

In our quest to understand the presence of life, it is helpful to have an understanding of death. Since death is the cessation of life, it gives clues into the essential elements of life itself. One problem with our definitions of life and death is seen in the case of stillborn babies. Are stillborn babies "dead babies" or "never-have-been-alive babies"? It is commonplace for physicians to speak of stillborn babies as babies who have died…

The fetus *looks* like a living human person. It *acts* like a human person. The embryo has the genetic structure of a human person. It has the vital signs of a living human person. The fetus has sexuality and movement. Often, it sucks its thumb, reacts to music, and kicks its legs. With this cumulative[90] evidence, it would seemingly require powerful evidence to the contrary to conclude that a prenatal baby is not a living human person.

Why do people resist this conclusion? The answer is prejudice. Indeed, prejudice is a powerful force in the debate concerning abortion. If we regard the embryo or fetus as a living human person, then the moral implications of destroying that person prior to birth are enormous! As long as we can convince ourselves that a fetus is not human until birth, we are relieved of those difficulties. Even if we conclude that an embryo is a living human person prior to birth, we have still not established that life begins at conception. All we have established is that life begins before birth. The clearest lines of demarcation[91] in the continuum[92] between conception and birth are the conception and birth themselves. If we grant that a fetus is a living human person merely five

---

90 **cumulative** – created by gradual additions.
91 **demarcation** –marking the boundary or limits of something.
92 **continuum** – continuous series of things that blend into each other so gradually and seamlessly that it is impossible to say where one becomes the next.

minutes—*even five seconds*—before birth, then birth cannot be the point when life begins. In my judgment, the evidence from science is as weighty as that inferred from the Bible that a fetus is a living human person prior to birth. If that is so, then we must locate the beginning of that life either at the point of conception or at some point between conception and birth.

From *Abortion: A Rational Look at an Emotional Issue*.

R. C. Sproul: Presbyterian theologian and teaching elder; president of Ligonier Academy of Biblical and Theological Studies; founder and chairman of Ligonier Ministries.

> *Paul tells us of the old Gentiles that they were "without natural affection" (Rom. 1:31). That which he aims at is that barbarous custom among the Romans, who oftimes, to spare the trouble in the education of their children and to be at liberty to satisfy their lusts, destroyed their own children from the womb, so far did the strength of sin prevail to obliterate the law of nature and to repel the force and power of it. Examples of this nature are common in all nations—amongst ourselves—of women murdering their own children through the deceitful reasoning of sin. And herein sin turns the strong current of nature, darkens all the light of God in the soul, controls all natural principles [that are] influenced with the power of the command and will of God. Yet this evil hath, through the efficacy of sin, received a fearful aggravation. Men have not only slain but cruelly sacrificed their children to satisfy their lusts. —John Owen*

> *Although unhesitatingly and uncompromisingly committed to the cause of child killing, [Lawrence] Tribe, a well-known professor of constitutional law at Harvard, is forced to admit that abortion can only be advocated by those who have jettisoned the last remaining remnants of biblical orthodoxy. He essentially—and accurately—defines the titanic struggle between pro-lifers and pro-choicers as the struggle between Christian absolutes and pagan absolutes. —George Grant*

> *Zeal [for Christ] will make a man hate everything that God hates, such as drunkenness, slavery, or infanticide, and long to sweep it from the face of the earth. —J.C. Ryle*

Proclamations of God's Word and Abortion
JOEL BEEKE

Proclamation 1

God created mankind in His own image. Most people intuitively know that human beings are on a different level than animals. Even the theory of evolution cannot completely erase the sense most people have of how sacred human life is. Animals are beautiful and valuable, but we would kill a grizzly bear to save a child without any qualms of conscience. We know that people are special.

The Bible explains this sense of the sanctity of human life when it says in Genesis 1:27, *"So God created man in his own image, in the image of God created he him; male and female created he them."* Men and women, whatever their age, have a special value far above the birds and beasts (Mat 10:31) because they are God's most special creation on earth. We should cherish and protect human beings, not just for their usefulness, but because they represent God's glory in a unique manner.

Proclamation 2

God rules life and death, ability and disability as the sovereign King. We also have a sense that it is not right to "play God" with other people's lives. We realize that we do not have the right to treat people as if we owned them and could dispose of them as we see fit. The Bible explains this by telling us that God is the King Who owns and rules all of His creation (Ps. 95:3-5). He alone has the sovereign right to do what He pleases with people (Dan. 4:35).

When God created the world, there was no death or pain; all was *"very good"* (Gen. 1:31). Death came through Adam's disobedience to God's Law (Gen. 2:17; Rom. 5:12). But even so, God retained His sovereignty over human life and death. *"The LORD killeth, and maketh alive"* (1 Sam. 2:6). He rules over human ability and disability. *"And the LORD said unto him, Who hath made man's mouth? or who maketh the dumb, or deaf, or the seeing, or the blind? have not I the LORD?"* (Ex. 4:11). So the Bible teaches us to receive each human life from God's hand, even if it is a child born with a handicap or into a difficult family situation. God has a wondrous way of bringing good out of evil (Gen. 50:20). We are to bow before His authority as the King of the universe and not try to play God with other people's lives.

Abortion trespasses into divine territory by taking into the hands of man what belongs to the Lord alone. It insults His sovereignty and foolishly grasps the authority to make decisions for which we do not have the necessary wisdom. Consider the following historical case: The father has syphilis, the mother has tuberculosis. They have already had four children—the first is blind, the second died, the third is deaf and dumb, and the fourth has tuberculosis. The mother is pregnant with her fifth child. Will you perform an abortion for them? If so, then you just killed Ludwig van Beethoven (1770-1827), a famous German composer and pianist! Playing God with human lives produces tragic results.

Proclamation 3

God forbids the killing of innocent human life. Even after the Fall, though man's heart was totally corrupted by sin (Gen. 6:5), God told us that remnants of the image of God remain (James 3:9); and therefore we must treat human life with great respect. God says in Genesis 9:6, *"Whoso sheddeth man's blood, by man shall his blood be shed: for in the image of God made he man."* The sixth of the Ten Commandments says, *"Thou shalt not kill"* (Ex. 20:13), which in context means we must not take innocent human life. To kill innocent people is to attack God, for they bear His sacred image.

Proclamation 4

God reveals the human personhood of the unborn child. God personally forms each child in the womb. Job said, *"The Spirit of God hath made me, and the breath of the Almighty hath given me life"* (Job 33:4). David exulted, *"Thou hast covered me in my mother's womb. I will praise thee; for I am fearfully and wonderfully made: marvelous are thy works; and that my soul knoweth right well"* (Ps. 139:13-14). What God makes in the womb is a "me"—a person who has a "soul."

David also confessed, *"Behold I was shapen in iniquity; and in sin did my mother conceive me"* (Ps. 51:5). From his conception in the womb, David was "in sin." Objects and animals cannot be sinners; they have no moral accountability. Only a person can be a sinner. So the sad reality that we are in a state of sin from conception proves that conception creates a human person. Abortion is an attack upon a human person with the intent to kill. It is premeditated murder.

Proclamation 5

God declares His judgment against the killers of the unborn. The Lord has a special compassion for the weak when they are oppressed by those more powerful than they are, whether it is the foreigner, the widow, or the orphan. He threatens deadly wrath against oppressors (Ex. 22:21-27). No one is more vulnerable than an unborn child is.

For this reason, God included this law in His legislation for Israel: *"If men strive, and hurt a woman with child, so that her fruit depart from her, and yet no mischief follow: he shall be surely punished, according as the woman's husband will lay upon him; and he shall pay as the judges determine. And if any mischief follow, then thou shalt give life for life"* (Ex. 21:22-23). *"Her fruit depart"* is literally "her offspring come out." The law envisions the accidental injury of a pregnant woman with the result of a miscarriage,[93] when two men are fighting. If God decreed the punishment of an *accidentally* induced abortion, how much more will He punish an *intentional* abortion? God abhors all crimes against women, but violence against pregnant women especially provokes Him to punish the offending nation (Amos 1:13).

This does not justify taking personal vengeance or acts of violence against abortion providers. But it does warn us that if our nation will not protect the innocent, then God will deal severely with our nation. Senator Jesse Helms[94] wrote, "The highest level of moral culture is that at which the people of a nation recognize and protect the sanctity of innocent human life… Great nations die when they cease to live by the great principles which gave them vision and strength to rise above tyranny and human degradation…No nation can remain free or exercise moral leadership when it has embraced the doctrine of death."

Proclamation 6: God calls sinners to repentance for forgiveness of sins. When we declare God's proclamations against abortion, we do so being painfully conscious that we all have sinned in many ways (Rom. 3:23). We speak as sinners who have found mercy with God, inviting other sinners to find the same mercy. For this purpose, God sent Christ to die for sinners and to rise again: *"Him hath God exalted with his right hand to be a Prince and a Saviour, for to give repentance to Israel, and forgiveness of sins"* (Acts 5:31).

In Christ Jesus, there is a promise of forgiveness to all who come to Him. But that promise is coupled with the command to repent (Luke 24:47). Repentance is God's gift for the salvation of a sinner by which a sinner, out of a sense of the evil of his sin and the goodness of God's mercy in Christ, turns from sin to God with grief for and hatred of his sin, and with full intent to obey God by His gracious help.

Perhaps you have been a party to abortion: a father who encouraged

---

93 For the discussion of an alternate view of this interpretation, see article 2, "The Silent Holocaust," pp. 7-10.

94 **Jesse Helms** (1921-2008) – five-term Republican United States Senator from North Carolina and a leading conservative. He served as chairman of the Senate Foreign Relations Committee from 1995 to 2001. The quotation is from a speech in the U.S. Senate on January 11, 1977.

the death of your child, a mother who submitted herself to the deadly instruments, a doctor or nurse who performed the procedure, a vocal supporter of abortion in public policy, or just a silent citizen who has allowed millions of children to die without voicing your protest. If this is the case, then you are guilty of bloodshed against the image of God.

But the Lord Jesus Christ [calls] you, *"Come now, and let us reason together, saith the LORD: though your sins be as scarlet, they shall be as white as snow; though they be red like crimson, they shall be as wool"* (Isa. 1:18). He stretches out His nail-pierced hands to you, calling you to "come" to Him, and promising, *"Let the wicked forsake his way, and the unrighteous man his thoughts: and let him return unto the LORD, and he will have mercy upon him; and to our God, for he will abundantly pardon"* (Isa. 55:1, 7).

From *Is Abortion Really So Bad?*, available from Chapel Library.

Joel R. Beeke: Pastor of Heritage Netherlands Reformed Congregation in Grand Rapids, MI; theologian, author, and president of Puritan Reformed Theological Seminary, where he is Professor of Systematic Theology and Homiletics.

> *An even more chilling development comes in the form of an article just published in the Journal of Medical Ethics. Professors Alberto Giubilini of the University of Milan and Francesca Minerva of the University of Melbourne and Oxford University, now argue for the morality and legalization of "after-birth abortion." These authors do not hide their agenda. They are calling for the legal killing of newborn children.*
>
> *Giubilini and Minerva now argue that newborn human infants lack the ability to anticipate the future, and thus that after-birth abortions should be permitted. The authors explain that they prefer the term "after-birth abortion" to "infanticide" because their term makes clear the fact that the argument comes down to the fact that the birth of the child is not morally significant. They propose two justifying arguments: First: "The moral status of an infant is equivalent to that of a fetus, that is, neither can be considered a 'person' in a morally relevant sense." Second: "It is not possible to damage a newborn by preventing her from developing the potentiality to be a person in the morally relevant sense." Thus: "The moral status of an infant is equivalent to that of a fetus in the sense that both lack the properties that justify the attribution of a right to life to an individual."*

Those assertions are as chilling as anything yet to appear in the academic literature of medical ethics. This is a straightforward argument for the permissibility of murdering newborn human infants. The authors make their argument with the full intention of seeing this transformed into public policy. Further, they go on to demonstrate the undiluted evil of their proposal by refusing even to set an upper limit on the permissible age of a child to be killed by "after-birth abortion." —Al Mohler

We have laws against homicide, and if the unborn child is recognized legally and morally as a human being, abortion would be rightly seen as murder. —Al Mohler

Molech Is Alive and Well

FRANKLIN E. (ED) PAYNE

> *And the* LORD *spake unto Moses, saying, Again, thou shalt say to the children of Israel, Whosoever he be of the children of Israel, or of the strangers that sojourn in Israel, that giveth any of his seed unto Molech; he shall surely be put to death: the people of the land shall stone him with stones. And I will set my face against that man, and will cut him off from among his people; because he hath given of his seed unto Molech, to defile my sanctuary, and to profane my holy name. And if the people of the land do any ways hide their eyes from the man, when he giveth of his seed unto Molech, and kill him not: Then I will set my face against that man, and against his family, and will cut him off, and all that go a whoring after him, to commit whoredom with Molech, from among their people. —Leviticus 20:1-5*

Molech was a god of the Ammonites to whom children were "passed through the fire." That is, they were sacrificed. Sacrifices are made to gods to obtain their favor and to gain prosperity, pleasure, and power.

Is abortion any different? More to the point: is abortion not child sacrifice? The reasons for abortion are clear. People want sexual pleasure (often as fornication and adultery) without the biological consequences. People want prosperity, but children cost a lot of money; and they interfere with activities that give power and prestige. Children cause many inconveniences to parents. Children require that women be homebound "slaves" (according to liberals). Thus, Molech is alive and well today. People do not believe that some deity will reward them for their child sacrifice, but they believe that they will gain rewards by the destruction of their children.

Let us be sure about God's position in this passage. Not only was the one who gave the child to be sacrificed to be stoned to death, but *anyone who knew of the act and allowed it to go unpunished* ("hid their eyes"). God's judgment rested not only upon the person, but also upon his family. Today, the large majority of our society "hides its eyes," while the government and the medical profession officially commits child sacrifice. Far worse, most who call themselves "Christians" condone the practice…And, physicians are the priests who commit this sacrifice.

The people of the United States ought to be frightened! God has not changed. He is *"the same yesterday, and to day, and for ever"* (Heb. 13:8). He *will* bring His judgments upon us…

Abortion Is a Symptom: A primary principle for medical practice is the distinction between symptoms and diseases. For example, a cough may indicate pneumonia, sinusitis, lung cancer, tuberculosis, or any number of other diseases. The same principle applies here. Abortion is not the disease: it is a symptom. The disease is *secular humanism*,[95] as it is commonly referred to. More specifically, it is an anti-God mentality that has no standard of right and wrong. The cure is not only to pass laws that prohibit abortion. The cure is regeneration or being "born again."[96] When that happens, [God changes] a person from being a secular humanist to a Bible believer.

Being anti-abortion is a non-negotiable ethic for true Christians. The practice is totally against the character of God and His design for the human race. Everywhere God is described as the God of life, not of death…The true definition of life is communion with God. Nowhere is the death of innocent people a biblical solution to any problem.

Further, He describes Himself as the God of the fatherless and calls for the special care of the fatherless (Deut. 14:29; Isa. 1:17; James 1:27). Certainly, today's unborn children are fatherless. The Supreme Court in its Roe v. Wade decision of 1973 disallowed the father [from] having any right to say what is or is not done with the unborn baby.[97] Not only does this law apply to babies conceived out of wedlock, but those conceived *within* marriage as well. Thus, the heart of marriage can be ripped out along with the unborn baby. This destruction of marriage was the reason that God's judgment was applied to families as well as individuals (Lev. 20:5).

The unborn are among the most defenseless of people. They cannot voice protest. They cannot run away from danger[98]…By contrast, God designed the unborn to be the most protected. Their nourishment is constant and dependable. Their environment is quite comfortable and unchanging. They do not have to interact with people and be hurt by them. They are well protected physically, often so well that the mother can be seriously injured, and they are not…

Abortion and the Family: We should understand that abortion represents as much, if not more so, a destruction of the family as destruction of human life. The most intimate human relationship is the "one flesh" nature of husband and wife (Gen. 2:24b; Matt. 19:1-10). The highest call for one human to care for another is that the husband should love his wife *"even as Christ also*

---

95 **secular humanism** – the belief that humanity is capable of morality and self-fulfillment without belief in God.
96 *See* FGB 202, *The New Birth*.
97 Curt Young, formerly Executive Director of the National Christian Action Council, first made the author aware that *Roe v. Wade* had the effect of making all children legally fatherless while in the womb.
98 As is clearly and violently portrayed in the video, *The Silent Scream*.

loved the church, and gave himself for it" (Eph. 5:25) and to nourish and cherish her as he does his own body (Eph. 5:28-29). The negative statement of this oneness is, of course, the Seventh Commandment: *"Thou shalt not commit adultery"* (Ex. 20:14).

Most abortions are the "cure" for pregnancies that are a result of sexual promiscuity. The extent of this promiscuity is directly correlated to the value placed upon God's design of sexuality for marriage. Certainly, the most "Christian" society will have some sexual immorality, but not openly and as prevalent as the one in which the family has been devalued. Both the man and the woman who are promiscuous make the statement that the limitation of sexuality to marriage is unimportant. Abortion, the destruction of the life created by that union, is a further denial of the value of the family into which the child would have been brought. The pregnancy that results from promiscuity does not have to end in abortion. The baby could be placed for adoption. Thus, abortion is not a consequence of promiscuity but an additional statement that the raising of a child in a family is unimportant. In reality, the mother acts in a way that considers her unborn child to be better off dead than being raised in a family!

Abortion causes further decline in the family. At times, the stressed mother may think toward her children, "I could have aborted you and avoided this trouble." Heaven forbid, but some even voice this thought! Husbands and wives are less fearful of adultery, knowing that abortion is an efficient and hidden "backup" to a consequent pregnancy. Further, as the number of children increases in a family, the temptation increases to prevent further stress on the family budget by the abortion of the next child.

Abortion assists the state in its control of the family. The biblical pattern is for grown children to take care of their parents when they are no longer able to take care of themselves (Mark 7:6-13). With no children, the elderly must depend upon the state to care for them, if they have not made sufficient provision for themselves (and most have not). Even with one or two children, the burden upon so few might be more than they are able to handle along with their own financial responsibilities…

The Social Consequences of Abortion: Babies, children, and the adults that they become are a source of knowledge and wealth for a society. Unfortunately, some think that the larger the population, the fewer the resources that are available on a per capita[99] basis. What is not considered are the resources of the growing population, especially in an industrial society. First, the goods and services necessary to raise these children to adulthood

---

99 **per capita** – for each person.

are considerable. Pregnant women have to have special clothes and medical care. Babies and children need clothes, food, and bigger houses. When they enter school, they need supplies and teachers. All these items create industries and jobs for large numbers of people.

By the time the children start school, they become buyers themselves. Their early impact may not be great, but the spendable income of today's teenagers is staggering. Then, when they marry and have their own children, they compound the goods and services necessary. As they enter the work force, they become producers. Their talents and knowledge increase efficiency and production. And, they become taxpayers!...It is ironic that babies are being aborted because of their financial liability to families and to the nation. These are short-term savings, if they are savings at all. In the long run, abortions are a considerable loss of human resources and productivity to a nation. As Christians, we should adopt the axiom[100] that any violation of God's laws has a severe economic consequence in the long run. Abortion in itself is heinous,[101] but its consequences extend far beyond the act alone. *"The wages of sin is death"* (Rom. 6:23)—both directly to the unborn child and indirectly to the economic and social health of a nation.

From "Abortion: The Killing Fields" in *Biblical Healing for Modern Medicine*.

Franklin E. (Ed) Payne, M.D.: American physician; taught Family Medicine at the Medical College of Georgia for 25 years; has written helpfully and extensively on the subjects of biblical-medical ethics with Hilton Terrell, PH.D, M.D. (www.bmei.org), worldview (www.biblicalworldview21.org), and biblical-Christian philosophy (www.biblicalphilosophy.org).

---

100 **axiom** – an established or generally accepted principle.
101 **heinous** – outrageously wicked.

Great Forgiveness for Great Sin
CHARLES HADDON SPURGEON (1834-1892)

> *In whom we have redemption through his blood, the forgiveness of sins, according to the riches of his grace. —Ephesians 1:7*

Sinner, if you trust in Christ, He will forgive you the blackest sin into which you have ever fallen. If—*God grant that it may not be true!*—the crime of murder should be on your conscience, if adultery and fornication should have blackened your very soul, if all the sins that men have ever committed, enormous and stupendous in their aggravation, should be rightly charged to your account, yet, remember that *"the blood of Jesus Christ his Son cleanseth us from all sin"* (1 John 1:7); and *"all that believe are justified from all things"* (Acts 13:39), however black they may be.

I like the way Luther[102] talks upon this subject, though he is sometimes rather too bold. He says, "Jesus Christ is not a sham savior for sham sinners, but He is a real Savior Who offers a real atonement for real sin, for gross crimes, for shameless offenses, for transgressions of every sort and every size." And a far greater One than Luther has said, *"Though your sins be as scarlet, they shall be as white as snow; though they be red like crimson, they shall be as wool"* (Isa. 1:18). I have set the door of mercy open widely, have I not? There is no one here who will dare to say, "Mr. Spurgeon said that I was too guilty to be forgiven!" I have said nothing of the kind. However great your guilt, though your sins, like the great mountains, tower above the clouds, the floods of divine mercy can roll over the tops of the highest mountains of iniquity and drown them all. God give you grace to believe this and to prove it true this very hour!

The greatness of God's forgiveness may be judged by the *freeness* of it. When a poor sinner comes to Christ for pardon, Christ does not ask him to pay anything for it, to do anything, to be anything, or to feel anything, but He freely forgives him. I know what you think: "I shall have to go through a certain penance of heart, at any rate, if not of body. I shall have to weep so much, or pray so much, or do so much, or feel so much." That is not what the gospel says. That is only your fancy. The gospel [says], *"Believe on the Lord Jesus Christ, and thou shalt be saved"* (Acts 16:31). Trust Jesus Christ, and the free pardon of sin is at once given without money and without price (Isa. 55:1).

Another thing that indicates its greatness is its *immediateness*. God will forgive you at once, as soon as you trust Christ. There was a daughter, well beloved by her father, who, in an evil hour, left her home and came to

---

102 **Martin Luther (1483-1546)** – German leader of the Protestant Reformation.

Chapter 9—Abortion: Great Forgiveness for Great Sin

London. Here, having no friends, she soon fell a prey to wicked men and became an utter wreck. A city missionary met with her, spoke faithfully to her about her sin, and the Holy Spirit brought her to the Savior's feet. The missionary asked for her father's name and address; and at last, she told him. But she said, "It is no use for you to write to him. I have brought such dishonor on my family that I am quite certain he would not reply to any letter." They wrote to the father and stated the case; and the letter that came back bore on the envelope, in large text hand, the word *Immediate*. Inside, he wrote, "I have prayed every day that I might find my child and am rejoiced to hear of her. Let her come home at once. I have freely forgiven her, and I long to clasp her to my bosom." Now, soul, if thou seekest mercy, this is just what the Lord will do with thee. He will send thee mercy marked *Immediate*, and thou shalt have it at once. I recollect how I found mercy in a moment, as I was told to look to Jesus, and I should be forgiven. I did look; and, swift as a lightning flash, I received the pardon of sin in which I have rejoiced to this very hour. Why should it not be the same with you, the blackest and worst sinner here, the most unfeeling and the least likely to repent? Lord, grant it; and Thou shalt have the praise!

Again, the greatness of God's forgiveness may be measured by the *completeness* of it. When a man trusts Christ and is forgiven, his sin is so entirely gone that it is as though it had never been. Your children bring home their copybooks without any blots in them; but if you look carefully, you can see where blots have been erased. But when the Lord Jesus Christ blots out the sins of His people, He leaves no marks of erasure: forgiven sinners are as much accepted before God as if they had never sinned.

Perhaps someone says, "You are putting the matter very strongly." I know I am, but not more strongly than the Word of God does! The Prophet Micah, speaking to the Lord under the inspiration of the Holy Spirit, says, *"Thou wilt cast all their sins into the depths of the sea"* (Mic. 7:19). Not into the shallows, where they might be dredged up again; but into the great deeps, as in the middle of the Atlantic… "What! All my sins gone?" Yes, they are all gone if thou believest in Jesus, for He cast them into His tomb where they are buried forever!…If I am in Christ Jesus, the verdict of *"No condemnation"* (Rom. 8:1) must always be mine, for who can condemn the one for whom Christ has died? No one, for *"whom he justified, them he also glorified"* (Rom. 8:30). If you have trusted your soul upon the atonement made by the blood of Christ, you are [forgiven]; you may go your way in peace, knowing that neither death nor hell shall ever divide you from Christ. You are His, and you shall be His forever and ever…

Now I close by showing you how really God forgives sin. I am sure He does; for I have proved it in my own case, and I have heard of many more like myself. I have known the Lord to take a man full of sin, renew him, and in a moment to make him feel—and feel it truly too—"God loves me!" He has cried, "Abba, Father." And he has begun to pray and has had answers to prayer. God has manifested His infinite grace to him in a thousand ways. By-and-by, that man has been trusted by God with some service for Him, as Paul and others were put in trust with the gospel, and as some of us also are. With some of us, the Lord has been very familiar and very kind and has blessed us with all spiritual blessings in Christ Jesus.

Now I have done when I have just said that, as these things are true, then nobody ought to despair. Come, sister, smooth those wrinkles out of your forehead. You have been saying, "I shall never be saved"; but you must not talk like that, for Christ's forgiveness of sin is *"according to the riches of his grace."* And, brother, are you in trouble because you have sinned against God? As He is so ready to forgive, you ought to be sorry that you have grieved such a gracious God. As He is so ready to forgive, let us be ready to be forgiven. Let us not leave this [subject], though the midnight hour is about to strike, until we have received this great redemption, this great forgiveness for great sin.

Thus have I preached the gospel to you! If you reject it, it is at your peril...I can say no more than this. There is pardon to be obtained by believing. Jesus Christ is fully worthy of your confidence. Trust Him now, and you shall receive full and free forgiveness. The Lord help you to do so, for Jesus Christ's sake! Amen.

From a sermon delivered on Lord's Day evening, December 31, 1876, at the Metropolitan Tabernacle, Newington.

Charles Haddon Spurgeon (1834-1892): Influential English Baptist preacher; born at Kelvedon, Essex, England.

Chapter 10
DUTIES OF SONS & DAUGHTERS

The breakdown of authority that we see in our present age is astonishing. This breakdown has a destructive impact on young people and it must not escape us. While the effects of this breakdown are numerous, the harm done to young people who reject the authority of their parents is perhaps the most disheartening and destructive. Quite simply, rejecting parental authority devastates the younger generation and puts them on a path to failure, heartache, and ultimately God's judgment.

Hollywood portrays children as wise and parents as stupid, and thus children must only obey when it suits them. Much of modern advertising tells us that acting young is better than being mature. In virtually every form of media, and in every venue, our culture encourages us to question authority. In any direction a child turns, he will find somebody ready to tell him to just do what seems right to him.

Thank God that He has not left us in the dark regarding the duties of sons and daughters. With crystal clarity, He has used simple language to explain how they should make their way through the minefields of authority in family life. When their inner impulse is to reject their parents' authority, the Lord is present with His steadying words and Spirit to rescue them from the path of destruction. God promises to bless them when they honor their fathers and mothers. He richly rewards sons and daughters who walk in His ways; He smoothes their paths and blesses their godly pursuits. He makes it go well with them spiritually. All of these things are explained in this chapter.

Parents, are you creating a culture of honor and obedience in your home? Let all the children and parents who read these words understand what a blessing it is when children honor and obey. Young person, is it well with you? Do you honor your parents and other biblical authorities? Do you obey? If it is not going well with you, don't look in the wrong place for the answer. Often the answer is clearer and simpler than we imagine.

—Scott Brown

A Prayer for Readers, Especially Sons and Daughters
J. G. PIKE (1784-1854)

My dear young friend, if a person could rise from the dead to speak to you, could come from the other world to tell you what he had seen there, how attentively would you listen to his discourse, and how much would you be affected by it! Yet a messenger from the dead could not tell you more important things than those to which I now beseech you to attend.

I come to entreat you to [believe in] GOD, to follow the divine REDEEMER now, and to walk in the pleasant path of early piety.[1] O that I could with all the fervor of a dying man beseech you to attend to your only great concerns! For of how little consequence is this poor transient[2] world to you who have an eternal world to mind![3] It is not to a trifle[4] that I call your attention, but to your life, your all, your eternal all, your God, your Savior, your heaven, your everything that is worth a thought or a wish! Do not let a stranger be more anxious than yourself for your eternal welfare. If you have been thoughtless hitherto, be serious now. It is time you were so. You have wasted years enough.

Think of Sir Francis Walsingham's[5] words: "While we laugh, all things are serious around us. *God* is serious, Who preserves us and has patience towards us. *Christ* is serious, Who shed His blood for us. The *Holy Spirit* is serious, when He strives with us. The *whole creation* is serious in serving God and us. *All* are serious in another world. How suitable then it is for man to be serious! And how can we be gay and trifling[6]?"

Do you smile at this grave address and say, "This is the cant of enthusiasm[7]"?...The friendly warning may be neglected and the truths of the Bible disbelieved, but death and eternity will soon force on the most careless heart a deep conviction that religion is the one thing needful. Yes, my young friend, one thing is needful. So said the Lord of life (Luke 10:42)—needful to you, to me, to all. The living neglect it, but the dead know its

---

1 **piety** – reverence and love for God.
2 **transient** – lasting a very short time.
3 **to mind** – to think about.
4 **trifle** – something of little importance.
5 **Sir Francis Walsingham (c. 1532-1590)** – English statesman.
6 **gay and trifling** – light-hearted and foolish.
7 **cant of enthusiasm** – language of religious fanaticism.

value. Every saint in heaven feels the worth of religion[8] through partaking of the blessings to which it leads. And every soul in hell knows its value by its want.[9] It is only on earth that triflers are to be found: will you be one of them? God forbid!

Read, I beseech you, this little [booklet] with serious prayer. Remember that it is your welfare that is sought. I wish you to be happy here and, when time is past, happy forever. Fain[10] would I persuade you to seek a Refuge in the skies and friends that never fail. I plead with you a more important cause than was ever conducted before an earthly judge. Not one that concerns time only, but that concerns a long eternity. Not one on which a little wealth or reputation depends; but one on which your eternal riches or eternal poverty, eternal glory or eternal shame, a smiling or a frowning God, an eternal heaven or an eternal hell are all depending. It is *your* cause I plead and not my own: shall I plead your cause to you in vain? O my God, forbid that I should!

I know, my young friend, how apt we are to read the most serious calls as if they were mere formal things, of little more consequence to us than the trifles recorded in a newspaper; but do not thus read this little [booklet]. Believe me: I am in earnest with you. Read, I entreat you, what follows as a serious message…from God for you.

Consider what will be your thoughts of the advice here given you a hundred years hence. Long before that time, you will have done with this world forever. Then your now vigorous and youthful body will be turned to dust and your name probably forgotten upon earth. Yet your immortal soul will be living in another world and far more sensible of joy or grief than it can possibly be now. Then, my young friend, what will you think of this friendly warning? How happy will you be if you have followed the advice it contains! Fancy[11] not that it will be then forgotten. Calls and mercies forgotten here must be remembered there, when every sin is brought to the sinner's memory…but *now* is your day of grace; then, another generation will have theirs.

Think again—while you are reading this, thousands are rejoicing in heaven that they in past years attended to such earnest calls. Once they were as careless as you may have been, but divine grace disposed them to listen to the Word of life. They regarded the warnings addressed to them. They

---

8 **religion** – *religion* in the author's sense means Biblical Christianity.
9 **want** – lack.
10 **fain** – willingly.
11 **fancy** – imagine.

found salvation. They are gone to rest. *Now*, with what pleasure may they recollect the fervent sermon or the little book that under God first awakened their attention and first impressed their hearts…Yes, think that while you are reading …millions of wretched souls in utter darkness and despair are cursing that desperate madness that led them to turn a deaf ear to such friendly warnings once addressed to them. O my young friend, I beseech you by the joys of saints in heaven and by the terrors of sinners in hell, trifle not with this affectionate call!

Consider further: If you were going [on] a journey, you would prepare for it. Would you not, if going to travel only one or two hundred miles? Were you thus far from home, would not your thoughts be often there? If obstructions lay in the way that threatened to prevent your ever returning, would you not exert all your skill and power to remove them? Are you indeed only a stranger and traveler upon earth? Are you only going forwards through a little span of time to an eternal world, and there to find an endless abode amidst the deepest sorrow or the most perfect joy? Do many things unite to hinder you from reaching the kingdom of heaven? Is this the case? Indeed it is. Will you go forward, thoughtless [of where] you are going? Thoughtless of what awaits you on your entrance [into] that unseen world—that unseen, unknown, endless world of joy unspeakable or of grief beyond expression?... It is *impossible* to be earnest enough with you. If you ever know the worth of true piety, you will be convinced that it is. [If we saw] thousands asleep on the brink of a precipice and some falling and dying every moment, could we too passionately endeavor to awaken those not yet undone?

O my young friend, if you have been a careless trifler with the Gospel of Christ, danger infinitely worse—*eternal* danger—threatens you! Awake! Awake! I beseech you [to] awake! Awake, before it is too late! Before eternity seals your doom!...Awake! I beseech you, and begin to mind that one thing that is so needful to you—food is not half so needful to the poor wretch perishing of hunger, nor help to him that is sinking in the sea or scorching in the flames!

Perhaps all [that] I urge to gain your attention is urged in vain. Shall it be so? Will you slight your God and make your own destruction sure? Will you be a crueler enemy to yourself than even devils themselves could possibly be to you? Alas! If you will, what must be your condition soon? But let me hope better of you and offer you one request: Look up to God…with me in the prayer that follows. Then beg His mercy on yourself:

A prayer for the divine blessing on this [booklet]: Ever blessed and most gracious God, Thy smile is life; Thy frown is death. Thou hast access to every heart and knowest every thought of every creature in Thy wide dominions. Look down from Thine eternal throne and teach one of the meanest[12] of Thy creatures to supplicate[13] Thy mercies. Without Thy love, we must be poor in the midst of plenty and wretched in the midst of worldly joy. In Thy love is pleasure though in the midst of pain and wealth in the midst of worldly poverty. He that knows Thee and loves Thee, though he die of want and hunger, is infinitely richer and happier than the king who rules the widest empire, but knows Thee not. Thou art our only happiness, yet we have not sought good in Thee. Thou art our bliss, yet have we bid Thee depart. Thou hast the first and most reasonable claim upon our hearts; yet by nature, those hearts are shut against Thee. But if Thou hast blessed him that indites[14] this prayer with the knowledge of Thyself, bless those who may read or utter it with the same heavenly knowledge.

Great God, Thou only knowest what is man—a fallen, miserable wretch, a willful child and slave of sin, a deserving heir of wrath and woe. Thy heavenly pity has opened for him [the] way of life, but how few are they who find it! And, ah! No hand but Thine can guide the sinner into that peaceful path. Hard is the heart Thy goodness does not melt—no rock so hard. Cold is the heart Thy kindness does not warm—no ice so cold. Yet, alas! Great God, such is naturally every human heart…But Thou hast power to soften the rock, melt the ice, and change the heart! And hast Thou not the desire? Merciful Maker…Thou hast said, *"Look unto me, and be ye saved, all the ends of the earth"* (Isa. 45:22). Thousands now in glory have experienced Thy saving power. The feeblest instruments can in Thy hand perform the mightiest works. A pebble and a sling can bring down to the dust Thy proudest foe. Now then, compassionate God, display Thy power to save. Grant that some who read this [booklet] may yield to its persuasions and earnestly regard their best concerns. By feeble instruments, Thou hast awakened many a thoughtless heart. If this be the feeblest of the feeble, yet magnify Thy power and mercy by making it to one soul (O, might it be to many!) a solemn and awakening call. Let some of its readers learn the end for which life was given. O let them not sleep the sleep of sin and death until awakened by judgment and destruction!

Gracious God, teach them that life is not given to be trifled and sinned away. By the power of the Gospel, *subdue* the stony heart and *break* the rock of ice. With a voice effectual as that which shall wake the dead, bid the dead

---

12 **meanest** – lowest.
13 **supplicate** – ask humbly in prayer.
14 **indites** – puts into words.

in sin arise and live. Bid the young sinner that may read this volume [to] flee from the wrath to come…God of mercy, by Thy conquering Spirit make this little [booklet], which in itself is feeble as a reed, powerful to lead to penitence, prayer, and conversion some youthful wanderer from the paths of peace. O Thou Who pitiest wretched men, teach the young readers…to pity themselves! Let them not by sin and folly make even immortality a curse. Let them not despise Thy gracious calls, nor trample on Thy dying love. Over them let not hell rejoice and heaven mourn; but let the angels that dwell in Thy presence and the saints that surround Thy throne exult over some penitent awakened by this feeble instrument—some youth embracing the Gospel of Thy Son and finding every good in Him.

Great God, grant this request! O let the sorrows of the Savior urge it! O let the intercession of the Savior obtain it! O let the influences of the Spirit accomplish what is thus desired!…Bestow Thy Spirit, O God of love! Bestow those blessed influences, O Thou Savior of mankind, Who hast received gifts for men! Bestow them, O Father and Lord of all, and bring some youthful sinner to the feet of Thy crucified Son! Though it be but one, grant that one may go to Him for life…Now, O God of grace, hear this supplication and teach the young reader with sincerity of heart to join in that which follows. Grant this, great God, for His sake Who died on Calvary below, Who lives, reigns, and pleads for man above, and Whose is the kingdom, the power, and the glory, forever and forever. Amen.

From *Persuasives to Early Piety*, reprinted by Soli Deo Gloria, a ministry of Reformation Heritage Books: www.heritagebooks.org.

J. G. Pike (1784-1854): Baptist minister; born in Edmonton, Alberta, Canada.

Honor Your Father and Mother
THOMAS WATSON (C. 1620-1686)

Honour thy father and thy mother: that thy days may be long upon the land which the LORD thy God giveth thee. —Exodus 20:12

Children are to show honor to their parents by a reverential[15] esteem of their persons. They must "give them a civil veneration."[16] Therefore, when the Apostle speaks of fathers of our bodies, he speaks also of giving them reverence (Heb. 12:9). This veneration or reverence must be shown:

1. Inwardly, by fear[17] mixed with love. *"Ye shall fear every man his mother, and his father"* (Lev. 19:3). In the commandment, the father is named first; here the mother is first named, partly to put honor upon the mother because, by reason of many weaknesses incident to her sex, she is apt to be more slighted by children. And partly because the mother endures more for the child.

2. Reverence must be shown to parents outwardly in both word and gesture. Reverence to parents in word relates to speaking directly *to* them or speaking *about* them to others. *"Ask on, my mother,"* said King Solomon to his mother Bathsheba (1 Kings 2:20). In speaking of parents, children must speak honorably. They ought to speak well of them, if they deserve well. *"Her children arise up, and call her blessed"* (Prov. 31:28). And, in case a parent betrays weakness and indiscretion, the child should make the best of it and by wise apologies cover his parent's nakedness.[18]

a. Children are to show reverence to their parents by submissive behavior…Joseph, though [he was] a great prince and his father had grown poor, bowed to him and behaved himself as humbly as if his *father* had been the prince and *he* the poor man (Gen. 46:29). King Solomon, when his mother came to him, *"rose up to meet her, and bowed himself unto her"* (1 Kings 2:19)…Oh, how many children are far from thus giving reverence to their parents! They despise their parents. They carry themselves with such pride and neglect towards them that they are a shame to religion and bring their parents' gray hairs with sorrow to the grave. "Cursed be he that setteth light by his father or his mother" (Deut. 27:16). If all that set light by their parents are cursed, how many children in our age are under a curse! If such as are disrespectful to parents live to have children, their own children will

---

15 **reverential** – respectful.
16 **civil veneration** – polite and profound respect.
17 **fear** – respect and reverence.
18 **cover…nakedness** – not literal nakedness as in Gen. 9:23, but covering his parent's faults.

be thorns in their sides; and God will make them read their sins in their punishment.

b. The second way of showing honor to parents is by careful obedience. *"Children, obey your parents in all things"* (Col. 3:20). Our Lord Christ herein set a pattern to children. He was subject to His parents (Luke 2:51). He, to whom angels were subject, was subject to His parents. This obedience to parents is shown three ways:

1. In hearkening to their counsel: *"My son, hear the instruction of thy father, and forsake not the law of thy mother"* (Prov. 1:8). Parents are, as it were, in the place of God. If they would teach you the fear of the Lord, you must listen to their words as oracles and not be as the deaf adder to stop your ears. Eli's sons hearkened not to the voice of their father but were called *"sons of Belial"*[19] (1 Sam. 2:12, 25). And as children must hearken to the counsel of their parents in spiritual matters, so in affairs that relate to this life as in the choice of a calling and in case of entering into marriage. Jacob would not dispose of himself in marriage—though he was forty years old—without the advice and consent of his parents (Gen. 28:1-2)…If [Protestant] parents should indeed counsel a child to match with one that is irreligious or Roman Catholic, I think the case is plain—and many of the learned are of opinion—that here the child may have a negative voice and is not obliged to be ruled by the parent. Children are to "marry in the Lord," not therefore with persons irreligious; for that is not to marry in the Lord (1 Cor. 7:39).

2. Obedience to parents is shown in complying with their commands. A child should be the parents' echo: when the father speaks, the child should echo back obedience. The Rechabites were forbidden by their father to drink wine. They obeyed him and were commended for it (Jer. 35:14). Children must obey their parents in all things (Col. 3:20). In things against the grain, to which they have most reluctance, they must obey their parents. Esau would obey his father when he commanded him to fetch him venison because it is probable he took pleasure in hunting. But [he] refused to obey him in a matter of greater concern: the choice of a wife. But though children must obey their parents *"in all things,"* yet, "It is with the limitation of things just and honest." *"Obey…in the Lord,"* that is, so far as the commands of parents agree with God's commands (Eph. 6:1). If they command against God, they lose their right of being obeyed. In this case, we must unchild ourselves.

3. Honor is to be shown to parents in relieving their wants. Joseph cherished his father in his old age (Gen. 47:12). It is but paying a just debt. Parents raise children when they are young, and children ought to nourish

---

[19] **Belial** – "sons of wickedness" or "of Satan"; hence, wicked, worthless fellows; scoundrels.

their parents when they are old…Such children, or monsters shall I say, are to blame who are ashamed of their parents when they are old and fallen into decay and [who] give them a stone when they ask for bread. When houses are shut up, we say the plague is there; when children's hearts are shut up against their parents, the plague is there. Our blessed Savior took great care for His mother. When on the cross, He charged His disciple John to take her home to him as his mother and see that she wanted nothing (John 19:26-27).

The *reasons* why children should honor their parents are [these]:

a. It is a solemn command of God. *"Honour thy father"*—as God's Word is the rule, so His will must be the reason of our obedience.

b. They deserve honor in respect of the great love and affection that they bear to their children. The evidence of that love [is] both in their care and in cost. Their care in bringing up their children is a sign their hearts are full of love to them. Parents often take more care of their children than for themselves. They take care of them when they are tender, lest, like wall fruit,[20] they should be nipped in the bud. As children grow older, the care of parents grows greater. They are afraid of their children falling when young and of worse than falls when they are older. Their love is evidenced by their cost (2 Cor. 12:14). They lay up and they lay out for their children. [They] are not like the raven or ostrich that are cruel to their young (Job 39:16). Parents sometimes impoverish themselves to enrich their children. Children never can equal a parent's love, for parents are the instruments of life to their children, and children cannot be so to their parents.

c. To honor parents is well-pleasing to the Lord (Col. 3:20). As it is joyful to parents, so it is pleasing to the Lord. Children! Is it not your duty to please God? In honoring and obeying your parents, you please God as well as when you repent and believe. That you may see how well it pleases God, He bestows a reward upon it: *"That thy days may be long upon the land which the LORD thy God giveth thee."* Jacob would not let the angel go until he had blessed him; and God would not part with this commandment until He had blessed it. Paul calls this *"the first commandment with promise"* (Eph. 6:2)… Long life is mentioned as a blessing. *"Thou shalt see thy children's children"* (Ps. 128:6). It was a great favor of God to Moses that, though he was a hundred and twenty years old, he needed no spectacles: *"His eye was not dim, nor his natural force abated"* (Deut. 34:7). God threatened as a curse to Eli that there should not be an old man in his family (1 Sam. 2:31). Since the flood, life is much abbreviated and cut short: to some the womb is their tomb. Others exchange their cradle for their grave. Others die in the flower of their age.

---

20 **wall fruit** – fruit grown on trees trained against a wall for shelter and warmth.

Death serves its warrant every day upon one or other. Now, when death lies in ambush continually for us, if God satisfies us with long life, saying (as in Ps. 91:16), *"With long life will I satisfy him,"* it is to be esteemed a blessing. It is a blessing when God gives a long time to repent, a long time to do service, and a long time to enjoy the comforts of relations.

Upon whom is this blessing of long life entailed but obedient children? *"Honour thy father...that thy days may be long."* Nothing sooner shortens life than disobedience to parents. Absalom was a disobedient son who sought to deprive his father of his life and crown. He did not live out half his days. The mule he rode upon, being weary of such a burden, left him hanging in the oak betwixt heaven and earth, so as not fit to tread upon the one or to enter into the other. Obedience to parents spins out the life. Nor does obedience to parents lengthen life only, but sweetens it. To live long and not to have a foot of land is a misery; but obedience to parents settles land of inheritance upon the child. *"Hast thou but one blessing, my father? bless me, even me also, O my father,"* said Esau (Gen. 27:38). Behold, God has more blessings for an obedient child than one. Not only shall he have a long life, but a fruitful land: and not only shall he have land, but land given in love—*"the land which the LORD thy God giveth thee."* You shall have the land not only with God's leave, but with His love. All these are powerful arguments to make children honor and obey their parents…

From *The Ten Commandments*, reprinted by The Banner of Truth Trust: www.banneroftruth.org.

Thomas Watson (c. 1620-1686): Nonconformist Puritan preacher and prolific author; actual place and date of birth unknown.

The Duties of Sons and Daughters to Their Parents
JOHN ANGELL JAMES (1785-1859)

> *The father of the righteous shall greatly rejoice: and he that begetteth a wise child shall have joy of him. Thy father and thy mother shall be glad, and she that bare thee shall rejoice.* —Proverbs 23:24-25

Consider well the relation you sustain to your parents. There is a natural connection between you, inasmuch as they are the instruments of your very existence: a circumstance which of itself seems to invest them…with an almost absolute authority over you. The commonness, the universality of the tie, takes off the mind from contemplating its closeness, its tenderness, its sanctity.[21] You are literally parts of them and cannot dwell for a moment upon your descent without being struck, one should think, with the amazing and solemn weight of obligation that rests upon you towards a father and a mother. But consider, there is not only a natural, but in reference to duty, an *instituted* connection between you. Jehovah Himself has interposed and—uniting the language of revelation with the dictates of reason [and] the force of authority to the impulse of nature—has called you to filial piety,[22] not only as a matter of feeling, but of principle. Study then the relationship: look narrowly and seriously at the connection subsisting between you. Weigh well the import of the word *parent*. Think how much is employed in it towards its appropriate object, how many offices it contains in itself—guardian, rider, teacher, guide, benefactor, provider. What then must be the obligations of a child! The following is a brief *summary* of filial duties:

1. You Ought to Love Your Parents

Love is the only state of mind from which all the other duties that you owe them can arise. By love, we mean complacency.[23] Surely, this is due to a father and mother. The very relation in which you stand to them demands this. If you are destitute of this, if you are without any propensity of heart towards them, you are in a strange and guilty state of mind. Until you are married or are in prospect of it, they ought in most cases to be the supreme objects of your earthly affections. It is not enough for you to be respectful and obedient and even kind; but, where there exist no [biblical] reasons for alienating your heart, you should be fond of them. It is of infinite importance that you should watch over the internal state of your mind and not suffer

---

21 **sanctity** – sacred, and therefore entitled to respect and reverence.
22 **filial piety** – a child's loyalty to parents and family.
23 **complacency** – (nowadays *complaisance*) the desire to please or comply with the wishes of.

dislike, alienation, or indifference, to extinguish your regards. Do not take up a prejudice against them nor allow an unfavorable impression to be made upon your mind. Respect and obedience, if they do not spring from love, are…very precarious[24] in their existence.

If you love them, you will delight to be in their company and take pleasure in being at home with them. It is painful to them to see that you are happier anywhere than at home and fonder of any other society than theirs. No companion should be so valued by you as a kind father or mother.

If you love them, you will strive in all things to please them. We are always anxious to please those whom we regard and to avoid whatever would give them pain. If we are careless whether we please or displease anyone, it is obviously impossible that we can have any affection for him or her. The essence of piety towards God is a deep solicitude[25] to please Him; and the essence of filial piety is a solicitude to please your parents. Young people, dwell upon this single, simple thought: a child's pleasure should be to please his parents. This is love and the sum of all your duty. If you would adopt this rule, if you would write this upon your heart, if you would make this the standard of your conduct, I might lay down my pen: for it includes everything in itself. O that you could be brought to reason and to resolve thus: "I am bound by every tie of God and man, of reason and revelation, of honor and gratitude to do all I can to make my parents happy by doing whatever will give them pleasure and by avoiding whatever will give them pain. By God's help, I will from this hour study and do whatever will promote their comfort. I will make my will to consist in doing theirs and my earthly happiness to arise from making them happy. I will sacrifice my own predilections[26] and be satisfied with their choice." Noble resolution, and just and proper! Adopt it, act upon it, and you will never repent of it. Do not have any earthly happiness that is enjoyed at the expense of theirs.

If you love them, you will desire their good opinion. We naturally value the esteem of those to whom we are attached: we wish to be thought highly of by them. If we are quite careless about their respect for us, it is a sure sign we have no regard for them. Children should be desirous and even anxious to stand high in the opinion of their parents. Nothing can be a more decisive proof of a bad disposition in a son or a daughter than their being quite indifferent what their parents think of them. All love must be gone in such a case as this, and the youth is in the road to rebellion and destruction…

---

24 **precarious** – dangerously lacking in stability.
25 **solicitude** – concern.
26 **predilections** – preferences.

2. Reverence is the Next Duty

"Honour," saith the commandment, *"thy father and thy mother"* (Ex. 20:12). This reverence has respect to your feelings, your words, and your actions. It consists in part of an inward consciousness of their superiority[27] and an endeavor to cherish a reverential frame of mind towards them as placed by God over you. There must be…a submission of the heart to their authority in a way of sincere and profound respect…If there be no reverence of the heart, it cannot be expected in the conduct. In all virtue, whether it be that higher kind that has respect to God or that secondary kind that relates to our fellow creatures, we must have a right state of heart: without this, virtue does not exist.

Your words should correspond with the reverential feelings of the heart. When speaking to them, your address, both in language and in tones, should be modest, submissive, and respectful, not loud, boisterous, impertinent, or even familiar.[28] For they are not your equals, but your superiors. If at any time you differ from them in opinion, your views should be expressed not with the flippancy and pertinaciousness[29] of disputants, but with the meek inquisitiveness of pupils. Should they reprove and even more sharply than you think is due, you must lay your hand upon your mouth and neither answer them again[30] nor show resentment. Your reverence for them should be so great as to impose a considerable restraint upon your speech in their company, for much is due to the presence of a parent. It is exceedingly offensive to hear a pert,[31] clamorous, talkative young person unchecked by the countenance of a father or mother and engaging much of the conversation of a party to himself. Young persons should always be modest and retiring in company, but more especially when their parents are there. You should also be careful about the manner of speaking of them to others. You should never talk of their faults… nor say anything that would lead others to think lightly or to suppose that *you* thought lightly of them. If they are attacked in their reputation, you are with promptitude[32] and firmness, though with meekness, to defend them as far as truth will allow; and even if the charge be true, to make all the excuses that veracity will permit and protest against the cruelty of degrading your parents in your presence.

Reverence should extend to all your behavior towards your parents. In all your conduct towards them, give them the greatest honor. Let it be

---

27 **superiority** – position of authority.
28 **familiar** – taking liberties with someone too freely because of constant association.
29 **pertinaciousness** – unyielding determination.
30 **answer…again** – talk back.
31 **pert** – disrespectful; sassy; too ready to express an opinion boldly.
32 **promptitude** – quickness; readiness of action.

observed by others that you pay them all possible respect, and let it also be seen by them when there is no spectator near. Your conduct should always be under restraint when they are within sight—not the restraint of dread, but of *esteem*...

3. The Next Duty is Obedience

"Children obey your parents," says the Apostle in his epistle to the Colossians. This is one of the most obvious dictates of nature. Even the irrational creatures are obedient by instinct and follow the signs of the parent beast, bird, or reptile. Perhaps there is no duty more generally acknowledged than this. Your obedience should begin early: the younger you are, the more you need a guide and a ruler. It should be *universal*: *"Children obey your parents,"* said the Apostle, *"in all things."*

The only exception to this is when their commands are, in the letter or spirit of them, opposed to the commands of God. In this case, as well as in every other, we must obey God rather than man. But even here your refusal to comply with the sinful injunction[33] of a parent, must be uttered in a meek and respectful manner, so that it shall be manifest [that] you are actuated[34] by pure, conscientious motives and not by a mere rebellious resistance of parental authority. Your obedience should have no other exception than that which is made by conscience: if your situation, inclination, and taste are out of the question, [these must be] set aside when opposed to parental authority.

Obedience Should Be Prompt

As soon as the command is uttered, it should be complied with. It is a disgrace to any child that it should be necessary for a father or a mother to repeat a command. You should even anticipate, if possible, their injunctions and not wait until their will is announced in words. A tardy obedience loses all its glory.

It Should Be Cheerful

A reluctant virtue is no virtue at all. Constrained and unwilling obedience is rebellion in principle: it is vice clothed in the garment of holiness. God loveth a cheerful giver, and so does man. A child retiring from a parent's presence muttering, sullen, and murmuring is one of the ugliest spectacles in creation: of what value is anything he does in such a temper as this?

---

33 **injunction** – command; directive.
34 **actuated** – motivated.

It Should Be Self-Denying

You must give up your own wills, sacrifice your own predilections, and perform the things that are difficult as well as those that are easy. When a soldier receives a command, although he may be at home in comfort and he is required at once to go into the field of danger, he hesitates not. He considers [that] he has no option. A child has no more room for the gratification of self-will than the soldier has: he must obey. It should be uniform. Filial obedience is generally rendered without much difficulty when the parents are present, but not always with the same unreservedness when they are absent.

Young people, you should despise the meanness and abhor the wickedness of consulting the wishes and obeying the injunctions of your parents only when they are there to witness your conduct. Such hypocrisy is *detestable*. Act upon nobler principles. Let it be enough for you to know what the will of a parent is—to ensure obedience even though continents laid and oceans rolled between you and your father. Carry this injunction with you everywhere: let the voice of conscience be to you instead of his voice, and the consciousness that God sees you be enough to ensure your immediate compliance. How sublimely simple and striking was the reply of the child who, upon being pressed in company to take something that his absent parents had forbidden him to touch, and who, upon being reminded that they were not there to witness him, replied, "Very true, but God and my conscience are here." Be it your determination to imitate this beautiful example…and obey in all things even your absent parents.

4. Submission to the Family Discipline and Rule is No Less Your Duty than Obedience to Commands

In every well-ordered family, there is a rule of government: there is subordination, system, discipline, reward, and punishment. To these, *all* the children must be in subjection. Submission requires that if at any time you have behaved so as to render parental chastisement necessary, you should take it patiently and not be infuriated by passion or excited to resistance. Remember that your parents are commanded by God to correct your faults, that they are actuated by love in performing this self-denying duty… Ingenuously[35] confess your faults and submit to whatever punishment their authority and wisdom may appoint. One of the loveliest sights in the domestic economy, next to that of a uniformly obedient child, is a disobedient one

---

35 **ingenuously** – honestly and straightforwardly.

brought to a right sense of his misconduct and quietly submitting to the penalty he has incurred. It is a proof both of strength of mind and of good disposition of heart to say, "I have done wrong, and it is [fitting that] I should bear chastisement."

In the case of elder children…it is exceedingly painful when a parent, in addition to the extreme pain that it costs him to administer reproof to such children, has to endure the anguish produced by their utter indifference, smiling contempt, sullen murmuring, or insolent replies. This conduct is the more guilty because the authors of it [have] arrived at an age when they may be supposed to have advanced so far in the growth of their understanding as to perceive how deeply laid are the foundations of the parental authority—in nature, reason, and revelation—and how necessary it is that the reins of parental discipline should not be relaxed. If then you have committed one error in deserving reproof, do not commit another in resenting it. Keep all still within, let not your passions rebel against your judgment, but suppress in a moment the rising tumult of the soul.

The conduct of some children after reproof is a deeper wound on the heart of a parent than that which preceded and deserved the reproof. On the other hand, I know not a greater mark of nobleness of mind, nor anything that tends to raise a young person higher in the esteem of a parent or to endear him more to a father's heart, than a humble submission to reproof and an ingenuous confession of his fault. A friend of mine had a son, long since gone to join the immortals, who, having one day displeased his father before his younger brothers and sisters, not only meekly submitted to parental rebuke, but when the family were assembled at the dinner table, rose before them all. After having confessed his fault and craved his father's forgiveness, [he] admonished the junior branches of the family to take warning by his example and be cautious never to distress their parents, whom they were under such obligations to love and respect. Nothing could be lovelier or more impressive than this noble act. He rose, by his apology, to a higher place in the regard and esteem of his parents and the family than he occupied even before his fault. Sullenness, impertinence, and obstinate resistance are meanness, cowardice, littleness compared with such an action as this, which combines a heroic magnanimity[36] with the profoundest humility.

Subjection also requires a due observance of the rules laid down for the maintenance of family order. In every well-ordered family, things are not left to chance, but regulated by fixed laws. There is a time for everything and everything in its time…Meals, prayer, going to bed, and rising in the

---

36 **magnanimity** – courageous nobility in mind and heart.

morning are all in their appointed season. To these rules, it is the obvious duty of every branch of the family to submit. The sons and daughters may be growing up or arrived at full age; this matters not. They must submit to the law of the house; and their age is an additional reason for their submission, as it supposes a maturity of judgment that enables them to perceive more clearly the grounds of all moral obligation. They may think the rules too strict; but if the parent has enacted them, they should be in subjection, and that, as long as they continue members of the little community, though it be almost to old age. It is also for the parent to decide what visitors shall be brought to the house: and it is in the highest degree unbecoming for a child to introduce, or even wish to attempt to introduce, any companion contrary to the known will of a parent. The same remark will apply to recreations: parents must determine this point; and no child that has the proper feelings of a child would desire to set up any amusements that the taste, and especially that the *conscience*, of a father or mother forbids. Instances have occurred of young people inviting such friends and joining with them in such diversions in the absence of their parents, as they know to be decidedly contrary to the law of the house. This is such an act of base and wicked rebellion against parental authority, and such an unprincipled disregard to parental comfort as language is too weak to characterize. Even the books that are brought into the house must be in accordance with the domestic rule. If the parent forbids the introduction of novels, romances, or any other books, a child in most cases should forego his own predilections and yield to an authority that he cannot resist without opposing the institute of nature and religion.

5. It is the Duty of Children to Consult Their Parents

They are the guides of your youth, your natural counselors, [and] the family oracle that you are ever to consult and the responses of which are to be received with pious reverence. Even if you have just reason to suspect the solidity and penetration of their judgment, it is due to the relation in which you stand to them to undertake nothing without laying the matter before them and obtaining their opinion. How much more ready should you be to do this where you have every reason to confide in their wisdom. You are young and *inexperienced*: the path of life is in a considerable degree untrodden by you, and contingencies are perpetually arising that you have yet acquired no experience to understand…They have travelled the road and know its turnings, its dangers, and its difficulties. Go to your parents then with every affair: consult them on the subject of companions, books, recreations. Let a father's or a mother's ear be the receptacle of all your cares. Have no secrets that you conceal from them. Especially consult with them on the subjects of trade and marriage. On the former, you perhaps need their [financial] assistance, and how can you expect this if you take not their advice as to the best way of employing their property? As to marriage…the Scripture has furnished us with many fine instances of the deference paid in patriarchal times by children to their parents. Isaac and Jacob both appear to have left the selection of their wives to their parents. Ruth, though a daughter-in-law, was willing to be guided entirely by Naomi. Ishmael asked his mother's advice. Sampson sought for his parents' consent. The simplicity of that age has departed; and in the advance of society, more of the power of selection now vests in the children. But it should not be exercised independently of parental advice. An old divine said thus to his sons: "When you are youths, choose your callings; when men, choose your wives, only take me along with you. It may be old men see farther than you"…With all this, you must take especial pains that your [faith in Christ] may be consistent and practical; visible in all your conduct and more particularly conspicuous in the kind, tender, and dutiful manner in which you discharge your obligations to them.

Such is the compendium[37] of filial duties. Let [sons and daughters] read them, study them, sincerely desire to perform them, and pray to Almighty God for the grace that is in Christ Jesus to assist them in discharging their obligations.

From *A Help to Domestic Happiness*, reprinted by Soli Deo Gloria, a ministry of Reformation Heritage Books: www.heritagebooks.org.

John Angell James (1785-1859): English Congregationalist preacher and author; born at Blandford, Dorsetshire, England.

---

37 **compendium** – a short, but comprehensive summary of a larger subject.

Some General Responsibilities of Children to Parents

JOHN BUNYAN (1628-1688)

There lies a duty upon children to their parents that they are bound both by the Law of God and nature conscientiously to observe: *"Children, obey your parents in the Lord: for this is right"* (Eph. 6:1). And again, *"Children, obey your parents in all things: for this is well pleasing unto the Lord"* (Col. 3:20).

General duties: There are these general things in which children should show forth that honor that is due to their parents from them.

First, they should always count them better than themselves. I observe a vile spirit among some children, and that is, they are apt to look down upon their parents and to have slighting[38] and scornful thoughts of them. This is worse than heathenish;[39] such a one has got just the heart of a dog or a beast, which will bite those that produced them and her that brought them forth.

OBJECTION: But my father is now poor, and I am rich, and it will be a disparagement,[40] or at least a hindrance to me, to show that respect to him as otherwise I might.

ANSWER: I tell you, you argue like an atheist and a beast and stand in this full…against the Son of God (Mark 7:9-13). Must a gift, and a little of the glory of the butterfly,[41] make you that you should not do for, and give honor to, your father and mother? *"A wise son maketh a glad father: but a foolish man despiseth his mother"* (Prov. 15:20). Though your parents be never so low, and you yourself never so high, yet he is your father, and she your mother; and they must be in your eye in great esteem: *"The eye that mocketh at his father, and despiseth to obey his mother, the ravens of the valley shall pick it out, and the young eagles shall eat it"* (Prov. 30:17).

Second, you should show honor to your parents by a willingness to help them with such necessaries and accommodations that they need. *"If any widow have children or nephews, let them learn first to shew piety at home, and to requite[42] their parents,"* says Paul, *"for that is good and acceptable before God"* (1 Tim. 5:4). And this rule Joseph observed to his poor father, though he himself was next [to] the king in Egypt (Gen. 47:12; 41:39-44).

But notice: let them *"requite their parents."* There are three things for which, as long as you live, you will be a debtor to your parents.

---

38 **slighting** – disrespectful; insulting.
39 **heathenish** – like heathens; uncivilized; unchristian.
40 **disparagement** – act that brings loss of dignity.
41 **a gift, and a little of the glory of the butterfly** – gift: talents given by God; glory: outward colorful and fancy adornments such as clothing.
42 **requite** – repay; reward.

1. For your existence in this world. They are [the ones] from whom, immediately[43] under God, you did receive it.

2. For their care to preserve you when you were helpless and could neither care for nor regard yourself.

3. For the pains they have taken with you to bring you up. Until you have children of your own, you will not be sensible of the pains, watchings, fears, sorrow, and affliction that they have gone under to bring you up; and when you know it, you will not easily yield that you have recompensed them for their favor to you. How often have they sustained you in your hunger, clothed your nakedness? What care have they taken that you might have the means to live and do well when they were dead and gone? They possibly have spared it from their own belly and back for you, and have also impoverished themselves, that you might live like a man. All these things should duly, and like a man, be considered by you; and care should be taken on your part to repay them. The Scripture says so, reason says so, and there be none but dogs and beasts that deny it. It is the duty of parents to lay up for their children; and the duty of children to repay their parents.

Third, therefore show, by all humble and son-like behavior, that you do to this day, with your heart, remember the love of your parents. Thus much for obedience to parents in general…

Duties If You Are Not Saved

Again, if your parents be godly and you wicked, as you are if you have not a second work or [spiritual] birth[44] from God upon you, then you are to consider that you are more strongly engaged to respect and honor your parents, not now only as a father in the flesh, but as godly parents; your father and mother are now made of God your teachers and instructors in the way of righteousness. Therefore, to allude to that of Solomon, *"My son, keep thy father's commandment, and forsake not the law of thy mother: Bind them continually upon thine heart, and tie them about thy neck"* (Prov. 6:20-21).

Now, to provoke you to consider this,

1. That this has been the practice always of those that are and have been obedient children; yes, of Christ Himself to Joseph and Mary, though He Himself was God blessed forever (Luke 2:51).

2. You have also the severe judgments of God upon those that have been disobedient, to awe you. As, 1) Ishmael, for mocking at but one good act of his father and mother, was thrust out of both his father's inheritance and

---

43 **immediately** – directly, without anything in between.
44 See FGB 202, *The New Birth*.

the kingdom of heaven, and that with God's approbation[45] (Gen. 21:9-14; Gal. 4:30). 2) Hophni and Phinehas, for refusing the good counsel of their father, provoked the great God to be their enemy: *"They hearkened not unto the voice of their father, because the LORD would slay them"* (1 Sam. 2:23-25). 3) Absalom was hanged, as I may say, by God Himself, for rebelling against his father (2 Sam. 18:9).

3. Besides, little do you know how heart-aching a consideration it is to your parents when they do but *suppose* you may be damned! How many prayers, sighs, and tears are there wrung from their hearts upon this account? Every misdeed of yours goes to their heart, for fear God should take an occasion by it to shut you up in hardness forever. How did Abraham groan for Ishmael? "O," said he to God, "that Ishmael might live before thee!" (Gen. 17:18). How were Isaac and Rebecca grieved for the misbehavior of Esau (Gen. 26:34-35)? And how bitterly did David mourn for his son who died in his wickedness? (2 Sam. 18:32-33).

4. Lastly, and can any imagine, but that all these prayers, sighs, etc., of your godly parents, will be to you the increase of your torments in hell if you die in your sins notwithstanding?

Duties If You Are Saved

Again, if your parents and you also be godly, how happy a thing is this? How should you rejoice that the same faith should dwell both in your parents and you? Your conversion, possibly, is the fruit of your parents' groans and prayers for your soul, and they cannot choose but [to] rejoice—rejoice with them. It is true in the salvation of a natural son, which is mentioned in the parable: *"This my son was dead, and is alive again; he was lost, and is found. And they began to be merry"* (Luke 15:24). Let, therefore, the consideration of this—that your parents have grace, as well as you—engage your heart so much the more to honor, reverence, and obey them.

You are better able now to consider the pains and care that your friends have been at, both for your body and soul; therefore strive to repay them. You have strength to answer in some measure the command; therefore do not neglect it. It is a double sin in a gracious son not to remember the commandment, yes, the first commandment with promise (Eph. 6:1-2). Take heed of giving your sweet parents one snappish word or behaving in any way unseemly towards them. Love them because they are your parents, because they are godly, and because you must be in glory with them.

---

[45] **approbation** – approval.

Duties If Your Parents Are Not Saved

Again, if you be godly and your parents wicked, as often it sadly falls out, then,

1. Let your heart yearn towards them: it is your parents that are going to hell!

2. As I said before to the wife as touching her unbelieving husband, so now I say to you: Take heed of a parroting[46] tongue. Speak to them wisely, meekly, and humbly; do for them faithfully without repining;[47] and bear with all child-like modesty their reproaches, their railing, and evil speaking. Watch [for] fit opportunities to lay their condition before them. O! how happy a thing would it be if God should use a child to bring his father to the faith! Then indeed might the father say, "With the fruit of my own body has God converted my soul." The Lord, if it be His will, convert our poor parents, that they, with us, may be the children of God.

From *Christian Behavior*, available from Chapel Library.

John Bunyan (1628-1688): English minister, preacher, and author; born at Elstow near Bedford, England.

> *Some of us owe a great deal to our [families], and all of you have reason to thank God that you are the son of such a one, or that you are the father of such a one, or the sister of such a one, or the brother of such a one. There is a special mercy, probably, in your domestic position; and if there is, do not cease to praise God that He has given you to be associated in life with those who are associated with Him! May our children be His children! May our friends be His friends! May our brothers be our Brothers in Christ! —C. H. Spurgeon*

---

46 **parroting** – repeating in a mechanical way like a parrot, therefore, disrespecting one's parents by mockingly repeating them.
47 **repining** – grumbling.

Children, Authority, and Society

DAVID MARTYN LLOYD-JONES (1899-1981)

Children, obey your parents in the Lord: for this is right. Honour thy father and mother; which is the first commandment with promise; that it may be well with thee, and thou mayest live long on the earth. —Ephesians 6:1-3

We are living in a world that is witnessing an alarming breakdown in the matter of discipline. Lawlessness is rampant. There is a breakdown in discipline in all these fundamental units of life—in marriage and in home relationships. A spirit of lawlessness is abroad, and things that were once more or less taken for granted are not only being queried[48] and questioned but are being ridiculed and dismissed. There is no question but that we are living in an age when there is a ferment of evil working actively in the whole of society. We can go further—and I am simply saying something that all observers of life are agreed about, whether they are Christians or not—and say that in many ways we are face to face with a total collapse and breakdown of what is called "civilization" and society. And there is no respect in which this is more evident and obvious than in this matter of the relationship of parents and children.

I know that much of what we are witnessing is probably a reaction from something that was far too common, unfortunately, at the end of the Victorian era and in the early years of this present century. I shall have more to say about that later, but I mention it now in passing in order to set out this problem clearly. There is no doubt a reaction against the stern, legalistic, and almost cruel Victorian type of father. I am not excusing the present position, but it is important that we understand it and try to trace its origin. But whatever the cause, there is no doubt that it is part and parcel of this collapse in the whole matter of discipline and law and order.

The Bible in its teaching and in its history tells us that this is something that always happens at a time of irreligion, at a time of godlessness. For instance, we have a notable example in what the Apostle Paul says about the world in the Epistle to the Romans in the second half of the first chapter from verse 18 to the end. There he gives an appalling description of the state of the world at the time when our Lord came into it. It was a state of sheer lawlessness. And in the various manifestations of that lawlessness which he lists, he includes this very matter we are now considering.

---

48 **queried** – doubted.

First, he says, *"God gave them over to a reprobate mind, to do those things which are not convenient*[49]*"* (1:28). Then follows the description: *"Being filled with all unrighteousness, fornication, wickedness, covetousness, maliciousness; full of envy, murder, debate,*[50] *deceit, malignity;*[51] *whisperers, backbiters, haters of God, despiteful, proud, boasters, inventors of evil things, disobedient to parents, without understanding, covenant-breakers, without natural affection,*[52] *implacable,*[53] *unmerciful…"* In that horrible list, Paul includes this idea of being disobedient to parents.

Again, in the Second Epistle to Timothy, probably the last letter he ever wrote, we find him saying in the third chapter, verse 1, *"In the last days perilous times shall come."* Then he states the characteristics of such times: *"For men shall be lovers of their own selves, covetous, boasters, proud, blasphemers, disobedient to parents, unthankful, unholy, without natural affection"*—that has gone—*"trucebreakers,*[54] *false accusers, incontinent,*[55] *fierce,*[56] *despisers of those that are good, traitors, heady,*[57] *highminded, lovers of pleasures more than lovers of God"* (2 Tim. 3:1-4).

In both instances, the Apostle reminds us that at a time of apostasy, at a time of gross godlessness and irreligion, when the very foundations are shaking, one of the most striking manifestations of the lawlessness is *"[disobedience] to parents."* So it is not at all surprising that he should call attention to it here, as he gives us illustrations of how the life that is *"filled with the Spirit"* of God manifests itself (Eph. 5:18). When will the civil authorities learn and realize that there is an indissoluble connection between godlessness and a lack of morality and decent behavior? There is an order in these matters. *"The wrath of God is revealed from heaven,"* says the Apostle in Romans 1:18, *"against all ungodliness and unrighteousness of men."* If you have ungodliness, you will always have unrighteousness. But the tragedy is that the civil authorities—irrespective of which political party is in power—all seem to be governed by modern psychology rather than by the Scriptures. They all are convinced that they can deal with unrighteousness directly, in and by itself. But that is impossible. Unrighteousness is always the result of

---

49 **are not convenient** – not proper; should not be done.
50 **debate** – quarreling; strife.
51 **malignity** – mean-spiritedness; evil done for the sake of evil.
52 **without natural affection** – hardhearted; without regard for others.
53 **implacable** – unwilling to negotiate the resolution of a problem; irreconcilable.
54 **trucebreakers** – *see* implacable.
55 **incontinent** – without self-control.
56 **fierce** – brutal; savage.
57 **heady** – reckless; thoughtless.

ungodliness. The only hope of getting back any measure of righteousness into life is to have a revival of godliness. That is precisely what the Apostle is saying to the Ephesians and to us…

Present conditions therefore demand that we should look at the Apostle's statement. I believe that Christian parents and children, Christian families, have a unique opportunity of witnessing to the world at this present time by just being different. We can be true evangelists by showing this discipline, this law and order, this true relationship between parents and children. We may be the means under God's hand of bringing many to a knowledge of the Truth. Let us therefore think of it in that way.

But there is a second reason why we all need this teaching. According to the Scriptures, it is not only needed by those who are not Christians in the way I have been indicating, but Christian people also need this exhortation because the devil often comes in at this point in a most subtle manner and tries to sidetrack us. In the fifteenth chapter of Matthew's Gospel, our Lord takes up this point with the religious people of His day because they were in a very subtle way evading one of the plain injunctions of the Ten Commandments. The Ten Commandments told them to honor their parents, to respect them, and to care for them; but what was happening was that some of those people, who claimed to be ultra-religious, instead of doing what the Commandment told them to do, said in effect, "Ah, I have dedicated this money that I have to the Lord. I therefore cannot look after you, my parents." This is how He puts it: *"But ye say, Whosoever shall say to his father or his mother, It is a gift, by whatsoever thou mightest be profited by me; and honour not his father or his mother, he shall be free"* (Matt. 15:5-6). They were saying, "This is Corban,[58] this is dedicated to the Lord. Of course, I would like to look after you and help you, and so on; but this has been dedicated to the Lord." In this way, they were neglecting their parents and their duties towards them…

Let us, then, in the light of these things notice how the Apostle states the matter. He starts—using the same principle as he used in the case of the married relationship—with the children. That is to say, he starts with those who are under obedience, those who are to be subject. He started with the wives and then went on to the husbands. Here he starts with the children and then goes on to the parents. He does so because he is illustrating this fundamental point: *"Submitting yourselves one to another in the fear of God"* (Eph. 5:21). The injunction is, *"Children, obey your parents."* Then he reminds them of the Commandment, *"Honour thy father and mother."*

---

58 **Corban** – among the ancient Hebrews, an offering given to God in performance of a vow.

In passing, we note the interesting point that here, once again, we have something that differentiates Christianity from paganism. The pagans in these matters did not link the mother with the father, but spoke of the father only. But the Christian position, as indeed the Jewish position as given by God to Moses, puts the mother *with* the father. The injunction is that children are to obey their parents; and the word *obey* means not only to listen to, but to listen as realizing that you are under authority…You not only listen, but you recognize your position of subservience;[59] and you proceed to put it into practice.

But it is most important that this should be governed and controlled by the accompanying idea—that of "honoring." *"Honour thy father and mother."* That means "respect," "reverence." This is an *essential* part of the Commandment. Children are not to give a mechanical and a grudging obedience. That is quite wrong. That is to observe the letter but not the spirit. That is what our Lord condemned so strongly in the Pharisees. No, they are to observe the spirit as well as the letter of the Law. Children are to reverence and to respect their parents, they are to realize the position as it obtains between them, and they are to rejoice in it. They are to regard it as a great privilege, and therefore they must go out of their way *always* to show this reverence and respect in their every action.

The Apostle's appeal implies that Christian children should be an entire contrast to godless children[60] who generally show lack of reverence for parents and ask, "Who are they?" "Why should I listen?" They regard their parents as "back numbers"[61] and speak of them disrespectfully. They assert themselves and their own rights and their "modernism" in this whole matter of conduct. That was happening in the pagan society out of which these Ephesians had come, as it is happening in the pagan society that is round and about us at this present time. We read constantly in the newspapers of how this lawlessness is coming in, and how children, so it is worded, "are maturing at an earlier age." There is no such thing, of course. Physiology does not change. What is changing is the mentality and the outlook leading to aggressiveness and a failure to be governed by biblical principles and biblical teaching. One hears of this on all hands—young people speaking disrespectfully to their parents, looking disrespectfully at them, flouting[62]

---

59 **subservience** – obedience to authority.
60 This is a reference to Western culture, not to various Eastern cultures in which children are still expected to respect their parents.
61 **back numbers** – the numbers of a magazine, periodical, etc., earlier than the current one; hence, one who is behind the times, out of date, or useless.
62 **flouting** – expressing contempt and scorn; laughing at with derision.

everything that they tell them, and asserting themselves and their own rights. It is one of the ugliest manifestations of the sinfulness and the lawlessness of this present age. Now, over and against all such behavior, the Apostle says, "Children, obey your parents; honor your father and mother, treat them with respect and reverence, show that you realize your position and what it means."

Let us look at the Apostle's reasons for giving the injunction. The first is—and I am taking them in this particular order for a reason that will emerge later—*"For this is right."* By this he means, "It is righteous"...What Paul means by "right," in other words, is this: he is going back to the whole order of creation laid down at the very beginning, away back in the Book of Genesis...He tells us that, with regard to this question of children, the principle is there at the beginning. It has always been so, it is a part of the order of nature, it is a part of the basic rule of life. This is something you find not only among human beings, it operates even among the animals. In the animal world, the mother cares for the young offspring that has just been born, looks after it, feeds it, and protects it...This is the order of nature. The young creature in its weakness and ignorance needs the protection, the guidance, the help, and the instruction that is given by the parent. So, says the Apostle, *"Obey your parents...for this is right."* Christians are not divorced from a natural order found everywhere in creation.

It is a regrettable thing that this needs to be said to Christians at all. How does it become possible that people can deviate at any point from something that is so patently obvious and belongs to the very order and course of nature? Even the wisdom of the world recognizes this. There are people around us who are not Christians at all, but they are firm believers in discipline and order. Why? Because the whole of life and the whole of nature indicate this. For an offspring to be rebellious against the parents and to refuse to listen and to obey is something ridiculous and foolish...It is *unnatural* for children not to obey their parents. They are violating something that is clearly a part of the whole warp and woof[63] of human nature, seen everywhere, from top to bottom. Life has been planned on this basis. If it were not, of course, life would soon become chaotic; and it would end its own existence.

"This is right!" There is something about this aspect of the teaching of the New Testament that seems to me to be very wonderful. It shows that you must not divide the Old Testament from the New Testament. There is nothing that displays more ignorance than for a Christian to say, "Of course, being a Christian now, I am not interested in the Old Testament." That is

---

63 **warp and woof** – the underlying structure on which something is built.

entirely wrong because, as the Apostle reminds us here, it is the God Who created at the beginning Who is the God Who saves. It is one God from beginning to end. God made male and female, parents and children, right through the whole of nature. He did it in that way, and life is to work along these principles. So the Apostle starts his exhortation by virtually saying: "This is right, this is basic, this is fundamental, this is part of the order of nature! Do not go back on that! If you do, you are denying your Christianity; you are denying the God who established life after this fashion and made it work according to these principles. Obedience is *right*."

But having spoken thus, the Apostle proceeds to his second point. This is not only right, he says, this is also *"the first commandment with promise."* *"Honour thy father and mother; which is the first commandment with promise."* He means that the honoring of parents is not only essentially right, but that it is actually one of the things that God pinpointed in the Ten Commandments. This is the Fifth Commandment: *"Honour thy father and thy mother"* (Ex. 20:12)...

What does the Apostle mean by the expression *"First commandment with promise"*? This is a difficult point, and we cannot be quite final in our answer. It obviously does not mean that this is the first commandment that has a promise attached to it, for it will be noticed that *none* of the other commandments have a promise attached to them at all. If it were true to say that commandments 6, 7, 8, 9, and 10 had promises attached to them, then it could be said, "Paul means of course that this is the 'first' of the commandments to which he attaches a promise." But there is not a promise attached to the others, so it cannot bear that meaning.

What then does it mean? It may mean that here in this fifth commandment we begin to have instruction with respect to our relationships to one another. Until then it has been our relationship to God, His Name, His Day, and so on. But here He turns to our relationships with one another, so it may be the first in that sense. Over and above that, however, it may mean that it is the first commandment, not so much in *order* as in *rank*, [and] that God was anxious to impress this upon the minds of the children of Israel to such an extent that He added this promise in order to enforce it. First, as it were, in *rank*, first in *importance*! Not that ultimately any one of these is more important than the others, for they are all important. Nevertheless, there is a relative importance.

I would therefore view it like this: this is one of those laws that, when neglected, leads to the collapse of society. Whether we like it or not, a breakdown in home life will eventually lead to a breakdown everywhere.

This is, surely, the most menacing and dangerous aspect of the state of society at this present time. Once the family idea, the family unit, the family life is broken up—once that goes, soon you will have no other allegiance. It is the most serious thing of all. And that is perhaps the reason why God attached this promise to it.

But I believe that there is even a further suggestion here. There is something about this relationship of children to parents that is unique in this sense: it points to a yet higher relationship. After all, God is our Father. That is the term He Himself uses; that is the term our Lord uses in His model prayer—*"Our Father which art in heaven"* (Matt. 6:9). The earthly father therefore is, as it were, a reminder of that other Father, the heavenly Father. In the relationship of children to parents, we have a picture of the relationship of all mankind originally to God. We are all "children" face to face with God. He is our Father, *"For we are also his offspring"* (Acts 17:28). So in a very wonderful way the relationship between the parent and the child is a replica and a picture, a portrayal, a preaching of this whole relationship that subsists especially between those who are Christian and God Himself… The whole relationship of father and child should always remind us of our relationship to God. In that sense, this particular relationship is unique…This relationship reminds us of God Himself as Father and ourselves as children. There is something very sacred about the family, about this relationship between parents and children. God, as it were, has told us so in the Ten Commandments. When He came to lay down this commandment, *"Honour thy father and mother,"* He attached a promise to it.

What promise? *"That it may be well with thee, and thou mayest live long on the earth."* There can be no doubt that, as the promise was originally given to the children of Israel, it meant the following: "If you want to go on living in this land of promise to which I am leading you, observe these commandments, this one in particular. If you want to have a time of blessedness and happiness in that Promised Land, if you want to go on living there under My blessing, observe these commandments, *especially* this one." There is no doubt that that was the original promise.

But now the Apostle generalizes the promise because he is dealing here with Gentiles as well as Jews who had become Christians. So he says in effect, "Now if you want everything to be well with you, and if you want to live a long and a full life on the earth, honor your father and mother." Does that mean that if I am a dutiful son or daughter I am of necessity going to live to great age? No, that does not follow. But the promise certainly means this: if you want to live a blessed life, a full life under the benediction of God, observe this commandment. He may choose to keep you for a long time on this earth as an example and illustration. But however old you may be when you leave this world, you will know that you are under the blessing and the good hand of God…

That brings us to the third and last point. You notice how the Apostle puts it: *"Children, obey your parents…Honour thy father and mother."* Nature dictates it, but not only nature: the Law dictates it. But we must go beyond that to—*Grace*! This is the order—Nature, Law, Grace. *"Children, obey your parents in the Lord."* It is important that we should attach that phrase "in the Lord" to the right word. It does not mean "Children, obey your *parents in the Lord."* It is, rather, *"Children, obey in the Lord your parents."* In other words, the Apostle is repeating the very thing he said in the case of husbands and wives. *"Wives, submit yourselves unto your own husbands as unto the Lord." "Husbands, love your wives, even as Christ also loved the church."* When we come to his words about servants we shall find him saying, *"Servants, be obedient to them that are your masters according to the flesh… as unto Christ."* That is what *"in the Lord"* means. In other words, this is the supreme reason. We are to obey our parents and honor them and respect them because it is a part of our obedience to our Lord and Savior Jesus Christ. Ultimately, that is why we are to do it…Do it *"as unto the Lord."* Obey your father and mother *"in the Lord."* That is the finest and greatest inducement of all. It gives Him pleasure; it is a proof of what He said; we are substantiating His teaching. He said He had come into the world to redeem us, to wash away our sins, to give us a new nature, to make us new men and women. "Well," says the Apostle, "prove it, show it in practice." Children, *show it* by obeying your parents: you will be unlike all other children! You will be unlike those arrogant, aggressive, proud, boastful, evil-speaking children that are round about you at the present time! *Show* that you are different, *show* that the Spirit of God is in you, *show* that you belong to Christ! You have a wonderful opportunity; and it will give Him great joy and great pleasure.

But let us go even further. *"Children, obey your parents,"* for this reason also: when He was in this world, He did so. This is what I find in Luke 2:51: *"And he went down with them, and came to Nazareth, and was subject unto them."* The words refer to the Lord Jesus at the age of twelve. He had been up to Jerusalem with Joseph and Mary. They were making their return journey, and they had travelled for a day before they discovered that He was not in the company. They went back and found Him in the Temple reasoning and debating and arguing with the doctors of the Law, and confuting and confounding them. They were staggered and amazed. And He said, *"Wist ye not that I must be about my Father's business?"* (Luke 2:49). He had this dawning realization at the age of twelve. But then we are told that He went back with them to Nazareth: *"He went down with them, and came to Nazareth, and was subject unto them."* The Son of God incarnate *submitting* Himself to Joseph and Mary! Though He had this consciousness within Him that He was in this world about His Father's business, He humbled Himself and was obedient unto His parents. Let us look at Him: let us realize that He was doing it primarily to please His Father in heaven, that He might fulfill His Law in every respect and leave us an example that we might follow in His steps.

From "Submissive Children" in *Life in the Spirit in Marriage, Home, & Work: An Exposition of Ephesians 5:18 to 6:9*, published by The Banner of Truth Trust. Used by permission. www.banneroftruth.org.

David Martyn Lloyd-Jones (1899-1981): Perhaps the greatest expository preacher of the 20th century; Westminster Chapel, London, 1938-68; born in Wales.

Sins of Children and Youth

J. G. PIKE (1784-1854)

> *Remember not the sins of my youth, nor my transgressions: according to thy mercy remember thou me for thy goodness' sake, O LORD. —Psalm 25:7*

My young friend, I entreat you to follow me while I point out to you some of those sins that undo multitudes. Among these evils, a thoughtless, inconsiderate spirit is in young persons, one of the most common and one of the most fatal. While open impiety[64] slays its thousands, this sinks its ten thousands to perdition.[65] A time is coming when you must consider your ways. From the bed of death or from the eternal world, you must take a review of life. But as you love your soul, defer not until that solemn period, which shall fix your eternal state, the momentous question, "How has my life been spent?" Look back on your past years. They are gone forever. But what report have they borne to heaven? What is the record made respecting them in the book of God? Will they rise up in the judgment against you? Possibly, you may not see many instances of flagrant[66] crime. But do you see nothing that conscience must condemn? Nothing that would fill you with alarm, if going this moment to the bar of your Maker? Perhaps you reply, "It is true, I cannot justify all the actions of my youthful years. Yet the worst that I see were but the frolics[67] of youth."

My friend, do they bear that name in heaven? Does your Judge view them in no worse a light? It has ever been the custom of this world to whitewash sin and hide its hideous deformity. But, know that what you pass over so lightly, your God abhors as sins—sins, the least of which, if not forgiven, would sink your soul to utter, endless woe. *"For the wrath of God is revealed from heaven against all ungodliness and unrighteousness"* (Rom. 1:18). He abhors the iniquities of youth, as well as of riper years. The sins of youth were the bitter things that holy Job lamented. *"For thou writest bitter things against me, and makest me to possess the iniquities of my youth"* (Job 13:26). And for deliverance from which David devoutly prayed, *"Remember not the sins of my youth, nor my transgressions: according to thy mercy remember thou me for thy goodness' sake, O LORD"* (Ps. 25:7).

Take then another review of life. Begin with childhood. In that early period, so often falsely represented as a state of innocence, the corruptions

---

64 **impiety** – lack of reverence for God; wickedness.
65 **perdition** – eternal damnation; hell.
66 **flagrant** – outrageously bad.
67 **frolics** – light-hearted activities; pranks.

of a fallen nature begin to appear. The early years of life are stained with falsehood, disobedience, cruelty, vanity, and pride. Can you recollect no instances in which your earlier years were thus polluted with actual sin? Can you bring to remembrance no occasion on which falsehood came from your lips? Or vanity, pride, or obstinacy was cherished in your heart? Or when cruelty to the meaner creatures[68] was your sport? Shrink not from the review: though painful, it is useful. It is far better to see and abhor your youthful sins in this world, where mercy may be found, than to have them brought to your remembrance when mercy is no more.

But you have passed the years of childhood. You have advanced one stage [further] in your journey to an endless world. Has sin weakened as your years increased? Have not some sinful dispositions ripened into greater vigor? Have not others that you knew not in your earlier years begun to appear? And does not increasing knowledge add new guilt to all your sins?

Among the prevailing iniquities of youth may be mentioned *pride*. This is a sin common to all ages, but it often peculiarly infects the young. God abhors it. *"But the proud he knoweth afar off"* (Ps. 138:6). *"God resisteth the proud, but giveth grace unto the humble"* (James 4:6). *"Every one that is proud in heart is an abomination to the LORD"* (Prov. 16:5). He hateth *"a proud look"* (Prov. 6:16-17). *"An high look, and a proud heart...is sin"* (Prov. 21:4). The proud are *"cursed"* (Ps. 119:21). Pride is the parent of many other vices. It puts on a thousand forms; yet unless subdued by religion, [it] is found in the palace and the cottage. You may see it displayed in the character of the young prodigal (Luke 15:19).

Has not this sin, which God so much abhors, crept into your heart? Perhaps it has made you haughty, when you should have been humble; obstinate, when you should have been yielding; revengeful, when you should have been forgiving. You thought it showed spirit to resent an injury or insult, instead of patiently bearing it like Him you call your Lord. Perhaps it has filled you with dissatisfaction, when you should have been all submission. You have thought it hard in the day of affliction that you should be so tried; and even if you stayed the murmur against God from passing your lips, have you not felt it in your heart?

Pride has probably led you to neglect the counsels of wisdom—to turn a deaf ear to those who wished you well forever. Vain of the ornaments of apparel—have you not bestowed more thought on the dress you should wear than on the salvation of your immortal soul? [Have you not] been more concerned about the shape of a coat or the fashion of a gown or a bonnet

---

68 **meaner creatures** – lowly animals.

than about life or death eternal? Perhaps you have been one of those who spend more time in surveying their own image in a glass[69] than in seeking the favor of their God. Ah! Did pride never lead you to this self-idolatry? Did it never, never fill you with vanity from the fancy of your possessing a pleasing face, or a lovely form, or manly vigor? Ah, foolish vanity! When you must so soon say to corruption, *"Thou art my father: to the worm, Thou art my mother, and my sister"* (Job 17:14). Yet, foolish as it is, was it never yours? "Where is there a face so disagreeable, that never was the object of self-worship in a glass? And where a body, however deformed, that never was set up as a favorite idol by the fallen spirit that inhabits it?"[70]

One of the most prevalent and most baneful[71] kinds of pride is that which I may term the pride of *self-righteousness*. Our Lord, in the parable of the Pharisee and Publican, gives a most striking description of this sin. The Pharisee boasts that he was not like others; that he had not committed such flagrant crimes as they; and that he practiced duties that they omitted. On this sandy foundation, his hope for eternity appears to have rested. Nothing like humility entered his heart; but in all the pride of fancied[72] virtue, he approached his God. This is the exact spirit of multitudes in the present day. And where young persons have been restrained from open immoralities, how commonly does it exist among them! It is pleaded, respecting them, "They are not like many profligate[73] youth around them! They have not given way to profaneness and lying, to drunkenness or dishonesty; but they have been kind and dutiful, tender and obliging, have good hearts, and are good young people." They may have lived all their lives careless of God and their souls, but this is not taken into account. Others commend them, and they are willing to believe these commendations. They please themselves with their fancied virtue [and] think themselves very good young persons. [They are] proud of this goodness [and] go forward to meet that God Who sees in them ten thousand crimes and Who abhors nothing more than the pride of *self-righteousness* in a creature polluted by daily iniquities.

Another common sin of the young is disobedience to parents. *"Honour thy father and mother…That it may be well with thee, and thou mayest live long on the earth"* (Eph. 6:2-3). This is the divine commandment. There is, it is true, one case in which even parents should not be obeyed: when their directions

---

69 **glass** – mirror.
70 John Fletcher, "An Appeal to Matter of Fact and Common Sense" in *The Whole Works of the Rev. John Fletcher*, Vol. 1(Devon: S. Thorne, 1835), 264.
71 **baneful** – exceedingly harmful.
72 **fancied** – imagined.
73 **profligate** – unrestrained by morality.

Chapter 10—Duties of Sons & Daughters: Sins of Children and Youth

and wishes are opposed to those of God. *"We ought to obey God rather than men"* (Acts 5:29), and to love the Redeemer more than parents themselves. Parents are commonly the tenderest of friends, and pious parents among the surest guides that the young and inexperienced can have to lead them to the footstool of God. Your interests are theirs. Your welfare *their* happiness. But ah! Has their kindness met with the return it demanded? Who, my young friend, so much deserve your obedience and affection as those who gave you being and who watched over your helpless infancy? The father, whose years have been spent in care for you; the mother, who tended you at her breast and led you through the days of childhood—have they received this obedience and affection from you?

Perhaps I address one whose disobedience and unkindness have wrung with grief the hearts of fond and pious parents and filled them with sorrow instead of gladness. Their desire has been to see you walking in the ways of God. For this, they have led you to His house. For this, their prayers have ascended in public and in private. This, by their early instructions and later admonitions, they have warned you to regard as the chief end of life, as that only concern that beyond all others should interest your attention and engage all your hearts. And now they see you negligent of God and religion. [They] mourn in secret that the child they love is still a child of Satan. Ah! Young man or young woman, if this be your case, God will bring you into judgment for all your abuse of precious privileges and all your neglect of parental instructions. The prayers, the tears, and the admonitions of your parents will awfully witness against you. Think not that if affectionate and kind to them you will much mitigate[74] the sorrows of truly pious parents. No. They will still mourn at the thought that the affectionate child they fondly love is not a child of God. It will grieve them to the heart to consider how near you are to endless destruction and how soon they must bid you an eternal farewell, when they go to that rest in which they have no hope of meeting you.

Ah! My young friend, if you slight religion, pious parents may leave you, mournfully saying in their dying hour, "Alas! Our beloved child, we shall see you no more. For our God you have not [trusted] as your God; our Savior you have not sought as your Savior. The heaven to which we go is a rest to which you have no title and which, dying as you are, you cannot enter!" Yes, bitterly will they mourn to think that with so much that is lovely in *their* view, there is nothing in you that is lovely in the sight of God. All that they esteem so pleasing in you must soon be buried in the deeps of hell.

---

74 **mitigate** – make less severe.

Another sin, not peculiar to the young, but awfully prevalent among them, is the waste of precious time. The Word of God reminds us that *"time is short"* (1 Cor. 7:29) and commands us to redeem the time (Eph. 5:16; Col. 4:5). The value of time is beyond our comprehension or expression… Time is given us to prepare for eternity. But, alas, how are its golden hours sinned and trifled away! Many young persons act as if they thought they had so much time before them that they may afford to squander some, when perhaps their wasted youth is their *all*—all in which they will ever have an opportunity of preparing for eternity, all in which they can "escape from hell, and fly to heaven."[75]

One of the most common ways in which time is worse than wasted is employing it on romances, plays, and novels. Novels are the poison of the age. The best of them tend to produce a baneful effeminacy[76] of mind. Many of them are calculated to advance the base designs of the licentious and abandoned on the young and unsuspecting. But, were they free from every other charge of evil, it is a most heavy one that they occasion a dreadful waste of that time that must be accounted for before the God of heaven. Let their deluded admirers plead the advantages of novel reading, if they will venture to plead the same before the worthy Judge eternal. If you are a novel reader, think the next time you take a novel into your hands, "How shall I answer to my tremendous Judge for the time occupied by this? When He shall say to me, 'I gave you so many years in yonder world to fit you for eternity. Did you converse with your God in devotion? Did you study His Word? Did you attend to the duties of life and strive to improve to some good end even your leisure hours?' Then, then shall I be willing to reply, 'Lord, my time was otherwise employed! Novels and romances occupied the leisure of my days, when—alas!—my Bible, my God, and my soul were neglected!" In this way and many others is time—that most precious blessing—squandered away. Does not conscience remind you of many leisure hours? Hours that, though thoughtlessly thrown away, would soon to you be worth more than mountains of gold or of pearl?

Willful neglect of the soul and eternity is another common sin of youth. Young persons presume on future life and grieve the Holy Spirit by delaying to regard the one thing needful (Luke 10:42). They trust in their youth. God reproves the folly and says, *"Boast not thyself of tomorrow; for thou knowest not what a day may bring forth"* (Prov. 27:1). Few will listen to the warning. Instead of doing so, they flatter themselves that they shall live for many years

---

75 Isaac Watts, *The Psalms of David*, Book 1, Hymn 88.
76 **baneful effeminacy** – ruinous, unmanly weakness.

Chapter 10—Duties of Sons & Daughters: Sins of Children and Youth

and think sickness, death, and judgment far from them. Hence, they neglect the soul and seem to imagine religion unsuitable or at least not needful for them. The blessed God calls on them in His Word. The crucified Savior bids them come to Himself, *"I love them that love me; and those that seek me early shall find me"* (Prov. 8:17). The ministers of the Gospel urge the advice upon them. Prayers are offered, tears shed for them—yet many persist in their own ways; and whatever they do, [they] will not remember their Creator in the days of their youth (Eccl. 12:1). My young friend, has this been your sin and folly? O, if it has, remember how many ways there are out of the world! How many diseases to cut short your days! God gives you time enough to secure salvation, but think not that He gives you any to spare.

An inordinate love of sensual pleasure and worldly gaieties is another most prevalent sin of youth. The Word of God describes those who live in pleasure as dead while they live (1 Tim. 5:6) and classes with the most abominably wicked those who are "lovers of pleasures more than lovers of God" (2 Tim. 3:4). Though such are the declarations of the Lord, yet pleasure, *pleasure* is the chief object of thousands of the young. Some pursue it in the gross and brutish paths of rioting[77] and drunkenness, of chambering and wantonness;[78] others [pursue it] in less profligate ways, but with hearts not less intent upon it. The card table, the dance, the horse race, the playhouse, the fair, the wake[79] are the scenes of their highest felicity.[80] My young men, has not this love of worldly pleasure dwelt in your heart? Perhaps you have not run into scandalous and disgraceful excesses; but have you not had a greater love to worldly pleasures than to God and religion? If you have, you but too surely bear that awful mark of being a child of destruction: you are a lover of pleasures more than a lover of God. Have not you been present at scenes of sinful amusement and guilty festivity? Have not you been as anxious as others have for those sensual delights that were most suited to your taste? And, while thus loving this world, have not you forgotten that which is to come? Have not you been more pleased with some shining bauble or glittering toy than with the blessings displayed in the Gospel? And been more earnest about a day of promised pleasure than about securing an eternity of pure celestial joy?

---

77 **rioting** – drunken merrymaking.
78 **chambering…wantonness** – sexual immorality and unbridled lust.
79 **wake** – the eve of a festival: in this use, *wake* primarily refers to the rule of the early church that certain feast-days should be preceded by services lasting through the night. When this rule had ceased to exist, the vigil continued to be an excuse for nighttime festivity. The word *wake* was extended to refer not only to the *eve* but also to the feast-day itself and the duration of the festivities.
80 **felicity** – happiness.

Think not that I mean to insinuate that the Christian should be the slave of melancholy. Far from it! None has so much reason to be cheerful as he who reads his title clear to heaven. But wide is the difference between the innocent cheerfulness and humble joy of the Christian and the vain pleasures of a foolish world. The truly religious have their delights, though they know that there is no room for mirthful trifling here.

Let conscience now answer, as in the sight of God: Has the love of worldly and sensual pleasure been cherished in your heart? If your situation has prevented your freely following the delights of sense, has the love of them dwelt within? If it has, though you should not have had the opportunity of indulging your worldly taste once in a month or a year, you are still in God's sight as much a lover of pleasures as if these had occupied every moment of your time…

The Apostle Paul, when enumerating some of the sins of mankind, concludes the dreadful list with that of their taking pleasure in the sins of others (Rom. 1:32). This, though one of the most awful, is one of the most common of human iniquities and abounds among none *more* than among the young. Young persons are often each other's tempters and destroyers. The lewd and profane tempt others to lewdness and profaneness. The thoughtless and [those addicted to social life] persuade others to imitate their levity and folly. As if it were not sufficient to have their own sins to account for, many thus make themselves partakers in the sins of others! And, as if it were not enough to ruin their *own* souls, many thus contract the guilt of assisting to destroy those of their companions and friends.

Have you never thus led others into sin? Perhaps some, who are now lost forever, may be lamenting in utter darkness and despair the fatal hour when they became acquainted with *you*. Have any learned of you to trifle with religion? To squander away their golden day of grace? To slight their God and choose perdition? If not by words, yet perhaps by a careless and irreligious example, you have taught them these dreadful lessons.

I have now named a few youthful iniquities, but think not that these things are all. No. Every sin to which our fallen nature is prone has been found not merely in those who, by years, were ripened in guilt; but in those also who were beginning the journey of life. And not to enumerate the darker crimes of the multitude who drink in iniquity like water, where, my young friend, is the youthful heart that never felt the rising emotions of those infernal passions: pride, envy, malice, or revenge? Where is the youthful tongue that never uttered a profane, wanton, or at least an unkind or slanderous word? Where is the youth, possessed of the forms of piety, that never mocked God,

"With solemn sounds upon a thoughtless tongue"? Where is the youthful ear that was never open to drink in with pleasure the conversation of the trifling and the foolish? And where the youthful eye that never cast a haughty, an angry, a wanton, or insulting glance? Are you the person? Can you appeal to the Searcher of hearts and rest your eternal hopes on the success of the appeal that love—unmingled love to God and man—has always dwelt in your bosom? That no resentful, envious, or unkind emotion, was ever for a moment harbored there? That a law of constant kindness has ever dwelt upon your lips? That only meekness, tenderness, and goodness have glanced from your eye? That your ear was never opened to hear with pleasure of a brother's shame? Can you make the appeal?

From *Persuasives to Early Piety*, reprinted by Soli Deo Gloria, a ministry of Reformation Heritage Books: www.heritagebooks.org.

J. G. Pike (1784-1854): Baptist minister; born in Edmonton, Alberta, Canada.

Nowadays, there are some children who seem to be at the head of the family, and the parents obey them in all things. This is very foolish and wrong; and when their children grow up and become their plague and curse, they will bitterly lament their folly in putting things out of joint and not keeping the house as God would have it kept: the children in their place and the father in his. —Charles Haddon Spurgeon

Children, Seek the Good Shepherd

ROBERT MURRAY M'CHEYNE (1813-1843)

> *He shall feed his flock like a shepherd: he shall gather the lambs with his arm, and carry them in his bosom, and shall gently lead those that are with young.* —Isaiah 40:11

Beloved children, Jesus is the Good Shepherd. His arm was stretched out on the cross, and His bosom was pierced with the spear. That arm is able to gather you, and that bosom is open to receive you. I pray for you every day that Christ may save you. He said to me, "Feed My lambs"; and I daily return the words to Him, "Lord, feed my lambs." In the bowels of Jesus Christ, I long after you all. I believe Christ has gathered some of you. But are no more to be gathered? Are no more green brands to be plucked from the burning? Will no more of you hide beneath the white robe of Jesus? Oh, come! For *"yet there is room"* (Luke 14:22). Lift up your hearts to God while I tell you something more of the Good Shepherd.

1. Jesus has a flock: Every shepherd must have a flock, and so has Christ. I once saw a flock in a valley near Jerusalem. The shepherd went before them and called the sheep, and they knew his voice and followed him. I said, "This is the way Jesus leads His sheep!" Oh, that I may be one of them!

a. Christ's flock is a little flock. Hear what Jesus says: "Fear not, little flock, for it is your Father's good pleasure to give you the kingdom" (Luke 12:32). *Pray* to be among the little flock. Look at the world—[billions of] men, women, and children of different countries, color, and language all journeying to the Judgment Seat! Is this Christ's flock? Ah, no! [Untold] millions never heard the sweet name of Jesus; and of the rest, the most see no beauty in the Rose of Sharon. Christ's is a little flock. Look at this town. What crowds press along the streets on a market-day! What a large flock is here! Is this the flock of Christ? No. It is to be feared that most of these are not the brothers and sisters of Christ. They do not bear His likeness. They do not follow the Lamb now and will not follow Him in eternity. Look round the Sabbath schools. What a number of young faces are there! How many beaming eyes! How many precious souls! Is this the flock of Christ? No, no. Most of you have hard and stony hearts. Most of you love pleasure more than [you love] God. Most of you love sin and lightly esteem Christ…I could weep when I think how many of you will live lives of sin, die deaths of horror, and spend an eternity in hell. Beloved children, pray that you may be like the one lily among many thorns—that you may be the few lambs in the midst of a world of wolves.

b. Christ's sheep are marked sheep. In almost every flock, the sheep are all marked in order that the shepherd may know them. The mark is often made with tar on the woolly back of the sheep. Sometimes it is the first letter of the owner's name. The use of the mark is that they may not be lost when they wander among other sheep. So it is with the flock of Jesus. Every sheep of His has two marks:

One mark is made with the blood of Jesus. Every sheep and lamb in Christ's flock was once guilty and defiled with sin, altogether become filthy. But every one of them has been drawn to the blood of Jesus and washed there. They are all like sheep that *"came up from the washing"* (Song 4:2). They can all say, *"Unto him that loved us, and washed us from our sins in his own blood"* (Rev. 1:5). Have you this mark? Look and see. You can never be in heaven unless you have it. Every one there has washed his robes and *"made them white in the blood of the Lamb"* (Rev. 7:14).

Another mark is made by the Holy Spirit. This is not a mark that you can see outside, like the mark on the white wool of the sheep. It is deep, deep in the bosom, where the eye of man cannot look. It is a new heart. *"A new heart also will I give you"* (Ezek. 36:26). This is the seal of the Holy Spirit that He gives to all them that believe. With infinite power, He puts forth His unseen hand and silently changes the heart of all that are truly Christ's. Do you have the new heart? You never will go to heaven without it. *"Now if any man have not the Spirit of Christ, he is none of his"* (Rom. 8:9). Beloved children, pray for these two marks of the sheep of Jesus—forgiveness through blood and a new heart. Oh, be in earnest to get them and to get them now. Soon the Chief Shepherd will come, and set the sheep on His right hand, and the goats on His left. Where will you be in that day?

c. Christ's sheep all flock together. Sheep love to go together. A sheep never goes with a wolf or with a dog, but always with the flock. Especially when a storm is coming down, they keep near one another. When the sky turns dark with clouds and the first drops of a thundershower are coming on, the shepherds say that you will see the sheep flocking down from the hills and all meeting together in some sheltered valley. They love to keep together. So it is with the flock of Jesus. They do not love to go with the world, but always one with another. Christian loves Christian. They have the same peace, the same Spirit, the same Shepherd, the same fold on the hills of immortality. Especially in the dark and cloudy day—such as our day is likely to be—the sheep of Christ are driven together to weep together. They love to pray together, to sing praise together, and to hide in Christ together… Little children, *"love one another"* (1 John 4:7). Make companions of those that fear God. Flee from all others. Who can take fire into [his] bosom and not be burned?...

2. What Jesus does for his flock:

a. He died for them. *"I am the good shepherd: the good shepherd giveth his life for the sheep"* (John 10:11). This is the chief beauty in Christ. The wounds that marred His fair body make Him altogether lovely in a needy sinner's eye. All that are now and ever shall be the sheep of Christ were once condemned to die. The wrath of God abode upon them. They were ready to drop into the burning lake. Jesus had compassion upon them, left His Father's bosom, emptied Himself, became a worm and no man, and died under the sins of many. *"While we were yet sinners, Christ died for us"* (Rom. 5:8). This is the grace of the Lord Jesus. Everyone in the flock can say, *"[He] loved me, and gave himself for me"* (Gal. 2:20).

b. He seeks and finds them. We would never seek Christ, if He did not seek us first. We would never find Christ, if He did not find us. *"For the Son of man is come to seek and to save that which was lost"* (Luke 19:10). I once asked a shepherd, "How do you find sheep that are lost in the snow?" "Oh," he said, "we go down into the deep ravines, where the sheep go in storms. There we find the sheep huddled together beneath the snow." "And are they able to come out when you take away the snow?" "Oh, no. If they had to take a single step to save their lives, they could not do it. So we just go in and carry them out." Ah, this is the very way Jesus saves lost sheep. He finds us in the deep pit of sin, frozen and dead. If we had to take a single step to save our souls, we could not do it. But He reaches down His arm and carries us out. This He does for every sheep He saves. Glory, glory, glory be to Jesus, the Shepherd of our souls!...

d. He feeds them. *"By me if any man enter in, he shall be saved, and shall go in and out, and find pasture"* (John 10:9). If Jesus has saved you, He will feed you. He will feed your *body*. *"I have been young, and now am old; yet have I not seen the righteous forsaken, nor his seed begging bread"* (Ps. 37:25)…He will feed your *soul*. He that feeds the little flower in the cleft of the craggy precipice, where no hand of man can reach it, will feed your soul with silent drops of heavenly dew.

I shall never forget the story of a little girl in Belfast, Ireland. She was at a Sabbath school and gained a Bible as a prize for her good conduct. It became to her a treasure indeed. She was fed out of it. Her parents were wicked. She often read to them, but they became worse and worse. This broke Eliza's heart. She took to her bed and never rose again. She desired to see her teacher. When he came, he said, "You are not without a companion, my dear child," taking up her Bible. "No," she replied,

Chapter 10—Duties of Sons & Daughters: Children, Seek the Good Shepherd

"Precious Bible? What a treasure, Does the Word of God afford!
All I want for life or pleasure, Food and medicine, shield and sword.
Let the world account me poor, Having this, I ask no more."[81]

She had scarcely repeated the lines when she hung back her head and died. Beloved children, this is the way Jesus feeds His flock. He is a tender, constant, almighty Shepherd. If you become His flock, He will feed you all the way to glory.

3. Jesus cares for [his] lambs. Every careful shepherd deals gently with the lambs of the flock. When the flocks are travelling, the lambs are not able to go far: they often grow weary and lie down. Now, a kind shepherd stoops down, puts his gentle arm beneath them, and lays them in his bosom. Such a shepherd is the Lord Jesus, and saved children are His lambs. He gathers them with His arm and carries them in His bosom. Many a guilty lamb He has gathered and carried to His Father's house. Some He has gathered out of this place that you and I once knew well.

Before He came into the world, Jesus cared for lambs. Samuel was a very little child, no bigger than the least of you when he was converted. He was girded with a linen ephod. His mother made him a little coat and brought it to him every year. One night as he slept in the holy place, near where the Ark of God was kept, he heard a voice cry, *"Samuel!"* He started up and ran to old Eli, whose eyes were dim, and said, *"Here am I; for thou calledst me."* And Eli said, *"I called not; lie down again."* He went and lay down, but a second time the voice cried, *"Samuel!"* He rose and went to Eli, saying, *"Here am I; for thou calledst me."* And Eli said, *"I called not, my son; lie down again."* A third time the holy voice cried, *"Samuel!"* He arose and went to Eli with the same words. Then Eli perceived that the Lord had called the child. Therefore, Eli said, *"Go, lie down: and it shall be, if he call thee, that thou shalt say, Speak, LORD; for thy servant heareth."* So he went and lay down. A fourth time—how often Christ will call on little children!—the voice cried, *"Samuel! Samuel!"* Then Samuel answered, *"Speak; for thy servant heareth."* Thus did Jesus gather this lamb with His arm and carried him in His bosom. For *"And Samuel grew, and the LORD was with him…for the LORD revealed himself to Samuel in Shiloh"* (1 Sam. 3:5-10; 19, 21).

Little children, of whom I travail in birth until Christ be formed in you, pray that the same Lord would reveal Himself to you. Some people say [that] you are too young to be converted and saved. But Samuel was not too young. Christ can open the eyes of a child as easily as of an old man. Yea, youth is the best time to be saved in. You are not too young to die, not too

---

81 John Newton, "Precious Bible! What a Treasure," *Olney Hymns* (1779).

young to be judged, and therefore not too young to be brought to Christ. Do not be contented to hear about Christ from your teachers. Pray that He would reveal Himself to you. God grant there may be many little Samuels amongst you.

Jesus cares for lambs still. The late Duke of Hamilton had two sons. The eldest [became sick with tuberculosis] when a boy, which ended in his death. Two ministers went to see him at the family seat near Glasgow, where he lay. After prayer, the youth took his Bible from under his pillow and turned to 2 Timothy 4:7-8: *"I have fought a good fight, I have finished my course, I have kept the faith: Henceforth there is laid up for me a crown of righteousness."* [He] added, "This, sirs, is all my comfort!" When his death approached, he called his younger brother to his bed and spoke to him with great affection. He ended with these remarkable words: "And now, Douglas, in a little time you will be a duke, but I shall be a king"…

Would you wish to be gathered thus? Go now to some lonely place—kneel down and call upon the Lord Jesus. Do not leave your knees until you find Him. Pray to be gathered with His arm and carried in His bosom. Take hold of the hem of His garment and say, "I must—I dare not—I will not let Thee go except Thou bless me."

From "To the Lambs of the Flock" in *Memoir and Remains of Robert Murray M'Cheyne*, reprinted by The Banner of Truth Trust: www.banneroftruth.org.

Robert Murray M'Cheyne (1813-1843): Scottish Presbyterian minister of St. Peter's Church, Dundee; born in Edinburgh, Scotland.

Why Sons and Daughters Need Faith in Christ
CHARLES WALKER (1791-1870)

My young reader…the writer speaks to you as a friend. Will you listen to what he says? Will you give your own mind to the study of this important subject? If you will do so earnestly, you may become wise unto salvation. Of persons of your age, God says in the Scriptures, *"Those that seek me early shall find me"* (Prov. 8:17).

You know that there is much said in the Bible about faith. You know that every person must have faith [in Christ], or he cannot be good and happy. The Bible says, *"But without faith it is impossible to please him"* (Heb. 11:6). If then you hope to please God, to have His blessing, and to dwell in His presence when you leave this world, you must have faith. So you see it is of the utmost importance that you should know what faith is…

You know that the Holy Bible is the Word of God. You know that in the Bible God speaks to us and tells us about many things that we should never have known if they had not been told us in that Holy Book. You know that God speaks to us in the Bible about Himself. He tells us who He is, where He dwells, what He has done, and what He will do. God tells us also what we are ourselves, what we have done, and what we must do if we would please Him. He tells us too about another world, a state of being beyond the grave—a place of happiness for the righteous and a place of misery for the wicked. God tells us further about Jesus Christ Who came into the world and died to save sinners, that they who believe in Christ shall be saved, and that they who believe not shall be damned. All this and very much more God makes known to us in the Bible.

Now I am ready to tell you what faith is: It is so believing what God has said as to do what He has commanded. Do you understand this? I want you [to] understand it. [I] will therefore express it in a little different language. Faith is believing what God has said. [It is believing] in such a manner as will lead you to do what He has bidden. This is a definition in general terms. And faith in this sense is applicable to all things that God has said in the Bible. It regards all that He has said of Himself, of His government, and of His Son Jesus Christ. It has respect to whatever God has commanded and whatever He has forbidden. But more particularly, Christian faith, or that faith by which a sinner is saved, may be explained in this manner: It is that belief or trust in Jesus Christ that will lead us to rely on Him alone for salvation. [This faith will lead us] to commit our souls, ourselves, our all to Him as the only Savior and to obey His commandments.

Chapter 10—Duties of Sons & Daughters: Why Sons and Daughters Need Faith in Christ

It is not enough to *say* that you believe the Bible or to *think* that you believe it if you do not obey it. It is not faith to have a kind of general belief that the Bible is the Word of God and that it is all true. Many have this kind of belief who have no true faith. If a man has true faith, he will not only believe what God has said in the Bible, but he will act as if he believed it. Nor is it enough to say that you believe Christ to be the only Savior if you do not follow Him. It is not faith in Christ merely to acknowledge Him as the only Redeemer. Thousands have this kind of belief who are utterly destitute of true faith. You will *obey* the Savior if you have true faith in Him. In the language of Jesus Himself, you will deny yourself and take up the cross and follow Him…The great object of the Christian's faith is the Lord Jesus Christ. He is the *only* Savior. And the only way in which we can be saved is by faith in Him. The Bible says, *"Believe on the Lord Jesus Christ, and thou shalt be saved, and thy house"* (Acts 16:31). It says also, *"He that believeth not shall be damned"* (Mark 16:16). It is plain, therefore, that our salvation depends on our having true faith in the Savior.

Now, you know what God has told us in the Holy Scriptures about His Son. You remember what the Bible says about the birth, life, and death of Jesus. Though He dwelt in heaven and was with God and was God (John 1:1), yet He…became a man. He was born of the Virgin Mary. He grew up like other children. *"Jesus increased in wisdom and stature, and in favour with God and man"* (Luke 2:52). When He was thirty years old, He began His ministry. He preached that all men must repent and believe in Him (Mark 1:15), or they can never enter the Kingdom of Heaven. He performed a great many wonderful miracles that proved that God was with Him and that He worked the works of God. His life was entirely holy, free from all manner of sin. His example was perfectly good…His teaching was wise and good. Even His enemies said, *"Never man spake like this man"* (John 7:46). He told all about the duties that mankind owe to each other and to God…At last, He permitted Himself to be taken and crucified by wicked men that, by His death, He might make an atonement for the sins of the world[82] (1 John 2:2) and prepare [the] way that all sinners who repent and believe in Him might be saved and be happy in heaven forever. After His death, He arose from the grave, appeared alive to His disciples, told them to *"Go…into all the world, and preach the gospel to every creature"* (Mark 16:15). Then He ascended into heaven in the sight of many of His friends, and there *"he ever liveth to make intercession"* (Heb. 7:25).

---

82 The world, that is, His people (John 1:21): Christ redeemed His people to God by His blood out of every kindred, tongue, people, and nation (Rev. 5:9).

This is a short account of what the Bible informs us concerning the Savior. Now God requires that we should believe this, and so believe it that it will rule our conduct and make us the followers and disciples of Jesus Christ…It is not enough for you to say that you do not dispute or deny what God says concerning His Son. It is not enough for you to *say* that you believe the Scriptural account of the Savior. If your belief is not of that kind that will govern your actions, if it does not lead you to do as the Savior bids you, if it does not make you His friend and disciple, it is not true faith in Him.

Now, my young reader, if you have read attentively and understood what you have read, you see that when you have true faith in Christ, you will trust yourself [into] His hands. You will look to Him alone for salvation. You will obey His commands and strive to be like Him…This is the faith that God speaks of in the Bible…Consider, my young friend, why you yourself need faith. It is because you are a sinner. Did you ever seriously think of this? You *are* a sinner. You have naturally a wicked heart, have disobeyed God, and [have] come into condemnation. The Bible says, *"He that believeth not is condemned already"* (John 3:18). The only way to escape this condemnation is by faith in Christ. He came to save *sinners*. He says, *"For the Son of man is come to seek and to save that which was lost"* (Luke 19:10). *You* are a lost one. You have wandered away from duty and from God; and you will perish forever if you are not saved by Jesus Christ. And this is the reason why you need faith in Him.

From *Repentance and Faith Explained to the Understanding of the Young*, reprinted by Solid Ground Christian Books: www.solid-ground-books.com.

Charles Walker (1791-1870): Congregational minister, burdened to teach God's truth to the young; born in Woodstock, Connecticut.

Children Walking in Truth

J.C. RYLE (1816-1900)

I rejoiced greatly that I found of thy children walking in truth, as we have received a commandment from the Father. —2 John 1:4

What does *"walking"* mean here? You must not think it means walking on your feet…It means, rather, our way of behaving ourselves—our way of living and going on. And shall I tell you why the Bible calls this *"walking"*? It calls it so because a man's life is just like a journey. From the time of our birth to the time of our death, we are always traveling and moving on. Life is a journey from the cradle to the grave, and a person's manner of living is on that account often called his "walk."

But what does *"walking in truth"* mean? It means walking in the ways of true Bible religion,[83] and not in the bad ways of this evil world. The world, I am sorry to tell you, is full of false notions and untruths, and especially full of untruths about religion. They all come from our great enemy, the devil. The devil deceived Adam and Eve in Eden and [caused] them [to] sin by telling them an untruth. He told them they would not die if they ate the forbidden fruit, and that was untrue. The devil is *always* at the same work now. He is *always* trying to make men, women, and children have false notions about God and about religion. He persuades them to believe that what is really evil is good, and what is really good is evil—that God's service is not pleasant, and that sin will do them no great harm. And, I grieve to say, vast numbers of people are deceived by him and believe these untruths.

But those persons who walk in truth are very different! They pay no attention to the false notions there are in the world about religion. They follow the true way that God shows us in the Bible. Whatever others may do, their chief desire is to please God and be His true servants. Now this was the character of the children spoken of in the text. John writes home to their mother and says, "I found them walking in truth."

Dear children, would you not like to know whether you are walking in truth yourselves? Would you like to know the marks by which you may find it out? Listen, every one of you, while I try to set these marks before you in order. Let every boy and girl come and hear what I am going to say.

1. I tell you, then, for one thing, that children who walk in truth know the truth about sin. What is sin? To break any command of God is sin. To do anything that God says ought not to be done is sin. God is very holy and very pure, and every sin that is sinned displeases Him exceedingly. But, in

---

83 **religion** – Biblical Christianity.

spite of all this, most people in the world, both old and young, think very little about sin. Some try to make out that they are not great sinners and do not often break God's commandments. Others say that sin is not so terrible a thing after all and that God is not so particular and strict as ministers say He is. These are two great and dangerous mistakes.

Children who walk in truth think very differently. They have no such proud and high feelings. They feel themselves full of sin, and it grieves and humbles them. They believe that sin is the abominable thing that God hates. They look upon sin as their greatest enemy and plague. They hate it more than anything on earth! There is *nothing* they so heartily desire to be free from as sin.

Dear children, there is the first mark of walking in truth. Look at it. Think of it. Do you hate sin?

2. I tell you for another thing that children who walk in truth love the true Savior of sinners and follow Him. There are few men and women who do not feel they need in some way to be saved. They feel that after death comes the judgment; and from that awful judgment they would like to be saved.

But, alas! Few of them will see that the Bible says there is only one Savior, even Jesus Christ. And few go to Jesus Christ and ask Him to save them. They trust rather in their own prayers, their own repentance, their own church going, their own regular attendance at sacrament, their own goodness, or something of the kind. But these things, although useful in their place, cannot save any one soul from hell. These are false ways of salvation. They cannot put away sin. They are not Christ. Nothing can save you or me but Jesus Christ Who died for sinners on the cross. Those only who trust entirely in Him have their sins forgiven and will go to heaven. These alone will find they have an Almighty Friend in the Day of Judgment. This is the true way to be saved.

Children who walk in truth have learned all this. If you ask them what they put their trust in, they will answer, "Nothing but Christ." They remember His gracious words: *"Suffer the little children to come unto me, and forbid them not"* (Mark 10:14). They try to follow Jesus as the lambs follow the good shepherd. And they love Him because they read in the Bible that He loved them and gave Himself for them. Little children, there is the second mark of walking in truth. Look at it. Think of it. Do you love Christ?

3. I tell you that children who walk in truth serve God with a true heart. I dare say you know it is very possible to serve God with outward service only. Many do so. They will put on a grave face and pretend to be serious while they do not feel it. They will say beautiful prayers with their lips and yet not mean what they say. They will sit in their places at church every Sunday and

Chapter 10—Duties of Sons & Daughters: Children Walking in Truth

yet be thinking of other things all the time—and such service is outward service and very wrong.

Bad children, I am sorry to say, are often guilty of this sin. They will say their prayers regularly when their parents make them, but not otherwise. They will seem to pay attention in church when the master's eye is upon them, but not at other times. Their hearts are far away.

Children who walk in truth are not so. They have another spirit in them. Their desire is to be honest in all they do with God and to worship Him in spirit and in truth. When they pray, they try to be in earnest and mean all the words they say. When they go to church, they try to be serious and to give their minds to what they hear. And it is one of their chief troubles that they cannot serve God more heartily than they do.

Little children, there is the third mark of walking in truth. Look at it. Think of it. Is your heart false or true?

4. I tell you, for a last thing, that children who walk in truth really try to do things that are right and true in the sight of God. God has told us very plainly what He thinks is right. Nobody can mistake this who reads the Bible with an honest heart. But it is sad to see how few men and women care for pleasing God. Many break His commandments continually and seem to think nothing of it. Some will tell lies, swear, quarrel, cheat, and steal. Others use bad words, break the Sabbath, never pray to God at all, and never read their Bibles. Others are unkind to their relations or idle or gluttonous or bad-tempered or selfish. *All* these things, whatever people may choose to think, are very wicked and displeasing to a holy God.

Children who walk in truth are always trying to keep clear of bad ways. They take no pleasure in sinful things of any kind, and they dislike the company of those who do them. Their great wish is to be like Jesus: holy, harmless, and separate from [sinful ways]. They endeavor to be kind, gentle, obliging, obedient, honest, truthful, and good in all their ways. It grieves them that they are not more holy than they are.

Little children, this is the last mark I shall give you of walking in truth. Look at it. Think of it. Are your doings right or wrong?

Children, you have now heard some marks of walking in truth. I have tried to set them plainly before you. I hope you have understood them. Knowing the truth about sin; loving the true Savior, Jesus Christ; serving God with a true heart; doing the things that are true and right in the sight of God—there they are, all four together. Think about them, I entreat you, and each ask yourself this question: "What am I doing at this very time? Am I walking in truth?"…

Trust all to Christ, and He will undertake to manage all that concerns your soul. Trust in Him at all times. Trust in Him in every condition—in sickness and in health, in youth and in age, in poverty and in plenty, in sorrow and in joy. Trust in Him, and He will be a Shepherd to watch over you, a Guide to lead you, a King to protect you, a Friend to help you in time of need. Trust in Him, and He says Himself, *"I will never leave thee, nor forsake thee"* (Heb. 13:5). He will put His Spirit into you and give you a new heart. He will give you power to become a true child of God. He will give you grace to keep down bad tempers, to no longer be selfish, to love others as yourself. He will make your cares more light and your work easier. He will comfort you in time of trouble. Christ can make those happy who trust in Him…Dear children, John was well aware of these things. He had learned them by experience. He saw this lady's children likely to be happy in this world, and no wonder he rejoiced!

From *Boys and Girls Playing*, reprinted by Soli Deo Gloria, a ministry of Reformation Heritage Books: www.heritagebooks.org.

J.C. Ryle (1816-1900): Anglican Bishop; born at Macclesfield, Cheshire County, England.

Let us learn to behold the goodness of God in all who have authority over us in order to submit ourselves to their obedience. —John Calvin

To the Children of Godly Parents
CHARLES HADDON SPURGEON (1834-1892)

> *My son, keep thy father's commandment, and forsake not the law of thy mother: bind them continually upon thine heart, and tie them about thy neck.* —Proverbs 6:20-21

I think that to any young man or any young woman either, who has had a godly father and mother, the best way of life that they can mark out for themselves is to follow the road in which their father's and mother's principle would conduct them. Of course, we make great advances on the old folks, do we not? The young men are wonderfully bright and intelligent, and the old people are a good deal behind them. Yes, yes—that is the way we talk before our beards have grown. Possibly, when we have more sense, we shall not be quite so conceited of it. At any rate, I, who am not very old and who dare not any longer call myself *young*, venture to say that, for myself, I desire nothing so much as to continue the traditions of my household. I wish to find no course but that which shall run parallel with that of those who have gone before me. And I think, dear friends, that you who have seen the holy and happy lives of Christian ancestors will be wise to pause a good deal before you begin to make a deviation, either to the right or to the left, from the course of those godly ones. I do not believe that he begins life in a way that God is likely to bless, and which he himself will in the long run judge to be wise, who begins with the notion that he shall upset everything—that all that belonged to his godly family shall be cast to the winds.

I do not seek to have heirlooms of gold or silver: but, though I die a thousand deaths, I can never give up my father's God, my grandsire's[84] God, and his father's God, and his father's God. I must hold this to be the chief possession that I have. I pray young men and women to think the same. Do not stain the glorious traditions of noble lives that have been handed down to you. Do not disgrace your father's shield; bespatter not the escutcheons[85] of your honored predecessors by any sins and transgressions on your part. God help you to [believe] that the best way of leading a noble life will be to do as they did who trained you in God's fear!

Solomon tells us to do two things with the teachings that we have learned of our parents. First, he says, *"Bind them continually upon thine heart,"* for they are worthy of loving adherence. Show that you love these things by binding them upon your heart. The heart is the vital point! Let godliness lie there.

---

84 **grandsire's** – grandfather's.
85 **escutcheons** – shields displaying the family coat of arms.

Love the things of God. If we could take young men and women and make them professedly religious without their truly loving godliness, that would be simply to make them hypocrites, which is not what we desire. We do not want you to *say* that you believe what you do not believe or that you rejoice in what you do not rejoice in. But our prayer—and, oh, that it might be your prayer, too!—is that you may be helped to bind these things about your heart. They are worth *living* for, they are worth *dying* for, and they are worth more than all the world besides— the immortal principles of the divine life that comes from the death of Christ. *"Bind them continually upon thine heart."*

Then Solomon, because he would not have us keep these things secret as if we were ashamed of them, adds, *"And tie them about thy neck,"* for they are worthy of boldest display. Did you ever see my Lord Mayor wearing his chain of office? He is not at all ashamed to wear it. And the sheriffs with their brooches: I have a lively recollection of the enormous size to which those ornaments attain; and they take care to wear them, too. Now then, you who have any love to God, tie your religion about your neck. Do not be ashamed of it! Put it on as an ornament. Wear it as the mayor does his chain. When you go into company, *never* be ashamed to say that you are a Christian. And if there is any company where you cannot go as a Christian, well, do not go there at all. Say to yourself, "I will not be where I could not introduce my Master. I will not go where He could not go with me." You will find that resolve to be a great help to you in the choice of where you will go and where you will not go. Therefore, bind it upon your heart; tie it about your neck. God help you to do this, and so to follow those godly ones who have gone before you!...

But *first*, believe in the Lord Jesus Christ! Trust yourselves wholly to Him, and He will give you grace to stand fast even to the end.

Delivered at the Metropolitan Tabernacle, Newington, on Lord's Day evening, March 27, 1887, reprinted by Pilgrim Publishers.

Charles Haddon Spurgeon (1834-1892): English Baptist and history's most widely read preacher, apart from those found in Scripture; born at Kelvedon, Essex, England.

Chapter 11
MODEST APPAREL

Should there be a dress code in your family or your church? This question is actually rhetorical; everyone already has a dress code. The more appropriate questions are these. First, what is your dress code? And second, where does your dress code come from?

We must acknowledge this inescapable reality: a dress code is either informed by culture, created from our own conscience, driven by preference, or governed by the Word of God. This is why dress codes are battle zones for the kingdom of darkness and the kingdom of light as we dress either to please God, ourselves or others. We must acknowledge that our very clothing choices will place us in the crossfire of bullets from culture, conscience, preference and the Word of God.

The subject of modesty also brings us to the matter of Christian liberty – a much misunderstood subject. In today's Christian world, "liberty" includes taking most of your clothes off at the beach. Is that what Scripture defines as liberty? Today, some believe it is Christian liberty for girls to dress like boys and boys to dress like girls. Is this a proper application of Christian liberty?

When we talk about clothing and modesty, we are speaking of something earthly that points to something spiritual. Clothing and modesty are "types." As found in Scripture, a type is something or someone that is a symbol of something else. In the same way that the adoption of a child here on earth is a picture of our spiritual adoption as God's sons and daughters, so our clothing is a picture of salvation. As God clothed Adam and Eve in the garden, so Christ clothes His sons and daughters with His righteousness.

Therefore, clothing has great meaning, demonstrating the glory of the gospel to cover our spiritual nakedness and signify that we are a holy people set apart, changed by God from the heart. Thus, we can say along with the prophet Isaiah, "my soul shall be joyful in my God; for He hath clothed me with the garments of salvation, He hath covered me with the robe of righteousness" (Isaiah 61:10).

Is Scripture sufficient to address our clothing choices? The answer of the authors in this chapter is *Yes*.

—Scott Brown

Thinking Like a Christian about Modest Apparel
ROBERT G. SPINNEY

The Christian's wardrobe is no small matter. The daily statements we make with our clothing—intentional or unintentional, interpreted correctly or incorrectly—are among the boldest statements we make. Our children, siblings, coworkers, classmates, and fellow church members cannot help but see our clothing. Everyone notices if we are sloppy or neat, simple or glamorous, provocative or modest. Clothing can both affect our self-image and shape other peoples' perceptions of us: that is why we spend gobs of money purchasing nice clothing. Thinking Christianly about clothing involves many issues…

We must first remove two obstacles that sometimes prevent Christians from even considering this subject: the belief that any discussion of clothing is inherently legalistic and the belief that such discussions are simply unnecessary. In many places today, simply to *raise* the subject of immodest clothing is to set off every legalism alarm in the building. This is regrettable.

We do not understand *holiness* if we think applying Colossians 3:17 (*"And whatsoever ye do in word or deed, do all in the name of the Lord Jesus"*) to the subject of clothing is somehow wrong. The person who says, "Jesus will not be Lord of my clothing" is little different from the person who says, "Jesus will not be Lord of my money."

Nor is it legalistic when God's people endeavor to obey God's instructions. D. Martyn Lloyd-Jones[1] put it well when he said that if the "grace" we have received does not help us to keep God's laws, then we have not really received grace. To be sure, Christians can handle the subject of immodest clothing in a clumsy, unbiblical, and grace-denying fashion. That *is* a problem. But surely, ignoring the subject is not the solution: by doing this, we imply there is no such thing as inappropriate clothing.

God's people cannot afford to ignore this issue. Why not? Because Christians who think unbiblically about this issue do not naturally gravitate toward more modest clothing. As is true with other aspects of living the Christian life, we never "drift forward." Holiness and spiritual maturity must be pursued (Heb. 12:14). That pursuit of godliness should be marked by diligence (2 Peter 1:10; 3:14). Our mind's default settings are not godly: renewing our minds produces spiritual transformation (Rom. 12:2).

---

[1] **David Martyn Lloyd-Jones** (1899-1981) – Welsh expository preacher at Westminster Chapel, London, England, 1938-68

Sometimes Christians dismiss the issue of modest clothing as *trivial*. It is not. After all, it was God Who noticed the first clothing ever invented, judged it inadequate, and intervened to replace it with apparel of His own making (Gen. 3:7, 21). And no one can deny that much of the clothing available in stores today is scandalously immodest. "If you're blind or from another planet," writes Barbara Hughes, "you may conceivably have missed the fact that modesty has disappeared. It is dead and buried! If you don't think so, go shopping with a teenager."[2]

A third issue also deserves attention at the outset of this discussion. Some God-fearing Christians dress immodestly, even though they have no wish to offend others, flaunt their sexuality, or turn heads with their skimpy apparel. These believers often sincerely *think* they are dressing modestly. The problem? They take their fashion cues from the world. They permit the clothing industry and entertainers to define both what is beautiful and what is appropriate apparel. The result? Stylish attire that runs afoul of biblical principles. Clothing that reflects the world's values can be immodest regardless of the wearers' motives. Innocent motives change nothing: unintentional immodesty and "immodesty out of ignorance" are still unbiblical immodesty. The Christian might truthfully say, "It is not my intention to dress sensually or seductively," and yet still dress inappropriately. Surely biblical principles—not worldly fashion designers, movie stars, and celebrities—should set the standards for proper clothing.

To whom is this booklet addressed? I suppose to every reader who wears clothing. However, it seems that we tend to direct messages like this at younger women. This strikes me as inappropriate. The message in this booklet is aimed primarily at husbands and fathers,[3] who are the God-ordained leaders of families. When I see a Christian teenager who is immodestly dressed, my first thought is, "Where is the father? Why is the father asleep at the wheel?" When a married Christian woman does not dress modestly, my first thought is, "Why is the husband so unconcerned with the Bible's teaching regarding modest clothing?" A man has a God-given responsibility to protect his wife and children. Immodest clothing invites the wrong kind of people to pay the wrong kind of attention to our family members. In addition, improper apparel is sometimes a way to express sensuality in an inappropriate (and public) manner. Men, we dare not ignore these matters.

Similarly, a man has a responsibility to protect others from the stumbling blocks that his wife and children may create with their immodest attire. This

---

2 Barbara Hughes, *Disciplines of a Godly Woman* (Wheaton: Crossway Books, 2001), 92.
3 **Editor's Note:** and pastors.

is true in all places and at all times, but it is especially true with regard to corporate church meetings. More than one Christian has asked me, "Why can't we have at least one safe haven from tight clothing, cleavage, bare shoulders, and short shorts? Why can't people be sure to dress modestly when they attend church meetings? I expect to be tempted by scandalous clothing when I go to a college campus, but God's people shouldn't have to face that kind of temptation at worship services. Can't Christians be more considerate of others?" That is a legitimate request. Men have an added responsibility: they should explain to their wives and older children how easily men are tempted to lust by immodest clothing. Our families may think that we never battle with sexual temptations. Tell your family the truth! I have spoken with Christian women who simply did not know that Christian men are tempted to sin by immodest clothing. Once they understood, they gladly dressed more modestly.

Has God given us instructions regarding clothing? The answer to this question is *yes*…The inspired Apostle writes in 1 Timothy 2:9, *"In like manner also, that women adorn themselves in modest apparel, with shamefacedness and sobriety; not with broided hair, or gold, or pearls, or costly array."* Perhaps the most obvious truth in this verse is one that is often denied today: God *does* care about our clothing…In 1 Timothy 2:9, modesty is specifically linked to *how* Christian women adorn themselves with clothing.

Every discussion of modest and immodest clothing at some point asks what could be called The Line Question: Where exactly is the line between acceptable and unacceptable clothing? How do I know where the line is? I will not cross the line, but could you please define precisely where the line exists? The word [*shamefacedness*] addresses The Line Question because the modest Christians say, "I don't want to get near the line! I may not know exactly where the line is between acceptable and unacceptable clothing, but I know approximately where it is . . . and I will stay away from it."

The word [*sobriety*]…speaks of exercising restraint over one's thoughts, preferences, and desires. The discreet Christian does not give free rein to his passions; he knows how to bridle his desires. The Bible is exposing something here that many simply do not want to admit: some use their clothing as non-verbal expressions of their own sensuality. They deliberately turn themselves into an object of lust: they walk into a room with the intention of turning heads. Instead of practicing self-control, they openly flaunt their sensuality with their apparel. Dressing [with sobriety] means we do not express our private sexual desires with our public clothing.

Why should believers practice self-control when it comes to their apparel? Indiscreet clothing surely affects others (by tempting them to sin). But both Christians and non-Christians have noticed how clothing affects the wearer as well. "Dress changes the manners," wrote the French *philosophe* Voltaire,[4] who was no friend of Christianity but nonetheless a shrewd observer of the human condition. The English writer Virginia Woolf[5] agreed: "There is much to support the view that it is clothes that wear us and not we them; we may make them take the mold of arm or breast, but they would mold our hearts, our brains, our tongues to their liking."

This is one of the intangible aspects of clothing that we have all experienced. Donning a new outfit or dressing sharply imparts a sense of confidence and positive self-esteem. By the same token, racy, provocative, and revealing clothing emboldens us to flaunt our sexuality. Christ's disciple must exercise self-control over his sexual passions, so he must also exercise self-control over apparel that would "mold his heart, brain, and tongue" in inappropriate directions. A built-in cultural application accompanies this command in 1 Timothy 2:9. Notice the verse's final words: *"not with braided hair and gold or pearls or costly garments."* This instructed Christian women not to imitate the outrageous dress and hairstyles that were commonplace among the Roman nobility. In Paul's day, some women wove precious gems into their hair to create hairstyles costing the modern equivalent of hundreds and even thousands of dollars. They also wore dazzling clothing that easily cost $10,000 in today's money. This was the unofficial uniform for Roman court women, a uniform that was distinctive and attention grabbing. At the same time, these Roman courtesans were notoriously immoral when it came to sexual matters. These women did not dress properly, modestly, and discreetly. Everyone knew that their lives were characterized by sexual impurity. God's Word says to Christians, "Do not imitate the appearance of these famous and immoral people. No flashiness, gaudiness, extravagance, and flaunting of wealth. No association with these court women of bad reputation. Do not regard these 'court women' as your fashion role models."

Consider the piercing words of Stephen M. Baugh, who is the professor of Greek and New Testament at Westminster West Theological Seminary. Baugh applies these final words in 1 Timothy 2:9 to modern readers: "Today, it is the equivalent of warning Christians away from imitation of styles set by promiscuous pop singers or actresses." That means that if we want to apply

---

4 **Voltaire** (1694-1778) – French writer and poet; a leading figure of the Enlightenment.
5 **Virginia Woolf** (1882-1941) – English author, associated with the Bloomsbury Group that influenced the growth of modernism.

this verse practically, Christian women should not imitate the appearances of salacious "Hollywood court women." The very next verse—1 Timothy 2:10—amplifies the Apostle's instruction. The Christian woman is to adorn herself not with improper clothing, *"but (which becometh women professing godliness) with good works."* The [word *professing*] is from a Greek word meaning to make a public announcement or to convey a message loudly. Our lives make public announcements. The godly woman's public announcement must consist of good works, not questionable clothing. What is the public function of a Christian's good works? Matthew 5:16 says that believers must live in such a manner that men see our good works and therefore glorify our Father Who is in heaven. Numerous verses state that the Christian's good deeds are valuable not only for the assistance they bring to men but also for what they demonstrate about God's glory (1 Peter 2:12; 3:1-6; Matt. 9:6-8). The implication here is that both good works and improper clothing have a Godward element: one provokes men to praise God while the other encourages men to demean Him. The upshot of 1 Timothy 2:10 is that God's reputation is at stake in our public professions. God's glory is more clearly seen when we abound in good works, but it is obscured and misunderstood when we make public announcements with improper clothing…It is not only *your* reputation that is at stake when you wear improper clothing: *God's reputation is also at stake.*

From *Dressed to Kill,* published by Tulip Books: www.tulipbooks.com.

Robert G. Spinney: Baptist minister and associate professor of history at Patrick Henry College, Purcellville, VA.

Christian Modesty Defined
JEFF POLLARD

In like manner also, that women adorn themselves in modest apparel, with shamefacedness and sobriety. —1 Timothy 2:9

What is modesty? Like the words love and faith, we often use the word modesty without grasping its Biblical meaning. Modern dictionaries offer definitions such as (1) Having or showing a moderate estimation of one's own talents, abilities, and value; (2) Having or proceeding from a disinclination[6] to call attention to oneself; retiring or diffident;[7] (3) Reserve or propriety in speech, dress, or behavior; (4) Free from showiness or ostentation;[8] unpretentious; (5) Moderate or limited in size, quantity, or range; not extreme: *a modest price; a newspaper with a modest circulation.*[9]

Noah Webster defines *modesty* as "that lowly temper which accompanies a moderate estimate of one's own worth and importance."[10] He adds, "In *females*, modesty has the like character as in males; but the word is used also as synonymous with chastity, or purity of manners. In this sense, modesty results from purity of mind, or from the fear of disgrace and ignominy fortified by education and principle. Unaffected *modesty* is the sweetest charm of female excellence, the richest gem in the diadem[11] of their honor."

According to these definitions then, modesty is a broad concept not limited to sexual connotation. This state of mind or disposition expresses a humble estimate of one's self before God. Modesty, like humility, is the opposite of boldness or arrogance. It does not seek to draw attention to itself or to show off in an unseemly way. Webster apparently links chastity with modesty because chastity means "moral purity in thought and conduct." Moral purity, like humility, will not exhibit sensuality any more than ostentation.

Underlying these definitions is a crucial point: modesty is not first an issue of clothing. It is primarily an issue of the *heart*. If the heart is right with God, it will govern itself in purity coupled with humility and will express itself modestly. Calvin observes, "Yet we must always begin with the dispositions; for where debauchery reigns within, there will be no chastity; and where

---

6 **disinclination** – an unwillingness to do something.
7 **retiring or diffident** – reluctant to draw attention to oneself or shy.
8 **ostentation** – display intended to attract notice or admiration.
9 *The American Heritage Dictionary of the English Language,* 3rd Ed.(Houghton Mifflin, 1992).
10 Noah Webster, *Noah Webster's First Edition of an American Dictionary of the English Language*(Anaheim, CA: Foundation for American Christian Education, 2006).
11 **diadem** – crown.

ambition reigns within, there will be no modesty in the outward dress."[12] He concludes, "Undoubtedly the dress of a virtuous and godly woman must differ from that of a strumpet…If piety must be testified by works, this profession ought also to be visible in chaste and becoming dress."[13] This applies not only to corporate worship, but to daily living also. Though it is true that one may dress modestly from a sinful and prideful motive, one cannot knowingly dress lavishly or sensually from a good one. Thus, the purity and humility of a regenerate heart internally must ultimately express itself by modest clothing externally.

Several words shed light on a biblical view of modesty. In 1 Timothy 2:9, the Apostle Paul commands women to *"adorn themselves in modest apparel, with shamefacedness and sobriety."* George Knight III says that the word translated *modest*[14] has "the general meaning of 'respectable,' 'honorable,' and when used in reference to women means elsewhere, as here, 'modest'."[15] He observes, "Adornment and dress is an area with which women are often concerned and in which there are dangers of immodesty or indiscretion."[16] Therefore, "Paul makes that the focal point of his warning and commands women 'to adorn themselves' in keeping with their Christian profession and life." Hence, modesty is an element of Christian character, and our dress should make the same "profession" that we do. Paul's directive implies that this is an *especially* dangerous matter for women.

According to Knight, *shamefacedness*[17] denotes "a state of mind or attitude necessary for one to be concerned about modesty and thus to dress modestly." It means "a moral feeling, reverence, awe, respect for the feeling or opinion of others or for one's own conscience and so shame, self-respect… sense of honor."[18] William Hendriksen says it "indicates a sense of shame, a shrinking from trespassing the boundaries of propriety."[19] This means that modesty knows the boundaries and desires to stay within them—it does not desire to show off.

---

12 John Calvin, *Calvin's Commentaries*, Vol. XXI, "The First Epistle to Timothy" (Grand Rapids: Baker Publishing Group, 1993), 66.
13 Ibid.
14 κόσμιος
15 George W. Knight III, *Commentary on the Pastoral Epistles*, NIGTC (Grand Rapids: Eerdmans, 1992), 134.
16 Ibid.
17 αἰδώς
18 Knight, *Pastoral Epistles*, 134.
19 William Hendriksen, *Thessalonians, Timothy, Titus*, NTC (Grand Rapids: Baker Publishing Group, 1979), 106.

Finally, *sobriety*[20] has among its meanings "the general one of 'good judgment, moderation, self-control,' which when seen as 'a feminine virtue' is understood as 'decency, chastity'."[21] Sobriety signifies "a command over bodily passions, a state of self-mastery in the area of the appetite. The basic meaning of the word has different nuances and connotations and represents 'that habitual inner self-government, with its constant rein on all the passions and desires, which would hinder the temptation to [immodesty] from arising'…in effect, Paul is saying that when such attitudes self-consciously control a woman's mind, the result is evident in her modest apparel."[22] Kelly says of shamefacedness and sobriety, "The former, used only here in the N.T., connotes feminine reserve in matters of sex. The latter…basically stands for perfect self-mastery in the physical appetites…As applied to women it too had a definitely sexual nuance."[23]

What then is Christian modesty? Since modesty possesses a range of meanings, we will draw our definition from the Biblical material: Christian modesty is the inner self-government, rooted in a proper understanding of one's self before God, which outwardly displays itself in humility and purity from a genuine love for Jesus Christ, rather than in self-glorification or self-advertisement.

I have taken the time to unfold these words a bit because some ministers believe Paul's words apply only to luxurious, expensive, or gaudy clothing in the worship services of Christ's church. Their point is that such clothing would "distract" in the worship services. However, they want to stop there and go no further. I whole-heartedly agree that this idea is included, but these men overlook or ignore the sexual aspect that is clearly in Paul's mind. "While his remarks conform broadly to the conventional diatribe[24] against female extravagance, what is probably foremost in his mind is the impropriety of women exploiting their physical charms on such occasions, and also the emotional disturbance they are liable to cause their male fellow-worshipers."[25] Knight explains that "the reason for Paul's prohibition of elaborate hair styles, ornate jewelry, and extremely expensive clothing becomes clear when one reads in the contemporary literature of the inordinate time, expense, and effort that elaborately braided hair and jewels demanded, not just as ostentatious display, but

---

20 σωφροσύνη
21 Knight, *Pastoral Epistles*, 134.
22 Ibid.
23 J. N. D. Kelly, *The Pastoral Epistles* (Peabody: Hendrickson Publishers, 1960), 66.
24 **diatribe** – a forceful verbal attack; a discourse directed against some person or work.
25 Kelly, *Pastoral Epistles*, 66.

also as the mode of dress of courtesans[26] and harlots…it is the excess and sensuality that Paul forbids."[27]

Excess *and* sensuality—both of these bear on modesty. Christian women must self-consciously control their hearts and passions, instead of arraying themselves elaborately, expensively, and/or sensuously. If they are modest, they will not draw attention to themselves in the wrong way. Their clothing will not say "SEX!" or "PRIDE!" or "MONEY!", but *"purity," "humility,"* and *"moderation."*

One more point: because the immediate context of Paul's epistle to Timothy regards the Christian's behavior in church, some claim that Paul limits his discussion to distractions in the church's worship, *not* principles of dress at all times. Again, I believe this entirely misses Paul's point. Christ's church is *"the pillar and ground of the truth"* (1 Tim. 3:15). Therefore, the principles we learn in the worship of God for ordering our lives should ultimately guide our daily living in the presence of God. Can one honestly conclude that a woman should dress modestly in the presence of men and God for corporate worship, only to dress pridefully and sensuously outside of church meetings? Knight's insight is keen here: "Therefore, Paul's instructions to women, like the preceding instructions to men, are related to the context of the gathered Christian community but are not restricted to it…women are always to live in accord with their profession of godliness, dressing modestly and discreetly."[28] We have then a Biblical directive for modest apparel that begins in the context of our corporate worship and that extends from there to our daily living.

Adapted from *Christian Modesty and the Public Undressing of America*, available from Chapel Library.

Jeff Pollard: An elder of Mount Zion Bible Church in Pensacola, Florida.

---

26 **courtesans** – prostitutes, especially those whose clients are wealthy or upper class.
27 Knight, *Pastoral Epistles*, 135.
28 Ibid., 131.

A Crying Sin of Our Age
ARTHUR W. PINK (1886-1952)

And why take ye thought for raiment? —Matthew 6:28

All care for apparel is not here forbidden. There is a lawful and godly concern, whereby we may labor honestly and in a sober manner for such clothing as is [suitable] for the station of life that divine providence has allotted us: such as is needful to the health and comfort of our bodies. That which is here prohibited is a carnal and inordinate care for clothing that arises either from distrust and fear of [lacking what is necessary] or from pride and discontentedness with such apparel as is [suitable] and necessary. It is the latter that is one of the crying sins of our age, when there is such a lusting after strange and costly garments, when such vast sums are wasted annually upon outward adornment, when there is such a making of a "god" out of fashion, when maids covet the finery of their mistresses, and when their mistresses waste so much time on the attiring of their bodies that ought to be spent upon more profitable duties. Well may all such seriously face the question, "Why take ye [such] thought for raiment?"

Why, we may well ask, has the pulpit for so long maintained a criminal silence, instead of condemning this flagrant sin? It is not one that only a few are guilty of, but is common to all classes and ages. Preachers were not ignorant that many in their own congregations were spending money they could ill afford in order to "keep up with the latest styles"—styles often imported from countries whose morals are notoriously corrupt. Why, then, has not the pulpit denounced such vanity and extravagance? Was it the fear of man, of becoming unpopular, which restrained them? Was it the sight of their own wives and daughters in silk stockings, fur coats, and expensive hats that hindered them? Alas, only too often the minister's family, instead of setting an example of sobriety, frugality,[29] and modesty, has given a lead to the community in worldliness and wastefulness. The churches have failed lamentably in this matter as in many others.

It may be that some preachers who read this article will be ready to say, "We have something better to do than give our attention to such things, a far more important message to deliver than one relating to the covering worn by the body." But such a rejoinder will not satisfy God, Who requires His servants to declare all His counsel and to keep back nothing that is profitable. If the Scriptures be read attentively, it will be found that they have not a little to say upon the subject of clothing, from the aprons of fig leaves made by our

---

29 **frugality** – economical in the use of anything.

first parents to the mother of harlots *"arrayed in purple and scarlet colour, and decked with gold and precious stones and pearls"* of Revelation 17. Has not the Most High said, *"The woman shall not wear that which pertaineth unto a man, neither shall a man put on a woman's garment: for all that do so are abomination unto the LORD thy God"* (Deut. 22:5)? No wonder His wrath is upon us when our streets are becoming filled with [unthinking] women wearing trousers.[30] No wonder so many church houses are being destroyed when their pulpits have so long been unfaithful!

"And why take ye thought for raiment? Consider the lilies of the field, how they grow; they toil not, neither do they spin" (Matt. 6:28). The scope of these words is wider than appears at first glance. As "raiment" must be taken to include all that is used for the adorning as well as covering of the body, so we are to learn from the "lilies" that which corrects every form of sin we may commit in connection with apparel, not only in distrusting God to supply us with what we need, but also our displeasing Him by setting our affections upon such trifles, by following the evil fashions of the world, or by disregarding His prohibitions. In sending us to learn of the flowers of the field, Christ would humble our proud hearts; for notwithstanding our intelligence, there are many important and valuable lessons to be learned even from these lowly and irrational creatures if only we have ears to hear what they have to say unto us.

"Consider the lilies of the field." This is brought in here to correct that inordinate care and that immoderate lusting that men and women have concerning raiment. It seems to us that part of the force of our Lord's design here has been generally missed and this through failure to perceive the significance of His following remarks. *"Wherefore, if God so clothe the grass of the field, which to day is, and to morrow is cast into the oven, shall he not much more clothe you?"* (Matt. 6:30). Thus, though the lily is such a lovely flower, nevertheless it is but "the grass of the field." Notwithstanding its beauty and delicacy, it belongs to the same order and stands upon the same level as the common grass that withers, dies, and is used (in oriental countries where there is no coal) for fuel. What ground or occasion then has the lily to be proud and vain? None whatever: it is exceedingly frail, it belongs to a very lowly order of creation, its loveliness quickly vanishes, its destiny is but the oven.

In what has just been pointed out, we may discover a forceful reason why we should not be unduly concerned about either our appearance or our raiment. Some are given gracefulness of body and comeliness of

---

30 Chapel Library understands that not all will hold the view of the author on this point.

feature, which, like the lilies, are much admired by those who behold them. Nevertheless, such people need to be reminded that they come only of the common stock, that they are of the same constitution and subject to the same experiences as their less favored fellows. Physical beauty is but skin deep, and the fairest countenance loses its bloom in a few short years at most. The ravages of disease and the effects of sorrow dim the brightest eye and mar the roundest cheek, and wrinkles will soon crease what before was so attractive. *"For all flesh is as grass, and all the glory of man as the flower of grass. The grass withereth, and the flower thereof falleth away"* (1 Peter 1:24), and the grave is the "oven" to which the handsomest equally with the ugliest are hastening.

In view of the brevity of life and fleetingness of physical charm, how groundless and foolish is pride over a handsome body! That beauty upon which we need to fix our hearts and unto which we should devote our energies is *"the beauty of holiness"* (1 Chron. 16:29), for it is a beauty that fadeth not away, is not transient[31] and disappointing, is not destroyed in the grave, but endureth for ever. And what is the beauty of holiness? It is the opposite of the hideousness of sin, which is likeness unto the devil. The beauty of holiness consists in conformity unto Him of Whom it is said, *"How great is his goodness, and how great is his beauty!"* (Zech. 9:17). This is not creature beauty, but divine beauty! Yet it is imparted to God's elect, for *"the king's daughter is all glorious within"* (Ps. 45:13). Oh, how we need to pray, *"Let the beauty of the LORD our God be upon us"* (Ps. 90:17), then shall we be admired by the holy angels.

Not only does the evanescent[32] beauty of the lily rebuke those who are proud of their physical comeliness, but it also condemns all who make an idol of costly or showy apparel. Alas, such a sorry wretch is fallen man that even when his food is assured (for the present, at any rate) he must perforce harass himself over the matter of clothes—not merely for warmth and comfort, but for display, to gratify a peacock vanity. This gives as much concern to the rich as worrying about food does to the poor. Then, *"consider the lilies of the field"*: they are indeed clothed with loveliness; yet how fleeting it is, and the oven awaits them! Does your ambition rise no higher than to be like unto them and to share their fate? Oh, heed that word, *"Whose adorning let it not be that outward adorning of plaiting the hair, and of wearing of gold, or of putting on of apparel; but let it be the hidden man of the heart, in that which is not corruptible, even the ornament of a meek and quiet spirit, which is in the sight of God of great price"* (1 Peter 3:3-4)…

---

31 **transient** – lasting a very short time.
32 **evanescent** – quickly fading or disappearing; vanishing like vapor.

Chapter 11—Modest Apparel: A Crying Sin of Our Age

"They toil not, neither do they spin." Here the Savior bids us to take note of how free from care the lilies are. They expend no labor in order to earn their clothing, as we have to do. This is proof that God Himself directly provides for them and decks them out so attractively. How forcibly does that fact press upon us the duty of contentment,[33] relying upon God's gracious providence without distracting care…Though no man under the pretense of relying on God's providence may live idly, neglecting the ordinary lawful means to procure things honest and needful, yet Christ here gives assurance to all who trust in Him and serve Him that, even though all means should fail them, He will provide things needful for them. If through sickness, injury, or old age we can no longer toil and spin, God will not suffer us to lack sufficient clothing.

"And yet I say unto you, That even Solomon in all his glory was not arrayed like one of these" (Matt. 6:29). In those words, Christ rebukes that folly of the vain that moves so many to make an idol of personal adornment…It should be pointed out that in making mention of the splendor of Solomon's royal apparel, He did not condemn the same…Though the Word of God reprehends[34] pride and superfluities[35] in attire, yet it allows unto princes and persons of high office the use of gorgeous and costly raiment…

How senseless it is to be conceited over fine attire and to be so solicitous[36] about our personal appearance! For when we have done everything in our power to make ourselves [brightly colored] and attractive, yet we come far short of the flowers of the field in their glorious array. What cloth or silk is as white as the lily, what purple can equal the violet, what scarlet or crimson is comparable with roses and other flowers of that color? The arts of the workman may indeed do much, yet they cannot equal the beauties of nature. If, then, we cannot [compete] with the herbs of the field that we trample under our feet and cast into the oven, why should we be puffed up with any showiness in our dress?…

Alas, so great is the depravity and perversity of man that he turns into an occasion of feeding his vanity and of self-display what ought to be a ground of humiliation and self-abasement. If we duly considered the proper and principal end of apparel, we should rather be humbled and abased when we put it on, than pleased with our gaudy attire. Clothing for the body is to cover the shame of nakedness that sin brought upon us. It was not ever thus,

---

33 *See* FGB 213, *Contentment,* available from Chapel Library.
34 **reprehends** – finds fault with.
35 **superfluities** – excessiveness.
36 **solicitous** – deeply concerned; extremely attentive.

for of our first parents before the Fall it is written, *"And they were both naked, the man and his wife, and were not ashamed"* (Gen. 2:25). Raiment, then, is a covering of our shame, the ensign of our sin, and we have no better reason to be proud of our apparel than the criminal has of his handcuffs or the lunatic of his straitjacket; for as they are badges of wrongdoing or insanity, so apparel is but the badge of our sin.

"Even Solomon in all his glory was not arrayed like one of these." The array of Solomon must indeed have been magnificent. Possessed of [limitless] wealth, owner of a fleet of ships that brought to him the products of many foreign countries, nothing was lacking to make his court one of outstanding splendor and pomp. No doubt on state occasions, he appeared in the richest and most imposing of clothes, yet deck himself out as finely as he might, he came far short of the beauty of the lilies. Rightly did Matthew Henry point out, "Let us therefore be more ambitious of the wisdom of Solomon in which he was outdone by none—wisdom to do our duty in our place—than the glory of Solomon in which he was outdone by the lilies. Knowledge and grace are the perfection of man, not beauty, much less fine clothes." To which we would add, let us seek to be *"clothed with humility"* (1 Peter 5:5) rather than lust after peacock feathers.

From *Studies in the Scriptures*, available from Chapel Library.

Arthur W. Pink (1886-1952): Pastor, itinerate Bible teacher, author; born in Nottingham, England.

Symptoms of Bodily Pride

JOHN BUNYAN (1628-1688)

WISEMAN: There are two sorts of pride: pride of *spirit* and pride of *body*. The first of these is thus made mention of in the Scriptures. *"Every one that is proud in heart is an abomination to the LORD"* (Prov. 16:5). *"An high look, and a proud heart, and the plowing of the wicked, is sin"* (Prov. 21:4). *"The patient in spirit is better than the proud in spirit"* (Eccl. 7:8). Bodily pride the Scriptures also mention: *"In that day the Lord will take away the bravery[37] of their tinkling ornaments about their feet, and their cauls,[38] and their round tires[39] like the moon, the chains, and the bracelets, and the mufflers,[40] the bonnets, and the ornaments of the legs, and the headbands, and the tablets,[41] and the earrings, the rings, and nose jewels, the changeable suits of apparel, and the mantles,[42] and the wimples,[43] and the crisping pins,[44] the glasses,[45] and the fine linen, and the hoods, and the vails"* (Isa. 3:18-23). By these expressions, it is evident that there is pride of *body*, as well as pride of *spirit*, and that both are sin, and so abominable to the Lord. But these texts Mr. Badman could never abide to read. They were to him as Micaiah was to Ahab: they never spake good of him, but evil (1 Kings 22:6-18).

ATTENTIVE: I suppose that it was not Mr. Badman's case alone to malign[46] those texts that speak against their vices. For I believe that most ungodly men, where the Scriptures are [concerned], have a secret antipathy[47] against those words of God that do most plainly and fully rebuke them for their sins.

WISEMAN: That is out of doubt. And by that antipathy, they show that sin and Satan are more welcome to them than are wholesome instructions of life and godliness.

ATTENTIVE: Well, but not to go off from our discourse of Mr. Badman, you say he was proud. But will you show me now some symptoms of one that is proud?

WISEMAN: Yes, that I will. First, I will show you some symptoms of pride of heart. Pride of heart is seen by outward things, as pride of body in

---

37 **bravery** – splendor; beauty.
38 **cauls** – headbands.
39 **round tires** – crescent shaped ornaments.
40 **mufflers** – veils or scarves.
41 **tablets** – perfume boxes.
42 **mantles** – outer tunics.
43 **wimples** – shawls.
44 **crisping pins** – instruments for curling hair; the Hebrew can mean "purse."
45 **glasses** – hand mirrors.
46 **malign** – to regard with bitter dislike.
47 **antipathy** – hostile feeling toward.

general is a sign of pride of heart; for all proud gestures of the body flow from pride of heart. Therefore Solomon saith, *"There is a generation, O how lofty are their eyes! and their eyelids are lifted up"* (Prov. 30:13). And again, there is *"that exalteth his gate,"* his going (Prov. 17:19). Now, these lofty eyes and this exalting of the gate is a sign of a proud heart; for both these actions come from the heart. For out of the heart comes pride in all the visible appearances of it (Mark 7:21-23).

But more particularly, 1. Heart pride is discovered by a stretched-out neck and by mincing[48] as they go. For the wicked, the proud, have a proud neck, a proud foot, a proud tongue, by which this their going is exalted. This is that which makes them look scornfully, speak ruggedly, and carry it huffingly[49] among their neighbors. 2. A proud heart is a persecuting one. *"The wicked in his pride doth persecute the poor"* (Ps. 10:2). 3. A prayerless man is a proud man (Ps. 10:4). 4. A contentious man is a proud man (Prov. 13:10). 5. The disdainful[50] man is a proud man (Ps. 119:51). 6. The man that oppresses his neighbor is a proud man (Ps. 119:122). 7. He that hearkeneth not to God's Word with reverence and fear is a proud man (Jer. 13:15, 17). 8. And he that calls the proud *happy* is, be sure, a proud man. All these are proud in heart, and this their pride of heart doth thus discover itself (Jer. 43:2; Mal. 3:15).

As to bodily pride, it is discovered—that is, *something* of it—by all the particulars mentioned before. For though they are said to be symptoms of pride of heart, yet they are symptoms of that pride by their showing of themselves in the body. You know diseases that are within are seen oft-times by outward and visible signs, yet by these very signs even the outside is defiled also. So all those visible signs of heart pride are signs of bodily pride also.

But to come to more outward signs. The putting on of gold, pearls, and costly array; the plaiting of the hair, the following of fashions, the seeking by gestures to imitate the proud, either by speech, looks, dresses, goings, or other fools' baubles,[51] of which at this time the world is full. All these and many more are signs of a proud heart, so of bodily pride also (1 Tim. 2:9; 1 Peter 3:3-5).

But Mr. Badman would not allow by any means that this should be called *pride*, but rather *neatness, handsomeness, comeliness, cleanliness*, etc. Neither would he allow that following of fashions was anything else, but because he would not be proud, singular, and esteemed fantastical[52] by his neighbors.

---

48 **mincing** – walking in a pretentious way with little steps.
49 **huffingly** – arrogantly.
50 **disdainful** – showing contempt or lack of respect.
51 **baubles** – showy trinkets or ornaments such as would please a child.
52 **fantastical** – bizarre.

ATTENTIVE: But I have been told that when some have been rebuked for their pride, they have turned it again upon the brotherhood of those by whom they have been rebuked, saying, "Physician, heal thy friends! Look at home among your brotherhood, even among the wisest of you, and see if you yourselves are clear, even you professors. For who is prouder than you professors? scarcely the devil himself!"

WISEMAN: My heart aches at this answer because there is too much cause for it. This very answer would Mr. Badman give his wife when she, as she would sometimes, reprove him for his pride. "We shall have," says he, "great amendments in living now, for the devil is turned a corrector of vice!" "For no sin reigneth more in the world," quoth he, "than pride among professors." And who can contradict him? Let us give the devil his due: the thing is too apparent for any man to deny. And I doubt not but the same answer is ready in the mouths of Mr. Badman's friends; for they may and do see pride display itself in the apparel and carriages of professors—one may say—almost as much as among any people in the land; the more is the pity. Ay, and I fear that even their extravagancies in this hath hardened the heart of many a one, as I perceive it did somewhat the heart of Mr. Badman himself. For my own part, I have seen many myself—*and those church members too*—so decked and bedaubed[53] with their fangles and toys[54] that when they have been at the solemn appointments of God in the way of His worship, I have wondered with what face such painted persons could sit in the place where they were without swooning. But certainly, the holiness of God and the pollution of themselves by sin must need be very far out of the minds of such people, what profession soever they make.

I have read of a whore's forehead, and I have read of Christian shamefacedness (Jer. 3:3; 1 Tim. 2:9). I have read of costly array and of that which becometh women professing godliness—with good works (1 Peter 3:1–3). But if I might speak, I know what I know and could say, and yet do no wrong, that which would make some professors stink in their places; but now I forbear (Jer. 23:15).

ATTENTIVE: Sir, you seem greatly concerned at this, but what if I shall say more? It is whispered that some good ministers have countenanced their people in their light and wanton apparel, yea, have pleaded for their gold and pearls, and costly array, etc.

---

53 **bedaubed** – covered with showy dress or ornaments in a coarse, tasteless manner.
54 **fangles and toys** – new fashions and trinkets.

WISEMAN: I know not what they have pleaded for, but it is easily seen that they tolerate, or at leastwise, wink and connive[55] at such things both in their wives and children. And so *"from the prophets of Jerusalem is profaneness gone forth into all the land"* (Jer. 23:15). When the hand of the rulers are chief in a trespass, who can keep their people from being drowned in that trespass (Ezra 9:2)?

ATTENTIVE: This is a lamentation and must stand for a lamentation.

WISEMAN: So it is, and so it must. And I will add, it is a shame, it is a reproach, it is a stumbling block to the blind! For though men be as blind as Mr. Badman himself, yet they can see the foolish lightness that must needs be the bottom of all these apish and wanton extravagancies. But many have their excuses ready, [namely], their parents, their husbands, and their breeding calls for it and the like…But all these will be but the spider's web when the thunder of the Word of the great God shall rattle from heaven against them—as it will at death or judgment. But I wish it might do it before. Alas! These excuses are but bare pretenses: these proud ones love to have it so. I once talked with a maid by way of reproof for her fond and gaudy garment. But she told me, "The tailor would make it so," when alas! Poor, proud girl: she gave order to the tailor so to make it. Many make parents, husbands, and tailors, etc., the blind to others; but their naughty hearts and their giving of way thereto is the original cause of all these evils.

From "The Life and Death of Mr. Badman," in *The Works of John Bunyan*, Vol. 3, reprinted by The Banner of Truth Trust, www.banneroftruth.org.

John Bunyan (1628-1688): English minister and one of the most influential writers of the 17th century; born at Elstow near Bedford, England.

Get the heart mortified, and that will mortify the clothing. —Vincent Alsop

---

55 **wink and connive** – shut one's eyes to the faults of.

Avoiding Immodest Fashions

VINCENT ALSOP (1630-1703)

> *And it shall come to pass in the day of the LORD'S sacrifice, that I will punish the princes, and the king's children, and all such as are clothed with strange apparel.* —Zephaniah 1:8

What distance ought we to keep in following the strange fashions of apparel that come up in the days wherein we live? That the present generation is lamentably intoxicated with novelties and as sadly degenerated from the gravity[56] of some former ages can neither be denied, concealed, defended, nor, I fear, reformed. What is more deplorable, some that wear the livery of a stricter profession[57] are carried away with the vanity. Even *"the daughters of Zion"* have caught the epidemical infection (Isa. 3:16)…Before I can give a direct and distinct answer, I must crave your patience that I may lay down these preliminaries:

Pride will be sure to perplex and entangle the controversy. For seeing a haughty heart will never confine its licentiousness to the narrow rule of God, it must widen the rule and stretch it to its own extravagancies. The lust that scorns to bow its crooked practices to the straight rule will not fail to bend the rule, if possible, to its *own* crooked practices…

The universality of the corruption, like a deluge, has overspread the face of the earth…Pride and profit, glory and gain have their distinct concernments in this controversy. To decry the silver shrines of Diana by which so many craftsmen get their livings must raise a heavy outcry against the opponent (Acts 19:23-27)…He must have a very hardy spirit that shall dare to cross the stream or stem the current of a prevailing luxuriancy.[58] So that to have a finger in this debate must engage him in Ishmael's fate—to have every man's hand lifted up against him, seeing [that] it is unavoidable that his hand must be set almost against every man (Gen. 16:12)…Yet charity will lend us one safe rule—that we impose a severer law upon ourselves and allow a larger indulgence to others. The rule of our own [conduct] should be with the strictest, but that by which we censure others, a little more with the largest…Let us then inquire,

For what ends does God appoint and nature require apparel? In the state of innocence and primitive integrity, nakedness was man's richest clothing. No ornament, no raiment was ever so decent as [when there] was

---

56 **gravity** – seriousness; dignity.
57 **livery…profession** – uniform of a person's servants; metaphorically of those who make the "stricter profession" of being the servants of the Lord Jesus.
58 **prevailing luxuriancy** – currently popular pleasure.

no ornament and no raiment. For as there was then no irregular[59] motion in the soul, so neither was there any in the body that might dye the cheeks with a blush or cover the face with shame. *"They were both naked, the man and his wife, and were not ashamed"* (Gen. 2:25).

But once they had violated the covenant and broken the law of their Creator, *shame*—the fruit and daughter of sin—seized their souls, and that in respect of God and of each other. The best expedient[60] that their confused and distracted thoughts could pitch upon was to stitch together a few fig leaves to make themselves aprons until God, commiserating[61] their wretched plight, provided better covering, more adequate to the necessity of nature, more comporting[62] with decency, that is, *"coats of skins"* (Gen. 3:7, 21).

The divine wisdom so admirably contrived that their apparel might serve as a standing memorial of their demerits that they might carry about them the continual conviction of their sin and its deserved punishment. For what less could they infer than that they deserved to die the death that innocent beasts must die to preserve and accommodate their lives? Also, their apparel was to direct their weak faith to the promised Seed, in Whom they might expect a better covering from a greater shame—that of their filthiness in the sight of God; in Him, I say, Whom those beasts probably slain in sacrifice typified…Now God appoints and nature requires apparel.

1. To hide shame and to cover nakedness. Clothing was given that our first parents and their posterity, in their exile from Paradise, might not become a perpetual "covering of the eyes" and a shame to each other. So it follows that whatever apparel or fashions of apparel either cross[63] or do not comply with this great design of God must be used sinfully. It also follows that as any apparel or fashions of apparel more or less cross or do not comply with this end, they are proportionately more or less sinful.

But our semi-Evites[64]—aware of danger from these conclusions to their [cleavage][65]—will readily reply that this will be of no great use to decide this controversy because it is not clear what parts of the body God has appointed to cover! Nor is it clear which of them may be uncovered without shame, seeing that some parts, such as the hands, the face, and the feet may be naked without sin to us or offense to others.

---

59 **irregular** – lawless.
60 **expedient** – means to an end; something done to achieve an objective quickly.
61 **commiserating** – expressing compassion for.
62 **comporting** – agreeable; in accord.
63 **cross** – contradict.
64 **semi-Evites** – women who wore apparel that exposed their shoulders or cleavage.
65 **cleavage** – the hollow between a woman's breasts exposed by low cut garments.

To this, I answer that the use of the parts and their designed ends are to be considered in this case. The use of the face is chiefly to distinguish the male from the female and one person from another. The use of the hands is to be instruments for work, business, and all manual operations. To cover or muffle up those parts ordinarily, whose ends and use require them to be uncovered, is to cross God's ends and design and so is sinful by consequence.

To uncover those parts promiscuously and expose them ordinarily to open view for which there can be no such good ends and uses assigned is sinful…Therefore, all apparel or fashions of apparel that expose those parts to view, of which exposing neither God nor nature have assigned any use, is sinful.

It is true, I confess, our first parents, in that hasty provision that they made for their shame, took care only for aprons. But God—Who had adequate conceptions of their wants and what was necessary to supply them of the rule of decency and what would fully answer it—provided *coats* for them so that the whole body (except as before stated) might be covered and its shame concealed.

2. Another end of apparel was to defend the body from the ordinary injuries of unseasonable seasons, from the common inconveniences of labor and travel, and from the emergent accidents that might befall them in their pilgrimage. The fall of man introduced excessive heat and cold spells. Adam and Eve were driven out of Paradise to wander and work in a wilderness that was now overgrown with briars, thorns, and thistles, the early fruits of the late curse. Clothes were assigned to them in this exigency[66] for a kind of defensive armor…So whatever modes of apparel do not comply with this gracious end of God in defending our bodies from those inconveniences are sinfully worn and used. It is a horrid cruelty to our frail bodies to expose them to those injuries against which God has provided a remedy, just to gratify pride or to humor our vanity…

3. To these I may add that when God made man his first suit of apparel, He took measure of him by that employment that He had cut out for him. Man's assigned work was labor, not to eat the bread of idleness, but first to earn it by the sweat of his brow. Though at first it was a curse, [this] is by grace converted into a blessing. Accordingly, God so adapted and accommodated his clothes to his body that they might not hinder readiness, expedition, industry, diligence, or perseverance in the works of his particular calling…

---

66 **exigency** – urgent need or necessity.

Chapter 11—Modest Apparel: Avoiding Immodest Fashions

4. There is yet another end of apparel, namely, the adorning of the body. In this, all our wanton fashionists[67] take sanctuary. Out of that which I may force them, or (so far as is sober and moderate) indulge them, I shall first premise a few observations and then lay down some conclusions. Let these few things be premised:

Ornaments, strictly taken as distinct from useful garments, do not come under the same appointment of God as necessary clothing. For, first, it is ordinarily sinful to wear no apparel [in public], but not so to wear no ornaments. Second, the necessity of nature requires one, but no necessity or end of nature requires the other. God's ends and nature's occasions may be secured and answered fully without these additional things. Ornaments, then, are…matters of *permission* rather than injunction.

Plain, simple apparel—a real ornament to the body—is a sufficient ornament to the body. For if nakedness is our shame, apparel that hides it is…its beautifying and adorning…

Ornaments are either natural or artificial. Natural ornaments are such as nature has provided, such as the hair given by God…to the woman to be her glory and her covering (1 Cor. 11:15). Artificial ornaments are such as are the product of ingenuity and witty invention. In these, as God has not been liberal, so man has been very prodigal.[68] Not content with primitive simplicity, he has sought out many inventions[69] (Eccl. 7:29).

It is evident that God allowed the Jews the use of artificial ornaments as distinct from necessary apparel. *"And Aaron said unto them, Break off the golden earrings, which are in the ears of your wives, of your sons, and of your daughters, and bring them unto me"* (Ex. 32:2)…Yet there was some difference between the indulgence granted to the male and that to the female. Dr. [Thomas] Fuller observes this from the order and placing of the words "wives, sons, and daughters,"[70] intimating that those sons were in their minority, "under covert parent,"[71] as he explains it in his work, *A Pisgah Sight*

---

67 **wanton fashionists** – lustful followers of fashion.
68 **prodigal** – recklessly wasteful.
69 **inventions** – things originated by a person's ingenuity; in this case, ornaments, etc.
70 Earrings were generally worn by Jewish women, as also by their male children, whilst as yet young and under their mother's command; "Break off the golden ear-rings which are in the ears of your wives, your sons, and your daughters" (Exo 32:2). Where, by sons, we understand little boys (therefore hemmed in the text with women on both sides), having their sex as yet scarcely discriminated by their habits. But whether men amongst them wore ear-rings is doubtful, and the negative most probable… (Fuller, *A Pisgah-sight of Palestine*, 533)
71 **undercovert parent** – under parental authority.

of Palestine.[72] This seems to be implied in Isaiah 61:10, where we find indeed the bridegroom's "ornaments," but only bride's "jewels," as if the masculine sex was restrained to a more manly and grave sort of ornaments, whereas females were allowed a greater degree of finery and gallantry.[73] And when God permitted the Jewish women to borrow from their neighbors jewels of silver and gold, the use was not limited to their sons and daughters, and grown men were not considered (Ex. 3:22), which is also evidently inferred from Judges 8:24, where the army conquered by Gideon is said to have worn golden earrings, for they were Ishmaelites. This clearly implies that their golden earrings were an ornament peculiar to the Ishmaelites, and not common to the Israelites.

Though there might be something typical or symbolic in the jewels worn by the Jewish women (as I conceive there was), yet the use of them was of common right to the females of their nations. Indeed, they were of ordinary use long before the Jewish polity[74] was settled. *"The man took a golden earring of half a shekel weight [a quarter of an ounce], and two bracelets for her [Rebecca] hands of ten shekels weight [five ounces] of gold"* (Gen. 24:22).

These things premised, I will now lay down these conclusions:

Conclusion 1

Whatever pretends to ornament, which is inconsistent with modesty, gravity, and sobriety and with whatever is according to godliness, is not ornament, but defilement. *Modesty* teaches us not to expose those parts to view that no necessity, no good end or use will justify. *Humility* teaches us to avoid curiosity[75] in decking a vile body that ere long must be a feast for worms. *Good husbandry*[76] will teach us not to lay out on the back what should feed the bellies of a poor family. *Holiness* will teach us not to keep such a stir about the outward man when the inward man is naked. *Charity* will teach us not to spend superfluously on your own carcass when so many of your Father's children lack necessary food and raiment. And *godly wisdom* will teach us not to trifle out those precious minutes between the comb and the glass, between curling hair and painting faces, which should be laid out on and for eternity.

---

72 Thomas Fuller, *A Pisgah-sight of Palestine and the Confines Thereof with the Historie of the Old and New Testament Acted Thereon* (London: William Tegg, 1869).
73 **gallantry** – adornment; elegant clothing.
74 **Jewish polity** – Jewish social and political society; nation of Israel.
75 **curiosity** – excessive attention given to unimportant matters.
76 **good husbandry** – good stewardship or management.

Chapter 11—Modest Apparel: Avoiding Immodest Fashions

Let me recommend [that] you read 1 Peter 3:2-4: *"While they behold your chaste conversation*[77] *coupled with fear. Whose adorning let it not be that outward adorning of plaiting the hair, and of wearing of gold, or of putting on of apparel; but let it be the hidden man of the heart, in that which is not corruptible, even the ornament of a meek and quiet spirit, which is in the sight of God of great price."* From this passage, these things offer themselves to your observation:

1. Plaiting the hair and wearing of gold or golden ornaments are not simply in and of themselves condemned, but only so far as they are either our *chief* ornament, or as we are too curious,[78] too costly, excessive, or expensive in them. For otherwise, the *"putting on of apparel,"* which is joined in the same thread and texture of the discourse and sentence, would be condemned also.

2. The rule for regulating these ornaments is that they be visibly consistent with a pure and reverent conduct. I say *visibly* consistent: it must be such pure and reverent conduct as may be beheld: *"While they behold your chaste conversation."* That pure vestal[79] fire of chastity that burns upon the altar of a holy heart must flame out and shine in chastity of words, actions, clothing, and adorning. For whenever God commands chastity, He commands whatever may feed and nourish it, manifest and declare it. He forbids whatever may endanger it—wound, weaken, blemish, or impair it.

3. Godly fear must be placed as a severe sentinel to keep strict guard over the heart so that nothing is admitted that may defile our own hearts, nothing steal out what may pollute another's. We must keep a watch over our own hearts and other men's eyes. [We must] neither lay a snare for the chastity of another nor a bait for our own. This "pure and reverent conduct" must be coupled with godly fear.

4. Holy fear and godly jealousy will have [plenty of work regarding] the matter of ornament. We must not err in our judgment, as if these outward adornings with gold or plaited hair were of such grand concern, nor err in our practice in an immoderate care and superfluous cost about them.

5. The rule must be that which Peter laid down as a pattern: *"For after this manner in the old time the holy women also, who trusted in God, adorned themselves"* (1 Peter 3:5). Note, first, that they must be *holy* women who are the standard of our imitation: not a painting Jezebel, nor a dancing Dinah, nor a flaunting Bernice, but a holy Sarah, a godly Rebecca, and a prudent Abigail. Second, they must be such as were *"in the old time,"* when pride was

---

77 **chaste conversation** – pure manner of life; hereafter, "pure and reverent conduct."
78 **curious** – careful as to the standard of excellence; precise (in a prideful way).
79 **vestal** – virginal; chaste.

pin-feathered,[80] not such as now, since lust grew fledged and high-flown[81]; such examples as the old time afforded, when plain cleanliness was counted as abundant elegance; such as the world's infancy produced, not such as an old, decrepit age recommends to us. Third, they must be such as could trust in God to deliver them from evil because they did not rush themselves into temptation. For it is hardly conceivable how any could trust in God to give them victory [when they] tempt and challenge the combat. How can any expect that divine grace could secure them from being overcome, when they by their enticing attire provoke others to assail their chastity? If, then, *"the daughters of Zion"* will be the heirs of Abraham's *faith*, they must approve themselves the followers of Sarah's *modesty*.

Conclusion 2

Nothing can justly pretend to be a lawful ornament that takes away the distinction that God has put between the two sexes. That law given in Deuteronomy 22:5 is of moral equity and perpetual obligation: *"The woman shall not wear that which pertaineth unto a man, neither shall a man put on a woman's garment: for all that do so are abomination unto the LORD thy God."* The Hebrew word translated *"that which pertaineth"* signifies any "vessel, instrument, utensil, garment, or ornament," military or civil, used for the discrimination of the sex, according to Henry Ainsworth[82] in his *Annotations on the Pentateuch*…God will therefore have the distinction between the sexes inviolably[83] observed in the outward apparel. This is a fence around the Moral Law to prevent those murders, adulteries, and promiscuous lusts that under those disguises would be more secretly and easily perpetrated…What particular form of apparel shall distinguish the one sex from the other must be determined by the custom of particular countries, provided that those customs do not thwart some general law of God, the rule of decency, the ends of apparel, or the directions of Scripture.

Yet there seems to be some distinctive ornament provided by God so that the difference between the sexes might not be left to the arbitrary customs and desultory humors[84] of men. An example would be the hair of the head and the manner of wearing it, or at least in the beard, which is ordinarily given to one sex and denied to the other. Hence, it seems probably

---

80 **pinfeathered** – having undeveloped feathers, hence, "in an early stage of development."
81 **grew fledged and high-flown** – developed feather and fit to fly, soaring high; hence, "grew up, becoming extravagantly prideful."
82 **Henry Ainsworth** (1571-1622) – English Nonconformist minister and scholar.
83 **inviolably** – sacredly; without violation.
84 **desultory humors** – irregular, disordered whims or inclinations.

that for women to crop their hair, or for men to nourish it to full length, is a contravention[85] to the discriminating badge and cognizance that the God of nature has bestowed upon them...

Conclusion 3

Nothing ought to be allowed for ornament that crosses the end of all apparel: that of covering nakedness...But among us, our English ladies will not acknowledge it to be any nakedness, any shame to have their breasts exposed. They pretend that the parts that decency requires to be covered, and in whose nakedness shame lies, are only those which the Apostle called *"less honorable"* or *"uncomely"* (1 Cor. 12:23).

To this, I answer, first, that no parts of the body are in themselves *"less honorable"* or *"uncomely."* Second, that the uncovering of any part will be so when no honorable use requires the uncovering. Thus, the prophet calls the uncovering of the locks, of the legs, the thigh the *"nakedness"* and *"shame"* of the Babylonians (Isa. 47:2-3). Though it is meant of a necessitated nakedness—which may be a reproach, but not a sin—yet, when that is done *voluntarily* which then was done *necessarily*, it will become both the sin *and* the reproach.

It is pleaded that what they do is *not* out of pride (to glory in the beauty of the skin), nor out of lust (to inveigle[86] others to become enamored at their beauty), but only to avoid the reproach of a morose singularity,[87] and a little, perhaps, to comply with what has been the vogue among the more genteel[88] and well-bred persons.

To remove this argument, first, it is a branch of holy singularity rather to be sober alone than mad for company. What Christian would not rather choose to lag behind than strain himself to keep pace with a hair-brained age in all its endless and irrational usages? And, second, compliance with a vain, humorsome[89] generation is so far from being an excuse that it is an aggravation of the vanity of the practice.

But these are only the umbrages[90] invented to palliate[91] the extravagance. The persuasive inducements lie much deeper, which, because we cannot in all make a judgment of, we must leave them to the censures of their own

---

85 **contravention** – violation.
86 **inveigle** – seduce; allure.
87 **morose singularity** – being different from others in an unsocial way in order to stand out.
88 **genteel** – fashionably elegant; of a social status above common people.
89 **vain, humorsome** – foolish; guided by whims.
90 **umbrages** – pretenses.
91 **palliate** – conceal.

Chapter 11—Modest Apparel: Avoiding Immodest Fashions

consciences. I dare not say that it is to allure or invite customers, though what does the open shop and sign at the door signify but that there is something for sale? Nor shall I tax the practice of ambition to show the fineness, clearness, and beauty of the skin; though, if it were so, I would ask who are concerned, I pray, to know what hue, what color it is of, but either their lawful husbands or their unlawful paramours[92]? In the meantime, it is all too plain that arrogance and impudence have usurped the place and produced the effect of primitive simplicity. Women are now almost naked, but are not at all ashamed.

From "What Distance Ought We to Keep, in Following the Strange Fashions of Apparel Which Come Up in the Days Wherein We Live?" in *Puritan Sermons 1659-1689*, reprinted by Richard Owen Roberts, Publishers.

Vincent Alsop (1630-1703): English Nonconformist minister; born in Northamptonshire, England.

Modesty and shamefacedness become women at all times, especially in times of public worship. The more of this is mixed with their grace and personage, the more beautiful they are both to God and men. —John Bunyan

If you want ornaments, here they are: here are jewels, rings, dresses, and all kinds of ornament. Men and women, ye may dress yourselves up until ye shine like angels. How can you do it? By dressing yourselves out in benevolence, in love to the saints, in honesty and integrity, in uprightness, in godliness, in brotherly-kindness, in charity. These are the ornaments that angels themselves admire, and that even the world will admire; for men must give admiration to the man or the woman who is arrayed in the jewels of a holy life and godly conversation. I beseech you, brethren, 'Adorn the doctrine of God our Savior in all things.' —Charles Haddon Spurgeon

---

92 **paramours** – lovers.

Accessories to Adultery

ROBERT G. SPINNEY

Christians have long connected immodest clothing to sexual immorality. Amazingly, that is challenged today. The person who points out the link between immorality and revealing clothing is sometimes thought to be expressing only his or her own personal weakness regarding sexual temptations. The wearer of skimpy clothing (and the skimpy clothing itself) is not perceived to be the problem; rather, the problem allegedly rests with the person who protests the skimpy clothing. (This is the same argument that militant feminists have long made, an argument we now hear Christians making: women should be free to wear whatever they want and any resulting problems are due to vulgar men.) This silences appeals for modest clothing: he who makes such appeals is deemed to be shifting the blame for his own lust. Thanks to socially acceptable immodesty, the person who challenges immodesty is accused of having a dirty mind.

But the old confessions and catechisms expose the emptiness of this contention. Long before bikinis, Speedos, short shorts, and strapless dresses, Christians realized the essential connection between sexual immorality and immodest clothing. Their comprehensive application of God's Word regarding sexual purity—*and their serious pursuit of holiness*—led them to denounce immodest clothing. The modern claim that no clothing is out-of-bounds for a Christian would have bewildered our spiritual forefathers…

[This article] is an appeal to obey the Seventh Commandment: *"Thou shalt not commit adultery"* (Ex. 20:14). [It] requires the preservation of both our own *and* our neighbor's sexual purity, a purity that should be displayed in our hearts as well as our behavior. Negatively, the commandment forbids unchaste thoughts, words, and actions. We violate it if our clothing expresses our own sexual lusts, promotes sexual immorality either in ourselves or in others, tacitly[93] (if perhaps unintentionally) sanctions unchastity and lusting, or tempts others to indulge in sexual sins.

Are you an accessory to adultery? Our legal system rightly recognizes that both murderers and accessories to murder are lawbreakers. Similarly, both adulterers and accessories to adultery are guilty of breaking God's Law.

If we wear clothing that encourages lust in someone else, then we are an accessory to lust. That makes us accessories to sin—regardless of our intentions. The Christian cannot say, "I'm not trying to be sexually provocative with my clothing. I have no immoral motives. Therefore,

---

93 **tacitly** – understood or implied without being expressed directly.

my clothing is modest." I will go further. As a husband and father, I am the head of my household. When I allow my family members to wear clothing that contributes to someone else's heart-level adultery, *I am guilty of promoting sin.*

This is one reason why both men *and* women must dress modestly. Men can promote lust in women just as women can promote sexually immoral thoughts in men. God's Word speaks clearly to the issue of becoming an accessory to sin. The Bible uses the phrase *stumbling block* [or *offenses*] where we usually use the word *accessory*.

What is a stumbling block? It is something that entices someone to sin. In Matthew 18:7-9, Jesus said, *"Woe unto the world because of offences [stumbling blocks]! for it must needs be that offences come; but woe to that man by whom the offence cometh! Wherefore if thy hand or thy foot offend thee, cut them off, and cast them from thee: it is better for thee to enter into life halt or maimed, rather than having two hands or two feet to be cast into everlasting fire. And if thine eye offend thee, pluck it out, and cast it from thee: it is better for thee to enter into life with one eye, rather than having two eyes to be cast into hell fire"*…In this passage, Jesus is primarily concerned that we examine ourselves and eliminate stumbling blocks that tempt us to sin. But we can also create hindrances and obstacles for other people—and woe to that man through whom the stumbling block comes! This concept applies to much more than clothing, but it certainly includes clothing.

Notice the extreme metaphors in this passage: Amputate your hand. Cut off your foot. Gouge out your eye. Of course, Jesus is not sanctioning self-mutilation. He is using figurative language to make a point: take drastic action to avoid hurting yourself or others spiritually. Do radical things to make sure obstacles do not hinder your pursuit of the Kingdom of God… Dressing modestly is a relatively small price.

I am stunned when I hear a Christian say, "If my clothing causes Greg to lust, that's *his* problem." That attitude is simply unbiblical. It is the same as saying, "I am not responsible for the moral stumbling blocks that I create with my clothing." To be sure, Greg's lust *is* his problem and is primarily his problem. But if your clothing makes you an accessory to lust—*a stumbling block*—then the Word of God says it has become your problem also. The Lord Jesus Christ Himself pronounces condemnation upon those people who encourage others to sin: woe to that man through whom the stumbling block comes! John MacArthur makes this very point in his discussion of 1 Timothy 2:9 and Matthew 18:7-9: "A woman characterized by this attitude [that is, modesty] will dress so as not to be the source of any temptation…A godly woman hates sin so much that she would avoid anything that would engender sin in anyone. Better to be dead than lead another believer into sin!"[94] Why do some Christians dress so as to make themselves "lusting events"? Often it is due to innocent ignorance. Many believers simply do not realize that other Christians are easily tempted to sin by immodest clothing. This is especially true for Christian women: they often do not understand that many Christian men experience great anguish of soul as they fight with sexual temptation. Without intending to, they wear clothing that is a stumbling block. Be mindful that Christian men are saints, not angels! Sisters, please love your brothers enough to avoid tempting them to sin. Margaret Buchanan is right when she writes, "By dressing in a provocative way, girls and women are actually sexually harassing men." This is true even when there is no deliberate intent to promote sensuality with one's clothing.

In other cases, however, the problem is not *innocent ignorance*; rather, it is unwillingness to honor God and love our neighbors with our clothing. The Bible declares that the Christian's body belongs to God, both by creation and by redemption (1 Cor. 6:19-20). Every square inch of a Christian's life is to be lived under Christ's Lordship and for God's glory—and this includes the Christian's apparel. "I can dress any way I want to" is simply not something a Christian can say.

Please hear your Lord when He says that drastic action must be taken to minimize temptations and stumbling blocks. This is a command, not a suggestion. (*See* 1 Cor. 8:9; 10:31-33.) Dressing modestly is simply one result of a godly and unselfish concern for others' well-being.

From *Dressed to Kill,* published by Tulip Publications.

Robert G. Spinney: Baptist minister and associate professor of history at Patrick Henry College, Purcellville, VA.

---

[94] John MacArthur, *1 Timothy* (Chicago: Moody Press, 1995), 80.

Your Clothing Reveals Your Heart

RICHARD BAXTER[95] (1615-1691)

The care that people have about [clothes],[96] the cost they bestow on superfluities, their desire to go with the highest of their rank, to say nothing of mutable[97] and immodest fashions, do show to what end they use it. I desire these kinds of people to think of these few things that I shall say to them.

This vanity of apparel is the certain effect of the vanity of your mind. You openly proclaim yourselves to be persons of a foolish, childish temper[98] and poor understanding: among the most ungodly people, they that have but common wisdom do look upon this vanity of inordinate apparel as quite below them. Therefore, it is commonly taken to be the special sin of women, children, and light-headed, silly, empty men. Those that have no inward worth to commend them to the world are silly souls indeed, if they think any wise folks will take a silken coat instead of it! Wisdom, holiness, and righteousness are the ornaments of man—*that* is his beauty that beautifieth his soul. Do you think that among wise men fine clothes will go instead of wisdom, virtue, or holiness? You may put as fine clothes upon a fool as upon a wise man; and will that, think you, make him pass for wise? When a gallant[99] came into the shop of Apelles,[100] that famous painter, to have his picture drawn, as long as he stood silent, the apprentices carried themselves reverently to him because he shone in gold and silver lace. But when he began to talk, they perceived that he was a *fool*. They left their reverence and all fell a-laughing at him.

When people see you in an extraordinary garb,[101] you draw their observation towards you; and one asketh, "Who is yonder that is so fine?" And another asks, "Who is yonder?" And when they perceive that you are more witless and worthless than other folks, they will but laugh at you and despise you. Excess in apparel is the very sign of folly that is hanged out to tell the world what you are, as a sign at an inn-door acquaints the passenger

---

95 **Editor's Note:** Chapel Library does not agree with Baxter's views of Christ's atonement and justification. The use of this article is not an endorsement of his other writings.

96 **Editor's Note:** The author's style of English is sometimes quite difficult for modern readers, even more so than other Puritan writers. The article has undergone more editing than usual in an effort to retain the power of his thought, but increasing its readability.

97 **mutable** – changing.

98 **temper** – character.

99 **gallant** – a man of fashion and pleasure, well-dressed and showy.

100 **Appelles** (4th century BC) – Greek painter, now known only from written sources, but was highly acclaimed throughout the ancient world.

101 **extraordinary garb** – exceptional fashions that provoke astonishment or admiration.

that there he may have entertainment...If I see people inordinately careful of their apparel, I must needs suspect that there is some special cause for it: all is not well where all this care and curiosity are necessary. And what is the deformity that you would hide by this? *Is it that of your mind?*...You tell all that see you that you are empty, silly souls—as plainly as a morris dancer[102] or a stage-player doth tell folks what he is by his attire...

You also make an open ostentation[103] of pride, lust, or both to all that look upon you.In other cases, you are careful to hide your sin and take it for a heinous injury if you are but openly told of it and reproved. How then comes it to pass that you are here so forward *yourselves* to make it known that you must carry the signs of it open in the world! Is it not a dishonor to rogues and thieves that have been burnt in the hand or forehead or must ride about with a paper pinned on their backs, declaring their crimes to all that see them, so that everyone may say, "Yonder is a thief, and yonder is a perjured[104] man"? Is it not much like it for you to carry the badge of pride or lust abroad with you in the open streets and meetings?

Why do you desire to be so fine, neat, or excessively comely? Is it not to draw the eyes and observations of men upon you? And to what end? Is it not to be thought either rich or beautiful or of a handsome person? To what end desire you these thoughts of men? Do you not know that this desire is pride itself? You must needs be somebody, and fain you would be observed and valued! Fain you would be noted to be of the best or highest rank that you can expect to be reckoned of—what is this but pride?

I hope you know that pride is the devil's sin, the firstborn of all iniquity, and that which the God of heaven abhors! It [would be] more credit for you in the eyes of men of wisdom to proclaim yourselves beggars, sots,[105] or idiots than to proclaim your pride! Too oft it shows a pang of *lust* as well as pride, especially in young persons. Few are as forward[106] to this sin as they. This bravery[107] and fineness are but the fruit of a procacious[108] mind: it is plainly a wooing, alluring act. It is not for nothing that they would [eagerly] be eyed and be thought comely or fair in others' eyes! They want something:

---

102 **morris dancer** – one who performed a grotesque dance in a fancy costume that had bells attached to it; they usually represented characters from the Robin Hood legend.
103 **ostentation** – display intended to attract notice or admiration.
104 **perjured** – guilty of uttering false statement while under an oath to tell the truth.
105 **sots** – those who stupefy themselves with alcohol; foolish, stupid people.
106 **forward** – zealous; eager.
107 **bravery** – showy apparel.
108 **procacious** – insolent; shameless.

you may conjecture *what!* Even married people—if they love their credit[109]—should take heed by such means of drawing suspicion upon themselves.

Sirs, if you are guilty of folly, pride, and lust, your best way is to seek of God an effectual *cure* and to use such means as tend to cure it, not such as tend to cherish it and increase it, as certainly fineness in clothing doth. But if you will not cure it, for shame conceal it. Do not tell everyone that sees you what is in your heart! What would you think of one that should go up and down the street telling all that meet him, "I am a thief" or "I am a fornicator?" Would you not think that he was a compound of foolery and knavery?[110] And how little do you come short of this that write upon your own backs, "Folly, pride, and lust!" or tell them by your apparel, "Take notice of me! I am foolish, proud, and lustful"?

If you are so silly as to think that bravery is a means of honor, you should withal consider that it is but a shameful begging of honor from those that look upon you, when you show them not anything to purchase or deserve it. Honor must be forced by desert[111] and worth, not by begging; for that is no honor that is given to the undeserving...Your bravery doth so openly show your desire of esteem and honor that it plainly tells all wise men that you are the *less* worthy of it. For the more a man desireth esteem, the less he deserves it.

You tell the world by your attire that you desire it—even as plainly and foolishly as if you should say to the folks in the streets, "I pray think well of me and take me for a handsome, comely person, and for one that is above the common sort." Would you not *laugh* at one that should make such a request to you? Why, what do you less when by your attire you beg estimation from them? For what, I pray you, *should* we esteem you? Is it for your clothes? Why, I can put a silver lace upon a mawkin[112] or a silken coat on a post or an ass. Is it for your comely bodies? Why, a wicked Absalom was beautiful, and the basest harlots have had as much of this as you! A comely body or beautiful face doth oft betray the soul, but *never* saveth it from hell. Your bodies are never the comelier for your dress, whatever they may seem. Is it for your virtues that you would be esteemed? Why pride is the greatest enemy to virtue, and as great a deformity to the soul as the pox is to the body. And he that will think you [more honest because of] a new suit or a silver lace doth know as little what honesty is as yourselves. For shame,

---

109 **credit** – reputation.
110 **compound...knavery** – mix of foolishness and trickery.
111 **desert** – conduct that deserves reward.
112 **mawkin** – mop.

therefore, give over begging for esteem, at least by such a means as inviteth all wise men to deny your suit.¹¹³ Either let honor come without begging or be without it.

Consider also that excess of apparel doth quite contradict the end that proud persons do intend it for. I confess it doth sometimes ensnare a fool and so accomplish the desires of the lustful, but it seldom attaineth the ends of the proud. Their desire is to be [more highly] esteemed, and almost all men do think the [less] of them. Wise men have more wit¹¹⁴ than to think the tailor can make a *wise* man or woman, or an *honest* man or woman, or a *handsome* man or woman. Good men pity them, lament their folly and vice, and wish them wisdom and humility. In the eyes of a wise and gracious man, a poor self-denying, humble, patient, heavenly Christian is worth a thousand of these painted posts and peacocks. And it so falls out that the ungodly themselves do frustrate the proud person's expectations. For as covetous men do not like covetousness in another because they would get most themselves, so proud persons like not pride in others because they would not have any to vie¹¹⁵ with them or overtop¹¹⁶ them and be looked upon and preferred before them…

Lastly, I beseech you, do not forget what it is that you are so carefully doing, and what those bodies are that you so adorn, are so proud of, and set out to the sight of the world in such bravery. Do you not know yourselves? Is it not a lump of warm and thick clay that you would have men observe and honor? When the soul that you neglect is once gone from them, they will be set out then in another garb. That little space of earth that must receive them must be defiled with their filthiness and corruption, and the dearest of your friends will have no more of your company, nor one smell or sight of you more, if they can choose. There is not a carrion¹¹⁷ in the ditch that is [more loathsome] than that gallant, painted corpse will be a little after death.

What are you in the mean time? Even bags of filth and living graves in which the carcasses of your fellow-creatures are daily buried and corrupt. There is scarce a day with most of you but some part of a dead carcass is buried in your bodies,¹¹⁸ in which, as in a filthy grave, they lie and corrupt—part of them turneth into your substance, and the rest is cast out [as dung]. Thus, you walk like painted sepulchers: your fine clothes are the adorned

---

113 **suit** – earnest endeavor to obtain something.
114 **wit** – good sense; wisdom.
115 **vie** – be in competition with; rival.
116 **overtop** – surpass.
117 **carrion** – dead, rotting flesh.
118 **but some part…bodies** – eating animal flesh.

covers of filth, phlegm, and dung. If you did but see what is within the proudest gallant, you would say the *inside* did much differ from the *outside*. It may be a hundred worms [inside, consuming] that beautiful damsel or adorned fool that set out themselves to be admired for their bravery! If a little of the [foulness] within do but turn to the scab or the smallpox, you shall see what a piece it was that was [accustomed] to have all that curious trimming.

Away, then, with these vanities—be not children all your days!…Be ashamed that ever you have been guilty of so much dotage,[119] as to think that people should honor you for a borrowed bravery, which you put off at night and on in the morning! O poor deluded dust and worms' meat! Lay by your dotage and know yourselves: look after that which may procure you deserved and perpetual esteem, and see that you make sure of the honor that is of God.

Away with deceitful [and showy] ornaments, and look after the inward real worth! Grace is not set out and honored by fine clothes, but clouded, wronged, and dishonored by excess. The inward glory is the real glory! The image of God must needs be the chiefest beauty of man: let *that* shine forth in the holiness of your lives, and you will be honorable indeed.

From "A Treatise of Self-Denial" in *Baxter's Practical Works*, Vol. 3, reprinted by Soli Deo Gloria, a ministry of Reformation Heritage Books: www.heritagebooks.org.

Richard Baxter (1615-1691): English Puritan preacher and theologian; born in Rowton, Shropshire, England.

---

119 **dotage** – folly; stupidity.

Too Much, Too Little, Too Tight

ROBERT G. SPINNEY

Creating a list of approved and unapproved clothing is a remedy that can be worse than the disease. I will explain. Sometimes God provides specific Bible commands and then clearly states how they are to be applied. But sometimes God gives principles and expects His people to make prayerful, Spirit-led, and Word-informed applications for themselves. With regard to clothing, God does the second. He does not give us exact wardrobe regulations; instead, He gives us principles. In addition, there is some sense in which cultural values play a role in determining if specific kinds of apparel are proper, modest, and discreet. The Puritan pastor Richard Baxter concluded his strong plea for modest clothing with a needed caution: "Custom and common opinion do put much of the signification upon fashions of apparel."[120] In other words, the standards of modesty are somewhat (but not entirely) determined by cultural context. I am not persuaded that the Apostle Peter dressed immodestly when he was "stripped for work" while fishing (John 21:7). John Calvin wrote that, strictly speaking, clothing is an "indifferent matter" that makes it "difficult to assign a fixed limit, how far we ought to go."[121]

Scriptural principles are eternally true; cultural applications may change. I can tell you with full Scriptural authority that God commands you to dress properly and decently, which means dressing in a manner consistent with God's command to be holy even as God Himself is holy (1 Peter 1:16). God requires you to dress modestly, which means you should not push the limits of moral acceptability when it comes to clothing. You are to dress discreetly, which means you must restrain your fleshly passions when it comes to apparel. You must not tempt others to sin with your clothing. In short, you must bring your wardrobe under the Lordship of Christ. "This at least will be settled beyond all controversy," said Calvin, in words immediately following his recognition that we must be cautious regarding specific clothing applications, "that everything in dress which is not in accordance with modesty and sobriety must be disapproved."[122]

As believers indwelt by the Holy Spirit and having minds transformed by the Bible, God calls us to apply these "modesty principles" to our daily living.

---

120 Richard Baxter, "The Christian Directory" in *Baxter's Practical Works,* Vol. 1 (Ligonier: Soli Deo Gloria, 1990), 394.
121 John Calvin, *Calvin's Commentaries*, Vol. XXI, "The First Epistle to Timothy" (Grand Rapids: Baker Publishing Group, 1993), 66.
122 Ibid, 66.

Some protest that these non-applied principles are insufficient. However, we should realize that there are several problems with creating specific and mandatory dress codes. To begin with, I suspect that most readers of this [article] affirm (as do I) the doctrine of Scripture's sufficiency: the Bible is sufficient for *all* things pertaining to life and godliness. Yet that same Bible consistently deals with the issue of modest clothing on the level of principle. The Bible itself does not provide us with a specific dress code. Apparently, the Holy Spirit deemed it not only adequate but best that God's Word speak to clothing issues on the level of principle. I am reluctant to go beyond what the Holy Spirit has done; I am reluctant to say that God's principles regarding modesty are insufficient. To be sure, pastors should suggest possible applications of these principles. God's servants must help God's people apply God's Word to real-life situations. I shall make such suggestions below.

Nevertheless, only *God's* principles are perfect and morally binding, while my personal applications of those principles may be incorrect. God's Word is infallible, but my applications of His Word are not. Immodest clothing is a problem, but it is also a problem if I go beyond the inspired Word of God and require men to obey my uninspired applications. What follows is an attempt at practical guidance in this area. These are *suggestions*: they are not commandments on the level of "thus saith the Lord." Do not regard them as extrabiblical rules, but rather as possible applications of biblical principles. Their author is a fallible man, a man who is also a father, husband, and redeemed-but-still-sinful Christian.

Immodest clothing usually falls into the categories of too much, too little, or too tight. Too much clothing refers to apparel that is extravagant, flamboyant,[123] or vainglorious.[124] It is clothing that says, "Look at me! I want to be the center of attention!" Such apparel need not be skimpy, but it functions like a siren or spotlight: it causes the wearer to stand out as a promoter of himself or some cause. It is clothing that demands attention or comment. Writing almost 500 years ago, John Calvin diagnosed the root of this problem: "Luxury and immoderate expense [in clothing] arise from a desire to make a display either for the sake of pride or of departure from chastity."[125] This desire to attract spectators sometimes results in a woman looking like the harlot of Proverbs 7. Perhaps the most obvious examples of *too much* are the clothes worn by entertainment industry celebrities. Such

---

123 **flamboyant** – noticeable because of bright colors or unusual style.
124 **vainglorious** – excessively prideful; desirous of attracting the admiration of others.
125 Calvin, *1 Timothy*, 66.

apparel is expensive and visually arresting, and it is usually accented by plenty of flashy jewelry. There is nothing sinful about a sequin or an earring; but at some point, the overall appearance is too loud and dazzling.

Certainly, clothing is too much when it presents a message that can be reasonably perceived as contrary to Christianity. Consider the current Goth fashions, which are becoming so popular they now appear in shopping malls' specialty shops. Thankfully, Goth clothing is often loose fitting and adequately covers the wearer's body. But Goth clothing proclaims a message: the Goth subculture is dark, rebellious, morbid, and obsessed with depression and death. Many people understandably make associations between Goth and the occult. Regardless of the wearer's intentions, Goth clothing sends a message that is at odds with Christianity. Such clothing is *too much*.

What is the opposite of too much? It is clothing that is tasteful but not eye-popping. Such apparel is not a means for displaying wealth or social status. Nor is it slovenly or grubby: appropriate clothing does not make the wearer stand out in a crowd of modestly clothed people, either by overdressing or underdressing. It does not send messages that are potentially harmful to the cause of Christ or that misrepresent Christianity. "Make not too great a matter of your clothing," wrote Richard Baxter, "Set not your hearts upon it. For that is a worse sign than the excess in itself."[126]

Too little clothing refers to clothing that fails to cover the wearer's body. Simply put, it shows too much skin. For women, this includes unbuttoned blouses or plunging necklines that reveal cleavage. It also includes clothing that bares a woman's shoulders, such as strapless dresses, spaghetti-strap dresses, and halter-tops. Many too little tops today deliberately expose bare skin at a woman's midriff and hips, and they are sometimes worn with too little pants that ride low on the hips. Short shorts and short skirts are likewise too little when they reveal women's thighs. Ditto for sheer see-through blouses that reveal undergarments and the body's outline. Ditto for women's "exercise tops" that are little more than bras worn in public. In the words of one man (as he considered current trends in apparel), "Never in the history of fashion has so little material been raised so high to reveal so much that needs to be covered so badly."

Some Christian women are surprised to discover that their bare shoulders or exposed thighs frequently trigger lust in men. Christian women think too highly of Christian men; they think we are immune to visually triggered lust. Not so. Sin means that even nice men can have nasty thoughts. If a Christian woman could read the minds of all the men as she walks into the

---

126 Baxter, *Directory*, 394.

church sanctuary with her bare shoulders or cleavage on display, she would never wear such clothing again. But most Christian men are afraid to admit publicly that it takes very little skin to tempt them to sin. They say nothing, and Christian women assume they are not lusting.

Men can wear too little as well. Several women once told me of a small-group Bible study that was scandalized by an indiscreet man and his too-short short pants. The participants' chairs were organized in a circle, and this clueless brother routinely wore extremely short and baggy shorts. Unbeknownst to him, he frequently exposed himself. The women often resigned themselves to concentrating not on the Bible study material but rather on looking away from this Christian man who was wearing too little.

The most obvious example of too little? Bathing suits.[127] A man would never walk through the shopping mall wearing only underwear, and a woman would never go to a restaurant wearing only her undergarments. However, we routinely expose our bodies like this with our skimpy bathing suits. We have no good reason for thinking that partial nudity is acceptable at the pool or beach…In addition, a surprising number of Christian weddings display women in too little dresses. In the name of elegance, bridal parties wear gowns that expose shoulders, reveal cleavage, and bare backs. We only used to see the "blushing bride" at weddings; now we see many at weddings blush as they witness immodestly dressed women in the ceremony.

Too tight refers to body-hugging clothing that clearly reveals the body's contours. I suspect that in conservative churches today, this is the most common kind of immodesty. Even today's non-skimpy and non-ostentatious clothing is often skintight, *especially* in the torso. Modesty is not simply covering flesh: it is concealing form. Some Christian women wear skirts in the interest of being modest, but then wear t-shirts or sweaters so tight that their bodies' contours are clearly displayed. This is too tight. Such tops often cling to the woman's torso and hips so that they function as what a previous generation would have called a body suit or a leotard. Christian women must understand that when tight tops reveal the shape of the waist, hips, or bust, men are sorely tempted to lust. One man put it this way: sometimes a woman's clothing is so tight that he can hardly breathe.

Dresses can be too tight as well. It is not true that dresses and skirts never tempt guys to lust: *just ask them*. Tight dresses can be just as scandalous as other kinds of clothing. (They used to be called *slinky* dresses.)…Can someone look at you and—thanks to your tight clothing—clearly discern

---

127 For further study of modesty and swimwear, see *Christian Modesty and the Public Undressing of America,* available from Chapel Library.

your body's shape? Is the outline of your buttocks obvious? Is the diameter of your thigh clearly displayed? Without much imagination, can someone tell what your body would look like unclothed? If yes, then your clothing is too tight. This kind of too tight clothing is more than just attractive: it is a stumbling block.

Unsure if your clothing is too much, too little, or too tight? Ask a godly individual to evaluate it. You may be surprised at how others see your apparel.

Beware of the "show me exactly where the line is" fallacy. Some Christians make the modest clothing issue more difficult than it needs to be. They think they must possess precise criteria whereby they can determine whether any given piece of clothing is modest or immodest. "I must know exactly where the line is," they think. "If I cannot know exactly what distinguishes modest from immodest clothing, then I cannot render any clothing judgments at all."

Thinking like this is logically flawed. It is simply not true that we must know *exactly* where a line is in order to know if something is clearly over the line. I do not know exactly where the U.S.-Canada border exists, but I know that I am clearly located on the U.S. side. I do not know exactly where the line exists between good singing and bad singing, but I know that my daughter is clearly on the good side of the line and I am clearly on the other side of it. In many areas of life, we do not know exactly where lines exist and yet understand their approximate locations…I cannot provide a precise definition of immodest clothing that will enable us to know exactly where the line is between modesty and immodesty. But I know immodesty when I see it. In other words, we do not need to know exactly what criteria distinguishes proper from improper clothing. "Modest clothing" and "immodest clothing" are not two clearly defined categories, and it is sometimes unclear whether a specific clothing item falls into one category or the other. A third category exists: clothing that is neither unambiguously modest nor obviously immodest. But the presence of a third "not sure about it" category need not prevent us from concluding that some clothing is undeniably immodest while other clothing is safely consistent with our Christian testimony. As for the questionable clothing that is neither clearly immodest nor clearly modest: recall the word [*shamefacedness*] in 1 Timothy 2:9 means a humble reluctance to trespass the boundaries of what is morally appropriate, a reluctance that makes the believer not bold when it comes to "testing the limits" of right behavior.

Chapter 11—Modest Apparel: Too Much, Too Little, Too Tight

From *Dressed to Kill*, published by Tulip Publishing.

Robert G. Spinney: Baptist minister and associate professor of history at Patrick Henry College, Purcellville, VA.

> *Take heed of being Satan's instrument in putting fire to the corruption of another. Some on purpose do it. Thus the whore perfumes her bed, paints her face. Idolaters, as whorish as the other, set out their temples and altars with superstitious pictures, embellished with all the cost that gold and silver can afford them to bewitch the spectator's eye. Hence, they are said to be inflamed with their idol (Isa. 57:5), as much as any lover with his minion in her whorish dress. And the drunkard—he enkindles his neighbor's lust, "[putting the] bottle to him" (Hab. 2:15). Oh! What a base work are these men employed about! By the law, it is death for any willfully to set fire on his neighbor's house: what then deserve they that set fire on the souls of men, and that no less than hell-fire? But it is possible thou mayest do it unawares by a less matter than thou dreamest on. A silly child playing with a lighted straw may set a house on fire, which many wise men cannot quench. And truly, Satan may use thy folly and carelessness to kindle lust in another's heart. Perhaps an idle, light speech drops from thy mouth, and thou meanest no great hurt; but a gust of temptation may carry this spark into thy friend's bosom and kindle a sad fire there. Wanton attire, perhaps [cleavage] and shoulders, which we will suppose thou wearest with a chaste heart and only because it is the fashion, yet may ensnare another's eye. Paul would not eat flesh while the world stood, if it made his brother to offend (1 Cor. 8:13). And canst thou dote on a foolish dress and immodest fashion, whereby many may offend, still to wear it? The soul, then, of thy brother is more to be valued surely than an idle fashion of thy raiment. —William Gurnall*

> *Costly apparel is like a prancing steed: he who will follow it too closely may have his brains knocked out for his folly or rather his empty skull shattered, for the brains have probably gone long before. —Vincent Alsop*

> *Look into the Gospel wardrobe. Christ has provided complete apparel to clothe you, as well as complete armor to defend you; and He commands you to put on both. —Vincent Alsop*

Our Royal Apparel
CHARLES HADDON SPURGEON (1834-1892)

And whom he justified, them he also glorified. —Romans 8:30

Let us begin…by considering what it is to be justified. If you wish for an answer in a few words, ask your children who have learned our catechism, and you have it: "Justification is an act of God's free grace, wherein he pardoneth all our sins, and accepteth us as righteous in his sight only for the righteousness of Christ imputed to us, and received by faith alone."[128] Perhaps, however, I had better unfold the truth in detail.

You will perceive by reading the connection and by a moment's reflection that the justification here meant is an act of God passed upon a person needing it, consequently passed upon a person who could not justify himself. [This is] a person naturally guilty of sin, being in a state of condemnation naturally, and needing to be lifted out of it by an act of justification of a divine order…Justification is an act of grace passed upon a sinner, upon one who has transgressed the Law and cannot be justified by it. He, therefore, needs [justification] in another way—a way out of his own reach, above his own doings, and coming as in the text from God Himself. For it says, "He justifies"…

Oh, sinner! However black thy sins may have been, thou mayest yet be justified. Though thy sins be as scarlet, they may yet be as wool. Though thou be red like crimson, thou mayest be white as snow (Isa. 1:18). It is written, *"[He] justifieth the ungodly"* (Rom. 4:5). Yes, the ungodly, such as thou hast been. Christ as a physician came not into the world for those who are whole, but for those who are sick. Justification is an act of grace that looks out for a sinner upon whom to exercise itself. May the eyes of grace find thee out [today], poor transgressor, and [declare thee righteous].

In the next place, justification is the result of sovereign grace and of sovereign grace alone. We are told, *"By the works of the law shall no flesh be justified"* (Gal. 2:16). And again, *"Justified freely by his grace through the redemption that is in Christ Jesus"* (Rom. 3:24). I cannot *earn* justification. Nothing that I can ever do can merit justification at the hands of God. I have so offended that all that is due to me is God's wrath, and that *forever*. If I shall ever be accounted just, it must be because God wills to make me just. It must be because out of His divine compassion, and for no other reason whatever, He looks upon me in my sin and misery, lifts me up from the dunghill of my ruin, and determines to wrap me about with the royal

---

128 *Spurgeon's Catechism*, Q. 32, available from Chapel Library.

Chapter 11—Modest Apparel: Our Royal Apparel

apparel of a righteousness that He has prepared. There is no justification, then, as an act of merit…Justification now comes as a priceless boon[129] from the liberal hand of God's grace.

Justification has for its matter and means the righteousness of Jesus Christ, set forth in His vicarious[130] obedience both in life and death. Certain modern heretics, who ought to have known better, have denied this; and because of ignorance, some in older times said that there was no such thing as the imputed righteousness[131] of Jesus Christ. He who denies this, perhaps unconsciously, cuts at the root of the Gospel system. I believe that this doctrine is involved in the whole system of substitution[132] and satisfaction; and we all know that substitution and a vicarious sacrifice are the very marrow of the Gospel of Christ.

The Law, like the God from Whom it came, is absolutely immutable and can be satisfied by nothing else than a complete and perfect righteousness, at once suffering the penalty for guilt incurred already, and working out obedience to the precept that still binds those upon whom penalty has passed. This was rendered by the Lord Jesus as the representative of His chosen and is the sole legal ground for the justification of the elect. As for me, I can never doubt that Christ's righteousness is mine, when I find that Christ Himself and all that He has belongs to me. If I find that He gives me everything, surely He gives me His righteousness among the rest.

What am I to do with that if not to wear it? Am I to lay it by in a wardrobe and not put it on? Well, sirs, let others wear what they will: my soul rejoices in the royal apparel. For me, the term *"the LORD our righteousness"* is significant and has a weight of meaning. Jesus Christ shall be my righteousness so long as I read the language of the Apostle, *"Who of God is made unto us wisdom, and righteousness, and sanctification, and redemption"* (1 Cor. 1:30). My dear brethren, do not doubt the imputed righteousness of Jesus Christ, whatever cavilers[133] may say. Remember that you must have a righteousness. The Law requires this. I do not read that the Law made with our first parents required suffering: it did demand it as a penalty after its breach. But the righteousness of the Law required not suffering, but obedience. Suffering would not release us from the duty of obeying. Lost souls in hell are still under the Law, and their woes and pangs if completely endured would never justify

---

129 **boon** – gift.
130 **vicarious** – done by one person as a substitute for another.
131 *See* FGB 191, *Imputed Righteousness.*
132 *See* FGB 207, *Substitution.*
133 **cavilers** – those who raise annoying petty objections.

them. Obedience, and obedience alone, can justify. Where can we have it but in Jesus our Substitute?

Christ comes to *magnify* the Law: how does He do it but by obedience? If I am to enter into life by the keeping of the commandments, as the Lord tells me in the nineteenth chapter of Matthew and the seventeenth verse, how can I except by Christ having kept them? And how can He have kept the Law except by obedience to its commands? The promises in the Word of God are not made to suffering; they are made to obedience. Consequently, Christ's sufferings, though they may remove the penalty, do not alone make me the inheritor of the promise. *"If thou wilt enter into life,"* said Christ, *"keep the commandments"* (Matt. 19:17). It is only Christ's keeping the commandments that entitles me to enter life. *"The LORD is well pleased for his righteousness' sake; he will magnify the law, and make it honourable"* (Isa. 42:21). I do not enter into life by virtue of His sufferings—those deliver me from death, those purge me from filthiness; but entering the enjoyments of the life eternal must be the result of obedience. As it cannot be the result of mine, it is the result of His, which is imputed to me. We find the Apostle Paul putting Christ's obedience in contrast to the disobedience of Adam: *"For as by one man's disobedience many were made sinners, so by the obedience of one shall many be made righteous"* (Rom. 5:19). Now this is not Christ's death merely, but Christ's active obedience, which is meant here: it is by *this* that we are [declared] righteous…For despite all the outcry of modern times against that doctrine, it is written in heaven and is a sure and precious truth to be received by all the faithful: we are justified by faith through the righteousness of Christ Jesus imputed to us. See what Christ has done in His living and in His dying, His acts becoming our acts and His righteousness being imputed to us, so that we are rewarded as if we were righteous, while He was punished as though He had been guilty.

This justification, then, comes to sinners as an act of pure grace, the foundation of it being Christ's righteousness. The practical way of its application is by faith. The sinner believeth God and believeth that Christ is sent of God. [He] takes Christ Jesus to be his only confidence and trust; and by that act, he becomes a justified soul. It is not by repenting that we are justified, but by *believing*; it is not by deep experience of the guilt of sin; it is not by bitter pangs and throes under the temptations of Satan; it is not by mortification of the body, nor by the renunciation of self; all these are good, but the act that justifieth is a look at Christ. We, having nothing, being nothing, boasting of nothing, but being utterly emptied, do look to Him Whose wounds stream with the life-giving blood. As we look to Him, we live and are justified by His life. There is life in a look at the crucified One—life in the sense of justification. He, who a minute before was in himself a condemned criminal fit only to be taken to the place from whence he came and to suffer divine wrath, is at once by an act of faith made an heir of God, joint heir with Jesus Christ, taken from the place of condemnation and put into the place of acceptance, so that now he dreads no more the wrath of God! The curse of God *cannot* touch him, for Christ was made a curse for him; as it is written, *"Cursed is every one that hangeth on a tree"* (Gal. 3:13).

Now concerning this great mercy of justification, let us say that it is instantaneous…The dying thief was as clean one moment after he had trusted in Christ as he was when he was with Christ in Paradise. Justification in heaven is not more complete than it is on earth. Nay, listen to me…Justification never alters in a child of God. God pronounces him guiltless, and guiltless he is. Jehovah justifies him, and neither his holiness can improve his righteousness nor his sins diminish it. He stands in Christ Jesus, the same yesterday, today, and forever, as accepted one moment as at another moment, as sure of eternal life at one instant as at another. Oh, how blessed is this truth: justified in a moment, and justified completely!

From a sermon delivered on Sunday morning, April 30, 1865, at the Metropolitan Tabernacle, Newington.

Charles Haddon Spurgeon (1834-1892): English Baptist minister; history's most widely read preacher (apart from those found in Scripture); born at Kelvedon, Essex.

> *Another thing that bespeaks a man or woman inclining to wantonness and uncleanness is adorning themselves in light and wanton apparel. The attire of a harlot is too frequently in our day the attire of professors—a vile thing that argueth much wantonness and vileness of affections. —John Bunyan*

A Return to Modest Apparel
JEFF POLLARD

For ye are bought with a price: therefore glorify God in your body, and in your spirit, which are God's. —1 Corinthians 6:20

Vincent Alsop observed, "That the present generation is lamentably intoxicated with novelties and as sadly degenerated from the gravity of former ages can neither be denied, nor concealed, nor defended nor, I fear, reformed...even 'the daughters of Zion' have caught the epidemical infection." Likewise, an epidemic of immodesty infects our churches today. The principles by which most swimwear fails the modesty test should be applied to everything we wear. We need to realize that some "coverings" do not really cover: tight clothing brings out the "body underneath" in the same way swimwear does. While we must not be ashamed of the body itself as if it were an evil thing, we must properly cover it to preserve chastity of mind and spirit, especially in the corporate worship of our holy God. Above all, we men must learn how to govern our hearts and eyes as well as to teach our wives and children the proper principles of modesty. Although women are vulnerable to wearing lavish or sensual apparel, their fathers and husbands are ultimately responsible for what the women in their homes wear. Christian men and women need to study this matter and fervently pray about it, for we truly need a return to a Biblical modesty.

Why do we dress the way we do? John Bunyan put the question this way: "Why are they for going with their...naked shoulders, and paps hanging out like a cow's bag? Why are they for painting their faces, for stretching out their neck, and for putting of themselves unto all the formalities which proud fancy leads them to? Is it because they would honor God? Because they would adorn the Gospel? Because they would beautify religion, and make sinners to fall in love with their own salvation? No, no, it is rather to please their lusts...I believe also that Satan has drawn more into the sin of uncleanness by the spangling[134] show of fine clothes than he could possibly have drawn unto it without them. I wonder what it was that of old was called the attire of a harlot: certainly it could not be more bewitching and tempting than are the garments of many professors this day." The same could be said today, dear reader. Examine your own heart. Why *do* you dress the way you do?

The cry of the Satanist is "Do what thou wilt shall be the whole of the law." The cry of the 60s was "Do your own thing!" The cry of the Feminists

---

134 **spangling** – sparkling.

is "It's my body, and I'll do what I want." The cry of the modern Evangelical is "It's my liberty, and I'll do what I want." Nevertheless, the declaration of Scripture is this: *"What? know ye not that your body is the temple of the Holy Ghost which is in you, which ye have of God, and ye are not your own? For ye are bought with a price: therefore glorify God in your body, and in your spirit, which are God's"* (1 Cor. 6:19-20). You are not your own, if you are a Christian. Your whole being—body and soul—is the purchased property of Jesus Christ; and the price paid for your body was the breaking of His: *"This is my body, which is broken for you"* (1 Cor. 11:24; Matt. 26:26). Your body belongs to Him! He redeemed it with His precious blood on the cross of Calvary. We must consider how we adorn His blood-bought property.

No doubt, some will cry at this point, "Ahhh! But this is legalism!" It is not legalism to urge God's children to cover themselves because modesty is the command of Scripture. The desire of the regenerate heart is to honor the Lord Jesus and to do whatever brings Him glory by keeping His commandments. *"He that hath my commandments, and keepeth them, he it is that loveth me...He that loveth me not keepeth not my sayings"* (John 14:21, 24). The glory of God and love for Christ should be the primary motives for everything we say, do, and think, which includes what we wear.

I have given you the Scriptures, and...I trust that these [articles] have provoked you to thought, as well as to love and good works. However, as mentioned above, if you find the definition of modesty inaccurate or the conclusions in [these articles] unbiblical, then wrestle and pray until the Lord gives you something better. But pray! For the love of Christ, pray! It is never legalism to call God's children to obey Him according to His Word!

Pray meditating on the very eternal purpose of Almighty God: *"For whom he did foreknow, he also did predestinate to be conformed to the image of his Son"* (Rom. 8:29). This earth, this whole universe exists for one reason alone: the God of grace intended to save His people from their sins and make them like His holy Son, Jesus Christ. He poured out His blood on the cross of Calvary to pay the debt for the sins of His people. By faith in Him alone, their sins are pardoned for all eternity. Christ saves them, cleanses them, and makes them like Himself. And what is He like? *"Holy, harmless, undefiled, separate from sinners"* (Heb. 7:26).

So then, how shall we properly govern ourselves with regard to this difficult issue? Let us consider these principles: 1) The glory of God must be our primary aim—*"glorify God in your body"* (1 Cor. 6:20); *"do all in the name of the Lord Jesus"* (Col. 3:17). 2) Love for Christ must be our motive: *"We love him, because he first loved us"* (1 John 4:19). 3) Remembering that we are the temple of the Holy Spirit and that we are not our own must be our corrective. *"Your body is the temple of the Holy Ghost which is in you…and ye are not your own"* (1 Cor. 6:19). 4) Love for others, the preservation of purity in them and us, and the desire not to provoke them to lust will be our resulting aim. *"Love worketh no ill to his neighbour: therefore love is the fulfilling of the law"* (Rom. 13:10).

May the God of mercy grant us repentance where we have sinned in this matter. Be honest with yourselves and your God, dear reader. Have you ever really given this issue serious consideration? Have any of you fervently asked the Lord how a holy child of God ought to dress? If not, I urge you to do so with all my heart. Repent of whatever worldliness you find in your hearts. Repent if you dress for the gazes of men and not for the glory of God.

Today many are again valiantly holding forth the Gospel of God's sovereign grace; they are plainly declaring in many quarters the glorious truth of salvation by faith alone through Christ alone. These wonderful, transforming truths should produce a holy, humble, and modest people, distinguishable from this lost and dying world. Hence, my fervent prayer is that we ardently love Jesus Christ and one another, that we strive together for the unity of the faith, and that we lead lives that magnify the saving grace of our blessed Redeemer. May we live soberly, righteously, and godly in this present world (Titus 2:11-14); and may we never deny these precious truths that we love by clinging to the forms and fashions of this present evil world and its sinful nakedness. Let us glorify God in our bodies, and in our spirits, which are His (1 Cor. 6:20). And for God's glory and the love of the Lord Jesus Christ, let us return to Christian modesty.

Adapted from *Christian Modesty and the Public Undressing of America*, published and available from Chapel Library.

Jeff Pollard: An elder of Mount Zion Bible Church in Pensacola, Florida.

Chapter 12
THOUGHTS FOR YOUNG PEOPLE

Would you rather be warned early or late of a coming disaster? All of us would want early warning. Why? If you can catch the problem early, you avoid much of the damage. Early counsel heeded pays dividends far out in the future.

Young people need early counsel as they prepare for adulthood in a fallen world. God must love young people very much, for He designed and commanded such a comprehensive methodology of care for them. He delivered detailed instructions to parents for teaching their young people. He commanded the older in the church to teach the younger (Titus 2:2-5); He gave them spiritual fathers and mothers and brothers and sisters in the church (1 Tim. 5:1-2); He gave them shepherds (pastors) in the church who know how to manage their own households well to teach them the Word of God (1 Tim. 3:1-5); and He commanded fathers to "bring them up in the nurture and admonition of the Lord" (Eph. 6:4).

The Bible says that children are like arrows that a warrior shoots at his enemies (Ps. 127:4). There are two characters in this verse: the warrior (parent) and the arrow (children). Children are arrows shot into the world, in order to bring glory to God on earth. They prosper. It goes well with them. They enjoy life. The arrows hit the target, and there is a ripple effect—truth and love grows all around them and the world gets to see a glimpse of what God is like.

In this chapter, you will find practical counsel and biblical wisdom for young people. These authors deal with nearly every major area of life, outlining the particular sins and temptations boys and girls will face as they fulfill the biblical vision for manhood and womanhood. They are experienced and knowledgeable saints. The counsel young people need today is no different from the youth of the past. Despite technological changes, nothing about the heart of young people has changed since these men wrote these lines.

—Scott Brown

Thoughts for Young People

ARCHIBALD ALEXANDER (1772-1851)

It is a matter of serious regret that young people[1] are commonly so little disposed to listen to the advice of the aged…But it is greatly to be desired that the lessons of wisdom taught by the experience of one set of men should be made available for the instruction of those who come after them. We have therefore determined to address a few short hints of advice to the rising generation on subjects of deep and acknowledged importance to all. But previously to commencing, we would assure them that it is no part of our object to interfere with their innocent enjoyments or to deprive them of one pleasure that cannot be shown to be injurious to their best interests. We wish to approach you, dear youth, in the character of affectionate friends, rather than in that of dogmatical[2] teachers or stern reprovers. We would therefore solicit[3] your patient, candid, and impartial attention to the following counsels:

Aim at consistency in your Christian character. There is a beauty in moral consistency that resembles the symmetry of a well-proportioned building, where nothing is deficient, nothing redundant.[4] Consistency can only be acquired and maintained by cultivating every part of the Christian character…We are not very frequently permitted to witness a character well-proportioned and nicely balanced in all its parts: while in one branch, there is vigor and even exuberance,[5] in another there may be the appearance of feebleness and sterility.[6] The man who is distinguished for virtues of a particular class is apt to be deficient in those that belong to a different class… Men are frequently found whose zeal blazes out ardently and conspicuously, so as to leave most others far back in the shade, while they are totally destitute of that humility, meekness, and brotherly kindness that form an essential part of the Christian character. Some people are conscientious and punctilious[7] in the performance of all the rites and external duties connected

---

1 **Editor's note:** Several articles in this chapter originally addressed young men, young women, or children. To render the articles more useful for all readers, the term *young people* often appears instead of those three designations. Similarly, *person* sometimes replaces *man*, *woman*, *boy*, and *girl*. This is no surrender to feminism: the Biblical counsel found in all the articles of this issue is profitable for either sex.
2 **dogmatical** – overbearing; dictatorial.
3 **solicit** – earnestly ask.
4 **redundant** – exceeding what is necessary.
5 **exuberance** – abundant productiveness.
6 **sterility** – barrenness; unproductiveness.
7 **punctilious** – showing great attention to detail or correct behavior.

with the worship of God. [Yet they] are inattentive to the obligations of strict justice and veracity[8] in their [dealings] with others. On the other hand, many boast of their morality and yet are notoriously inattentive to the duties of the Christian faith.[9]

Real Christians, too, are often chargeable with inconsistency. [This] arises from a lack of clear discernment of the rule of moral conduct in its application to particular cases. While the general principles of duty are plain and easily understood by all, the ability to discriminate between right and wrong in many complicated cases is extremely rare. This delicate and correct perception of moral relations can only be acquired by the divine blessing… It is too commonly taken for granted that Christian morals are a subject so easy that all close study of it is unnecessary. This is an injurious mistake! Many of the deficiencies and inconsistencies of Christians are owing to a lack of clear and correct knowledge of the exact rule of moral conduct. On no subject will you find a greater diversity of opinion than concerning the lawfulness or unlawfulness of particular practices. Even good men are often thrown into difficulty and doubt respecting the proper course to be pursued.

But while many cases of inconsistency arise from ignorance of the exact standard of rectitude,[10] more must be attributed to heedlessness and forgetfulness. Men do not act sufficiently from principle, but too much from custom, from fashion, and from habit. Thus, many actions are performed without any inquiry into their moral character…

Another cause of the inconsistency so commonly observed is the prevalence[11] that certain passions or appetites may obtain in the time of temptation. The force of the internal principles of evil is not perceived when the objects and circumstances favorable to their exercise are absent. As the venomous adder seems to be harmless while chilled with cold, but soon manifests his malignity when brought near the fire, so sin often lies hid in the bosom as though it were dead until some exciting cause draws it forth into exercise. Then the person is surprised to find the strength of his own passions above anything that he had before conceived. Thus, in certain circumstances, people often act in a way altogether contrary to the general tenor of their conduct. It is by no means a fair inference from a single act of irregularity that the person who is guilty of it has acted hypocritically in

---

8 **veracity** – truthfulness.
9 **Editor's note:** The author's original word here is *religion*. In light of the broad and often confusing uses of *religion* in the present day, the terms *Christian faith*, *Christianity*, and *faith in Christ* usually replace *religion* and *religious* in this issue.
10 **rectitude** – morally correct behavior; righteousness.
11 **prevalence** – effective power; influence.

all the apparent good actions of his former life. The true explanation is that principles of action that he has commonly been able to govern and restrain acquire—in some unguarded moment or under the power of some strong temptation—a force that his good principles are not at that moment strong enough to oppose. The person who is usually correct and orderly may thus be overtaken in a fault. As all are liable to the same frailties, there should exist a disposition to receive and restore offending Christians when they give sufficient evidence of penitence.[12]

Man at his best estate in this world is an inconsistent creature. The only persons in whom this defect is not observed are the people who by grace live near to God and exercise a constant jealousy and vigilance over themselves. But when faith is weak and inconstant, great inconsistencies will mar the beauty of Christian character. Young people ought, therefore, to begin early to exercise this vigilance and to keep their hearts with all diligence, lest they be ensnared by their own passions and overcome by the power of temptation.

I counsel you then, my young friends, to aim at consistency. Cultivate assiduously[13] every part of the Christian character, so that there may appear a beautiful proportion in your virtue…To preserve consistency, it is necessary to be well acquainted with the weak points in our own character, to know something of the strength of our own passions, and to guard beforehand against the occasions and temptations that would be likely to cause us to act inconsistently with our Christian profession…According to that of the wise man, *"He that is slow to anger is better than the mighty; and he that ruleth his spirit than he that taketh a city"* (Prov. 16:32)…Learn then, my young friends, to bridle your passions and govern your temper from your earliest days…

Let your [relationships with others] be marked by a strict and conscientious regard to truth, honor, justice, kindness, and courtesy…Be honest, be upright, sincere, people of your word, faithful to every trust, kind to everybody, respectful where respect is due, generous according to your ability, grateful for benefits received, and delicate in the mode of conferring favors…Let your conduct and conversation be characterized by frankness and candor, by forbearance, and a spirit of indulgence and forgiveness. In short, *"All things whatsoever ye would that men should do to you, do ye even so to them"* (Matt. 7:12)…

Govern your tongue. It is probable [that] more sin is committed and more mischief done by this small member than in all other ways. The faculty

---

12 **penitence** – repentance.
13 **assiduously** – with care and persistence; diligently.

of speech is one of our most useful endowments, but it is exceedingly liable to abuse. He who knows how to bridle his tongue is, therefore, in Scripture denominated *"a perfect man"* (James 3:2). Again, of him who seemeth *"to be religious, and bridleth not his tongue,"* it is declared, *"This man's religion is vain"* (James 1:26). The words that we utter are a fair index of the moral state of the mind. *"For by thy words,"* says our Lord, *"thou shalt be justified, and by thy words thou shalt be condemned"* (Matt. 12:37). Not only are sins of the tongue more *numerous* than others, but some of them are the most heinous of which man can be guilty—even that one sin that has no forgiveness is a sin of the tongue (Matt. 12:32).

Not only should all profaneness, obscenity, and falsehood be put far away, but also you should continually endeavor to render your conversation useful. Be ever ready to communicate knowledge, to suggest profitable ideas, to recommend virtue and religion, to rebuke sin, and to give glory to God. Beware of evil speaking. A habit of detraction[14] is one of the worst that you can contract and is always indicative of an envious and malignant heart. Instead of prostituting this active and useful member to the purposes of slander, employ it in defending the innocent and the injured.

Permit me to suggest the following brief rules for the government of the tongue. Avoid [talking too much]: *"In the multitude of words there wanteth not sin"* (Prov. 10:19). If you have nothing to communicate that can be useful, be silent. Think before you speak …Especially, be cautious about uttering anything in the form of a promise without consideration. Be conscientiously regardful of truth…Never speak what will be likely to excite bad feelings of any kind in the minds of others. Be ready on all suitable occasions to give utterance to good sentiments, especially such as may be useful to the young. Listen respectfully to the opinions of others, but never fail to give your testimony—modestly but firmly—against error. *"Let your speech be always with grace, seasoned with salt…Let no corrupt communication proceed out of your mouth, but that which is good to the use of edifying, that it may minister grace unto the hearers"* (Col. 4:6; Eph. 4:29).

Keep a good conscience. If wickedness had no other punishment than the stings of conscience that follow evil actions, it would be reason enough to induce every considerate person to avoid that which is productive of so much pain. No misery of which the human mind is susceptible is so intolerable and so irremediable[15] as remorse of conscience. And it is liable to be renewed as often as the guilty action is distinctly [remembered]. It is true

---

14 **detraction** – making comments that damage someone's reputation.
15 **irremediable** – impossible to cure or put right.

[that] the conscience, by means of error and repeated resistance to its dictates, may become callous—*"seared with a hot iron"* (1 Tim. 4:2). But this apparent death of moral sensibility is no more than a *sleep*. At an unexpected time and in the most inconvenient circumstances, conscience may be aroused and may exert a more tremendous power than was ever before experienced... Joseph's brethren seemed to have almost forgotten their unnatural and cruel conduct in selling him as a slave into a foreign country. But when many years had elapsed and they found themselves environed with difficulties and dangers in that very land, the remembrance of their crime painfully rushed upon their minds. [It] extorted mutual confessions of their guilt from them. *"God,"* said they, *"hath found out the iniquity of thy servants...And they said one to another, We are verily guilty concerning our brother, in that we saw the anguish of his soul, when he besought us, and we would not hear; therefore is this distress come upon us"* (Gen. 44:16; 42:21).

Men often endeavor to escape from the stings of a guilty conscience by a change of place, but the remedy is ineffectual. The transgressor may traverse the widest ocean, transcend the loftiest mountains, and bury himself in the dark recesses of the desert, but he cannot fly so far nor conceal himself so effectually as to escape from his tormentor. In some cases, the agonies of remorse have been so intolerable that the guilty perpetrator of great wickedness has preferred *"strangling, and death"* (Job 7:15) to a miserable life and has rushed uncalled into the presence of his Judge...But what man is there who has not committed sins, the recollection of which gives him sensible pain? And such acts often stand out in strong relief in the retrospect of the past. No effort can obliterate such things from the memory. We may turn away our eyes from the disagreeable object, but the painful idea will return!...

When I counsel you, my young friends, to keep a good conscience, I mean that you should...endeavor to obtain this inestimable blessing by an application to *"the blood of sprinkling"* (Heb. 12:24). Until the soul is justified[16] and sin pardoned, there can be no true peace of conscience. While the Law remains unsatisfied for us and denounces vengeance against us for our sins, what in the universe can give us peace? But when by faith, the soul apprehends the atonement[17] and sees that it is commensurate[18] to all the demands of the Law and that in the cross, justice is not only satisfied but also gloriously illustrated, it is at once relieved from the agony of guilt. [Then] *"the peace of*

---

16 **justified** – declared righteous by God through faith in Jesus Christ.
17 **atonement** – reconciliation with God through the death and resurrection of Jesus Christ.
18 **commensurate** – in proportion; corresponding in extent.

God, which passeth all understanding" pervades the soul (Phil. 4:7). The great secret of genuine peace is, therefore, living faith in the blood of Christ…

Learn to bear affliction with fortitude and resignation…Christ Himself suffered while in the world and has left His followers a perfect example of holy fortitude and filial submission to the will of God. When sorely pressed with the inconceivable load of our sins, so that His human soul could not have sustained it unless supported by the divine nature, His language was, *"Not my will, but thine, be done"* (Luke 22:42). Those afflictions allotted to the people of God are necessary parts of salutary[19] discipline, intended to purify them from the dross of sin and to prepare them for the service of God here and the enjoyment of God in the world to come. They are to them, therefore, not penal judgments, but Fatherly chastisement. Though not *"joyous, but grievous"* for the present, *"it yieldeth the peaceable fruit of righteousness"* (Heb. 12:11)…That to which I would bring my youthful readers is a state of mind prepared for adversity, whatever kind it may be that they may not be taken by surprise when calamity falls upon them. When the dark day of adversity arrives, be not dismayed; but put your trust in the Lord and look to Him for strength to endure whatever may be laid upon you. Never permit yourselves to entertain hard thoughts of God because of any of His dispensations.[20] They may be dark and mysterious, but they are all wise and good. What we cannot understand now, we shall be privileged to know hereafter. Exercise an uncomplaining submission to the will of God as developed in the events of Providence. Believe steadfastly that all things are under the government of wisdom and goodness. Remember that whatever sufferings you may be called to endure, they are always less than your sins deserve. Consider that these afflictive dispensations are fraught with rich, spiritual blessings. They are not only useful but also *necessary*. We should perish with a wicked world if a kind Father did not make use of the rod to reclaim us from our wanderings. Besides, there is no situation in which we can more glorify God than when in the furnace of affliction…And when schooled in adversity, you will be better qualified to sympathize with the children of sorrow and better skilled in affording them comfort…

Cherish and diligently cultivate genuine piety.[21] *"The fear of the LORD is the beginning of wisdom"* (Ps. 111:10; Prov. 9:10). Early piety is the most beautiful spectacle in the world. Without piety, all your morality, however useful to men, is but a shadow. It is a branch without a root. Religion, above

---

19 **salutary** – calculated to bring remedy; producing good effects.
20 **dispensations** – acts of divine ordering and arrangements of events.
21 **piety** – habitual reverence and obedience to God; godliness.

every other acquisition, enriches and adorns the mind of man. It is especially congenial with the natural susceptibilities[22] of the youthful mind. The vivacity[23] and versatility of youth, the tenderness and ardor of the affections in this age exhibit piety to the best advantage. How delightful it is to see the bosoms of the young swelling with the lively emotions of pure devotion! How beautiful is the [repentant tear] of holy joy that glistens in the eye of tender youth! Think not, dear young people, that true religion will detract from your happiness. It is a reproach cast upon your Maker to indulge such a thought. It cannot be. A God of goodness never required anything of His creatures that did not tend to their true felicity.[24] Piety may indeed lead you to exchange the pleasures of the theater and ballroom for the purer joys of the Church and prayer meeting. It may turn your attention from books of mere idle fancy and fiction to the Word of God, which to a regenerated soul is found to be sweeter than honey and more excellent than the choicest gold; but this will add to your happiness rather than diminish it. We would then affectionately and earnestly exhort and entreat you, *"Remember now thy Creator in the days of thy youth"* (Eccl. 12:1). This will be your best security against all the dangers and temptations to which you are exposed…Dear youth, be wise, and secure an inheritance among the saints in light. God [calls] you to be reconciled. Christ [calls] you (Matt. 11:28)…The doors of the church will be opened to receive you. The ministers of the Gospel and all the company of believers will hail your entrance and will welcome you to the precious ordinances of God's house. Finally, remember that *"now is the accepted time; behold, now is the day of salvation"* (2 Cor. 6:2).

Seek divine direction and aid by incessant fervent prayer. You need grace to help you every day. Your own wisdom is folly, your own strength weakness, and your own righteousness altogether insufficient. *"It is not in man that walketh to direct his steps"* (Jer. 10:23). But if you lack wisdom, you are permitted to ask; and you have a gracious promise that you shall receive. Whatever we need will be granted if we humbly and believingly ask for it. *"Ask, and it shall be given you; seek, and ye shall find; knock, and it shall be opened unto you"* (Matt. 7:7)…

Faith and prayer are our chief resources under all the various and heavy afflictions of this life. When all other refuges fail, God will hide His people who seek Him in His secret pavilion and shelter them under the shadow of His wings. Prayer is essential to the existence and growth of the spiritual

---

22 **susceptibilities** – tendencies to be easily influenced; impressionable.
23 **vivacity**–liveliness.
24 **felicity** – happiness.

life. It is the breath of the new man. By this means, he obtains quick relief from innumerable evils and draws down from heaven blessings of the richest and sweetest kind. Possess your minds fully of the persuasion that prayer is efficacious,[25] when offered in faith and with importunity,[26] to obtain the blessings that we need. God has made Himself known as a Hearer of prayer: yea, He has promised that we shall have, as far as may be for His glory and our good, whatever we ask...That man who has access to a throne of grace will never lack anything that is really needful. *"The LORD will give grace and glory: no good thing will he withhold from them that walk uprightly"* (Ps. 84:11)...I need not be afraid, therefore, to counsel the young to cultivate the spirit of prayer and to be constant in its exercise. *"Pray without ceasing... [continue] instant in[27] prayer"* (1 Thess. 5:17; Rom. 12:12). Often, too, in the performance of this duty, a taste of heaven is brought down to earth; and the pious worshipper anticipates in some degree those joys that are ineffable[28] and eternal. Moreover, prayer will be your most effectual guard against sin and the power of temptation: "And Satan trembles when he sees the weakest saint upon his knees."[29]

I conclude my counsels to the young by a serious and affectionate recommendation to everyone who reads these pages: make immediate preparation for death. I know that light-hearted youth are unwilling to hear this subject mentioned. There is nothing that casts a greater damp upon their spirits than the solemn fact that death must be encountered and that no earthly possessions or circumstances can secure us from becoming his victims on any day. But if it is acknowledged that this formidable evil is inevitable and that the tenure by which we hold our grasp of life is very fragile, why should we act so unreasonably and—*I may say*—[so] madly as to shut our eyes against the danger?...Do you ask what preparation is necessary? I answer, reconciliation with God and a [fitness] for the employments and enjoyments of the heavenly state. Preparation for death includes repentance towards God for all our sins, trust in the Lord Jesus Christ and reliance on His atoning sacrifice, regeneration of heart, and reformation of life; and finally, a lively exercise of piety, accompanied with a comfortable assurance of the divine favor. In short, genuine and lively piety forms the essence of the needed preparation. With this, your death will be safe and your

---

25 **efficacious** – able to produce the intended result.
26 **importunity** – insistence.
27 **continueinstant in** – be devoted to; persist in.
28 **ineffable** – incapable of being expressed; too great to be described in words.
29 From the hymn "Exhortation to Prayer" by William Cowper (1731-1800).

happiness after death secure. But to render a deathbed not only safe but also comfortable, you must have a strong faith and clear evidence that your sins are forgiven and that you have passed from death unto life. Be persuaded then, before you give sleep to your eyes, to commence your return unto God, from Whom like lost sheep you have strayed. *"Prepare to meet thy God"* (Amos 4:12). *"Therefore be ye also ready: for in such an hour as ye think not the Son of man cometh"* (Matt. 24:44).

Seek deliverance from the fear of death by a believing application to Him Who came on purpose to deliver from this bondage. With His presence and guidance, we need fear no evil, even while passing through the gloomy valley and shadow of death. He is able by His rod and His staff to comfort us and to make us conquerors over this last enemy.

From *Thoughts on Religious Experience*, reprinted by The Banner of Truth Trust: www.banneroftruth.org.

Archibald Alexander (1772-1851): American Presbyterian theologian, first professor of Princeton Seminary; born in Augusta County, VA.

General Counsels for Young People
J.C. RYLE (1816-1900)

For one thing, try to get a clear view of the evil of sin. Young people, if you did but know what sin is and what sin has done, you would not think it strange that I exhort you as I do. You do not see it in its true colors. Your eyes are naturally blind to its guilt and danger, and hence you cannot understand what makes me so anxious about you. Oh, let not the devil succeed in persuading you that sin is a small matter!

Think for a moment what the Bible says about sin—how it dwells naturally in the heart of every man and woman alive (Eccl. 7:20; Rom. 3:23)—how it defiles our thoughts, words, and actions, and that continually (Gen. 6:5; Matt. 15:19)—how it renders us all guilty and abominable in the sight of a holy God (Isa. 64:6; Hab. 1:13)—how it leaves us utterly without hope of salvation if we look to ourselves (Ps. 143:2; Rom. 3:20)—how its fruit in this world is shame and its wages in the world to come, death (Rom. 6:21-23). Think calmly of all this…

Think what an awful change sin has worked on all our natures. Man is no longer what he was when God formed him out of the dust of the ground. He came out of God's hand upright and sinless (Eccl. 7:29). In the day of his creation he was, like everything else, *"very good"* (Gen. 1:31). And what is man now? A fallen creature, a ruin, a being that shows the marks of corruption all over: his heart like Nebuchadnezzar, degraded and earthly, looking down and not up; his affections like a household in disorder, calling no man master, all extravagance and confusion; his understanding like a lamp flickering in the socket, impotent to guide him, not knowing good from evil; his will like a rudderless ship, tossed to and fro by every desire and constant only in choosing any way rather than God's. Alas, what a wreck is man compared to what he might have been! Well may we understand such figures being used as blindness, deafness, disease, sleep, death, when the Spirit has to give us a picture of man as he is. And man as he is, remember, was so made by sin.

Think too what it has cost to make atonement for sin and to provide a pardon and forgiveness for sinners. God's own Son must come into the world and take upon Him our nature in order to pay the price of our redemption and deliver us from the curse of a broken Law. He, Who was in the beginning with the Father and by Whom all things were made, must suffer for sin—the just for the unjust—must die the death of a malefactor[30] before the way to

---

30 **malefactor** – criminal.

heaven can be laid open to any soul. See the Lord Jesus Christ despised and rejected of men, scourged, mocked, and insulted; behold Him bleeding on the cross of Calvary; hear Him crying in agony, *"My God, my God, why hast thou forsaken me?"* (Matt. 27:46); mark how the sun was darkened and the rocks rent at the sight; *then* consider, young people, what the evil and guilt of sin must be.

Think, also, what sin has done already upon the earth. Think how it cast Adam and Eve out of Eden, brought the flood upon the old world, caused fire to come down on Sodom and Gomorrah, drowned Pharaoh and his host in the Red Sea, destroyed the seven wicked nations of Canaan, scattered the twelve tribes of Israel over the face of the globe. Sin alone did all this.

Think, moreover, of *all* the misery and sorrow that sin has caused and is causing at this very day. Pain, disease, and death—strife, quarrels, and divisions—envy, jealousy, and malice—deceit, fraud, and cheating—violence, oppression, and robbery—selfishness, unkindness, and ingratitude—all these are the fruits of sin. Sin is the parent of them all. Sin has so marred and spoiled the face of God's creation.

Young people, consider these things, and you will not wonder that we preach as we do. Surely, if you did but think of them, you would break with sin forever. Will you play with poison? Will you sport with hell?[31] Will you take fire in your hand? Will you harbor your deadliest enemy in your bosom? Will you go on living as if it mattered nothing whether your own sins were forgiven or not—whether sin had dominion over you or you over sin? Oh, awake to a sense of sin's sinfulness and danger! Remember the words of Solomon: *"Fools,"* none but fools, *"make a mock at sin"* (Prov. 14:9).

Hear, then, the request that I make of you this day: pray that God would teach you the real evil of sin. As you would have your soul saved, arise and pray.

For another thing, seek to become acquainted with our Lord Jesus Christ. This is indeed the principal thing in religion. This is the cornerstone of Christianity. Until you know this, my warnings and advice will be useless; and your endeavors, whatever they may be, will be in vain. A watch without a mainspring is not more unserviceable than is religion without Christ.

But let me not be misunderstood. It is not the mere *knowing* Christ's name that I mean: it is knowing His mercy, grace, and power—the knowing Him not by the hearing of the ear, but by the experience of your hearts. I want you to know Him by *faith*. I want you, as Paul says, to know *"the power of his resurrection…being made conformable unto his death"* (Phil. 3:10). I want

---

31 *See* FGB 211 *Hell*, available from Chapel Library.

you to be able to say of Him, "He is my peace and my strength, my life and my consolation, my Physician and my Shepherd, my Savior and my God."

Why do I make such a point of this? I do it because in Christ alone *"all fullness [dwells]"* (Col. 1:19), because in Him alone there is full supply of all that we require for the necessities of our souls. Of ourselves, we are all poor, empty creatures—empty of righteousness and peace, empty of strength and comfort, empty of courage and patience, empty of power to stand or go on or make progress in this evil world. It is in Christ alone that all these things are to be found—grace, peace, wisdom, righteousness, sanctification, and redemption. It is just in proportion as we live upon Him that we are strong Christians. It is only when self is nothing and Christ is all our confidence, it is then only that we shall do great exploits. Then only are we armed for the battle of life and shall overcome. Then only are we prepared for the journey of life and shall get forward. To live on Christ, to draw all from Christ, to do all in the strength of Christ, to be ever looking unto Christ—this is the true secret of spiritual prosperity. *"I can do all things,"* says Paul, *"through Christ which strengtheneth me"* (Phil. 4:13).

Young people, I set before you Jesus Christ this day as the treasury of your souls. I invite you to begin by going to Him if you would so run as to obtain. Let this be your first step: go to Christ. Do you want to consult friends? He is the best friend: *"A friend that sticketh closer than a brother"* (Prov. 18:24). Do you feel unworthy because of your sins? Fear not: His blood cleanseth from all sin. He says, *"Though your sins be as scarlet, they shall be as white as snow; though they be red like crimson, they shall be as wool"* (Isa. 1:18). Do you feel weak and unable to follow Him? Fear not: He will give you power to become sons of God. He will give you the Holy Ghost to dwell in you and seal you for His own: a new heart will He give you, and a new spirit will He put within you. Are you troubled or beset with peculiar infirmities? Fear not: there is no evil spirit that Jesus cannot cast out; there is no disease of soul that He cannot heal. Do you feel doubts and fears? Cast them aside: *"Come unto me,"* He says (Matt. 11:28). *"Him that cometh to me I will in no wise cast out"* (John 6:37). He knows well the heart of a young person. He knows your trials and your temptations, your difficulties and your foes…He can be touched with the feeling of your infirmities (Heb. 4:15); for He suffered Himself, being tempted. Surely, you will be without excuse if you turn away from such a Savior and Friend as this.

Hear the request I make of you this day: if you love life, seek to become acquainted with Jesus Christ.

For another thing, never forget that nothing is as important as your soul. Your soul is eternal. It will live forever. The world and all that it contains shall pass away—firm, solid, beautiful, well-ordered as it is, the world shall come to an end. *"The earth also and the works that are therein shall be burned up"* (2 Peter 3:10). The works of statesmen, writers, painters, architects, are all short-lived: your soul will outlive them all. The angel's voice shall proclaim one day, *"There should be time no longer"* (Rev. 10:6). But that shall never be said of your souls.

Try, I beseech you, to realize the fact that your soul is the one thing worth living for. It is the part of you that ought always to be first considered. No place, no employment that injures your soul is good for you. No friend, no companion who makes light of your soul's concerns deserves your confidence. The man who hurts your person, your property, your character does you but temporary harm. He is the true enemy who contrives to damage your soul.

Think for a moment what you were sent into the world for. Not merely to eat, drink, and indulge the desires of the flesh—not merely to dress out your body and follow its lusts whithersoever they may lead you—not merely to work, sleep, laugh, talk, enjoy yourselves, and think of nothing but time. No! You were meant for something higher and better than this. You were placed here to train for eternity. Your body was only intended to be a house for your immortal spirit. It is flying in the face of God's purposes to do as many do—to make the soul a servant to the body, and not the body a servant to the soul.

Young people, God is no respecter of persons (Acts 10:34). He regards no man's coat, purse, rank, or position. He sees not with man's eyes. The poorest saint that ever died in a workhouse is nobler in His sight than the richest sinner that ever died in a palace. God does not look at riches, titles, learning, beauty, or anything of the kind. One thing only God does look at, and that is the immortal soul. He measures all men by one standard, one measure, one test, one criterion, and that is the state of their souls.

Do not forget this. Keep the interests of your soul in view—morning, noon, and night. Rise up each day desiring that it may prosper. Lie down each evening inquiring of yourself whether it has really got on…Set your immortal soul before your mind's eye; and when men ask you why you live as you do, answer them in this spirit, "I live for my soul." Believe me, the day is fast coming when the soul will be the one thing men will think of, and the only question of importance will be this: "Is my soul lost or saved?"

For another thing, determine as long as you live to make the Bible your guide and adviser. The Bible is God's merciful provision for sinful man's soul, the map by which he must steer his course if he would attain eternal life. All that we need to know in order to make us peaceful, holy, or happy is there richly contained. If young people would know how to begin life well, let them hear what David says: *"Wherewithal shall a young man cleanse his way? by taking heed thereto according to thy word"* (Ps. 119:9).

Young people, I charge you to make a habit of reading the Bible and not to let the habit be broken. Let not the laughter of companions, let not the bad customs of the family you may live in, let *none* of these things prevent your doing it. Determine that you will not only have a Bible, but also make time to read it too…It is the book from which King David got wisdom and understanding. It is the book that young Timothy knew from his childhood. Never be ashamed of reading it. Do not despise the Word (Prov. 13:13).

Read it with *prayer* for the Spirit's grace to make you understand it… Read it *reverently*, as the Word of God, not of man, believing implicitly that what it approves is right and what it condemns is wrong. Be very sure that every doctrine that will not stand the test of Scripture is false. This will keep you from being tossed to and fro and carried about by the dangerous opinions of these latter days. Be very sure that every practice in your life that is contrary to Scripture is sinful and must be given up. This will settle many a question of conscience and cut the knot of many a doubt. Remember how differently two kings of Judah read the Word of God: Jehoiakim read it, at once cut the writing to pieces, and burned it on the fire (Jer. 36:23). Why? Because his heart rebelled against it, and he was resolved not to obey. Josiah read it, at once rent his clothes, and cried mightily to the Lord (2 Chron. 34:19). And why? Because his heart was tender and obedient. He was ready to do anything that Scripture showed him was his duty. O that you may follow the last of these two and not the first!

And read it *regularly*. This is the only way to become *"mighty in the scriptures"* (Acts 18:24). A hasty glance at the Bible now and then does little good. At that rate, you will never become familiar with its treasures or feel the sword of the Spirit fitted to your hand in the hour of conflict. But get your mind stored with Scripture by diligent reading, and you will soon discover its value and power. Texts will rise up in your hearts in the moment of temptation. Commands will suggest themselves in seasons of doubt. Promises will come across your thoughts in the time of discouragement. Thus you will experience the truth of David's words, *"Thy word have I hid in mine heart, that I might not sin against thee"* (Ps. 119:11); and of Solomon's words, *"When thou goest, it shall lead thee; when thou sleepest, it shall keep thee; and when thou awakest, it shall talk with thee"* (Prov. 6:22).

I dwell on these things more because this is an age of reading. Of making many books there seems no end, though few of them are really profitable. There seems a rage for cheap printing and publishing. Newspapers of every sort abound; the tone of some that have the widest circulation tells badly for the taste of the age. Amidst the flood of dangerous reading, I plead for my Master's book—I call upon you not to forget the book of the soul. Let not newspapers, novels, and romances be read while the prophets and Apostles lie despised. Let not the exciting and licentious swallow up your attention, while the edifying and the sanctifying can find no place in your mind.

Young people, give the Bible the honor due to it every day you live. Whatever you read, read that first. And beware of bad books: there are plenty in this day. Take heed what you read. I suspect there is more harm done to souls in this way than most people have an idea is possible. Value all books in proportion as they are agreeable to Scripture. Those that are nearest to it are the best, and those that are farthest from it and most contrary to it, the worst.

For another thing, never make an intimate friend of anyone who is not a friend of God. Understand me—I do not speak of acquaintances. I do not mean that you ought to have nothing to do with any but true Christians. To take such a line is neither possible nor desirable in this world. Christianity requires no man to be discourteous. But I do advise you to be very careful in your choice of friends…Never be satisfied with the friendship of anyone who will not be useful to your soul.

Believe me: the importance of this advice cannot be overrated. There is no telling the harm that is done by associating with godless companions and friends. The devil has few better helps in ruining a person's soul. Grant him this help, and he cares little for all the armor with which you may be armed against him. Good education, early habits of morality, sermons, books, regular homes, letters of parents—all, he knows well, will avail you little if you will only cling to ungodly friends. You may resist many open temptations, refuse many plain snares; but once take up a bad companion, and he is content. The awful chapter that describes Amnon's wicked conduct about Tamar almost begins with these words, *"But Amnon had a friend…a very subtil man"* (2 Sam. 13:3).

You must recollect [that] we are all creatures of imitation: precept may teach us, but it is example that draws us. There is that in us all that we are always disposed to catch the ways of those with whom we live. The more we like them, the stronger does the disposition grow. Without our being aware of it, they influence our tastes and opinions: we gradually give up what they dislike and take up what they like, in order to become more close friends with them. And, worst of all, we catch their ways in things that are wrong far quicker than in things that are right. Health, unhappily, is not contagious, but disease is. It is far easier to catch a chill than to impart a glow—to make each other's religion dwindle away than grow and prosper.

Young people, I ask you to lay these things to heart. Before you let anyone become your constant companion, before you get into the habit of telling him everything, and going to him in all your troubles and all your pleasures—before you do this, just think of what I have been saying. Ask yourself, "Will this be a useful friendship to me or not?"

"Evil communications" do indeed *"corrupt good manners"* (1 Cor. 15:33). I wish that text were written in hearts as often as it is in copybooks.[32] Good friends are among our greatest blessings: they may keep us back from much evil, quicken us in our course, speak a word in season, draw us upward, and draw us on. But a bad friend is a positive misfortune, a weight continually dragging us down and chaining us to earth. Keep company with an irreligious man, and it is more than probable you will in the end become like him. That is the general consequence of all such friendships. The good go down to the bad, and the bad do not come up to the good…

I dwell the more upon this point because it has more to do with your prospects in life than at first sight appears. If ever you marry, it is more than probable you will choose a wife among the connections of your friends. If Jehoshaphat's son Jehoram had not formed a friendship with Ahab's family, he would most likely not have married Ahab's daughter. And who can estimate the importance of a right choice in marriage? It is a step that, according to the old saying, "either makes a man or mars him." Your happiness in both lives may depend on it. Your wife must either help your soul or harm it: there is no medium. She will either fan the flame of religion in your heart or throw cold water upon it and make it burn low…He that findeth a good wife indeed *"findeth a good thing"* (Prov. 18:22). But if you have the least wish to find one, be very careful how you choose your friends.

Do you ask me what kind of friends you shall choose? Choose friends who will benefit your soul: friends whom you can really respect; friends whom you would like to have near you on your death-bed; friends who love the Bible and are not afraid to speak to you about it; friends such as you will not be ashamed of owning at the coming of Christ and the Day of Judgment.[33] Follow the example that David sets you: he says, *"I am a companion of all them that fear thee, and of them that keep thy precepts"* (Ps.

---

32 **copybooks** – books containing models of good penmanship; used in teaching penmanship.
33 *See* FGB 210 *Day of Judgment*.

119:63). Remember the words of Solomon: *"He that walketh with wise men shall be wise: but a companion of fools shall be destroyed"* (Prov. 13:20). But depend on it: bad company in the life that now is, is the sure way to procure worse company in the life to come.

From *Thoughts for Young Men,* available from Chapel Library.

J.C. Ryle (1816-1900): Anglican Bishop; born at Macclesfield, Cheshire County, England.

As a general rule, young men and women who have the high privilege of Christian parentage and training do not see the love of God in it. They often kick against it and wish they did not have to endure what they regard as a great hardship. That is the way we used to think of it in the days of our ignorance. But, now that God has opened our eyes, we can see the love of God in it all. We see how He has orchestrated things for our benefit.
—Charles Haddon Spurgeon

Youth Warned Against Sin

JOHN ANGELL JAMES (1785-1859)

> *Rejoice, O young man, in thy youth; and let thy heart cheer thee in the days of thy youth, and walk in the ways of thine heart, and in the sight of thine eyes: but know thou, that for all these things God will bring thee into judgment.* —Ecclesiastes 11:9

Without pretending to say that the youth of this generation are more corrupt than those of former times were, I will assert that their moral interests are now exposed from various causes to imminent[34] peril. The improvement and diffusion[35] of modern education have produced a bold and independent mode of thinking, which, though it be in itself a benefit, requires a proportionate degree of Christian restraint to prevent it from degenerating into lawless licentiousness.[36] It is also probable that of late years, parents have relaxed the salutary rigor of domestic discipline in compliment to the improved understanding of their children. Trade and commerce are now so widely extended that our youth are more from beneath their parents' inspection than formerly and consequently more exposed to the contaminating influence of evil company. The habits of society in general are becoming more expensive and luxurious. In addition to all this, the secret but zealous efforts of infidelity[37] to circulate works, which by attempting to undermine revealed religion aim to subvert the whole fabric of morals, have most alarmingly increased irreligion and immorality. But whatever be the causes, the fact to me is indubitable[38] that multitudes of the young people of the present day are exceedingly corrupt and profane. Such a state of things rouses and interests all my feelings as a father, a minister, and a patriot. I am anxious for my own children, as well as for the youth of my flock, my town, and my country.

You are to be the fathers, young men, of the next generation. Most solicitous[39] do I feel that you should transmit the Christian faith and not vice to posterity. Listen then with seriousness to what I shall this evening advance from motives of pure and faithful affection.

I shall direct your attention to that solemn portion of sacred Scripture that you will find in Ecclesiastes 11:9…No one was more capable of forming a

---

34 **imminent** – about to happen; approaching.
35 **diffusion** – spreading abroad.
36 **licentiousness** – disregard for morality; preoccupation with lustful desires.
37 **infidelity** – atheism.
38 **indubitable** – too obvious to be doubted.
39 **solicitous** – eager; desirous.

correct opinion on this subject than Solomon, since no man ever commanded more resources of earthly delight than he did or ever more eagerly availed himself of the opportunities that he possessed…His testimony, therefore, is to be considered not as the cynical declamation of an ascetic,[40] who had never tasted sensual indulgence, but as that of a man who had drunk the cup to its dregs and who found those dregs to be wormwood, gall, and poison… (Ps. 75:8; Lam. 3:19)

The text properly explained consists of an ironical[41] address. Under a seeming permission, this language contains a very strong and pointed prohibition. It is as if the writer had said, "Thoughtless and sensual young person, who hast no idea of happiness but as arising from animal indulgence, and who art drinking continually the intoxicating cup of worldly pleasure, pursue thy course if thou art determined on this mode of life. Gratify thy appetites. Indulge all thy passions. Deny thyself nothing—eat, drink, and be merry. Disregard the admonitions of conscience. Trample underfoot the authority of revelation, but think not that thou shalt always prosper in the ways of sin or carry forever that air of jollity[42] and triumph. The day of reckoning is at hand, when for all these things thou wilt be called into judgment. God now witnesses and takes account of all thy ways and will one day call thee to His bar and reward thee according to thy doings."

It is implied in this address that young people are much addicted to sensual pleasure. This has been the case with every generation and in every country. It is too common not only for the young themselves, but even for their seniors and their sires to justify or palliate[43] their vicious excesses. We [do] not infrequently hear the abominable adage,[44] "Youth for pleasure, age for business, and old age for religion." It is not possible for language to utter or mind to conceive a more gross or shocking insult to God than this. [It] is saying in effect, "When I can no longer enjoy my lusts or pursue my gains, then I will carry to God a body and soul worn out in the service of sin, Satan, and the world." The monstrous wickedness and horrid impiety of this idea is enough, one should think, to shock and terrify the most confirmed and careless sinner in existence when put clearly to him.

Many things tend to cherish in the youthful breast and to justify in the estimation of young people the love of sensual pleasure. At their age, care

---

40 **cynical…ascetic** – bitter, emotional speech of one that practices extreme self-denial.
41 **ironical** – meaning the opposite of what is expressed.
42 **jollity** – merrymaking; cheerfulness.
43 **palliate** – partially excuse.
44 **adage** – old saying.

sits lightly on the heart, the passions are strong, the imagination is lively, the health is good, and the social impulse is felt in all its energy. The attractions of company are powerful. This, they imagine, is the halcyon[45] time for them to take their fill of pleasure. They think that they shall be steady enough by and by when the season of youth is past and that sobriety, morality, and religion will all come in the proper order of nature. Worldly pleasure, decked in the voluptuous[46] attire and the meretricious[47] ornaments of a harlot, appears to their heated imagination with all the attractive charms of a most bewitching beauty. They yield themselves at once to her influence and consider her as abundantly able to afford them all the happiness they desire. Their great concern is to gratify their senses. The soul and all her vast concerns is neglected for the pleasures of fleshly appetites and is condemned to the degradation of acting as a mere waiting maid to minister to the enjoyment of the body.

Young people, can you justify, either at the bar of reason or revelation, such an appropriation of the morning of your existence, of the best and loveliest portion of your life? If there is indeed a God who made and preserves you, is it reasonable that the season of youth should be passed in a manner hateful in His sight? Is this the way to ensure His blessing on your future days?...Where is it said that young people may innocently walk in all kinds of sensual indulgences? On what page of the book of God's truth do you find these allowances for the excesses of youth, which you make for yourselves and ill-judging friends make for you? *"Woe unto them that rise up early in the morning, that they may follow strong drink; that continue until night, till wine inflame them! And the harp, and the viol, the tabret, and pipe, and wine, are in their feasts: but they regard not the work of the LORD, neither consider the operation of his hands"* (Isa. 5:11-12). This is the testimony of the Lord, delivered as much against the sins of youth as those of riper years. And is it not mentioned amongst other vices by St. Paul that men should be *"lovers of pleasures more than lovers of God"* (2 Tim. 3:4)?...There is not one duty of true godliness binding upon you in future years that does not rest with all its authority upon you [now]. Is youth the season for sinful pleasure then? Is this best and most influential portion of your existence to be deliberately given up to vice? That is a dreadful idea, repugnant alike to reason and revelation.

If sensual pleasure be pursued as the object of youthful years, see how it will influence all your pursuits. Where young people live in this way, it

---

45 **halcyon** – happy and carefree.
46 **voluptuous** – sensuous; suggestive of unrestrained pleasure of the senses.
47 **meretricious** – gaudy; befitting a prostitute.

directs their reading, which is not pious or improving, but light, trifling, and polluting. Inflammatory novels, stimulating romances, lewd poetry, immoral songs, satires against religious characters, and arguments against revelation are in general the works consulted by corrupt and vicious youth. By these, they become still more vicious. Never did the press send forth streams of greater pollution than at this time. Authors are to be found, of no mean talents, who pander to every corruption of the youthful bosom. Almost every vice has its high priest to burn incense on its altar and to lead its victims, decked with the garlands of poetry or fiction, to their ruin.

The recreations and amusements of young people who live in sinful pursuits are of the same nature as their reading, conversation, and company—polluted and polluting. They generally frequent the theater. The theater—that corrupter of public morals, that school where nothing good and everything bad is learned, that resort of the vicious and seminary of vice, that broad and flowery avenue to the bottomless pit. Here young people find no hindrances to sin, no warnings against irreligion, no mementos of judgment to come. On the contrary, [they find] everything to inflame their passions, to excite their criminal desires, and to gratify their appetites for vice. The language, the music, and the company are all adapted to a sensual taste and calculated to demoralize the mind.[48] Multitudes of once comparatively innocent and happy youths have to date their ruin for both worlds from the hour when their feet first trod within the polluted precincts of a theater. Until then they were ignorant of many of the ways of vice… When, therefore, a young person acquires and gratifies a taste for theatrical representations, I consider his moral character in imminent peril…

---

48 It is by no means the author's intention to affirm that all who frequent the theater are vicious [*depraved, evil*] persons. Far be it from him to prefer an accusation as extensive and unfounded as this. No doubt, many amiable and moral persons are among the admirers of dramatic representation. That they receive no contamination from the scenes they witness or the language they hear is no stronger proof that the stage is not immoral in its tendency and effects than that there is no contagion in the plague because some constitutions resist the infection. That persons fenced in by every conceivable moral defense and restraint should escape uninjured is saying little. But even in their case, I will contend that the mind is not altogether uninjured. Is it possible for an imperfect moral creature (and such are the best of us), to hear the irreverent appeals to heaven, the filthy allusions, the anti-Christian sentiments that are uttered during the representation of even our purest plays and hear these for amusement without some deterioration of mental purity?…If it were admitted that occasionally some one person had been improved by theatrical satires on vice (though, by the way, to laugh at vice is not the best way of becoming virtuous), will they not confess that for this one case of improvement, a thousand cases of ruin could be found? (J. A. James, *Youth Warned*)

Who shall depict, in proper colors, the crime of seducing and then abandoning an innocent female? Yet how common it is! She—poor, wretched victim—[is] the dupe of promises never intended to be fulfilled, and at length deserted as a worthless, ruined thing...[if] her betrayer feels a pang of remorse, his pity comes too late for her. It cannot restore the peace that with felon hand he stole from a bosom that was serene until he invaded its tranquility. It cannot repair the virtue he corrupted. It cannot build up the character he demolished...The seducer, I admit, is less guilty than the murderer, but how much less? The latter extinguishes life at once, the former causes it to waste away by slow degrees...The latter hazards his own life in the commission of the crime, the former exposes himself to no personal risk. The latter is visited with the heaviest sentence that the justice of the country can inflict, but the seducer can revel in impunity and can go on from conquering to conquer in his desolating career. [He can] defy all justice but that of heaven. Yes, the guilty and polluted wretch will be greeted in fashionable and moral society with the same welcome as before, though he comes to it with the guilt of female ruin fresh upon his soul...If any individual shall glance on these passages who is guilty of this great transgression, let him ponder on his guilt, and never cease through life to weep for his sin, looking for pardon through the blood of Christ... Pause, young man! Oh! Pause before you resolve to ruin two souls at once and produce an entanglement of sin and misery that eternity itself shall never unravel.[49]

Amidst all your sinful jollity, are you happy, young people, in your sins?... Add up, young people, all the pains of vice—the anxiety that precedes and the remorse that follows it, the stings of conscience and the reproaches of friends, the fear of being detected, and the shame of detection when it has taken place—and say if they do not far overbalance the pleasures of sin... What you need, young people, is regeneration of heart by the Holy Ghost. You must be born again of the Spirit and be renewed in the spirit of your mind. You must have a new heart, a holy bias, a spiritual disposition...You must be brought to fear God as your habitual principle of action and to love Him supremely as the master passion of your soul. Under a deep conviction of sin, you must have *"repentance toward God, and faith toward our Lord Jesus Christ"* (Acts 20:21). You must be justified by faith and have peace with God through our Lord Jesus Christ.

---

[49] I would not throw the blame of seduction entirely on my own sex. There are not a few to whom Solomon's description of the female tempter will apply in this age. (J. A. James, *Youth Warned*)

You must be sanctified by the truth and Spirit of God. Without holiness no man shall see the Lord (Heb. 12:14). The grace of God that brings salvation must teach you not only to deny ungodliness and worldly lusts, but to live soberly, righteously, and godly, in the present evil world (Titus 2:12). Morality alone will not do…It will improve your temporal interests as people; it will lessen your condemnation as sinners, but it will not entitle you to the character of Christians here, nor will it be followed by glory, honor, immortality, and eternal life hereafter. It is extremely probable that if you are satisfied with being moral, to the neglect of piety, you may not long retain even your virtue. Temptations may assail you, too powerful for anything short of that faith in Christ that engages Omnipotence for our defense. In one unguarded moment, you may become the victims of those spiritual enemies that lie in wait to deceive you. God alone can preserve you…

Sin is deceitful, young people…Vice first is pleasing, then it grows easy, then delightful, then frequent, then habitual, then confirmed; then the man is impenitent, then he is obstinate, then he resolves never to repent, and then he is damned.

"Let the wicked forsake his way, and the unrighteous man his thoughts: (and for his encouragement I would add,) *and let him return unto the LORD, and he will have mercy upon him; and to our God, for he will abundantly pardon"* (Isa. 55:7). With the Lord, there is mercy that He may be feared and plenteous redemption that He may be sought unto. Even yet, God waiteth to be gracious. Jesus Christ is *"able also to save them to the uttermost that come unto God by him"* (Heb. 7:25). Pause, consider, repent, believe, and be holy.

From a sermon preached in Carrs Lane Meeting House.

John Angell James (1785-1859): English Congregationalist preacher and author; born at Blandford, Dorsetshire, England.

Persuasions to Sober-mindedness

MATTHEW HENRY (1662-1714)

Young men likewise exhort to be sober minded. —Titus 2:6

Doctrine: it is the great duty of all young people to be sober-minded. I shall endeavor to show you…what it is that we press upon you when we exhort you to be sober-minded. I shall keep to the original word used in my text and the various significations of it. It is the same word that is used to set forth the third part of our Christian duty and is put first of the three lessons that the grace of God teacheth us: to *"live soberly"* (Titus 2:12). In another place, it is put last of three excellent Christian graces: God hath given us the spirit *"of power, and of love, and of a sound mind"* (2 Tim. 1:7)…Give this exhortation its full latitude, and it speaks to you that are young these [following] things:

You must be considerate and thoughtful, not rash and heedless.[50] To be sober-minded is to make use of our reason in reasoning with ourselves and in communing with our own hearts. [It means] to employ those noble powers and capacities by which we are distinguished from and dignified above the beasts for those great ends for which we were endued with them. [This is so] that we may not receive the grace of God in them in vain (2 Cor. 6:1), but being rational creatures may act rationally…as becomes us. You learned to talk when you were children: when will you learn to think—*to think seriously?*…When once you come to see the greatness of that God with Whom you have to do and the weight of that eternity you are standing upon the brink of, you will see it is time to think!

[It is] high time to look about you! Learn to think not only of what is just before you, which strikes the senses and affects the imagination, but also of the causes, consequences, and reasons of things. [Learn] to discover truths—to compare them with one another, to argue upon them and apply them to yourselves, and to bring them to a head. [Do not] fasten upon that which doth come first into your minds, but upon that which *should* come first and that deserves to be first considered. Multitudes are undone because they are *unthinking*. Inconsideration[51] is the ruin of thousands, and many a precious soul perisheth through mere carelessness. *"Now therefore thus saith the LORD of hosts; Consider your ways"* (Hag. 1:5). Retire into your own souls: begin an acquaintance with them. It will be the most profitable acquaintance you can fall into and will turn to the best account…Take time to think, desire to be alone now and then, and let not solitude and retirement be uneasiness to

---

50 **rash and heedless** – reckless and paying no attention.
51 **inconsideration** – thoughtlessness; failing to be considerate of others.

you. For you have a heart of your own that you may talk with, and a God nigh unto you with Whom you may have a pleasing communion.

Learn to think freely. God invites you to do so. *"Come now, and let us reason together"* (Isa. 1:18). We desire not [that] you should take things upon trust, but inquire impartially into them as the noble Bereans, who searched the Scriptures daily, whether those things were so that the Apostles told them (Acts 17:11). Pure Christianity and serious godliness [do not] fear the scrutiny of a free thought, but despise the impotent malice of a prejudiced one...

Learn to think for yourselves—to think of yourselves, to think with application. Think what you are and of what you are capable. Think Who made you, what you were made for, [and] for what end you were endowed with the powers of reason...[Think] therefore whether it be not time—*high time*—for the youngest of you to begin to have faith in Christ and to enter in at the strait gate (Matt. 7:13-14).

[As for] your particular actions...consider what you do *before* you do it that you may not have occasion to repent of it afterwards. Do nothing rashly...Ponder the path of your feet that it may be a straight path. Some people take pride in being careless. Tell them of such and such a thing that they were warned about, [and] they turn it off with this excuse: for their part, they never heed. They mind not what is said to them, nor [have they] thought of it since. So they glory in their shame. But [do not be] thus negligent...There begins to be hope for young people when they begin to set their hearts to all those things that are testified unto them and to think of them with the reason of men and the concern they deserve.

You must be cautious and prudent, not willful and heady.[52] The word in the text is the same that is rendered *"to be discreet"* (Titus 2:5). You must not only think rationally; but when you have done so, you must act wisely...Walk circumspectly:[53] look before you, look about you, look under your feet, and pick your way—*"not as fools, but as wise"* (Eph. 5:15). When he set out in the world, David's purpose was, *"I will behave myself wisely in a perfect way,"* and his prayer was, *"[Lord,] when wilt thou come unto me?"* (Ps. 101:2). Accordingly, we find his purpose performed and his prayer answered: *"David behaved himself wisely in all his ways; and the LORD was with him"* (1 Sam. 18:14)...

Put away childish follies with other childish things, and do not think and speak as children all your days...It is the wisdom of the prudent to

---

52 **willful and heady** – determined to have one's own way; headstrong.
53 **circumspectly** – cautiously; carefully.

Chapter 12—Thoughts for Young People: Persuasions to Sober-mindedness

understand his own way, his own business, [and] not to censure[54] other people's. This wisdom will in all cases be profitable to direct what measures, what steps to take…"My son, be wise…*Wisdom is the principal thing; therefore get wisdom: and with all thy getting get understanding*" (Prov. 27:11; 4:7)… Say not, "I will do so and so. I am resolved…whatever may be said to the contrary! I will walk in the way of *my* heart and in the sight of *my* eyes, whatever it cost me." Never have any will but what is guided by wisdom … Consult with those that are wise and good. Ask them what they would do if they were in your case, and you will find that *"in the multitude of counsellors there is safety"* (Prov. 11:14)…

But would you be wise?—not only to be thought so, but really *be* so? Study the Scriptures. By them, you will get more understanding than the ancients will, than all your teachers will (Ps. 119:99-100). Make your observations upon the carriage and miscarriage[55] of others that you may take a pattern by those that do well and take warning by those that do ill. Look upon both and receive instruction.

But especially be earnest with God in prayer for wisdom as Solomon was. The prayer was both pleasing and prevailing in heaven. If any person, if any young person, *"lack wisdom"* and is sensible that he lacks it, he is directed what to do—his way is plain. *"Let him ask of God"* (James 1:5). He is encouraged to do it, *"For the LORD giveth wisdom."* He has it to give (Prov. 2:6). He delights to give it! He gives liberally. He has a particular eye to young people in the dispensing of this gift, for His Word was written to give to the young man *"knowledge and discretion[56]"* (Prov. 1:4)…There is an express promise to everyone that seeks aright that he shall not seek in vain. It is not a promise with a "peradventure,"[57] but with the greatest assurance: *"It shall be given him"* (James 1:5). To all true believers, Christ Himself is and shall be made of God wisdom (1 Cor. 1:30).

You must be humble and modest,[58] not proud and conceited…It is an observation I have made upon what little acquaintance I have had with the world: I have seen more young people ruined by *pride* than perhaps by any one lust whatsoever. Therefore, let me press this upon you with all earnestness: it is a caution introduced with more than ordinary solemnity. *"For I say, through the grace given unto me, to every man that is among you."*

---

54 **censure** – harshly criticize.
55 **carriage and miscarriage** – behavior and misbehavior.
56 **discretion** – wisdom coupled with a sense of caution.
57 **peradventure** – perhaps; maybe.
58 **modest** – having a moderate estimate of oneself.

Chapter 12—Thoughts for Young People: Persuasions to Sober-mindedness

What is the word that is thus declared to be of divine original and universal concern? It is this: that no man *"think of himself more highly than he ought to think; but to think soberly"* (Rom. 12:3).

Keep up low thoughts of yourselves, of your endowments both outward and inward, of your attainments and improvements, and all your performances—all the things you call merits and excellencies …Let not the handsome glory in their beauty, nor the ingenious[59] in their wit. For there cannot be a greater allay[60] to their glory than to have it said, such and such are comely and witty, but they *know* it …Delight more to say and do what is praiseworthy than to be praised for it. For *"what hast thou that thou didst not receive"* (1 Cor. 4:7)? And what hast thou received that thou hast not abused? Why then dost thou boast?

Keep up a quick and constant sense of your own manifold defects and infirmities. [Consider] how much there is in you, how much is said and done by you every day that you have reason to be ashamed of and humbled for… Dwell much upon humbling considerations and those that tend to take down your high opinion of yourselves. Keep up a humble sense of your necessary and constant dependence upon Christ and His grace, without which you are nothing and will soon be worse than nothing.

Think not yourselves too wise, too good, too old to be reproved for what is amiss, and to be taught to do better. When you are double and treble[61] the age you are, yet you will not be too old to learn and increase in learning. *"If any man think that he knoweth any thing, he knoweth nothing yet as he ought to know"* (1 Cor. 8:2). Therefore, he that seems to be wise—seems so to himself, seems so to others, *"let him become a fool, that he may be wise"* (1 Cor. 3:18)… Be not confident of your own judgment, nor opinionated, nor look upon those with contempt that do not think as you do…Be ashamed of nothing but sin…There cannot be a greater disgrace to you than loose walking. Nor above the exercises of religion, as if it were a thing below you to pray, hear the Word, and join in acts of devotion. For it is really the greatest honor you can do yourselves thus to honor God…

You must be temperate and self-denying, not indulgent of your appetites. It is the same word in the text that is translated "temperate" in verse 2 and is one of the lessons that the aged men must learn. Some think it properly signifies "a moderate use of meat and drink"…Let me therefore warn young men to dread the sin of drunkenness. Keep at a distance from

---

59 **ingenious** – clever.
60 **allay** – diminishing.
61 **treble** – triple.

it. Avoid all appearances of it and approaches towards it. It has slain its thousands, its ten thousands of young people. [It] has ruined their health, brought diseases upon them, and cut them off in the flower of their days. How many fall unpitied sacrifices to this base lust!...You should tremble to think how fatal the consequences of it are—how unfit it renders you for the service of God at night, yea, and for your own business the next morning...and yet that is not the worst: it extinguishes convictions and sparks of devotion and provokes the Spirit of grace to withdraw. It will be the sinner's eternal ruin if it be not repented of and forsaken in time. The Word of God hath said it, and it shall not be unsaid; it cannot be gainsaid[62] that drunkards *"shall not inherit the kingdom of God"* (1 Cor. 6:9)...If you saw the devil putting the cup of drunkenness into your hand, I dare say, you would not take it out of his. You may be sure the temptation to it comes from him. Therefore, [you] ought to dread it as much as if you saw it. If you saw poison put into the glass, you would not drink it. And if it be provoking to God and ruining to your souls, it is worse than poison. There is worse than death: there is hell in the cup. Will you not then refuse it?...Perhaps you have given up your names to the Lord Jesus at His table: dare you partake of the cup of the Lord and the cup of devils? Let Christians that are made to our God kings and priests take to themselves the lesson that Solomon's mother taught him: *"It is not for kings, O Lemuel, it is not for kings"* (Prov. 31:4). So it is not for Christians to drink wine but with great moderation, *"lest they drink, and forget the law"*—forget the Gospel (Prov. 31:4, 5)...Learn betimes[63] to relish the delights that are rational and spiritual, and then your mouths will be out of taste to those pleasures that are brutal and belong only to the animal life. Be afraid, lest by indulging the body and the lusts of it, you come by degrees to the black character of those that were *"lovers of pleasure more than lovers of God"* (2 Tim. 3:4). The body is made to be a servant to the soul, and it must be treated accordingly. We must give it, as we must to our servants, that which is just and equal. Let it have what is fitting, but let it not be suffered to domineer...deny yourselves. So you will make it easy to yourselves and will the better bear the common calamities of human life, as well as sufferings for righteousness' sake. Those that would approve themselves good soldiers of Jesus Christ must endure hardness, must inure[64] themselves to it (2 Tim. 2:3).

---

62 **gainsaid** – contradicted.
63 **betimes** – early.
64 **inure** – become hardened; become accustomed.

Chapter 12—Thoughts for Young People: Persuasions to Sober-mindedness

You must be mild and gentle, not indulgent of your passions.[65] The word here used signifies moderation, such a soundness of mind as is opposed to frenzy and violence…Young people are especially apt to be hot and furious, to resent injuries, and to study revenge…Therefore, the passion is ungoverned because the pride is unmortified. They are fond of liberty, and therefore cannot bear control. [They are] wedded to their own opinion, and therefore cannot bear contradiction. [Yet they] are all in a flame presently if anyone cross *them*…Learn betimes to bridle your anger, to guard against the sparks of provocation that they may not fall into the tinder. If the fire be kindled, put it out presently by commanding the peace in your own souls and setting a watch before the door of your lips. And when at any time you are affronted—or think yourselves so—aim not at the wit of a sharp answer that will stir up anger, but at the wisdom and grace of a soft answer that will turn away wrath (Prov. 15:1)…To all the arguments that reason suggests for meekness, Christianity adds (1) the authority of the God that made us, forbidding rash anger as heart murder; (2) the example of the Lord Jesus Christ that bought us and bids us learn of Him to be meek and lowly in heart; (3) the consolations of the Spirit that have a direct tendency to make us pleasant to ourselves and others; and (4) our experiences of God's mercy and grace in forbearing and forgiving us. Shall this divine and heavenly institution come short of their instructions in plucking up this root of bitterness that bears gall and wormwood? [Shall it not make] us peaceful, gentle, and easy to be entreated, which are the bright and blessed characters of the wisdom from above (James 3:17)?

If you suffer your passions to [gain power] now [while] you are young, they will be in danger of growing more and more headstrong and of making you perpetually uneasy. But if you get dominion over them now, you will easily keep dominion and so keep the peace in your hearts and houses. Through the grace of God, it will not be in the power even of sickness or old age to make you peevish, to sour your temper, or embitter your spirits. Put on therefore among the ornaments of your youth, *"as the elect of God, holy and beloved, bowels of mercies, kindness, humbleness of mind, meekness, longsuffering"* (Col. 3:12). Your age is made for love: let *holy* love therefore be a law to you.

You must be chaste and reserved,[66] not wanton and impure.[67] Both the Greek fathers and philosophers use the word for *chastity*. When it is here

---

65 **passions** – overpowering emotions, such as love, joy, hatred, anger, revenge, etc.
66 **chaste and reserved** – sexually pure and marked by self-restraint.
67 **wanton and impure** – sexually immoral and defiled by sin.

made the particular duty of young men, this signification of the word must certainly be taken for the *"works of the flesh [which] are manifest...Adultery, fornication, uncleanness, [and] lasciviousness"* (Gal. 5:19). [They] are particularly called *"youthful lusts"* (2 Tim. 2:22). And against those, in Christ's name, I am here to warn all you that are young. For God's sake and for your own precious soul's sake, flee these youthful lusts! Dread them as you would a devouring fire or a destroying plague and keep at a distance from them. Abstain from all appearances of these sins: hating even the garment spotted with the flesh, even *"the attire of an harlot"* (Prov. 7:10). Covet not to know these depths of Satan, but take pride in being ignorant of the way of the adulterous woman. See all temptations to uncleanness coming from the unclean spirit, that roaring lion who goes about continually, thus seeking to devour young people (1 Peter 5:8). O that you would betimes conceive a detestation and abhorrence of this sin…Put on a firm and steady resolution in the strength of the grace of Jesus Christ never to defile yourselves with it. [Remember] what the Apostle prescribes as that which ought to be the constant care of the unmarried—to be holy both in body and spirit and so to please the Lord (1 Cor. 7:34).

Take heed of the beginnings of this sin, lest Satan in anything get advantage against you…How earnestly doth Solomon warn his young man to take heed of the baits, lest he be taken in the snares of the evil woman! *"Remove thy way far from her,"* saith he. For he that would be kept from harm must keep out of harm's way! *"Come not nigh the door of her house"* (Prov. 5:8). Go on the other side of the street as thou wouldst if it were a house infected, lest *"thou mourn at the last, when thy flesh and thy body are consumed, and say, How have I hated instruction, and my heart despised reproof"* (Prov. 5:11-12). Pray earnestly to God for His grace to keep you from this sin and that it may be sufficient for you…Get your hearts purified by the Word of God and sanctified by divine love! For how else shall young people cleanse their way, but by *"taking heed thereto according to [the] word"* (Ps. 119:9)?

Make a covenant with your eyes that they may not be the inlets of any impure thoughts or the outlet of any impure desires (Job 31:1). Pray David's prayer, *"Turn away mine eyes from beholding vanity"* (Ps. 119:37) that you may never look and lust.

Modesty[68] is the hedge of chastity, and it is the ornament of your age. Therefore, be sure to keep that up. Let your dress and carriage be very modest, such as speaks [of] *"your chaste conversation[69] coupled with fear"* (1

---

68 See *Christian Modesty and the Public Undressing of America*, available from Chapel Library.
69 **chaste conversation** – pure and respectful behavior.

Peter 3:2). Make it to appear that you know how to be pleasant and cheerful without transgressing even the strictest rules of modesty…

You must be content and easy, not ambitious and aspiring…A sober mind is that which accommodates itself to every estate of life and every event of providence, so that whatever changes happen, it preserves the possession and enjoyment of itself. You that are young must learn betimes to reconcile yourselves to your lot. Make the best of that which is because it is the will of God [that] it should be as it is. What pleaseth Him ought to please us. He knows what is fit to be done and [what is] fit for us better than we do. Let this check all disquieting, discontented thoughts. Should it be according to thy mind? Shalt thou who art but of yesterday control Him, quarrel with Him, or prescribe to Him, Whose counsels were of old from everlasting? It is folly to direct the divine disposals, but wisdom to acquiesce[70] in them.

He Who *"determined the times before appointed, and the bounds of [men's] habitation"* (Acts 17:26) ordered what our rank and station should be in the world, what parents we should be born of, what lot we should be born to, and what our make and capacity of mind and body should be…Some are born to wealth and honor, others to poverty and obscurity. Some seem made and marked by…the God of nature to be great and considerable, while others seem doomed to be little and low all their days…fret [not] at the place God's providence has put you in. Make yourselves easy in it and make the best of it, as those who are satisfied that all is well that God doth—not only in general, but also in particular: all is well that He doth with you. Now you are young: possess your minds with a reverence for the divine providence—its sovereignty, wisdom, and goodness…Reckon your lot best made when you have the Lord to be the portion of your inheritance and your cup (Ps. 16:5). Then say, *"The lines are fallen unto me in pleasant places"* (Ps. 16:6). That is best for you, which is best for your souls. In that, you must soberly rest satisfied…Let young people be modest,[71] moderate, and sober-minded in their desires and expectations of temporal good things, as becomes those who see through them and look above and beyond them to the things not seen that are eternal (2 Cor. 4:18).

You must be grave and serious, and not frothy and vain[72]…I put this last of the ingredients of this sober-mindedness because it will have a very great influence upon all the rest. We should gain our point entirely with young people if we could but prevail with them to be serious. It is serious piety

---

70 **acquiesce** – to remain in quiet submission.
71 **modest** – humble.
72 **frothy and vain** – having no depth of character and silly.

Chapter 12—Thoughts for Young People: Persuasions to Sober-mindedness

we would bring them to…Not that we would oblige young people never to be merry or [that we] had any ill-natured design upon them to make them melancholy. No, religion allows them to be cheerful! It is your time: make your best of it. Evil days will come, of which you will say, *"I have no pleasure in them"* (Eccl. 12:1). When the cares and sorrows of this world increase upon you, and we would not have you to anticipate those evil days…God expects to be served by us with joyfulness and with gladness of heart for the abundance of all things (Deut. 28:47). It is certain that none have such good reason to be cheerful as godly people have! None can be so upon better grounds or with a better grace, so justly or so safely. I have often said—and I must take all occasions to repeat it—that a holy, heavenly life, spent in the service of God and in communion with Him, is without doubt the most pleasant, comfortable life anyone can live in this world.

But that which I would caution you against under this head is vain and carnal mirth—that mirth, that laughter of the fool—of which Solomon saith, *"It is mad…what doeth it?"* (Eccl. 2:2). Innocent mirth is of good use in its time and place. It will revive the spirit and fit you for business. *"A merry heart doeth good like a medicine"* (Prov. 17:22), but then it must be *used* like a medicine. [It] must be taken physically only when there is occasion for it and not constantly like our daily bread…Allow yourselves in mirth as far as will consist with sober-mindedness and no further. Be merry and wise: never let your mirth transgress the laws of piety, charity, or modesty, nor entrench upon your time for devotion and the service of God…

When Christ was here upon earth, healing all manner of sickness and all manner of disease, there was no one sort of patients that He had greater numbers of than such as were lunatic. Their lunacy was the effect of their being possessed with the devil. It was the miserable case of many young people. We find parents making complaints of this kind concerning their children: one has a daughter, another has a son, grievously vexed with a devil. But Christ healed them all, dispossessed Satan, and so restored them to the possession of their own souls. It is said of some whom He thus relieved that they then sat at the feet of Jesus *"clothed, and in [their] right mind"* (Luke 8:35). [*In…right mind*] is the word used in [Titus 2:6 for "sober-minded"]. As far as sin reigns in you, Satan reigns; and your souls are in his possession. By casting out devils, Christ gave a specimen and indication of the great design of His Gospel and grace, which was to cure men of their spiritual frenzy by breaking the power of Satan in them. O that you would therefore apply yourselves to Him, submit to the Word of His grace, pray for the Spirit of His grace. By this it will appear that both these have had their due influence upon you, if you sit at the feet of Jesus in your right mind—*in a sober mind*. And indeed, you never come to your right mind until you do sit down at the feet of Jesus to learn of Him and be ruled by Him. You are never truly *rational* creatures until in Christ you become *new* creatures.

From *"Sober Mindedness Recommended to the Young"* in The Miscellaneous Works of the Rev. Matthew Henry, Vol. 1, published by Robert Carter and Brothers, 1855.

Matthew Henry (1662-1714): Presbyterian preacher, author, and commentator; born at Broad Oak, on the borders of Flintshire and Shropshire, England.

Brothers and Sisters

JOHN ANGELL JAMES (1785-1859)

No family can be happy where a right feeling is lacking on the part of brothers and sisters. Nothing can be a substitute for this defect, and it is of great importance that all young people should have this set in a proper light before them. Many households are a constant scene of confusion, a perpetual field of strife, and an affecting spectacle of misery, through the quarrels and ill will of those, who as flesh of each other's flesh and blood of each other's blood ought to have towards each other no feeling but that of love. [They ought] to use no words but those of kindness…

The general principles that are to regulate the discharge of these duties and on which indeed they rest are the same in reference to all seasons of life. Love, for instance, is equally necessary whether brothers and sisters are sporting[73] together in the nursery, dwelling together as young men and women beneath the parental roof, or descending the hill of life at the head of separate establishments and families of their own…Children of the same parents who are lacking in love are lacking in the first virtue of a brother and a sister as such…

Brothers and sisters should make it a study to promote each other's happiness. They should take pleasure in pleasing each other, instead of each being selfishly taken up in promoting his own separate enjoyment…Envy in children is likely to grow into a most baleful and malignant disposition.[74] They should never take each other's possessions away. [They should] always be willing to lend what cannot be divided and to share what [can be] divided. Each must do all he can to promote the happiness of the whole. They should never be indifferent to each other's sorrows, much less laugh at and sport with each other's tears and griefs. It is a lovely sight to see one sibling weeping because another is in distress…

Brothers and sisters should never accuse each other to their parents nor like to see each other punished. An informer is a hateful and detestable character. But an informer against his brother or sister is the most detestable of all spies. If, however, one should see another doing that which is wrong and which is known to be contrary to the will of their parents, he should first in a kind and gentle manner point out the wrong and give an intimation[75] that if it be not discontinued, he shall be obliged to mention it.

---

73 **sporting** – playing.
74 **baleful and malignant disposition** – harmful and evil character.
75 **intimation** – an act of making something known in an indirect way; a hint.

Chapter 12—Thoughts for Young People: Brothers and Sisters

If the warning be not taken, it is then manifestly his duty to acquaint their parents with the fact.

Brothers and sisters must not tease or torment one another. How much domestic uneasiness sometimes arises from this source! One of the siblings, perhaps, has an infirmity, weakness of temper, awkwardness of manner, or personal deformity; the rest—instead of pitying—tease and torment the unhappy individual…Is this promoting their mutual comfort? As to fighting, quarrelling, or calling ill names—this is so utterly disgraceful that it is a deep shame upon those siblings who live in such practices…

A family of grown-up siblings should be the constant scene of uninterrupted harmony. Love guided by ingenuity [should put] forth all its power to please by those mutual good offices and minor acts of beneficence[76] of which every day furnishes the opportunity. While they cost little in the way of either money or labor, [they] contribute so much to the happiness of the household. One of the most delightful sights in our world…is a domestic circle where the parents are surrounded by their children—the daughters being employed in elegant or useful work and the elder brother reading some instructive and improving volume for the benefit or entertainment[77] of the whole.

Brothers and sisters, seek your happiness in each other's society. What can the brother find in the circle of dissipation[78] or amongst the votaries of intemperance[79] to compare with this? What can the sister find amidst the concert of sweet sounds that has music for the soul compared with this domestic harmony? Or in the glitter and fashionable confusion and mazy dance of the ballroom, compared with these pure, calm, [private] joys, which are to be found at the fireside of a happy family? What can the theater yield that is comparable with this?…

It is of great importance to the pleasant [relationship] of brothers and sisters that each should pay particular attention to the cultivation[80] of the temper. I have known all the comfort of a family destroyed by the influence of one passionate or sullen[81] disposition. Where such a disposition unhappily exists, the subject of it should take pains to improve it. The other branches of the family, instead of teasing, irritating, or provoking it, should exercise

---

76 **beneficence** – doing good.
77 **entertainment** – holding a person's attention agreeably.
78 **circle of dissipation** – crowd who waste money and energy indulging in sensual pleasure.
79 **votaries of intemperance** – those who enthusiastically pursue excessive use of alcohol.
80 **cultivation** – improvement.
81 **passionate or sullen** – hot-tempered or showing hostility by refusal to talk.

all possible forbearance.⁸² With ingenious⁸³ kindness, [they should] help their unfortunate relative in the difficult business of self-control.

Mutual respect should be shown by brothers and sisters. All coarse, vulgar, degrading terms, and modes of address should be avoided. Nothing but what is courteous [should be] either done or said. The [relationship] of such relatives should be marked…by the politeness of good manners, blended with all the tenderness of love. It is peculiarly requisite also, that while this is maintained at home, there should not be disrespectful neglect in company. It is painful for a sister to find herself more neglected than [a total] stranger and thus exposed to others as one in whom her brother feels no interest.

Brothers ought not to be tyrants over their sisters, even in lesser matters. [They ought not to] expect from them the [cringing submissiveness] of slaves. The poor girls are sometimes sadly treated and rendered miserable by the caprice,⁸⁴ freaks,⁸⁵ and iron yoke of some insolent and lordly boy. Where the parents are living, they ought not to suffer such oppression. Let all young women beware of such a despot: he that is a tyrant to his sister is sure to be a tyrant also to a wife…

The responsibility of elder brothers and sisters, especially that of the first-born, is great indeed. The younger branches of the family look up to them as examples, and their example has great influence—in some cases greater than that of the parent. It is the example of one [who is] more upon a level with themselves, more near to them, more constantly before them than that of the parent. On these accounts, [it is] more influential. It is, therefore, of immense consequence to their juniors how these conduct themselves. If they are bad, they are likely to lead all the rest astray. If good, they may have great power in leading them aright. They bring companions, books, recreations before the rest that are proper or improper according as their own taste is.

It is a most distressing spectacle to see an elder brother or sister training up younger ones by his own conduct and precept in the ways of wickedness. Such a youth is an awful character. Like Satan, he goeth about seeking whom by his temptations he may destroy (1 Peter 5:8). But worse, in some respects, [he is] more wicked and more cruel than his prototype:⁸⁶

---

82 **forbearance** – patient self-control.
83 **ingenious** *or* **ingenuous** – noble; honorably straightforward.
84 **caprice** – a sudden change of mind without apparent motive; a whim.
85 **freaks** – unpredictable or unaccountable changes of mind or behavior.
86 **prototype** – the original person of which another is a copy; in this context, Satan.

he marks out his own brother as the victim of his cruelty and the dupe of his wiles.[87] Whole families have in some cases been schooled in iniquity by one unprincipled elder son. What will such a brother have to answer for in the Day of Judgment! What will be his torment in hell, when the souls of those whom he has ruined shall be near him and by their ceaseless reproaches become his eternal tormentors!

In other cases, what a blessing to a family a steady, virtuous, and pious[88] elder brother or sister has been! Many a weak and sickly mother has given daily thanks to God for a daughter, who by her attentions was a kind of second mother to the younger members of the family, for whom she did her uttermost to train them up in her own useful and holy habits. Many a father has felt with equal gratitude the blessing of having in his firstborn son not only a help to himself in the cares of business, but in the work of education—a son who lent all the power of an amiable[89] and religious example to form the characters of his younger brothers.

Let such young persons consider their responsibility. At the same time, let those who are their juniors in the family consider their duty. If they have a good example in their elder brothers and sisters, they should make it not only the object of attention and admiration, but also of imitation. On the other hand, if, unhappily, the conduct of their seniors be bad, let them not follow them in their evil course. Let no threats, no bribes, no persuasions induce them to comply with the temptation to do what is wrong.

I will now suppose the case of one or more branches of the family who are brought by divine grace to be partakers of true religion. [I will] point out what their duty is to the rest and what the duty [is] of the rest to them. In reference to the former, it is manifestly their solemn and irrevocable[90] obligation to seek by every affectionate, Scriptural, and judicious effort the real conversion of those of the family who are yet living without heartfelt religion. O how often has the leaven of piety, when by divine mercy and power it has been laid in the heart of one of the family, spread through nearly the whole household. How often has fraternal love, when it has soared to its sublimest[91] height—with a heaven-kindled ambition aimed at the loftiest object that benevolence can possibly pursue by seeking the salvation of a brother's soul—secured its prize and received its rich reward.

---

87 **dupe...wiles** – victim of his tricks or deceit.
88 **pious** – godly.
89 **amiable** – friendly; kind.
90 **irrevocable** – not able to be changed or reversed.
91 **sublimest** – highest; noblest.

Chapter 12—Thoughts for Young People: Brothers and Sisters

Young people, whose hearts are under the influence of piety, but whose hearts also bleed for those who, though they are the children of the same earthly parent, are not yet the children of your Father in heaven, I call upon you by all the love you bear your brothers and sisters—by all the affection you bear for your parents—by all the higher love you bear to God and Christ—seek by every proper means the conversion of those who, though bound to you by the ties of nature, are not yet united by the bond of grace. Make it an object with you to win their souls. Pray for it constantly. Put forth in your own example all the beauties of holiness. Seek for the most undeviating consistency, since a single [lack] of this would only strengthen the prejudice you are anxious to subdue. Let them see your faith in Christ in your conscientiousness, your joy, your humility, your meekness, your love.

In all the general duties of life, be more than ordinarily exact. Win their affections by the kindest and most conciliating[92] conduct. Avoid all consciousness of superiority. Attempt not to scold them out of their sins. Avoid the language of reproach. Draw them with the cords of love, for they are the bands of a man. Now and then, recommend to their perusal a valuable book. When they are absent, write to them on the subject of faith in Christ; but at the same time, do not disgust them by boring them with [it]. Seize favorable opportunities, and wisely improve them. Point them to eminently happy, consistent, and useful Christians. Comply with all their wishes that are lawful, but give not up one atom of your consistency. Pliancy[93] on your part to meet their tastes and pursuits, if they are contrary to God's Word, will only disgust them: mild firmness will secure their respect. And crown all with earnest prayer for that grace without which no means can be successful. How knowest thou but thou shalt gain thy brother? And O what a conquest!

From *A Help to Domestic Happiness,* reprinted by Soli Deo Gloria, a ministry of Reformation Heritage Books: www.heritagebooks.org.

John Angell James (1785-1859): English Congregationalist preacher and author; born in Blandford Forum, Dorset, England.

Salvation is priceless, let it come when it may; but oh! an early salvation has a double value in it. —Charles Haddon Spurgeon

---

92 **conciliating** – regaining by pleasant behavior.
93 **pliancy** – being easily persuaded.

Standing Fast or Falling Away?
THOMAS VINCENT (1634-1678)

> *Being confident of this very thing, that he which hath begun a good work in you will perform it until the day of Jesus Christ. —Philippians 1:6*

You have heard that the good work that God has begun in the day of grace He will perform until the day of Christ. Yet, lest any should abuse this doctrine and turn the grace of God into wantonness—lest any should, by presuming that the good work has begun in them and thence concluding that they shall never fall away, presume also to indulge themselves in sin and hence take occasion to give way unto licentiousness—I shall add a serious caution unto all, especially to young professors…

Motives to Keep from Apostasy[94] and Backsliding[95]

Some have and [some] may fall and apostatize from the ways of God, who have made a high profession of faith in Christ [and have] attained great illumination, gifts, and tastes of spiritual things. These may have been thought—by others and themselves too—to have stood as surely as any. Therefore, all who think they stand, especially you who are young professors, should take heed lest you fall. The Apostle tells Timothy that Demas had forsaken him, having loved this present world (2 Tim. 4:10). Before that, he tells of Hymenaeus and Alexander, who had put away a good conscience, [had] made shipwreck of the faith, and had learned to blaspheme (1 Tim. 1:19-20). The Apostle Peter speaks in 2 Peter 2:20-22 of some who had escaped the pollutions of the world through the knowledge of Christ, who now were entangled again and overcome. [He says] this was according to the old proverb: *"The dog is turned to his own vomit again; and the sow that was washed to her wallowing in the mire."* Our Savior tells us in His explication[96] of the Parable of the Sower (Matt. 13:20-21) that he who received the Word in stony places is he who hears the Word and receives it with joy. Yet not having any root in himself, he only endures for a while: when tribulation arises because of the Word, by and by he is offended. Indeed, such as have true grace can never totally fall…but many may have that which is *like* true grace and may fall totally from it. They may lose that which they seem to have…

Besides the sin of apostasy itself, which is so heinous, such as are guilty of it usually grow worse than they were before in all kinds of licentious

---

94 *See* FGB 205, *Apostasy.*
95 *See* FGB 197, *Backsliding.*
96 **explication** – a detailed explanation.

conduct. *"When the unclean spirit is gone out of a man, [and returneth again]... he...taketh with himself seven other spirits more wicked than himself, and they enter in and dwell there, and the last estate of that man is worse than the first"* (Matt. 12:43-45). Apostates are the firstborn children of the devil, and the lusts of their father they will do. He dwells in them and rules over them, and they are ready at his motion for any wickedness. Besides uncleanness,[97] debauchery,[98] mischief, villainy,[99] oaths, and blasphemy, such persons usually have the most desperate enmity against God and godliness. Of all others, [they] prove the greatest persecutors of the saints...I do not remember ever hearing or reading of an apostate who has been converted...

Though God will not allow you totally to fall from grace if the good work is in truth begun in you, yet, without great heed, you may fall into great decay of grace...You may, instead of the sweet meltings for sin that you have, grow insensible and contract a great stupidity and hardness of heart. Instead of your pliableness and readiness to spiritual duties, you may contract listlessness and indisposition[100]...Instead of your meek and gentle temper, you may grow peevish and passionate.[101] Instead of your uprightness of heart and your single eye to God's glory, you may spoil most of your duties with hypocrisy. Instead of self-denial and temperance, you may indulge yourself and grow licentious in a great measure. You may lose much of your contentment, patience, and fear of God that you now have. Your hungering desire after Christ may be abated.[102] Your now strong faith may become feeble. Your flames of love may be quenched, the flame quite gone; and only some coals or sparks remain imperceivable under the ashes. Your hopes of heaven may be lost, as to the liveliness and delightful working of them. Therefore, beware lest you fall... You may be kept from falling if you look well to your standing. Whatever your danger is, God can keep you and hold up your goings in His paths so that your footsteps do not slip. *"Now unto him that is able to keep you from falling, and to present you faultless before the presence of his glory with exceeding joy"* (Jude 1:24)...And I shall add that it is more easy (besides the honor brought hereby unto God, and the inexpressible benefit and comfort to yourselves) to stand, not to fall and then to arise and get up when you are fallen. It is no easy thing to recover out of a backsliding state. Such as backslide very much do not usually, easily, or presently recover themselves.

---

97 **uncleanness** – moral impurity.
98 **debauchery** – excessive indulgence in sensual pleasures.
99 **villainy** – evil or wrongdoing of a foul, infamous, or shameful nature.
100 **listlessness and indisposition** – lack of interest and unwillingness.
101 **peevish and passionate** – irritable and hot-tempered.
102 **abated** – reduced in intensity.

Chapter 12—Thoughts for Young People: Standing Fast or Falling Away?

Directions to Keep from Apostasy and Backsliding

Look to it that the good work is indeed begun in your hearts—that you have grace of the right kind. If you should prove unsound in the main points, rotten at the core, false-hearted hypocrites—notwithstanding all your profession—you are in great danger of total apostasy…It is only true grace that is of an establishing nature. *"It is a good thing that the heart be established with grace"* (Heb. 13:9). Only the truly gracious are built upon the Rock of Ages where they are safe. However they may be shaken by troubles and temptations, yet they shall never be utterly cast down and quite overturned…

Stand Not in Your Own Strength

None have fallen more foully than the presumptuous self-confident…Let your confidence and strength be in the Lord. *"Be strong in the grace that is in Christ Jesus"* (2 Tim. 2:1). Have recourse to Him for grace to help in every need and under every assault and temptation that you have to sin. Christ is able to give aid. It is His office to give aid, and He is ready to do so. He pities you when you are tempted and is touched *"with the feeling of [your] infirmities"* (Heb. 4:15). He has [called] you to come unto Him and has promised that He will bruise Satan under your feet shortly (Rom. 16:20). In the meantime, His grace shall be sufficient for you (2 Cor. 12:9).

Beware of worldly-mindedness, so that you are not swallowed up with worldly business and encumbered with the affairs of this life. I am sure this will cause a great decay in the power of godliness. If the world, because of your callings, has most of your time, take heed that it has not all. Reserve some time every day for exercises of faith, and let them have most of your hearts…Endeavor to get the world crucified to you, and your hearts crucified to it. Make use of the cross of Christ in order hereunto, and take frequent view of the transcendent glory and happiness of the other world, which will disgrace the world in your esteem.

Stand Continually Upon Your Watch

Beware of sin in the beginning of it. Do not so much as entertain sin in your minds with any pleasing, delightful thoughts. Refrain from secret sins;[103] otherwise, your feet will slide up before you are aware. Take heed of the least degree of apostasy: observe your hearts when they begin to go off from God, and endeavor with all speed to recover and rise again when you feel yourselves beginning to fall…

---

103 *See* FGB 209 *Secret Sins*.

Set God always before your eyes as David did…[He] tells us that because God was at his right hand, he should not be moved (Ps. 16:8). Temptations to sin will little move you when you actually look to and consider God's eye upon you…*"How then can I do this great wickedness, and sin against God?"* (Gen. 39:9).

Labor for a Strong and Fervent Love to God

Many waters cannot quench the fire of this love. While your hearts are mounting upwards in this flame unto God, you are not in such danger of falling down and giving ear unto temptations that would draw you into sin. Labor to dwell in the love of God and the love of one another. Hereby you will dwell in God and God in you (1 John 4:16). And while you dwell in God, you cannot fall from Him.

Be much in secret conversation with God in meditation, contemplation, short and secret prayers. Go often to your knees when you are alone: there bewail[104] sin and pray for the mortification of your special corruptions. Secret duties seriously, diligently, and constantly performed are both an evidence of sincerity and a great preservative against apostasy.

Lastly, and chiefly, labor for much of the grace of faith and put it forth into daily exercise. *"By faith ye stand"* (2 Cor. 1:24). If you would resist the devil, you must be steadfast in faith (1 Peter 5:8-9). If you would quench his fiery darts you must get on and hold up the shield of faith (Eph. 6:16). If you would be kept by the power of God, it must be through faith unto salvation (1 Peter 1:5). Such as draw back unto perdition, [do so] through unbelief. Such as hold out, it is through faith to the saving of their souls (Heb. 10:39).

From *"Cautionary Motives and Directions unto Youths Professing Religion to Keep Them from Apostasy and Backsliding"* in The Good Work Begun, reprinted by Soli Deo Gloria, a ministry of Reformation Heritage Books: www.heritagebooks.org.

Thomas Vincent (1634–1678): English Puritan minister and author; born in Hertford, Hertfordshire, England.

---

104 **bewail** – express great sorrow for.

No Excuses: Believe the Gospel

CHARLES HADDON SPURGEON (1834-1892)

> *Son of man, behold, they of the house of Israel say, The vision that he seeth is for many days to come, and he prophesieth of the times that are far off.*
> —Ezekiel 12:27

Men display great ingenuity in making excuses for rejecting the message of God's love. They display marvelous skill, not in seeking salvation, but in fashioning reasons for refusing it. They are dexterous[105] in avoiding grace and in securing their own ruin. They hold up first this shield and then the other to ward off the gracious arrows of the Gospel of Jesus Christ, which are only meant to slay the deadly sins that lurk in their bosoms.

The evil argument that is mentioned in the text has been used from Ezekiel's day right down to the present moment. It has served Satan's turn in ten thousand cases. By its means, men have delayed themselves into hell. The sons of men, when they hear of the great atonement made upon the cross by the Lord Jesus and are bidden to lay hold upon eternal life in Him still say concerning the Gospel, *"The vision that he seeth is for many days to come, and he prophesieth of times that are far off."* That is to say, they pretend that the matters whereof we speak are not of immediate importance and may safely be postponed. They imagine that religion is for the weakness of the dying and the infirmity of the aged, but not for healthy men and women. They meet our pressing [call], "All things are now ready, come ye to the supper," with the reply, "Religion is meant to prepare us for eternity, but we are far off from it as yet. [We] are still in the heyday[106] of our being. There is plenty of time for those dreary preparations for death. Your religion smells of the vault and the worm. Let us be merry while we may! There will be room for more serious considerations when we have enjoyed life a little or have become established in business or can retire to live upon our savings…You prophesy of things that are for many days to come and of times that are far off." Very few young people may have *said*…this, but that is the secret thought of many. With this, they resist the admonition of the Holy Ghost, Who saith, *"To day if ye will hear his voice, harden not your hearts"* (Heb. 3:15; 4:7). They put off the day of conversion as if it were a day of tempest and terror and not as it really is—a day most calm, most bright—the bridal of the soul with heaven.

---

105 **dexterous** – skillful.
106 **heyday** – the period when excited feeling is at its height.

Chapter 12—Thoughts for Young People: No Excuses: Believe the Gospel

Let every unconverted person recollect that God knows what his excuse is for turning a deaf ear to the voice of a dying Savior's love. You may not have spoken it to yourself as to put it into words: you might not even dare to do so, lest your conscience should be too much startled—but God knows it all. He sees the hollowness, the folly, and the wickedness of your excuses. He is not deceived by your vain words, but makes short work with your apologies for delay…God knows the frivolity of your plea for delay. He knows that you yourself are doubtful about it and dare not stand to it to give it anything like a solemn consideration. Very hard do you try to deceive yourself into an easy state of conscience concerning it. But in your inmost soul, you are ashamed of your own falsehoods. By the aid of the Holy Spirit, my business at this time is to deal with your consciences and to convince you yet more thoroughly that delay is unjustifiable. For the Gospel has present demands upon you, and you must not say, *"The vision that he seeth is for many days to come, and he prophesieth of the times that are far off."*

Granted for a moment that the message we bring to you has most to do with the future state, yet even then, the day is not far off. Neither is there so great a distance between now and then that you can afford to wait. Suppose that you are spared for threescore years and ten. Young man, suppose that God spares you in your sins until the snows of many winters shall whiten your head. Young woman, suppose that your now youthful countenance shall still escape the grave until wrinkles are upon your brow—still, *how short your life will be!* You, perhaps, think seventy years a long period. But those who are seventy, in looking back, will tell you that their age is an hand's breadth. I, who am but forty, feel at this time that every year flies more swiftly than the last; months and weeks are contracted into twinklings of the eye. The older one grows, the shorter one's life appears. I do not wonder that Jacob said, *"Few and evil have the days of the years of my life been"* (Gen. 47:9), for he spake as an extremely old man. Man is short-lived compared with his surroundings; he comes into the world and goes out of it as a meteor flashes through yonder skies that have remained the same for ages…Stand by some giant rock that has confronted the tempests of the ages, and you feel like the insect of an hour…Therefore do not say, "These things are for a far-off time." For even if we could guarantee to you the whole length of human existence, it is but a span…

You, young men and women, cannot be certain that you shall reach middle life. Let me check myself! What am I talking of? You cannot be certain that you will see this year out and hear the bells ring in a new year! Yea, close upon you as tomorrow is, boast not yourselves of it. It may never come!

Should it come, you know not what it may bring forth to you—perhaps a coffin or a shroud. Ay, and this very night, when you close your eyes and rest your head upon your pillow, reckon not too surely that you shall ever again look on that familiar chamber or go forth from it to the pursuits of life. It is clear, then, that the things that make for your peace are not matters for a far-off time. The frailty of life makes them necessities of this very hour. You are not far from your grave! You are nearer to it than when this discourse began: some of you are far nearer than you think you are.

To some this rejection comes with remarkable emphasis, for your occupation has enough of danger about it every day to furnish death with a hundred roads to convey you to his prison-house in the sepulcher. Can you look through a newspaper without meeting with the words *total* or *sudden death*? Travelling has many dangers, and even to cross the street is perilous. Men die at home; and when engaged about their lawful callings, many are met by death. How true is this of those who go down to the sea in ships or descend into the bowels of the earth in mines! Indeed, *no* occupations are secure from death. A needle can kill as well as a sword. A scald, a burn, a fall may end our lives, quite as readily as a pestilence or a battle. Does your business lead you to climb a ladder? It is no very perilous matter, but have you never heard of one who missed his footing and fell, never to rise again? You work amidst the materials of a rising building: have you never heard of stones that have fallen and have crushed the workers?...Notwithstanding all that can be done by sanitary laws, fevers are not unknown, and deadly strokes that fell men to the ground in an instant, as a butcher slays an ox, are not uncommon. Death has already removed many of your former companions...The arrow of destruction has gone whizzing by your ear to find another mark: have you never wondered that it spared *you*?...How can you say, when we talk to you about preparing to die, that we are talking about things that are far off? Dear souls, do not be so foolish. I implore you [to] let these warnings lead you to [faith in Christ]. Far be it from me to cause you needless alarm—but *is it* needless? I am sure I love you too well to distress you without cause—but *is there* not cause enough? Come now, I press you most affectionately: answer me and say, does not your own reason tell you that my anxiety for you is not misplaced? Ought you not at once to lay to heart [the] Redeemer's call and obey [the] Savior's appeal? The time is short! Catch the moments as they fly and hasten to be blest.

Remember also, once again, that even if you knew that you should escape from accident, fever, and sudden death, yet there is one grand event that we too often forget, which may put an end to your day of mercy [suddenly]. Have you never heard that Jesus Christ of Nazareth was crucified on Calvary, died on the cross, and was laid in the tomb? Do you not know that He rose again the third day and that after He had spent a little while with His disciples, He took them to the top of the Mount of Olives and there before their eyes ascended into heaven, a cloud hiding Him from their view? Have you forgotten the words of the angels, who said, *"This same Jesus, which is taken up from you into heaven, shall so come in like manner as ye have seen him go into heaven"* (Acts 1:11)? Jesus will certainly come a second time to judge the world. Of that day and of that hour knoweth no man—no, not the angels of God. He will come as *"a thief in the night"* to an ungodly world (1Thess. 5:2; 2 Peter 3:10); they shall be *"eating and drinking, and marrying and giving in marriage"* (Matt. 24:38), just as they were when Noah entered into the ark. They knew not until the flood came and swept them all away! In a moment—we cannot tell when: perhaps it may be ere next the words escape my lips—a sound far louder than any mortal voice will be heard above the clamors of worldly traffic, ay, and above the roaring of the sea! That sound as of a trumpet will proclaim the Day of the Son of Man. *"Behold, the bridegroom cometh; go ye out to meet him"* (Matt. 25:6) will sound throughout the Church! And to the world, there will ring out this clarion[107] note: *"Behold, he cometh with clouds; and every eye shall see him, and they also which pierced him"* (Rev. 1:7). Jesus may come tonight. If He were to do so, would you then tell me that I am talking of far-off things? Did not Jesus say, *"Behold, I come quickly"* (Rev. 3:11)! And has not His Church been saying, *"Even so, come, Lord Jesus"* (Rev. 22:20)? His tarrying may be long to us, but to God it will be brief. We are to stand hourly watching and daily waiting for the coming of the Lord from heaven. Oh, I pray you do not say that the Lord delayeth His coming, for that was the language of the wicked servant who was cut in pieces! It is the mark of the mockers of the last days, [who] say, *"Where is the promise of his coming?"* (2 Peter 3:4). Be ye not mockers, lest your bands be made strong. But listen to the undoubted voice of prophecy and of the Word of God: *"Behold, I come quickly"* (Rev. 22:7, 12). *"Be ye therefore ready also: for the Son of man cometh at an hour when ye think not"* (Luke 12:40)…

We are sent to plead with you, young men and women, and tenderly to remind you that at this hour you are acting unjustly and unkindly towards your God. He made you, and you do not serve Him. He has kept you alive, and you are not obedient to Him. He has sent the Word of His Gospel to you, and you have not received it. He has sent His only begotten Son, and you have despised Him…Child of mercy, erring child of the great Father

---

107 **clarion** – loud and clear.

of spirits, canst thou bear to live forever at enmity with the loving Father? "Would He forgive me?" say you. What makes you ask the question? Is it that you do not know how good He is?...Say no longer that we are talking of things of a far-off time!

I have to remind you, however, of much more than this, namely, that you are...in danger. Because of your treatment of God and your remaining an enemy to Him, He will surely visit you in justice and punish you for your transgressions. He is a just God, and every sin committed is noted in His book. There it stands recorded against His Judgment Day. The danger you are in is that you may this moment go down into the pit, and...may bow your head in death and appear before your Maker in an instant to receive the just reward of your sins. We come to tell you that there is immediate pardon for all the sins of those who will believe in the Lord Jesus Christ! If you will believe in Jesus, your sins, which are many, are all forgiven you.

Know ye not the story (ye have heard it many a time) that the Lord Jesus took upon Himself the sins of all who trust Him? [He] suffered in their room and stead the penalty due to their sins. He was our substitute,[108] and as such He died, the just for the unjust, to bring us to God. He laid down His life...that *"whosoever believeth in him should not perish, but have everlasting life"* (John 3:16). Will you refuse the salvation so dearly purchased but so freely presented? Will you not [believe on Him] here and now? Can you bear the burden of your sins? Are you content to abide for a single hour in peril of eternal punishment? Can you bear to be slipping down into the open jaws of hell as you now are? Remember God's patience will not last forever; long enough have you provoked Him...It is a wonder that you do not sink at once to destruction. For this cause, we would have you pardoned now and made free from divine wrath now. The peril is immediate; the Lord grant that so the rescue may be.

Do I hear you say, "But may pardon be had at once? Is Jesus Christ a present Savior? We thought that we might perhaps find Him when we came to die or might obtain a hope of mercy after living a long life of seeking." It is not so. Free grace proclaims immediate salvation from sin and misery. Whosoever looks to Jesus at this very moment shall have his sins forgiven. At the instant he believes in the Lord Jesus, the sinner shall cease to be in danger of the fires of hell. The moment a man turns his eye of faith to Jesus Christ, he is saved from the wrath to come. We preach present salvation to you and the present comfort of that present salvation, too.

---

108 *See* FGB 207 *Substitution.*

The Gospel that we preach to you will also bring you present blessings. In addition to present pardon and present justification, it will give you present regeneration, present adoption, present sanctification, present access to God, present peace through believing, and present help in time of trouble; and it will make you even for this life doubly happy. It will be wisdom for your way, strength for your convictions, and comfort for your sorrows…Young men and women, in preaching to you the Gospel, we are preaching that which is good for *this* life as well as for the life to come. If you believe in Jesus you will be saved now, on the spot, and you will now enjoy the unchanging favor of God, so that you will go your way henceforth not to live as others do, but as the chosen of God, beloved with special love, enriched with special blessings, to rejoice every day until you are taken up to dwell where Jesus is. Present salvation is the burden of the Lord's message to you. Therefore, it is not true, but infamously false, that the vision is for many days to come and the prophecy for times that are far off. Is there no reason in my pleadings? If so, yield to them. Can you answer these arguments? If not, I pray you cease delaying. Again would I implore the Holy Spirit to lead you to immediate [repentance and faith in Christ].

From a sermon delivered on Thursday evening, March 19, 1874, at the Metropolitan Tabernacle, Newington.

Charles Haddon Spurgeon (1834-1892): English Baptist minister; history's most widely read preacher (apart from those found in Scripture); born at Kelvedon, Essex.

Chapter 13
THE LORD'S DAY
INCREASING DELIGHT IN YOUR
FAMILY THROUGH A DAY OF DELIGHT

What does the Sabbath have to do with the family? Exodus 20 and Deuteronomy 5, make it clear that the responsibility for keeping the Sabbath is a family matter. Fathers and mothers are charged to see to it, that everyone in their homes and businesses observe this day of rest. Yes, God desires to govern time in the weekly rhythms of families.

We pray that this chapter will help transform the Sabbath into the day of delight for which it was designed. We also submit it as a testimony regarding the importance of Sabbath keeping in the days of the new covenant.

For those who have a new heart, the Lord's Day truly is "a market-day of the soul." It is designed to serve as a taste of glory divine and of the eternal rest that awaits all of God's elect. It is a way that God has ordained to increase the delight of His people, to re-fashion the thinking of the church, and to revive and set it on a course of justice and righteousness.

This chapter begins with Arthur W. Pink, who gives us a glimpse of the origin of the six-days-of-work and one-day-of-rest pattern that God established in His almighty work of creation. J. C. Ryle offers a multitude of Scriptures from the Old and New Testaments that lay the groundwork for the seventh-day Sabbath and the first-day-of-the-week Lord's Day. Thomas Boston gives a brief exposition of the fourth commandment, while Benjamin B. Warfield lays a biblical foundation for observing the Lord's Day. Why do Christians worship on Sunday instead of Saturday? Archibald A. Hodge helps us to understand the biblical and historical shift from the Sabbath to the Lord's Day. Ezekiel Hopkins then gives us a brief glimpse of how we worship on the Lord's Day in public, while William S. Plumer teaches us that our Lord's Day responsibilities reach into the home. Apart from worship in public and at home, what kind of works should we do on the Lord's Day? Ezekiel Hopkins explains works of piety, necessity, and charity. Thomas Case wisely counsels us in honoring the Father, the Son, and the Holy Spirit on the day of worship. And, finally, Jonathan Edwards makes clear that the Lord's Day was not given to us to be a burden, but a time of most precious enjoyment—truly a market-day of the soul.

—Scott Brown

Established at Creation

ARTHUR W. PINK (1886-1952)

And on the seventh day God ended his work which he had made; and he rested on the seventh day from all his work which he had made. And God blessed the seventh day, and sanctified it: because that in it he had rested from all his work which God created and made.—Genesis 2:2-3

This passage records the institution of the Sabbath.[1] Lest any should wish to cavil[2] because the word sabbath is not found in Genesis 2:2-3, we call attention to the fact that in Exodus 20:11 Jehovah Himself expressly terms that first "seventh day" the "sabbath day": "For in six days the LORD made heaven and earth, the sea, and all that in them is, and rested the seventh day: wherefore the LORD blessed the sabbath day, and hallowed[3] it."

The second chapter of Genesis opens with the words, "Thus the heavens and the earth were finished, and all the host of them." And then, the very next thing we read of is the institution of the Sabbath rest. Thus, to institute the Sabbath was God's first act after the earth had been made fit for human habitation! Let us now point out four things in connection with this first Scripture in which the Sabbath is referred to.

1. The primal[4] Sabbath was a rest day. Emphasis is laid upon this feature by the repetition in thought that is found in the two parts of Genesis 2:2. First, on the seventh day, "God ended his work which he had made"; second, "And he rested on the seventh day from all his work which he had made." Therefore, the prime element and basic truth connected with the Sabbath is rest. Before raising the question as to why God "rested," let us offer a few words upon the nature of His rest.

It has been said repeatedly by a certain class of expositors[5] that this rest

---

1 The Sabbath [did not] originate with Moses or with any sinner. It was an ordinance in Eden. So that the first whole day that man ever spent on earth was in the observance of this holy day. "The Sabbath is but one day younger than man; ordained for him, in the state of his uprightness and innocence that, his faculties being then holy and excellent, he might employ them, especially on that day, in the singular and most spiritual worship of God his Creator" (Ezekiel Hopkins). When, for his sins, man was driven out of Paradise, God permitted him to carry with him two institutions, established for his good before his fall. Which of these institutions is the greatest mercy to our world, or which is the dearest to the heart of a good man, I will not undertake to say. One of them is marriage, the other the Sabbath day. (William Plumer, The Law of God, 294-295)
2 **cavil** – find fault without good reason.
3 **hallowed** – set apart as sacred; made or declared holy.
4 **primal** – belonging to the earliest stage; original.
5 **expositors** – persons that explain the meaning or intent of a text.

of God consisted of His satisfaction in the work of His hands, that it was God looking out in complacency over His fair creation. But, we are told that this "rest" of God did not last for long: it was rudely broken by the entrance of sin; and ever since man fell [into sin,] God has been "working," John 5:17 being appealed to in proof. That such a definition of the "rest" of God in Genesis 2:2 should have been received by a large number of the Lord's people, only goes to show how few of them ever do much thinking or studying for themselves. It also proves how the most puerile[6] interpretations of Scripture are likely to be accepted, providing they are made by reputable teachers, who on other matters are worthy of respect. Finally, it demonstrates what a real need there is for every one of us to humbly, prayerfully, and diligently bring everything we read and hear to a rigid examination in the light of Holy Scripture.

That God's "rest" in Genesis 2:2 was not the complacence of the Creator prior to the entrance of sin is unequivocally[7] evidenced by the fact that Satan had fallen before the time contemplated in that verse. How could God look abroad upon creation with divine contentment when the highest creature of all had become the basest and blackest of sinners? How could God find satisfaction in all the works of His hands when the anointed cherub had apostatized,[8] and in his rebellion had dragged down with him "the third part" of the angels (Rev 12:4)? No, this is manifestly untenable.[9] Some other definition of God's "rest" must therefore be sought.

Now, we need to pay very close attention to the exact wording here (as everywhere). Genesis 2:2 does not say (nor does Exodus 20:10) that God rested from all work, for that was not true. Genesis 2:2 is careful to say, "On the seventh day God ended his work which he had made," and, "He rested on the seventh day from all his work which he had made." And this brings out and calls attention to the basic feature and primal element in the Sabbath: it is a resting from the activities commonly pursued during the six working days. But the Sabbath day is not appointed as a day for the cessation of all activities—to remain in bed and sleep through that day would not be spending the Sabbath as God requires it to be spent…What we now press upon the reader is the fact that, according to Genesis 2:2, the Sabbath rest consists of resting from the labors of the working week.

Genesis 2:2 does not state that on the seventh day God did no work, for,

---

6 **puerile** – childish; immature.
7 **unequivocally** – plainly.
8 **apostatized** – abandoned the faith one had believed in.
9 **untenable** – not able to be defended against objection.

as we have said, that would not have been true. God did work on the seventh day, though His activities on the seventh day were of a different nature from the ones in which He had been engaged during the preceding days. And herein we see not only the marvelous accuracy of Scripture, but the perfect example God here set before His creatures; for as we shall yet see, there are works suited to the Sabbath. For God to have ceased all work on that first seventh day in human history would have meant the total destruction of all creation. God's providential working could not cease, or no provision would be made for the supply of His creatures' wants. "All things" needed to be "upheld" (Heb 1:3), or they would have passed back into nonentity.[10]

Let us fix it firmly in our minds that rest is not inertia.[11] The Lord Jesus has entered into "rest" (Heb 4:10); yet He is not inactive, for He ever liveth "to make intercession." And when the saints shall enter their eternal rest, they shall not be inactive; for it is written, "And his servants shall serve him" (Rev 22:3). So here with God. His rest on that first day was not a rest of total inactivity. He rested from the work of creation and restoration, but He then began (and has never ceased) the work of Providence[12]—the providing of supplies for His myriad creatures.

But now the question arises, Why did God rest on the seventh day? Why did He so order it that all the works recorded in Genesis 1 were completed in six days, and that then He rested? Certainly, it was not because the Creator needed rest, for "the Creator of the ends of the earth, fainteth not, neither is weary" (Isa 40:28). Why, then, did He "rest," and why is it so recorded on the top of the second page of Holy Writ? Surely, there can be only one answer: as an example for man! Nor is this answer merely a logical or plausible inference of ours. It rests on divine authority. It is based directly upon the words of none other than the Son of God, for He expressly declared, "The sabbath was made for man" (Mar 2:27): made not for God, but for man. Nothing could be plainer, nothing simpler, nothing more unequivocal.

2. The next thing that we would carefully note in this initial reference to the Sabbath is that Genesis 2:3 tells us this day was blessed by God: "And God blessed the seventh day." The reason why God blessed the seventh day was not because it was the seventh, but because "in it he had rested." Hence, when the Sabbath law was written upon the tables of stone, God did not say,

---

10 **nonentity** – non-existence.
11 **inertia** – inactivity; unwillingness to move.
12 **Providence** – What are God's works of providence? A: God's works of providence are His most holy, wise, and powerful preserving and governing all His creatures and all their actions. (Spurgeon's Catechism, Q. 11)

"Remember the seventh day to keep it holy," but, "Remember the sabbath day, to keep it holy." And again, He did not say, "He blessed the seventh day and hallowed it," but "the LORD blessed the sabbath day, and hallowed it."

But why should He? Why single out the seventh day thus? Young's Concordance defines the Hebrew word for blessed here as "to declare blessed." But why should God have "declared" the seventh day blessed, for there is no hint that He pronounced any of the other days blessed. Surely, it was not for the mere day's sake. Only one other alternative remains: God declared the seventh day blessed because it was the Sabbath day; and because He would have every reader of His Word know, right at the beginning, that special divine blessing marks its observance. This at once refutes a modern heresy and removes an aspersion[13] that many cast upon God. The Sabbath was not appointed to bring man into bondage. It was not designed to be a burden, but a blessing! And if history demonstrates anything, it demonstrates beyond a peradventure that the family or nation that has kept the Sabbath day holy has been markedly blest of God; and contrariwise, that the family or nation that has desecrated the Sabbath has been cursed of God. Explain it as we may, the fact remains.

3. Genesis 2:3 teaches us that the Sabbath was a day set apart for sacred use. This comes out plainly in the words, "And God blessed the seventh day and sanctified it"…The prime meaning (according to its scriptural usage) of the Hebrew word rendered "sanctified" and "hallowed" is "to set apart for sacred use." This shows that here in Genesis 2:3 we have something more than a historical reference to the resting of God on the seventh day, and something more, even, than God setting an example before His creatures. The fact that we are told God "sanctified" it proves conclusively that here we have the original institution of the Sabbath, the divine appointment of it for man's use and observance. As exemplified by the Creator Himself, the Sabbath day is separated from the six preceding days of manual labor.

4. Let us call attention to a notable omission in Genesis 2:3. If the reader will turn to Genesis 1, he will find that at the close of each of the six working days, the Holy Spirit says, "And the evening and the morning were…" (see Gen. 1:5, 8, 13, 19, 23, 31). But here in Genesis 2:2-3 we do not read, "And the evening and the morning were the seventh day"; nor are we told what took place in the eighth day. In other words, the Holy Spirit has not mentioned the ending of the "seventh day." Why is this? There is a reason for every omission in Scripture, a divine reason, and there is a reason why the Holy Spirit omitted the usual formula at the close of the seventh day. We

---

13 **aspersion** – damaging, abusive speech regarding someone's character.

suggest that this omission is a silent but most significant intimation that the observance of the Sabbath never would end—it was to be perpetuated as long as time should last.

Before we proceed further, let it be said that Genesis 2 contains nothing whatever that enables us to determine which day of our week this primal "seventh day" was. We have absolutely no means of knowing whether that original seventh day fell on a Saturday, a Sunday, or any other day of the week, for the simple reason that we are quite unable to ascertain on which day that first week began. All we do know—and it is all that is necessary for us to know—is that the seventh day was the day that followed six days of manual work…

Ere passing from Genesis 2, let us duly weigh the fact that this notice of the divine institution of the Sabbath is placed almost at the very beginning of Holy Writ. Nothing takes precedence save the brief announcement in the first two verses of Genesis 1 and the description of the six days' work of creation…This at once impresses us with the great importance that God Himself places upon the Sabbath and its observance. Before a single page of human history is chronicled, before a single act of Adam is described, the Holy Spirit places before us the institution of the Sabbath! Does not this signify, plainly, that the observance of the Sabbath—the sanctifying of a seventh day—is a primary duty! Moreover, are we not thereby plainly warned that failure to keep the Sabbath day holy is a sin of the first magnitude!

From The Holy Sabbath, available from Chapel Library.

A.W. Pink (1886-1952): Pastor, itinerate Bible teacher, author; born in Nottingham, England, UK.

Biblical Thoughts About the Lord's Day

J.C. RYLE (1816-1900)

I ask the attention of all professing Christians, while I try to say a few plain words on the subject of the Sabbath. I have no new argument to advance. I can say nothing that has not been said, and said better too, a hundred times before. But at a time like this, it becomes every Christian writer to cast in his mite into the treasury of truth. As a minister of Christ, a father of a family, and a lover of my country, I feel bound to plead in behalf of the old English Sunday. My sentence is emphatically expressed in the words of Scripture: let us "keep it holy." My advice to all Christians is to contend earnestly for the whole day against all enemies, both without and within. It is worth a struggle…

Let me, in the first place, consider the authority on which the Sabbath stands. I hold it to be of primary importance to have this point clearly settled in our minds. Here is the very rock on which many of the enemies of the Sabbath make shipwreck. They tell us that the day is "a mere Jewish ordinance," and that we are no more bound to keep it holy than to offer sacrifice. They proclaim to the world that the observance of the Lord's Day rests upon nothing but Church authority and cannot be proved by the Word of God.

Now, I believe that those who say such things are entirely mistaken. Amiable and respectable as many of them are, I regard them in this matter as being thoroughly in error. Names go for nothing with me in such a case. It is not the assertion of a hundred divines—living or dead—that will make me believe black is white or reject the evidence of plain texts of Scripture… The grand question is, "Were their thoughts worth credit?—were they right or wrong?"

My own firm conviction is that the observance of a Sabbath Day is part of the eternal Law of God. It is not a mere temporary Jewish ordinance. It is not a manmade institution of priestcraft.[1] It is not an unauthorized imposition[2] of the Church. It is one of the everlasting rules that God has revealed for the guidance of all mankind. It is a rule that many nations without the Bible have lost sight of and buried, like other rules, under the rubbish of superstition and heathenism. But it was a rule intended to be binding on all the children of Adam.

What saith the Scripture? This is the grand point after all. What public

---

1 **priestcraft** – influence and work of priests.
2 **imposition** – making something required by a rule.

opinion says or newspaper writers think matters nothing. We are not going to stand at the bar of man when we die. He that judgeth us is the Lord God of the Bible. What saith the Lord?

1. I turn to the history of creation. I read there, "God blessed the seventh day, and sanctified it" (Gen 2:3). I find the Sabbath mentioned in the very beginning of all things. There are five things that were given to the father of the human race in the day that he was made. God gave him a dwelling place, a work to do, a command to observe, a help meet to be his companion, and a Sabbath Day to keep. I am utterly unable to believe that it was in the mind of God that there ever should be a time when Adam's children should keep no Sabbath.

2. I turn to the giving of the Law on Mount Sinai. I there read one whole commandment out of ten devoted to the Sabbath Day, and that the longest, fullest, and most minute of all (Exo 20:8–11). I see a broad, plain distinction between these Ten Commandments and any other part of the Law of Moses. It was the only part spoken in the hearing of all the people; and after the Lord had spoken it, the Book of Deuteronomy expressly says, "He added no more" (Deu 5:22). It was delivered under circumstances of singular solemnity and accompanied by thunder, lightning, and an earthquake. It was the only part written on tables of stone by God Himself. It was the only part put inside the ark. I find the law of the Sabbath side by side with the law about idolatry, murder, adultery, theft, and the like. I am utterly unable to believe that it was meant to be only of temporary obligation.

3. I turn to the writings of the Old Testament Prophets. I find them repeatedly speaking of the breach[3] of the Sabbath side by side with the most heinous[4] transgressions of the Moral Law (Eze 20:13, 16, 24; 22:8, 26). I find them speaking of it as one of the great sins that brought judgments on Israel and carried the Jews into captivity (Neh 13:18; Jer 17:19-27). It seems clear to me that the Sabbath, in their judgment, is something far higher than the washings and cleansings of the ceremonial law. I am utterly unable to believe, when I read their language, that the Fourth Commandment was one of the things one day to pass away.

4. I turn to the teaching of our Lord Jesus Christ when He was upon earth. I cannot discover that our Savior ever let fall a word in discredit of any one of the Ten Commandments. On the contrary, I find Him declaring at the outset of His ministry that He came not to "destroy the law…but to fulfil," and the context of the passage where He uses these words satisfies

---

3 **breach** – breaking.
4 **heinous** – extremely wicked.

me that He was not speaking of the ceremonial law, but the moral (Mat 5:17). I find Him speaking of the Ten Commandments as a recognized standard of moral right and wrong: "Thou knowest the commandments" (Mar 10:19). I find Him speaking eleven times on the subject of the Sabbath, but it is always to correct the superstitious additions that the Pharisees had made to the Law of Moses about observing it and never to deny the holiness of the day. He no more abolishes the Sabbath than a man destroys a house when he cleans off the moss or weeds from its roof. Above all, I find our Savior taking for granted the continuance of the Sabbath when He foretells the destruction of Jerusalem. "Pray ye," He says to the disciples, "that your flight be not in the winter, neither on the sabbath day" (Mat 24:20). I am utterly unable to believe, when I see all this, that our Lord did not mean the Fourth Commandment to be as binding on Christians as the other nine.

5. I turn to the writings of the apostles. I there find plain speaking about the temporary nature of the ceremonial law and its sacrifices and ordinances. I see them called "carnal" and "weak." I am told they are a "shadow of good things to come" (Heb 10:1)—"a schoolmaster to bring us to Christ" (Gal 3:24), and "imposed on them until the time of reformation" (Heb 9:10). But I cannot find a syllable in their writings that teaches that any one of the Ten Commandments is done away. On the contrary, I see St. Paul speaking of the Moral Law in the most respectful manner, though he teaches strongly that it cannot justify us before God. When he teaches the Ephesians the duty of children to parents, he simply quotes the Fifth Commandment: "Honour thy father and mother; (which is the first commandment with promise)" (Rom 7:12; 13:8; Eph 6:2; 1Ti 1:8). I see St. James and St. John recognizing the Moral Law as a rule, acknowledged and accredited among those to whom they wrote (Jam 2:10; 1Jo 3:4). Again, I say that I am utterly unable to believe that when the apostles spoke of the Law, they only meant nine commandments and not ten.

6. I turn to the practice of the apostles, when they were engaged in planting the Church of Christ. I find distinct mention of their keeping one day of the week as a holy day (Act 20:7; 1Co 16:2). I find the day spoken of by one of them as "the Lord's day" (Rev 1:10). Undoubtedly, the day was changed: it was made the first day of the week in memory of our Lord's resurrection, instead of the seventh—but I believe the apostles were divinely inspired to make that change, and at the same time wisely directed to make

no public decree about it.⁵ The decree would only have raised a ferment⁶ in the Jewish mind and caused needless offence; the change was one that it was better to effect gradually, and not to force on the consciences of weak brethren. The change did not interfere with the spirit of the Fourth Commandment in the smallest degree: the Lord's Day, on the first day of the week, was just as much a day of rest after six days' labor, as the seventh-day Sabbath had been. But why we are told so pointedly about the "first day of the week" and the "Lord's Day," if the apostles kept no one day more holy than another, is to my mind wholly inexplicable.

7. I turn, in the last place, to the pages of unfulfilled prophecy. I find there a plain prediction that in the last days, when the knowledge of the Lord shall cover the earth, there shall still be a Sabbath. "From one sabbath to another, shall all flesh come to worship before me, saith the LORD" (Isa 66:23). The subject of this prophecy no doubt is deep. I do not pretend to say that I can fathom all its parts, but one thing is very certain to me: in the glorious days to come on the earth, there is to be a Sabbath, and a Sabbath not for the Jews only, but for "all flesh." And when I see this, I am utterly unable to believe that God meant the Sabbath to cease between the first coming of Christ and the second. I believe He meant it to be an everlasting ordinance in His Church.

I ask serious attention to these arguments from Scripture. To my own mind, it appears very plain that wherever God has had a church, in Bible times, God has also had a Sabbath Day. My own firm conviction is that a church without a Sabbath would not be a church on the model of Scripture.

Let me close this part of the subject by offering two cautions, which I consider are eminently required by the temper of the times.

For one thing, let us beware of undervaluing the Old Testament. There has arisen of late years a most unhappy tendency to slight and despise any religious argument that is drawn from an Old Testament source, and to regard the man who uses it as a dark, benighted, and old-fashioned person. We shall do well to remember that the Old Testament is just as much inspired as the New and that the religion of both Testaments is in the main, and at the root, one and the same. The Old Testament is the gospel in the bud; the New Testament is the gospel in full flower. The Old Testament is

---

5 The Jews had a regard for their Sabbath above almost anything in the laws of Moses… Therefore, Christ dealt very tenderly with them in this point. Other things of this nature we find very gradually revealed. Christ had many things to say, as we are informed, which yet He said not because they could not as yet bear them and gave this reason for it: it was like putting new wine into old bottles (Joh 16:12).—Jonathan Edwards

6 **ferment** – agitation; excitement.

the gospel in the blade; the New Testament is the gospel in full ear. The Old Testament saints saw many things through a glass darkly, but they looked to the same Christ by faith and were led by the same Spirit as ourselves. Let us, therefore, never listen to those who sneer at Old Testament arguments. Much infidelity begins with an ignorant contempt of the Old Testament.

For another thing, let us beware of despising the law of the Ten Commandments. I grieve to observe how exceedingly loose and unsound the opinions of many men are upon this subject. I have been astonished at the coolness with which even clergymen sometimes speak of them as a part of Judaism, which may be classed with sacrifices and circumcision. I wonder how such men can read them to their congregations every week! For my own part, I believe that the coming of Christ's gospel did not alter the position of the Ten Commandments one hair's breadth. If anything, it rather exalted and raised their authority. I believe that, in due place and proportion, it is just as important to expound and enforce them, as to preach Christ crucified. By them is the knowledge of sin. By them, the Spirit teaches men their need of a Savior. By them, the Lord Jesus teaches His people how to walk and please God. I suspect it would be well for the Church if the Ten Commandments were more frequently expounded in the pulpit than they are. At all events, I fear that much of the present ignorance on the Sabbath question is attributable to erroneous views about the Fourth Commandment.

From "The Sabbath" in Knots Untied, in the public domain.

J.C. Ryle (1816-1900): English Anglican Bishop and author; born at Macclesfield, Cheshire County, UK.

The Fourth Commandment

THOMAS BOSTON (1676-1732)

> *Remember the sabbath day, to keep it holy. Six days shalt thou labour, and do all thy work: But the seventh day is the sabbath of the LORD thy God: in it thou shalt not do any work, thou, nor thy son, nor thy daughter, thy manservant, nor thy maidservant, nor thy cattle, nor thy stranger that is within thy gates: For in six days the LORD made heaven and earth, the sea, and all that in them is, and rested the seventh day: wherefore the LORD blessed the sabbath day, and hallowed it.*
> —Exodus 20:8-11

This command respects the time of worship and is the last of the first table, set to join both together, the Sabbath being the bond of all religion. In the words we have,

1. THE COMMAND: It is delivered two ways.

1st, positively: "Remember the sabbath day, to keep it holy." Sabbath signifies rest or cessation from labor. There is a threefold rest or Sabbath spoken of in Scripture: (1) temporal; (2) spiritual, which is an internal soul-rest in ceasing from sin (Heb 4:3); (3) eternal, celebrated in heaven (Heb 4:9, 11), where the saints rest from their labors. It is the first of these, the weekly Sabbath that is here meant. Observe here, (1) Our duty with respect to the Sabbath is to keep it holy. God has made it holy, set it apart for holy exercises, and we must keep it holy, spending it in holy exercises. (2) The quantity of time to be observed as a Sabbath of rest [is] a day—a whole day of twenty-four hours, and one day in seven. They must observe a seventh day after six days' labor, wherein all our work must be done, put by hand, so as nothing of it may remain to be done on the Sabbath. (3) A note of remembrance put upon it: [this] imports that this precept should be diligently observed, special regard paid to it, and due honor put upon this sacred day.

2nd, negatively: Where observe (1) what is forbidden here: the doing of any work that may hinder the sanctifying of this day. (2) To whom the command is directed and who must observe it: magistrates, to whom belong the gates of the city; and masters of families, to whom belong the gates of the house. They must observe it themselves and cause others to observe it.

2. THE REASONS ANNEXED TO THIS COMMAND. None of the commands are thus delivered, both positively and negatively, as this is. And that imports, (1) God is in a special manner concerned for the keeping of the Sabbath, it being that on which all religion depends. Accordingly, as it is observed or disregarded, so it readily goes with the other parts of religion.

(2) People are most ready to halve the service of this day, either to look on resting from labor as sufficient or to look on the work of the day as over when the public work is over. (3) There is less light of nature for this command than the rest: for though it is naturally moral that there should be a sabbath, yet it is but positively moral that this should be one day in seven, depending entirely on the will of God…

First, I am to show that this command requireth the keeping holy to God such set times as He hath appointed in His Word. The Jews under the Old Testament had several days beside the weekly Sabbath that by divine appointment were to be kept as holy days. By virtue of this command, they were to observe them, even as by virtue of the second they were to observe the sacrifices and other parts of the Old Testament instituted worship. But these days are taken away under the gospel by the coming of Christ.

But that which this command requires in the first place is the keeping holy of a sabbath to God: whatever be the day, God determines it, whether the seventh in order from the creation, as under the Old Testament, or the first, as under the New. And so the command is "Remember the sabbath day to keep it holy," not "Remember the seventh day." Thus, the keeping of a sabbath is a moral duty binding all persons in all places of the world.

For it is a moral duty and by the natural law required that as God is to be worshipped—not only internally, but externally, not only privately, but publicly—so there must be some special time designed and set apart for this, without which it cannot be done. And so the very pagans had their sabbaths and holidays. This is the first thing imported[1] here: a sabbath is to be kept.

Another thing imported here is that it belongs to God to determine the Sabbath, or what day or days He will have to be kept holy. He says not, "Remember to keep holy a sabbath day," or "a day of rest," leaving it to men what days should be holy and what not; but, "Remember the sabbath day," supposing the day to be already determined by Himself. So that we are bound to set time appointed in His Word.

And this condemns men's taking on themselves, whether churches or states, to appoint holidays to be kept that God has not appointed in His Word. Consider, (1) This command puts a peculiar honor on the Sabbath above all other days: "Remember the sabbath day." But when men make holidays of their own to be kept holy, the day appointed of God is spoiled of its peculiar honor, and there is no peculiar honor left to it (Eze 43:8). Yea, in practice, they go before it: men's holidays, where they are regarded, are more regarded than God's day. (2) This command says, "Six days shalt

---

1 **imported** – brought in; introduced.

thou labour." Formalists say, "There are many of these six days thou shalt not labor, for they are holy days. If these words contain a command, who can countermand it? If but a permission, who can take away that liberty that God has left us?" As for fast-days or thanksgiving days occasionally appointed that are not holy days, the worship is not made to wait on the days as on sabbaths and holidays, but the days on the worship that God by His providence requires. Consequently, there must be a time for performing these exercises. (3) It belongs only to God to make a holy day. For who can sanctify a creature but the Creator or time but the Lord of time? He only can give the blessing: why should they that cannot bless it then sanctify a day? The Lord abhors holy days devised out of men's own hearts (1Ki 12:33). (4) What reason is there to think that when God has taken away from the Church's neck a great many holy days appointed by Himself, He has left the gospel-church to be burdened with as many, nay, and more of men's invention than He Himself had appointed?

Secondly, this command requires one day in seven to be kept as a holy sabbath unto the Lord. "Six days shalt thou labour, and do all thy work: But the seventh day is the sabbath of the LORD thy God." Thus, the Lord determines the quantity of time that is to be His own, in a peculiar manner, that is, the seventh part of our time. After six days working, a seventh is to be a sabbath. This is moral, [obligating] all persons in all ages, and not a ceremony abrogated[2] by Christ. (1) This command of appointing one day in seven for a sabbath is one of the commands of that Law, consisting of ten commands, which…[was] written on tables of stone, to show the perpetuity of it, and of which Christ says, "Think not that I am come to destroy the law, or the prophets: I am not come to destroy, but to fulfil. For verily I say unto you, Till heaven and earth pass, one jot or one tittle shall in no wise pass from the law, till all be fulfilled. Whosoever therefore shall break one of these least commandments, and shall teach men so, he shall be called the least in the kingdom of heaven: but whosoever shall do and teach them, the same shall be called great in the kingdom of heaven" (Mat 5:17-19). (2) It was appointed and given of God to Adam in innocence before there was any ceremony to be taken away by the coming of Christ (Gen 2:3). (3) All the reasons annexed to this command are moral, respecting all men, as well as the Jews to whom the ceremonial law was given. And we find strangers obliged to the observation of it, as well as the Jews; but they were not so to ceremonial laws. (4) Jesus Christ speaks of it as a thing perpetually to endure, even after the Jewish Sabbath was over and gone (Mat 24:20). Although the

---

2 **abrogated** – abolished authoritatively; done away with.

Sabbath of the seventh day in order from the creation was changed into the first day, yet still it was kept a seventh day.

Thirdly, the day to be kept holy is one whole day—not a few hours, while the public worship lasts, but a whole day. There is an artificial day between sun rising and sun setting (Joh 11:9) and a natural day of twenty-four hours (Gen 1), which is the day here meant. This day we begin in the morning, immediately after midnight; and so does the Sabbath begin, and not in the evening, as is clear, if ye consider, (1) John 20:19: "Then the same day at evening, being the first day of the week," where ye see that the evening following, not going before this first day of the week, is called the evening of the first day. (2) Our Sabbath begins where the Jewish Sabbath ended; but the Jewish Sabbath did not end towards the evening, but towards the morning: "In the end of the sabbath, as it began to dawn toward the first day of the week" (Mat 28:1). (3) Our Sabbath is held in memory of Christ's resurrection, and it is certain that Christ rose early in the morning of the first day of the week.

Let us therefore take the utmost care to give God the whole day—spending it in the manner He has appointed—and not look on all the time, besides what is spent in public worship, as our own, which is too much the case in these degenerate times wherein we live.

From The Works of Thomas Boston, Vol. 2, in the public domain.

Thomas Boston (1676-1732): Scottish Presbyterian minister and theologian; born in Duns, Berwickshire, Scotland.

Foundations of The Lord's Day

BENJAMIN B. WARFIELD (1851-1921)

When we wish to remind ourselves of the foundations of the Sabbath in the Word of God, it is naturally to the Decalogue[1] that we go first. There we read the fundamental commandment that underlay the Sabbath of which our Lord asserted Himself to be the Lord, and the divine authority and continued validity of which He recognized and reaffirmed when He announced Himself Lord of the Sabbath established by it.

The Ten Commandments were, of course, given to Israel; and they are couched in language that could only be addressed to Israel. They are introduced by a preface adapted and doubtless designed to give them entrance into the hearts of precisely the Israelitish people, as the household ordinances of their own God—the God to Whom they owed their liberation from slavery and their establishment as a free people: "I am the LORD thy God, which have brought thee out of the land of Egypt, out of the house of bondage" (Exo 20:2). This intimacy of appeal specifically to Israel is never lost throughout the whole document. Everywhere it has just Israel in mind, and in every part of it, it is closely adapted to the special circumstances of Israel's life. We may, therefore, read off from its texts many facts about Israel…We may learn from it also that Israel was a people to whom the Sabbath was already known, and which needed not to be informed, but only to be reminded of it: "Remember the sabbath day" (Exo 20:8).

Nothing can be clearer, then, than that the Ten Commandments are definitely addressed to the Israelitish people and declare the duties peculiarly incumbent[2] upon them, unless it be even clearer that these duties, declared thus to be peculiarly incumbent upon the Israelitish people, are not duties peculiar to that people. Samuel R. Driver[3] describes the Ten Commandments as "a concise but comprehensive summary of the duties of the Israelite towards God and man…" It does not appear but that this is a very fair description of them. They are addressed to the Israelite. They give him a concise but comprehensive summary of his duties towards God and man. But the Israelite, too, is a man. And it ought not to surprise us to discover that the duties of the Israelite towards God and man, when summarily stated, are just the fundamental duties that are owed to God and man by every man, whether Greek or Jew, circumcision or uncircumcision,

---

1 **Decalogue** – Ten Commandments.
2 **incumbent** – necessary as obligation or duty.
3 **Samuel Rolles Driver** (1846-1914) – English theologian and Hebrew scholar.

barbarian, Scythian, bond or free. Such, at all events, is, in fact, the case. There is no duty imposed upon the Israelite in the Ten Commandments that is not equally incumbent upon all men everywhere. These commandments are but the positive publication to Israel of the universal human duties, the common morality of mankind.

It was not merely natural but inevitable that in this positive proclamation of universal human duties to a particular people, a special form should be given their enunciation[4] specifically adapting them to this particular people in its peculiar circumstances; and it was eminently desirable that they should be so phrased and so commended as to open a ready approach for them to this particular people's mind and to bring them to bear with special force upon its heart. This element of particularity embedded in the mode of their proclamation, however, has no tendency to void these commandments of their intrinsic[5] and universal obligation. It only clothes them with an additional appeal to those to whom this particular proclamation of them is immediately addressed. It is not less the duty of all men to do no murder, not to commit adultery, not to steal, not to bear false witness, not to covet a neighbor's possession that the Israelite too is commanded not to do these things and is urged to withhold himself from them by the moving plea that he owes a peculiar obedience to a God Who has dealt with him with distinguishing grace. And it is not less the duty of all men to worship none but the one true God and Him only with spiritual worship; not to profane His name nor to withhold from Him the time necessary for His service or refuse to reverence Him in His representatives that these duties are impressed especially on the heart of the Israelite by the great plea that this God has shown Himself in a peculiar manner His God. The presence of the Sabbath commandment in the midst of this series of fundamental human duties, singled out to form the compact core of the positive morality divinely required of God's peculiar people is rather its commendation to all peoples of all times as an essential element in primary human good conduct.

It is clearly this view of the matter that was taken by our Lord…He tells us explicitly that His mission as regards the Law was not to abrogate it, but "to fulfil it," that is to say, "to fill it out," complete it, develop it into its full reach and power. The Law, He declares in the most solemn manner, is not susceptible of being done away with, but shall never cease to be authoritative and obligatory. "For verily I say unto you" (Mat 5:18), He says, employing for the first time in the record of His sayings that have come down to us, this

---

4 **enunciation** – formal declaration.
5 **intrinsic** – belonging to something as a basic and essential feature of what it is.

formula of solemn asseveration:⁶ "Till heaven and earth pass, one jot or one tittle shall in no wise pass from the law, till all be fulfilled." So long as time endures, the Law shall endure in full validity, down to its smallest details… Now, the Law of which our Lord makes this strong assertion of its ever-abiding validity includes, as one of its prominent constituent parts, just the Ten Commandments. For, as He proceeds to illustrate His statements from instances in point, showing how the Law is filled out, completed by Him, He begins by adducing instances⁷ from the Ten Commandments: "Thou shalt not kill" (Mat 5:21); "Thou shalt not commit adultery" (Mat 5:27). It is with the Ten Commandments clearly in His mind, therefore, that He declares that no jot or tittle of the Law shall ever pass away, but it all must be fulfilled.

Like Master, like disciple: There is an illuminating passage in the Epistle of James in which the Law is so adverted to⁸ as to throw a strong emphasis on its unity and its binding character in every precept of it. "For whosoever shall keep the whole law," we read, "and yet offend in one point, he is guilty of all" (Jam 2:10)…If then, we keep the Law, indeed, in general but fail in one precept, we have broken not that precept only, but the whole Law of which that precept is a portion…Now, the matter of special interest to us is that James illustrates this doctrine from the Ten Commandments. It is the same God, he declares, Who has said, "Thou shalt not commit adultery, and thou shalt not kill." If we do not commit adultery but kill, we are transgressors of the holy will of this God, expressed in all the precepts and not merely in one. It is obvious that James might have taken any others of the precepts of the Decalogue to illustrate his point—the Fourth as well as the Sixth or Seventh. The Decalogue evidently lies in his mind as a convenient summary of fundamental duty; and he says in effect that it is binding on us all, in all its precepts alike, because they all alike are from God and publish His holy will.

An equally instructive allusion to the Decalogue meets us in Paul's letter to the Romans (Rom 13:8-10). Paul is dwelling on one of his favorite themes—love as the fulfilment of the Law. "Love worketh no ill to his neighbour," he says, "Love worketh no ill to his neighbour" (Rom 13:10). For, all the precepts of the Law—he is thinking here only of our duties to our fellowmen—are summed up in the one commandment, "Love worketh no ill to his neighbour" (Rom 13:9). To illustrate this proposition, he enumerates some of the relevant precepts. They are taken from the second table of the Decalogue: "Thou shalt not commit adultery, Thou shalt not

---

6 **asseveration** – forcible, definite declaration.
7 **adducing instances** – bringing forward examples for consideration.
8 **adverted to** – referred to.

kill, Thou shalt not steal, Thou shalt not bear false witness, Thou shalt not covet" (13:9). Clearly, the Ten Commandments stand in Paul's mind as a summary of the fundamental principles of essential morality and are, as such, of eternal validity. When he declares that love is the fulfilment of these precepts, he does not mean, of course, that love supersedes them, so that we may content ourselves with loving our neighbor and not concern ourselves at all with the details of our conduct toward him. What he means is the precise contrary of this: he who loves his neighbor has within him a spring of right conduct towards his neighbor, which will make him [eager] to fulfil all his duties to him. Love does not abrogate but fulfils the Law.

Paul was not the originator of this view of the relation of love to the Law. Of his Master before him we read, "Jesus said unto him, Thou shalt love the Lord thy God with all thy heart, and with all thy soul, and with all thy mind. This is the first and great commandment" (Mat 22:37-38). "And the second is like unto it, Thou shalt love thy neighbour as thyself. On these two commandments hang all the law and the prophets" (Mat 22:39-40)… Love, again, means not the abrogation but the fulfilment of the law.

It cannot be necessary to multiply examples. Nothing could be clearer than that our Lord and the writers of the New Testament treated the Ten Commandments as the embodiment—in a form suited to commend them to Israel—of the fundamental elements of essential morality, authoritative for all time and valid in all the circumstances of life. All the references made to them have as their tendency not to discredit them, but to cleanse them from the obscuring accretions[9] of years of more or less uncomprehending and unspiritual tradition, and penetrating to their core, to throw up into high light their purest ethical content. Observe how our Lord deals with the two commandments—"Thou shalt not kill, thou shalt not commit adultery"—in the passage near the beginning of the Sermon on the Mount, to which we have already had occasion to allude. Everything external and mechanical in the customary application of these commandments is swept away at once; the central moral principle is seized with firmness and…is developed without hesitation into its uttermost manifestations. Murder, for example, is discovered in principle already in anger, and not in anger only, but even in harsh language—adultery, in the vagrant[10] impulses of the mind and senses, and in every approach to levity[11] in the treatment of the marriage tie. There

---

9 **obscuring accretions** – made unclear and difficult to understand by increasing layers of tradition.
10 **vagrant** – straying; wandering.
11 **levity** – lack of care in making and breaking promises; unbecoming freedom of conduct.

is no question here of abrogating these commandments or of limiting their application. One might say rather that their applications are immensely extended, though "extended" is not quite the right word—say rather, deepened. They seem somehow to be enriched and ennobled in our Lord's hands, made more valuable and [fertile], increased in beauty and splendor. Nothing really has happened to them. But our eyes have been opened to see them as they are—purely ethical precepts, declaring fundamental duties and declaring them with that clean absoluteness that covers all the ground.

We have no such formal commentary from our Lord's lips on the Fourth Commandment. But we have the commentary of His life, and that is quite as illuminating and to the same deepening and ennobling effect. There was no commandment that had been more overlaid in the later Jewish practice with mechanical incrustations.[12] Our Lord was compelled, in the mere process of living, to break His way through these and to uncover to the sight of man ever more and more clearly the real Law of the Sabbath—the Sabbath that was ordained of God, and of which He, the Son of Man, is Lord. Thus, we have from Him a series of crisp declarations, called out as occasion arose, the effect of which in the mass is to give us a comment on this commandment altogether similar in character to the more formal expositions of the Sixth and Seventh Commandments.

Among these, such a one as this stands out with great emphasis: "It is lawful to do good on the Sabbath day." And this will lead us naturally to this broad proclamation: "My Father worketh hitherto, and I work" (Joh 5:17). Obviously, the Sabbath, in our Lord's view, was not a day of sheer idleness: inactivity was not its mark. Inactivity was not the mark of God's Sabbath when He rested from the works that He creatively made. Up to this very moment, He has been working continuously; and, imitating Him, our Sabbath is also to be filled with work. God rested, not because He was weary or needed an intermission in His labors, but because He had completed the task He had set for Himself (we speak as a man) and had completed it well. "And God saw every thing that he had made, and, behold, it was very good... God ended his work which he had made" (Gen 1:31, 2:2). He was now ready to turn to other work. And we, like Him, are to do our appointed work—"Six days shalt thou labour, and do all thy work" (Exo 20:9)—and then, laying it well aside, turn to another task. It is not work as such, but our own work from which we are to cease on the Sabbath. "Six days shalt thou labor and do all thy work," says the commandment; or, as Isaiah puts it: "If thou turn away thy foot from the sabbath" (that is, from trampling it down), "from

---

12 **mechanical incrustations** – legalistic, hard crusty layers of tradition.

doing thy pleasure on my holy day" (that is the way we trample it down); "and call the sabbath a delight, the holy (day) of the LORD, honourable; and shalt honour him, not doing thine own ways, nor finding thine own pleasure, nor speaking thine own words: Then shalt thou delight thyself in the LORD; and I will cause thee to ride upon the high places of the earth, and feed thee with the heritage of Jacob thy father: for the mouth of the LORD hath spoken it" (Isa 58:13-14).

In one word, the Sabbath is the Lord's Day, not ours; and on it is to be done the Lord's work, not ours; that is our "rest"…Rest is not the true essence of the Sabbath or the end of its institution; it is the means to a further end, which constitutes the real Sabbath "rest." We are to rest from our own things that we may give ourselves to the things of God.

The Sabbath came out of Christ's hands, we see then, not despoiled[13] of any of its authority or robbed of any of its glory, but rather enhanced in both authority and glory. Like the other commandments, it was cleansed of all that was local or temporary in the modes in which it had hitherto been commended to God's people in their isolation as a nation and stood forth in its universal ethical content. Among the changes in its external form that it thus underwent was a change in the day of its observance. No injury was thus done the Sabbath as it was commended to the Jews, rather a new greatness was brought to it. Our Lord, too, following the example of His Father, when He had finished the work that it had been given Him to do, rested on the Sabbath—in the peace of His grave. But He had work yet to do. And, when the first day of the new week dawned, which was the first day of a new era—the era of salvation—He rose from the Sabbath rest of the grave and made all things new. As C. F. Keil beautifully puts it, "Christ is Lord of the Sabbath (Mat 12:8), and after the completion of His work, He also rested on the Sabbath. But He rose again on Sunday; and through His resurrection, which is the pledge to the world of the fruits of His redeeming work, He has made this day the Lord's Day for His Church, to be observed by [her] till the Captain of [her] salvation shall return, and having finished the judgment upon all His foes to the very last shall lead [her] to the rest of that eternal Sabbath, which God prepared for the whole creation through His own resting after the completion of the heaven and the earth."[14] Christ took the Sabbath into the grave with Him and brought the Lord's Day out of the grave with Him on the resurrection morn.

---

13 **despoiled** – stripped.
14 **Carl Friedrich Keil** (1807-1888) and Franz Delitzsch (1813-1890), Commentary on the Old Testament, vol. 1, 400; Keil and Delitzsch were Lutheran commentators.

Chapter 13—The Lord's Day: Foundations of The Lord's Day

It is true enough that we have no record of a commandment of our Lord's requiring a change in the day of the observance of the Sabbath. Neither has any of the apostles to whom He committed the task of founding His Church given us such a commandment. By their actions, nevertheless, both our Lord and His apostles appear to commend the first day of the week to us as the Christian Sabbath. It is not merely that our Lord rose from the dead on that day: a certain emphasis seems to be placed precisely upon the fact that it was on the first day of the week that He rose. This is true of all the accounts of His rising. Luke, for example, after telling us that Jesus rose "on the first day of the week" (Luk 24:1) on coming to add the account of His appearing to the two disciples journeying to Emmaus, throws what almost seems to be superfluous[15] stress on that also having happened "on that very day." It is in John's account, however, that this emphasis is most noticeable. "The first day of the week," he tells us, "cometh Mary Magdalene early" to find the empty tomb. And then, a little later: "Then the same day at evening, being the first day of the week," Jesus showed Himself to His assembled followers…After thus pointedly indicating that it was on the evening of precisely the first day of the week that Jesus first showed Himself to His assembled disciples, John proceeds equally sharply to define the time of His next showing Himself to them as "after eight days." That is to say, it was on the next first day of the week that "again his disciples were within" (Joh 20:26), and Jesus manifested Himself to them. The appearance is strong that our Lord, having crowned the day of His rising with manifestations, disappeared for a whole week to appear again only on the next Sabbath…There is an appearance, at least, that the first day of the week was becoming under this direct sanction of the risen Lord the appointed day of Christian assemblies.

That the Christians [had been driven early] to separate themselves from the Jews (see Acts 19:9) and had soon established regular times of "the assembling of ourselves together," we know from an exhortation in the Epistle to the Hebrews (Heb 10:25). A hint of Paul's suggests that their ordinary day of assembly was on the first day of the week (1Co 16:2). It is clear from a passage in Acts 20:7 that the custom "upon the first day of the week, when the disciples came together to break bread" was so fixed in the middle of the period of Paul's missionary activity that, though in haste, he felt constrained to tarry a whole week in Troas that he might meet with the brethren on that day…We learn from a passing reference in the Apocalypse (1:10) that the designation "the Lord's day" had already established itself in Christian usage…With such suggestions behind us, we cannot wonder that

---

15 **superfluous** – beyond what is required; unnecessary.

the Church emerges from the Apostolic Age with the first day of the week firmly established as [her] day of religious observance…

If we wish, however, fully to apprehend how Paul was accustomed to Christianize and universalize the Ten Commandments while preserving nevertheless intact their whole substance and formal authority, we should turn over the page and read this: "Children, obey your parents in the Lord: for this is right. Honour thy father and mother; (which is the first commandment with promise;) That it may be well with thee, and thou mayest live long on the earth" (Eph 6:1-3). Observe, first, how the Fifth Commandment is introduced here as the appropriate proof that obedience to parents is right. Having asserted it to be right, Paul adduces the commandment that requires it. Thus, the acknowledged authority of the Fifth Commandment as such in the Christian Church is simply taken for granted. Observe, secondly, how the authority of the Fifth Commandment—thus assumed as unquestionable—is extended over the whole Decalogue. For this commandment is not adduced here as an isolated precept: it is brought forward as one of a series in which it stands on equal ground with the others, differing from them only in being the first of them that has a promise attached to it—"which is the first commandment with promise." Observe, thirdly, how everything in the manner in which the Fifth Commandment is enunciated in the Decalogue that gives it a form and color adapting it specifically to the Old Dispensation is quietly set aside and a universalizing mode of statement substituted for it: "That it may be well with thee, and thou mayest live long on the earth" (Eph 6:3). All allusion to Canaan—the land that Jehovah, Israel's God, had promised to Israel—is eliminated and with it all that gives the promise or the commandment to which it is annexed any appearance of exclusive application to Israel. In its place is set a broad declaration valid not merely for the Jew who worships the Father in Jerusalem, but for all those true worshippers everywhere who worship Him in spirit and in truth (Joh 4:24). This may seem the more remarkable because Paul, in adducing the commandment, calls special attention to this promise, and that in such a manner as to appeal to its divine origin. It is quite clear that he was thoroughly sure of his ground with his readers [Gentiles]. And that means that the universalizing reading of the Ten Commandments was the established custom of the Apostolic Church.

Can we doubt that as Paul, and the whole Apostolic Church with him, dealt with the Fifth Commandment, so he dealt with the Fourth? That he preserved to it its whole substance and its complete authority, but eliminated from it, too, all that tended to give it a local and temporary reference? And why should this not have carried with it, as it certainly seems to have carried with it, the substitution for the day of the God of Israel (Who brought His people out of the land of Egypt, out of the house of bondage) the day of the Lord Jesus (Who brought them out of worse bondage than that of Egypt by a greater deliverance, a deliverance of which that from Egypt was but a type)? Paul would be dealing with the Fourth Commandment precisely as he deals with the Fifth, if he treated the shadow-Sabbath as a matter of indifference and brought the whole obligation of the commandment to bear upon keeping holy to the Lord the new Lord's Day, the monument of the second and better creation.

That this was precisely what he did, and with him the whole Apostolic Church, there seems no room to question. And the meaning of that is that the Lord's Day is placed in our hands by the authority of the apostles of Christ, under the undiminished sanction of the eternal Law of God.

From Sunday: The World's Rest Day, in the public domain.

Benjamin Breckinridge Warfield (**1851-1921**): Presbyterian professor of theology at Princeton Seminary; born near Lexington, KY, USA.

From Sabbath to Lord's Day

ARCHIBALD A. HODGE (1823-1886)

Remember the sabbath day, to keep it holy. —Exodus 20:8

The object of this [article] is simply to state the grounds upon which the faith of the universal Church rests when, while recognizing the Fourth Commandment as an integral part of the supreme, universal, and unalterable Moral Law, she affirms that the first day of the week has for this purpose—and for obvious reasons—been substituted for the seventh by the authority of the inspired apostles and, therefore, of Christ Himself.

1. Observe that the particular day of the week on which the Sabbath is to be kept, although fixed for revealed reasons by the will of God at the creation, never was or could be of the essence of the institution itself. The command to observe the Sabbath is essentially as moral and immutable as the commands to abstain from stealing, killing, or adultery. It has, like them, its ground in the universal and permanent constitution and relations of human nature. It was designed to meet the physical, moral, spiritual, and social wants of men; to afford a suitable time for the public moral and religious instruction of the people and the public and private worship of God; and to afford a suitable period of rest from the wear and tear of secular labor. That a certain proper proportion of time—regularly recurring and observed in common by the community of Christian people and of Christian nations—should be appointed and its observance rendered obligatory by divine authority is therefore the very essence of the institution. These essential elements are found unchanged under both dispensations.[1]

The Sabbath, as divinely ordained in the Old Testament, is just what all men need today. It was commanded that all should cease from worldly labor and keep the time holy in devoting it to the worship of God and the good of men. The services of the temple were redoubled;[2] and, afterward, the instructions and worship of the synagogue were introduced. It was granted to the people and to their servants and beasts as a privilege, not as a burden (Deu 5:12-15). It was always kept by the Jews and after them by the early Christians, as a festival, and not as a fast.[3]

In later years, it was—like all other parts of God's revealed will—overlaid

---

1 **under both dispensations** – dispensations, as used here, means "periods of time," and in this context, the phrase means "under the Old and New Covenants."
2 **redoubled** – increased
3 **Joseph Bingham** (1668-1723), Antiquities of the Christian Church, vol. 2, bk. 20, ch. 3; Smith's Dictionary of the Bible, Art. "Sabbath."

with pharisaical and rabbinical carnal interpretations and additions. From all these, Christ purged it, as He did the rest of the Law. He came "to fulfill all righteousness"; therefore, He kept the Sabbath religiously and taught His disciples, while disregarding the glosses[4] of the Pharisees, to keep it in its essential spiritual sense as ordained by God. He declared that "the Sabbath was made for man" (Mar 2:27), the genus homo,[5] and consequently is both binding on all men for all time and adapted to the nature and wants of all men under all historical conditions.

On the other hand, it is evident that the particular day set apart is not in the least of the essence of the institution and that it must depend upon the positive will of God, which of course may substitute one day instead of another on suitable occasions for adequate reasons.

2. The introduction of a new dispensation, which a preparatory and particularistic nation-system [Israel] is to be replaced by a permanent and universal one [the Church], embracing all nations to the end time, is certainly such a suitable occasion. The Moral Law, expressed in the Ten Commandments written by the finger of God on stone and made the foundation of His throne between the cherubim and the condition of His covenant, must remain. The types, the special municipal laws of the Jews, and whatever is unessential in Sabbath or other permanent institutions must be changed.

3. The amazing fact of the resurrection of the Lord Jesus on the first day of the week constitutes evidently adequate reason for appointing that instead of the seventh day to be the Christian Sabbath. The Old Testament is introduced with an account of the genesis of the heaven and earth, and the old dispensation first grounds itself upon the relation of God as Creator of the universe and of man.

The New Testament is introduced with an account of the genesis of Jesus Christ and reveals the incarnate Creator as our champion, victorious over sin and death. The recognition of God as Creator is common to every theistic[6] system; the recognition of the resurrection of the incarnate God is peculiar to Christianity. The recognition of God as Creator is involved and conserved in the recognition of the resurrection of Christ, while the latter article of faith carries with it also the entire body of Christian faith and hope and life. The fact of the resurrection consummates the process

---

4 **glosses** – deceptive interpretations.
5 **genus homo** – genus = scientific classification of one or more species; in this context, homo = human beings.
6 **theistic** – pertaining to belief in the existence of a god or gods.

of redemption as far as it is objective to the Church. It is the reason of our faith, the ground of our hope, [and] the pledge of our personal salvation and of the ultimate triumph of our Lord as the Savior of the world. It is the keystone of historical Christianity and, consequently, of all living theism[7] in the civilized world. The essential qualification of an apostle was that he was an eyewitness of the resurrection. Their doctrine was summed up as a preaching of "Jesus and the resurrection" (Act 1:22, 4:2, 17:18, 23:6, 24:21).

4. During His life, Jesus had affirmed that He was "Lord also of the Sabbath day" (Mar 2:28). After His resurrection, He signalized the first day of the week, and not the seventh, by His revelation. On the day He rose, He appeared to His disciples on five different occasions. Withdrawing Himself during the interval, [He] reappeared on the following "first day of the week,"[8] His disciples being assembled and Thomas with them: "Then the same day at evening, being the first day of the week, when the doors were shut where the disciples were assembled for fear of the Jews, came Jesus and stood in the midst, and saith unto them, Peace be unto you" (Joh 20:19). The day of Pentecost falling that year on the "first day of the week," the disciples were again found assembled by mutual understanding: "And when the day of Pentecost was fully come, they were all with one accord in one place... And they were all filled with the Holy Ghost, and began to speak with other tongues, as the Spirit gave them utterance" (Act 2:1, 4); and the promised gift of the Holy Ghost descended upon them. The Lord, after many years, appeared unto John in Patmos and granted him the great closing Revelation on the "Lord's day": "I was in the Spirit on the Lord's day, and heard behind me a great voice, as of a trumpet" (Rev 1:10), which all the early Christians understood to signify the weekly festival dedicated to the resurrection of the Lord.

The record is also full of evidence that the members of all the apostolic churches were in the habit of assembling in their respective places at regular times for the purpose of common worship (1Co 11:17, 20; 14:23-26; Heb 10:25). That these assemblies were held on the "first day of the week" is certain from the action of Paul at Troas: "And we sailed away from Philippi after the days of unleavened bread, and came unto them to Troas in five days; where we abode seven days. And upon the first day of the week, when the disciples came together to break bread, Paul preached unto them, ready

---

7 **theism** – belief in the existence of God.
8 **first day of the week** – (Greek = μιᾷ τῶν σαββάτων) The assertion of the seventh day Sabbatarians that this phrase should be translated "one of the Sabbaths" is absurd. σαββάτων (sabbatōn) is neuter and cannot agree [grammatically] with the feminine μιᾷ (mia).

to depart on the morrow; and continued his speech until midnight" (Act 20:6-7). So also his orders to the churches of Corinth and Galatia: "Now concerning the collection for the saints, as I have given order to the churches of Galatia, even so do ye. Upon the first day of the week let every one of you lay by him in store, as God hath prospered him, that there be no gatherings when I come" (1Co 16:1-2). The change was then certainly made, as we can trace by an unbroken and consistent chain of testimonies from the time of the apostles to the present. The motives for the change assigned by the early Christian Fathers are known to have operated upon the apostles and are perfectly congruous[9] with all that is recorded of their characters, lives, and doctrines. The change, therefore, had the sanction of the apostles and, consequently, the authority of the "Lord of the Sabbath" Himself.

5. From the time of John, who first gave the institution its best and most sacred title—"Lord's Day"—there is an unbroken and unexceptional chain of testimonies that the "first day of the week" was observed as the Christian's day of worship and rest. For a long time, the word Sabbath continued to be applied exclusively to the seventh day. From habit, and in conformity to the natural sentiments of the Jewish converts, the early Christians long continued to observe both days. They kept every seventh day except the Sabbath before Easter, when the Lord lay in the grave, as they did every first day, as a festival. Afterward for a time, [Romanism], in opposition to Judaism, kept it as a fast. They held public religious services upon it. But the day was no longer considered sacred; labor was never suspended nor legally interdicted.[10] On the other hand, any tendency to return to its ancient observance as a strictly holy day, as in any sense sacred, as the first day of the week was maintained to be, was discountenanced[11] as an abandoning the freedom of the gospel and a returning to the ceremonial [practices] of the Jews.

The early Christians called their own day, for which they asserted preeminence and exclusive obligation, "the Lord's Day," "the first day of the week," "the eighth day"; and, in their communication with the heathen, they came to call it, as we have done in correspondence with ancient secular usage, "dies solis"—"Sunday." A comparison of the passages in which these designations are used by the early Christians makes it absolutely certain that they signify the same day, since they are all defined as applying to the day after the Jewish Sabbath or to the day on which Christ rose from the dead.

---

9 **congruous** – in agreement or harmony.
10 **interdicted** – forbidden.
11 **discountenanced** – looked on with disfavor.

Ignatius,[12] an immediate friend of the apostles, martyred at Rome not more than fifteen years after the death of John, in his Epistle to the Magnesians, chapter 9, says, "Those who have come to the possession of new hope, no longer observing the Sabbath (seventh day), but living in the observance of the Lord's Day, on which also our life has sprung up again, by Him and by His death." He calls the Lord's Day "the queen and chief of all the days" (of the week).

The author of the Epistle of St. Barnabas, writing a little before or at latest not long after the death of the apostle John, says, chapter 15, "We celebrate the eighth day with joy, on which, too, Jesus rose from the dead."

Justin Martyr[13] says, "On the day called Sunday is an assembly of all who live either in cities or in the rural districts, and the memoirs of the apostles and the writings of the prophets are read…because it is the first day on which God dispelled the darkness and the original state of things and formed the world, and because Jesus Christ our Savior rose from the dead upon it." "Therefore it remains the chief and first of days." The testimony continues uniform and unbroken…

Tertullian,[14] writing at the close of the second century, says, "On the Lord's Day, Christians, in honor of the resurrection of the Lord…must avoid everything that would cause anxiety, and defer all worldly business, lest they should give place to the devil."

Athanasius[15] says explicitly, "The Lord transferred the sacred observance (from the Sabbath) to the Lord's Day."

The author of the sermons de Tempore[16] says: "The apostles transferred the observance of the Sabbath to the Lord's Day; and therefore from the evening of the Sabbath to the evening of the Lord's Day, men ought to abstain from all country-work and secular business, and only attend divine service"…

The testimony of all the great Reformers and all historical branches of the modern Christian Church agree…(1) Luther,[17] Calvin,[18] and other Reformers taught that the Sabbath was ordained for the whole human race

---

12 **Ignatius of Antioch** (c. 35/50-c. 110) – early Christian theologian and martyr; student of John the Apostle.
13 **Justin Martyr** (c. 100-c. 165) – early Christian apologist and martyr.
14 **Tertullian** (c. 155-220) – early Latin theologian and apologist from Carthage, Africa.
15 **Athanasius** (c. 295-373) – Greek bishop of Alexandria, Egypt; defender of the deity of Christ.
16 **sermons de Tempore** – festival sermons.
17 **Martin Luther** (1483-1546) – German theologian and leader of the Reformation.
18 **John Calvin** (1509-1564) – French-born Swiss Protestant reformer.

at the creation, [and] (2) that it was in its essential features designed to be of universal and perpetual obligation…

The change of the day by the apostolic Church [is] proved by historical testimony [of the early church and of the Reformers], to which much might be added if space permitted, but against which no counter-evidence exists. This, as well as the passages above cited, proves that the change was effected by the authority of the apostles and, hence, by the authority of Christ. With the apostles preaching "Jesus and the resurrection" and observing and appointing the first day of the week for religious services, God bore "witness both with signs and wonders and divers miracles and gifts of the Holy Ghost" (Heb 2:4). Ever since the great Pentecostal Lord's Day, this day has been observed by God's true people and blessed by the Holy Ghost. It has been recognized and graciously used as an essential and pre-eminent means of building up the kingdom of Christ and effecting the salvation of His seed. And this divine acknowledgement has been in every age and nation in direct proportion to the faithful consecration of the day to its spiritual purpose. It is not possible that either a superstitions will-worship or an ignorant misconception should have been crowned with uniform and discriminating seals of divine [approval] through eighteen hundred years.

From The Sabbath: The Day Changed; the Sabbath Preserved, in the public domain.

Archibald Alexander Hodge (1823-1886): American Presbyterian pastor, theologian, and principal of Princeton Seminary; born in Princeton, NJ, USA.

The Lord's Day in Public

EZEKIEL HOPKINS (1634-1690)

Consider what duties you are to be engaged in [for] the public and solemn worship of God on this day. For in them, a great and principal part of the sanctification of it doth consist.

This I mention in the first place as most preferable. For, certainly, as long as—through the mercy of God—we have the public and free dispensation[1] of the gospel, we ought not to slight nor turn our backs upon this visible communion of the Church. [Rather we should] honor and own the freedom of the gospel by our constant attendance on the dispensations of it, lest, despising the mercy of God in giving them to us so publicly, we provoke Him…Now the public duties that are necessary to the right sanctifying of the Lord's Day are these:

1. Affectionate prayer, in joining with the minister, who is our mouth unto God as well as God's mouth unto us. For, as he is entrusted to deliver [God's] sovereign will and commands, so likewise to present our requests unto the throne of His grace. We ought heedfully to attend to every petition, to dart it up to heaven with our most earnest desires, and to close and seal it up with our affectionate Amen—"So be it." For, though it be the minister alone that speaks, yet it is not the minister alone that prays, but the whole congregation by him and with him. Whatsoever petition is not accompanied with thy most sincere and cordial affections, it is as much mocking of God as if thine own mouth had uttered it without the concurrence[2] of thy heart. [This] is most gross hypocrisy. Consider what promises are made to particular Christians when they pray singly and by themselves: "Whatsoever ye shall ask the Father in my name, he will grant it you" (Joh 15:16; 16:23). What great prevalence,[3] then, must the united prayers of the saints have when they join interests and put all the favor that each of them hath at the Throne of Grace into one common stock! When we come to the public prayers, we are not to come as auditors, but as actors: we have our part in them. And every petition that is spread before God ought to be breathed from our very hearts and souls. If we affectionately perform [this], we may have good assurance that what is ratified by so many votes and suffrages[4] here on earth

---

1 **dispensation** – act of distributing or dispensing; here, through preaching and literature.
2 **concurrence** – agreement.
3 **prevalence** – influence; effective power.
4 **votes and suffrages** – prayers and intercessions.

shall likewise be confirmed in heaven. For our Savior hath told us, "That if two of you shall agree on earth as touching any thing that they shall ask, it shall be done for them of my Father which is in heaven" (Mat 18:19).

2. Our reverent and attentive hearing of the Word of God, either read or preached, is another public duty necessary to the sanctification of the Lord's Day. This was observed also in the times of the Law, before Christ's coming into the world: "For Moses of old time hath in every city them that preach him, being read in the synagogues every sabbath day" (Act 15:21). Their synagogues were built for this very purpose: as their temple was the great place of their legal and ceremonial worship, so these were for their moral and natural worship. In the temple, they chiefly sacrificed; in their synagogues, they prayed, read, and heard. Every town and almost every village had one erected in it, as now our churches are, where the people on the Sabbath day assembled and had some portion of the Law read and expounded to them. Much more ought we to give our attendance on this holy ordinance now, in the times of the gospel, since a greater measure of spiritual knowledge is required from us, and the mysteries of salvation are more clearly declared unto us. And may that tongue wither and that mouth be forever silenced that shall dare to utter anything in contempt and vilifying[5] of this holy ordinance! Such excellent things are spoken of the preaching of the gospel! It is "the power of God" (1Co 1:18). It is the salvation of "them that believe" (1Co 1:21). It is the sweet "savour of his knowledge" (2Co 2:14). Certainly, whosoever disparageth[6] it, rejecteth against himself the counsel of God and neglects the only appointed means for the begetting of faith and for the obtaining of eternal salvation! For "faith cometh by hearing, and hearing by the word of God" (Rom 10:17).

3. Another public duty pertaining to the sanctifying of the Lord's Day is singing of Psalms. For this day being a festival unto God, a day of spiritual joy and gladness, how can we better testify our joy than by our melody? "Is any merry?" saith St. James, "let him sing psalms" (Jam 5:13). And, therefore, let profane spirits deride this how they please; yet, certainly, it is a most heavenly and spiritual duty. The holy angels and the spirits of just men in heaven are said to sing Eternal Hallelujahs unto the Great King! And if our Lord's Day be typical of heaven and the work of the Lord's Day represents to us the everlasting work of these blessed spirits, how can it be better done than when we are singing forth the praises of Him that sits upon the throne and of the Lamb our Redeemer? This is to join with the heavenly

---

5 **vilifying** – speaking or writing about with slanderous or abusive language.
6 **disparageth** – refer disapprovingly or contemptuously to somebody or something.

choir in their heavenly work and to observe a Lord's Day here, like that eternal Sabbath there, as the imperfection of earth can resemble the glory and perfection of heaven.

4. Another public duty belonging unto the sanctifying of the Lord's Day is the administration of the [ordinances], especially that of the Lord's Supper. And therefore it is mentioned, "And upon the first day of the week, when the disciples came together to break bread," that is, to partake of the Holy Communion of the body and blood of Christ, "Paul preached unto them" (Act 20:7), which intimates that the primary intent of their assemblies was to receive the Lord's Supper. Upon occasion of this, the apostle instructed them by preaching. It is most evident by all the records of the Church that it was the apostolic and primitive custom to partake of this most holy ordinance every Lord's Day and that their meetings were chiefly designed for this, to which were annexed prayer and preaching. I am afraid, Sirs, that one of the great sins of our age is not only the neglect and contempt of this ordinance by some, but the seldom celebrating it by all. The apostle, where he speaks of this holy institution, intimates that it should be frequently dispensed and participated: "As often as ye eat this bread, and drink this cup" (1Co 11:26). Although this ordinance be too seldom administered, let us consider what dishonor [some show to] Christ, [when they] totally withdraw themselves from it or very rarely partake of it. I shall no longer insist upon this, but leave it to God and your own consciences; for, certainly, if either persuasion or demonstration itself could prevail against resolution, enough hath been said many times [before] to spare me the labor of making this complaint any more.

And, thus much, concerning the sanctification of the Lord's Day, in the public duties of His worship and service.

From The Works of Ezekiel Hopkins, Vol. 1, in the public domain.

Ezekiel Hopkins (1634-1690): Anglican minister and author; born in Sandford, Crediton, Devonshire, UK.

The Lord's Day at Home
WILLIAM S. PLUMER (1802-1880)

The prophet Jeremiah puts prayerless families and the heathen in the same category. If God's wrath falls on the latter, it will certainly descend on the former. The language the prophet uses is truly startling: "Pour out thy fury upon the heathen that know thee not, and upon the families that call not on thy name" (Jer 10:25). Such families[1] are truly heathenish[2] in their dispositions and practices.

Perhaps there never was a godly pastor who did not feel that the cultivation of family religion[3] was very important to the success of his ministry and to the progress of true piety—who did not regret the neglect of it as a sad injury to the cause of God. But what is the cultivation of family religion? It consists,

1. In a devout reading, hearing, and studying of the Scriptures. The Word of God is able to make us wise unto salvation, and Timothy knew it from a child. We should acquaint ourselves and all our household with the sacred volume because it is the Word of God, because it is as fit to be read and spoken of in the family as anywhere else, and because we are specially commanded to teach all its truths to our children in the most familiar manner (2Ti 3:15; Deu 4:9, 6:7; Psa 78:4).

2. A portion should be spent in praising God for His mercies. Where it can be done to edification, families should sing God's praises. If it is impossible to sing them,…read [a] sacred hymn.

3. To these should be added prayer, including adoration, thanksgiving, confession, and supplication.

4. Religious conversation guided and conducted by the head of the family, consisting of familiar explanations. This commandment also requires Scripture and catechetical[4] instruction. In these endeavors to maintain domestic piety,[5] all the family as far as possible should unite. Some may be too young. Others may be sick, but none should be absent except for good cause. Servants should be kindly invited to unite with the rest of the family,

---

1 **families** – clans; "This noun is used in a wider sense than the English term family usually conveys. The word for the inhabitants of one house is usually house, household…[Family] most often refers to a circle of relatives with strong blood ties." (Harris, Archer, Waltke, eds., Theological Wordbook of the Old Testament, 947)
2 **heathenish** – pagan; not acknowledging the God of the Bible.
3 See FGB 188, Family Worship, available from CHAPEL LIBRARY.
4 **catechetical** – relating to Christian instruction through questions and answers.
5 **domestic piety** – godliness in the home.

and comfortable seats should be provided for all. What a blessed sight is that, when the pious head of a family, "with solemn air," says, "Let us worship God,"[6] and then devoutly reads the Bible and sings the praises of the Most High…

Great care should be taken that this family religion should be attended to at the most fitting time and not at hours so early as to make it necessary for the members of a household to neglect their private devotions in the morning, nor so late in the evening as to render it certain that children and others will be drowsy and, of course, unedified. That this whole matter may be truly useful, family worship and attention to family religion should be [as follows:]

1. Stated and regular: No light or trivial cause should be allowed to postpone or hinder it.

2. It should be decorous,[7] orderly, quiet, and serious. If it fails in this respect, it can scarcely edify any one. All trifling behavior should be carefully avoided.

3. It should be cheerful, not austere and morose.[8] God, Who loves a cheerful giver (2Co 9:7), no less loves a cheerful worshipper. Everything said and done should be suited to secure attention and to awaken an interest in the service.

4. Therefore, tediousness[9] should be avoided. A wise man regardeth both time and judgment. Where exhaustion begins, edification ceases. It would often prevent weariness, if there was more variety in conducting Sabbath day instruction and worship. Prayers, expositions, and remarks should be short and comprehensive.

5. But we should avoid both the appearance and reality of being hasty and of attending to this matter as though we were desirous of finishing it as speedily as possible.

6. Family instruction and worship should take proper notice of family mercies and afflictions. Such are continually occurring. But we should be very careful not to wound the feelings of even the youngest or most ignorant. It is seldom well to lecture one member of a family for personal faults in the presence of others.

7. In this matter, widows, who are the heads of families, should remember that they are held responsible for the order and religious education of their

---

6 From The Cotter's Saturday Night by Scottish poet Robert Burns (1759-1796).
7 **decorous** – characterized by conformity to the recognized standards of behavior.
8 **austere and morose** – stern in manner and gloomy.
9 **tediousness** – long and tiresome.

Chapter 13—The Lord's Day: The Lord's Day at Home

households…

8. It is sometimes asked, what should pious[10] wives and mothers do when husbands and fathers are absent? The correct answer is, "Take [their] place and see to it that God is honored in the house."

9. But what shall wives and mothers do when husbands and fathers—even when at home and well—decline to give proper religious instruction and to conduct family worship? In answer, it may be stated that it is not the duty of the wife to assume the husband's place, and therefore she may not in his presence, with an air of authority over him, convene[11] the family and give instruction. But though she is not the head of her husband, yet, with him and under him, she is the head of the rest of the family. She ought to assemble her children and servants in some suitable apartment and there teach them and unite with them in suitable acts of devotion. This course has often been followed by the happiest con¬sequences.

10. As the great object of all religious instruction and worship is to please God and secure His blessing, so let great care be taken that whatever is done be sincere, humble, and fervent. A heartless form is idle; yea, it is worse. Be zealous, not cold.

The following considerations show the propriety[12] and obligation of family religion:

(1) The very heathen, who profess and practice any form of religion, do, without exception, maintain some form of domestic religion. Though they call not on the name of Jehovah, yet they call upon their gods, and teach their children to do the same. This certainly argues a strong presumption that family religion is a dictate of nature. It is only in countries nominally [13]Christian that we find men failing to cultivate some form of devotion at home…

(2) The condition of every family calls for such instruction and devotion. We are very ignorant. Every appliance[14] is necessary to diffuse light into our darkened understandings. Every family has wants,[15] which should lead it to unite in prayer. Every family has mercies, which demand a united song. Every family has trials, where each should shed with the rest the tear of sympathy. Afflicted souls can find no better way to staunch[16] their bleeding wounds

---

10 **pious** – godly.
11 **convene** – bring together.
12 **propriety** – quality of being proper.
13 **nominally** – in name only, not really.
14 **appliance** – thing applied as a means to an end.
15 **wants** – needs.
16 **staunch** – stop the flow.

than thus to unite in solemn acts of worship. Sometimes a household is threatened with some dire calamity. Then, what is more proper than united petitions to Him, Who is Lord of all, to avert the dreaded evil?

(3) The maintenance of domestic religion has a happy effect on the peace and order of families. If one is absent, sick, or peculiarly afflicted, how it awakens and strengthens proper affection in the rest to speak of that one, to utter words of kindness to turn, and to pray for his return or deliverance! How many little heart-burnings and jealousies are thus extinguished. How sweet is the sight, when old and young quietly and lovingly meet and put away all else that they may speak, hear, think, pray, and praise before the Father of their spirits! There can hardly be an unamiable, disobliging[17] family, whose habit is to make common confession of sin, common acknowledgments of mercies, and common supplications for needed blessings, attended with the correct understanding of God's mind and will. They may lack much that the world calls courtliness.[18] But of the politeness that consists in "real kindness, kindly expressed," such a family can hardly be destitute. There is real love there. Every act of joint devotion strengthens it. Temptation may assail it. It may even be temporarily interrupted; but it will seldom or never be destroyed. Such bonds as these are the ligaments of the whole social system…A nation made up of such families can never be [worthy of hatred]. It is an alarming fact that during the nineteenth century, infidelity[19] has directed its most formidable enginery[20] against the family institution and against family religion.

(4) The primitive church, and indeed every thriving evangelical church, has set us an example in this matter, which it cannot be safe to despise. Church history informs us that after their private devotions, the members of the family in primitive times met for united prayer, the reading of the Scriptures, the recital of doctrinal and practical sentiments and mutual edification generally. This indeed, to some extent, was done every day. Each day was also closed by similar devotions. But the Lord's Day abounded in them.

(5) This maintenance of family religion is eminently useful. It has nearly every advantage attending every possible method of teaching. It gives a little at a time and repeats it often. It is varied in its modes. It cuts up ignorance by the roots…

---

17 **unamiable, disobliging** – unfriendly, deliberately unhelpful.
18 **courtliness** – the elegance of manners befitting a royal court.
19 **infidelity** – atheism.
20 **enginery** – figuratively, artillery.

(6) Family instruction and worship are of great importance in promoting pure and undefiled religion in the world. When Richard Baxter[21] settled in Kidderminster, there were but few devout families. Consequently, iniquity abounded. But as the spirit of religion revived, so did family worship, until at last, in some whole streets, not one family was found [in which] God was not honored by even daily worship…

(7) Besides the solemn passage already cited from Jeremiah, other Scriptures show that pious men did not neglect family religion. Of Abraham, God said, "I know him, that he will command his children and his household after him, and they shall keep the way of the LORD, to do justice and judgment" (Gen 18:19). Joshua said, "for me and my house, we will serve the LORD" (Jos 24:15). David says, "I will behave myself wisely in a perfect way. O when wilt thou come unto me? I will walk within my house with a perfect heart" (Psa 101:2). Solomon says, "The curse of the LORD is in the house of the wicked: but he blesseth the habitation of the just" (Pro 3:33).

Let family religion be maintained in all its purity and power, cost what it may. But this has never been done where families have slighted the Lord's Day. Stowell [wrote,] "It may be seriously questioned whether any one duty is so lamentably neglected among all classes of professing Christians, as the domestic observance of the Sabbath."

From The Law of God, Sprinkle Publications, www.sprinklepublications.net.

William S. Plumer (1802-1880): American Presbyterian minister and author; born in Greensburg, PA, USA.

---

21 **Richard Baxter (1615-1691)** – Nonconformist Puritan preacher and theologian.

Piety, Necessity, and Charity
EZEKIEL HOPKINS (1634-1690)

When we devote ourselves to [God] service and worship, meditating on His excellency, magnifying and praising His mercy, and invoking His holy name, we then hallow this day and give unto God that which is God's. Thus, you see what it is to sanctify the Lord's Day: both as God hath done it—by dedication—and as man ought to do it—by observation. But the great difficulty is in what manner the Lord's Day ought to be sanctified and kept holy: whether or not we are bound to the same strict and vigorous observation of our Christian Sabbath, as the Jews were of theirs under the economy of Moses.

To this I answer in general: as our Sabbath is not the very same with theirs, but only [similar], bearing a fit proportion to it, so, likewise, our sanctification of the Lord's Day—for thus I would rather call it than the Sabbath—is not, in all particulars the same that was required from the Jews. [It] bears a proportion to it in those things that are not ceremonial nor burdensome to our Christian liberty.

But, more particularly: The sanctifying of this day consists, partly, in abstaining from those things whereby it would be profaned; and, partly, in the performance of those things that are required of us and tend to promote the sanctity and holiness of it...Notwithstanding this rest and cessation from labor that is required from us on the Lord's Day, yet there are three sorts of works that may and ought to be performed on it, how great soever our bodily labor may be in doing them. And they are works of piety, works of necessity, and works of charity.

1. Works of piety are to be performed on the Lord's Day, yea, on this day especially, as being the proper works of the day. And such are not only those that consist in the internal operations of the soul, as heavenly meditations and spiritual affections; but such also as consist in the external actions of the body, as oral prayer, reading of the Scriptures, and preaching of the Word. Yea, on this day are ministers chiefly employed in their bodily labor and spending of their spirits: yet it is far from being a profanation of the Lord's Day, for holy works are most proper for holy days. And not only are such works to be performed on the Lord's Day, but they were enjoined also on the Jewish Sabbath. And therefore saith our Savior, "Have ye not read in the law, how that on the sabbath days the priests in the temple profane the sabbath, and are blameless?" (Mat 12:5). This word, therefore, of profaning the Sabbath is not to be understood of a formal profanation, as if they did that which was

unlawful to be done on that day. [This was] only of a material profanation, that is, they labored hard in killing and flaying, dividing and boiling, and burning the sacrifices in the temple. Had they not been instituted parts of God's worship, [they would have] been profanations of the Sabbath. But, being commanded by God, [they] were so far from being profanations that they were sanctifications of that day…So that it appears that works of piety or works immediately tending to piety may lawfully be performed with the strictest observation of the Lord's Day.

2. Not only works of piety, but works of necessity—and of great convenience—may also be done on the Lord's Day. And [these] are such without which we cannot subsist or not well subsist. Therefore, we may quench a raging fire; prevent any great and notable damage that would happen either to our persons or estates…without being guilty of the violation of this day…And not only those works that are of absolute necessity, but those likewise that are of great convenience may lawfully be done on the Lord's Day: such as kindling of fire, preparing of [food], and many other particulars too numerous to be mentioned. We find our Savior defending His disciples against the exceptions of the Pharisees for plucking the ears of corn, rubbing them in their hands, and eating them on the Sabbath Day (Mat 12:1-8). Only let us take this caution: we [should not] neglect the doing of those things until the Lord's Day that might be well done before and then plead necessity or convenience for it. For, if the necessity or convenience were such as might have been foreseen, our Christian prudence and piety ought to have provided for it before this holy day, so that we might wholly attend the immediate service of God in it, with as few avocations and impediments[1] as are possible.

3. Another sort of works that may and ought to be done on the Lord's Day are the works of charity and mercy. For, indeed, this day is instituted for a memorial of God's great mercy towards us. Therefore, in it, we are obliged to show charity and mercy: charity towards men and mercy to the very beasts themselves. Therefore, although the observation of the Sabbath was so strictly enjoined [upon] the Jews, yet was it to give place to the works of mercy whenever a poor beast did but stand in need of it. So Matthew 12:11: "What man shall there be among you, that shall have one sheep, and if it fall into a pit on the sabbath day, will he not lay hold on it, and lift it out?" So, again, Luke 13:15: "Doth not each one of you on the sabbath loose his ox or his ass from the stall, and lead him away to watering?"…Works of mercy, therefore, are to be done even to beasts themselves, whatsoever labor may

---

1 **avocations and impediments** – distractions and hindrances.

be required to the doing of them. How much more, then, [should we do] works of charity to men like ourselves! [This] charity is to be shown either to their souls or their bodies, for both many times are extremely miserable. To their souls in instructing, advising, exhorting, reproving, comforting, and counselling of them, praying for them—and if in anything they have offended us, freely forgiving them. This, indeed, is a work of charity proper for the Lord's Day, a work highly acceptable unto God and the best way that can be to sanctify it.

Neither are we to forbear any work of charity to their bodies and outward man. [For this reason,] we find how severely our Savior rebukes the superstitious hypocrisy of the Pharisees, who murmured against Him as a Sabbath-breaker because He had healed some of their infirmities on the Sabbath Day: "The ruler of the synagogue answered with indignation, because that Jesus had healed on the sabbath day, and said unto the people, There are six days in which men ought to work: in them therefore come and be healed, and not on the sabbath day." See how our Lord takes him up: "Thou hypocrite, doth not each one of you on the sabbath loose his ox?... Ought not this woman, being a daughter of Abraham, be loosed from this bond on the sabbath day?" (Luk 13:14-16)…Certainly, it is a right Sabbath-Day's work to do good and to put ourselves to any work and labor that may tend to the saving of life, easing of pain, or healing of the diseases and sickness of our brother…The strict and punctual observation of the Sabbath is to give place, whenever the [urgent need] or good of our neighbor doth require it; for God prefers mercy before sacrifice.

Thus, you see what rest is required from us on the Lord's Day and what works may be done on it, without any violation of the Law or profanation of the day.

From "An Exposition of the Ten Commandments" in The Works of Ezekiel Hopkins, Vol. 1, in the public domain.

Ezekiel Hopkins (1634-1690): Anglican minister and author; born in Sandford, Crediton, Devonshire, UK.

Honoring God on His Day

THOMAS CASE (1598-1682)

If thou turn away thy foot from the sabbath, from doing thy pleasure on my holy day; and call the sabbath a delight, the holy of the LORD, honourable; and shalt honour him, not doing thine own ways, nor finding thine own pleasure, nor speaking thine own words: Then shalt thou delight thyself in the LORD; and I will cause thee to ride upon the high places of the earth, and feed thee with the heritage of Jacob thy father: for the mouth of the LORD hath spoken it.—Isaiah 58:13-14

The verb in the Hebrew, "And shalt honour [or glorify] him"—may be rendered "honour it" or "honour him." But the sense seems to incline to the latter—"him," rather than "it." The day having had its title of veneration[1] put upon it before—"honourable"—this may more properly belong to God, even to the whole blessed and glorious Trinity,[2] requiring at the hands of every one that enjoyeth this blessed privilege of a Sabbath that they ascribe[3] the honor and glory of it unto God. And that is done, (1) When we make divine authority the sole ground of our separating and sanctifying the whole day to His peculiar service and worship, without alienating[4] any part or parcel of that holy time to our own carnal uses and purposes. "Keep the sabbath day to sanctify it"—there is the duty. "As the Lord thy God hath commanded thee"—there is the authority (Deu 5:12). (2) When, as we make God's command our ground, we make God's glory our [goal]. When we make it our design to set up God—Father, Son, and Holy Ghost in all His glorious and infinite perfections—in our adorations and admirations upon His holy day. And that is done in a special manner, when we make it the great business of a Sabbath to ascribe to each glorious person in the Trinity the glory of His proper work and operation, whereby He challengeth a title to and interest in the Sabbath. For example,

(1) When we ascribe to God the Father the glory of the stupendous work of creation. And that is done by a due contemplation of all His glorious attributes, shining forth in this beautiful structure of heaven and earth, celebrated by the royal Psalmist in Psalm 19:1: "The heavens declare the glory of God; and the firmament sheweth his handywork." The transcendent

---

1 **veneration** – reverence; deep respect.
2 See FGB 231, The Triune God, available from CHAPEL LIBRARY.
3 **ascribe** – assign a quality or character to.
4 **alienating** – transferring to the ownership of another.

excellences of the glorious Jehovah are conspicuous[5] and illustrious in this admirable theatre of the world, that is to say,

First, His power in creating all things out of nothing, and that by a word of His mouth.

Secondly, His wisdom in making all things in such a beautiful and exact manner and order. As the great physician [Galen][6] said of the body of man, "No man can come after God and say, 'This might have been better' "; so in the fabric of heaven and earth, neither man nor angels can say, "Here is a defect, and there is a redundancy.[7] It had been better [if] there had been more suns and fewer stars, more land, and less sea, etc." No, when the divine prophet had stood and in his most serious contemplation looked through the creation, he could spy out nothing that could have been otherwise, but breaks out in admiration, "O LORD, how manifold are thy works! in wisdom hast thou made them all" (Psa 104:24). He could see nothing from one end of the universe to another, but what speaks infinite perfection: "In wisdom hast thou made them all!" And as the omnipotence and wisdom of God is magnified in the creation, so also,

Thirdly, His bounty in bestowing all this visible creation upon man for his use and benefit. As one saith, "God made man last that He might bring him, as a father brings his son, into an house ready furnished." This is one branch of our honoring God, when we ascribe to God the Father the glory of the work of creation.

2. When we ascribe to God the Son the glory of His most glorious work of redemption. Wherein these particulars are wonderful:

His ineffable[8] incarnation: "Without controversy, great is the mystery of godliness, God manifest in the flesh" (1Ti 3:16), that is, the invisible God made visible in a body of flesh. This was a mystery indeed: a Son in heaven without a mother and a Son on earth without a father!

Christ's stupendous being "made under the law" (Gal 4:4). Behold, He that made the Law, was made under the Law—under the ceremonial law that He might abolish it! Under the Moral Law, the preceptive[9] power of it that He might fulfil it, so that every believer might have a "righteousness" that he may call his own (Rom 10:4), [and] the maledictive[10] power of it that

---

5 **conspicuous** – clearly visible; easy to be seen.
6 **Aelius Galenus or Galen** (129-c. 200/16) – Greek physician, surgeon, and philosopher in the Roman Empire; the quote is from his The Usefulness of the Parts of the Body.
7 **redundancy** – something not needed or useful.
8 **ineffable** – too great to be described in words.
9 **preceptive** – expressing a command.
10 **maledictive** – characterized by curses.

He might take it away (Gal 3:13).

Christ's work of redemption was principally transacted by His death and passion. For therein He laid down "the price of redemption," which was "his own precious blood" (Act 20:28; 1Pe 1:18-19).

This great work and mystery of our redemption was perfectly consummated in Christ's glorious resurrection. Wherein He "spoiled principalities and powers, he made a shew of them openly, triumphing over them" (Col 2:15)…Christ, rising from the dead like a conqueror, led death, the grave, hell, and the devil in chains after Him. [Christ did this] as conquerors in war were wont[11] to lead their vanquished enemies—whom they had taken prisoners—in chains of captivity after them, exposing them to the public scorn of all spectators.

Thus, we are to ascribe the glory of the work of redemption to Jesus Christ the Son of God; and thereby do honor God in our sanctifying of His holy Sabbath.

3. We likewise glorify the Holy Ghost when we ascribe to Him the honor of the work of sanctification.[12] Whether we look upon it in that first miraculous effusion[13] of the Spirit that our Lord Jesus, as the King and Head of His Church, did first purchase by the blood of His cross,[14] and afterward ascended into heaven and obtained of His Father when He took possession of His kingdom and did abundantly pour down upon the apostles, other officers, and members of His evangelical church in the day of Pentecost (Act 2:1-4), which was (as it were) the sanctification of the whole gospel Church at once in the first-fruits; or whether we understand that work of sanctification, which successively is wrought by the Holy Ghost in every individual elect child of God, happily begun in their…conversion and mightily upheld and carried on in the soul to the dying day, this is a glorious work. [It consists] in these two glorious branches of it: mortification[15] of corruption, which, before the Holy Ghost hath [finished in us], shall end in the total annihilation of the body of sin (that blessed privilege groaned for so much by the blessed apostle [in] Rom 7:24); and the erecting of a beautiful fabric of grace, holiness in the soul, which is the very "image" of

---

11 **wont** – accustomed; in the habit of doing.
12 **sanctification** – Sanctification is the work of God's free grace, whereby we are renewed in the whole man after the image of God, and are enabled more and more to die unto sin, and live unto righteousness. (Spurgeon's Catechism, Q. 34) See FGB 215, Sanctification; catechism and FGB are available from CHAPEL LIBRARY.
13 **effusion** – pouring out.
14 See FGBs 225, The Work of Christ, 226 Christ upon the Cross, 227 Atonement.
15 **mortification** – putting to death; see FGB 201, Mortification.

Chapter 13—The Lord's Day: Honoring God on His Day

God—an erection of more transcendent wonder and glory than [His] six-days' workmanship [in creation]—that the Holy Ghost doth "uphold" and will perfectly [do so] unto the day of Christ (Heb 1:3). This is the great end and design of the Sabbath and of the ordinances of the gospel, according to the Word that the great Maker and Appointer of Sabbaths speaketh: "I gave them my sabbaths, to be a sign between me and them, that they might know that I am the LORD that sanctify them" (Eze 20:12).

Here, then, is the third branch of our sanctifying the Sabbath, namely, the ascribing to God the Holy Ghost the glory of the work of sanctification.

This is proper work for Christians in the intervals and void spaces between the public ordinances: to sit down and first seriously and impartially to examine the work of grace in our souls (1) for the truth of it [and] (2) for the growth of it. Then, if we can give God and our own consciences some Scriptural account concerning this matter, [we should] humbly fall down and put the crown of praise upon the head of free grace, which hath made a difference where it found none. And so much for this text at this time.

From "Of Sabbath Sanctification" in Puritan Sermons 1659-1689, in the public domain.

Thomas Case (1598-1682): English Presbyterian minister and member of the West-minster Assembly; born in Kent, England, UK.

A Most Precious Enjoyment

JONATHAN EDWARDS (1703-1758)

Let us be thankful for the institution of the Christian Sabbath. It is a thing wherein God hath shown His mercy to us and His care for our souls. He shows that He by His infinite wisdom is contriving for our good. Christ teaches us that the Sabbath was made for man: "The sabbath was made for man, and not man for the sabbath" (Mar 2:27). It was made for the profit and for the comfort of our souls.

The Lord's Day is a day of rest: God hath appointed that every seventh day we should rest from all our worldly labors. Instead of that, He might have appointed the hardest labors for us to go through, some severe hardships for us to endure. It is a day of outward, but especially of spiritual, rest. It is a day appointed of God that His people thereon may find rest unto their souls; that the souls of believers may rest and be refreshed in their Savior. It is a day of rejoicing: God made it to be a joyful day to the Church…They that receive and improve the Sabbath aright, call it a delight and honorable (Isa 58:13-14). It is a pleasant and a joyful day to them; it is an image of the future heavenly rest of the Church: "There remaineth therefore a rest" (or sabbatism, as it is in the original) "to the people of God. For he that is entered into his rest, he also hath ceased from his own works, as God did from his. Let us labour therefore to enter into that rest" (Heb 4:9-11).

The Christian Sabbath is one of the most precious enjoyments of the visible Church. Christ showed His love to His Church in instituting it; and it [is appropriate for] the Christian Church to be thankful to her Lord for it. The very name of this day—the Lord's Day or Jesus' day—should endear it to Christians, as it intimates the special relation it has to Christ and the design of it, which is the commemoration of our dear Savior and His love to His Church in redeeming it.

Be exhorted to keep this day holy. God hath given such evidences that this is His mind, that He will surely require it of you, if you do not strictly and conscientiously observe it. And if you do thus observe it, you may have this comfort in the reflection upon your conduct: (1) that you have not been superstitious in it, but have done as God hath revealed it to be His mind and will in His Word that you should do; and (2) that in so doing you are in the way of God's acceptance and reward.

Here let me lay before you the following motives to excite you to this duty:

1. By a strict observation of the Lord's Day, the name of God is honored,

and that in such a way as is very acceptable to Him. "If thou…call the sabbath a delight, the holy of the LORD, honourable; and shalt honour him" (Isa 58:13). God is honored by it, as it is a visible manifestation of respect to God's holy Law and a reverencing of that which has a peculiar relation to God Himself…If a person, with evident strictness and care, observe the Sabbath, it is a visible manifestation of a conscientious regard to God's declaration of His mind, and [this is] a visible honor done to His authority.

By a strict observance of the Sabbath, the face of religion is kept up in the world. If it were not for the Sabbath, there would be but little public and visible appearance of serving, worshipping, and reverencing the supreme and invisible Being. The Sabbath seems to have been appointed very much for this end, viz.,[1] to uphold the visibility of [Christianity] in public…By how much greater the strictness is with which the Sabbath is observed and with how much more solemnity the duties of it are observed among a people, by so much the greater is the manifestation among them of respect to the Divine Being.

This should be a powerful motive with us to the observation of the Sabbath. It should be our study above all things to honor and glorify God. It should be the great thing with all that bear the name of Christian to honor their great God and King…

2. That which is the business of the Lord's Day is the greatest business of our lives, viz., that of religion. To serve and worship God is that for which we were made and for which we had our being given us. Other business, which is of a secular nature and on which we are wont[2] to attend on week days, is but subordinate and ought to be subservient to the higher purposes and ends of religion. Therefore, surely we should not think much of devoting one-seventh part of our time to be wholly spent in this business and to be set apart to exercise ourselves in the immediate duties of religion.

(3) Let it be considered that all our time is God's. Therefore, when He challenges of us one day in seven, He challenges His own. He doth not exceed His right: He would not have exceeded it if He had challenged a far greater proportion of our time to be spent in His immediate service. But He hath mercifully considered our state and our necessities here; and, as He hath consulted the good of our souls in appointing a seventh day for the immediate duties of religion, so He hath considered our outward necessities and hath allowed us six days for attendance on our outward affairs. What unworthy treatment therefore will it be of God, if we refuse to allow Him

---

1 **viz.** – Latin = videlicet: that is; namely.
2 **wont** – accustomed; in the habit.

Chapter 13—The Lord's Day: A Most Precious Enjoyment

even the seventh day!

4. As the Lord's Day is a day that is especially set apart for religious exercises, so it is a day wherein God especially confers His grace and blessing. As God hath commanded us to set it apart to have converse with Him, so hath He set it apart for Himself to have converse with us. As God hath commanded us to observe the Sabbath, so God observes the Sabbath too… His eyes are open upon it. He stands ready then especially to hear prayers, to accept of religious services, to meet His people, to manifest Himself to them, to give His Holy Spirit and blessing to those who diligently and conscientiously sanctify it.

That we should sanctify the Lord's Day, as we have observed, is according to God's institution. God in a sense observes His own institutions, i.e., [He] is wont to cause them to be attended with a blessing. The institutions of God are His appointed means of grace; and with His institutions, He hath promised His blessing: "In all places where I record my name, I will come unto thee, and I will bless thee" (Exo 20:24). For the same reason, we may conclude that God will meet His people and bless them, waiting upon Him not only in appointed places, but at appointed times and in all appointed ways…God hath made it our duty, by His institution, to set apart this day for a special seeking of His grace and blessing. [Therefore,] we may argue that He will be especially ready to confer His grace on those who thus seek it. If it is the day on which God requires us especially to seek Him, we may argue that it is a day on which especially He will be found. That God is ready on this day especially to bestow His blessing on them that keep it aright is implied in that expression of God's blessing the Sabbath day (Gen 2:3)…So here is great encouragement for us to keep holy the Sabbath, as we would seek God's grace and our own spiritual good. The Sabbath day is an accepted time, a day of salvation, a time wherein God especially loves to be sought and loves to be found. The Lord Jesus Christ takes delight in His own day: He delights to honor it. He delights to meet with and manifest Himself to His disciples on it, as He showed before His ascension by appearing to them from time to time on this day. He delights to give His Holy Spirit on this day, as He intimated by choosing it as the day on which to pour out the Spirit in so remarkable a manner on the primitive church (Act 2:1-4), and on which to give His Spirit to the apostle John (Rev 1:10).

Of old, God blessed the seventh day or appointed it to be a day whereon especially He would bestow blessings on His people, as an expression of His own joyful remembrance of that day and of the rest and refreshment that He had on it: "Wherefore the children of Israel shall keep the Sabbath…for

Chapter 13—The Lord's Day: A Most Precious Enjoyment

in six days the LORD made heaven and earth, and on the seventh day he rested, and was refreshed" (Exo 31:16-17).

But how much more reason has Christ to bless the day of His resurrection, to delight to honor it, and to confer His grace and blessed gifts on His people on this day. It was a day whereon Christ rested and was refreshed in a literal sense. It was a day of deliverance from the chains of death, the day of His finishing that great and difficult work of redemption, which had been upon His heart from all eternity; the day of His [vindication] by the Father; the day of the beginning of His exaltation, and of the fulfilment of the promises of the Father; the day when He had eternal life, which He had purchased, put into His hands. On this day, Christ doth indeed delight to distribute gifts, blessings, joy, and happiness, and will delight to do the same to the end of the world.

O therefore, how well is it worth our while to improve this day, to call upon God and seek Jesus Christ! Let awakened sinners be stirred up by these things to improve the Lord's Day, as they would lay themselves most in the way of the Spirit of God. Improve this day to call upon God, for then He is near. Improve it for reading the Holy Scriptures and diligently attending His Word preached; for then is the likeliest time to have the Spirit accompanying it. Let the saints who are desirous of growing in grace and enjoying communion with Christ improve the Lord's Day in order to it.

From "The Perpetuity and Change of the Sabbath" in The Works of Jonathan Edwards, Vol. 2, in the public domain.

Jonathan Edwards (1703-1758): American Congregational preacher and theologian; born in East Windsor, Connecticut Colony, USA.

Appendix A

THEMES AND HISTORY OF THE FREE GRACE BROADCASTER

The *Free Grace Broadcaster* is a quarterly digest of classic Christian sermons and articles, each issue focusing on a different theme. The *Broadcaster* is useful for personal study, discipleship, family worship, and sermon preparation. These 48 page booklets are available in print and by download from *www.ChapelLibrary.org*.

Themes of Available Issues

Apostasy (#205)

Aspects of Repentance (#156)

Assurance and Perseverance (#179)

Backsliding (#197)

Biblical Parenthood (#204, also in Spanish)

Blood of Christ, The (#155)

Christ The Mediator (#183)

Comfort in Affliction (#217)

Communion/Union with Christ (#164)

Contentment (#213)

Conversion (#195)

Covetousness (#167)

Cross of Jesus Christ, The (#176)

Day of Judgment (#210)

Death Is Coming: Flee from the Wrath of God (#180)

Duties of Sons & Daughters (#208, also in Spanish)

Evangelism (#151)

Evil Tongue, The (#152)

Faith (#157)

Faithfulness of God, The (#169, also in Spanish)

Family Worship (#188)

Fear of God, The (#182)

Forgiveness (#184)

Glory of Christ, The (#162)

God of All Comfort, The (#194)

God's Warnings (#178)

Godly Home, The (#170, also in Spanish)

Godly Manhood (#192)

Good Works (#199)

Gospel, The (#198)

Heaven (#181)

Hell (#211)

Holy Spirit, The (#154)

Hope (#186)

Hypocrisy (#193)

Idolatry (#189)

Imputed Righteousness (#191)

Justification (#187, also in Spanish)

Love (#159)

Love Not the World (#163)

Love of the Spirit, The (#173)

Loving One Another (#206)

Majesty of God, The (#171, also in Spanish)

Marriage (#200)

Modest Apparel (#216)

Mortification (#201)

New Birth, The (#202)

Persecution (#185)

Prayer (#153)

Pride and Humility (#168)

Repentance (#203)

Resurrection, The (#175)

Revival (#166)

Sanctification (#215)

Satan and His Deception (#161)

Scripture, The (#150)

Secret Sins (#209)

Self-denial (#218)

Sin of Unbelief (#174)

Substitution (#207)

Suffering (#158)

Temptation (#160)

Thankfulness (#190)

Thoughts for Young People (#212)

Trinity, The (#165)

Union with Christ (#214)

Uniqueness of the God-Man (#172)

Virtuous Womanhood (#196)

Worship (#177)

Appendix B

HISTORY

Pastor W. F. Bell of Canton, Georgia, began the *Free Grace Broadcaster* in September of 1970. The first 49 issues were published six times per year under the title *The Word of Truth*. Then, in November of 1975, issue 50 carried the name *Free Grace Broadcaster* with the significant subtitle (from the Baptist preacher Samuel Medley, 1738-1799):

"Our Purpose: To humble the pride of man, to exalt the grace of God in salvation, and to promote real holiness in heart and life."

Every edition since has been devoted to fulfilling this purpose. These early issues included articles from the pens of Pastors Bell, Glen Berry, Ferrell Griswold, Henry Mahan, Conrad Murrell, and also J. C. Philpot, Arthur W. Pink, J.C. Ryle, and C. H. Spurgeon.

In May 1988 with issue 125, Pastor Bell asked Mt. Zion Bible Church's pastor, L.R. Shelton, Jr., to assume the editing, printing, and distribution of the *FGB* because his mailing list had grown to more than 3,000 subscribers. These subscribers were combined with that of Chapel Library, and by faith Pastor Shelton printed 10,000 copies of issue 125! By 1991, 15,000 copies were printed. By God's grace, the 200th issue had a print run of 27,000, including 16,500 subscribers in North America, 2,000 sent in bulk to churches, 3,000 for the Free Quarterly Offer and follow-up requests during the quarter, 1,000 for our stock, 1,000 sent to other ministries who share complimentary copies with their constituents, and 3,500 sent to 13 international distributors who maintain subscriptions in their own countries.

The *FGB* became a quarterly in January of 1989 with issue 127. Pastor Shelton loved the old writers; he cut his teeth on Lloyd-Jones, Pink, and Spurgeon. When the Lord's people donated for a new printing press, by January 1990 the FGB listed 18 available Spurgeon sermon booklets (they now number 95). Today, the Chapel Library catalog is filled with tracts and booklets that first appeared as articles in the *FGB* during this era. January 1993 issue 143 came with a new title font, which has remained to this day. Significantly, with issue 150 in November 1994, the *FGB* included **articles all related to one theme**. This increased its value immensely because God's people could now feast on the best of what older writers had to say on one relevant topic!

Working behind the scenes, Mike Snyder ably assisted Pastor Shelton Jr. in the editing for many years. Pastor Jeff Pollard became the third primary editor of the *FGB* when he moved to Pensacola in August 2002 from Providence Baptist Church of Ball, Louisiana. He and Pastor Shelton co-edited two issues before Pastor Shelton passed away in January 2003. Since then, Pastor Pollard has sought to make each issue a more **extensive presentation** of the facets of the theme at hand: what it is, what it means, and how it affects the lives of the saints. We believe this increases its value still further because it has now become a more in-depth tool for discipleship, training, and sermon preparation, in addition to its role in encouraging the saints in discipleship and personal devotions. As such, it is proving very significant in the training of native pastors worldwide.

The ***FGB Spanish Edition*** first appeared in 2009 with the addition of international distributors in Mexico and Spain.

Chapel Library makes issues since #150 available for **download worldwide** without charge. And in North America, these also may be ordered in print from the website of Literature Catalog.

Appendix C

ABOUT CHAPEL LIBRARY

Sending Christ-Centered Messages from Prior Centuries Worldwide

Chapel Library sends Christ-centered messages from prior centuries worldwide. It operates under the authority of *Mount Zion Bible Church,* a small, evangelical, Bible-teaching, independent church in Pensacola, Florida. The authors have stood the test of time and therefore are not subject to contemporary trends. These include *Spurgeon* (Baptist), *Bonar* (Presbyterian), *Ryle* (Anglican), *Bunyan* (Independent), *Pink,* the *Puritans,* and many others. The focus is the grace of God through Jesus Christ, our Lord and Savior.

The printing ministry began in 1978. The Prison Ministry started mailing free Bibles to inmates in 1984. Chapel Library was added by God's grace in 1987, the *Free Grace Broadcaster* in 1988, the Bible Institute in 1995, the website in 1996, and the International Distributors in 2004.

In North America, we send materials to individuals in moderate quantities postage paid and free of charge. We also send large quantities without charge to prisons, missions, and overseas pastors. Larger quantities to churches and others are available at our costs. We are a faith ministry, depending upon the Lord to meet all our needs. We never ask for donations, share our mailing list, or send promotional mailings.

The ministries include the following:

Printing: Distributing tracts, booklets, and paperbacks printed in our own facilities.

Tape Ministry: Audio tapes from our library of over 6,000 messages and books on tape.

Prison Ministry: Serving inmates and chaplains throughout North America.

Bible Institute: More than 35 study courses utilizing proven authors of the past.

Two magazines: *Free Grace Broadcaster* and Pink's *Studies in the Scriptures*, sent quarterly without charge in North America.

Missions: Sending Christ-centered materials from prior centuries to pastors and missionaries worldwide without charge.

Internet Ministry &**John Bunyan Archive**: Downloadable sermons, literature, MP3 audio, & Bunyan's complete works.

There are more than **800 titles** in all. In addition, more than 100 titles have been translated into **Spanish**. Several other languages are also available, including Portuguese and Russian.

Sample Titles
(*t*–tract, *b*–booklet, *p*–paperback, *s*–Spanish also available)

All of Grace—Charles Haddon Spurgeon (p)
Appointment You Will Keep, An—Joel Beeke (t)
Are You Born Again? ˢ—J.C. Ryle (t)
Atonement, The—John Murray (b)
Attributes of God—Arthur W. Pink (p)
Biblical Repentance ˢ—L.R. Shelton, Jr. (b)
Biblical View of Self-esteem—Jay Adams (b)
Blood of Jesus, The—William Reid (b)
Bondage of the Will, The—Martin Luther (b)
Calvin on Self-Denial—John Calvin (b)
Canons of Dort (b)
Catechism with Proofs, A—Charles Haddon Spurgeon*b* (b)
Charity and Its Fruits—Jonathan Edwards (b)
Church Discipline—John Owen (b)
Christ's Sympathies to Weary Pilgrims—Octavius Winslow (b)
Christian Behavior—John Bunyan (b)
Christian's Warfare, The—Robert McCheyne (t)
Compel Them to Come In—Charles Haddon Spurgeon (b)

Deny Yourself (biographies)—Steve Gallagher (b)
Divine Guidance—B.A. Ramsbottom (b)
Divine Sovereignty & Human Responsibility—J.I. Packer (b)
Duties of Parents, The—J.C. Ryle (b)
Earnest Warning against Lukewarmness—C.H. Spurgeon (b)
Effective Prayer—Charles Haddon Spurgeon (b)
Evolution or Creation? (b)
Faith's Freedom with God—Ralph Erskine (b)
Fleeing Out of Sodom—Jonathan Edwards (b)
From Tradition to Truth ˢ—Richard Bennett (b)
God's Indisputable Sovereignty (b)
God's Way of Peace—Horatius Bonar (p)
God's Way of Holiness—Horatius Bonar (p)
Greasy the Robber ˢ—Lukesh (b)
Heaven, A World of Love—Jonathan Edwards (b)
Holiness—Joel Beeke (b)
Holiness, Part 1—J.C. Ryle (p)
Honey Out of the Rock ˢ—Thomas Willcox (b)
Hour with George Mueller, An (b)
How to Die to Selfishness—G.D. Watson (b)
Imminent Danger to Our Nation—John Newton (b)
Is Christ Your Lord? ˢ—Arthur W. Pink (t)
Is the Bible Reliable?—John Piper (b)
Just God, A ˢ—Charles Haddon Spurgeon (t)
Justification, the Law, the Righteousness of Christ—Hodge (b)
Letter to a Friend re. Lordship Salvation—John Piper (b)
Letters of Samuel Rutherford—Samuel Rutherford (b)
Lord Our Righteousness, The—George Whitefield (b)
Luther's Conversion—Horatius Bonar (t)
Man's Will – Free Yet Bound—Walter Chantry (b)
Minister's Self-Watch, The—Charles Haddon Spurgeon (b)
Mirage Shall Become a Pool, The—D.M. Lloyd-Jones (b)
Mute Christian under the Smarting Rod—Thomas Brooks (b)
Only Savior, The—Erroll Hulse (b)
Pilgrim's Progress (condensed)—John Bunyan (b)

Pilgrim's Progress in Pictures ˢ (condensed)—John Bunyan (b)
Postmodernism—Erroll Hulse (b)
Prayer of Jabez, The—Charles Haddon Spurgeon (b)
Proverbs—Charles Bridges (b)
Pure in Heart, The—Thomas Watson (b)
Rare Jewel of Christian Contentment—Jeremiah Burroughs (b)
Real Faith—George Mueller (t)
Robbery Committed – Restitution Made—Ebenezer Erskine (b)
Salvation Is of the Lord—Charles Haddon Spurgeon (t)
Sanctification—J.C. Ryle (t)
Satisfied with the Scriptures—Geoff Thomas (b)
Scriptures and the World—Arthur W. Pink (b)
Self or Christ: Which Is It?—Horatius Bonar (t)
Sinners in the Hands of an Angry God ˢ—Jonathan Edwards (b)
Sovereignty of God—Arthur W. Pink (p)
Sovereignty of God in Providence—John Reisinger (b)
Spurgeon Gems—Charles Haddon Spurgeon (b)
Story of the Puritans, The—Erroll Hulse (b)
Ten Indictments against the Modern Church—Paul Washer (b)
Timely Warning—Charles Haddon Spurgeon (t)
Thoughts for Young Men ˢ—J.C. Ryle (b)
Treasures of Bonar—Horatius Bonar (b)
Treasury of David, The—Charles Haddon Spurgeon (b)
True Prayer – True Power ˢ—Charles Haddon Spurgeon (b)
Useless Kinds of Religion—J.C. Ryle (t)
Vanity of Thoughts, The—Thomas Goodwin (t)
What Is a Biblical Christian? ˢ—Al Martin (b)
What the Bible Says About… ˢ (t)
When the Salt Loses Its Savour—Maurice Roberts (b)
White Devil, The (unbelief)—John Bunyan (t)
Words to Winners of Souls—Horatius Bonar (b)